2024 Release

Organizational Behavior

Steven L. McShane
Interconnected Knowledge

Mary Ann Von Glinow
Florida International University

Mc Graw Hill

M: ORGANIZATIONAL BEHAVIOR

This book is printed on acid-free paper.

1 2 3 4 5 6 7 8 9 LMN 29 28 27 26 25 24

ISBN 978-1-266-95558-7
MHID 1-266-95558-5

Cover Image: *Thomas Barwick/Getty Images*

mheducation.com/highered

about the Authors

Steven L. McShane

Courtesy of Donna McClement

Steven L. McShane has held tenured positions as Professor at Simon Fraser University's Faculty of Business Administration (Canada) and Winthrop Professor of Management at the University of Western Australia Graduate School of Management and Business School. He has been Conjoint Professor at Newcastle Business School, University of Newcastle (Australia) and Adjunct Professor at Gustavson School of Business, University of Victoria (Canada). He has also taught organizational behavior in the IMBA program at the Antai College of Economics and Management at Shanghai Jiao Tong University in Shanghai, China. Steve is currently head of Interconnected Knowledge, which he founded two decades ago.

Steve earned his PhD from Michigan State University, where he specialized in organizational behavior and labor relations. He also holds a Master's of Industrial Relations from the University of Toronto and an undergraduate degree from Queen's University in Canada. Steve is a past president of the Administrative Sciences Association of Canada (the Canadian equivalent of the Academy of Management) and served as Director of Graduate Programs in Simon Fraser University's business faculty. He has also conducted executive programs with many organizations. Steve has received awards for his teaching quality and innovation, and he has high ratings from students in Perth, Shanghai, Singapore, Manila, Vancouver, and other cities where he has taught.

Along with coauthoring *M: Organizational Behavior,* 2024 Release, Steve is lead coauthor of *Organizational Behavior,* Tenth Edition (2024); *Canadian Organizational Behaviour,* Eleventh Edition (2021), which is the leading organizational behavior book in Canada; and *Organisational Behaviour: Asia Pacific,* Sixth Edition (2019), which has twice been awarded the best tertiary textbook in Australia. He is also coauthor of editions or translations of his organizational behavior books in other countries. Steve has published several dozen articles and conference papers on workplace values, training transfer, organizational learning, exit-voice-loyalty, employee socialization, wrongful dismissal, media bias in business magazines, and other diverse topics.

Steve enjoys spending his leisure time hiking, swimming, body board surfing, canoeing, skiing, and traveling with his wife and their two daughters and partners.

Mary Ann Von Glinow

Mary Ann Von Glinow

Dr. Von Glinow is a Knight Ridder Eminent Scholar Chair in International Management at Florida International University and is senior editor for the *Journal of International Business Studies (JIBS).* She served as 2010 to 2012 president of the Academy of International Business (AIB) and the 1994–1995 president of the Academy of Management (AOM). Previously on the Marshall School faculty of the University of Southern California, she has an MBA and a PhD in management science from Ohio State University, and is a Fellow of the Academy of Management, the Academy of International Business, and the Pan-Pacific Business Association. She sits on 13 editorial review boards and numerous international panels and teaches in executive programs in Latin America, Asia, and the United States.

Dr. Von Glinow has authored over 100 journal articles and 13 books, most of which have been translated into Chinese, Hindi, and Spanish. Her book on organizational learning capability won a Gold Book Award from the Ministry of Economic Affairs in Taiwan in 2002. She is the 2005 recipient of the Academy of Management's Distinguished Service Award, one of the highest honors bestowed by the Academy.

Mary Ann has consulted widely and is on the board of directors of several organizations, including the advisory board to Volvo-Geely in China. She is actively involved in several animal welfare organizations and received the 1996 Humanitarian Award of the Year from Miami's Adopt-a-Pet.

Dedication

Dedicated with love and devotion to Donna, and to our wonderful daughters, Bryton and Madison

–S.L.M.

Dedicated to Zack, Emma, Googun, Blue, Chloe, Jackson, and Boomer

–M.A.V.G.

Brief Contents

Contents

part one Introduction 2

Ground Picture/Shutterstock

part two Individual Behavior and Processes 30

Jacob Lund/Shutterstock

StudioByTheSea/Shutterstock

Zamrznuti tonovi/Shutterstock

fizkes/Shutterstock

fizkes/Shutterstock

Fredrick Kippe/Alamy Stock Photo

What's New
in the 2024 Release

M: Organizational Behavior, 2024 Release, has received considerable updating. Many chapters have new conceptual content; a few chapters have new subtopics. All chapters have new opening vignettes and in-text examples, along with new or revised OB Theory to Practice features and factoids. The most substantial conceptual changes have occurred in Chapter 1 (Introduction to the Field of Organizational Behavior), Chapter 3 (Perceiving Ourselves and Others in Organizations), Chapter 8 (Communicating in Teams and Organizations), and Chapter 13 (Organizational Culture).

Diversity, Equity, and Inclusion

M: Organizational Behavior, 2024 Release, describes contemporary knowledge and practices regarding diversity, equity, and inclusion (DEI). The topic is fully introduced in Chapter 1, which describes these concepts; summarizes how they are practiced in organizations, and identifies their benefits, challenges, and moral imperative. Chapter 3 explains the authentic self, how self-concept awareness and acceptance allows people of all identities to be fully themselves while contributing to the organization, and how inclusion in informal workplace groups is an important part of everyone's self-concept. Equity (the "E" in DEI) is detailed in Chapter 5 as part of the more complete topic of organizational justice. Chapter 9 explains how social networks can create a more inclusive workplace, such as through employee resource groups. Chapter 13 discusses the potential advantages of diverse subcultures and introduces the emerging debate about whether "culture fit" inherently undermines diversity, equity, and inclusion, in contrast to "culture add."

The authors personally researched, selected, and wrote all of this content (i.e., no artificial intelligence program or ghost writers were involved). We believe this integrated and human-originated approach provides a more cohesive body of knowledge and ensures that the examples are relevant, recent, and engaging. Here are the key changes we've made to each chapter of this 2024 Release.

Chapter 1: Introduction to the Field of Organizational Behavior

- The topic of diversity, equity, and inclusion (DEI) has been significantly revised and updated, including a description of the inclusive workplace, its importance for supporting a diverse workforce, and ways to maintain an inclusive workplace at the individual and collective level.
- This 2024 Release significantly updates content on personal strategies to improve work–life integration and, in particular, ways to practice boundary management across roles.
- The section on individual behavior and performance (MARS model) now includes habits as one of three aspects of ability.
- The discussion on why OB is important for students has been updated, including new survey results and an updated associated exhibit on the top-ranked skills that employers seek in job applicants.
- The topics of organizations as open systems and the reasons why human capital increases organizational effectiveness have been updated.
- The systematic research anchor has updated analysis on why organizational leaders overlook evidence-based knowledge, as well as ways to minimize these problems.
- The topic of remote and hybrid work arrangements has been updated with information about current trends, as well as more details about jobs best suited to remote work.
- The topic of maintaining work attendance now refers to both the negative and potentially positive consequences of presenteeism.
- The three types of role perceptions are now described more distinctly.
- New exhibit on the three types of individual performance.
- New OB Theory to Practice on applying DEI at RingCentral.
- New chapter-opening vignette looks at employee–employer differences in preferences for remote, hybrid, and in-office work arrangements.
- Revised factoid on "Mind the MARS Gap."

Chapter 2: Individual Differences: Personality and Values

- The topic of MBTI and Jungian theory in the workplace has been updated with more discussion about both the strengths and weaknesses of this personality model.

- This 2024 Release includes more details about ways to support ethical values and practices.
- The discussion about how dark triad personality characteristics affect workplace behavior has been revised and streamlined.
- New OB Theory to Practice on how Hartford Financial Services Group supports ethical behavior.
- New chapter-opening vignette examines how job applicants pay attention to their personal values when assessing new employment opportunities.
- Revised factoid on the value of personal values at work.
- Revised factoid on ethics in the workplace.

Chapter 3: Perceiving Ourselves and Others in Organizations

- The attribution process topic has been revised to reflect how the three attribution rules are actually described in the original and subsequent scholarly literature. This 2024 Release also presents a new exhibit depicting how the three attribution rules operate.
- The section on improving perceptions revises and streamlines the limitations of awareness of perceptual biases. It also has a new subheading on the limitations and contingencies of self-awareness as a strategy to improve perceptions.
- Specific forms of perceptual organization are identified.
- The topic of stereotype threat has been updated to further clarify how this phenomenon operates.
- New OB Theory to Practice on being your authentic self at work.
- New chapter-opening vignette describes how FedEx executives may have engaged in the self-serving attribution error.
- Revised factoid on positive self-evaluation in the workplace.
- Revised factoid on first impressions in job applications.

Chapter 4: Workplace Emotions, Attitudes, and Stress

- This book pioneered the inclusion of emotions in several OB topics (perceptions, attitudes, motivation, decisions). This 2024 Release continues this development with minor rewriting about how people regulate their emotions.
- The EVLN model includes some rewriting on the meaning of voice and loyalty.
- The cognitive dissonance topic has some revision for better clarity.
- New in-text examples have been added, notably on the topics of emotional intelligence and the service profit chain model.
- New OB Theory to Practice on emotional intelligence training for law enforcement officers.
- New OB Theory to Practice on reducing stress through forest therapy.
- New chapter-opening vignette on how employees in several organizations have fun in the workplace.
- Revised factoid on stress in the workplace.

Chapter 5: Employee Motivation

- The two social job characteristics (social interaction requirement and social feedback) are more distinctly presented.
- The learned needs topic now briefly refers to the priming and self-concept effects.
- New chapter-opening vignette on how KKR and CGI motivate employees through an ownership culture.
- New factoid on the motivational potential of jobs.
- Revised factoid on how well (or poorly) companies motivate employees through performance-to-outcome expectancies.

Chapter 6: Decision Making and Creativity

- The topic of decision choice maximization now describes conditions in which decision paralysis is avoided or minimized when a large number of alternatives are presented.
- The employee involvement model now identifies five contingencies by distinguishing the two risks of potential conflict in that process.
- A few other topics have minor rewriting of content or examples, including problems with problem identification, problems with information processing, and the representativeness heuristic.
- New OB Theory to Practice on how Ubisoft supports creative thinking.
- Revised exhibit on employee involvement contingencies and outcomes.
- New chapter-opening vignette details the problem identification error at Ullrich Water Treatment Plant, which subsequently required residents in Austin, Texas, to boil their water for three days.
- Revised factoid on using intuition or data analysis in organizational decision making.
- Revised factoid on challenges to instilling creativity in organizations.

Chapter 7: Team Dynamics

- This book previously provided a substantial update about elements of team processes and team design. This 2024 Release continues this development with minor rewriting on team diversity, complementary team mental models, and improving team processes through team building.
- The self-directed teams topic includes new in-text examples along with minor rewriting.
- New OB Theory to Practice on how teams, particularly diverse teams, improve financial investment advice and broker research.
- New OB Theory to Practice on how Shopify supports remote teams through "hangouts" and "bursts."
- Revised OB Theory to Practice on proclamations by four organizations about the importance of teamwork.
- New chapter-opening vignette on how Norwegian law firm Advokatfirmaet Thommessen AS supports teamwork.
- Revised factoid on the importance of effective teamwork behaviors in college graduates and coworkers.

Chapter 8: Communicating in Teams and Organizations

- This book has been at the forefront of new research and practices on the rapid development of digital communication in the workplace. This 2024 Release continues that leadership with updated information and analysis of multiple digital channel trends over the past decade.
- The communication channels section has a new subtopic on digital nonverbal communication, which particularly looks at workplace communication using emojis.
- The section on communication channels has been significantly reorganized and conceptually updated.
- Several other updates and rewriting occur throughout this chapter, but particularly on social media in the workplace, influences on effective encoding and decoding, improving communication through workspace design, and problems with digital written communication.
- New OB Theory to Practice on the benefits and risks of emojis in workplace communication.
- New OB Theory to Practice on how companies are improving communicating efficiency and reducing "Zoom fatigue" by cancelling meetings and introducing "Async Weeks."
- New exhibit on body language miscommunication by job interviewers.
- Significantly updated exhibit on the changing use of digital communication channels among knowledge workers in organizations.
- New chapter-opening vignette describes how installing an enterprise communication platform helped CBI Health to become a more unified organization with improved communication and a stronger corporate culture.
- Revised factoid on the support and effectiveness of internal communication in organizations.

Chapter 9: Power and Influence in the Workplace

- The topic on the consequences of power provides more detail about the consequences of independent versus interdependent power.
- Two contingencies of power—visibility and discretion—have been rewritten with updated content and examples.
- The topics of impression management, the dark side of social networks, and organizational politics have received minor rewriting.
- New OB Theory to Practice on how a women's employee resource group at Franklin Electric supports networking and inclusion.
- New OB Theory to Practice on strategies for minimizing organizational politics.
- Substantially revised and updated OB Theory to Practice presents advice by career and marketing experts on developing your personal brand.
- New chapter-opening vignette in which several executives explain why and how employees should engage in upward influence (manage their boss).
- Revised factoid on dysfunctional influence through assertiveness.
- Revised factoid on the problems with office politics.

Chapter 10: Conflict and Negotiation in the Workplace

- The logical fallacy of argumentum ad hominem is described as a characteristics of relationship conflict.
- The section on task conflict and relationship conflict has minor rewriting to further clarify these approaches to conflict.
- The topics of differentiation (a source of conflict) and gathering information in negotiations have received minor rewriting and updating.
- New OB Theory to Practice on how interdependence and scarce resources fuel conflict in shared workspaces.
- New OB Theory to Practice on three ways to minimize conflict through casual encounters in the workplace.
- New chapter-opening vignette about conflict at sports apparel company Under Armour.
- Revised factoid on conflict episodes in the workplace.
- Revised factoid on the tendency of people to steer clear of (i.e., avoid) workplace conflict.
- Revised factoid on the effectiveness of managers as third-party conflict handlers.

Chapter 11: Leadership in Organizational Settings

- This 2024 Release revises the writing and content on task-oriented and people-oriented leadership, path–goal theory contingencies, and the leadership attributes of drive and integrity.
- New chapter-opening vignette presents Ceridian co-CEO Leagh Turner's observations about engaging in transformational versus managerial leadership.
- Revised factoid on how employees perceive and rate their managers.
- Revised factoid on how well (or poorly) organizational leaders present a clear, inspiring vision for the organization's future.
- Revised factoid on employee evaluations of the honesty and integrity of their organizational leaders.

Chapter 12: Designing Organizational Structures

- The topic of matrix organizational structures has been revised and updated, including a description of the matrix structure at Shiseido.

- The topic of coordination through informal communication has updated writing on liaison roles, concurrent engineering, and agile teams.
- Two topics in the section on departmentalization—simple structure and the current geographic divisional organizational structure at McDonald's—have been revised.
- New OB Theory to Practice describes how Airbnb became more effective by reverting to a functional structure from a divisional organizational structure.
- New exhibit depicts a simplified adaptation of the matrix organizational structure at Shiseido.
- Updated exhibit on recommended, actual, estimated, and enforced spans of control in specific companies or jurisdictions.
- Updated exhibit on the types of divisional organizational structure (specifically, a new company example for the geographic divisional structure).
- New chapter-opening vignette describes how Samsung is flattening its organizational structure to support greater creativity and agility.
- Revised factoid on the problem with coordination through micromanagement.

Chapter 13: Organizational Culture

- The attraction–selection–attrition topic has a new subtopic that describes and analyzes the recent debate about "culture fit" versus "culture add."
- The organizational socialization section more clearly delineates the four inherent conflicts between employers and job applicants when exchanging information during preemployment socialization.
- The organizational culture concept has been revised to include norms as an element of that concept.
- Several topics have minor revision of concepts and/or updating of examples, including the content of organizational culture, organizational language as an artifact of culture, organizational culture and business ethics, and strengthening culture through workforce stability and communication.
- New exhibit shows the four inherent conflicts between employers and job applicants during preemployment socialization.
- Revised exhibit on the elements and artifacts of organizational culture.
- New OB Theory to Practice describes the award-winning onboarding process developed at Singapore-based mobile network operator Circles.Life.
- New chapter-opening vignette explains why the founder of Bill.com appreciates the digital software company's subcultures, not just its dominant organizational culture.
- Revised factoid on the importance of organizational culture.
- Revised factoid on the corporate culture risks in mergers and acquisitions.
- Revised factoid highlights how much job applicants and employers pay attention to corporate culture fit during the hiring process.

Chapter 14: Organizational Change

- Negative valance of change as a source of resistance to change has been revised with examples and greater detail about that concept.
- The force field analysis model topic now notes that the unfreezing and refreezing metaphor was introduced after Kurt Lewin's original model.
- More detail and examples have been provided regarding ways to refreeze the desired conditions in the change process.
- New OB Theory to Practice describes how the CEO of Rotork Controls created an urgency for change and determined which employee groups would be most resistant to change.
- New chapter-opening vignette on how UK mobile network provider EE relied on communication to support organizational change.
- Revised factoid on employee and company readiness for organizational change.
- Revised factoid on the challenges of resistance to organizational change.

Digital Resources

Evergreen

Content and technology are ever-changing, and it is important that you can keep your course up to date with the latest information and assessments. That's why we want to deliver the most current and relevant content for your course, hassle-free.

McShane, *Organizational Behavior* is moving to an Evergreen delivery model, which means it has content, tools, and technology that is updated and relevant, with updates delivered directly to your existing McGraw Hill Connect® course. Engage students and freshen up assignments with up-to-date coverage of select topics and assessments, all without having to switch editions or build a new course.

Reflecting the Diverse World Around Us

McGraw Hill believes in unlocking the potential of every learner at every stage of life. To accomplish that, we are dedicated to creating products that reflect, and are accessible to, all the diverse, global customers we serve. Within McGraw Hill, we foster a culture of belonging, and we work with partners who share our commitment to equity, inclusion, and diversity in all forms. In McGraw Hill Higher Education, this includes, but is not limited to, the following:

- Refreshing and implementing inclusive content guidelines around topics including generalizations and stereotypes, gender, abilities/disabilities, race/ethnicity, sexual orientation, diversity of names, and age.
- Enhancing best practices in assessment creation to eliminate cultural, cognitive, and affective bias.
- Maintaining and continually updating a robust photo library of diverse images that reflect our student populations.

- Including more diverse voices in the development and review of our content.
- Strengthening art guidelines to improve accessibility by ensuring meaningful text and images are distinguishable and perceivable by users with limited color vision and moderately low vision.

Application-Based Activities in McGraw Hill Connect®

Prepare students for the real world with Application-Based Activities in Connect©. These highly interactive, assignable exercises boost engagement and provide a safe space to apply concepts learned to real-world, course-specific problems. Each Application-Based Activity involves the application of multiple concepts, providing the ability to synthesize information and use critical thinking skills to solve realistic scenarios.

ReadAnywhere® App

Read or study when it's convenient with McGraw Hill's free ReadAnywhere® app. Available for iOS and Android smartphones or tablets, give users access to McGraw Hill tools including the eBook and SmartBook® or Adaptive Learning Assignments in McGraw Hill Connect®. Students can take notes, highlight, and complete assignments offline—all their work will sync when connected to Wi-Fi. Students log in with their Connect© username and password to start learning—anytime, anywhere!

OLC-Aligned Courses

Implementing High-Quality Instruction and Assessment through Preconfigured Courseware

In consultation with the Online Learning Consortium (OLC) and our certified Faculty Consultants, McGraw Hill has created preconfigured courseware using OLC's quality scorecard to align with best practices in online course delivery. This turnkey courseware contains a combination of formative assessments, summative assessments, homework, and application activities, and can easily be customized to meet an individual instructor's needs and desired course outcomes. For more information, visit https://www.mheducation.com/highered/olc.

Polling

Every learner has unique needs. Uncover where and when you're needed with the new Polling tool in McGraw Hill Connect®! Polling allows you to discover where students are in real time. Engage students and help them create connections with your course content while gaining valuable insight during lectures. Leverage polling data to deliver personalized instruction when and where it is needed most.

Proctorio

Remote Proctoring & Browser-Locking Capabilities

Remote proctoring and browser-locking capabilities, hosted by Proctorio within Connect©, provide control of the assessment environment by enabling security options and verifying the identity of the student.

Seamlessly integrated within Connect, these services allow instructors to control the assessment experience by verifying identification, restricting browser activity, and monitoring student actions.

Instant and detailed reporting gives instructors an at-a-glance view of potential academic integrity concerns, thereby avoiding personal bias and supporting evidence-based claims.

Test Builder in Connect

Available within McGraw Hill Connect®, Test Builder is a cloud-based tool that enables instructors to format tests that can be printed, administered within a Learning Management System, or exported as a Word document. Test Builder offers a modern, streamlined interface for easy content configuration that matches course needs, without requiring a download.

Test Builder allows you to:

- access all test bank content from a particular title.
- easily pinpoint the most relevant content through robust filtering options.
- manipulate the order of questions or scramble questions and/or answers.
- pin questions to a specific location within a test.
- determine your preferred treatment of algorithmic questions.
- choose the layout and spacing.
- add instructions and configure default settings.

Test Builder provides a secure interface for better protection of content and allows for just-in-time updates to flow directly into assessments.

Writing Assignment

Available within McGraw Hill Connect®, the Writing Assignment tool delivers a learning experience to help students improve written communication skills and conceptual understanding. Assign, monitor, grade, and provide feedback on writing more efficiently and effectively.

Create

Your Book, Your Way

McGraw Hill's Content Collections Powered by Create® is a self-service website that enables instructors to create custom course materials—print and eBooks—by drawing upon McGraw Hill's comprehensive, cross-disciplinary content. Choose what you want from our high-quality textbooks, digital products, articles, cases, and more. Combine it with your own content quickly and easily, and tap into other rights-secured, third-party content such as cases, articles, readings, cartoons, and labs. Content can be arranged in a way that makes the most sense for your course, and you can select your own cover and include the course name and school information as well. Choose the best format for your course: color print, black-and-white print, or eBook. The eBook can be included in your Connect course and is available on the free ReadAnywhere® app for smartphone or tablet access as well. When you are finished customizing, you will receive a free digital copy to review in just minutes! Visit McGraw Hill Create®—www.mcgrawhillcreate.com—today and begin building!

McGraw Hill GO

McGraw Hill GO is an easy-to-use, quick-to-set-up eBook+ that lives within the LMS. GO equips instructors and students with essential course materials: trusted, assignable content and auto-graded chapter questions that sync directly into the LMS. GO makes it easier to keep up with progress and direct attention where it matters.

McGraw Hill connect®

A complete course platform

Connect enables you to build deeper connections with your students through cohesive digital content and tools, creating engaging learning experiences. We are committed to providing you with the right resources and tools to support all your students along their personal learning journeys.

65%

Less Time Grading

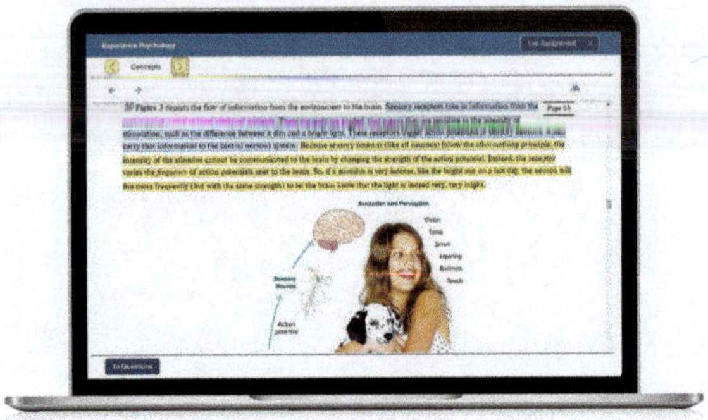

Laptop: Getty Images; Woman/dog: George Doyle/Getty Images

Every learner is unique

In Connect, instructors can assign an adaptive reading experience with SmartBook® 2.0. Rooted in advanced learning science principles, SmartBook 2.0 delivers each student a personalized experience, focusing students on their learning gaps, ensuring that the time they spend studying is time well spent. **mheducation.com/highered/connect/smartbook**

Study anytime, anywhere

Encourage your students to download the free ReadAnywhere® app so they can access their online eBook, SmartBook® 2.0, or Adaptive Learning Assignments when it's convenient, even when they're offline. And since the app automatically syncs with their Connect account, all of their work is available every time they open it. Find out more at **mheducation.com/readanywhere**

"I really liked this app—it made it easy to study when you don't have your text-book in front of you."

Jordan Cunningham, a student at *Eastern Washington University*

Effective tools for efficient studying

Connect is designed to help students be more productive with simple, flexible, intuitive tools that maximize study time and meet students' individual learning needs. Get learning that works for everyone with Connect.

SUPPORT AT every step

Education for all

McGraw Hill works directly with Accessibility Services departments and faculty to meet the learning needs of all students. Please contact your Accessibility Services Office, and ask them to email **accessibility@mheducation.com**, or visit **mheducation.com/about/accessibility** for more information.

Affordable solutions, added value

Make technology work for you with LMS integration for single sign-on access, mobile access to the digital textbook, and reports to quickly show you how each of your students is doing. And with our Inclusive Access program, you can provide all these tools at the lowest available market price to your students. Ask your McGraw Hill representative for more information.

Solutions for your challenges

A product isn't a solution. Real solutions are affordable, reliable, and come with training and ongoing support when you need it and how you want it. Visit **supportateverystep.com** for videos and resources both you and your students can use throughout the term.

Updated and relevant content

Our new Evergreen delivery model provides the most current and relevant content for your course, hassle-free. Content, tools, and technology updates are delivered directly to your existing McGraw Hill Connect® course. Engage students and freshen up assignments with up-to-date coverage of select topics and assessments, all without having to switch editions or build a new course.

PART 1

1 Introduction to the Field of Organizational Behavior

Ground Picture/Shutterstock

Learning Objectives

After reading this chapter, you should be able to:

LO1-1 Define organizational behavior and organizations.

LO1-2 Explain why organizational behavior knowledge is important for you and for organizations.

LO1-3 Describe the anchors on which organizational behavior knowledge is based.

LO1-4 Summarize the workplace trends of diversity, equity, and inclusion; work–life integration; and remote work.

LO1-5 Diagram the MARS model and describe the four factors that directly influence individual behavior and performance.

LO1-6 Summarize the five types of individual behavior in organizations.

organizational behavior (OB) The study of what people think, feel, and do in and around organizations

Soon after becoming rehired as CEO of Walt Disney Co., Bob Iger adopted a return-to-office (RTO) policy whereby employees must work on-site Monday through Thursday each week. Starbucks employees received similar news; those within commuting distance must work in the office three specific days each week. "Partners, it's time for us to come back to the office—to do this Mission-critical work face-to-face, and in person," urged CEO Howard Schultz.

The pandemic dramatically reconfigured how and where employees perform their work. Disney, Starbucks, and other businesses are now trying to manage how much—and whether—employees should work from home (WFH) rather than on-site. Disney's Bob Iger believes the company's RTO policy will boost creativity. "In a creative business like ours, nothing can replace the ability to connect, observe, and create with peers that comes from being physically together," he explains. Starbuck's Howard Schultz argues that RTO will improve team cohesion and strengthen the organization's culture. "While we have built transactive connection and on-screen skills through COVID, we have lost a true human connection. We need to rebuild that."

Companies that implement strict RTO policies face several challenges, however. Critics point out that the pro-RTO arguments either ignore the full spectrum of benefits and problems with remote versus in-person work, or are misaligned with the evidence. Another barrier is that 80 percent of remote-capable employees want and expect their employer to allow flexible hybrid work arrangements (i.e., employees can choose their remote and on-site schedule).

For example, most Apple employees say they are dissatisfied with the technology company's RTO policy requiring everyone to work on-site three designated days each week. Some high-profile staff have quit over the policy. And after 15 consecutive years as one of Glassdoor's 100 best companies to work for in America, Apple was recently dropped from the list. "In the last year for Apple, the return to office push has been met with mixed responses from employees," observes Glassdoor's lead economist.[1]

WELCOME TO THE FIELD OF ORGANIZATIONAL BEHAVIOR!

Remote work. Creativity. Team work and collaboration. Productivity. Organizational culture. Employee attitudes and turnover. These are just a few of the many organizational behavior topics related to the dramatic reconfiguration of how and where people perform work. In every sector of the economy, organizations need to employ skilled and motivated people who can be creative, work in teams, and maintain a healthy lifestyle. They need leaders with foresight and vision, who support innovative work practices, and who make decisions that consider the interests of multiple stakeholders. In other words, the best companies succeed through applying the concepts and practices that we discuss in this organizational behavior book.

Our purpose is to help you understand what goes on in organizations. We examine the factors that make companies effective, improve employee well-being, and drive successful collaboration among coworkers. We look at organizations from numerous and diverse perspectives, from the deepest foundations of employee thoughts and behavior (personality, self-concept, attitudes, etc.) to the complex interplay between the organization's structure, culture, and the external environment. Along this journey, we emphasize why things happen and what you can do to predict and guide organizational events.

We begin this chapter by introducing you to the field of organizational behavior (OB) and its historical origins. This is followed by details about why OB is important for your career and why organizations depend on OB knowledge to survive and thrive. An integrative model of organizational behavior is presented, which illustrates the interconnectedness of OB topics and serves as a road map to guide you through this book. We then describe the philosophical anchors that guide the development of organizational behavior knowledge. This is followed by an overview of three emerging features of the workplace environment: workplace diversity, equity, and inclusion; work-life integration; and remote work. The latter part of this chapter introduces the MARS model, which outlines the four direct drivers of individual behavior and performance. The final section identifies the five main types of individual behavior.

LO1-1 Define organizational behavior and organizations.

What Is Organizational Behavior?

Organizational behavior (OB) is the study of what people think, feel, and do in and around organizations. It looks at employee behaviors, decisions, perceptions, and emotions. It examines how individuals and teams in organizations interact with one another. OB also extends to the study of how organizations interact with their external environments, such as serving or collaborating with customers, suppliers, and communities. OB researchers systematically study these topics at multiple levels of analysis, namely, at the level of the individual, team (including interpersonal), and organization.[2]

The definition of organizational behavior begs the question: What are organizations? **Organizations** are groups of people who work interdependently toward some purpose.[3] Notice that organizations are not buildings or government-registered entities. In fact, many organizations exist with neither physical walls nor government documentation to confer their legal status.[4]

One key feature of all organizations is that they consist of human beings who interact with one another in an *organized* way.
Image Source

One key feature of all organizations is that they are collective entities.[5] They consist of human beings—typically, but not necessarily, employees—who interact with one another in an *organized* way. This organized relationship requires communication, coordination, and collaboration to achieve organizational objectives. As such, all organizational members have degrees of interdependence; they accomplish goals by sharing materials, information, or expertise with coworkers.

A second key feature of organizations is that their members have a collective sense of purpose. This collective purpose isn't always well defined or agreed upon. Companies typically have vision and mission statements, but they are sometimes out of date or don't describe what employees and leaders actually try to achieve. Still, some sense of collective purpose does exist, even if it is implicit or informally understood. Otherwise, an organization would be nothing more than an assemblage of people without direction or unifying force.

Although the field of OB has recent origins, experts in other fields have been studying organizations for many centuries. The Greek philosopher Plato (400 BC) philosophized about the essence of leadership, and the Chinese philosopher Confucius (500 BC) extolled the virtues of ethics and leadership. Economist Adam Smith (1700s) discussed the benefits of job specialization and division of labor. German sociologist Max Weber (early 1900s) wrote about rational organizations, the work ethic, and charismatic leadership. Around the same time, industrial engineer Frederick Winslow Taylor proposed systematic ways to organize work processes and motivate employees through goal setting and rewards.[8]

> A company is one of humanity's most amazing inventions . . . [It's] this abstract construct we've invented, and it's incredibly powerful.[6]
>
> —Steve Jobs, Apple and Pixar Animation Studios cofounder

Historical Foundations of Organizational Behavior

Organizational behavior emerged as a distinct field sometime around the early 1940s.[7] During that decade, a few researchers began describing their research as organizational (rather than sociological or psychological). And by the late 1940s, Harvard University had changed the name of its MBA human relations course to "Organizational Behavior."

Political scientist Mary Parker Follett (1920s) offered new ways of thinking about constructive conflict, team dynamics, power, and leadership. Throughout the 1930s and 1940s, Harvard professor Elton Mayo and his colleagues in the new "human relations" school of management pioneered research on employee attitudes, formal team dynamics, informal groups, and supervisor leadership style. Telecommunications executive and Harvard associate Chester Barnard (1930s) wrote insightful views regarding organizational communication, coordination, leadership and authority, organizations as open systems, and team dynamics.[9] This brief historical tour demonstrates that OB has been around for a long time; however, it wasn't organized into a unified discipline until around World War II.

organizations Groups of people who work interdependently toward some purpose

LO1-2 Explain why organizational behavior knowledge is important for you and for organizations.

WHY ORGANIZATIONAL BEHAVIOR IS IMPORTANT

You are likely reading this as part of a required course in organizational behavior. Apart from degree or diploma requirements, why should you learn the ideas and practices discussed in this book? After all, who ever heard of a career path leading to a "vice president of OB" or a "chief OB officer"? Our answer to this question comes in two parts: why OB is important for you personally and why OB is important for organizations generally.

Why OB Is Important for You

Throughout our careers teaching undergraduate, graduate, and executive programs, we (the authors of this book) have found that students with work experience identify organizational behavior as one of the most valued courses. Why? Because organizational behavior knowledge and skills are critical to everyone's career, and people become more aware of its value through work experience. Whether you are a sales professional, technical specialist, or senior executive, you need to make sound decisions, interact effectively with other people, understand social networks and power dynamics, and apply other OB concepts.[10]

The importance of organizational behavior is evident in numerous surveys that ask employers to identify the most important skills and knowledge they look for in new hires. Technical skills are important, of course, particularly for highly specialized jobs and professions. But the skills and knowledge that employers tend to rank above anything else are the topics found in this and other organizational behavior books.

Exhibit 1.1 lists the most important skills identified by employers in four recent major surveys. One of the top-ranked skills is problem solving (along with critical thinking and analytic skills), which relates to several OB topics, particularly decision making and perceptions. A second important skill for new hires is teamwork (as well as interpersonal skills). This book includes an entire chapter on team dynamics; the topic also relates to managing conflict, influencing others, managing emotions, and other themes. Communication is the third skill appearing on all four lists. Along with an entire chapter on communication, the topic is interwoven with influence, conflict management, leadership, organizational change, and other OB topics.

Other critical skills that employers look for in new hires are adaptability, work ethic, and resiliency. Adaptability is discussed later in this chapter as one of the three types of individual performance; it also connects with creativity, teamwork behavior, and organizational change. Work ethic refers to self-motivation as well as specific personality traits. Resiliency, the capacity to recover from setbacks, is discussed in the context of work-related stress. Overall, these and other surveys suggest that OB offers a core foundation of knowledge and skill development for your success in organizations.[11]

Better Personal Theories to Comprehend, Predict, and Influence Along with providing the specific knowledge and skills identified in these surveys, the field of organizational

Exhibit 1.1 Most Important Skills for New Hires

NACE Job Outlook Survey (United States)	QS Global Skills Gap Report (Global)	Business Council of Canada Skills Survey (Entry-level hires list)	Hays Soft Skills Employer Survey (Australia and New Zealand)
• Problem solving • Ability to work in a team • Strong work ethic • Analytic/ quantitative skills • Communication skills (written)	• Problem solving • Teamwork • Communication • Adaptability • Interpersonal skills	• Collaboration, teamwork, interpersonal skills • Communication skills • Problem-solving skills • Resiliency • Analytical capabilities	• Teamwork • Problem solving • Communication • Adaptability • Critical thinking

Sources: "The Global Skills Gap Report 2019" (London: QS Quacquarelli Symonds, September 2019); Morneau Shepell, "Investing in a Resilient Canadian Workforce: 2020 Business Council Skills Survey" (Ottawa: Business Council of Canada, August 2020); "The Unexpected Soft Skill Employers Need Today (Australia) (New Zealand)," Press release (Sydney: Hays, June 29, 2021); "Employers Seek Key Attributes on College Grads' Resumes as Their Focus on GPA Wanes," News Release (Bethlehem, PA: National Association of Colleges and Employers, November 2, 2022).

organizational effectiveness An ideal state in which an organization has a good fit with its external environment, effectively transforms inputs to outputs through human capital, and satisfies the needs of key stakeholders

open systems The view that organizations depend on the external environment for resources, affect that environment through their output, and consist of internal subsystems that transform inputs to outputs

human capital The knowledge, skills, abilities, creative thinking, and other valued resources that employees bring to the organization

Organizational behavior knowledge helps you to refine your personal theories, so you can understand, predict, and influence organizational events.
Chaay Tee/Shutterstock

behavior helps you to adopt better personal theories so you can more effectively comprehend, predict, and influence organizational events.[12] Comprehending and predicting workplace behavior is valuable because everyone has an inherent drive to make sense of the world around them. The personal theories individuals develop for this purpose are sometimes accurate, often overgeneralized, and occasionally wrong. Even some ideas that appear to be "common sense" may be inaccurate or oversimplified.[13] Through systematic research, the field of organizational behavior has developed theories that will help you to improve the accuracy of your personal theories.

Probably the greatest value of OB knowledge for you personally is to get things done by influencing others.[14] By definition, organizations are people who work together to accomplish work-related goals. A toolkit of OB knowledge and skills is therefore vital to motivate ourselves and coworkers, make better decisions, build effective teams, resolve workplace conflicts, and work successfully with others in a host of other ways. No matter what career path you choose, OB concepts play an enormously important role in helping you to work more effectively within organizations.

Organizational Behavior Is for Everyone You may have noticed that we haven't mentioned "managers" in this discussion on why OB is important for you. Effective management (and leadership) does depend on OB concepts and practices, but this book pioneered the broader view that OB is valuable for everyone who works in and around organizations. Whether you are a software engineer, customer service representative, foreign exchange analyst, or chief executive officer, you need to understand and apply organizational behavior topics that are discussed in this book. In fact, OB knowledge is probably more valuable than ever before because employees increasingly need to be proactive, self-motivated, and able to work effectively with coworkers without management intervention. In the words of one forward-thinking OB writer almost a half century ago: Everyone is a manager.[15]

Why OB Is Important for Organizations

Along with benefiting you as an individual, the field of organizational behavior is vital to the organization's survival and success.[16] For instance, the best 100 companies to work for in America (i.e., companies with the highest levels of employee satisfaction) enjoy significantly higher financial performance than other businesses within the same industry. Hospitals with higher levels of employee motivation (engagement) have lower inpatient mortality rates; other types of firms with motivated staff tend to have higher sales and profitability. Studies also report a positive relationship between the quality of leadership and the company's financial performance. Employee motivation, leadership, performance-based rewards, and other specific OB variables are also important "positive screens" for selecting companies with the highest and most consistent long-term investment returns.[17]

Almost all organizational behavior theories have the implicit or explicit objective of making organizations more effective.[18] In fact, **organizational effectiveness** is considered the "ultimate dependent variable" in organizational behavior.[19] Organizational performance, success, competitiveness, and excellence are variations or components of organizational effectiveness. Organizations are effective when they have a good fit with their external environment, effectively transform inputs to outputs through human capital, and satisfy the needs of key stakeholders.[20] Let's look at these elements to understand how OB knowledge improves organizational effectiveness.

Organizations as Open Systems One of the fundamental views in organizational behavior is that organizations are **open systems**.[21] This means that organizations are dependent on the external environment for resources (inputs), consist of internal subsystems that transform inputs to outputs, and affect the environment through those outputs (see Exhibit 1.2). The external environment includes the physical and social setting in which the organization operates. The word *open* describes this permeable relationship between the organization and its environment, whereas *closed systems* operate without dependence on or interaction with an external environment.

Inputs include raw materials, job applicants, financial funding, information, and equipment. The environment also

Exhibit 1.2 Organizations as Open Systems

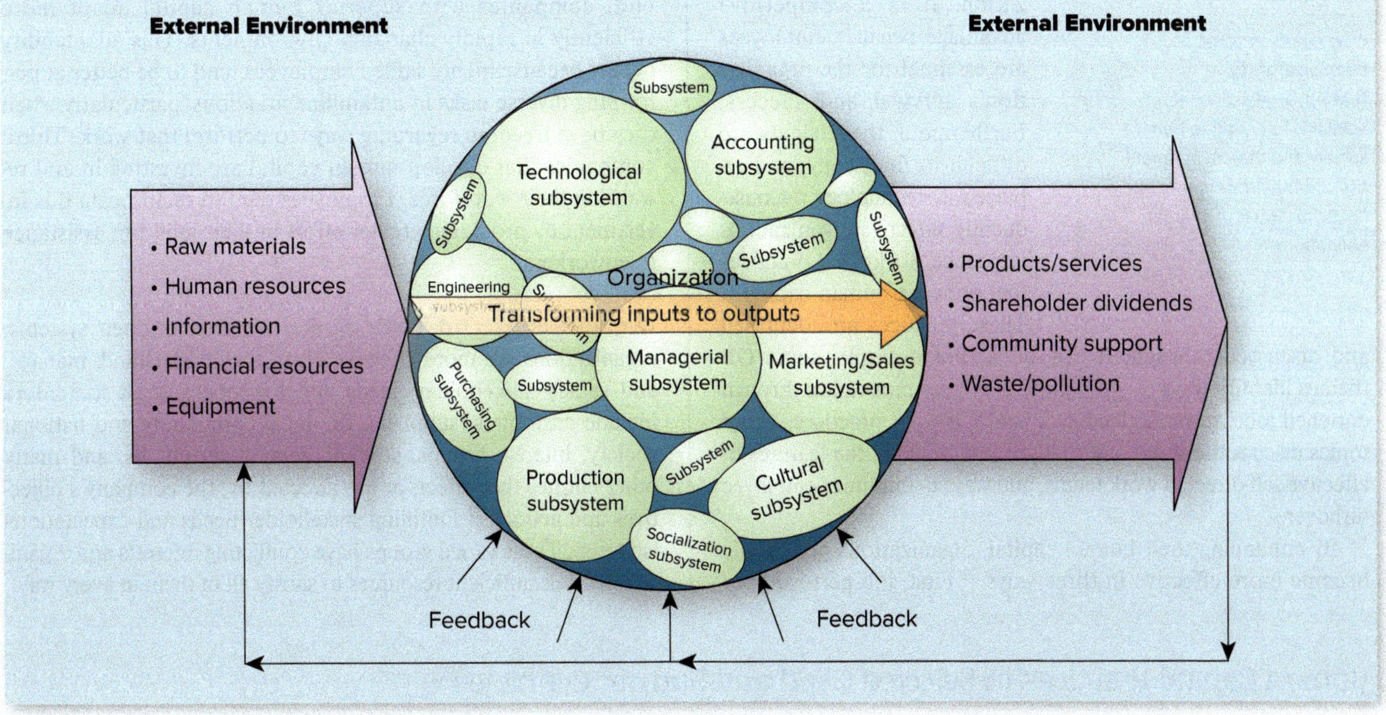

consists of laws, cultural norms, and other expectations that place demands on how organizations should operate. Organizations transform inputs to outputs through internal subsystems. Furthermore, they depend on the external environment to receive outputs created throughout the transformation process. Some outputs (e.g., products and services) may be valued by the external environment; other outputs (e.g., employee layoffs, pollution) are undesirable by-products. Organizations also receive feedback from the external environment regarding the value of their outputs, the availability of future inputs, and the appropriateness of the transformation process.

As open systems, organizations are effective when they maintain a good "fit" with their external environment.
Palto/iStock/Getty Images

The open systems view points to two ways that OB knowledge supports organizational effectiveness. First, it helps the organization to maintain a good "fit" with the external environment.[22] A good fit exists when the organization's inputs, processes, and outputs are aligned with the resources available in the external environment and with the needs and expectations of that environment. Several OB topics discuss the organization's fit or alignment with the external environment. For example, we discuss how specific organizational structures, organizational cultures, and leadership behaviors are more appropriate for some environments than for others.

Second, OB theories identify ways for companies to develop and maintain effective transformation processes. Organizations consist of numerous subsystems (departments, teams, technological processes, etc.) that transform the incoming resources into outputs. OB theories offer guidance on this matter, such as how internal subsystems coordinate with one another.[23] For instance, we discuss the conditions for teams to perform effectively, how employees influence each other, and how successful companies improve coordination through a strong organizational culture.

Human Capital as the Organization's Competitive Advantage Human capital is the most important ingredient in the organization's process of transforming inputs to outputs. **Human capital** refers to the knowledge, skills, abilities, creativity,

stakeholders Individuals, groups, and other entities that affect, or are affected by, the organization's objectives and actions

corporate social responsibility (CSR) Organizational activities intended to benefit society and the environment beyond the firm's immediate financial interests or legal obligations

and other valued resources that employees bring to the organization. It is a competitive advantage because employees are essential for the organization's survival and success. Furthermore, their talents are difficult to find, copy, and replace with technology.[24] Consequently, effective organizations introduce workplace practices that enhance human capital.[25]

These practices are identified and discussed throughout this book. For example, some OB themes identify ways to strengthen employee motivation through enriched jobs, rewards, feedback, and fair work practices. Other topics discuss the value of employee involvement, the features of effective self-directed work teams, and ways to minimize employee turnover.

By enhancing their human capital, organizations potentially become more effective in three ways.[26] First, job performance tends to improve as employees acquire more skills and knowledge, which, in turn, improves the organization's success. Second, companies with superior human capital adapt more efficiently in rapidly changing environments. This adaptability occurs because highly skilled employees tend to be better at performing diverse tasks in unfamiliar situations, particularly when they have freedom regarding ways to perform that work. Third, companies that develop human capital are investing in and rewarding their workforce. Employees tend to reciprocate this investment by providing greater effort in their jobs and assistance to coworkers.

Organizations and Their Stakeholders As open systems, organizations are more effective when they understand, manage, and satisfy stakeholder needs and expectations. **Stakeholders** include customers, suppliers, the local community and national society, interest groups, stockholders, governments, and many other entities that affect, or are affected by, the company's objectives and actions.[27] Fulfilling stakeholder needs and expectations isn't easy. These varied groups have conflicting interests and organizations lack sufficient resources to satisfy all of them in every way.

Human Capital Practices in Selected OECD and Partner Countries[28]

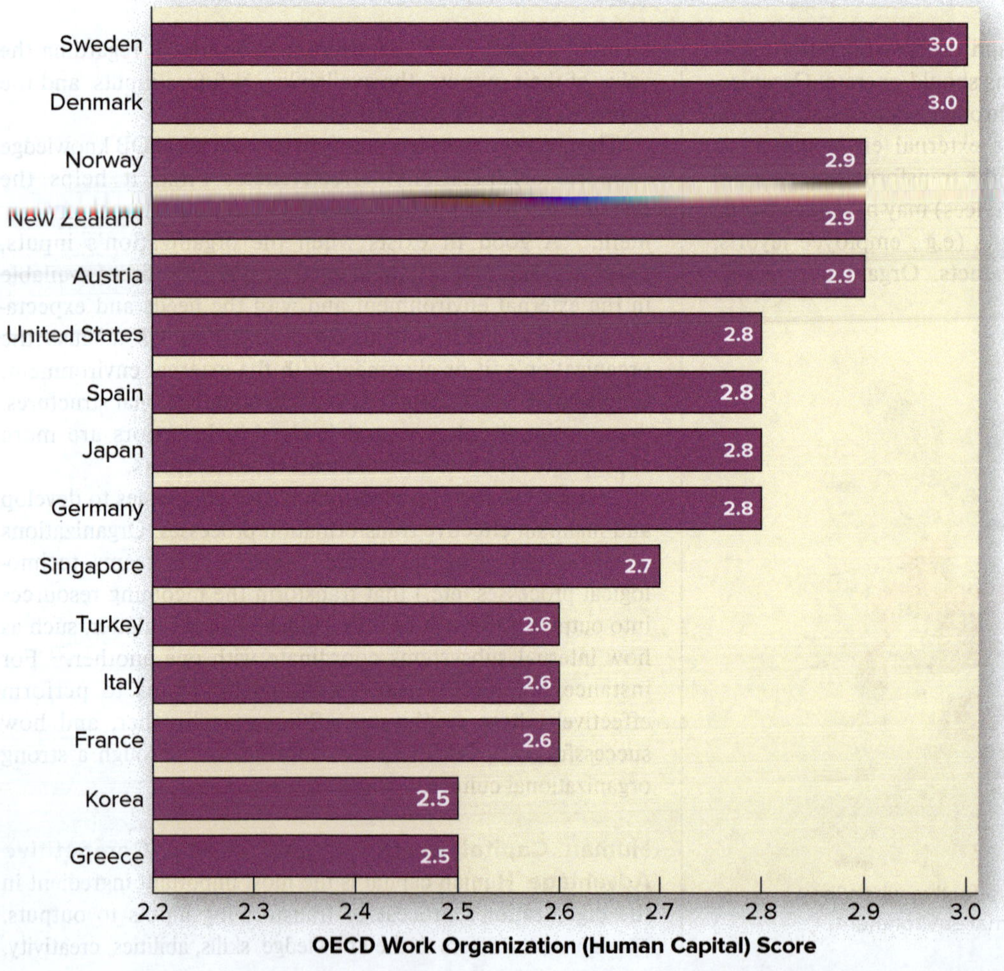

Average composite score on work organization (human capital) practices reported by employees in selected countries. Higher scores indicate a higher incidence of human capital practices in that country. This scale represents "work organization" practices, which exclude rewards but include work flexibility/autonomy, planning one's own work, cooperating and sharing information with coworkers, and training others. Data were collected from more than 215,000 adults in OECD and partner countries with a minimum 4,000 respondents per country. This chart shows a subset of the 34 countries measured in the study.

Several organizational behavior topics provide guidance to maintain favorable stakeholder relations.[29] In particular, OB research has identified several factors that influence the prioritization of stakeholders, including stakeholder power, how executives perceive the organization's environment, the organization's culture, and the personal values of the corporate board and executive team.

> Corporate social responsibility applies the triple bottom line; organizations strive to be financially successful as well as to improve society and the environment.

One topic that is closely aligned with stakeholders is corporate social responsibility. **Corporate social responsibility (CSR)** consists of organizational activities intended to benefit society and the environment beyond the firm's immediate financial interests or legal obligations.[30] It is the view that companies have a contract with society, in which they must serve stakeholders beyond stockholders and customers. This is known as the triple-bottom-line philosophy. Firms that adopt the triple bottom line aim to survive and be profitable in the marketplace (economic), but they also intend to maintain or improve conditions for society (social) as well as the physical environment. Companies with a positive CSR reputation tend to have better financial performance, more loyal employees, and better relations with customers, job applicants, and other stakeholders.[31]

Connecting the Dots: An Integrative Model of Organizational Behavior

So far, we have explained how organizational behavior benefits you as well as the organization. This discussion also reveals that OB is a diverse and interconnected field of knowledge. Exhibit 1.3 is an integrative road map to help you navigate the various organizational behavior topics throughout this book. It is a meta-model—a model that connects more specific OB models and concepts. As such, this exhibit gives you a bird's-eye view of the book and its various topics, so you can more easily see how they fit together.

As Exhibit 1.3 illustrates, individual inputs and processes influence individual outcomes, which, in turn, have a direct influence on the organization's effectiveness. For example, how well organizations transform inputs to outputs and satisfy key stakeholders is dependent on how well employees perform their jobs and make logical and creative decisions. Individual inputs, processes, and outcomes are identified in the two left-side boxes of our integrative OB model and are the center of attention in Part 2 of this book. We will learn about personality and values—two important individual characteristics—and later examine self-concept, perceptions, emotions, attitudes, and motivation.

Exhibit 1.3 An Integrative Model of Organizational Behavior

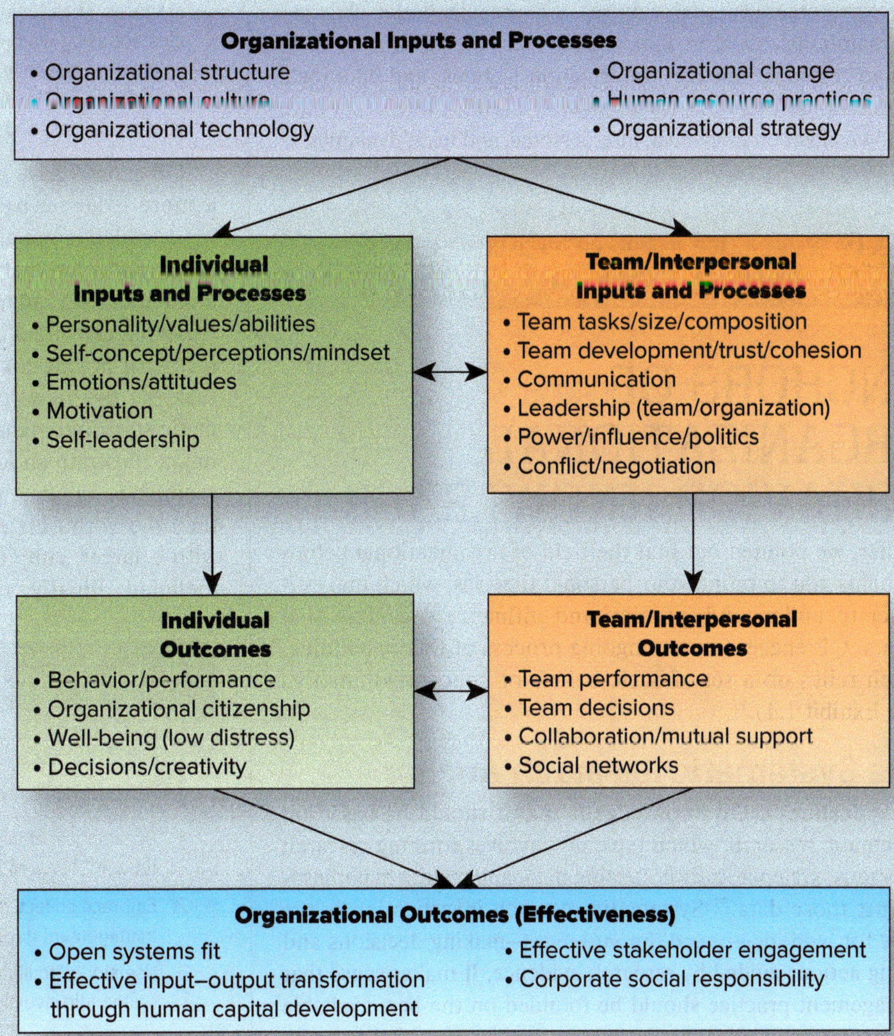

evidence-based management The practice of making decisions and taking actions based on research evidence

Part 3 of this book directs our attention to team and interpersonal inputs, processes, and outcomes. These topics are found in the two boxes on the right side of Exhibit 1.3. The chapter on team dynamics (Chapter 7) offers an integrative model showing that team inputs influence team processes, which then affect team performance and other outcomes. Later chapters in Part 3 examine specific interpersonal and team processes listed in Exhibit 1.3, including communication, power and influence, conflict, and leadership.

Exhibit 1.3 illustrates that team processes and outcomes affect individual processes and outcomes. As an example, an individual's personal well-being is partly affected by the mutual support received from team members and other coworkers. The opposite is also true; individual processes affect team and interpersonal dynamics in organizations. For instance, self-concept among individual team members influences the team's cohesion.

The top area of Exhibit 1.3 highlights the macro-level influence of organizational inputs and processes on both teams and individuals. These organizational-level variables—including organizational structure, organizational culture, and organizational change—are mainly discussed in Part 4. However, we will also refer to human resource practices, information systems, and additional organizational-level variables throughout this book where they have a known effect on individual, interpersonal, and team dynamics.

LO1-3 Describe the anchors on which organizational behavior knowledge is based.

ANCHORS OF ORGANIZATIONAL BEHAVIOR KNOWLEDGE

Earlier, we pointed out that the field of organizational behavior helps you to refine your personal theories, which makes it easier to understand, predict, and influence organizational events. OB engages in an ongoing process of theory-building, which relies on a set of basic beliefs or conceptual anchors (see Exhibit 1.4).[32]

The Systematic Research Anchor

A key feature of OB knowledge is that it should be based on systematic research, which typically involves forming research questions, systematically collecting data, and testing hypotheses against those data.[33] Systematic research investigation is the basis for **evidence-based management**—making decisions and taking actions guided by research evidence. It makes sense that management practice should be founded on the best available systematic knowledge, yet corporate leaders often fail to make evidence-based decisions.[34]

Here are several explanations why organizations fail to apply evidence-based management:[35]

1. Organizational decision makers are bombarded with ideas from consultant reports, guru websites, and other sources that are popular, visually appealing, and accessible. In contrast, most OB research is found in relatively obscure journal articles that have restricted access and, consequently, low readership.
2. Management fads often gain public attention because their sources are rewarded for being persuasive, not for having a strong evidence-based foundation. In contrast, OB researchers are usually rewarded for carefully testing the validity of their theories, not for convincing the public that their research findings are important.
3. Organizational decision makers sometimes ignore or dismiss evidence-based knowledge that contradicts their preconceived beliefs. This problem is caused by perceptual errors and decision-making biases that we discuss in this book.
4. Good OB research is necessarily generic rather than relevant to a specific situation or industry. Leaders therefore have the difficult task of figuring out which theories are relevant to their unique situation.
5. Leaders often exhibit herd mentality when choosing new organizational practices. They tend to embrace ideas that their peers at other companies are using even when those trendy practices lack evidence of their validity or relevance. Following the herd gives decision makers more confidence in the fad and that their reputation is protected if the intervention falls short of expectations.

OB experts have proposed a few simple suggestions to create a more evidence-based organization.[36] First, be skeptical of hype, which is apparent when so-called experts say the idea is "new," "revolutionary," and "proven." In reality, most management ideas are adaptations, evolutionary, and never proven (research can either disprove or provide evidential support for a theory or practice; it can't make something "proven"). Second, seek out the views of several expert sources, not lone charismatic stars and management gurus. Third, an example or story might illustrate an idea, but it does not validate that idea. An example is one data point, which could be the exception rather than the norm. Instead, rely on more systematic investigation with a larger sample, preferably with some quantitative data included. Finally, resist the temptation to engage in herd

OB THEORY TO PRACTICE

Creating an Evidence-Based Management Organization

1. Be skeptical of hyped management practices ("new," "revolutionary," "proven").
2. Embrace collective expertise, not lone charismatic stars or management gurus.
3. Use stories to illustrate, not as evidence; instead, rely on systematic investigation.
4. Avoid engaging in herd behavior with popular trends and ideologies.

Exhibit 1.4 Anchors of Organizational Behavior Knowledge

Systematic research anchor	Study organizations using systematic research methods
Practical orientation anchor	Ensure that OB theories are useful in organizations
Multidisciplinary anchor	Import knowledge from other disciplines, not just create its own knowledge
Contingency anchor	Recognize that the effectiveness of an action may depend on the situation
Multiple levels of analysis anchor	Understand OB events from three levels of analysis: individual, team, organization

behavior. People with clearer and more confident self-concepts are less likely to follow the herd. Herd behavior is also minimized by involving other people with diverse backgrounds in the decision or project.

The Practical Orientation Anchor

OB theories are interesting, but they also need to be useful in practice, whether for executive teams or for the rest of us in everyday work activities.[37] This is consistent with our statement earlier in this chapter that almost all organizational behavior theories have the implicit or explicit objective of making organizations more effective. The true "impact" of an OB theory is how well it finds its way into organizational life and becomes a valuable asset for improving the organization's effectiveness. OB theories offer specific advice on how to energize employees, improve customer service through employee attitudes, create more effective teams, determine the best communication channel for a specific situation, build a strong corporate culture, determine when to involve others in your decisions, handle conflict effectively, and so forth. After reading this book, you will have a toolkit of theories that are not only interesting; they also have practical value in organizations and elsewhere.

The Multidisciplinary Anchor

Another organizational behavior anchor is that the field should welcome theories and knowledge from other disciplines, not just from its own isolated research base. For instance, psychological research has aided our understanding of individual and interpersonal behavior. Sociologists have contributed to our knowledge of team dynamics, organizational socialization, organizational power, and other aspects of the social system. OB knowledge has also benefited from knowledge in newer fields such as communications, marketing, and information systems.

This practice of borrowing theories from other disciplines is inevitable. Organizations have central roles in society, so they are studied in many social sciences.[38] Furthermore, organizations consist of people who interact with one another, so there is an inherent intersection between OB and most disciplines that study human beings. However, by relying too much on theories developed in other fields, OB faces the risk of lagging rather than leading in knowledge production. In contrast, OB-bred theories allow researchers to concentrate on the quality and usefulness of the theory and be the first to understand and apply that knowledge.[39]

The Contingency Anchor

OB research embraces the contingency anchor: the effect of one variable on another variable often depends on the characteristics of the situation or people involved. The workplace and its inhabitants are complex, so a particular action may have different consequences under different conditions. An action rarely has the same outcome in every situation.[40] Contingencies are identified in many OB theories. For example, later in this chapter we discuss how the success of remote work depends on specific characteristics of the employee, job, and organization. Of course, it would be so much simpler if we could rely on "one best way" theories, in which a particular concept or practice has the same results in every situation. OB experts do try to keep theories as simple as possible, but most theories need to apply the contingency anchor.

People and their work environments are complex, so a particular action may have different consequences under different conditions (the contingency anchor).
Elnur/Shutterstock

surface-level diversity The observable demographic or physiological differences in people, such as their race, ethnicity, biological sex, age, and physical disabilities

deep-level diversity Differences in the psychological characteristics of employees, including personalities, beliefs, values, and attitudes

inclusive workplace A workplace that values people of all identities and allows them to be fully themselves while contributing to the organization

The Multiple Levels of Analysis Anchor

Organizational behavior recognizes that what goes on in organizations can be placed into three levels of analysis: individual, team (including interpersonal), and organization. In fact, advanced empirical research carefully identifies the appropriate level of analysis for each variable in the study and then measures at that level of analysis. For example, team norms and cohesion are measured as team variables, not as characteristics of individuals within each team.

Although OB research and writing pegs each variable within one of these levels of analysis, most variables are understood best by thinking of them from all three levels of analysis.[41] Communication is located in this book as a team (interpersonal) process, for instance, but it also includes individual and organizational processes. Therefore, you should try to think about each OB topic at the individual, team, and organizational levels, not just at one of these levels.

LO1-4 Summarize the workplace trends of diversity, equity, and inclusion; work–life integration; and remote work.

THE EMERGING WORKPLACE LANDSCAPE

Organizations are experiencing unprecedented change. Rapid and disruptive technological developments, changing workforce characteristics and expectations, global competition, and many other factors have substantially altered business strategy and everyday workplace activities. The field of organizational behavior plays a vital role in guiding organizations through this continuous turbulence. In this section, we look at three emerging workplace developments: diversity, equity, and inclusion (DEI); work–life integration; and remote work.

Workplace Diversity, Equity, and Inclusion (DEI)

An important feature of successful organizations is that they continuously strive for DEI. *Diversity* refers to heterogeneity of the organization's workforce. Most people initially think about **surface-level diversity**, that is, the observable demographic and other overt differences among members of a group, such as their race, ethnicity, biological sex, age, and physical capabilities.[42] Surface-level diversity in the United States and many other countries has increased substantially over the past few decades.

However, workforce diversity also exists in psychological characteristics, including personalities, beliefs, values, and attitudes.[43] We can't directly see this **deep-level diversity**, but it is evident in a person's words, decisions, and actions. Some deep-level diversity is associated with surface-level attributes. For example, males and females tend to have somewhat different preferences regarding conflict-handling styles, ethical principles, and approaches to communicating with other people in various situations.

An **inclusive workplace**, another component of DEI, refers to how well the organization values diversity and allows people of all identities to be fully themselves while contributing to the organization.[44] At the individual level, an inclusive workplace enables people of all backgrounds to feel psychologically safe, engaged, valued, authentic, listened to, and respected. At a collective level, an inclusive workplace gives diverse groups voice through formal structures as well as everyday processes, such as representation in teams and casual gatherings. It also continually assesses recruitment, rewards, social and information networks, and other organizational systems to ensure that they do not inappropriately favor some groups over others. An inclusive workplace is essential for maintaining a diverse workforce because it is inherently more receptive to and supportive of people with different surface- and deep-level characteristics.

Employee resource groups (ERGs, also called affinity groups) are increasingly popular and successful formal structures for supporting workplace inclusion. ERGs represent many ethnicities, sexual orientations, ages, abilities, and other identities and interests among employees within the organization. These voluntary employee-led groups provide support and education about diversity, equity, inclusion, and social issues. They are also an ongoing conduit of feedback and advice to the company's leadership regarding organizational policies and practices.[45]

One other component of DEI is *equity,* which is about treating everyone fairly. But more correctly, DEI is about *organizational justice* (not just equity), as we will discuss fully in Chapter 5. Organizational justice takes many forms. It involves applying appropriate rules to decide how the organization's benefits (e.g., rewarding employees) and burdens (e.g., workload) are distributed to employees. It includes how well the organization applies appropriate procedural rules when making these decisions, such as being consistent, neutral, and receptive to information from employees. Organizational justice also includes treating employees politely, respectfully, and honestly.

Diversity, equity, and inclusion have become prominent topics because they offer significant benefits for the organization and its employees.[46] Teams with high informational diversity (members have different knowledge and skills) tend to be more creative and make better decisions compared to teams with less informational diversity. A workforce with surface-level and deep-level diversity is also more representative of most communities, so companies are better able to recognize and address the

OB THEORY TO PRACTICE

Supporting Diversity, Equity, and Inclusion (DEI) at RingCentral

The people at RingCentral recognize that workforce diversity requires much more than hiring people from different backgrounds. "Companies need to focus on fostering inclusion—finding ways for all employees to have their voices heard and grow more opportunities for diversity at all levels of the organization," explains Jedd Ong, diversity program manager at the Silicon Valley provider of cloud-based communications and collaboration for businesses.

RingCentral supports diversity, equity, and inclusion (DEI) in many ways. It actively hires people who are both collaborative and cosmopolitan. It encourages employees to participate in volunteer activities that help diverse groups in the community. RingCentral's inclusive culture is also anchored in its employee resource groups, employee-led structures that provide support, networking, and education about diversity, equity, and inclusion. A few of these have definable titles, such as The Rainbow Room (LGBTQ), BE@R (Black Employees at RingCentral), HUGS (Help & Understanding Group Support), and EnviRingmentalists.

RingCentral points to its DEI culture and practices as a competitive advantage. DEI helps the telecommunications firm to more effectively understand and connect with its global clients. "We're committed to developing an inclusive workforce, ensuring our employees are as diverse as the customers we serve," the company states in its annual impact report. The company's inclusive culture also amplifies its creative potential. "If you have people of different backgrounds and different experiences, they come to the table with new ideas," says Evie Goldstein, senior UX content designer on RingCentral's innovation team.

Hero Images Inc./Alamy Stock Photo

> **The many benefits of an inclusive workplace depend on leadership, team structure, psychological safety norms, and employees' personal values.**

needs of customers, suppliers, future employees, and other stakeholders. However, the many benefits of a diverse and inclusive workplace are contingent on several factors, such as leadership, team structure, psychological safety norms, and employees' personal values.[47]

Diversity also poses a few challenges.[48] Employees with diverse backgrounds usually take longer to perform together effectively due to slower development of fluid communication, coordination, and cooperation (see Chapter 7). Some forms of diversity also increase the risk of dysfunctional conflict, which reduces information sharing and satisfaction with coworkers (see Chapter 10). These issues sometimes produce a curvilinear relationship between team diversity and performance. For example, one study reported that innovation performance in research teams increased with employees' cross-national geographic diversity, but only up to a point; teams with very high geographic diversity had lower performance.

Overall, diversity, equity, and inclusion are competitive advantages for organizations, particularly when the potential challenges are managed. In addition, companies that apply DEI practices are, in essence, striving to be more ethical. They also nurture a culture of respect that, in turn, improves cooperation and coordination among employees and increases their job satisfaction and organizational commitment. DEI also improves the quality of hiring and promotion, which provides a higher level of human capital.

Work–Life Integration

Before the digital age, most employees would finish work after eight or nine hours at the office or factory and could separate their personal time from their employment. Few people had complete separation of these roles, of course. Employees either brought paperwork home or thought about workplace issues long after their official work day had ended. Even so, the past is a stark contrast to the situation today in which information technology tethers a large percentage of employees to work on a 24/7 schedule. Globalization has contributed to this blending of work and nonwork because employees need to be "on-call" with coworkers, suppliers, and clients who live in different time zones around the planet.

Work–life integration occurs by satisfying the demands and experiencing the positive emotions of our multiple roles, which are inherently integrated because the resources generated and consumed by one role enhance or starve other roles.
Chaponta/Shutterstock

Little wonder that one feature employees value in a job is the ability to manage work-life integration.[49] **Work–life integration** refers to the degree that people are effectively engaged in their various work and nonwork roles and have a low degree of role conflict across those life domains.[50] This phrase has replaced *work-life balance,* which incorrectly implies that work and nonwork roles are completely separate and opposing partitions (like a balance of a scale). "There is no such thing as work-life balance," says Lisa Sterling, executive vice president and chief people officer at Perceptyx, which provides employee surveys and people analytics. "You've got to get to a point at which work and life integrate, and you figure out organizationally and individually how to make those two things work together."[51]

To understand work-life integration, consider that each of us has multiple roles and associated self-concepts, such as accountant, parent, friend, manager, and sports fan (see Chapter 3). Work-life integration occurs by satisfying the demands and experiencing the positive emotions of our various segments of life. These roles are inherently integrated because the resources generated and consumed by one role enhance or starve other roles.[52] People with a fulfilling home life, for example, develop social support, positive moods, relaxation, and other resources that can enrich their work and other roles. Similarly, the resources gained at work—such as new skills, financial rewards, and feelings of success—contribute to home and other nonwork roles.

Unfortunately, many people don't experience resource enrichment across roles. Instead, the heavy demands of one role deplete personal resources, which starve other roles. Employees who spend most waking hours performing or thinking about their job—whether at the workplace, at home, or on vacation—have insufficient time and energy remaining for other aspects of their lives. They experience what is widely known as *work-life conflict.* In short, a person's work roles and nonwork roles are inherently integrated because the physical, cognitive, and emotional resources produced or consumed by one role potentially enrich or undermine the success and enjoyment of other roles.

Practicing Work–Life Integration How do individuals and organizations maximize work-life integration?[53] One strategy is to literally integrate two or more roles. An increasingly popular trend is to conduct meetings during an exercise walk. Some companies encourage staff to bring their dogs to work, which is both comforting and requires an occasional break to walk the four-legged friend. On-site child care is a form of integration because it allows employees to switch from work to parent roles

OB THEORY TO PRACTICE

Strategies to Improve Work–Life Integration

Work–Life Integration Strategy	Description	Example
Integrate multiple roles	Find ways to perform work and nonwork activities simultaneously or proximally.	Have a meeting with a coworker while doing exercise that allows conversation (e.g., walking).
Flexible work scheduling	Establish work (and nonwork) roles that allow work time to have variable time frames.	Seek jobs and companies that allow you to vary your start and finish times as well as work remotely on some days.
Align roles with personal attributes	Choose work and nonwork roles that are sufficiently compatible with each other and with your personality and values.	Assess your personality and values, then choose work and life activities that are compatible with those personal attributes.
Boundary management	Establish methods that prevent your work roles from encroaching on time and attention devoted to your nonwork roles.	1. Schedule time blocks. 2. Create physical role spaces. 3. Apply technological boundaries. 4. Communicate role boundary expectations.

throughout the day. These integration efforts are not always effective, but they illustrate that blending work and nonwork roles is more viable than we previously understood.

A second work-life integration strategy occurs through flexible work scheduling.[54] For instance, you might remotely attend a meeting from home in the evening with coworkers who live in other time zones, then arrive at work late the next morning after doing a few household chores. Companies that have introduced return-to-office (RTO) policies, as the opening of this chapter described, restrict this form of work-life integration. This restriction partly explains why the majority of employees who can work from home oppose RTO policies. Organizations also have parental and other personal leave benefits to support higher demands at home in the short term.

A third work-life integration strategy is to ensure that your various work and nonwork roles are sufficiently compatible with each other and with your personal characteristics. In other words, your job, family life, sports activities, and so forth should align with your personality and values and have some similarity to each other. This relates to self-concept consistency, which we discuss in Chapter 3.

Although work is integrated with other life roles, a fourth strategy is to engage in some degree of "boundary management" across those roles. Here are four types of boundary management to support work-life integration:[55]

1. *Scheduling time blocks.* A common boundary management tactic is actively blocking out time for work versus other life roles. For example, some people strictly end their work day at a specific hour, and they set aside specific blocks of time each week to engage in family, leisure, fitness, and other nonwork events. A few companies support this tactic by closing offices and shutting down work-related resources.
2. *Creating physical role spaces.* This involves assigning specific physical locations to specific roles. Some people perform work only at the office, and rarely bring work materials home. Employees who routinely work at home might have a dedicated "home office" and limit interruptions from family and other nonwork sources in that space. Physical locations are usually designed to facilitate the role (desk, equipment, etc.), but they also create a "mental fence" to separate that role from other roles.
3. *Applying technological boundaries.* Technologies often blur work and nonwork boundaries, but they can also manage those boundaries. Employee shut off work-related devices during nonwork hours. Digital calendars distinguish work from nonwork events, so work notifications are turned off during nonwork hours. Some governments have assisted technological boundary management by passing legislation (France) or creating an employment code of practice (Ireland) giving employees the right to ignore company messages after regular work hours (called the "right to disconnect").
4. *Communicating role boundary expectations.* This involves advising others of role-related boundaries, such as by activating automated phone and digital messages to signal that the individual is away for a set time. Several organizations and a few governments (e.g., Portugal) support this form of boundary management by prohibiting work-related communication (except in extreme emergencies) after the regular workday.

> I never wrote anything in the office—too many distractions.[57]
>
> —David Ogilvy, founder of Ogilvy, known as the "Father of Advertising"

work–life integration The degree that people are effectively engaged in their various work and nonwork roles and have a low degree of role conflict across those life domains

remote work Any arrangement whereby an individual performs organizational tasks while located away from the employer's physical premises, usually connected through various forms of information technology

Remote Work

Another significant workplace transformation in recent years has been the increasing number of people and amount of time working remotely. **Remote work** is any arrangement whereby an individual performs organizational tasks while located away from the employer's physical premises. Approximately half of the American workforce is employed in remote-capable jobs—their work can be performed away from the employer's site. Remote employees are rarely isolated; they are typically connected through various forms of digital technology to coworkers, clients, and the company's systems. The most common form of remote work is working from home (WFH), formerly known as *telecommuting* or *teleworking.* However, some people are digital nomads; they work while traveling (or travel while working) throughout the world.[56]

Before the COVID-19 pandemic, a small percentage of American employees in remote-capable jobs performed WFH one or more days each week. Estimates vary, but early in the pandemic about 60 percent of the workforce and almost all remote-capable employees in the United States and many other countries worked remotely most of the time. As the pandemic waned, fewer of these employees were fully remote, while on-site and hybrid work arrangements increased. *Hybrid work* refers to working remotely at some times and at the company's premises at other times. Some companies, such as Automattic, GitLab, Emsisoft, and Sonatype have a completely remote workforce. These *distributed organizations* have no physical premises. Instead, they recruit, train, support, retain, and lead employees who rarely (if ever) meet in person.

This chapter opened by describing organizations that have imposed return-to-office (RTO) policies. These mandates will further reduce the degree of remote work, but most RTO policies continue to support hybrid work arrangements. One large survey estimates that about one-fifth of remote-capable employees in the United States currently work remotely almost all the time, slightly more than half have hybrid work arrangements, and one-quarter perform work on-site at all times.[58]

Exhibit 1.5 Potential Benefits and Risks of Remote Working

Potential Benefits	Potential Risks
• Better employee work–life integration • Attractive benefit for job applicants • Low employee turnover • Higher employee productivity • Reduced greenhouse gas emissions • Reduced corporate real estate and office costs	• More social isolation • Lower team cohesion • Weaker organizational culture • Higher stress due to home space and roles

Remote Work Benefits and Risks The opening vignette to this chapter highlighted the fact that remote work remains a contentious practice, particularly among some corporate leaders. This is because remote work presents both benefits and risks for organizations as well as remote workers (see Exhibit 1.5).[59] Several contingencies also enhance and undermine its effectiveness. One benefit is that remote workers usually experience better work–life integration because they have more time (no commuting time) and somewhat more control to juggle work with nonwork obligations. Work–life integration is more difficult, however, when employees lack sufficient workspace and privacy at home, and when they have increased family responsibilities on days when working from home.

Job applicants rate remote work as a highly attractive job feature. Turnover also tends to be lower among employees who are able to work from home. Research also indicates that remote workers have higher productivity than other employees, likely because they experience less stress and tend to convert some of the former commuting time into work time. Working remotely also improves productivity by enabling employees to perform their jobs at times when natural disasters (the COVID-19 pandemic, dangerous weather conditions) limit access to the company's premises.[60]

Due to less commuting, remote work offers considerable financial benefits for employees, including less unpaid time traveling, vehicle use, fuel costs, and other commuting expenses.[61] With less commuting, remote work also benefits society in the form of lower greenhouse gas emissions and less need for taxpayer-funded transportation infrastructure. Companies also benefit from lower real estate costs.

Remote work also has several potential disadvantages or risks, a few of which were identified by CEOs at Walt Disney and Starbucks in the opening vignette to this chapter.[62] People who regularly or mostly work from home report higher levels of social isolation, including weaker relationships with coworkers. They also receive less word-of-mouth information, which may have implications for promotional opportunities and workplace relations. Teams potentially suffer from lower cohesion. Organizations risk having a weaker culture when most employees work from home most days.

Contingencies of Remote Work Success The success of remote working depends on several characteristics of the employee, job, and organization.[63] Employees who work effectively from home typically have high self-motivation, self-organization, and need for autonomy. They also tend to have a lower need for regular social interaction or are able to fulfill their social needs from sources outside the workplace. Given the importance of technology in remote work arrangements, employees who perform well under these conditions have good information technology skills.

Some jobs and tasks are more suitable for remote work. Remote work jobs should require fairly low interdependence with other jobs, because coordination and communication are more challenging in remote than face-to-face work settings. Also, jobs are best suited for remote work if resources required to perform the work can be transported home or are available digitally. A third job characteristic is that task performance is measurable.

At the organizational level, remote work tends to be more successful when rewards and promotions are determined by performance and other measurable contributions rather than by

Remote work tends to be more successful when employers help remote workers maintain sufficient cohesion with their team and psychological connectedness with the organization.
fizkes/Shutterstock

MARS model of individual behavior A model depicting the four variables-motivation, ability, role perceptions, and situational factors—that directly influence an individual's voluntary behavior and performance

presence in the office (face time). Companies also help remote workers maintain sufficient cohesion with their team and psychological connectedness with the organization. This occurs through regular supportive communication with the supervisor and teammates. Visual communication channels, such as video conferences with cameras turned on, also improve personal relatedness. Companies also need to arrange occasions when teams and larger work units assemble in-person to engage in meaningful projects as well as social events.

LO1-5 Diagram the MARS model and describe the four factors that directly influence individual behavior and performance.

MARS MODEL OF INDIVIDUAL BEHAVIOR AND PERFORMANCE

For most of the past century, experts have investigated the direct predictors of individual behavior and performance.[64] One of the earliest formulas was *performance* = *person* × *situation*, where *person* includes individual characteristics and *situation* represents external influences on the individual's behavior. Another frequently mentioned formula is *performance* = *ability* × *motivation*.[65] Sometimes known as the "skill-and-will" model, this formula elaborates two specific characteristics within the person that influence individual performance. Some organizational studies use the *ability-motivation-opportunity (AMO)* model, which refers to the three variables but with a limited interpretation of the situation. Along with ability, motivation, and situation, researchers have identified a fourth key direct predictor of individual behavior and performance: role perceptions (the individual's expected role obligations).[66]

These four variables–motivation, ability, role perceptions, and situational factors–are represented in the **MARS model** of individual behavior and performance (see Exhibit 1.6). *MARS* is the acronym for these four concepts.[67] All four variables are essential influences on an individual's voluntary behavior and performance; if any one of them is low in a given situation, the employee is less likely to engage in the behavior or will perform it poorly. For example, motivated salespeople with clear role perceptions and sufficient resources (situational factors) will not perform their jobs as well if they lack sales skills and related knowledge (ability).

Exhibit 1.6 MARS Model of Individual Behavior and Results

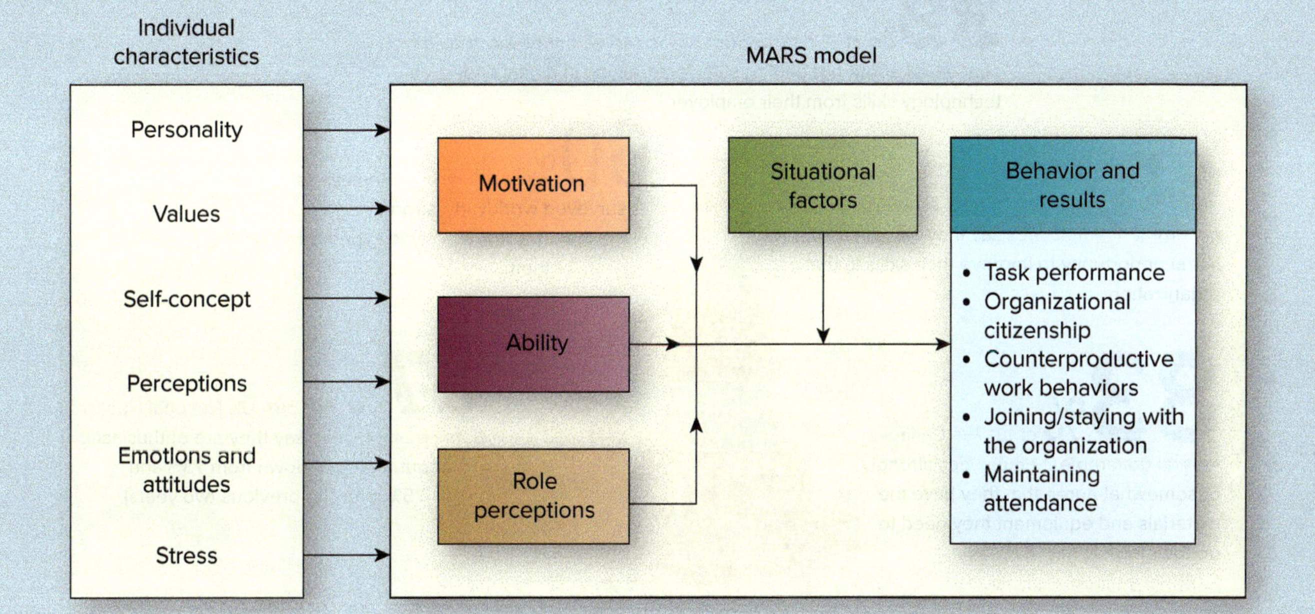

Motivation, ability, and role perceptions are clustered together in the model because they are located within the person. Situational factors are external to the individual but still affect one's behavior and performance.[68] The four MARS variables are the direct predictors of employee performance, customer service, team behaviors (cooperation, coordination, etc.), ethical behavior, and all other forms of voluntary behavior in the workplace. Let's look at each of the four elements in the MARS model.

Employee Motivation

Motivation represents the forces within a person that affect the direction, intensity, and persistence of effort for voluntary behavior.[69] *Direction* refers to the path along which people steer their effort. In other words, motivation is goal-directed, not random. People have choices about what they are trying to achieve and at what level of quality, quantity, and so forth. They are motivated to arrive at work on time, finish a project today rather than tomorrow, or aim for many other targets.

The second element of motivation, called *intensity,* is the amount of effort allocated to the goal. Intensity is how much people push themselves to complete a task. Two employees might be motivated to finish their project within the next few hours (direction), but only one of them puts forth enough effort (intensity) to achieve this goal. The third element of motivation is *persistence,* which refers to the length of time that the individual continues to exert effort toward an objective. Employees sustain their effort until they reach their goal or give up beforehand.

To help remember these three elements of motivation, consider the metaphor of driving a car in which the thrust of the motor is your effort. Direction refers to where you steer the car, intensity is how much you put your foot down on the accelerator, and persistence is for how long you drive toward your destination. Remember that motivation is a force that exists within individuals; it is not their actual behavior. Thus, direction, intensity, and persistence are cognitive (thoughts) and emotional conditions that directly cause us to move.

Ability

Employee abilities have a well-known influence on behavior and task performance. **Ability** includes the natural aptitudes, learned capabilities, and habits required to successfully complete a task.[70]

- *Aptitudes* are the natural (inborn) physical or cognitive talents that help employees learn specific tasks more quickly and perform them better. For example, finger dexterity is an aptitude by which individuals learn more quickly and potentially achieve higher performance at picking up and handling small objects with their fingers. Employees with high finger dexterity are not necessarily better than others at first; instead, they usually learn the skill faster and potentially reach a higher level of performance.
- *Learned capabilities* include the skills and knowledge that people acquire through training, practice, and other forms of learning. Learned capabilities tend to wane over time if they are not regularly put to use.
- *Habits* are tendencies to engage in specific behaviors in response to contextual cues and enacted with little conscious awareness or reflection.[71] Unlike other learned capabilities, habits are triggered by situational cues with minimal or no consciously motivated thought. This automaticity develops over time as the behavior is repeated and rewarded in specific contexts. Between one-third and one-half of our daily behaviors are habitual. Organizations train employees to develop habits, particularly for situations requiring quick action without careful deliberation (e.g., emergencies, military responses).

Mind the MARS Gap on Ability, Role Perceptions, and Situational Factors[72]

39% of 52,195 workers across 44 countries say they're concerned about not getting sufficient training in digital and technology skills from their employer.

68% of 557,778 U.S. federal government employees say they are given a real opportunity to improve their skills in the organization.

60% of 2.2 million employees surveyed worldwide strongly agree that they know what is expected of them.

83% of 181,754 Canadian federal government employees strongly or somewhat agree that they have the materials and equipment they need to do their job.

67% 648,594 UK National Health Service employees say they are enthusiastic about their job (down from 73% and 75% over the previous two years).

(Photo): Maren Wischnewski/Alamy Stock Photo

An individual's performance and well-being depend on how closely their abilities match the job requirements. One matching strategy is to hire people who already have the required abilities. For example, companies determine the suitability of job applicants through past work references, work samples, and various selection tests. A second strategy is to train employees who lack specific knowledge or skills needed for the job.[73] The third person-job matching strategy is to redesign the job so that employees are given tasks only within their current abilities. For example, a complex task might be simplified—some aspects of the work are transferred to others—so new employees are assigned only tasks that they are currently able to perform. As newcomers become more competent at these tasks, other tasks are added back into the job.

Role Perceptions

Along with motivation and ability, employees require accurate **role perceptions** to perform their jobs well. Role perceptions refer to how clearly people understand what is expected of them in their organizational roles. These perceptions range from role clarity to role ambiguity. Role clarity exists when the individual:

1. Understands the specific duties or consequences for which the employee is accountable. Employees have poor role perceptions when they are responsible for tasks that were never mentioned as part of their job responsibilities.
2. Understands company expectations of task scheduling priority and performance criterion priority. Task scheduling priority refers to which jobs should be completed before performing other tasks. Performance criterion priority refers to the relative importance of performance dimensions, such as how many customers to serve in an hour (quantity) versus how well each customer should be served (quality).
3. Understands the preferred behaviors or procedures for accomplishing tasks. Role ambiguity exists when an employee is skilled at performing a task in multiple ways, but is unsure which way the company prefers.

Role perceptions are important because they represent how well employees know where to direct their effort.[74] Employees with role clarity perform work more accurately and efficiently, whereas those with role ambiguity waste considerable time and energy performing the wrong tasks or in the wrong way. Furthermore, role clarity is essential for coordination with coworkers and other stakeholders. This improves team performance and ensures that everyone performs their work safely. Finally, role clarity motivates employees because they have a higher belief that their effort will produce the expected outcomes. In other words, people are more confident when they know what is expected of them.

motivation The forces within a person that affect the direction, intensity, and persistence of effort for voluntary behavior

ability The natural aptitudes, learned capabilities, and habits required to successfully complete a task

role perceptions The degree to which a person understands the job duties assigned to or expected of them

Situational Factors

Individual behavior and performance also depend on the situation, which is any context beyond the employee's immediate control.[75] One influence of the situation is as a constraint or facilitator of behavior and performance.[76] Employees who are motivated and skilled and know their role obligations will nevertheless perform poorly if they lack time, budget, physical work facilities, and other resources. The second influence is that the work situation provides cues to guide and motivate people. For example, companies install barriers and warning signs in dangerous areas. These workplace features are situational factors that alert employees to avoid the nearby hazards.

OB THEORY TO PRACTICE

Walmart Employees Improve Role Perceptions through Virtual Reality Training[77]

Through virtual reality training, Walmart employees are improving their role clarity for everyday situations. An employee slips on VR goggles and acts out the role while classmates view a projection of the same scene. The Black Friday scenario, for example, shows long lines, confused shoppers, a toddler standing on a shopping cart seat, and a manager searching for lost keys.

The instructor coaches employee role perceptions by asking the class to prioritize what should be done and to describe the preferred behaviors for each incident. For example, Walmart has a preferred way to correct the child's risky behavior in the shopping cart (*hint:* don't tell the child directly). "Black Friday is a busy, hectic day for everyone," says Sandi Hughes, a Walmart employee in St. Petersburg, Florida. "With the VR, an associate can feel how it can play out."

Julio Cortez/AP Images

task performance The individual's voluntary goal-directed behaviors that contribute to organizational objectives; includes proficient, adaptive, and proactive task performance

proficient task performance How well employees perform the work efficiently and accurately

adaptive task performance How well employees modify their thoughts and behavior to align with and support a new or changing work process or work setting

proactive task performance How well employees take the initiative to anticipate and introduce new work patterns that benefit the organization

organizational citizenship behaviors (OCBs) Various forms of cooperation and helpfulness to others that support the organization's social and psychological context

LO1-6 Summarize the five types of individual behavior in organizations.

TYPES OF INDIVIDUAL BEHAVIOR

The four elements of the MARS model–motivation, ability, role perceptions, and situational factors–affect all voluntary workplace behaviors and performance. There are many varieties of individual behavior, but most can be organized into the five categories described in this section: task performance, organizational citizenship behaviors, counterproductive work behaviors, joining and staying with the organization, and maintaining work attendance.

Task Performance

Task performance refers to the individual's voluntary goal-directed behaviors that contribute to organizational objectives.[78] Most jobs require incumbents to complete several tasks. For example, foreign exchange traders at Morgan Stanley must be able to identify and execute profitable trades, work cooperatively with clients and coworkers, assist in training new staff, and work on special software and digital equipment without error. All tasks involve working with people, data, things, and ideas.[79] Foreign exchange traders, for instance, mainly work with data (e.g., performing technical analysis of trends) but also with people (e.g., sharing information with coworkers and clients) and ideas (interpreting charts and company reports).

There are three types of task performance (see Exhibit 1.7).[80] **Proficient task performance** refers to how well employees perform the work efficiently and accurately. It involves accomplishing the assigned work at or above the expected standards of quality, quantity, and other indicators of effectiveness. **Adaptive task performance** refers to how well employees modify their thoughts and behavior to align with and support a new or changing work process or work setting. In essence, adaptive task performance is about how well employees respond to change in the workplace and in their job duties. **Proactive task performance** refers to how well employees take the initiative to anticipate and introduce new work patterns that benefit the organization. Proactive performance is about anticipating change, and leading that change in oneself, coworkers, and the workplace to achieve what is perceived to be a better future for the organization.

Organizational Citizenship Behaviors

Organizational citizenship behaviors (OCBs) are various forms of cooperation and helpfulness to others that support the organization's social and psychological context.[81] Most OCBs are directed toward individuals, such as assisting coworkers with their work problems, adjusting your work schedule to accommodate coworkers, showing genuine courtesy toward coworkers, and sharing your work resources (supplies, technology,

Exhibit 1.7 Three Types of Task Performance in the Workplace

Proficient task performance	Adaptive task performance	Proactive task performance
How well employees perform the work efficiently and accurately	How well employees modify their thoughts and behavior to align with and support a new or changing work process or work setting	How well employees take the initiative to anticipate and introduce new work patterns that benefit the organization

(*Left*): Volha Hlinskaya/123RF; (*Middle*): Fred Ho Yeow Hui/Shutterstock; (*Right*): malika.1028/Shutterstock.

Most organizational citizenship behaviors involve cooperating with and helping coworkers, such as adjusting your work schedule to accommodate theirs, sharing your work resources with them, and showing genuine courtesy toward them.
fizkes/Shutterstock

staff) with coworkers. Some OCBs represent cooperation and helpfulness toward the organization, such as supporting the company's public image, offering ideas beyond those required for your own job, attending events that support the organization, and keeping up with new developments in the organization. Some organizational citizenship behaviors are discretionary (employees don't have to perform them), whereas other OCBs are job requirements even if they aren't explicitly stated in job descriptions.[82]

OCBs can have a significant effect on individual, team, and organizational effectiveness.[83] High-OCB employees receive more support from coworkers, which, in turn, supports their own task performance. OCBs also increase team performance because members depend on one another. However, engaging in OCBs can have negative consequences.[84] OCBs take time and energy away from performing tasks, so employees who give more attention to OCBs risk lower career success in companies that reward task performance. Also, employees who frequently perform OCBs tend to have higher work-life conflict because their attention to OCBs takes time away from nonwork obligations.

Counterproductive Work Behaviors

Organizational behavior is interested in all workplace behaviors, including dysfunctional activities collectively known as **counterproductive work behaviors (CWBs).** CWBs are voluntary behaviors that have the potential to directly or indirectly harm the organization or its stakeholders.[85] This concept includes a wide array of intentional and unintentional behaviors, such as harassing coworkers, creating unnecessary conflict, deviating from preferred work methods (e.g., shortcuts that undermine work quality), being untruthful, stealing, sabotaging work, and wasting resources. CWBs are not minor concerns; research suggests that they can substantially undermine the organization's effectiveness.

counterproductive work behaviors Voluntary behaviors that have the potential to directly or indirectly harm the organization

Joining and Staying with the Organization

Companies suffer and potentially fail if they can't hire and retain enough people with the right skills and knowledge to perform the work.[86] This isn't a hypothetical statement. During times of economic growth, companies have been unable to keep up with demand because they can't hire enough qualified people. Even when companies are able to hire enough qualified staff, they need these employees to stay with the company.[87] Earlier in this chapter, we explained that human capital is the organization's main source of competitive advantage. The importance of human capital is particularly apparent when employees quit. Those who leave remove valuable knowledge, skills, and relationships with coworkers and external stakeholders, all of which take time for new staff to acquire. Other problems with employee turnover are discussed in later chapters, such as its adverse effect on customer service, team development, and corporate culture strength. Employee turnover does open up positions for workforce renewal and remove people who engaged in counterproductive work behaviors. But overall, turnover usually has a negative influence on organizational effectiveness.

Maintaining Work Attendance

Along with attracting and retaining employees, organizations need everyone to be available to perform their work, either onsite or remotely. Unscheduled absenteeism can lead to increased workloads or overtime among coworkers, lower performance by temporary staff filling the vacant positions, poorer coordination in the work process, poorer customer service, and potentially more workplace accidents.[88]

What are the main causes of absenteeism and lateness?[89] Much absenteeism is due to situational factors, such as personal illness, family demands (e.g., sick children), and bad weather. Other absenteeism occurs because employees are motivated to distance themselves from workplace bullying, difficult customers, boring work, and other stressful conditions. Absenteeism is also higher in organizations with generous sick leave because it minimizes the financial loss of taking time away from work. Absenteeism also varies from one employee to the next due to their personality and personal values. Finally, studies report that absenteeism is higher in teams with strong absence norms, meaning that team members tolerate and even expect coworkers to take time off.

Although most companies focus on minimizing absenteeism, a related issue is *presenteeism*—showing up for work when unwell, injured, preoccupied by personal problems, or faced with dangerous conditions getting to work.[90] The current debate is whether presenteeism is, on balance, positive or negative for the individual and organization. The "positive" view argues that working rather than being absent fulfills psychological needs, interaction with coworkers provides social support and distraction from one's ailments, and illnesses or injuries are seldom so severe that the employee is unable to work. The "negative" view is that employees tend to be less productive, may reduce the productivity of interdependent coworkers, and may worsen their own health and increase health and safety risks for coworkers.

Presenteeism is more common among employees with low job security (such as new and temporary staff), employees who lack sick leave pay or similar financial buffers, and those whose absence would immediately affect many people. Personality characteristics also motivate some people to show up for work when others would gladly recover at home.[91]

THE JOURNEY BEGINS

This chapter introduced you to the field of organizational behavior, described the emerging landscape of organizations, and explained why OB is important for you and for organizations. It also introduced the foundations of individual behavior and performance as well as the main types of individual behavior. But this is only the beginning of our journey. Throughout this volume, we will help you to learn new ways of thinking about how people work in and around organizations. We begin this process in Chapter 2 through Chapter 6 by looking at personality, values, and other individual differences that indirectly predict individual behavior through the MARS model.

Study Checklist

Connect® is available for *M: Organizational Behavior*. Additional resources include:

✓ Exercises:

- **Case Analysis:** Apply concepts within the context of a real world situation.
- **Click and Drag:** Helps make the connection between theory and application through matching, ranking, or grouping activities.
- **Video Case:** See management in action through interactive videos.
- **Self-Assessment:** Designed to promote student self-awareness and reflection, these research based surveys contain detailed feedback for students.
- **Application-Based Activities:** These highly interactive, application- and analysis-based exercises allow students to take on specific roles to complete management related tasks within a real-world context.

✓ **SmartBook 2.0™**—Smartbook 2.0 is an adaptive learning solution that provides personalized learning to individual student needs, continually adapts to pinpoint knowledge gaps and focuses learning on concepts requiring additional study. It fosters more productive learning, takes the guesswork out of what to study, and helps students better prepare for class.

©Nalthawat Jamnapa/123RF

Notes

1. A. Rozentals, "Council Post: In-Office Vs. Remote Vs. Hybrid Work Two Years Later: The Impact On Employee Efficiency," *Forbes*, March 18, 2022; J. Corrigan, "Apple Exec Departs over Return-to-Office Policy," *Human Resource Director (USA)*, May 9, 2022; B. Wigert and S. Agrawal, "Returning to the Office: The Current, Preferred and Future State of Remote Work," *Gallup Workplace*, August 31, 2022; A. Semenova, "BlackRock Ordering Staff to Return to the Office Three Days per Week," *Yahoo! News*, September 6, 2022; C. Huston, "Disney Remote Work: Bob Iger Memo Says Employees Should Be In Office," *The Hollywood Reporter*, January 9, 2023; A. Jackson, "For the First Time in over a Decade, Apple and Meta Aren't on Glassdoor's 100 Best Places to Work List," *CNBC Make It*, January 11, 2023; H. Schultz, "Message to Starbucks Support Partners: Returning to Each Other and to the Office," *Starbucks Stories* (blog), January 11, 2023.
2. M. Warner, "Organizational Behavior Revisited," *Human Relations* 47 (1994): 1151–66; R. Westwood and S. Clegg, "The Discourse of Organization Studies: Dissensus, Politics, and Paradigms," in *Debating Organization: Point-Counterpoint in Organization Studies*, ed. R. Westwood and S. Clegg (Malden, MA: Wiley-Blackwell, 2003), 1–42.
3. D. Katz and R.L. Kahn, *The Social Psychology of Organizations* (New York: Wiley, 1966), Chap. 2; R.N. Stern and S.R. Barley, "Organizations as Social Systems: Organization Theory's Neglected Mandate," *Administrative Science Quarterly* 41 (1996): 146–62.
4. L.E. Greiner, "A Recent History of Organizational Behavior," in *Organizational Behavior*, ed. S. Kerr (Columbus, OH: Grid, 1979), 3–14; J. Micklethwait and A. Wooldridge, *The Company: A Short History of a Revolutionary Idea* (New York: Random House, 2003).
5. T. Lawson, "The Nature of the Firm and Peculiarities of the Corporation," *Cambridge Journal of Economics* 39, no. 1 (2015): 1–32.
6. B. Schlender, "The Three Faces of Steve," *Fortune*, November 9, 1998, 96–101.
7. L.E. Greiner, "A Recent History of Organizational Behavior," in *Organizational Behavior*, ed. S. Kerr (Columbus, OH: Grid, 1979), 3–14; "A Field Is Born," *Harvard Business Review* 86, no. 7/8 (2008): 164; P.R. Lawrence, "The Key Job Design Problem Is Still Taylorism," *Journal of Organizational Behavior* 31, no. 2/3 (2010): 412–21; L.W. Porter and B. Schneider, "What Was, What Is, and What May Be in OP/OB," *Annual Review of Organizational Psychology and Organizational Behavior* 1 (2014): 1–21.

8. T. Takala, "Plato on Leadership," *Journal of Business Ethics* 17 (1998): 785–98; J.A. Fernandez, "The Gentleman's Code of Confucius: Leadership by Values," *Organizational Dynamics* 33, no. 1 (2004): 21–31; A.M. Blake and J.L. Moseley, "Frederick Winslow Taylor: One Hundred Years of Managerial Insight," *International Journal of Management* 28, no. 4 (2011): 346–53; J.W. Stutje, ed., *Charismatic Leadership and Social Movements: The Revolutionary Power of Ordinary Men and Women, International Studies in Social History* (New York: Berghahn Books, 2012).

9. C.D. Wrege, "Solving Mayo's Mystery: The First Complete Account of the Origin of the Hawthorne Studies–The Forgotten Contributions of C. E. Snow and H. Hibarger" (paper presented at the Academy of Management Proceedings, August 1976), 12–16; P. Graham, ed., *Mary Parker Follett: Prophet of Management* (Boston: Harvard Business School Press, 1995); J.H. Smith, "The Enduring Legacy of Elton Mayo," *Human Relations* 51, no. 3 (1998): 221–49; R. Busse and M. Warner, "The Legacy of the Hawthorne Experiments: A Critical Analysis of the Human Relations School of Thought," *History of Economic Ideas* 25, no. 2 (2017): 91–114; G.M. Nelson, "Mary Parker Follett–Creativity and Democracy," *Human Service Organizations: Management, Leadership & Governance* 41, no. 2 (2017): 178–85.

10. The extent to which OB influences career success depends on course pedagogy as well as the practical value of the OB concepts covered in the course. In fact, OB scholars have an ongoing debate about the practical relevance of OB research. See, for example: J.M. Bartunek and S.L. Rynes, "Academics and Practitioners Are Alike and Unlike: The Paradoxes of Academic-Practitioner Relationships," *Journal of Management* 40, no. 5 (2014): 1181–201; K. Božič, A.A. Bachkirov, and M. Černe, "Towards Better Understanding and Narrowing of the Science-Practice Gap: A Practitioner-Centered Approach to Management Knowledge Creation," *European Management Journal* 40, no. 4 (2022): 632–44; D. Gioia, "On the Road to Hell: Why Academia Is Viewed as Irrelevant to Practicing Managers," *Academy of Management Discoveries* 8, no. 2 (2022): 174–79.

11. The skills identified in these recent surveys are almost identical to those reported in a recent review of more than two dozen surveys on employability skills of higher education graduates. See M. Osmani et al., "Graduates Employability Skills: A Review of Literature against Market Demand," *Journal of Education for Business* 94, no. 7 (2019): 423–32.

12. G. Loewenstein, "The Psychology of Curiosity: A Review and Reinterpretation," *Psychological Bulletin* 116, no. 1 (1994): 75–98; C. Kidd and B.Y. Hayden, "The Psychology and Neuroscience of Curiosity," *Neuron* 88, no. 3 (November 2015): 449–60, https://doi.org/10.1016/j.neuron.2015.09.010; M. Livio, *Why?: What Makes Us Curious* (New York: Simon and Schuster, 2017).

13. R.L. Priem and J. Rosenstein, "Is Organization Theory Obvious to Practitioners? A Test of One Established Theory," *Organization Science* 11, no. 5 (2000): 509–24.

14. R.S. Rubin and E.C. Dierdorff, "How Relevant Is the MBA? Assessing the Alignment of Required Curricula and Required Managerial Competencies," *Academy of Management Learning & Education* 8, no. 2 (2009): 208–24; Y. Baruch and O. Lavi-Steiner, "The Career Impact of Management Education from an Average-Ranked University: Human Capital Perspective," *Career Development International* 20, no. 3 (2015): 218–37.

15. M.S. Myers, *Every Employee a Manager* (New York: McGraw Hill, 1970).

16. For example, see: M.C. Díaz-Fernández, M.R. González-Rodríguez, and B. Simonetti, "Top Management Team's Intellectual Capital and Firm Performance," *European Management Journal* 33, no. 5 (2015): 322–31; S. Hauff, D. Alewell, and N.K. Hansen, "Further Exploring the Links between High-Performance Work Practices and Firm Performance: A Multiple-Mediation Model in the German Context," *German Journal of Human Resource Management* 32, no. 1 (2018): 5–26; J. Harter et al., "Increased Business Value for Positive Job Attitudes during Economic Recessions: A Meta-Analysis and SEM Analysis," *Human Performance* 33 (2020): 1–24; R.G. Badgett, L. Jonker, and S. Xirasagar, "Hospital Workforce Engagement and Inpatient Mortality Rate: Findings from the English National Health Service Staff Surveys," *Journal of General Internal Medicine* 35, no. 12 (2020): 3465–70.

17. A. Edmans, "The Link Between Job Satisfaction and Firm Value, with Implications for Corporate Social Responsibility," *Academy of Management Perspectives* 26, no. 4 (2012): 1–19; S. Abhayawansa and J. Guthrie, "Drivers and Semantic Properties of Intellectual Capital Information in Sell-Side Analysts' Reports," *Journal of Accounting & Organizational Change* 12, no. 4 (2016): 434–71; E. Symitsi, P. Stamolampros, and G. Daskalakis, "Employees' Online Reviews and Equity Prices," *Economics Letters* 162 (2018): 53–55; A. Krausert et al., "Investor Perspectives: People Data and Reporting" (London: Chartered Institute of Personnel and Development, March 2019); G. Filbeck, X. Zhao, and M. Warnaka, "Glassdoor's Best Places to Work Internationally: Are They Best for Shareholders?," *International Journal of Finance & Economics* 27, no. 4 (2022): 4350–63.

18. In 1961, Harvard business professor Fritz Roethlisberger proposed that the field of OB is concerned with human behavior "from the points of view of both (a) its determination . . . and (b) its improvement." See P.B. Vaill, "F. J. Roethlisberger and the Elusive Phenomena of Organizational Behavior," *Journal of Management Education* 31, no. 3 (2007): 321–38. The centrality of organizational effectiveness in OB research is also discussed in: B.S. Georgopoulos and A.S. Tannenbaum, "A Study of Organizational Effectiveness," *American Sociological Review* 22 (1957): 534–40; S.A. Mohrman, C.B. Gibson, and A.M. Mohrman Jr., "Doing Research That Is Useful to Practice: A Model and Empirical Exploration," *Academy of Management Journal* 44 (2001): 357–75; J.P. Walsh et al., "On the Relationship between Research and Practice," *Journal of Management Inquiry* 16, no. 2 (2007): 128–54; M. Beer, "Making a Difference: Developing Actionable Knowledge for Practice and Theory," *The Journal of Applied Behavioral Science* 56, no. 4 (2020): 506–20.

19. R.H. Hall, "Effectiveness Theory and Organizational Effectiveness," *Journal of Applied Behavioral Science* 16, no. 4 (1980): 536–45; K. Cameron, "Organizational Effectiveness: Its Demise and Re-Emergence through Positive Organizational Scholarship," in *Great Minds in Management*, ed. K.G. Smith and M.A. Hitt (New York: Oxford University Press, 2005), 304–30.

20. A.A. Amirkhanyan, H.J. Kim, and K.T. Lambright, "The Performance Puzzle: Understanding the Factors Influencing Alternative Dimensions and Views of Performance," *Journal of Public Administration Research and Theory* 24, no. 1 (2014): 1–34.

21. Chester Barnard gives one of the earliest descriptions of organizations as systems interacting with external environments and that are composed of subsystems. See C. Barnard, *The Functions of the Executive* (Cambridge, MA: Harvard University Press, 1938), esp. Chap. 6. Also see F.E. Kast and J.E. Rosenzweig, "General Systems Theory: Applications for Organization and Management," *Academy of Management Journal* 15, no. 4 (1972): 447–65; P.M. Senge, *The Fifth Discipline: The Art and Practice of the Learning Organization* (New York: Doubleday Currency, 1990); G. Morgan, *Images of Organization*, 2nd ed. (Newbury Park: Sage, 1996); A. de Geus, *The Living Company* (Boston: Harvard Business School Press, 1997).

22. D. Katz and R.L. Kahn, *The Social Psychology of Organizations* (New York: Wiley, 1966), Chap. 2; J. McCann, "Organizational Effectiveness: Changing Concepts for Changing Environments," *Human Resource Planning* 27, no. 1 (2004): 42-50; A.H. Van de Ven, M. Ganco, and C.R. Hinings, "Returning to the Frontier of Contingency Theory of Organizational and Institutional Designs," *Academy of Management Annals* 7, no. 1 (2013): 391-438.

23. K.E. Weick, *The Social Psychology of Organizing* (Reading, MA: Addison-Wesley, 1979); J.L. Claggett and E. Karahanna, "Unpacking the Structure of Coordination Mechanisms and the Role of Relational Coordination in an Era of Digitally Mediated Work Processes," *Academy of Management Review* 43 (2018): 704-22; R.M. Burton and B. Obel, "The Science of Organizational Design: Fit between Structure and Coordination," *Journal of Organization Design* 7, no. 5 (2018).

24. J. Barney, "Firm Resources and Sustained Competitive Advantage," *Journal of Management* 17, no. 1 (1991): 99-120.

25. P. Tharenou, A.M. Saks, and C. Moore, "A Review and Critique of Research on Training and Organizational-Level Outcomes," *Human Resource Management Review* 17, no. 3 (2007): 251-73; D.Y. Jeong and M. Choi, "The Impact of High-Performance Work Systems on Firm Performance: The Moderating Effects of the Human Resource Function's Influence," *Journal of Management & Organization* 22, no. 3 (2016): 328-48; F.S. Bentley, R.R. Kehoe, and H. Chung, "Investing for Keeps: Firms' Prepandemic Investments in Human Capital Decreased Workforce Reductions Associated with COVID-19 Financial Pressures," *Journal of Applied Psychology* 106, no. 12 (2021): 1785-804.

26. R.R. Kehoe and P.M. Wright, "The Impact of High-Performance Human Resource Practices on Employees' Attitudes and Behaviors," *Journal of Management* 39, no. 2 (2013): 366-91; B. Fabi, R. Lacoursière, and L. Raymond, "Impact of High-Performance Work Systems on Job Satisfaction, Organizational Commitment, and Intention to Quit in Canadian Organizations," *International Journal of Manpower* 36, no. 5 (2015): 772-90; J.G. Meijerink, S.E. Beijer, and A.C. Bos-Nehles, "A Meta-Analysis of Mediating Mechanisms between Employee Reports of Human Resource Management and Employee Performance: Different Pathways for Descriptive and Evaluative Reports?," *The International Journal of Human Resource Management* 32, no. 2 (2021): 394-442.

27. R.E. Freeman, J.S. Harrison, and A.C. Wicks, *Managing for Stakeholders: Survival, Reputation, and Success* (New Haven, CT: Yale University Press, 2007); B.L. Parmar et al., "Stakeholder Theory: The State of the Art," *Academy of Management Annals* 4, no. 1 (2010): 403-45; S. Sachs and E. Rühli, *Stakeholders Matter: A New Paradigm for Strategy in Society* (Cambridge: Cambridge University Press, 2011); A. Baughen, C. Oswick, and R. Oswick, "Rethinking 'Organizational Effectiveness' as a Core Premise of Organization Development: Beyond Narrow Organizational Interests and Towards Wider Soulful Interventions," *Journal of Change Management* 20, no. 4 (2020): 333-41.

28. OECD, *Skills Matter: Further Results from the Survey of Adult Skills*, OECD Skills Studies (Paris: OECD Publishing, June 2016). Also from Annex A, spreadsheet data file associated with tables in the OECD publication.

29. A. Santana, "Three Elements of Stakeholder Legitimacy," *Journal of Business Ethics* 105 (2012): 257-65; D. Crilly and P. Sloan, "Autonomy or Control? Organizational Architecture and Corporate Attention to Stakeholders," *Organization Science* 25 (2014): 339-55; M. Hall, Y. Millo, and E. Barman, "Who and What Really Counts? Stakeholder Prioritization and Accounting for Social Value," *Journal of Management Studies* 52 (2015): 907-34; D. Weitzner and Y. Deutsch, "Understanding Motivation and Social Influence in Stakeholder Prioritization," *Organization Studies* 36 (2015): 1337-60.

30. H. Aguinis and A. Glavas, "What We Know and Don't Know about Corporate Social Responsibility: A Review and Research Agenda," *Journal of Management* 38 (2012): 932-68; T. Meynhardt and P. Gomez, "Building Blocks for Alternative Four-Dimensional Pyramids of Corporate Social Responsibilities," *Business & Society* 58 (2019): 404-38.

31. A.B. Carroll and K.M. Shabana, "The Business Case for Corporate Social Responsibility: A Review of Concepts, Research and Practice," *International Journal of Management Reviews* 12 (2010): 85-105; J. Kim and J. Kim, "Corporate Sustainability Management and Its Market Benefits," *Sustainability* 10 (2018): 1455; M. Ong et al., "When Corporate Social Responsibility Motivates Employee Citizenship Behavior: The Sensitizing Role of Task Significance," *Organizational Behavior and Human Decision Processes* 144 (2018): 44-59; B. Lis, "Corporate Social Responsibility's Influence on Organizational Attractiveness: An Investigation in the Context of Employer Choice," *Journal of General Management* 43 (2018): 106-14.

32. Most of these anchors are mentioned in J.D. Thompson, "On Building an Administrative Science," *Administrative Science Quarterly* 1, no. 1 (1956): 102-11.

33. This anchor has a colorful history dating back to critiques of business schools in the 1950s. Soon after, systematic research became a mantra for many respected scholars. See, for example, J.D. Thompson, "On Building an Administrative Science," *Administrative Science Quarterly* 1, no. 1 (1956): 102-11.

34. J. Pfeffer and R.I. Sutton, *Hard Facts, Dangerous Half-Truths, and Total Nonsense* (Boston: Harvard Business School Press, 2006); D.M. Rousseau and S. McCarthy, "Educating Managers from an Evidence-Based Perspective," *Academy of Management Learning & Education* 6, no. 1 (2007): 84-101; R.B. Briner and D.M. Rousseau, "Evidence-Based I-O Psychology: Not There Yet," *Industrial and Organizational Psychology* 4, no. 1 (2011): 3-22.

35. J. Hamet and F. Maurer, "Is Management Research Visible Outside the Academic Community?" *M@n@gement* 20, no. 5 (2017): 492-516; E. Barends and D.M. Rousseau, *Evidence-Based Management: How to Use Evidence to Make Better Organizational Decisions* (London: Kogan Page Publishers, 2018), Chap. 4; W. Zhang et al., "The Neural Basis of Herding Decisions in Enterprise Clustering: An Event-Related Potential Study," *Frontiers in Neuroscience* 13 (2019): 1175; A. Vedadi, M. Warkentin, and A. Dennis, "Herd Behavior in Information Security Decision-Making," *Information & Management* 58, no. 8 (2021): 103526.

36. J. Pfeffer and R.I. Sutton, *Hard Facts, Dangerous Half-Truths, and Total Nonsense* (Boston: Harvard Business School Press, 2006); D.M. Rousseau, "The Realist Rationality of Evidence-Based Management," *Academy of Management Learning & Education* 19, no. 3 (2020): 415-24.

37. M. Bartunek and J. McKenzie, eds., *Academic-Practitioner Relationships: Developments, Complexities and Opportunities* (New York: Routledge, 2017); J. Hamet and S. Michel, "Rigor, Relevance, and the Knowledge 'Market,'" *European Business Review* 30, no. 2 (2018): 183-201; H. Aguinis et al., "A Pluralist Conceptualization of Scholarly Impact in Management Education: Students as Stakeholders," *Academy of Management Learning & Education* 18, no. 1 (2019): 11-42; G. Sharma and P. (Tima) Bansal, "Cocreating Rigorous and Relevant Knowledge," *Academy of Management Journal* 63, no. 2 (2020): 386-410; Z. Simsek, N. Li, and J.L. Huang, "Turbocharging Practical Implications in Management Studies," *Journal of Management* 48, no. 5 (2022): 1083-102.

38. P.H. Kim, R.E. Ployhart, and C.B. Gibson, "Editors' Comments: Is Organizational Behavior Overtheorized?" *Academy of Management Review* 43, no. 4 (2018): 541-45.

39. M.N. Zald, "More Fragmentation? Unfinished Business in Linking the Social Sciences and the Humanities," *Administrative Science Quarterly* 41 (1996): 251–61; C. Oswick, P. Fleming, and G. Hanlon, "From Borrowing to Blending: Rethinking the Processes of Organizational Theory Building," *Academy of Management Review* 36, no. 2 (2011): 318–37; B.M. Staw, "Stumbling Toward a Social Psychology of Organizations: An Autobiographical Look at the Direction of Organizational Research," *Annual Review of Organizational Psychology and Organizational Behavior* 3, no. 1 (2016): 1–19.

40. H.L. Tosi and J.W. Slocum Jr., "Contingency Theory: Some Suggested Directions," *Journal ofManagement* 10 (1984): 9–26; C.M. Christensen and M.E. Raynor, "Why Hard-Nosed Executives Should Care about Management Theory," *Harvard Business Review* (2003): 66–74; C.E.J. Härtel and J.M. O'Connor, "Contextualizing Research: Putting Context Back into Organizational Behavior Research," *Journal of Management & Organization* 20, no. 4 (2014): 417–22. For excellent critique of the "one best way" approach in early management scholarship, see P.F. Drucker, "Management's New Paradigms," *Forbes* (1998): 152–77.

41. D.M. Rousseau and R.J. House, "Meso Organizational Behavior: Avoiding Three Fundamental Biases," in *Trends in Organizational Behavior*, ed. C.L. Cooper and D.M. Rousseau (Chichester: Wiley, 1994), 13–30.

42. D.A. Harrison et al., "Time, Teams, and Task Performance: Changing Effects of Surface- and Deep-Level Diversity on Group Functioning," *Academy of Management Journal* 45, no. 5 (2002): 1029–46; W.J. Casper, J.H. Wayne, and J.G. Manegold, "Who Will We Recruit? Targeting Deep- and Surface-Level Diversity with Human Resource Policy Advertising," *Human Resource Management* 52, no. 3 (2013): 311–32; J.E. Mathieu et al., "A Review and Integration of Team Composition Models: Moving toward a Dynamic and Temporal Framework," *Journal of Management* 40, no. 1 (2014): 130–60.

43. J. Qin, N. Muenjohn, and P. Chhetri, "A Review of Diversity Conceptualizations: Variety, Trends, and a Framework," *Human Resource Development Review* 13, no. 2 (2014): 133–57; M. del Carmen Triana et al., "The Relationship Between Team Deep-Level Diversity and Team Performance: A Meta-Analysis of the Main Effect, Moderators, and Mediating Mechanisms," *Journal of Management Studies* 58, no. 8 (2021): 2137–79.

44. B.M. Ferdman, "Paradoxes of Inclusion: Understanding and Managing the Tensions of Diversity and Multiculturalism," *The Journal of Applied Behavioral Science* 53, no. 2 (2017): 235–63; A.E. Randel et al., "Inclusive Leadership: Realizing Positive Outcomes through Belongingness and Being Valued for Uniqueness," *Human Resource Management Review* 28, no. 2 (2018): 190–203; L.M. Shore, J.N. Cleveland, and D. Sanchez, "Inclusive Workplaces: A Review and Model," *Human Resource Management Review* 28, no. 2 (2018): 176–89; M.V. Norman and K.M. Johnson, "The Importance of Employee Inclusion: Lessons for HR Managers," *Strategic HR Review* 21, no. 1 (2022): 20–24.

45. T.M. Welbourne, S. Rolf, and S. Schlachter, "The Case for Employee Resource Groups: A Review and Social Identity Theory-Based Research Agenda," *Personnel Review* 46, no. 8 (2017): 1816–34; E.G. Foldy, "Employee Resource Groups: What We Know about Their Impact on Individuals and Organizations," *Academy of Management Proceedings* 2019 (August 2019): 10633.

46. C.-M. Lu et al., "Effect of Diversity on Human Resource Management and Organizational Performance," *Journal of Business Research* 68, no. 4 (2015): 857–61; Y. Zhang and M.-Y. Huai, "Diverse Work Groups and Employee Performance: The Role of Communication Ties," *Small Group Research* 47, no. 1 (2016): 28–57; J. Wang et al., "Team Creativity/Innovation in Culturally Diverse Teams: A Meta-Analysis," *Journal of Organizational Behavior* 40, no. 6 (2019): 693–708; M. del C. Triana et al., "The Relationship Between Team Deep-Level Diversity and Team Performance: A Meta-Analysis of the Main Effect, Moderators, and Mediating Mechanisms," *Journal of Management Studies* 58, no. 8 (2021): 2137–79.

47. Q. Roberson, O. Holmes, and J.L. Perry, "Transforming Research on Diversity and Firm Performance: A Dynamic Capabilities Perspective," *Academy of Management Annals* 11 (2017): 189–216; Y.R.F. Guillaume et al., "Harnessing Demographic Differences in Organizations: What Moderates the Effects of Workplace Diversity?," *Journal of Organizational Behavior* 38 (2017): 276–303; N. Luanglath, M. Ali, and K. Mohannak, "Top Management Team Gender Diversity and Productivity: The Role of Board Gender Diversity," *Equality, Diversity and Inclusion: An International Journal* 38 (2019): 71–86.

48. T. Kochan et al., "The Effects of Diversity on Business Performance: Report of the Diversity Research Network," *Human Resource Management* 42 (2003): 3–21; S.T. Bell et al., "Getting Specific about Demographic Diversity Variable and Team Performance Relationships: A Meta-Analysis," *Journal of Management* 37, no. 3 (2011): 709–43; S.M.B. Thatcher and P.C. Patel, "Group Faultlines: A Review, Integration, and Guide to Future Research," *Journal of Management* 38, no. 4 (2012): 969–1009; P. Choudhury and M.R. Haas, "Scope versus Speed: Team Diversity, Leader Experience, and Patenting Outcomes for Firms," *Strategic Management Journal* 39, no. 4 (2018): 977–1002; E. Seo, H. Kang, and J. Song, "Blending Talents for Innovation: Team Composition for Cross-Border R&D Collaboration within Multinational Corporations," *Journal of International Business Studies* 51, no. 5 (2020): 851–85.

49. J. Hyman, "New Research Reveals Employees Value Well-Being over Climbing the Ladder," *Work Life by Atlassian* (blog), July 19, 2021; Y. Bizouati-Kennedy, "42% of Gen Z Prioritize Work-Life Balance Over Other Job Perks, Survey Says," *GOBankingRates,* September 15, 2021; D. Klinghoffer, "Hybrid Tanked Work-Life Balance. Here's How Microsoft Is Trying to Fix It," *Harvard Business Review* (December 8, 2021).

50. J.H. Greenhaus and L.L. ten Brummelhuis, "Models and Frameworks Underlying Work–Life Research: Challenges and Opportunities," in *Handbook of Work-Life Integration Among Professionals: Challenges and Opportunities*, ed. D.A. Major and R.J. Burke (Cheltenham: Edward Elgar Publishing, 2013), 14–34; M.J. Sirgy and D.-J. Lee, "Work-Life Balance: An Integrative Review," *Applied Research in Quality of Life* 13, no. 1 (2018): 229–54.

51. Katie Clarey, "Work-Life Balance? There's No Such Thing," *HR Dive*, December 18, 2018.

52. L.L. ten Brummelhuis and A.B. Bakker, "A Resource Perspective on the Work-Home Interface: The Work–Home Resources Model," *American Psychologist* 67 (2012): 545–56; A. Li, A. Butler, and J. Bagger, "Depletion or Expansion? Understanding the Effects of Support Policy Use on Employee Work and Family Outcomes," *Human Resource Management Journal* 28 (2018): 216–34; N.P. Rothbard, A.M. Beetz, and D. Harari, "Balancing the Scales: A Configurational Approach to Work-Life Balance," *Annual Review of Organizational Psychology and Organizational Behavior* 8 (2021): 73–103.

53. S.D. Friedman, *Leading the Life You Want: Skills for Integrating Work and Life* (Boston: Harvard Business Press, 2014); A.M. Foreman et al., "Dogs in the Workplace: A Review of the Benefits and Potential Challenges," *International Journal of Environmental Research and Public Health* 14 (2017): 498; K. Lockwood, "Achieving Work-Life Integration in this New World of Work," *Forbes*, April 18, 2018; I. Damen et al., "Understanding Walking Meetings: Drivers and Barriers," in *Proceedings of the 2020 CHI Conference on Human Factors in Computing Systems*, CHI '20 (New York: Association for Computing Machinery, 2020), 1–14;

H.E. Kling et al., "Walking Meeting Effects on Productivity and Mood Among White-Collar Workers: Evidence From the Walking Meeting Pilot Study," *Journal of Occupational and Environmental Medicine* 63, no. 2 (2021): e75; J.F. Caringal-Go et al., "Work-Life Balance Crafting during COVID-19: Exploring Strategies of Telecommuting Employees in the Philippines," *Community, Work & Family* 25, no. 1 (2022): 112–31.

54. E.E. Kossek and R.J. Thompson, "Workplace Flexibility: Integrating Employer and Employee Perspectives to Close the Research–Practice Implementation Gap," in *The Oxford Handbook of Work and Family*, ed. T.D. Allen and L.T. Eby (New York: Oxford University Press, 2016), 255–70; M. Beatson, "Megatrends: Flexible Working" (London: Chartered Institute of Personnel and Development, January 15, 2019).

55. G.E. Kreiner, E.C. Hollensbe, and M.L. Sheep, "Balancing Borders and Bridges: Negotiating the Work-Home Interface via Boundary Work Tactics," *Academy of Management Journal* 52, no. 4 (2009): 704–30; N.P. Rothbard and A. Ollier-Malaterre, "Boundary Management," in *The Oxford Handbook of Work and Family*, ed. T.D. Allen and L.T. Eby (New York: Oxford University Press, 2016), 109–24; T. Karabinski et al., "Interventions for Improving Psychological Detachment from Work: A Meta-Analysis," *Journal of Occupational Health Psychology* 26, no. 3 (2021): 224–42; "Code of Practice for Employers and Employees on the Right to Disconnect" (Dublin: Government of Ireland Workplace Relations Commission, March 2021); T.D. Allen et al., "Boundary Management and Work-Nonwork Balance While Working from Home," *Applied Psychology* 70, no. 1 (2021): 60–84.

56. A. Felstead and G. Henseke, "Assessing the Growth of Remote Working and Its Consequences for Effort, Well-Being and Work-Life Balance," *New Technology, Work and Employment* 32, no. 3 (2017): 195–212; B.Y. Thompson, "The Digital Nomad Lifestyle: (Remote) Work/Leisure Balance, Privilege, and Constructed Community," *International Journal of the Sociology of Leisure* 2, no. 1 (2019): 27–42; "Working from Home during the COVID-19 Pandemic: How Rates in Canada and the United States Compare," Economic and Social Reports (Ottawa: Statistics Canada, August 24, 2022); B. Wigert and S. Agrawal, "Returning to the Office: The Current, Preferred and Future State of Remote Work," *Gallup Workplace*, August 31, 2022.

57. R. Sutherland, H. Matthews, and S. Tatam, "Ogilvy on Managed Remote Working: Building a Sustainable Way of Working" (London: Ogilvy UK, March 20, 2020).

58. A. Mann and A. Adkins, "America's Coming Workplace: Home Alone," *Gallup Business Journal*, March 15, 2017; "Gartner Forecasts 51% of Global Knowledge Workers Will Be Remote by the End of 2021," Press Release (Stamford, Conn.: Gartner, June 22, 2021); "Remote Work Persisting and Trending Permanent," *Gallup Inc.* October 13, 2021; "State of Remote Work 2022" (Boston: Owl Labs, October 2022); B. Wigert and S. Agrawal, "Returning to the Office: The Current, Preferred and Future State of Remote Work," *Gallup Workplace*, August 31, 2022.

59. T.D. Allen, T.D. Golden, and K.M. Shockley, "How Effective Is Telecommuting? Assessing the Status of Our Scientific Findings," *Psychological Science in the Public Interest* 16, no. 2 (2015): 40–60; M. Charalampous et al., "Systematically Reviewing Remote E-Workers' Well-Being at Work: A Multidimensional Approach," *European Journal of Work and Organizational Psychology* 28, no. 1 (2019): 51–73; T.A. Beauregard, K.A. Basile, and E. Canonico, "Telework: Outcomes and Facilitators for Employees," in *The Cambridge Handbook of Technology and Employee Behavior*, ed. R.N. Landers (Cambridge: Cambridge University Press, 2019), 511–43; B. Wang et al., "Achieving Effective Remote Working During the COVID-19 Pandemic: A Work Design Perspective," *Applied Psychology* 70, no. 1 (2021): 16–59.

60. R.S. Gajendran and D.A. Harrison, "The Good, the Bad, and the Unknown about Telecommuting: Meta-Analysis of Psychological Mediators and Individual Consequences," *Journal of Applied Psychology* 92, no. 6 (2007): 1524–41; M. Brittany Harker and R. MacDonnell, "Is Telework Effective for Organizations?" *Management Research Review* 35 (2012): 602–16; P. Choudhury, C. Foroughi, and B. Larson, "Work-from-Anywhere: The Productivity Effects of Geographic Flexibility," *Strategic Management Journal* 42, no. 4 (2021): 655–83; T. Galanti et al., "Work from Home during the COVID-19 Outbreak," *Journal of Occupational and Environmental Medicine* 63, no. 7 (2021): e426–32; A. Rozentals, "Council Post: In-Office Vs. Remote Vs. Hybrid Work Two Years Later: The Impact on Employee Efficiency," *Forbes*, March 18, 2022.

61. E.E. Kossek and R.J. Thompson, "Workplace Flexibility: Integrating Employer and Employee Perspectives to Close the Research–Practice Implementation Gap," in *The Oxford Handbook of Work and Family*, ed. T.D. Allen and L.T. Eby (New York: Oxford University Press, 2016), 255–70; H. Hambly and J. (Donghoon) Lee, "The Rural Telecommuter Surplus in Southwestern Ontario, Canada," *Telecommunications Policy* 43 (2019): 278–86.

62. C.A. Bartel, A. Wrzesniewski, and B.M. Wiesenfeld, "Knowing Where You Stand: Physical Isolation, Perceived Respect, and Organizational Identification among Virtual Employees," *Organization Science* 23, no. 3 (2011): 743–57; E.E. Kossek, R.J. Thompson, and B.A. Lautsch, "Balanced Workplace Flexibility: Avoiding the Traps," *California Management Review* 57, no. 4 (2015): 5–25.

63. T.A. O'Neill, L.A. Hambley, and G.S. Chatellier, "Cyberslacking, Engagement, and Personality in Distributed Work Environments," *Computers in Human Behavior* 40 (2014): 152–60; N.W. Van Yperen, E.F. Rietzschel, and K.M.M. De Jonge, "Blended Working: For Whom It May (Not) Work," *PLoS ONE* 9, no. 7 (2014): e102921; S.J. Perry, C. Rubino, and E.M. Hunter, "Stress in Remote Work: Two Studies Testing the Demand-Control-Person Model," *European Journal of Work and Organizational Psychology* 27, no. 5 (2018): 577–93; T.A. Beauregard, K.A. Basile, and E. Canonico, "Telework: Outcomes and Facilitators for Employees," in *The Cambridge Handbook of Technology and Employee Behavior*, ed. R.N. Landers, 1st ed. (Cambridge: Cambridge University Press, 2019), 511–43; A.M. Evans et al., "Extroversion and Conscientiousness Predict Deteriorating Job Outcomes during the COVID-19 Transition to Enforced Remote Work," *Social Psychological and Personality Science* 13, no. 3 (2022): 781–91.

64. L.L. Thurstone, "Ability, Motivation, and Speed," *Psychometrika* 2, no. 4 (1937): 249–54; N.R.F. Maier, *Psychology in Industry*, 2nd ed. (Boston: Houghton Mifflin, 1955); V.H. Vroom, *Work and Motivation* (New York: Wiley, 1964); J.P. Campbell et al., *Managerial Behavior, Performance, and Effectiveness* (New York: McGraw Hill, 1970).

65. R.S. Dalal, D.P. Bhave, and J. Fiset, "Within-Person Variability in Job Performance: A Theoretical Review and Research Agenda," *Journal of Management* 40, no. 5 (2014): 1396–436; S. Aryee et al., "Developing and Leveraging Human Capital Resource to Promote Service Quality: Testing a Theory of Performance," *Journal of Management* 42, no. 2 (2016): 480–99.

66. E.E. Lawler III and L.W. Porter, "Antecedent Attitudes of Effective Managerial Performance," *Organizational Behavior and Human Performance* 2 (1967): 122–42; O.-P. Kauppila, "So, What Am I Supposed to Do? A Multilevel Examination of Role Clarity," *Journal of Management Studies* 51, no. 5 (2014): 737–63.

67. Only a few sources have included all four factors. These include J.P. Campbell and R.D. Pritchard, "Motivation Theory in Industrial and Organizational Psychology," in *Handbook of Industrial and Organizational Psychology*, ed. M.D. Dunnette (Chicago: Rand McNally, 1976), 62–130; T.R. Mitchell, "Motivation: New Directions for Theory, Research, and Practice," *Academy of Management Review* 7, no. 1 (1982): 80–88; G.A.J. Churchill et al., "The Determinants of Salesperson Performance: A Meta-Analysis," *Journal of Marketing Research* 22, no. 2 (1985): 103–18; R.E. Plank and D.A. Reid, "The Mediating Role of Sales Behaviors: An Alternative Perspective of Sales Performance and Effectiveness," *Journal of Personal Selling & Sales Management* 14, no. 3 (1994): 43-56. The "MARS" acronym was coined by senior officers in the Singapore Armed Forces during a senior officer program taught by Steve McShane.

68. Technically, the model proposes that situation factors moderate the effects of the three within-person factors. For instance, the effect of employee motivation on behavior and performance depends on (is moderated by) the situation.

69. G.P. Latham and C.C. Pinder, "Work Motivation Theory and Research at the Dawn of the Twenty-First Century," *Annual Review of Psychology* 56 (2005): 485-516; G.P. Latham, *Work Motivation: History, Theory, Research, and Practice*, revised ed. (Thousand Oaks, CA: Sage, 2012), 7.

70. L.M. Spencer and S.M. Spencer, *Competence at Work: Models for Superior Performance* (New York: Wiley, 1993); R.A. Roe, "Using Competences in Employee Development," in *Wiley Blackwell Handbook of the Psychology of Training, Development, and Performance Improvement*, ed. K. Kraiger et al. (Chichester: Wiley, 2014), 303–35; P.R. Sackett et al., "Individual Differences and Their Measurement: A Review of 100 Years of Research," *Journal of Applied Psychology* 102 (2017): 254–73.

71. W. Wood, J.M. Quinn, and D.A. Kashy, "Habits in Everyday Life: Thought, Emotion, and Action," *Journal of Personality and Social Psychology* 83, no. 6 (2002): 1281–97; W. Wood and D. Rünger, "Psychology of Habit," *Annual Review of Psychology* 67 (2016): 289–314; D.L. Lorenzetti et al., "Strategies for Improving Physician Documentation in the Emergency Department: A Systematic Review," *BMC Emergency Medicine* 18, no. 1 (2018): 36; K. Miyahara, T.G. Ransom, and S. Gallagher, "What the Situation Affords: Habit and Heedful Interrelations in Skilled Performance," in *Habits: Pragmatist Approaches from Cognitive Science, Neuroscience, and Social Theory*, ed. F. Caruana and I. Testa (Cambridge: Cambridge University Press, 2020), 120–36.

72. *The Interserve Society Report* (Reading: Interserve, January 30, 2015); J. Harter, "Obsolete Annual Review: Gallup's Advice" (Washington, DC: Gallup, Inc., September 28, 2015); Randstad, "Prospects for Older Workers Shrink While the Skills Gap Widens," *Randstad Workmonitor* (Amsterdam, The Netherlands: Randstad Holding NV, June 2016); TINYpulse, *The Tinypulse 2015 Employee Engagement & Organizational Culture Report: The Era of Personal and Peer Accountability* (Seattle: TINYpulse, February 2016); Gallup Inc., *State of the American Workplace* (Washington, DC: Gallup, February 23, 2017).

73. P. Tharenou, A.M. Saks, and C. Moore, "A Review and Critique of Research on Training and Organizational-Level Outcomes," *Human Resource Management Review* 17, no. 3 (2007): 251–73; Y. Kim and R.E. Ployhart, "The Effects of Staffing and Training on Firm Productivity and Profit Growth Before, During, and After the Great Recession," *Journal of Applied Psychology* 99, no. 3 (2014): 361–89; M. Choi and H.J. Yoon, "Training Investment and Organizational Outcomes: A Moderated Mediation Model of Employee Outcomes and Strategic Orientation of the HR Function," *International Journal of Human Resource Management* 26, no. 20 (2015): 2632–51.

74. E.C. Dierdorff, R.S. Rubin, and D.G. Bachrach, "Role Expectations as Antecedents of Citizenship and the Moderating Effects of Work Context," *Journal of Management* 38, no. 2 (2012): 573–98; A. Newman, B. Allen, and Q. Miao, "I Can See Clearly Now: The Moderating Effects of Role Clarity on Subordinate Responses to Ethical Leadership," *Personnel Review* 44, no. 4 (2015): 611–28.

75. W.H. Cooper and M.J. Withey, "The Strong Situation Hypothesis," *Personality and Social Psychology Review* 13, no. 1 (2009): 62–72; N.A. Bowling et al., "Situational Strength as a Moderator of the Relationship between Job Satisfaction and Job Performance: A Meta-Analytic Examination," *Journal of Business and Psychology* 30, no. 1 (2015): 89–104; T.A. Judge and C.P. Zapata, "The Person–Situation Debate Revisited: Effect of Situation Strength and Trait Activation on the Validity of the Big Five Personality Traits in Predicting Job Performance," *Academy of Management Journal* 58, no. 4 (2015): 1149–79; J.F. Rauthmann and R.A. Sherman, "Situation Change: Stability and Change of Situation Variables between and within Persons," *Frontiers in Psychology* 6 (January 6, 2016): 1938.

76. L.H. Peters and E.J. O'Connor, "Situational Constraints and Work Outcomes: The Influences of a Frequently Overlooked Construct," *Academy of Management Review* 5, no. 3 (1980): 391–97; G. Johns, "Commentary: In Praise of Context," *Journal of Organizational Behavior* 22 (2001): 31–42; C.E.J. Härtel and J.M. O'Connor, "Contextualizing Research: Putting Context Back into Organizational Behavior Research," *Journal of Management & Organization* 20, no. 4 (2014): 417–22.

77. L. Mirabella, "Walmart Employees Get Real Look at Retail World; Virtual Reality Technology Prepares Supervisors for Situations That Might Arise," *Baltimore Sun*, December 3, 2017; H. Shively, "Area Stores Training Employees Using Virtual Reality," *TCA Regional News*, November 12, 2018; S. DiNatale, "What's It Like to Train for Walmart's Black Friday? Local Stores Use Virtual Reality Goggles," *Tampa Bay Times*, November 13, 2018.

78. R.D. Hackett, "Understanding and Predicting Work Performance in the Canadian Military," *Canadian Journal of Behavioural Science* 34, no. 2 (2002): 131–40; J.P. Campbell and B.M. Wiernik, "The Modeling and Assessment of Work Performance," *Annual Review of Organizational Psychology and Organizational Behavior* 2, no. 1 (2015): 47–74.

79. L. Tay, R. Su, and J. Rounds, "People-Things and Data-Ideas: Bipolar Dimensions?" *Journal of Counseling Psychology* 58, no. 3 (2011): 424–40.

80. M.A. Griffin, A. Neal, and S.K. Parker, "A New Model of Work Role Performance: Positive Behavior in Uncertain and Interdependent Contexts," *Academy of Management Journal* 50, no. 2 (2007): 327–47; S.K. Baard, T.A. Rench, and S.W.J. Kozlowski, "Performance Adaptation: A Theoretical Integration and Review," *Journal of Management* 40, no. 1 (2014): 48–99; D.K. Jundt, M.K. Shoss, and J.L. Huang, "Individual Adaptive Performance in Organizations: A Review," *Journal of Organizational Behavior* 36, no. S1 (2015): S53–S71; J.A. Carpini, S.K. Parker, and M.A. Griffin, "A Look Back and a Leap Forward: A Review and Synthesis of the Individual Work Performance Literature," *Academy of Management Annals* 11, no. 2 (2017): 825–85; S.K. Parker, Y. Wang, and J. Liao, "When Is Proactivity Wise? A Review of Factors That Influence the Individual Outcomes of Proactive Behavior," *Annual Review of Organizational Psychology and Organizational Behavior* 6 (2019): 221–48; S. Park and S. Park, "Employee Adaptive Performance and Its Antecedents: Review and Synthesis," *Human Resource Development Review* 18, no. 3 (2019): 294–324.

81. D.W. Organ, "Organizational Citizenship Behavior: It's Construct Clean-up Time," *Human Performance* 10 (1997): 85–97; J.A. LePine, A. Erez, and D.E. Johnson, "The Nature and Dimensionality of Organizational Citizenship Behavior: A Critical Review and Meta-Analysis," *Journal of Applied Psychology* 87 (2002): 52–65; N.P. Podsakoff et al., "Consequences of Unit-Level Organizational Citizenship Behaviors: A Review and Recommendations for Future Research," *Journal of Organizational Behavior* 35, no. S1 (2014): S87–S119.

82. E.W. Morrison, "Role Definitions and Organizational Citizenship Behavior: The Importance of the Employee's Perspective," *Academy of Management Journal* 37, no. 6 (1994): 1543–67; N. Podsakoff et al., "Individual- and Organizational-Level Consequences of Organizational Citizenship Behaviors: A Meta-Analysis," *Journal of Applied Psychology* 94, no. 1 (2009): 122–41; E.C. Dierdorff, R.S. Rubin, and D.G. Bachrach, "Role Expectations as Antecedents of Citizenship and the Moderating Effects of Work Context," *Journal of Management* 38, no. 2 (2012): 573–98.

83. S.B. Mackenzie, N.P. Podsakoff, and P.M. Podsakoff, "Individual- and Organizational-Level Consequences of Organizational Citizenship Behaviors," in *The Oxford Handbook of Organizational Citizenship Behavior*, ed. P.M. Podsakoff, S.B. MacKenzie, and N.P. Podsakoff (New York: Oxford University Press, 2018); C.J.C. de Geus et al., "Organizational Citizenship Behavior in the Public Sector: A Systematic Literature Review and Future Research Agenda," *Public Administration Review* 80, no. 2 (2020): 259–70.

84. M.C. Bolino, A.C. Klotz, and W.H. Turnley, "The Unintended Consequences of Organizational Citizenship Behaviors for Employees, Teams, and Organizations," in *The Oxford Handbook of Organizational Citizenship Behavior*, ed. P.M. Podsakoff, S.B. Mackenzie, and N.P. Podsakoff (New York: Oxford University Press, 2018), 185–202.

85. B. Marcus et al., "The Structure of Counterproductive Work Behavior: A Review, a Structural Meta-Analysis, and a Primary Study," *Journal of Management* 42, no. 1 (2016): 203–33; R.S. Dalal and N.C. Carpenter, "The Other Side of the Coin?: Similarities and Differences between Organizational Citizenship Behavior and Counterproductive Work Behavior," in *The Oxford Handbook of Organizational Citizenship Behavior*, ed. P.M. Podsakoff, S.B. MacKenzie, and N.P. Podsakoff (New York: Oxford University Press, 2018), 69–90.

86. The relationship between employee turnover and firm performance is actually very low, but this is due to moderators and is stronger for some forms of firm performance. See: J.I. Hancock et al., "Meta-Analytic Review of Employee Turnover as a Predictor of Firm Performance," *Journal of Management* 39, no. 3 (2013): 573–603.

87. T.-Y. Park and J. Shaw, "Turnover Rates and Organizational Performance: A Meta-Analysis," *Journal of Applied Psychology* 98, no. 2 (2013): 268–309; J.I. Hancock et al., "Meta-Analytic Review of Employee Turnover as a Predictor of Firm Performance," *Journal of Management* 39, no. 3 (2013): 573–603; J.G. Messersmith et al., "Turnover at the Top: Executive Team Departures and Firm Performance," *Organization Science* 25, no. 3 (2014): 776–93; B.C. Holtom and T.C. Burch, "A Model of Turnover-Based Disruption in Customer Services," *Human Resource Management Review* 26, no. 1 (2016): 25–36.

88. D.A. Harrison and J.J. Martocchio, "Time for Absenteeism: A 20-Year Review of Origins, Offshoots, and Outcomes," *Journal of Management* 24, no. 3 (1998): 305–50; M.A. Herrmann and J.E. Rockoff, "Worker Absence and Productivity: Evidence from Teaching," *Journal of Labor Economics* 30, no. 4 (2012): 749–82; V. Čikeš, H. Maškarin Ribarić, and K. Črnjar, "The Determinants and Outcomes of Absence Behavior: A Systematic Literature Review," *Social Sciences* 7, no. 8 (2018): 120.

89. W. Beemsterboer et al., "A Literature Review on Sick Leave Determinants (1984–2004)," *International Journal of Occupational Medicine and Environmental Health* 22, no. 2 (2009): 169–79; C. M. Berry, A. M. Lelchook, and M. A. Clark, "A Meta-Analysis of the Interrelationships between Employee Lateness, Absenteeism, and Turnover: Implications for Models of Withdrawal Behavior," *Journal of Organizational Behavior* 33, no. 5 (2012): 678–99; M. Miraglia and G. Johns, "The Social and Relational Dynamics of Absenteeism from Work: A Multilevel Review and Integration," *Academy of Management Annals* 15, no. 1 (2021): 37–67.

90. G. Johns, "Presenteeism in the Workplace: A Review and Research Agenda," *Journal of Organizational Behavior* 31, no. 4 (2010): 519–42; R.K. Skagen and A.M. Collins, "The Consequences of Sickness Presenteeism on Health and Wellbeing over Time: A Systematic Review," *Social Science & Medicine* 161 (2016): 169–77; S.A. Ruhle et al., "'To Work, or Not to Work, That Is the Question'–Recent Trends and Avenues for Research on Presenteeism," *European Journal of Work and Organizational Psychology* 29, no. 3 (2020): 344–63; M. Karanika-Murray and C. Biron, "The Health-Performance Framework of Presenteeism: Towards Understanding an Adaptive Behaviour," *Human Relations* 73, no. 2 (2020): 242–61.

91. G. Johns, "Attendance Dynamics at Work: The Antecedents and Correlates of Presenteeism, Absenteeism, and Productivity Loss," *Journal of Occupational Health Psychology* 16, no. 4 (2011): 483–500; D. Baker-McClearn et al., "Absence Management and Presenteeism: The Pressures on Employees to Attend Work and the Impact of Attendance on Performance," *Human Resource Management Journal* 20, no. 3 (2010): 311–28; R. Pohling et al., "Work-Related Factors of Presenteeism: The Mediating Role of Mental and Physical Health," *Journal of Occupational Health Psychology* 21, no. 2 (2016): 220–34.

PART 2

2 Individual Differences: Personality and Values

Jacob Lund/Shutterstock

Learning Objectives

After reading this chapter, you should be able to:

LO2-1 Define personality and discuss how the Big Five personality factors relate to workplace behavior and performance.

LO2-2 Describe the dark triad personality and identify its effects on behavior in organizations.

LO2-3 Summarize psychological types in the Myers–Briggs Type Indicator (MBTI) and discuss the usefulness of this model in organizations.

LO2-4 Summarize Schwartz's model of individual values and discuss the conditions where values influence behavior.

LO2-5 Describe four ethical principles and discuss three factors that influence ethical behavior.

LO2-6 Describe five values commonly studied across cultures.

personality The relatively enduring pattern of thoughts, emotions, and behaviors that characterize a person, along with the psychological processes behind those characteristics

Most people think about their personal values when assessing a job offer or deciding to change employers or careers. "One of the first things I do when I find a job opening, in addition to making sure it aligns with my skills and interests, is research the company, its culture and its values," says Erin Lewis, social media analyst at BCW Global in Atlanta. "Even if the job description sounds fantastic, if the company doesn't align with my personal values or have evidence of a larger purpose, I quickly move on."

Charlotte Bella also includes personal values in her job hunting checklist. "Each role I've had I've made a point of constantly checking: am I learning enough; am I pushing myself enough and most importantly; am I working for a company that aligns to my values?" says the senior product manager at Booking.com in Manchester, UK. For example, Bella describes a time when she worked at a charity but moved to another company mainly because it gave her more technology experience. "However, I quickly realized our goals and values were not aligned so I researched companies where I could get the tech experience but also be somewhere that I felt I belonged (and which is why I'm at Booking.com today!)."

"We know that a key driver for determined job seekers is finding companies that align with their values," says Emil Yeargin, head of talent and recruiting at online payroll platform Gusto in San Francisco. Yeargin urges companies to go beyond describing the transactional aspects of hiring (pay, job duties, employee–employer legal obligations, etc.) so they connect with applicants' personal values. "They must focus instead on creating a values-based interview experience."[1]

Personal values have a powerful influence on our attitudes, decisions, and behavior. This chapter takes a close look at personal values as well as personality, which are the two most stable foundations of individual behavior. We begin by describing the personality concept, the five-factor personality model, the personality dark triad, and the Jungian personality theory applied by the Myers–Briggs Type Indicator (MBTI). In the section on personal values, we describe Schwartz's values circumplex model, explain how personal values influence workplace decisions and behavior, and introduce the concept of values congruence. Next, we examine ethical values and the mechanisms through which they influence a person's decisions and behavior. The final section of this chapter describes several cross-cultural values and explains their relevance to organizational behavior.

LO2-1 Define personality and discuss how the Big Five personality factors relate to workplace behavior and performance.

PERSONALITY AND THE FIVE-FACTOR MODEL IN ORGANIZATIONS

On any given day in almost every workplace, we usually mention either our own or someone else's personality. **Personality** refers to the relatively enduring pattern of thoughts, emotions, and behaviors that characterize a person, along with the psychological processes behind those characteristics.[2] In essence, it is the bundle of characteristics that make our thoughts and actions similar to or different from other people. We estimate an individual's personality by what they say or do, and we infer the person's internal states—including thoughts and emotions—from these observable behaviors.

People engage in a wide range of behaviors in their daily lives, yet close inspection of those actions reveals discernible patterns called *personality traits*.[3] Traits are broad concepts that

An individual's personality is estimated by what they say or do, and we infer the person's internal states—including thoughts and emotions—from these observable behaviors.
Elnur/123RF

allow us to label and understand individual differences. For example, some of your friends are probably quite talkative whereas others tend to be quieter. Some people like to take risks whereas others are risk-averse. Each trait implies that there is something within the person, rather than environmental influences alone, that predicts this behavioral tendency. Studies have found that an individual's personality traits measured in childhood predict many behaviors and outcomes in adulthood, including educational attainment, employment success, marital relationships, illegal activities, and health-risk behaviors.[4]

Personality is based on behavioral tendencies, but it does not imply that the individual acts the same way in all situations. Such consistency would be considered abnormal because it indicates a person's insensitivity to social norms, reward systems, and other external conditions.[5] People temporarily vary their behavior to suit the situation, even if that behavior is at odds with their personality. For example, talkative people remain relatively quiet in a library where "no talking" rules are explicit and strictly enforced. But even there, personality differences are apparent because talkative people tend to do more chatting in libraries relative to how much other people talk in that setting.

> One regrets the loss even of one's worst habits. . . . They are such an essential part of one's personality.[6]
>
> —Oscar Wilde, author (from *The Picture of Dorian Gray*)

What Causes Personality: Nature versus Nurture

Personality is shaped by both nature and nurture, although the relative importance of each continues to be debated and studied.[7] *Nature* refers to our genetic or hereditary origins—the genes that we inherit from our parents. Studies of identical twins reveal that heredity has a very large effect on personality; up to 50 percent of variation in behavior and 30 percent of temperament preferences can be attributed to a person's genetic characteristics. In other words, genetic code not only determines our eye color, skin tone, and physical shape; it also significantly affects our attitudes, decisions, and behavior.

Personality is also shaped by *nurture*—our socialization, life experiences, and other forms of interaction with the environment. Personality develops and changes mainly from childhood to young adulthood, typically stabilizing by around age 30. However, some personality changes continue to occur later in life. For instance, a few traits (openness to experience, social vitality) increase through to young adulthood, then decline in later years, whereas other traits (agreeableness, conscientiousness) tend to increase through to late life. Our personality can also change somewhat due to the job we work in over a long time period. Even migrating to another culture can change our personality to some extent.[8]

The main explanation for why personality becomes more stable by adulthood is that we form a clearer and more rigid self-concept. This increasing clarity of "who we are" anchors our behavior with the help of our *executive function.* This is the part of the brain that monitors and regulates goal-directed behavior to keep it consistent with our self-concept. Our self-view becomes clearer and more stable with age, which increases the stability and consistency of our personality and behavior.[9] We discuss self-concept in more detail in Chapter 3. The main point here is that personality is not completely determined by heredity; life experiences, particularly early in life, also shape each individual's personality traits.

Five-Factor Model of Personality

Sociable, anxious, curious, dependable, suspicious, talkative, adventurous, and hundreds of other personality traits have been described over the years, so experts have tried to organize them into smaller clusters. The most researched and respected clustering of personality traits is the five-factor model, also known as the *Big Five.*[10] Several decades ago, personality experts identified more than 17,000 words that describe an individual's personality. These words were distilled down to five broad personality factors, each with a cluster of specific traits. Similar results were found in studies of different languages, suggesting that the five-factor model is fairly robust across cultures. These Big Five factors, represented by the handy acronym *CANOE* (or *OCEAN*), are outlined in Exhibit 2.1 and described next.

- **Conscientiousness.** Characterizes people who are organized, dependable, goal-focused, thorough, disciplined, methodical, and industrious. People with low conscientiousness tend to be careless, disorganized, and less thorough.
- **Agreeableness.** Describes people who are trusting, helpful, good-natured, considerate, tolerant, selfless, generous, and flexible. People with low agreeableness tend to be uncooperative and intolerant of others' needs as well as more suspicious and self-focused.
- **Neuroticism.** Refers to people who tend to be anxious, insecure, self-conscious, depressed, and temperamental. In contrast, people with low neuroticism (high emotional stability) are poised, secure, and calm.
- **Openness to experience.** Characterizes people who are imaginative, creative, unconventional, curious, nonconforming, autonomous, and aesthetically perceptive. Those with low scores on this factor tend to be more resistant to change, less open to new ideas, and more conventional and fixed in their ways.
- **Extraversion.** Describes people who are outgoing, talkative, energetic, sociable, and assertive. The opposite is *introversion*, which applies to those who are quiet, cautious, and less interactive with others. Extraverts get their energy from other people and things around them, whereas introverts get their energy more from personal reflection on concepts and ideas. Introverts do not necessarily lack social skills. Instead, they are more inclined to direct their interests to ideas than to social events. Introverts feel more comfortable being alone than do extraverts.

Exhibit 2.1 Five-Factor Model of Personality

Personality factor	People with higher scores on this factor tend to be more:
Conscientiousness	Organized, dependable, goal-focused, thorough, disciplined, methodical, industrious
Agreeableness	Trusting, helpful, good-natured, considerate, tolerant, selfless, generous, flexible
Neuroticism	Anxious, insecure, self-conscious, depressed, temperamental
Openness to experience	Imaginative, creative, unconventional, curious, nonconforming, autonomous, perceptive
Extraversion	Outgoing, talkative, energetic, sociable, assertive

connect

SELF-ASSESSMENT 2.1: What Is Your Big Five Personality?

connect

SELF-ASSESSMENT 2.2: Are You Introverted or Extraverted?

Five-Factor Model and Work Performance Personality mainly affects behavior and performance through motivation, specifically by influencing the individual's direction and intensity of effort (i.e., what goals they choose to reach and how much effort they apply to reach those goals). Consequently, all of the Big Five factors predict one or more types of employee behavior and performance to some extent.

Exhibit 2.2 highlights which Big Five personality factors best predict the three types of task performance as well as organizational citizenship and counterproductive work behaviors (see Chapter 1).[11] Conscientiousness stands out as the best overall personality predictor of proficient task performance for most jobs. The specific conscientiousness traits of industriousness (achievement, self-discipline, purposefulness) and dutifulness are the best predictors of proficient task performance. Conscientious employees set higher personal goals for themselves and are more persistent. They also engage in more organizational citizenship and in less counterproductive work behavior. Conscientiousness is a weak predictor of adaptive (responding to change) and proactive performance (taking initiative toward new work patterns). In fact, two specific conscientiousness traits—orderliness and dependability—tend to suppress adaptivity.

Extraversion is the second best overall personality predictor of proficient task performance but is a much weaker predictor than is conscientiousness. Among the specific traits within the extraversion factor, assertiveness and positive emotionality are the strongest predictors of proficient task performance. Assertiveness is also a strong predictor of adaptive and proactive performance. Assertive employees tend to have a "take charge" approach to situations, which is consistent with adapting to change and proactively initiating change. Extraversion is associated with influencing others and being comfortable in social settings, which (along with being assertive) explains why effective leaders and salespeople tend to be somewhat more extraverted than the general population.

Agreeableness is positively associated with organizational citizenship and negatively associated with counterproductive work behaviors.[12] The reason is that employees with high

five-factor model (FFM) of personality The five broad dimensions representing most personality traits: conscientiousness, emotional stability, openness to experience, agreeableness, and extraversion

conscientiousness A personality dimension describing people who are organized, dependable, goal-focused, thorough, disciplined, methodical, and industrious

agreeableness A personality dimension describing people who are trusting, helpful, good-natured, considerate, tolerant, selfless, generous, and flexible

neuroticism A personality dimension describing people who tend to be anxious, insecure, self-conscious, depressed, and temperamental

openness to experience A personality dimension describing people who are imaginative, creative, unconventional, curious, nonconforming, autonomous, and aesthetically perceptive

extraversion A personality dimension describing people who are outgoing, talkative, sociable, and assertive

Exhibit 2.2 Big Five Personality and Work Performance

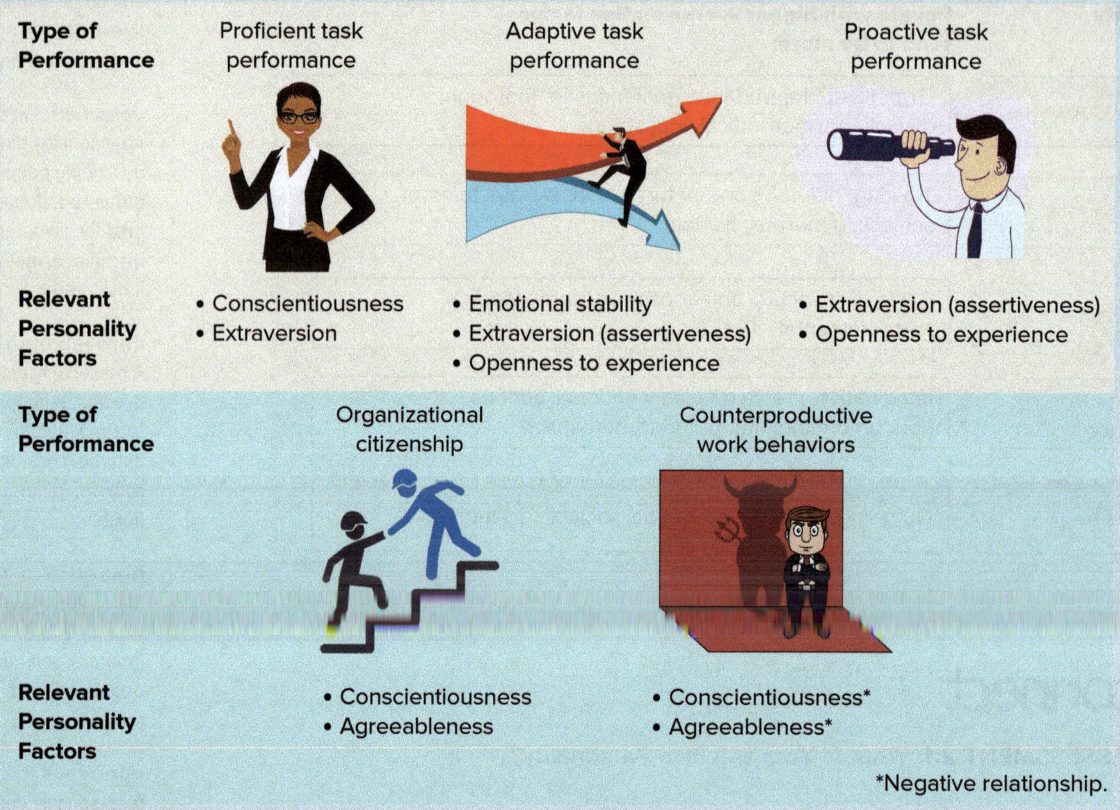

(Top-left): Volha Hlinskaya/123RF; *(Top-center):* Fred Ho Yeow Hui/Shutterstock; *(Top-right):* malika.1028/Shutterstock; *(Bottom-left):* Aha-Soft/Shutterstock; *(Bottom-right):* Sign N Symbol Production/Shutterstock

connect

SELF-ASSESSMENT 2.3: Can You Identify Personality Traits from Blogging Words?

agreeableness are motivated to be cooperative, sensitive, flexible, and supportive. Agreeableness does not predict proficient or proactive task performance very well, mainly because it is associated with lower motivation to set goals and achieve results. However, employees with higher (but not too high) agreeableness tend to improve team performance through better knowledge sharing and motivation to help the team. Agreeableness also has a positive effect on friendliness behavior in customer service jobs.[13]

Openness to experience is a weak predictor of proficient task performance, but it is one of the best personality predictors of adaptive and proactive performance. The main reason is that employees with higher openness scores have more curiosity, imagination, and tolerance of change.[14] These traits also explain why openness to change is associated with successful performance in creative work.

Emotional stability (low neuroticism) is one of the best personality predictors of adaptive performance.[15] The main explanation is that employees with higher emotional stability cope better with the ambiguity and uncertainty of change. In contrast, those with higher neuroticism view change as a threat, so they tend to avoid change and experience more stress when faced with workplace adjustments. These characteristics would suggest that emotional stability also predicts proactive performance, but the limited research has reported mixed results.

Caveats When Applying the Five-Factor Model The five-factor model of personality is well established, but we need to alert you to a few misconceptions. First, the "perfect employee" isn't the individual with the highest scores on all of the Big Five personality factors. Part of the problem may be that the labels and structure of the Big Five factors have a strong linear bias (high is good, low is bad). But research indicates that the relationship between some Big Five factors and performance is nonlinear. For instance, employees with moderate extraversion perform better in sales jobs than those with high or low extraversion.[16]

Second, some behaviors are predicted better by a specific personality trait than by the overall Big Five factor for that trait.

For example, the specific extraversion traits of assertiveness and positive emotionality predict proficient task performance better than the overall extraversion factor.

> Some behaviors are predicted better by a specific personality trait than by the overall Big Five factor for that trait.

Third, personality isn't completely static. As we explained earlier, an individual's personality does stabilize around age 30, but some Big Five factors tend to increase or decrease as we age. Some personality factors also change over a long time when our environment significantly changes.

Fourth, although the five-factor model captures a large portion of the domain we call *personality,* it doesn't represent all of it.[17] There are several perspectives or approaches to personality, each of which has a somewhat different view or emphasis. For example, the next section of this chapter looks at two other models of personality that only partially overlap with the Big Five factors.

L02-2 Describe the dark triad personality and identify its effects on behavior in organizations.

OTHER PERSONALITY CONCEPTS: THE DARK TRIAD AND MBTI TYPES

The Dark Triad

When personality experts developed the five-factor model, they deliberately excluded words with noticeably positive or negative valence, such as *humble* (positive) or *sinister* (negative). More recently, researchers re-examined the emotionally charged words that were previously excluded. Out of these studies has emerged a cluster of three socially undesirable personality traits—Machiavellianism, narcissism, and psychopathy—called the **dark triad.**[18] Although these traits are distinct, they have a common "dark core" consisting of either low humility/honesty or a tendency to malevolently undermine others to maximize one's own gains.[19]

- **Machiavellianism.** People with high Machiavellianism (*high-Machs*) demonstrate a strong motivation to get what they want at the expense of others. They believe that deceit is a natural and acceptable way to achieve their goals; indeed, they take pleasure in misleading, outwitting, and otherwise controlling others. High-Machs routinely use lies, manipulation, exploitation, and other undesirable influence tactics. They have a cynical disregard for moral principles, believe that getting more than one deserves is acceptable, and seldom empathize with or trust coworkers.[20]
- **Narcissism.** This personality trait is evident in people who have an obsessive belief in their superiority and entitlement. Along with their grandiose, inflated self-view, narcissists have an excessive need for attention, so they aggressively engage in self-promotion, exhibitionism, and other attention-seeking behaviors. They can be initially charming, but are intensely envious of others. This envy is eventually apparent in their arrogance, schadenfreude (deriving pleasure from another person's misfortune), callous disregard for others' feelings (i.e., low empathy), and exploitation of others for personal aggrandizement.[21]
- **Psychopathy.** Considered the most sinister personality trait in the dark triad, psychopathy refers to social predators who ruthlessly dominate and manipulate others, yet without empathy or any feelings of remorse or anxiety. They are selfish self-promoters who use superficial charm (called the "mask" of psychopathy), yet engage in antisocial, impulsive, and often fraudulent thrill-seeking behavior. These people callously do as they please and take what they want.[22]

The Dark Triad in the Workplace Machiavellianism, narcissism, and psychopathy may seem like they belong in textbooks on criminology or medieval politics, not organizational behavior. Yet these traits are gaining attention because they are prevalent throughout the workplace. As one personality researcher warned in his keynote address to a national police association: "Not all psychopaths are in prison. Some are in the board room."[23]

These three traits produce numerous dysfunctional outcomes in organizational settings.[24] Dishonesty is a core characteristic of the dark triad, so people with these traits are more likely to lie and deceive others at work. Similarly, they malevolently

dark triad A cluster of three socially undesirable (dark) personality traits: Machiavellianism, narcissism, and psychopathy

Machiavellianism A personality trait of people who demonstrate a strong motivation to achieve their own goals at the expense of others, who believe that deceit is a natural and acceptable way to achieve their goals, who take pleasure in outwitting and misleading others using crude influence tactics, and who have a cynical disregard for morality

narcissism A personality trait of people with a grandiose, obsessive belief in their superiority and entitlement, a propensity to aggressively engage in attention-seeking behaviors, an intense envy of others, and tendency to exhibit arrogance, callousness, and exploitation of others for personal aggrandizement

psychopathy A personality trait of people who ruthlessly dominate and manipulate others without empathy or any feelings of remorse or anxiety, use superficial charm, yet are social predators who engage in antisocial, impulsive, and often fraudulent thrill-seeking behavior

Dishonesty is a core characteristic of the dark triad, so people with these traits are more likely to lie and deceive others at work.
Ranta Images/Shutterstock

undermine others to maximize their own gains. This is the essence of **organizational politics** (see Chapter 9), which is about using influence tactics for personal gain at the expense of others and the interests of the entire organization. Political tactics produce a host of dysfunctional outcomes, ranging from employee stress and dissatisfaction to unproductive use of organizational resources.

Counterproductive work behaviors, such as taking company property from work without permission or deliberately working slowly to get overtime, are predicted by the dark triad to some extent, but they are more closely associated with specific Big Five factors (low agreeableness and low conscientiousness) that were identified earlier in Exhibit 2.1. Instead, dark triad traits are more strongly associated with serious white-collar crimes. The dark triad is also associated with bullying and other forms of workplace aggression.

People with dark triad personality traits tend to make decisions that produce poorer absolute and risk-adjusted investment returns. In particular, those with high psychopathy take excessive risks, due to their overconfidence and disregard for consequences.[25]

The dark triad has a complex relationship with other forms of task performance and career success. People with these traits are dysfunctional team members in the long term because, by definition, they don't trust coworkers and focus on their own goals at the expense of team goals.[26] At the same time, dark triad employees are known to help others in the short run when it serves their self-interest.

People who possess dark triad personality traits aren't always worse off. They have a manipulative political skill, which some supervisors rate favorably in job performance. Being manipulative also occasionally helps employees move into more central (and therefore powerful) positions in informal employee networks. Narcissistic CEOs tend to have higher direct pay as well as a larger gap in pay from other members of the executive team.[27]

LO2-3 Summarize psychological types in the Myers–Briggs Type Indicator (MBTI) and discuss the usefulness of this model in organizations.

Jungian Personality Theory and the Myers–Briggs Type Indicator

The five-factor model of personality has the most research support, but it is not the most popular personality test in practice. That distinction goes to Carl Jung's theory of psychological types, which is measured through the **Myers–Briggs Type Indicator (MBTI)** (see Exhibit 2.3).

Nearly a century ago, Swiss psychiatrist Carl Jung suggested that personality is mainly represented by the individual's preferences regarding perceiving and judging information.[28] Jung explained that the perceiving function—how people prefer to gather information—occurs through two competing orientations: *sensing (S)* and *intuition (N)*. Sensing involves perceiving information directly through the five senses; it relies on an organized structure to acquire factual and preferably quantitative details. In contrast, intuition relies more on insight and subjective experience to see relationships among variables. Sensing types focus on the here and now, whereas intuitive types focus more on future possibilities.

Jung also proposed that the judging function—how people prefer making decisions based on what they have perceived—consists of two competing processes: *thinking (T)* and *feeling (F)*. People with a thinking orientation rely on rational cause-effect logic and systematic data collection to make decisions. Those with a strong feeling orientation, on the other hand, give more weight to their emotional responses to the options presented, as well as to how those choices affect others. Jung noted that in addition to the four core processes of sensing, intuition, thinking, and feeling, people differ in their level of extraversion-introversion, which was introduced earlier as one of the Big Five personality traits.

The MBTI extends Jung's list of personality traits described previously by also measuring Jung's broader categories of *perceiving* and *judging,* which represent a person's attitude toward the external world. People with a perceiving orientation are open, curious, and flexible. They like to keep their options open and to adapt spontaneously to events as they unfold. Judging types prefer order and structure and want to resolve problems quickly.

connect

SELF-ASSESSMENT 2.4: How Machiavellian Are You?

Jungian Theory in the Workplace Is Carl Jung's theory of psychological types useful in

organizational politics Use of influence tactics for personal gain at the perceived expense of others and the organization

Myers-Briggs Type Indicator (MBTI) An instrument designed to measure the elements of Jungian personality theory, particularly preferences regarding perceiving and judging information

Exhibit 2.3 Jungian and Myers–Briggs Type Indicator Types

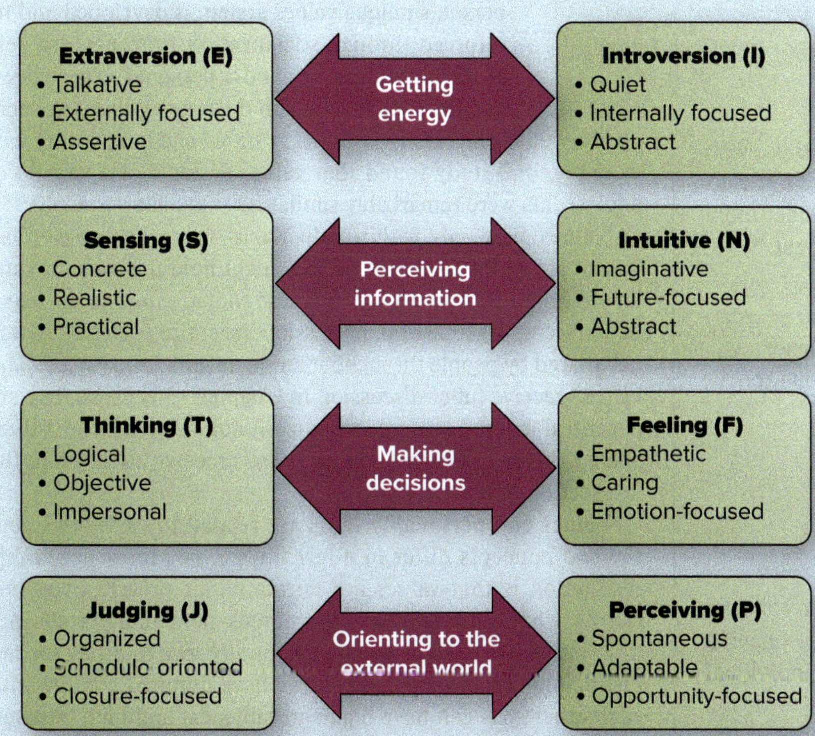

Sources: Adapted from an exhibit found at http://www.16-personality-types.com. Based on data from CPP, Inc., Sunnyvale, CA 94086 from *Introduction to Type and Careers* by Allen L. Hammer.

organizations? Given the popularity of the MBTI, many business leaders think so. However, popularity is not a proxy for validity. In fact, Jungian theory and the MBTI fail to pass several important quality standards.[29]

One problem is that Jung's theory was developed from observation of patients but never received subsequent systematic validation. The MBTI was also created with little or no empirical validation, and its forced choice binary (either-or) scale items causes interpretation and reliability problems. Consequently, the MBTI is not recommended for hiring or promotion decisions. Studies suggest that it also has questionable value in predicting leadership effectiveness or how well a team develops.[30]

The MBTI should not be used for employment selection and promotion decisions, but it may be helpful in career counseling and executive coaching.
Trinette Reed/Blend Images LLC

Some theoretical assumptions of Jungian theory and the MBTI are contrary to research evidence (e.g., personality is caused by both nature and nurture). Several issues have been identified with the theory's "types." Some broadly defined "types" are ambiguously defined, some don't seem to be sufficiently distinct from one another, and some opposing pairs of types are not necessarily opposites. Another conceptual problem is that Jungian theory and the MBTI dichotomize people into distinct groups (e.g., thinking versus feeling types). In reality, people are located across a continuous range, many of whom are around the middle of that range (between types). This explains why test-takers are likely to have different results at different times when boxed into one of the two categories.

In spite of these major limitations, the MBTI remains popular for career counseling and executive coaching, and it has some characteristics in its favor.[31] Jungian theory is modeled around perceiving and deciding, which are logical extensions of how people interact with their environment, whereas these processes are less explicit in the five-factor personality model. One of the most popular Big Five personality factors, extraversion-introversion, originated decades earlier from Carl Jung's theory of psychological types.

Another positive feature of Jungian theory (and the MBTI) is that it recognizes both the strengths and limitations of each type in different situations. In contrast, the five-factor personality

connect

SELF-ASSESSMENT 2.5: Are You a Sensing or Intuitive Type?

model views people with higher scores as better than those with lower scores on each personality factor. This may be a restrictive view of personality and makes the Big Five model more difficult to apply for coaching and personal development.[32]

LO2-4 Summarize Schwartz's model of individual values and discuss the conditions where values influence behavior.

VALUES IN THE WORKPLACE

We began this chapter by reporting that people tend to consider their personal values when assessing job offers. The opening vignette also provided an example in which an individual changed jobs because their personal values clashed with the company's dominant values or coworkers' values. **Values** are stable, evaluative beliefs that guide our preferences for outcomes or courses of action in a variety of situations.[33] Values are normative or prescriptive—they tell us what we "ought" to do. They are perceptions about what is good or bad and, consequently, influence our motivation, decisions, and actions in various situations. Some values also serve as a moral compass because they help us to evaluate what is right or wrong in line with universal virtues and societal norms. Values also provide justification for past decisions and behavior.

People arrange values into a hierarchy of preferences, called a *values system.* Some individuals value new challenges more than they value conformity. Others value personal success more than the well-being of others. Each person's unique values system is developed and reinforced through socialization from parents, religious institutions, friends, personal experiences, and the society in which that person lives. As such, an individual's hierarchy of values is stable and long-lasting. For example, one study found that values systems of a sample of adolescents were remarkably similar 20 years later as adults.[34]

Personal values serve as a moral compass; they influence our motivation, decisions, and actions in various situations.
GaudiLab/Shutterstock

Values exist only within individuals—we call them *personal values.* However, groups of people might hold the same or similar values, so we tend to ascribe these *shared values* to the team, department, organization, profession, or entire society. The values shared by people throughout an organization (*organizational values*) receive fuller discussion in Chapter 13 because they are a central component of organizational culture. The values shared across a society (*cultural values*) receive attention in the last section of this chapter.

Values and personality traits are related to each other, but the two concepts differ in a few ways.[35] The most noticeable distinction is that values are normative or prescriptive—they tell us what we *ought* to do—whereas personality traits are descriptive—they tell us what we naturally *tend* to do. A second distinction is that personality traits have minimal conflict with each other—you can have high agreeableness and high introversion, for example—whereas some values are opposed to other values. As an example, someone who values excitement and challenge would have difficulty also valuing stability and moderation. Third, although personality and values are both partly determined by heredity, values are influenced more by socialization whereas heredity has a stronger influence on an individual's personality traits.

Types of Values

Values come in many forms, and experts on this topic have conducted considerable attention to organizing them into clusters. By far, the most widely accepted model of personal values is Schwartz's values circumplex, developed and tested by social psychologist Shalom Schwartz and his colleagues.[36] This model clusters 57 values into 10 broad categories that are organized into the circular model (circumplex) shown in Exhibit 2.4. The 10 categories include universalism, benevolence, tradition, conformity, security, power, achievement, hedonism, stimulation, and self-direction. Each category is a cluster of several specific values (not shown in the exhibit). For example, conformity includes the values of politeness, honoring parents, self-discipline, and obedience.

The 10 broad values categories are further clustered into four quadrants. One quadrant, called *openness to change,* refers to the extent to which a person is motivated to pursue innovative ways. It includes the values categories of self-direction (creativity, independent thought), stimulation (excitement and challenge), and hedonism (pursuit of pleasure, enjoyment, gratification of desires). The opposing quadrant is *conservation,* which is the extent to which a person is motivated to preserve the status quo.

values Relatively stable, evaluative beliefs that guide a person's preferences for outcomes or courses of action in a variety of situations

Exhibit 2.4 Schwartz's Values Circumplex

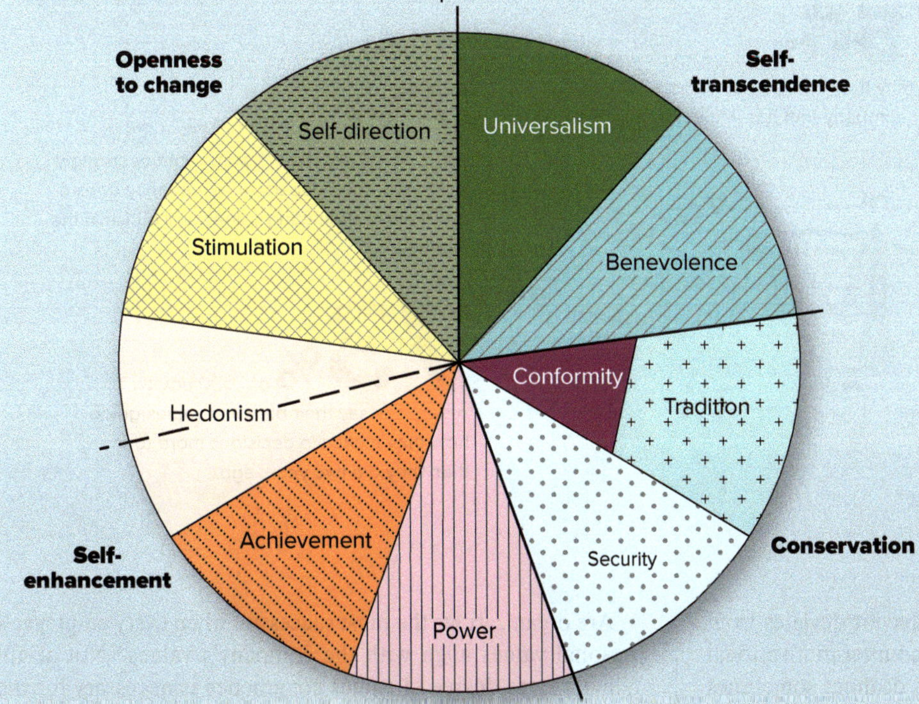

Sources: S.H. Schwartz, "Universals in the Content and Structure of Values: Theoretical Advances and Empirical Tests in 20 Countries," *Advances in Experimental Social Psychology* 25 (1992): 1–65; S.H. Schwartz and K. Boehnke, "Evaluating the Structure of Human Values with Confirmatory Factor Analysis," *Journal of Research in Personality* 38, no. 3 (2004): 230–55; Academic Rss. Inc.

The conservation quadrant includes the values categories of conformity (adherence to social norms and expectations), security (safety and stability), and tradition (moderation and preservation of the status quo).

The third quadrant in Schwartz's circumplex model, called *self-enhancement,* refers to how much a person is motivated by self-interest. This quadrant includes the values categories of achievement (pursuit of personal success), power (dominance over others), and hedonism (a values category shared with openness to change). The opposite of self-enhancement is *self-transcendence,* which refers to motivation to promote the welfare of others and nature. Self-transcendence includes the values categories of benevolence (concern for others in one's life) and universalism (concern for the welfare of all people and nature).

> It's not hard to make decisions when you know what your values are.[38]
>
> —attributed to Roy O. Disney, Walt Disney Company cofounder

connect

SELF-ASSESSMENT 2.6: What Are Your Dominant Values?

Values and Individual Behavior

Personal values influence decisions and behavior in at least three ways.[37]

- *Values influence the attractiveness of choices.* Our decisions are guided by personal values because those values generate positive or negative feelings (valences) toward the available choices. We experience more positive feelings toward choices that are aligned with our values and negative feelings toward alternatives that are contrary to our values. If stimulation is at the top of your values hierarchy, for instance, then jobs that offer new experiences will appeal to you more than jobs that have predictable and stable tasks.
- *Values frame our perceptions of reality.* We are constantly bombarded with stimuli from our surroundings. Personal values influence whether we notice something as well as how we interpret it (see Chapter 3). Our decisions and actions are affected by how we perceive those situations.
- *Values help regulate the consistency of behavior.* People are motivated to act consistently with their personal values and other aspects of their self-concept. If achievement is a key feature of your self-view and public image, then you are motivated to act in ways that are consistent with that value. The more clearly a behavior is aligned with a specific value that identifies us, the more motivated we are to engage in that behavior.

Personal values motivate behavior to some extent, but this connection isn't as strong as we might like to believe.[39] One reason for this "disconnect" between personal values and individual behavior is the situation. Personal values motivate us to engage in specific behavior, but the MARS model points out that the situation can prevent us from engaging in values-consistent behavior. For example, individuals with strong self-transcendent values are motivated to engage in recycling and other environmentally friendly behaviors, but lack of recycling facilities prevents or severely limits this behavior.

The Value of Personal Values at Work[40]

55% of 7,700 Millennials in 29 countries say their personal values/morals have a high degree of influence on their decision making at work.

18% of 600 corporate board directors in Australia identify "values" (leaders and employees aligned with company values) as the most important measure of the company's long-term success (2nd most important factor, following customer satisfaction/loyalty).

56% of 1,178 employed Americans say they wouldn't consider a job at a company that has values they disagree with.

73% of 187,519 Canadian federal government employees somewhat or strongly agree that their department or agency does a good job of promoting values and ethics in the workplace.

73% of 1,000 adult Americans say their personal values guide how they make life decisions more today than they did two years ago.

(Photo): Mattjeacock/iStock/Getty Images

A second reason why an individual's behavior deviates from personal values is the presence of strong countermotivational forces. Employees caught in illegal business dealings sometimes attribute their unethical activities to pressure from management to achieve their performance target at any cost.

A third reason why decisions and behavior are inconsistent with our personal values is that we don't actively think about them much of the time.[41] Values are abstract concepts, so their relevance is not obvious in many situations. Furthermore, many daily decisions and actions occur routinely and habitually, so we don't actively evaluate their consistency with our values. We do consciously consider our values in some situations, of course, such as realizing how much we value security when deciding whether to perform a risky task. But many daily events do not trigger values awareness, so we act without their guidance. We literally need to be reminded of our values so they can guide our decisions and actions.

Values Congruence

Values tell us what is right or wrong and what we ought to do. This evaluative characteristic affects how comfortable we are with specific organizations and individuals. The key concept here is *values congruence,* which refers to how similar a person's values hierarchy is to the values hierarchy of another entity, such as the employee's team or organization. When personal values are congruent with the organization's values, employees tend to have higher job satisfaction, loyalty, and organizational citizenship. They also have less stress and are less likely to quit. Furthermore, employees are more likely to make decisions that are compatible with organizational expectations when their personal values are congruent with the organization's shared values.[42]

Are organizations the most successful when every employee's personal values align with the company's values? Not at all! While a large degree of values congruence is necessary for the reasons just noted, organizations also benefit from some level of incongruence. Employees with diverse values offer different perspectives, which potentially lead to better decision making. Also, too much congruence can create a "corporate cult" that potentially undermines creativity, organizational flexibility, and business ethics (see Chapter 13).

LO2-5 Describe four ethical principles and discuss three factors that influence ethical behavior.

ETHICAL VALUES AND BEHAVIOR

Judging from its many accolades, Hartford Financial Services Group (The Hartford) gives business ethics a very high priority. For the past dozen years, the Connecticut-headquartered firm has been recognized as one of the World's Most Ethical Companies. It is also one of America's 100 most JUST companies, based on how well it serves employees, customers, communities, the environment, and stockholders. The Hartford is also one of two companies recently added to the elite list of Catalyst award winners, in recognition of its successful stewardship of organizational diversity, equity, and inclusion (DEI). Only 100 firms globally over the past quarter century have earned the Catalyst award. "The Hartford's

The State of Ethics in the Workplace[43]

60% of 557,778 U.S. federal government employees say their organization's senior leaders maintain high standards of honesty and integrity.

70% of 10,000 employees surveyed across 13 countries say that senior management takes ethics seriously in their organization.

33% of 5,006 American employees say they have experienced pressure to compromise their organization's ethics standards.

76% of 1,000 working Americans say their organization has strong, effective and ethical management and governance practices (71% of Canadians say this).

18% of 10,000 employees surveyed across 13 countries say that during the past year they were aware of employer or coworker conduct that violated the law or the firm's ethical standards.

(Photo): pathdoc/Shutterstock

ethics Moral principles (human good) or societal norms that determine whether actions are right or wrong and outcomes are good or bad

utilitarianism An ethical principle stating that the only moral obligation is to seek the greatest good for the greatest number of people

distributive justice An ethical principle stating that appropriate decision criteria should be applied to calculate how various benefits and burdens are distributed

ethic of care An ethical principle stating that everyone has a moral obligation to help others within their relational sphere to grow and self-actualize

values guide our actions," explains The Hartford's Chairman and CEO Christopher Swift. "Our stakeholders–customers, partners, shareholders, employees and regulators–know they can count on us to uphold the highest standards of ethics and compliance."[44]

The Hartford's global reputation highlights the importance of ethical values and behavior. **Ethics** refers to moral principles (human good) or societal norms that determine whether actions are right or wrong and outcomes are good or bad.[45] This definition recognizes that ethics and values overlap. Both are normative or prescriptive beliefs (determining what is good or bad), but values are personal preferences whereas ethics have a foundation in societal norms or univers al principles of "human good." For example, some people value work that provides stimulation (excitement and challenge), but this is a personal preference, not a societal norm. In contrast, most people value freedom of speech, which is both a personal value and a societal norm (i.e., an ethical principle).

Four Ethical Principles

Most ethical issues are associated with four ethical principles: utilitarianism, individual rights, distributive justice, and the ethic of care.[46] Your personal values might sway you more toward one principle than the others, but all four should be actively considered when making decisions that have ethical implications.

- **Utilitarianism.** This principle says the only moral obligation is to seek the greatest good for the greatest number of people. It advocates choosing the option that produces the highest satisfaction to those affected. One problem is that utilitarianism requires a cost–benefit analysis, yet many outcomes aren't measurable. Another problem is that utilitarianism focuses only on outcomes, whereas the means of achieving those outcomes may be considered unethical by other principles.
- *Individual rights.* This principle says that everyone has the same set of natural rights, such as freedom of speech, freedom of movement, the right to physical security, and the right to fair trial. The individual rights principle includes human rights that everyone is granted as a moral norm of society. One problem with this principle is that some individual rights may conflict with the rights of other people. Stockholders' right to be informed about corporate activities may ultimately conflict with an executive's right to privacy, for example.
- **Distributive justice.** This principle says that appropriate decision criteria rules should be applied to calculate how various benefits and burdens are distributed. These distribution criteria might be based on equality (everyone gets the same benefits and burdens), equity (they vary with one's contribution), or need (more benefits for those who most need them). The main problem with the distributive justice principle is that it is difficult to agree on the value of benefits and burdens and on the contribution or need of the people affected. We discuss distributive justice further in Chapter 5.
- **Ethic of care.** This principle states that everyone has a moral obligation to help others within their relational sphere to grow and self-actualize.[47] Thus, caring for others is a fundamental characteristic of humanity and an ethical virtue. Ethic of care includes being attentive to others' needs, using one's abilities to give care to others, and being responsive to (having empathy for) the person receiving care. This principle is found in writing about how organizations should serve stakeholders and how leaders should serve employees (see servant leadership in Chapter 11).[48]

> **It takes many good deeds to build a good reputation and only one bad one to lose it.**
>
> —Attributed to Benjamin Franklin

Moral Intensity, Moral Sensitivity, and Situational Influences

Three factors influence ethical conduct in the workplace: the moral intensity of the issue, the individual's moral sensitivity, and situational influences.[49]

Moral Intensity **Moral intensity** is the degree to which an issue demands the application of ethical principles. Decisions with high moral intensity have strong ethical implications that usually affect many people, so the decision maker needs to carefully apply ethical principles to make the best choice. Moral intensity specifically depends on four conditions: (a) the probability that the decision will have good or bad consequences, (b) the severity of those consequences, (c) the number of people who will experience those consequences, and (d) the level of agreement by others that the decision has good or bad consequences.[50]

Moral Sensitivity **Moral sensitivity** (also called *ethical sensitivity*) is a characteristic of the person, namely their ability to detect a moral dilemma and estimate its relative importance.[51] People with high moral sensitivity can more quickly and accurately estimate the moral intensity of the issue. This awareness does not necessarily translate into more ethical behavior; it just means that people with higher moral sensitivity are more likely to know when unethical decisions and behavior occur.

Moral sensitivity regarding a moral dilemma is higher among those with expertise on that topic or who have experienced similar incidents in the past.
voronaman/Shutterstock

Several factors are associated with a person's moral sensitivity.[52]

- *Expertise or knowledge of prescriptive norms and rules.* Occupational training and other learning increases awareness of illegal or otherwise unethical activities. For example, accountants are more morally sensitive regarding specific accounting procedures than are people who have not been trained in this profession.
- *Previous experience with specific moral dilemmas.* Past incidents likely generate internal cues that trigger awareness of future ethical dilemmas with similar characteristics.
- *Ability to empathize with those affected by the decision.* Moral sensitivity tends to be higher among people who more easily understand and are sensitive to the feelings, thoughts, and situations of others (called *empathy*, which we discuss in Chapter 3).
- *A strong self-view of being a morally sensitive person.*[53] Employees who strongly define themselves by their moral character (called their *moral identity*) put more energy into maintaining ethical conduct, which includes being more alert to the moral intensity of each decision and situation.
- *A high degree of situational mindfulness.*[54] *Mindfulness* refers to a person's receptive and impartial attention to and awareness of the present situation as well as to one's own thoughts and emotions in that moment. Mindfulness increases moral sensitivity because it involves actively monitoring the environment as well as being sensitive to our responses to that environment.

Situational Factors In addition to moral intensity and moral sensitivity, ethical conduct is influenced by the situation in which the conduct occurs.[55] In particular, some employees say they experience pressure from their manager and others that motivates them to lie to customers, breach regulations, or otherwise act unethically. Situational factors do not justify unethical conduct. Rather, we need to be aware of these factors so organizations can reduce their influence.

Supporting Ethical Behavior

Organizations have introduced various structures and processes to support ethical conduct. The most common strategy is to develop and communicate a code of ethical conduct—a statement about desired practices, rules of conduct, and philosophy about the organization's relationship to its stakeholders and the environment.[56] These codes are supposed to motivate and guide employee behavior, signal the importance of ethical conduct, and build the firm's trustworthiness to stakeholders. Ethics codes seem to improve the company's ethical image and increase employees' ethics awareness and intentions. But these codes alone have limited effect on ethical behavior; they work only in combination with other structural ethics initiatives.

A second strategy is to train and regularly evaluate employees about their knowledge of proper ethical conduct. Many large firms annually educate and test employees' awareness of company rules and practices concerning important ethical issues such as giving gifts and receiving sensitive information about competitors or governments.

A third strategy to improve ethical conduct is to establish an ethics hotline operated by an independent organization, through which employees can anonymously or confidentially report suspicious behavior or receive guidance about a current ethical dilemma. A few very large businesses also employ ombudspersons who receive information confidentially from employees and actively investigate possible wrongdoing.

Compliance-focused initiatives represent a fourth structural ethics category. These include rewarding ethical conduct, punishing unethical conduct, and evaluating ethical attitudes and behavior in performance appraisals. The effectiveness of these activities is mixed, partly because rewards and punishment can have unintended effects on employee behavior.[57]

Likely the most powerful way to improve ethical conduct is to instill a set of shared values that reinforces ethical conduct. As we describe in Chapter 13 (organizational culture), an ethical culture is supported by the conduct and vigilance of corporate leaders. By acting with the highest moral standards, leaders not only gain support and trust from followers, but they also role-model the ethical standards that employees are more likely to follow.[58]

moral intensity The degree to which an issue demands the application of ethical principles

moral sensitivity A person's ability to recognize the presence of an ethical issue and determine its relative importance

LO2-6 Describe five values commonly studied across cultures.

VALUES ACROSS CULTURES

Values differ not only among individuals and across organizations; they also vary across societies. We introduce five values that have been studied across cultures: individualism, collectivism, power distance, uncertainty avoidance, and achievement-nurturing orientation. Exhibit 2.5 summarizes these values and lists a sample of countries that have high, medium, or low emphasis on these values.

OB THEORY TO PRACTICE

Supporting Ethical Behavior at The Hartford[59]

Hartford Financial Services Group (The Hartford) has several structures and processes to support ethical conduct.

Ethics Code. The Hartford's Code of Ethics and Business Conduct "guides employees to choose a course of action consistent with The Hartford's core values in all operations and business services."

Guidance for making ethical decisions. The Hartford provides an overall Ethical Decision Aid to help employees determine whether a decision or action might be unethical. It also provides employees with Decision Aids for specific issues, such as conflict of interest, keeping records, and receiving gifts and entertainment.

Ethics training and certification. New employees learn The Hartford's code of ethics. Managers complete ethics courses, such as managing with integrity. The company holds an annual Ethics and Compliance Week, highlighting important ethical topics through panel discussions and in-house blogs written by company leaders. The code of ethics booklet presents ethical dilemma incidents (with answers). Employees certify annually that they have read and agree to comply with the code of ethics.

Communicating ethics concerns. The Hartford employees are encouraged to report ethical misconduct or seek clarification on ethical concerns. These communication avenues include: (a) talk to a manager, (b) contact the employee relations unit, (c) contact the compliance officer, (d) contact the chief ethics and compliance officer, and (e) contact EthicsPoint (The Hartford's 24/7 outside service provider to whom employees can share concerns anonymously).

Ombudsperson. The Hartford has an ombudsperson who provides guidance to employees regarding ethical matters. However, the ombudsperson is not a formal channel for reporting ethical concerns.

Ethical culture. The Hartford conducts a companywide survey of employees to assess how well the firm maintains an ethical culture. In the most recent survey, 96 percent of employees believe The Hartford is committed to ethical business decisions and conduct.

Exhibit 2.5 Five Cross-Cultural Values

Value	Sample Countries	Representative Beliefs/Behaviors in "High" Cultures
Individualism	High: United States, Chile, Canada, South Africa Medium: Japan, Denmark Low: Taiwan, Venezuela	Defines self more by one's uniqueness; personal goals have priority; decisions have low consideration of effect on others; relationships are viewed as more instrumental and fluid.
Collectivism	High: Israel, Taiwan Medium: India, Denmark Low: United States, Germany, Japan	Defines self more by one's in-group membership; goals of self-sacrifice and harmony have priority; behavior regulated by in-group norms; in-group memberships are viewed as stable with a strong differentiation with out-groups.
Power distance	High: India, Malaysia Medium: United States, Japan Low: Denmark, Israel	Reluctant to disagree with or contradict the boss; managers are expected and preferred decision makers; perception of dependence on (versus interdependence with) the boss.
Uncertainty avoidance	High: Belgium, Greece Medium: United States, Norway Low: Denmark, Singapore	Prefer predictable situations; value stable employment, strict laws, and low conflict; dislike deviations from normal behavior.
Achievement-nurturing orientation	High: Austria, Japan Medium: United States, Brazil Low: Sweden, Netherlands	Focus on outcomes (versus relationships); decisions based on contribution (equity versus equality); low empathy or showing emotions (versus strong empathy and caring).

Sources: Individualism and collectivism descriptions and results are from the meta-analysis reported in D. Oyserman, H.M. Coon, and M. Kemmelmeier, "Rethinking Individualism and Collectivism: Evaluation of Theoretical Assumptions and Meta-Analyses," *Psychological Bulletin*, 128 (2002): 3–72. The other information is from G. Hofstede, *Culture's Consequences*, 2nd ed. (Thousand Oaks, CA: Sage, 2001).

Individualism and Collectivism

Individualism is the extent to which we value independence and personal uniqueness. Highly individualist people value personal freedom, self-sufficiency, control over their own lives, and appreciation of the unique qualities that distinguish them from others. Americans, Chileans, Canadians, and South Africans generally exhibit high individualism, whereas Taiwan and Venezuela are countries with low individualism.[60] **Collectivism** is the extent to which we value our duty to groups to which we belong and to group harmony. Highly collectivist people define themselves by their group memberships, emphasize their personal connection to others in their in-groups, and value the goals and well-being of people within those groups.[61] Low collectivism countries include the United States, Japan, and Germany, whereas Israel and Taiwan have relatively high collectivism.

Contrary to popular belief, individualism is not the opposite of collectivism. In fact, the two concepts are typically uncorrelated.[62] For example, cultures that highly value duty to one's group do not necessarily give a low priority to personal freedom and uniqueness. People across all cultures define themselves by both their uniqueness and their relationship to others. It is an inherent characteristic of everyone's self-concept, which we discuss in the next chapter. Some cultures emphasize either personal uniqueness or group obligations, but both have a place in a person's values and self-concept.

McGraw Hill connect

SELF-ASSESSMENT 2.7: How Much Do You Value Individualism and Collectivism?

Power Distance

People with high **power distance** value unequal power.[63] Those in higher positions expect obedience to authority; those in lower positions are comfortable receiving commands from their superiors without consultation or debate. People with high power distance prefer to resolve differences through formal procedures rather than direct informal discussion. In contrast, people with low power distance view the relationship with their boss as one of interdependence, not dependence, so they expect their boss to share power and consult with them before decisions affecting them are made. People in India and Malaysia tend to have high power distance, whereas people in Denmark and Israel generally have low power distance. Americans collectively have medium-low power distance.

individualism A cross-cultural value describing the degree to which people in a culture emphasize independence and personal uniqueness

collectivism A cross-cultural value describing the degree to which people in a culture emphasize duty to groups to which they belong and to group harmony

power distance A cross-cultural value describing the degree to which people in a culture accept unequal distribution of power in a society

uncertainty avoidance A cross-cultural value describing the degree to which people in a culture tolerate ambiguity (low uncertainty avoidance)

achievement-nurturing orientation Cross-cultural value describing the degree to which people in a culture emphasize competitive versus cooperative relations with other people

Mc Graw Hill connect

SELF-ASSESSMENT 2.8: What Is Your Level of Power Distance?

Uncertainty Avoidance

Uncertainty avoidance is the degree to which people tolerate ambiguity (low uncertainty avoidance) or feel threatened by ambiguity and uncertainty (high uncertainty avoidance). Employees with high uncertainty avoidance value structured situations in which rules of conduct and decision making are clearly documented. They usually prefer direct rather than indirect or ambiguous communications. Uncertainty avoidance tends to be high in Belgium and Greece and very high in Japan. It is generally low in Denmark and Singapore. Americans collectively have medium-low uncertainty avoidance.

Achievement-Nurturing Orientation

Achievement-nurturing orientation reflects a competitive versus cooperative view of relations with other people.[64] People with a high achievement orientation value assertiveness, competitiveness, and materialism. They appreciate people who are tough, and they favor the acquisition of money and material goods. In contrast, people in nurturing-oriented cultures emphasize relationships and the well-being of others. They focus on human interaction and caring rather than competition and personal success. People in Sweden, Norway, and the Netherlands have a very low achievement orientation (i.e., high nurturing orientation). In contrast, very high achievement orientation scores have been reported in Japan and Austria. The United States is located a little above the middle of the range on achievement-nurturing orientation.

Caveats about Cross-Cultural Knowledge

Cross-cultural organizational research has gained considerable attention over the past two decades, partly due to increased globalization and cultural diversity within organizations. Our knowledge of cross-cultural dynamics has blossomed, and many of these findings will be discussed in other chapters, such as leadership, conflict, and influence. However, we also need to raise a few warning flags about cross-cultural knowledge. One problem is that too many studies have relied on small, convenient samples (such as students attending one university) to represent an entire culture.[65] The result is that many cross-cultural studies draw conclusions that might not generalize to the cultures they intended to represent.

A second caveat is that cross-cultural research and writing continues to rely on a major study conducted almost four decades ago of 116,000 IBM employees across dozens of countries. That study helped ignite subsequent cross-cultural research, but its findings are becoming outdated as values in some cultures have shifted over the years.[66]

A third concern is that cross-cultural studies often assume that each country has one culture.[67] In reality, the United States

Cultural diversity exists within many countries; for example, personal values and personalities vary somewhat across regions within the United States.
Ollyy/Shutterstock

and many other countries have become culturally diverse. For example, Americans of African heritage have significantly higher individualism than those of European and Hispanic heritage, whereas Americans with Asian heritage have the lowest individualism among these demographic groups.[68] Several studies also report variations in personal values and personality traits across geographic regions within the United States.[69]

Study Checklist

Connect® is available for *M: Organizational Behavior.* Additional resources include:

✓ Exercises:

- **Case Analysis:** Apply concepts within the context of a real-world situation.
- **Click and Drag:** Helps make the connection between theory and application through matching, ranking, or grouping activities.
- **Video Case:** See management in action through interactive videos.
- **Self-Assessment:** Designed to promote student self awareness and reflection, these research based surveys contain detailed feedback for students.
- **Application-Based Activities:** These highly interactive, application- and analysis-based exercises allow students to take on specific roles to complete management-related tasks within a real-world context.

✓ **SmartBook 2.0™**—Smartbook 2.0 is an adaptive learning solution that provides personalized learning to individual student needs, continually adapts to pinpoint knowledge gaps and focuses learning on concepts requiring additional study. It fosters more productive learning, takes the guesswork out of what to study, and helps students better prepare for class.

©Natthawat Jamnapa/123RF

Notes

1. E. Lewis, "For Attracting Top Talent, Purpose Must Come First," *PR Daily*, April 26, 2022; E. Yeargin, "Hiring Practices Are the New Litmus Test for Company Values," *TLNT-Talent Management & HR* (blog), August 3, 2022; R. Hesno, "How I Became a Senior Product Manager: Charlotte Bella, Booking.Com," *Prolific North (Manchester UK)*, October 18, 2022.
2. The definition presented here is based on: D.C. Funder, *The Personality Puzzle* (New York: W W Norton & Company, 2016); C.S. Carver and M.F. Scheier, *Perspectives on Personality*, 8th ed. (Hoboken, N.J.: Pearson Education, 2017). Both of these books recognize the varied perspectives of and approaches to personality. Several recent articles also recognize and attempt to address this conceptual diversity, such as: D. Cervone and B.R. Little, "Personality Architecture and Dynamics: The New Agenda and What's New about It," *Personality and Individual Differences* 136 (2019): 12–23; E. Jayawickreme, C.E. Zachry, and W. Fleeson, "Whole Trait Theory: An Integrative Approach to Examining Personality Structure and Process," *Personality and Individual Differences* 136 (2019): 2–11.
3. J. Anglim and P. O'Connor, "Measurement and Research Using the Big Five, HEXACO, and Narrow Traits: A Primer for Researchers and Practitioners," *Australian Journal of Psychology* 71, no. 1 (2019): 16–25.
4. B.W. Roberts and A. Caspi, "Personality Development and the Person-Situation Debate: It's Déjà Vu All over Again," *Psychological Inquiry* 12, no. 2 (2001): 104–9; N.A. Turiano et al., "Personality and Substance Use in Midlife: Conscientiousness as a Moderator and the Effects of Trait Change," *Journal of Research in Personality* 46, no. 3 (2012): 295–305; C.R. Gale et al., "Neuroticism and Extraversion in Youth Predict Mental Wellbeing and Life Satisfaction 40 Years Later," *Journal of Research in Personality* 47, no. 6 (2013): 687–97; M. Pluess and M. Bartley, "Childhood Conscientiousness Predicts the Social Gradient of Smoking in Adulthood: A Life Course Analysis," *Journal of Epidemiology and Community Health* 69, no. 4 (2015): 330–38; M. Blatný et al., "Personality Predictors of Successful Development: Toddler Temperament and Adolescent Personality Traits Predict Well-Being and Career Stability in Middle Adulthood," *PLoS ONE* 10, no. 4 (2015): e0126032.
5. W. Mischel, "Toward an Integrative Science of the Person," *Annual Review of Psychology* 55 (2004): 1–22; T.A. Judge and C.P. Zapata, "The Person–Situation Debate Revisited," *Academy of Management Journal* 58, no. 4 (2015): 1149–79; R.P. Tett, M.J. Toich, and S.B. Ozkum, "Trait Activation Theory: A Review of the Literature and Applications to Five Lines of Personality Dynamics Research," *Annual Review of Organizational Psychology and Organizational Behavior* 8 (2021): 199–233.
6. O. Wilde, *The Picture of Dorian Gray* (New York: Barnes & Noble, 2003), 340.
7. T. Vukasović and D. Bratko, "Heritability of Personality: A Meta-Analysis of Behavior Genetic Studies," *Psychological Bulletin* 141, no. 4 (2015): 769–85, https://doi.org/10.1037/bul0000017; W. Bleidorn, "What Accounts for Personality Maturation in Early Adulthood?" *Current Directions in Psychological Science* 24, no. 3 (2015): 245–52; T.J.C. Polderman et al., "Meta-Analysis of the Heritability of Human Traits Based on Fifty Years of Twin Studies," *Nature Genetics* 47, no. 7 (2015): 702–9; L. Penke and M. Jokela, "The Evolutionary Genetics of Personality Revisited," *Current Opinion in Psychology* 7 (2016): 104–9; M.-T. Lo et al., "Genome-Wide Analyses for Personality Traits Identify Six Genomic Loci and Show Correlations with Psychiatric Disorders," *Nature Genetics* 49, no. 1 (2017): 152–56, https://doi.org/10.1038/ng.3736.

8. R. Mıttus et al., "Within-Trait Heterogeneity in Age Group Differences in Personality Domains and Facets: Implications for the Development and Coherence of Personality Traits," *PLoS ONE* 10, no. 3 (2015): e0119667; M. Liu and J.L. Huang, "Cross-Cultural Adjustment to the United States: The Role of Contextualized Extraversion Change," *Frontiers in Psychology* 6 (2015); S. Tasselli, M. Kilduff, and B. Landis, "Personality Change: Implications for Organizational Behavior," *Academy of Management Annals* 12 (2018): 467–93; W. Bleidorn, C.J. Hopwood, and R.E. Lucas, "Life Events and Personality Trait Change," *Journal of Personality* 86 (2018): 83–96; P.T. Costa, R.R. McCrae, and C.E. Löckenhoff, "Personality Across the Life Span," *Annual Review of Psychology* 70 (2019): 423–48.

9. R.F. Baumeister, B.J. Schmeichel, and K.D. Vohs, "Self-Regulation and the Executive Function: The Self as Controlling Agent," in *Social Psychology: Handbook of Basic Principles*, ed. A.W. Kruglanski and E.T. Higgins (New York: Guilford, 2007), 516–39; K. Murdock, K. Oddi, and D. Bridgett, "Cognitive Correlates of Personality: Links between Executive Functioning and the Big Five Personality Traits," *Journal of Individual Differences* 34, no. 2 (2013): 97–104; P. Baggetta and P.A. Alexander, "Conceptualization and Operationalization of Executive Function," *Mind, Brain, and Education* 10, no. 1 (2016): 10–33.

10. R.R. McCrae, J.F. Gaines, and M.A. Wellington, "The Five-Factor Model in Fact and Fiction," in *Handbook of Psychology*, ed. I.B. Weiner, 2nd ed., vol. 5 (Hoboken, N. J.: John Wiley & Sons, 2013), 65–91.

11. P.R. Sackett and P.T. Walmsley, "Which Personality Attributes Are Most Important in the Workplace?," *Perspectives on Psychological Science* 9, no. 5 (2014): 538–51; L.M. Penney, E. David, and L.A. Witt, "A Review of Personality and Performance: Identifying Boundaries, Contingencies, and Future Research Directions," *Human Resource Management Review* 21, no. 4 (2011): 297–310; T. Judge et al., "Hierarchical Representations of the Five-Factor Model of Personality in Predicting Job Performance: Integrating Three Organizing Frameworks with Two Theoretical Perspectives," *Journal of Applied Psychology* 98, no. 6 (2013): 875–925; J. Huang et al., "Personality and Adaptive Performance at Work: A Meta-Analytic Investigation," *Journal of Applied Psychology* 99, no. 1 (2014): 162–79; Y. He, M.B. Donnellan, and A.M. Mendoza, "Five-Factor Personality Domains and Job Performance: A Second Order Meta-Analysis," *Journal of Research in Personality* 82 (2019): 103848; M.P. Wilmot et al., "Extraversion Advantages at Work: A Quantitative Review and Synthesis of the Meta-Analytic Evidence," *Journal of Applied Psychology* 104, no. 12 (2019): 1447–70.

12. R.D.S. Chiaburu et al., "The Five-Factor Model of Personality Traits and Organizational Citizenship Behaviors: A Meta-Analysis," *Journal of Applied Psychology* 96, no. 6 (2011): 1140–66; D.S. Chiaburu, I.-S. Oh, and S.V. Marinova, "Five-Factor Model of Personality Traits and Organizational Citizenship Behavior: Current Research and Future Directions," in *The Oxford Handbook of Organizational Citizenship Behavior*, ed. P.M. Podsakoff, S.B. Mackenzie, and N.P. Podsakoff (New York: Oxford University Press, 2018), 203–20.

13. R.F. Hurley, "Customer Service Behavior in Retail Settings: A Study of the Effect of Service Provider Personality," *Journal of the Academy of Marketing Science* 26 (1998): 115–27; M.A.G. Peeters et al., "Personality and Team Performance: A Meta-Analysis," *European Journal of Personality* 20 (2006): 377–96; J.L. Huang and A.M. Ryan, "Beyond Personality Traits: A Study of Personality States and Situational Contingencies in Customer Service Jobs," *Personnel Psychology* 64 (2011): 451–88; B.H. Bradley et al., "Team Players and Collective Performance: How Agreeableness Affects Team Performance Over Time," *Small Group Research* 44 (2013): 680–711.

14. A. Neal et al., "Predicting the Form and Direction of Work Role Performance from the Big 5 Model of Personality Traits," *Journal of Organizational Behavior* 33, no. 2 (2012): 175–92.

15. J.L. Huang et al., "Personality and Adaptive Performance at Work," *Journal of Applied Psychology* 99, no. 1 (2014): 162–79.

16. H. Le et al., "Too Much of a Good Thing: Curvilinear Relationships between Personality Traits and Job Performance," *Journal of Applied Psychology* 96, no. 1 (2011): 113–33; G. Blickle et al., "Extraversion and Job Performance: How Context Relevance and Bandwidth Specificity Create a Non-Linear, Positive, and Asymptotic Relationship," *Journal of Vocational Behavior* 87 (2015): 80–88; P.L. Curşeu et al., "Personality Characteristics That Are Valued in Teams: Not Always 'More Is Better'?," *International Journal of Psychology* 54, no. 5 (2019): 638–49.

17. J. Anglim and P. O'Connor, "Measurement and Research Using the Big Five, HEXACO, and Narrow Traits: A Primer for Researchers and Practitioners," *Australian Journal of Psychology* 71, no. 1 (2019): 16–25.

18. D.L. Paulhus and K.M. Williams, "The Dark Triad of Personality: Narcissism, Machiavellianism, and Psychopathy," *Journal of Research in Personality* 36, no. 6 (2002): 556–63; J.M. LeBreton, L.K. Shiverdecker, and E.M. Grimaldi, "The Dark Triad and Workplace Behavior," *Annual Review of Organizational Psychology and Organizational Behavior* 5, no. 1 (2018): 387–414; S.M. Spain, "The Dark Side of Personality," in *Leadership, Work, and the Dark Side of Personality*, ed. S.M. Spain (Academic Press, London 2019), 41–93; R. Rogoza and J. Cieciuch, "Dark Triad Traits and Their Structure: An Empirical Approach," *Current Psychology: A Journal for Diverse Perspectives on Diverse Psychological Issues* 39, no. 4 (2020): 1287–1302. A fourth trait–sadism–has recently been suggested, but it is early days to add this as a dark tetrad to our discussion.

19. D.N. Jones and D.L. Paulhus, "Differentiating the Dark Triad Within the Interpersonal Circumplex," in *Handbook of Interpersonal Psychology*, ed. L.M. Horowitz and S. Strack (Hoboken, NJ: John Wiley & Sons, Inc., 2012), 249–67; A. Book et al., "Unpacking More 'Evil': What Is at the Core of the Dark Tetrad?," *Personality and Individual Differences* 90 (2016): 269–72; M. Moshagen, B.E. Hilbig, and I. Zettler, "The Dark Core of Personality," *Psychological Review* 125 (2018): 656–88; G. Hodson et al., "Is the Dark Triad Common Factor Distinct from Low Honesty-Humility?," *Journal of Research in Personality* 73 (2018): 123–29.

20. R. Christie and F. Geis, *Studies in Machiavellianism* (New York: Academic Press, 1970); S. R. Kessler et al., "Re-Examining Machiavelli: A Three-Dimensional Model of Machiavellianism in the Workplace," *Journal of Applied Social Psychology* 40, no. 8 (2010): 1868–96; E. O'Boyle et al., "A Meta-Analysis of the Dark Triad and Work Behavior: A Social Exchange Perspective," *Journal of Applied Psychology* 97, no. 3 (2012): 557–79.

21. Z. Krizan and O. Johar, "Envy Divides the Two Faces of Narcissism," *Journal of Personality* 80, no. 5 (2012): 1415–51.

22. C.J. Patrick, "Psychopathy as Masked Pathology," in *Handbook of Psychopathy*, 2nd ed. (New York: The Guilford Press, 2018), 3–21.

23. Cited in: S.F. Smith and S.O. Lilienfeld, "Psychopathy in the Workplace: The Knowns and Unknowns," *Aggression and Violent Behavior* 18, no. 2 (2013): 204–18.

24. S.F. Smith and S.O. Lilienfeld, "Psychopathy in the Workplace: The Knowns and Unknowns," *Aggression and Violent Behavior* 18, no. 2 (2013): 204–18; H.L. DeShong, D.M. Grant, and S.N. Mullins-Sweatt, "Comparing Models of Counterproductive Workplace Behaviors: The Five-Factor Model and the Dark Triad," *Personality and Individual Differences* 74 (2015): 55–60; A. Harrison, J. Summers, and B. Mennecke, "The Effects of the Dark Triad on Unethical Behavior," *Journal of Business Ethics* 153, no. 1 (2018): 53–77; J.R. Van Scotter and K. De Déa Roglio, "CEO Bright and Dark Personality: Effects on Ethical Misconduct," *Journal of Business Ethics* 164, no. 3 (2020): 451–75.

25. D.N. Jones, "Risk in the Face of Retribution: Psychopathic Individuals Persist in Financial Misbehavior among the Dark Triad," *Personality and Individual Differences, The Dark Triad of Personality,* 67 (2014): 109–13; L. ten Brinke, A. Kish, and D. Keltner, "Hedge Fund Managers With Psychopathic Tendencies Make for Worse Investors," *Personality and Social Psychology Bulletin* 44, no. 2 (2018): 214–23.

26. M.A. Baysinger, K.T. Scherer, and J.M. LeBreton, "Exploring the Disruptive Effects of Psychopathy and Aggression on Group Processes and Group Effectiveness," *Journal of Applied Psychology* 99, no. 1 (2014): 48–65, https://doi.org/10.1037/a0034317; A.G. Nassif, "Heterogeneity and Centrality of 'Dark Personality' within Teams, Shared Leadership, and Team Performance: A Conceptual Moderated-Mediation Model," *Human Resource Management Review* 29, no. 4 (2019): 100675.

27. C.A. O'Reilly et al., "Narcissistic CEOs and Executive Compensation," *The Leadership Quarterly* 25 (2014): 218–31; K.J. Templer, "Dark Personality, Job Performance Ratings, and the Role of Political Skill: An Indication of Why Toxic People May Get Ahead at Work," *Personality and Individual Differences* 124 (2018): 209–14; W. Hart, K. Richardson, and G.K. Tortoriello, "Meet Your Public Relations Team: People with Dark Traits May Help You Manage Your Image," *Personality and Individual Differences* 134 (2018): 164–73; D.K. Marcus, J. Preszler, and V. Zeigler-Hill, "A Network of Dark Personality Traits: What Lies at the Heart of Darkness?," *Journal of Research in Personality* 73 (2018): 56–62.

28. C.G. Jung, *Psychological Types,* trans. H.G. Baynes (Princeton, NJ: Princeton University Press, 1971); I.B. Myers, *The Myers-Briggs Type Indicator* (Palo Alto, CA: Consulting Psychologists Press, 1987).

29. D.A. Johnson and D.R. Saunders, "Confirmatory Factor Analysis of the Myers-Briggs Type Indicator-Expanded Analysis Report," *Educational and Psychological Measurement* 50, no. 3 (1990): 561–71; R.M. Capraro and M.M. Capraro, "Myers-Briggs Type Indicator Score Reliability across Studies: A Meta-Analytic Reliability Generalization Study," *Educational and Psychological Measurement* 62 (2002): 590–602; D. Pittenger, "Cautionary Comments Regarding the Myers-Briggs Type Indicator," *Consulting Psychology Journal: Practice and Research* 57 (2005): 210–21; R. Randall, M. Isaacson, and C. Ciro, "Validity and Reliability of the Myers-Briggs Personality Type Indicator: A Systematic Review and Meta-Analysis," *Journal of Best Practices in Health Professions Diversity* 10, no. 1 (2017): 1–27; R. Stein and A.B. Swan, "Evaluating the Validity of Myers-Briggs Type Indicator Theory: A Teaching Tool and Window into Intuitive Psychology," *Social and Personality Psychology Compass* 13, no. 2 (2019): e12434.

30. J. Michael, "Using the Myers-Briggs Type Indicator as a Tool for Leadership Development? Apply with Caution," *Journal of Leadership & Organizational Studies* 10 (2003): 68–81; B.S. Kuipers et al., "The Influence of Myers-Briggs Type Indicator Profiles on Team Development Processes," *Small Group Research* 40, no. 4 (2009): 436–64; F.W. Brown and M.D. Reilly, "The Myers-Briggs Type Indicator and Transformational Leadership," *Journal of Management Development* 28, no. 10 (2009): 916–32; A. Luse et al., "Personality and Cognitive Style as Predictors of Preference for Working in Virtual Teams," *Computers in Human Behavior* 29, no. 4 (2013): 1825–32. One recent review offers counterarguments to many of the MBTI problems presented here. See: P. Moyle and J. Hackston, "Personality Assessment for Employee Development: Ivory Tower or Real World?," *Journal of Personality Assessment* 100, no. 5 (2018): 307–17.

31. R.B. Kennedy and D.A. Kennedy, "Using the Myers-Briggs Type Indicator in Career Counseling," *Journal of Employment Counseling* 41, no. 1 (2004): 38–44; S.J. Armstrong, E. Cools, and E. Sadler-Smith, "Role of Cognitive Styles in Business and Management: Reviewing 40 Years of Research," *International Journal of Management Reviews* 14, no. 3 (2012): 238–62.

32. J.B. Lloyd, "Unsubstantiated Beliefs and Values Flaw the Five-Factor Model of Personality," *Journal of Beliefs & Values* 36, no. 2 (2015): 156–64.

33. B.M. Meglino and E.C. Ravlin, "Individual Values in Organizations: Concepts, Controversies, and Research," *Journal of Management* 24, no. 3 (1998): 351–89; S. Hitlin and J.A. Pilavin, "Values: Reviving a Dormant Concept," *Annual Review of Sociology* 30 (2004): 359–93; L. Sagiv et al., "Personal Values in Human Life," *Nature Human Behaviour* 1, no. 9 (2017): 630–39; S. Arieli, L. Sagiv, and S. Roccas, "Values at Work: The Impact of Personal Values in Organisations," *Applied Psychology* 69, no. 2 (2020): 230–75.

34. D. Lubinski, D.B. Schmidt, and C.P. Benbow, "A 20-Year Stability Analysis of the Study of Values for Intellectually Gifted Individuals from Adolescence to Adulthood," *Journal of Applied Psychology* 81 (1996): 443–451; M. Vecchione et al., "Stability and Change of Basic Personal Values in Early Adulthood: An 8-Year Longitudinal Study," *Journal of Research in Personality* 63 (2016): 111–22; R. Sundberg, "Value Stability and Change in an ISAF Contingent," *Journal of Personality* 84, no. 1 (2016): 91–101.

35. L. Parks and R.P. Guay, "Personality, Values, and Motivation," *Personality and Individual Differences* 47, no. 7 (2009): 675–84; L. Parks-Leduc, G. Feldman, and A. Bardi, "Personality Traits and Personal Values: A Meta-Analysis," *Personality and Social Psychology Review* 19, no. 1 (2015): 3–29; L. Sagiv and S.H. Schwartz, "Personal Values Across Cultures," *Annual Review of Psychology* 73, no. 1 (2022): 517–46.

36. S.H. Schwartz, "Universals in the Content and Structure of Values: Theoretical Advances and Empirical Tests in 20 Countries," *Advances in Experimental Social Psychology* 25 (1992): 1–65; S.H. Schwartz and K. Boehnke, "Evaluating the Structure of Human Values with Confirmatory Factor Analysis," *Journal of Research in Personality* 38 (2004): 230–55; I. Borg, A. Bardi, and S.H. Schwartz, "Does the Value Circle Exist Within Persons or Only Across Persons?," *Journal of Personality* 85 (2017): 151–62; P.H.P. Hanel, L.F. Litzellachner, and G.R. Maio, "An Empirical Comparison of Human Value Models," *Frontiers in Psychology* 9 (September 25, 2018): 01643.

37. N.T. Feather, "Values, Valences, and Choice: The Influence of Values on the Perceived Attractiveness and Choice of Alternatives," *Journal of Personality and Social Psychology* 68, no. 6 (1995): 1135–51; L. Sagiv, N. Sverdlik, and N. Schwarz, "To Compete or to Cooperate? Values' Impact on Perception and Action in

Social Dilemma Games," *European Journal of Social Psychology* 41, no. 1 (2011): 64–77; S.H. Schwartz and T. Butenko, "Values and Behavior: Validating the Refined Value Theory in Russia," *European Journal of Social Psychology* 44, no. 7 (2014): 799–813.

38. This frequently cited quotation (and its less common cousin "When your values are clear to you, making decisions becomes easier.") has over the past dozen years been attributed to Roy E. Disney, who was a Walt Disney executive and board member, son of Roy O. Disney, and nephew of Walt Disney. Roy E. Disney was well-known for emphasizing personal values in his decisions. In books and articles before 2009, however, this quotation was attributed to Roy. O. Disney (or simply to Roy Disney), who cofounded Walt Disney company with his brother Walt Disney and was Roy E. Disney's father. None of the books or articles presenting this quotation provided its source. The earliest mention we could find of this quotation referring to "values" is in the 1987 book *Company Policy Statements* (pp. 223–25). But this popular quotation might actually be a creative re-writing of the following statement attributed to Roy O. Disney in the 1940 edition of the periodical *Metal Finishing* (p. 38): "It's not hard to make decisions when you know what your options are."

39. G.R. Maio et al., "Addressing Discrepancies between Values and Behavior: The Motivating Effect of Reasons," *Journal of Experimental Social Psychology* 37, no. 2 (2001): 104–17; A. Bardi and S.H. Schwartz, "Values and Behavior: Strength and Structure of Relations," *Personality and Social Psychology Bulletin* 29, no. 10 (2003): 1207–20; L. Sagiv, N. Sverdlik, and N. Schwarz, "To Compete or to Cooperate? Values' Impact on Perception and Action in Social Dilemma Games," *European Journal of Social Psychology* 41, no. 1 (2011): 64–77; K.M. Sheldon and L.S. Krieger, "Walking the Talk: Value Importance, Value Enactment, and Well-Being," *Motivation and Emotion* 38 (2014): 609–19.

40. "The 2016 Deloitte Millennial Survey: Winning Over the Next Generation of Leaders" (New York: Deloitte Touche Tohmatsu, January 2016); "Creating Value and Balancing Stakeholder Needs: The Board's Role," AICD-KPMG Survey: Australian Governance Summit 2019 (Sydney: Australian Institute of Company Directors, March 1, 2019); "2020 Public Service Employee Survey Results for the Public Service" (Ottawa: Government of Canada, Treasury Board of Canada Secretariat, January 2021); "The Rise of Values Investing: Schwab's Modern Wealth Survey Finds Values Are Driving Spending, Saving & Investing Decisions of Americans More Than Ever," Press Release (Westlake, TX: Charles Schwab, May 18, 2022); "For Employees, Shared Values Matter More Than Policy Positions," Press Release (Provo, UT, and Seattle: Qualtrics, June 2, 2022).

41. E. Dreezens et al., "The Missing Link: On Strengthening the Relationship between Values and Attitudes," *Basic and Applied Social Psychology* 30, no. 2 (2008): 142–52; S. Arieli, A.M. Grant, and L. Sagiv, "Convincing Yourself to Care about Others: An Intervention for Enhancing Benevolence Values," *Journal of Personality* 82, no. 1 (2014): 15–24.

42. M.L. Verquer, T.A. Beehr, and S.H. Wagner, "A Meta-Analysis of Relations between Person–Organization Fit and Work Attitudes," *Journal of Vocational Behavior* 63 (2003): 473–89; J.W. Westerman and L.A. Cyr, "An Integrative Analysis of Person–Organization Fit Theories," *International Journal of Selection and Assessment* 12, no. 3 (2004): 252–61; J.R. Edwards and D.M. Cable, "The Value of Value Congruence," *Journal of Applied Psychology* 94, no. 3 (2009): 654–77; A.L. Kristof-Brown et al., "Collective Fit Perceptions: A Multilevel Investigation of Person–Group Fit with Individual-Level and Team-Level Outcomes," *Journal of Organizational Behavior* 35, no. 7 (2014): 969–89. We use the phrase "values congruence" (plural, NOT the singular "value congruence") because values operate as a set, not individually. Also, "value" is easily confused with the economic concept of worth of something relative to price.

43. "Ethics at Work: 2021 International Survey of Employees" (London: Institute of Business Ethics, November 2021); "2022 Global Business Ethics Survey" (Vienna, VA: Ethics & Compliance Initiative, May 2022); "2022 Federal Employee Viewpoint Survey" (Washington, DC: United States Federal Government, Office of Personnel Management, November 2022); "Employers Care More about Customers than Employees: Worker Survey," Press Release (Toronto: Argyle Public Relations, December 15, 2022).

44. "The Hartford Named One of 'World's Most Ethical Companies' for 13th Time by Ethisphere," Press Release (Hartford, Conn.: The Hartford, March 15, 2022); "2023 Catalyst Award Winners to Be Honored at Annual DEI Conference & Dinner," Press Release (New York: Catalyst, January 19, 2023); "The Hartford Named One of America's Most 'JUST' Companies for Fifth Year" (Hartford, Conn.: The Hartford), accessed February 13, 2023.

45. This definition and discussion carefully integrates the ongoing debate about ethics as virtues (human good) versus norms and expectations of society (or specific entities such as a profession). See: D. Melé, *Business Ethics in Action: Managing Human Excellence in Organizations*, 2nd ed. (London: Macmillan Education, 2019), Chap. 2.

46. P.L. Schumann, "A Moral Principles Framework for Human Resource Management Ethics," *Human Resource Management Review* 11(2001): 93–111; J.A. Boss, *Analyzing Moral Issues*, 6th ed. (New York: McGraw-Hill, 2013), Chap. 1; A. Gustafson, "In Defense of a Utilitarian Business Ethic," *Business and Society Review* 118, no. 3 (2013): 325–60.

47. J.C. Tronto, *Moral Boundaries: A Political Argument for an Ethic of Care* (Psychology Press, 1993), Chap. 5; P.M. Linsley, "Application of an Ethic of Care to Business," in *Handbook of Virtue Ethics in Business and Management*, ed. A.J.G. Sison, G.R. Beabout, and I. Ferrero, International Handbooks in Business Ethics (Dordrecht: Springer Netherlands, 2017), 307–19.

48. D. Engster, "Care Ethics and Stakeholder Theory," in *Applying Care Ethics to Business*, ed. M. Hamington and M. Sander-Staudt (Dordrecht: Springer Netherlands, 2011), 93–110; G.J. Lemoine, C.A. Hartnell, and H. Leroy, "Taking Stock of Moral Approaches to Leadership: An Integrative Review of Ethical, Authentic, and Servant Leadership," *Academy of Management Annals* 13 (2018): 148–87; J. Nicholson and E. Kurucz, "Relational Leadership for Sustainability: Building an Ethical Framework from the Moral Theory of 'Ethics of Care,'" *Journal of Business Ethics* 156 (2019): 25–43.

49. For analysis of these predictors of ethical conduct, see J.J. Kish-Gephart, D.A. Harrison, and L.K. Treviño, "Bad Apples, Bad Cases, and Bad Barrels: Meta-Analytic Evidence about Sources of Unethical Decisions at Work," *Journal of Applied Psychology* 95, no. 1 (2010): 1–32.

50. T.M. Jones, "Ethical Decision Making by Individuals in Organizations: An Issue-Contingent Model," *Academy of Management Review* 16 (1991): 366–95; T. Barnett, "Dimensions of Moral Intensity and Ethical Decision Making: An Empirical Study," *Journal of Applied Social Psychology* 31, no. 5 (2001): 1038–57; T.T. Moores, H.J. Smith, and M. Limayem, "Putting the Pieces Back Together: Moral Intensity and Its Impact on the Four-Component Model of Morality," *Business and Society Review* 123, no. 2 (2018): 243–68.

51. K. Weaver, J. Morse, and C. Mitcham, "Ethical Sensitivity in Professional Practice: Concept Analysis," *Journal of Advanced Nursing* 62, no. 5 (2008): 607–18; L.J.T. Pedersen, "See No Evil: Moral Sensitivity in the Formulation of Business Problems," *Business Ethics: A European Review* 18, no. 4 (2009): 335–48; M.I. Kraaijeveld, J. (Hans) Schilderman, and E. van Leeuwen, "Moral Sensitivity Revisited," *Nursing Ethics* 28, no. 2 (2021): 179–89; D. Schmocker et al., "Moral Sensitivity in Business: A Revised Measure," *Current Psychology* 42, no. 12 (2023): 10277–91.

52. D. You, Y. Maeda, and M.J. Bebeau, "Gender Differences in Moral Sensitivity: A Meta-Analysis," *Ethics & Behavior* 21, no. 4 (2011): 263–82; A.H. Chan and H. Cheung, "Cultural Dimensions, Ethical Sensitivity, and Corporate Governance," *Journal of Business Ethics* 110, no. 1 (2012): 45–59; J.R. Sparks, "A Social Cognitive Explanation of Situational and Individual Effects on Moral Sensitivity," *Journal of Applied Social Psychology* 45, no. 1 (2015): 45–54; S.J. Reynolds and J.A. Miller, "The Recognition of Moral Issues: Moral Awareness, Moral Sensitivity and Moral Attentiveness," *Current Opinion in Psychology* 6 (2015): 114–17.

53. J. Boegershausen, K. Aquino, and A. Reed II, "Moral Identity," *Current Opinion in Psychology* 6 (2015): 162–66.

54. N. Ruedy and M. Schweitzer, "In the Moment: The Effect of Mindfulness on Ethical Decision Making," *Journal of Business Ethics* 95, no. 1 (2010): 73–87.

55. M.H. Bazerman and F. Gino, "Behavioral Ethics: Toward a Deeper Understanding of Moral Judgment and Dishonesty," *Annual Review of Law and Social Science* 8, no. 1 (2012): 85–104; M. Knoll et al., "Examining the Moral Grey Zone: The Role of Moral Disengagement, Authenticity, and Situational Strength in Predicting Unethical Managerial Behavior," *Journal of Applied Social Psychology* 46, no. 1 (2016): 65–78; "2022 Global Business Ethics Survey" (Vienna, VA: Ethics & Compliance Initiative, May 2022).

56. M. Kaptein, "Ethics Programs and Ethical Culture: A Next Step in Unraveling Their Multi-Faceted Relationship," *Journal of Business Ethics* 89, no. 2 (2009): 261–81; G. Svensson et al., "Ethical Structures and Processes of Corporations Operating in Australia, Canada, and Sweden: A Longitudinal and Cross-Cultural Study," *Journal of Business Ethics* 86, no. 4 (2009): 485–506; M. Kirsten, R. Wordsworth, and M. du-Plessis, "More Does Not Always Mean Better: Do More Comprehensive Ethics Management Programmes Result in Better Outcomes?," *African Journal of Business and Economic Research* 12, no. 2/3 (2017): 149–76; M. Constantinescu and M. Kaptein, "Ethics Management and Ethical Management: Mapping Criteria and Interventions to Support Responsible Management Practice," in *Research Handbook of Responsible Management*, ed. O. Laasch et al. (Cheltenham, UK: Edward Elgar Publishing, 2020), 115–74.

57. S. Román and J.-L. Munuera-Alemán, "Determinants and Consequences of Ethical Behaviour: An Empirical Study of Salespeople," *European Journal of Marketing* 39 (2005): 473–95; P. Ruiz et al., "Level of Coherence among Ethics Program Components and Its Impact on Ethical Intent," *Journal of Business Ethics* 128, no. 4 (2015): 725–42; A. Nygaard et al., "Leading by Example: Values-Based Strategy to Instill Ethical Conduct," *Journal of Business Ethics* 145, no. 1 (2017): 133–39.

58. L.-Z. Wu et al., "CEO Ethical Leadership and Corporate Social Responsibility: A Moderated Mediation Model," *Journal of Business Ethics* 130, no. 4 (2015): 819–31; C. Lapointe, L. Langlois, and D. Tanguay, "How Are You Managing, Ethically Speaking? A Typology Proposal of Ethical Culture," *Canadian Journal of Educational Administration and Policy* 194 (2020): 64–77.

59. "Ethics. Every Day. Everyone. Everywhere," Code of Ethics and Business Conduct (Hartford, Conn.: The Hartford, April 2021); "The Hartford Named One of 'World's Most Ethical Companies' for 13th Time by Ethisphere," Press Release (Hartford, Conn.: The Hartford, March 15, 2022); "2021 Sustainability Highlight Report: Forward as One" (Hartford, Conn.: The Hartford, July 2022).

60. Individualism and collectivism information is from the meta-analysis by Oyserman et al., not the earlier findings by Hofstede. See D. Oyserman, H.M. Coon, and M. Kemmelmeier, "Rethinking Individualism and Collectivism: Evaluation of Theoretical Assumptions and Meta-Analyses," *Psychological Bulletin* 128 (2002): 3–72. Consistent with Oyserman et al., a recent study found high rather than low individualism among Chileans. See A. Kolstad and S. Horpestad, "Self-Construal in Chile and Norway," *Journal of Cross-Cultural Psychology* 40, no. 2 (2009): 275–81.

61. F.S. Niles, "Individualism–Collectivism Revisited," *Cross-Cultural Research* 32 (1998): 315–41; C.P. Earley and C.B. Gibson, "Taking Stock in Our Progress on Individualism–Collectivism: 100 Years of Solidarity and Community," *Journal of Management* 24 (1998): 265–304; C.L. Jackson et al., "Psychological Collectivism: A Measurement Validation and Linkage to Group Member Performance," *Journal of Applied Psychology* 91, no. 4 (2006): 884–99.

62. D. Oyserman, H.M. Coon, and M. Kemmelmeier, "Rethinking Individualism and Collectivism: Evaluation of Theoretical Assumptions and Meta-Analyses," *Psychological Bulletin* 128 (2002): 3–72; H. Vargas and M. Kemmelmeier, "Ethnicity and Contemporary American Culture: A Meta-Analytic Investigation of Horizontal–Vertical Individualism–Collectivism," *Journal of Cross-Cultural Psychology* 44, no. 2 (2013): 195–222; Y. Kashima, P.G. Bain, and A. Perfors, "The Psychology of Cultural Dynamics: What Is It, What Do We Know, and What Is Yet to Be Known?" *Annual Review of Psychology* 70, no. 1 (2019): 499–529.

63. G. Hofstede, *Culture's Consequences: Comparing Values, Behaviors, Institutions, and Organizations across Nations*, 2nd ed. (Thousand Oaks, CA: Sage, 2001).

64. G. Hofstede, *Culture's Consequences: Comparing Values, Behaviors, Institutions, and Organizations across Nations*, 2nd ed. (Thousand Oaks, CA: Sage, 2001). Hofstede used the terms *masculinity* and *femininity* for *achievement* and *nurturing orientation*, respectively. We (along with other writers) have adopted the latter two terms to minimize the sexist perspective of these concepts. Also, readers need to be aware that achievement orientation is assumed to be opposite of nurturing orientation, but this opposing relationship might be questioned.

65. V. Taras, J. Rowney, and P. Steel, "Half a Century of Measuring Culture: Review of Approaches, Challenges, and Limitations Based on the Analysis of 121 Instruments for Quantifying Culture," *Journal of International Management* 15, no. 4 (2009): 357–73.

66. N. Jacob, "Cross-Cultural Investigations: Emerging Concepts," *Journal of Organizational Change Management* 18, no. 5 (2005): 514–28; V. Taras, B.L. Kirkman, and P. Steel, "Examining the Impact of Culture's Consequences: A Three-Decade, Multilevel, Meta-Analytic Review of Hofstede's Cultural Value Dimensions," *Journal of Applied Psychology* 95, no. 3 (2010): 405–39.

67. R.L. Tung and A. Verbeke, "Beyond Hofstede and GLOBE: Improving the Quality of Cross-Cultural Research," *Journal of International Business Studies* 41, no. 8 (2010): 1259–74.

68. D. Oyserman, H.M. Coon, and M. Kemmelmeier, "Rethinking Individualism and Collectivism: Evaluation of Theoretical Assumptions and Meta-Analyses," *Psychological Bulletin* 128 (2002): 3–72. However, a recent meta-analysis found only minor differences across ethnic groups. See J.H. Vargas and M. Kemmelmeier, "Ethnicity and Contemporary American Culture: A Meta-Analytic Investigation of Horizontal–Vertical Individualism–Collectivism," *Journal of Cross-Cultural Psychology* 44, no. 2 (2013): 195–222.

69. J.A. Vandello and D. Cohen, "Patterns of Individualism and Collectivism across the United States," *Journal of Personality and Social Psychology* 77, no. 2 (1999): 279–92; B. MacNab, R. Worthley, and S. Jenner, "Regional Cultural Differences and Ethical Perspectives within the United States: Avoiding Pseudo-Emic Ethics Research," *Business and Society Review* 115, no. 1 (2010): 27–55; J. Lun, B. Mesquita, and B. Smith, "Self- and Other-Presentational Styles in the Southern and Northern United States: An Analysis of Personal Ads," *European Journal of Social Psychology* 41, no. 4 (2011): 435–45; P.J. Rentfrow et al., "Divided We Stand: Three Psychological Regions of the United States and Their Political, Economic, Social, and Health Correlates," *Journal of Personality and Social Psychology* 105, no. 6 (2013): 996–1012.

3 Perceiving Ourselves and Others in Organizations

Learning Objectives

After reading this chapter, you should be able to:

LO3-1 Describe the self-concept characteristics and processes, and explain how each affects an individual's behavior and well-being.

LO3-2 Outline the perceptual process and discuss the effects of categorical thinking and mental models in that process.

LO3-3 Discuss how stereotyping; attribution; self-fulfilling prophecy; and the halo, false-consensus, recency, and primacy effects influence the perceptual process.

LO3-4 Discuss three ways to improve perceptions, with specific application to organizational situations.

self-concept An individual's self-beliefs and self-evaluations

FedEx Corp recently announced declining shipping volumes and profits, and it attributed the poor results to an economic slowdown. Several investment analysts weren't impressed with that explanation, saying that FedEx's executive team should have taken some personal responsibility for the company's financial problems rather than rely completely on an external attribution.

The slowing economy had been known for several months, yet Fedex apparently didn't adjust its business to those earlier signals. Similarly, experts had long ago predicted declining post-pandemic demand for delivery services as people ventured back into stores and spent more on travel and leisure than on goods. According to one Credit Suisse analyst, FedEx's inability to anticipate these changing conditions is a symptom of internal problems, possibly that the company is getting too complex. "The burden of proof now sits with management," the analyst reproached.[1]

When companies experience poor sales and profits, executives scramble for explanations, preferably ones that cast the blame on others rather than themselves. The FedEx announcement seems to be one example of this self-serving bias. Company executives and the rest of us make internal and external attributions all the time, but this perceptual process is far from perfect. This chapter describes how people engage in several perceptual processes, such as making internal and external attributions. Each of these cognitive activities is vital for interacting with the world around us as well as for understanding ourselves. However, each perceptual process can also lead to misperceptions.

We begin this chapter by examining self-concept—how we perceive ourselves—and how that self-perception affects our decisions and behavior. We then turn our attention to perceptions of others in organizational settings, beginning with how we select, organize, and interpret information. Next, we examine several specific perceptual processes, such as stereotyping, attribution, and self-fulfilling prophecy. The final section of this chapter discusses potentially effective ways to improve perceptions in the workplace.

LO3-1 Describe the self-concept characteristics and processes, and explain how each affects an individual's behavior and well-being.

SELF-CONCEPT: HOW WE PERCEIVE OURSELVES

Self-concept refers to an individual's self-beliefs and self-evaluations.[2] It is the "Who am I?" and "How do I feel about myself?" that people ask themselves and that guide their decisions and actions. When contemplating a career in a particular occupation, for example, we compare our perceptions of that job with our current (perceived self) and desired (ideal self) images of ourselves. We also evaluate our current and desired abilities to determine whether there is a good fit with that type of work. Our self-concept is defined at three levels: individual, relational, and collective. Specifically, we view ourselves in terms of our personal traits (individual self); connections to friends and coworkers (relational self); and membership in teams, organizations, social groups, and other entities (collective self).[3]

Self-Concept Complexity, Consistency, and Clarity

An individual's self-concept can be described by three characteristics: complexity, consistency, and clarity (see Exhibit 3.1). *Complexity* refers to the number of distinct and important roles

> **Whenever two people meet there are really six people present. There are the two people as they see themselves, the two people as they see each other, and the two people as they really are.[4]**
>
> —Restated from Oliver Wendell Holmes Sr., medical scholar and author (in *The Autocrat of the Breakfast-Table*, 1858)

Exhibit 3.1 Self-Concept Characteristics and Processes

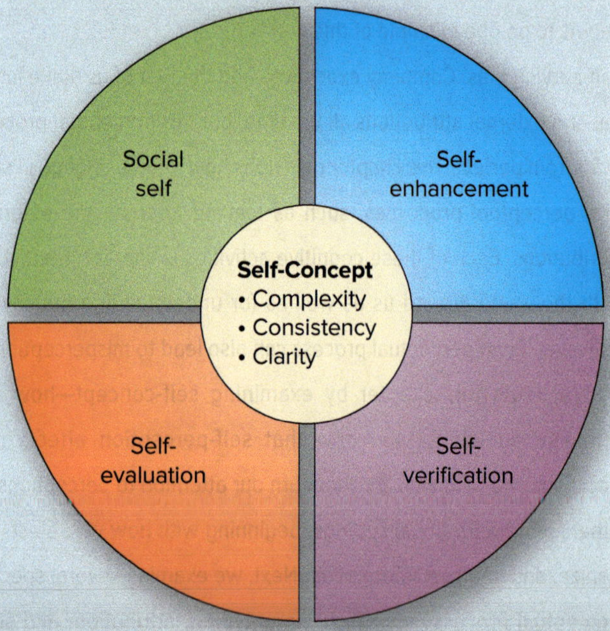

or identities that people perceive about themselves.[5] Everyone has multiple self-views because they see themselves in different roles at various times (student, friend, daughter, sports fan, etc.). People are generally motivated to increase their complexity (called *self-expansion*) as they seek out new opportunities and social connections. Your self-concept becomes more complex, for example, as you move from being an accountant to a manager because you have acquired additional roles.

Self-concept complexity is defined by more than just the person's number of identities; it is also defined by the separation of those identities. An individual with several identities might still have low self-concept complexity when those identities are highly interconnected, such as when they are all work related (manager, engineer, family income earner). Complexity is higher when the multiple identities have a low correlation with one another, such as when you have a successful career but also carve out sufficient time and focus to be a dedicated parent, a helpful neighbor, and a talented mountain biker.

Although people have multiple selves, only some of those identities dominate their attention at any one time.[6] A particular self-view (parent, manager, etc.) is usually domain specific; it is more likely to be activated in some settings than in others. People shift their self-concept more easily when the activated self-view is important and compatible with the situation. For instance, as employees travel from home to work, they can usually shift their self-view from being a parent to being an executive because each role is important and fits into the home and work contexts, respectively. In contrast, some individuals struggle to focus on their occupational self-concept when working from home (remote work).

Consistency, the second self-concept characteristic, is the degree to which a person's identities (a) require similar personal attributes and (b) are compatible with the person's actual attributes. Low consistency occurs when some self-views require personal attributes that conflict with attributes required for other self-views, such as when a safety-conscious engineer also has a self-view as a risk-oriented snowboarder. Low consistency also occurs when an individual's dominant self-views are incompatible with their actual personal attributes. As an example, low consistency would occur when someone has a self-concept as a highly creative individual yet has moderately low openness-to-experience personality and values. In contrast, high consistency among self-views and with personal attributes can have a positive synergistic effect across roles. For instance, your passion as an amateur marathon runner might give you better knowledge and role modeling as a physician.[7]

Clarity, the third characteristic of self-concept, refers to the degree to which a person's self-concept is clear, confidently defined, and stable.[8] People with high self-concept clarity are confident about "who I am," can describe their identities to others, and provide the same description of themselves across time.

OB THEORY TO PRACTICE

Being Your Authentic Self at Work

Most companies don't encourage employees to reveal their multiple "selves" at work, only their work-related identity. "Being yourself at work—and bringing the title of mom, wife, sister, and friend into the office typically comes at a price," complains Cathy Thorpe, CEO of home nursing care service Nurse Next Door. "It means becoming a chameleon, a reflection of your surroundings, changing how you behave depending on where you are."

In contrast, Nurse Next Door has torn down the hierarchy, empowered its employees, and encouraged them to bring their whole selves to work. "We don't want them to change who they are when they step through our doors," Thorpe explains. "At home or at the office, you should feel free to be yourself—no matter where you're standing.[9]

Life images/Shutterstock

Connect

SELF-ASSESSMENT 3.1: How Much Does Work Define Your Self-Concept?

Self-concept clarity increases with age because personality and values become relatively stable by adulthood and people develop better self-awareness through life experiences. Self-concept clarity also increases with consistency across the individual's multiple selves. This makes sense because low consistency produces ambiguity about a person's underlying characteristics. Someone whose self-view includes the opposing (low consistency) roles as a cautious engineer and a risk-oriented snowboarder, for instance, would have difficulty clearly or confidently defining themselves.[10]

Effects of Self-Concept Characteristics on Well-Being and Behavior Psychological well-being tends to be higher among people with fairly distinct multiple selves (complexity) that are well established (clarity) and require similar personal attributes that are compatible with the individual's character (consistency).[11] Self-concept complexity protects our self-esteem when some roles are threatened or damaged. A complex self is similar to a ship with several compartments that can be sealed off from one another. If one compartment of the ship is damaged, the other compartments remain intact so the ship remains afloat. A complex self offers the same benefits. If one identity is damaged by events–job loss, for example–the person's mental health stays afloat because the other selves remain intact. In contrast, people with low complexity, including those whose multiple selves are highly interconnected, suffer severe loss when they experience failure because these events affect a large part of themselves.

People tend to have better psychological well-being when their multiple selves are in harmony with one another and with their personality and values (high consistency).
alphaspirit/Shutterstock

People also tend to have better well-being when their multiple selves are in harmony with one another and with their personality and values (high consistency).[12] Self-concept complexity helps people adapt, but too much variation causes internal tension and conflict. Well-being also tends to increase with self-concept clarity. People who are unsure of their self-views are more easily influenced by others, experience more stress when making decisions, and feel more threatened by social forces that undermine their self-confidence and self-esteem.[13]

Self-concept complexity, consistency, and clarity have both positive and negative influences on individual behavior and performance.[14] Employees with complex identities tend to have more adaptive decision making and performance. This likely occurs because multiple selves generate more diverse experiences and role patterns, so these employees can more easily alter their thinking and behavior to suit new tasks and work environments. A second benefit is that self-concept complexity often produces more diverse social networks, which gives employees access to more resources and social support to perform their jobs.

Against these benefits is the problem that highly complex self-concepts require more effort to maintain and juggle, which can be stressful and less efficient. Low complexity self-concepts, on the other hand, require less effort and resources to develop. For example, people who define themselves mainly by their work (low complexity) tend to have better job performance due to their longer work hours, more investment in skill development, and more concentration on work. They also have lower absenteeism and turnover.

Self-concept clarity tends to improve performance and is considered vital for leadership roles.[15] Clarity also provides a more discernible career path, which enables people to direct their effort more efficiently toward career success. Another benefit is that people with high self-concept clarity feel less threatened by interpersonal conflict, which increases their ability to resolve conflicts through constructive problem-solving behaviors. However, those with very high clarity may have role inflexibility, with the result that they cannot adapt to changing job duties or environmental conditions.

Along with the three self-concept characteristics, Exhibit 3.1 illustrates four processes that shape self-concept and motivate a person's decisions and behavior. Let's look at each of these four "selves": self-enhancement, self-verification, self-evaluation, and social self (social identity).

Self-Enhancement

People are inherently motivated to perceive themselves, and to be perceived by others, as above average in important ways, such as being competent, attractive, lucky, ethical, and

self-enhancement A person's inherent motivation to have a positive self-concept (and to have others perceive them favorably), such as being competent, attractive, lucky, ethical, and important

self-verification A person's inherent motivation to confirm and maintain the individual's existing self-concept

self-efficacy A person's belief that they have the ability, motivation, correct role perceptions, and favorable situation to complete a task successfully.

locus of control A person's general belief about the amount of control they have over personal life events

valuable.[16] This phenomenon, called **self-enhancement**, occurs when individuals rate themselves above average, believe that they have a better-than-average probability of success, and attribute their successes to personal motivation or ability while blaming the situation for their mistakes. People don't believe they are above average in all circumstances, only for things that are important to them and are relatively common rather than rare.[17]

People are inherently motivated to perceive themselves, and to be perceived by others, as above average in important ways.
Spark Studio/Getty Images

Self-enhancement has both positive and negative consequences in organizational settings.[18] On the positive side, individuals tend to experience better mental and physical health when they amplify their self-concept. Overconfidence also generates a "can-do" attitude (which we discuss later in this section of the chapter) that motivates persistence in difficult or risky tasks. On the negative side, self-enhancement causes people to overestimate future returns in investment decisions and to engage in unsafe behavior, such as dangerous driving. It also accounts for executives repeating poor decisions, launching misguided corporate diversification strategies, and acquiring excessive corporate debt.

> The deepest urge in human nature is the desire to be important.[19]
>
> —John Dewey, educational philosopher

Self-Verification

Individuals try to confirm and maintain their existing self-concept.[20] This process, called **self-verification,** stabilizes an individual's self-view, which in turn provides an important anchor that guides the individual's thoughts and actions. Employees actively communicate their self-concept so coworkers understand it and provide verifying feedback when observed. For example, you might let coworkers know that you are a very organized person; later, they compliment you on occasions where you have indeed been very organized. Unlike self-enhancement, self-verification includes seeking feedback that is not necessarily flattering (e.g., "I'm a numbers person, not a people person"). Experts continue to debate whether and under what conditions people prefer information that supports self-enhancement or self-verification.[21] Do we prefer compliments rather than accurate critique about weaknesses that we readily acknowledge? The answer is likely complex; we enjoy compliments, but less so if they are significantly contrary to our self-view.

Self-verification is associated with several OB topics.[22] First it affects the perceptual process that we describe later in this chapter. Specifically, employees are more likely to remember information that is consistent with their self-concept and nonconsciously screen out information (particularly negative information) that seems inconsistent with it. Second, people with high self-concept clarity will consciously dismiss feedback that contradicts their self-view. Third, employees prefer interacting with others who affirm their self-concept, and this affects how well they get along with their boss and team members.

Self-Evaluation

Almost everyone strives to have a positive self-concept, but some people have a more positive evaluation of themselves than do others. This *self-evaluation* is mostly defined by three elements: self-esteem, self-efficacy, and locus of control.[23]

Self-Esteem Self-esteem represents a comprehensive self-evaluation. It is the extent to which individuals like, respect, and are satisfied with themselves. People have degrees of self-esteem for each of their various roles, such as being a good student, a good driver, and a good parent. From these multiple self-appraisals, they form an overall evaluation of themselves, known as their global self-esteem. Those with high self-esteem are less influenced by others, tend to persist in spite of failure, and have a higher propensity to think logically.[24]

Not Enough Positive Self-Evaluation in the Workplace[25]

88% of more than 2,400 American workers across several job groups (finance, technology, marketing, legal, etc.) say they are confident about their current skill set and marketability.

81% of 557,778 U.S. Federal government employees say the employees in their work unit treat them as a valued member of the team.

11% of 1,000 full-time U.S. workers say they do not feel valued at all by their organization.

32% of 1,200 U.S. and 1,200 U.K. employees say that within the past year they have felt unqualified for their current job.

38% of 2,995 school staff in the UK say they feel confident in their role.

(Photo): Ljupco Smokovski/Shutterstock

SELF-ASSESSMENT 3.2: How Much General Self-Efficacy Do You Have?

Self-Efficacy **Self-efficacy** refers to a person's belief that they can successfully complete a task.[26] Those with high self-efficacy have a "can-do" attitude. They believe they possess the energy (motivation), ability, clear expectations (role perceptions), and resources (situational factors) to perform the task. In other words, self-efficacy is an individual's perception regarding the MARS model in a specific situation. Self-efficacy is often task specific, but it also can be more generalized. People have a general self-efficacy when they believe they can be successful across a variety of situations.[27] Those with higher general self-efficacy have a more positive overall self-evaluation.

Locus of Control **Locus of control** is defined as a person's general beliefs about the amount of control they have over personal life events.[28] Individuals with an internal locus of control believe that life events are caused mainly by their personal characteristics (i.e., motivation and abilities). Those with an external locus of control believe events are due mainly to fate, luck, or conditions in the external environment. Locus of control is a generalized belief that varies to some extent with the situation. People with an external locus of control generally believe that life's outcomes are beyond their control, but they also believe they have control over the results of tasks they perform often. An individual's locus of control tendency is most apparent in new situations because their ability to control events is uncertain.

People with an internal locus of control have a more positive self-evaluation. They also tend to perform better in most employment situations, are more successful in their careers, earn more money, and are better suited for leadership positions. Internals also are more satisfied with their jobs, cope better in stressful situations, and are more motivated by performance-based reward systems.[29]

SELF-ASSESSMENT 3.3: What Is Your Locus of Control?

The Social Self

We began this topic by stating that an individual's self-concept exists at three levels: individual, relational, and collective. These three levels recognize two opposing human motives that influence how people view themselves.[30]

- *Motivation to be distinctive and different from other people.* The individual self, called *personal identity* or *internal self-concept,* fulfills the need for distinctiveness because it involves defining ourselves by our personality, values, abilities, qualifications, achievements, and other personal attributes. Everyone has a unique combination of personal characteristics, and we embrace this uniqueness to some degree. For instance, an unusual skill or accomplishment that distinguishes you from your coworkers is part of your personal identity.
- *Motivation for inclusion and assimilation with other people.* The relational and collective self-concepts fulfill the fundamental drive for affiliation because they involve both interaction and interdependence with others.[31] Human beings are social animals; we have an inherent drive to be associated with others and to be recognized as part of social communities. This drive to belong motivates all individuals to define themselves to some degree by their interpersonal and collective relationships, a definition known as their *social identity* or *external self-concept.*

Exhibit 3.2 Social Identity Theory Example

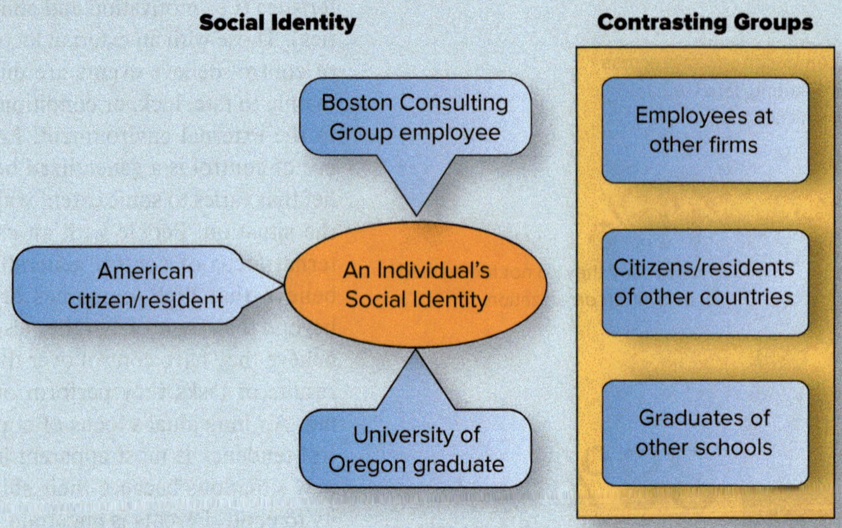

Social identity is the foundation of **social identity theory**, which says that people define themselves by the groups to which they belong or have an emotional attachment.[32] For instance, someone might have a social identity as an American citizen, a University of Oregon alumnus, and an employee at Boston Consulting Group (see Exhibit 3.2).

Social identity is a complex combination of many memberships arranged in a hierarchy of importance. One factor determining importance is how easily you are identified as a member of the reference group, such as by your biological sex, age, and ethnicity. A second factor is your minority status in a group. It is difficult to ignore your age in a class where most other students are another age cohort, for example. In that context, biological sex tends to become a stronger defining feature of your social identity than it is in social settings where there are many people of the same sex.

The group's status is another important social identity factor because association with the group makes us feel better about ourselves (i.e., self-enhancement). Medical doctors usually define themselves by their profession because of its high status. Some people describe themselves by where they work ("I work at Microsoft") because their employer has a good reputation. Others never mention where they work because their employer is noted for poor relations with employees or has a poor reputation in the community.[33]

Everyone tries to balance personal and social identities to some degree, but the priority for uniqueness (personal identities) versus relatedness (social identities) differs from one person to the next. People whose self-concepts are heavily defined by social rather than personal identities are more motivated to abide by team norms and more easily influenced by peer pressure. Those who place more emphasis on personal identities, on the other hand, speak out more frequently against the majority and are less motivated to follow the team's wishes. Furthermore, expressing disagreement with others is a sign of distinctiveness and can help employees form a clearer self-concept, particularly when that disagreement is based on differences in personal values.[34]

People whose self-concepts are heavily defined by social rather than personal identities are more motivated to abide by team norms and are more easily influenced by peer pressure.
andresr/Getty Images

Self-Concept and Organizational Behavior

Self-concept has become a hot topic in the social sciences and is starting to bloom in organizational behavior research.[35] This section briefly noted that self-concept influences human perceptions, decision making, motivation, stress, team dynamics, leadership development, and several other OB topics. Consequently, we will refer to self-concept later in this chapter and in many other topics throughout this book.

LO3-2 Outline the perceptual process and discuss the effects of categorical thinking and mental models in that process.

PERCEIVING THE WORLD AROUND US

We spend considerable time perceiving ourselves, but most of our perceptual energy is directed toward the outer world. Whether as a forensic accountant, mechanical engineer, or senior executive, we need to make sense of our surroundings and to manage the conditions that challenge the accuracy of those perceptions. **Perception** is the process of receiving information about and making sense of the world around us. It includes determining which information to notice, as well as how to categorize and interpret it within the framework of our existing knowledge.

The perceptual process generally follows the steps shown in Exhibit 3.3. Perception begins when environmental stimuli are received through our senses. We are continually bombarded by external stimuli. Most are screened out; the rest are organized and interpreted. The process of attending to some information received by our senses and ignoring other information is called **selective attention.** Selective attention is influenced by characteristics of the person or object being perceived, particularly size, intensity, motion, repetition, and novelty. For example, a small, flashing red light on a nurses' workstation console is immediately noticed because it is bright (intensity), flashing (motion), a rare event (novelty), and has symbolic meaning that a patient's vital signs are failing. Notice that selective attention also is influenced by the context in which the target is perceived. For instance, selective attention is triggered by things or people who might be out of context, such as someone with a foreign accent in a setting where most people have a local accent.

Characteristics of the perceiver also influence selective attention, usually without the perceiver's awareness.[36] When information is received through the senses, our brain quickly and nonconsciously assesses whether it is relevant or irrelevant to us and then attaches emotional markers (worry, happiness, boredom) to the retained information.[37] Emotional markers help us to store information in memory; those emotions are later reproduced when recalling the perceived information. The selective attention process is far from perfect, however. The Greek philosopher Plato acknowledged this imperfection long ago when he wrote that we see reality only as shadows reflecting against the rough wall of a cave.[38]

social identity theory A theory stating that people define themselves by the groups to which they belong or have an emotional attachment

perception The process of receiving information about and making sense of the world around us

selective attention The process of attending to some information received by our senses and ignoring other information

confirmation bias The process of screening out information that is contrary to our decisions, beliefs, values, and assumptions, while more readily accepting confirming information

Exhibit 3.3 Model of the Perceptual Process

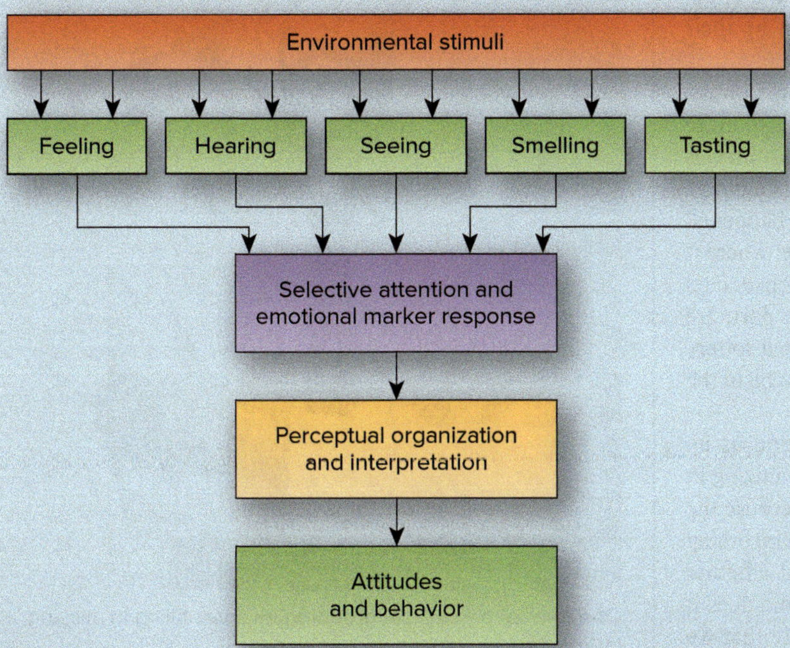

One selective attention bias is the effect of our assumptions and expectations about future events. You are more likely to notice a particular coworker's email among the daily avalanche of messages when you are expecting to receive that email (even more so if it is important). Unfortunately, expectations and assumptions also cause us to screen out potentially important information. In one study, students were asked to watch a 30-second video clip in which several people passed around two basketballs. Students in one group were instructed simply to watch the video clip. Most of them readily noticed a person dressed in a gorilla suit walking among the players for nine seconds and stopping to thump their chest. Students in a second group were asked to count the number of times one of the two basketballs was passed around. Only half of the people in this latter group noticed the intruding gorilla.[39]

Another selective attention problem, called **confirmation bias,** is the nonconscious tendency for people to screen out information that is contrary to their decisions, beliefs, values, and assumptions, while more readily accepting information that confirms those elements.[40] When we make important decisions, such as investing in a costly project, we tend to pay attention to information that supports that decision, ignore information that questions the wisdom of the decision, and more easily recall the supportive than the opposing information. Confirmation bias is a well-known perceptual problem in which law enforcement professionals form a theory too early in an investigation.[41]

> Theory like mist on eyeglasses. Obscure facts.[42]
>
> —Robert Ellis and Helen Logan (screenwriters of the film *Charlie Chan in Egypt*, 1935)

another individual's trustworthiness after viewing a facial image for as little as 50 milliseconds (1/20th of a second). In fact, our opinion regarding whether we like or trust a stranger is about the same whether we see the person's face for a minute or a fraction of a second.[46] Collectively, these studies reveal that selective attention, perceptual organization, and interpretation operate very quickly and to a large extent without our awareness.

Perceptual Organization and Interpretation

We pay attention to a tiny fraction of the stimuli received by the senses. Even so, the human brain applies various perceptual grouping strategies to further reduce the huge volume and complexity of selected information. Perceptual grouping occurs mostly without our awareness, yet it is the foundation for making sense of things and fulfilling our need for cognitive closure.

The dominant form of perceptual grouping is **categorical thinking**—the mostly nonconscious process of organizing people and objects into preconceived categories that are stored in our long-term memory.[43] Similarity is a widely used categorization principle in social settings; we group people together based on their observable similarity, such as biological sex, age, race, or clothing style. Proximity is another organizing principle.[44] When entering a room with many people, you quickly discern clusters rather than a random distribution of bodies, particularly when individuals seem to be interacting with each other. Quite often, we soon realize that organizing people in that room by their proximity is far from precise.

Another form of perceptual grouping involves filling in missing information about people or places. Everyone wants to make sense of what goes on around them, so they rely on past images and experiences to understand similar situations. This cognitive process occurs when making assumptions about what happened at a meeting that we didn't attend (e.g., who was there, where it was held). A related form of perceptual organization occurs when people tend to see patterns that, for the most part, are random events. A well-known example is expecting that lottery numbers recently drawn several times in a row will also be in the next winning lottery ticket.[45]

The process of "making sense" of the world around us involves interpreting incoming information, not just organizing it. This happens as quickly as selecting and organizing because the previously mentioned emotional markers are tagged to incoming stimuli, which are essentially quick judgments about whether that information is good or bad for us. How much time does it take to make these quick judgments? Studies estimate that we make reliable (but not necessarily accurate) judgments about

SELF-ASSESSMENT 3.4: How Much Perceptual Structure Do You Need?

Mental Models To engage in almost any activity and achieve goals, we need road maps of the environments in which we live. These road maps, called **mental models**, are knowledge

One form of perceptual grouping involves filling in missing information about people or places.
Romolo Tavani/Shutterstock

structures that we develop to describe, explain, and predict the world around us.[47] They consist of visual or relational images in our mind, such as what the classroom looks like or what happens when we submit an assignment late. Mental models partly rely on the process of perceptual grouping to make sense of things; they fill in the missing pieces, including the causal connection among events. For example, you have a mental model about attending a class lecture or seminar, including assumptions or expectations about where the instructor and students arrange themselves in the room, how they ask and answer questions, and so forth. In other words, you create a mental image of a class in progress.

Mental models are important for sense making, yet they also make it difficult to see the world in different ways. For example, accounting professionals tend to see corporate problems from an accounting perspective, whereas marketing professionals see the same problems from a marketing perspective. Mental models also block our recognition of new opportunities.

How do we change mental models? That's a tough challenge. After all, we developed these knowledge structures from several years of experience and reinforcement. One way to minimize the perceptual problems caused by mental models is to be aware of and frequently question them. We also need to question our assumptions, which are often based on mental models. Working with people from diverse backgrounds is another way to break out of existing mental models. Colleagues from different cultures and areas of expertise tend to have different mental models, so working with them makes our own assumptions more obvious.

LO3-3 Discuss how stereotyping; attribution; self-fulfilling prophecy; and the halo, false-consensus, recency, and primacy effects influence the perceptual process.

SPECIFIC PERCEPTUAL PROCESSES AND PROBLEMS

Within the general perceptual process are specific subprocesses and associated perceptual errors. In this section of the chapter, we examine several of these perceptual processes and biases as well as their implications for organizational behavior, beginning with the most widely known one: stereotyping.

Stereotyping in Organizations

Stereotyping is the perceptual process of characterizing an identifiable group by specific traits and automatically assigning those traits to individuals we believe are members of that group.[48] The assigned traits tend to be difficult to observe, such as personality traits and abilities, but they also can include physical characteristics and a host of other qualities. If we learn that someone is a professor, for example, we implicitly assume the person is probably also intelligent and absent-minded.

Stereotypes are formed to some extent from personal experience, but they are mainly provided to us through media images (e.g., movie characters) and other cultural prototypes. Consequently, stereotypes are shared beliefs across an entire society and often across several cultures, rather than beliefs that differ from one person to the next. Most stereotypes have one or more kernels of truth; they are more likely to characterize people within the group than the rest of us.[49] Even so, stereotypes embellish or distort those small kernels of truth and include other features that are completely false.

Why People Stereotype People engage in stereotyping because, as a form of categorical thinking, it is usually a nonconscious "energy-saving" process that simplifies our understanding of the world. It is easier to remember features of a stereotype than the constellation of characteristics unique to each person we meet. A second reason is that we have an innate need to understand and anticipate how others will behave. We don't have much information when first meeting someone, so we rely on stereotypes to fill in the missing pieces. The higher the perceiver's need for cognitive closure, the higher their reliance on stereotypes.[50]

A third explanation for stereotyping is that it is motivated by the observer's own need for social identity and self-enhancement. Earlier in this chapter we explained that people define themselves by the groups to which they belong or have an emotional

categorical thinking Organizing people and objects into preconceived categories that are stored in our long-term memory

mental models Visual and relational images that we develop in our mind to describe, explain, and predict the world around us

stereotyping The perceptual process of characterizing an identifiable group by specific traits and automatically assigning those traits to individuals perceived as members of that group

> **Social identity and self-enhancement motivate us to engage in the stereotyping process of categorization, homogenization, and differentiation.**

stereotype threat Occurs when a situation sensitizes a person to their social group's negative stereotype (usually competence), which increases their stress, distraction, and effort to avoid the negative trait to such an extent that they are more likely to display the undesirable trait

attribution process The perceptual process of determining whether an observed behavior or event is caused largely by internal (personal characteristics) or external (situational) factors

attachment. They are also motivated to maintain a positive self-concept. This combination of social identity and self-enhancement leads to the process of categorization, homogenization, and differentiation, all of which are the foundations of stereotyping:[51]

- *Categorization.* Social identity is a comparative process, and the comparison begins by categorizing people into distinct groups. By viewing someone (including yourself) as a Texan, for example, you remove that person's individuality and, instead, see them as a prototypical representative of the group called Texans. This categorization then distinguishes Texans from people who live in, say, California or Maine.
- *Homogenization.* To simplify the comparison process, we tend to think that people within each group are very similar to one another. For instance, we surmise that Texans collectively have similar attitudes and characteristics, whereas Californians collectively have their own set of characteristics. Of course, every individual is unique, but we often lose sight of this fact when thinking about our social identity and how we compare to people in other social groups.
- *Differentiation.* Along with categorizing and homogenizing people, we tend to assign more favorable characteristics to people in our groups than to people in other groups.[52] This differentiation is motivated by self-enhancement because being in a "better" group produces higher self-esteem. Differentiation is often subtle, but when out-group members threaten our self-concept, we are particularly motivated (often without our awareness) to assign negative stereotypes to them.

Problems with Stereotyping Everyone engages in stereotyping, yet it is highly inaccurate. Most features of a stereotype are distorted and embellished to such an extent that they describe very few people in the group. Even though a stereotype often has kernels of truth, that information doesn't describe everyone—often less than the majority—in the category. As a result, stereotyping leads to perceptual biases. For instance, the traditional accountant stereotype (boring, cautious, calculating) perhaps describes a few accountants, but it is certainly not characteristic of all, or even most, people in this profession. Nevertheless, when someone is categorized as an accountant, the nonobservable stereotypical features of accountants are transferred to that individual, even though we have no evidence that the person actually has those characteristics.

Most features of a stereotype are distorted and embellished to such an extent that they describe very few people in the group.
wavebreakmedia/Shutterstock

A second problem is that stereotypes produce **stereotype threat.** This condition occurs when a situation sensitizes a person to their social group's negative stereotype (usually competence), which increases their stress, distraction, and effort to avoid the negative trait to such an extent that they are more likely to display the undesirable trait.[53] Stereotype threat occurs in specific situations, such as when members of the stereotyped group are a minority in a social setting in which those attending are evaluated. People in that group experience more stress, are distracted by the salient negative stereotype, try to push the negative image from their mind, and actively try to avoid confirming the undesirable trait. Unfortunately, this consumes so much cognitive effort that the individuals perform poorly, thereby confirming the stereotype. Stereotype threat also can weaken self-efficacy; it is difficult to be confident in your ability when your group's stereotype suggests otherwise.

For example, females perform worse on math and science tests when sensitized to the generally false but widely held belief that they underperform males in these subjects. Females also tend to have lower scores when they are a small percentage of the group being tested. Females achieve much higher scores when the associated stereotype is not salient, such as when taking the test with many females in the class. Almost anyone can be affected by stereotype threat, but studies have particularly observed it for females, some minority groups, and people in older age groups.

A third problem with stereotyping is that it lays the foundation for unfair discrimination. Most of this perceptual bias occurs as *unintentional (systemic) discrimination*, whereby decision makers rely on stereotypes to establish notions of the "ideal" person in specific roles. Those who differ from the ideal tend to receive a less favorable evaluation than those who fit the occupational stereotype.

Unintentional systemic discrimination is particularly evident in employment and salary decisions. Consider the following example: Science faculty from several research intensive universities were given the fictitious application materials of either a male or female undergraduate student who was applying for a science laboratory manager job. The applications were identical other than the name and sex of the applicant, yet the male applicant received significantly higher ratings than the female applicant on competence and likelihood of being hired. The science faculty recommended a salary for the male applicant that was, on average, 15 percent higher than they recommended for the female applicant. Female faculty exhibited as much sex bias as the male faculty.[54]

> **Stereotype *activation* is automatic and nonconscious, but we can minimize stereotype *application*—the extent to which we rely on that information.**

Another negative consequence of stereotyping is *intentional discrimination* or *prejudice,* in which people hold unfounded negative attitudes toward people belonging to a particular stereotyped group.[55] Systemic discrimination is implicit, automatic, and unintentional, whereas intentional discrimination deliberately puts the target person at an unfair disadvantage.

If stereotyping is such a problem, shouldn't we try to avoid this process altogether? Unfortunately, it's not that simple. Most experts agree that categorical thinking (including stereotyping) is an automatic and nonconscious process. Specialized training programs can minimize stereotype activation to some extent, but for the most part the process is hardwired in our brain cells.[56] Also remember that stereotyping helps us in several valuable (although fallible) ways described earlier: minimizing mental effort, filling in missing information, and supporting our social identity.

Stereotype *activation* is automatic and nonconscious, but the good news is that we can minimize stereotype *application*—the extent to which we rely on that information. In other words, we automatically categorize people and assign stereotypic traits to them, but we can consciously minimize our reliance on that stereotypic information.[57] Later in this chapter, we identify ways to minimize stereotype application and other perceptual biases.

Attribution Theory

An important perceptual process in organizational settings is how people assess the causes of behavior or events. The **attribution process** evaluates whether an observed behavior or event seems to be caused mainly by the person (internal factors) or by one or more "entities" in the person's environment (external factors).[58] Internal factors include the individual's characteristics (ability, personality, motivation, etc.) whereas external factors include entities outside the person, such as the tools being used, presence or help from coworkers, the physical setting, and luck. If someone doesn't show up for an important meeting, for instance, we infer either internal attributions (the coworker is forgetful, lazy, etc.) or external attributions (traffic, a family emergency, etc.) to make sense of the person's absence.

Two attribution rules—distinctiveness and consensus—influence whether we believe an individual's behavior or performance are caused mainly by internal or external factors. A third attribution rule (consistency) influences our confidence in that attribution belief. Exhibit 3.4 illustrates how the distinctiveness and consensus attribution rules influence our perception of an internal or external attribution, and how consistency affects our confidence in that attribution. To explain these attribution rules, we'll use the example of an employee who makes poor-quality products on a specific machine (the external entity).[59]

- *Distinctiveness:* This rule refers to whether the individual's response is similar (low distinctiveness) or different (high distinctiveness) in the presence of different entities (e.g., different tools, customers, physical setting, etc.). In our example, high distinctiveness occurs if the employee makes poor-quality products on this machine but makes good-quality products on other machines. Low distinctiveness occurs if the employee makes poor-quality products on this machine and on other machines.
- *Consensus:* This rule refers to whether other people have the same response as the individual (high consensus) or a different response from the individual (low consensus) in the presence of the entity. In our example, high consensus occurs if other employees also make poor-quality products on this machine, whereas low consensus occurs if other employees make good-quality products on this machine.
- *Consistency:* The consistency rule refers to whether the individual's response is the same over time in the presence of the entity, and in whatever way the entity is presented. In our example, high consistency occurs if the employee always makes poor-quality products on this machine over time and in various situations (such as whether the manager is watching, or whether the machine is moved to another location). Low consistency occurs if the quality of the employee's work on this machine (and on other machines) varies from poor to good over time and in different situations.

Now, let's use these rules to decide whether to make an internal or external attribution about the employee's poor-quality products on a specific machine. We would form an internal attribution about the poor-quality products on this machine (i.e., caused by the employee's lack of ability or motivation) if the individual also makes poor-quality products on the other machines (low distinctiveness) and other employees make good-quality products on this machine (low consensus). Furthermore, we would have high confidence in this internal attribution if the employee consistently makes poor-quality products on this machine as well as on the other machines. If the quality of products the individual makes on this and other machines is inconsistent (sometimes good quality, sometimes poor quality), then we would have low confidence about attributing the cause of the poor quality products to characteristics of the employee.

We would form an external attribution (something about this machine is causing the poor-quality products) if the employee makes good-quality products on other machines (high distinctiveness) and other employees make poor-quality products on this machine (high consensus). Furthermore, we would have high confidence in this external attribution if the employee consistently makes poor-quality products on this machine whereas the person consistently makes good-quality products on other machines. We would have low confidence about this external attribution if this individual sometimes makes good-quality

Exhibit 3.4 Attribution Theory Rules

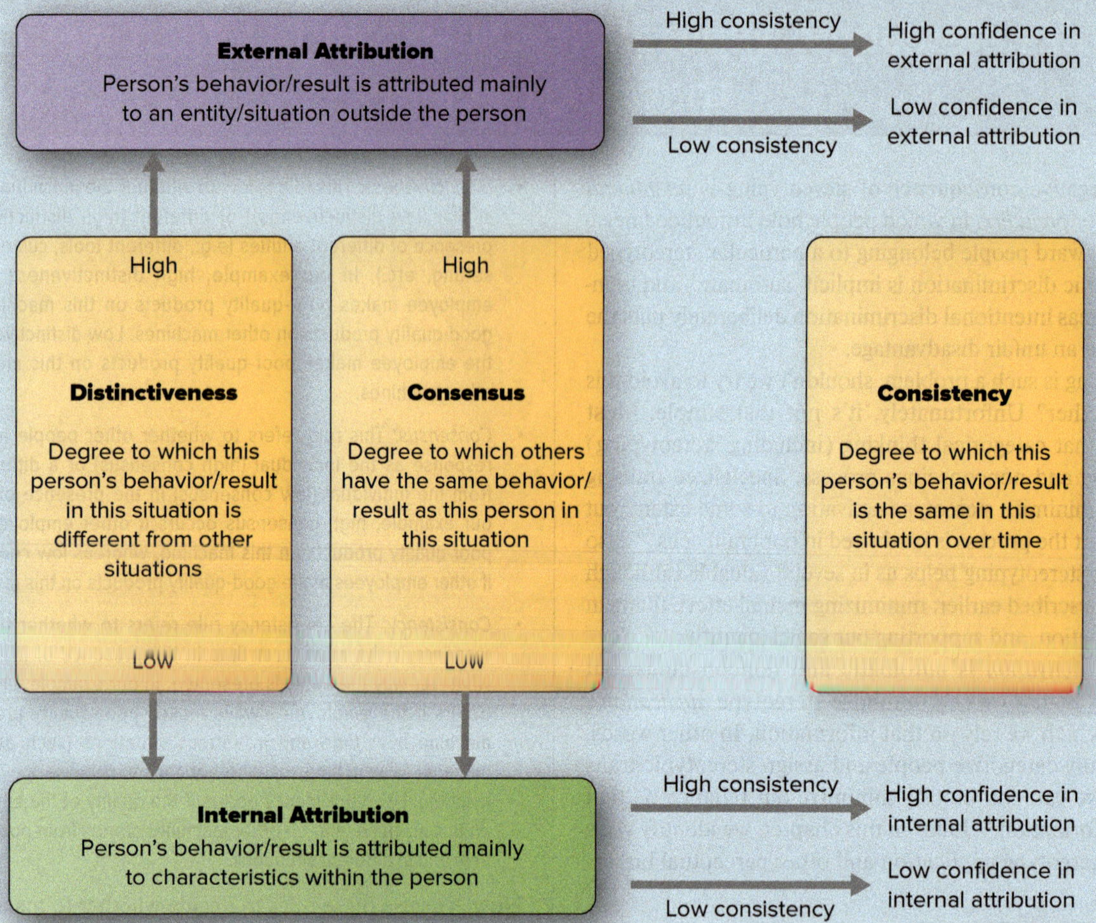

products and sometimes makes poor-quality products on this and on other machines (i.e., low consistency).

The attribution process is valuable because it helps to diagnose workplace problems, to improve organizational justice (such as assigning praise or blame), to work more effectively with others, and ultimately to improve organizational effectiveness.[60] Suppose a coworker didn't complete their task on a team project. You would evaluate this situation differently if you believed the coworker was lazy or lacked sufficient skill (an internal attribution) than if you believed the poor performance was due to lack of time or resources available to the coworker (an external attribution). We also react differently to attributions of our own behavior and performance. Students who make internal attributions about their poor grades, for instance, have lower self-efficacy and are more likely to drop out of their programs than if they make external attributions about those grades.[61]

Attribution Errors The attribution process is susceptible to errors. One such error is **self-serving bias**—the tendency to attribute our failures to external entities more than to internal factors (our own characteristics), and to attribute our successes more to internal than to external factors.[62] Simply put, we take credit for our successes and blame others or the situation for our mistakes. This bias was highlighted in the opening story to this chapter about FedEx's recent external attribution of its declining shipping volumes and profits. It is also evident in financial reports, where executives tend to overweight their personal qualities as reasons for the company's success and to emphasize external factors (competitors, weather, government regulations, etc.) as reasons why the company's performance fell below expectations.[63]

Self-serving bias is partly a deliberate influence tactic (impression management, see Chapter 10) to reframe how others view the situation, and partly the individual's perceptual distortion of the situation caused by self-enhancement (i.e., they actually believe problems weren't caused by their personal attributes).

Another attribution error, **fundamental attribution error** (also called *correspondence bias*), is the tendency to overemphasize internal causes of another person's behavior and to discount or ignore external causes of their behavior.[64] We are more likely to attribute a coworker's late arrival for work to lack of motivation rather than to situational constraints (such as traffic congestion). This occurs because observers can't easily see the

self-serving bias The tendency to attribute our favorable outcomes to internal factors and our failures to external factors

fundamental attribution error The tendency to see the person rather than the situation as the main cause of that person's behavior

self-fulfilling prophecy The perceptual process in which our expectations about another person cause that person to act more consistently with those expectations

The attribution process is valuable because it helps to diagnose workplace problems, to improve organizational justice, to work more effectively with others, and ultimately to improve organizational effectiveness.
Wavebreakmedia Ltd UC4/Alamy Stock Photo

external factors that constrain another person's behavior. Also, people like to think that human beings (not the situation) are the prime sources of their behavior. Although fundamental attribution error does occur, recent reviews suggest it may be less common than previously thought. It can often be minimized by giving those making attributions more information about the situation and warning them about this attribution error.[65]

Self-Fulfilling Prophecy

Self-fulfilling prophecy occurs when our expectations about another person cause them to act in a way that is consistent with those expectations. In other words, our perceptions can influence reality. Exhibit 3.5 illustrates the four steps in the self-fulfilling prophecy process using the example of a supervisor and a subordinate.[66] First, the supervisor forms expectations about the employee's future behavior and performance. These expectations are sometimes inaccurate because first impressions are usually formed from limited information. Second, the supervisor's expectations influence their behavior toward employees. In particular, employees who the supervisor expects will do well (high-expectancy employee) receive more emotional support through nonverbal cues (e.g., more smiling and eye contact from the boss), more frequent and valuable feedback and reinforcement, more challenging goals, better training, and more opportunities to demonstrate good performance.[67]

The third step in self-fulfilling prophecy includes two effects of the supervisor's behavior on the employee. One effect is that a high-expectancy employee learns more skills and knowledge than does a low-expectancy employee because of better training

Exhibit 3.5 The Self-Fulfilling Prophecy Cycle

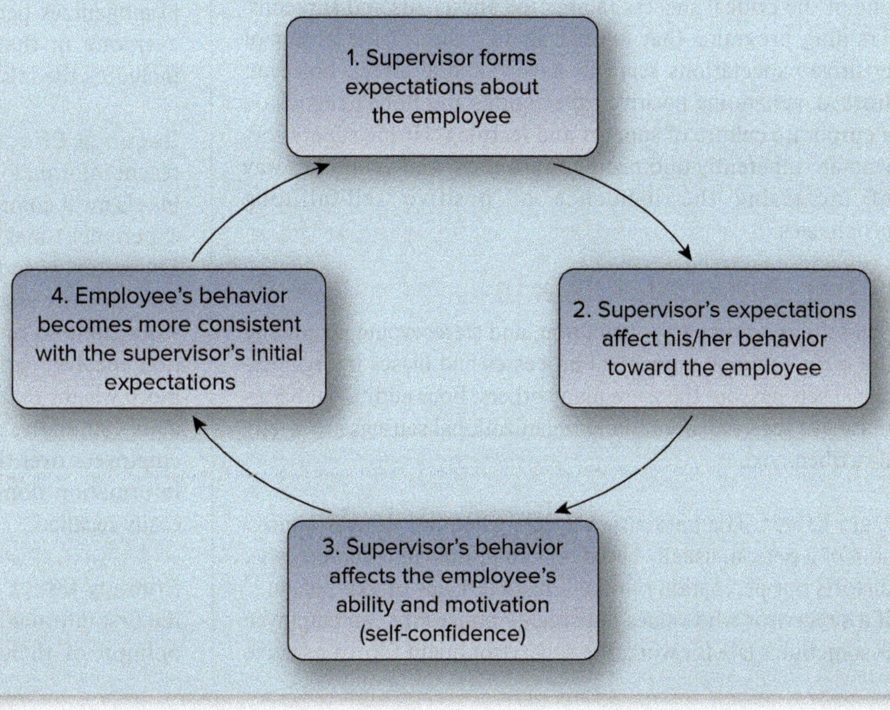

halo effect A perceptual error whereby our general impression of a person, usually based on one prominent characteristic, colors our perception of other characteristics of that person

false-consensus effect A perceptual error in which we overestimate the extent to which others have beliefs and characteristics similar to our own

recency effect A perceptual error in which the most recent information dominates our perception of others

primacy effect A perceptual error in which we quickly form an opinion of people based on the first information we receive about them

Johari Window A model and process of self-awareness and mutual understanding that encourages disclosure and feedback to increase our own open area and reduce the blind, hidden, and unknown areas

and more practice opportunities. The other effect is that the high-expectancy employee becomes more self-confident, which results in stronger motivation and willingness to set challenging goals.[68] In the final step, high-expectancy employees are more motivated and skilled, resulting in better performance, while the opposite is true of low-expectancy employees. An analysis of dozens of leader intervention studies over the years found that self-fulfilling prophecy is one of the most powerful leadership effects on follower behavior and performance.[69]

Contingencies of Self-Fulfilling Prophecy Self-fulfilling prophecy has a stronger effect at the beginning of a relationship, such as when employees are first hired. It is also stronger when several people (rather than just one person) hold the same expectations of the individual. In other words, we might be able to ignore one person's doubts about our potential but not the collective doubts of several people. The self-fulfilling prophecy effect is also stronger among people with a history of low achievement. These people tend to have lower self-esteem, so they are more easily influenced by others' opinions of them.[70]

The main lesson from the self-fulfilling prophecy literature is that leaders need to develop and maintain positive, yet realistic, expectations toward all employees. Communicating realistic hope and optimism is so important that it has been identified as one of the critical success factors for physicians and surgeons. Training programs that make leaders aware of the power of positive expectations seem to have minimal effect, however. Instead, generating positive expectations and hope depends on a corporate culture of support and learning. Hiring supervisors who are inherently optimistic toward their staff is another way of increasing the incidence of positive self-fulfilling prophecies.[71]

Other Perceptual Effects

Self-fulfilling prophecy, attribution, and stereotyping are among the most common perceptual processes and biases in organizational settings, but there are many others. Four additional biases that have received attention in organizational settings are briefly described next.

Halo Effect The **halo effect** occurs when our general impression of a person, usually based on one prominent characteristic, distorts our perception of other characteristics of that person.[72] If a supervisor who values punctuality notices that an employee is sometimes late for work, the supervisor might form a negative overall opinion of the employee and evaluate that person's other performance dimensions unfavorably as well. The halo effect is most likely to occur when important information about the other person is unavailable or we are not sufficiently motivated to search for it. Instead, we use our general impression of the person to fill in the missing information.

False-Consensus Effect The **false-consensus effect** (also called *similar-to-me effect*) occurs when people overestimate the extent to which others have similar beliefs or behaviors to their own.[73] Employees who are thinking of quitting their jobs overestimate the percentage of coworkers who also are thinking about quitting, for example. The false-consensus effect occurs partly because we are comforted by the belief that others are similar to us, particularly regarding less acceptable or divisive behavior. A second explanation is that we tend to spend more time with people who have similar views, and frequent interaction with like-minded people causes us to overestimate how common those views are throughout the company or society.

Confirmation bias is a third explanation for the false-consensus effect. We are more likely to notice and remember people whose views are similar to our own and ignore or forget about incidents in which individuals express views that oppose our own. A fourth explanation is that our social identity process homogenizes people within groups, so we tend to think that everyone in that group has similar opinions and behavior, including the false-consensus attitude or behavior.

Recency Effect The **recency effect** occurs when the most recent information dominates our perceptions.[74] This perceptual bias is most common when people (especially those with limited experience) make a decision involving complex information. For instance, auditors need to digest large volumes of information for their assessments about financial documents. They are susceptible to recency effect because the most recent information received prior to rendering their judgment may receive more weight than information received at the beginning of the audit. Similarly, when supervisors evaluate the performance of employees over the previous year, the most recent performance information dominates the evaluation because it is the most easily recalled.

Primacy Effect The **primacy effect** is our tendency to rely on the first information we receive about people to quickly form an opinion of them.[75] This perceptual bias is captured in the

First Impressions Count in Job Applications[76]

77% of 1,138 employers say they reject résumés with typos or bad grammar (75% and 76% of HR and general managers in two other surveys also say this).

26% of 205 U.S. human resources managers say that using informal greetings (such as "Hi!") in applicant cover letters are a serious problem.

Some Résumé Gaffes

- "References will be **made up** on request."
- "My last employer **fried me** for no reason."
- "**Exorcising** my sense of humor every day."
- "I have a keen eye for **derail**."
- "I'm **attacking** my resume for you to review."
- "Hope to hear from you, **shorty**."

70% of 205 U.S. human resources managers say they would reject a candidate for not including a cover letter in their job application.

47% of 2,800 employers in several countries say they won't bother to take a second look at a generic résumé (not customized to the advertised job).

25% of 2,800 employers in several countries say they spend less than one minute looking at a résumé. (23% in an earlier survey take less than 30 seconds.)

(Photo): Cornelius Krishna Tedjo/Shutterstock

well-known statement: First impressions are lasting impressions. We rapidly organize and interpret new information to fulfill our inherent need to make sense of the situation and, in particular, to trust others. The problem is that first impressions—particularly negative first impressions—are difficult to change. After categorizing someone, we tend to select subsequent information that supports our first impression and screen out information that opposes that impression.

LO3-4 Discuss three ways to improve perceptions, with specific application to organizational situations.

IMPROVING PERCEPTIONS

We can't bypass the perceptual process, but we should try to minimize perceptual biases and distortions. Three potentially effective ways to improve perceptions include awareness of perceptual biases, self-awareness, and meaningful interaction.

Awareness of Perceptual Biases

One of the most obvious and widely practiced ways to reduce perceptual biases is by knowing that they exist. For example, traditional diversity awareness training programs try to minimize discrimination by making people aware of systemic discrimination as well as prejudices that occur through stereotyping. Performance management training attempts to increase manager awareness of halo and primacy effect when evaluating employee performance. Awareness of perceptual biases can reduce biases to some extent by making people more mindful of their thoughts and actions, but the effect is often limited.[77]

There is minimal support for awareness training to reduce self-fulfilling prophecy, halo, or primacy effects. Diversity awareness training can improve cultural sensitivity when the trainees are motivated to learn and the program mainly describes the other culture (rather than judge the attendees' culture). However, the good intentions of these programs can evaporate quickly in organizations that lack an inclusive culture. Worse, teaching people to reject incorrect stereotypes has the unintended effect of reinforcing rather than reducing reliance on those stereotypes. For instance, students in one study showed more bias against older people after watching a video encouraging them to be less biased against older people! Another problem is that diversity training is ineffective for people with deeply held prejudices against those groups.[78]

Improving Self-Awareness

A more successful way to minimize perceptual biases is by increasing self-awareness.[79] This approach potentially reduces perceptual biases by making people more open-minded and nonjudgmental toward others. They become more aware of their own beliefs, values, and attitudes and, from that insight, are more mindful of biases in their own decisions and behavior. But how do we become more self-aware? One approach is to complete formal tests, such as the Implicit Association Test (IAT), that attempt to detect implicit biases the individual may have toward specific groups.[80] These tests are typically accompanied by training programs that teach participants strategies to maintain awareness and minimize application of these biases.

A second approach to reducing perceptual biases through increased self-awareness is by applying the **Johari Window**.[81] Developed by psychologists Joseph Luft and Harry Ingram (hence the name "Johari"), this model of self-awareness and mutual understanding divides information about you into four

contact hypothesis A theory stating that the more we interact with someone, the less prejudiced or perceptually biased we will be against that person

empathy The ability to understand another person's situation or viewpoint (perspective taking), be sensitive to their thoughts and feelings, and experience their emotions

"windows"—open, blind, hidden, and unknown—based on whether your own values, beliefs, and experiences are known to you and to others (see Exhibit 3.6). The *open area* includes information about you that is known both to you and to others. The *blind area* refers to information that is known to others but not to you. For example, your colleagues might notice that you are self-conscious and awkward when meeting the company's chief executive, but you are unaware of this fact. Information known to you but unknown to others is found in the *hidden area*. Finally, the *unknown area* includes your values, beliefs, and experiences that are buried so deeply that neither you nor others are aware of them.

The main objective of the Johari Window is to increase the size of the open area so that both you and your colleagues are aware of your perceptual tendencies and limitations. This objective is partly accomplished by reducing the hidden area through *disclosure*—informing others of your beliefs, feelings, and experiences that may influence the work relationship. The open area also increases through *feedback* from others about your behavior. Feedback reduces your blind area because, according to several studies, people near you are good sources of information about many of your traits and behaviors.[82] Finally, the combination of disclosure and feedback occasionally produces revelations about you in the unknown area.

Limitations and Contingencies of Self-Awareness Programs The Johari Window, nonconscious bias tests, and associated training programs improve self-awareness under some conditions, but self-awareness feedback alone does not automatically make participants less biased.[83] Instead, the effectiveness of these programs depends on a few contingencies. First, the usefulness of self-awareness feedback depends on participant acceptance of that information. Some people are inherently more receptive than are others to unflattering personal information. Receptivity also depends on the way the feedback and associated self-awareness training are presented (e.g., nonthreatening, non-accusing, confidential).

Second, self-awareness program effectiveness depends on how well participants are taught specific strategies to apply this awareness. Implicit biases include stereotyping which, as we explained earlier in this chapter, activate automatically and are therefore difficult to prevent.[84] Some interventions (such as meaningful interaction, which we discuss next) may eventually reduce automatic activation of social biases. But for self-awareness interventions, participants need to learn how to block the application of those activated biases. They need to become more aware of situations in which implicit biases are activated and apply strategies that neutralize those biases in decisions and behavior.

Finally, programs that attempt to improve self-awareness of perceptual biases can sometimes have the adverse effect of reinforcing rather than reducing reliance on those stereotypes, resulting in less favorable interactions.[85] This is the same problem we mentioned earlier about programs that only try to improve awareness of perceptual biases. Both types of programs may cause people to become more sensitized and self-conscious when interacting with people who are the target of that bias. Fortunately, this problem wanes with more frequent and meaningful interaction with members of other social groups.

Exhibit 3.6 Johari Window Model of Self-Awareness and Mutual Understanding

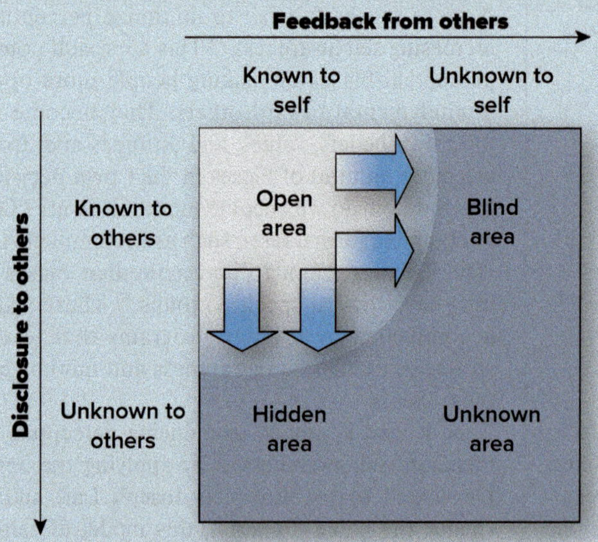

Source: Based on J. Luft, *Of Human Interaction* (Palo Alto, CA: National Press Books, 1969).

Meaningful Interaction

Increasing awareness of perceptual biases and increasing awareness of our own biases are somewhat limited because they focus on beliefs about perceptual biases rather than direct experiences. *Meaningful interaction* is a potentially powerful approach to improving self-awareness and mutual understanding because it involves direct interaction with others.[86] Meaningful interaction is any activity in which people engage in valued (meaningful, not trivial) activities. The activities might be work related, such as when senior executives work alongside frontline staff. Or the activities might occur outside the workplace, such as when sales staff from several countries and cultures participate in outdoor challenges.

Meaningful interaction is founded on the **contact hypothesis**, which states that, under specific conditions, people who interact with one another will be less perceptually biased because they have a more personal understanding of the other person and their group.[87] Simply spending time with members of other groups can improve this understanding to some extent. However, meaningful interaction is strongest when people work closely and frequently with one another on a shared goal that requires mutual cooperation and reliance. Furthermore, everyone should have equal status in that context, should be engaged in a meaningful task, and should have positive experiences with one another during those interactions.

Meaningful interaction tends to improve mutual understanding and reduce biases when people work closely and frequently with one another on a shared meaningful goal that requires mutual cooperation and reliance.
Rawpixel/123RF

Meaningful interaction reduces dependence on stereotypes because it diminishes psychological distance, improves our knowledge about individuals, and helps us to observe their unique attributes in action.[88] This process also potentially improves empathy toward others. **Empathy** refers to the ability to understand another person's situation or viewpoint (perspective taking), be sensitive to their thoughts and feelings, and experience their emotions.[89] People empathize when they visualize themselves in the other person's place as if they are the other person. This perceptual experience is cognitive, emotional, and experiential.

Empathizing reduces attribution errors by improving our sensitivity to the external causes of another person's performance and behavior. However, empathizing is more effective through meaningful interaction; otherwise, empathizing relies more on stereotypes than actual observations of the other person.[90]

Mc Graw Hill connect

SELF-ASSESSMENT 3.5: How Strong Is Your Perspective Taking (Cognitive Empathy)?

Mc Graw Hill connect

SELF-ASSESSMENT 3.6: How Strong Is Your Emotional Empathy?

Study Checklist

Connect® is available for *M: Organizational Behavior*. Additional resources include:

✓ Exercises:

- **Case Analysis:** Apply concepts within the context of a real-world situation.
- **Click and Drag:** Helps make the connection between theory and application through matching, ranking, or grouping activities.
- **Video Case:** See management in action through interactive videos.
- **Self-Assessment:** Designed to promote student self-awareness and reflection, these research-based surveys contain detailed feedback for students.
- **Application-Based Activities:** These highly interactive, application- and analysis-based exercises allow students to take on specific roles to complete management related tasks within a real-world context.

✓ **SmartBook 2.0™**—Smartbook 2.0 is an adaptive learning solution that provides personalized learning to individual student needs, continually adapts to pinpoint knowledge gaps and focuses learning on concepts requiring additional study. It fosters more productive learning, takes the guesswork out of what to study, and helps students better prepare for class.

©Natthawat Jamnapa/123RF

Notes

1. D. Berman, "FedEx Is Flashing a Recession Warning Sign—But There Are Reasons to View It with Skepticism," *The Globe and Mail*, September 16, 2022; L. Stebbins and J. Rizzo, "FedEx's Bleak Warning Could Reflect Global Economy—and Company's Own Shortcomings," *CNBC*, September 21, 2022.
2. J. Schaubroeck, Y.J. Kim, and A.C. Peng, "The Self-Concept in Organizational Psychology: Clarifying and Differentiating the Constructs," in *International Review of Industrial and Organizational Psychology* (New York: Wiley, 2012), 1–38; J.J. Skowronski and C. Sedikides, "Evolution of Self," in *Encyclopedia of Evolutionary Psychological Science*, ed. T.K. Shackelford and V.A. Weekes-Shackelford (Cham: Springer International Publishing, 2018), 1–10.
3. L. Gaertner et al., "A Motivational Hierarchy within: Primacy of the Individual Self, Relational Self, or Collective Self?," *Journal of Experimental Social Psychology* 48, no. 5 (2012): 997–1013; A.D. Nehrlich et al., "Individual Self > Relational Self > Collective Self—But Why? Processes Driving the Self-Hierarchy in Self- and Person Perception," *Journal of Personality* 87, no. 2 (2019): 212–30.
4. O.W. Holmes, *The Autocrat of the Breakfast-Table* (Boston: Phillips, Sampson, 1858), 58–59. This quotation, which Steve McShane slightly rewrote to remove sexist language, has a long and convoluted history. Pioneering psychology professor William James is almost always cited as the source, yet there is no evidence that he wrote this statement or anything similar. The first attribution of this quotation to William James may have been a 1958 *RAND Memoranda* publication (p. 925), and later in *Reader's Digest* (1962). Even if James did publish something similar, it is a highly condensed version of the humorous discussion of "six persons" that Oliver Wendell Holmes Sr. published decades before James began his career. Most likely, a RAND Corporation editor crafted this quotation from vague memory of Holmes's story and misattributed William James as the author because one of Holmes's characters in the story was "James." We cite Holmes as the source because he wrote the story from which this quotation is derived.
5. E.J. Koch and J.A. Shepperd, "Is Self-Complexity Linked to Better Coping? A Review of the Literature," *Journal of Personality* 72, no. 4 (2004): 727–60; A.R. McConnell, "The Multiple Self-Aspects Framework: Self-Concept Representation and Its Implications," *Personality and Social Psychology Review* 15, no. 1 (2011): 3–27; L.F. Emery, C. Walsh, and E.B. Slotter, "Knowing Who You Are and Adding to It: Reduced Self-Concept Clarity Predicts Reduced Self-Expansion," *Social Psychological and Personality Science* 6, no. 3 (2015): 259–66.
6. C.M. Brown et al., "Between Two Selves: Comparing Global and Local Predictors of Speed of Switching between Self-Aspects," *Self and Identity* 15, no. 1 (2016): 72–89.
7. C.D. Bataille and H.C. Vough, "More Than the Sum of My Parts: An Intrapersonal Network Approach to Identity Work in Response to Identity Opportunities and Threats," *Academy of Management Review* 47, no. 1 (2022): 93–115.
8. J.D. Campbell et al., "Self-Concept Clarity: Measurement, Personality Correlates, and Cultural Boundaries," *Journal of Personality and Social Psychology* 70, no. 1 (1996): 141–56.
9. J. Austin, "Why We Don't Bring Our Whole Selves to Work," *Work Life by Atlassian* (blog), January 8, 2020; A. Rivera-Beckstrom and E. Van Dam, "The Importance of Authenticity in the Workplace," 2021 Leadership Development Survey (Boston: Simmons University, Institute for Inclusive Leadership, July 2021); C. Thorpe, "The Future Of The Workplace: No Egos, No Ladders," *LinkedIn Pulse* (blog), June 20, 2022.
10. J. Lodi-Smith and B.W. Roberts, "Getting to Know Me: Social Role Experiences and Age Differences in Self-Concept Clarity During Adulthood," *Journal of Personality* 78, no. 5 (2010): 1383–410; H. Adam et al., "The Shortest Path to Oneself Leads around the World: Living Abroad Increases Self-Concept Clarity," *Organizational Behavior and Human Decision Processes* 145 (2018): 16–29.
11. E.J. Koch and J.A. Shepperd, "Is Self-Complexity Linked to Better Coping? A Review of the Literature," *Journal of Personality* 72, no. 4 (2004): 727–60; A.T. Church et al., "Relating Self-Concept Consistency to Hedonic and Eudaimonic Well-Being in Eight Cultures," *Journal of Cross-Cultural Psychology* 45, no. 5 (2014): 695–712, https://doi.org/10.1177/0022022114527347; A.W. Hanley and E.L. Garland, "Clarity of Mind: Structural Equation Modeling of Associations between Dispositional Mindfulness, Self-Concept Clarity and Psychological Well-Being," *Personality and Individual Differences* 106 (2017): 334–39, https://doi.org/10.1016/j.paid.2016.10.028; M. Parise et al., "Self-Concept Clarity and Psychological Adjustment in Adolescence: The Mediating Role of Emotion Regulation," *Personality and Individual Differences* 138 (2019): 363–65, https://doi.org/10.1016/j.paid.2018.10.023.
12. A.T. Brook, J. Garcia, and M.A. Fleming, "The Effects of Multiple Identities on Psychological Well-Being," *Personality and Social Psychology Bulletin* 34, no. 12 (2008): 1588–600; A.T. Church et al., "Relating Self-Concept Consistency to Hedonic and Eudaimonic Well-Being in Eight Cultures," *Journal of Cross-Cultural Psychology* 45, no. 5 (2014): 695–712.
13. J.D. Campbell, "Self-Esteem and Clarity of the Self-Concept," *Journal of Personality and Social Psychology* 59, no. 3 (1990).
14. S. Hannah et al., "The Psychological and Neurological Bases of Leader Self-Complexity and Effects on Adaptive Decision-Making," *Journal of Applied Psychology* 98, no. 3 (2013): 393–411; S.J. Creary, B.B. Caza, and L M. Roberts, "Out of the Box? How Managing a Subordinate's Multiple Identities Affects the Quality of a Manager-Subordinate Relationship," *Academy of Management Review* 40, no. 4 (2015): 538–62.
15. C. Peus et al., "Authentic Leadership: An Empirical Test of Its Antecedents, Consequences, and Mediating Mechanisms," *Journal of Business Ethics* 107, no. 3 (2012): 331–48; B. Mittal, "Self-Concept Clarity: Exploring Its Role in Consumer Behavior," *Journal of Economic Psychology* 46 (2015): 98–110; P. Uğurlar and D.U. Wulff, "Self-Concept Clarity Is Associated with Social Decision Making Performance," *Personality and Individual Differences* 197 (2022): 111783.
16. C.L. Guenther and M.D. Alicke, "Deconstructing the Better-Than-Average Effect," *Journal of Personality and Social Psychology* 99, no. 5 (2010): 755–70; S. Loughnan et al., "Universal Biases in Self-Perception: Better and More Human Than Average," *British Journal of Social Psychology* 49 (2010): 627–36; D.L. Ferris and C. Sedikides, "Self-Enhancement in Organizations," in *The Self at Work: Fundamental Theory and Research*, ed. D.L. Ferris, R.E. Johnson, and C. Sedikides (New York: Routledge, 2018), 91–118.
17. D.A. Moore, "Not So above Average after All: When People Believe They Are Worse Than Average and Its Implications for Theories of Bias in Social Comparison," *Organizational Behavior and Human Decision Processes* 102, no. 1 (2007): 42–58; E. Zell et al., "The Better-than-Average Effect in Comparative Self-Evaluation: A Comprehensive Review and Meta-Analysis," *Psychological Bulletin* 146, no. 2 (2020): 118–49.

18. D. Gosselin et al., "Comparative Optimism among Drivers: An Intergenerational Portrait," *Accident Analysis & Prevention* 42, no. 2 (2010): 734-40; P.M. Picone, G. Battista Dagnino, and A. Minà, "The Origin of Failure: A Multidisciplinary Appraisal of the Hubris Hypothesis and Proposed Research Agenda," *Academy of Management Perspectives* 28, no. 4 (2014): 447-68; G. Chen, C. Crossland, and S. Luo, "Making the Same Mistake All over Again: CEO Overconfidence and Corporate Resistance to Corrective Feedback," *Strategic Management Journal* 36, no. 10 (2015): 1513-35; M. Dufner et al., "Self-Enhancement and Psychological Adjustment: A Meta-Analytic Review," *Personality and Social Psychology Review* 23, no. 1 (2019): 48-72.

19. This quotation has been cited since the 1930s, yet we were unable to find it in any of Dewey's writing. The earliest known reference to this quotation is Dale Carnegie's famous self-help book, where the statement is attributed to Dewey. See D. Carnegie, *How to Win Friends and Influence People*, 1st ed. (New York: Simon & Schuster, 1936), 43-44 (p. 19 in later editions).

20. D.M. Cable and V.S. Kay, "Striving for Self-Verification during Organizational Entry," *Academy of Management Journal* 55, no. 2 (2012): 360-80; S. Talaifar and W.B. Swann, "Self-Verification Theory," in *Encyclopedia of Personality and Individual Differences*, ed. V. Zeigler-Hill and T.K. Shackelford (Cham: Springer International Publishing, 2020).

21. T. Kwang and W.B. Swann, "Do People Embrace Praise Even When They Feel Unworthy? A Review of Critical Tests of Self-Enhancement versus Self-Verification," *Personality and Social Psychology Review* 14, no. 3 (2010): 263-80.; G.S. Preuss and M.D. Alicke, "My Worst Faults and Misdeeds: Self-Criticism and Self-Enhancement Can Co-Exist," *Self and Identity* 16, no. 6 (2017): 645-63; A. Ashokkumar and W.B. Swann, "The Saboteur within: Self-Verification Strivings Can Make Praise Toxic," in *Psychological Perspectives on Praise*, ed. E. Brummelman (Abingdon UK: Routledge, 2020), 11-18.

22. M.R. Leary, "Motivational and Emotional Aspects of the Self," *Annual Review of Psychology* 58, no. 1 (2007): 317-44; A. Meister, K.A. Jehn, and S.M.B. Thatcher, "Feeling Misidentified: The Consequences of Internal Identity Asymmetries for Individuals at Work," *Academy of Management Review* 39, no. 4 (2014): 488-512; T.-Y. Kim, X. Lin, and S.-P. Kim, "Person-Organization Fit and Friendship from Coworkers: Effects on Feeling Self-Verified and Employee Outcomes," *Group & Organization Management* 44, no. 4 (2019): 777-806; J. Lee Cunningham et al., "Seeing Oneself as a Valued Contributor: Social Worth Affirmation Improves Team Information Sharing," *Academy of Management Journal* 64, no. 6 (2021): 1816-41.

23. We have described three components of core self-evaluation. The remaining component is the personality trait emotional stability, which was described in Chapter 2. However, personality is a behavior tendency, whereas core self-evaluation includes only "evaluation-focused" variables. Some also question whether locus of control is part of self-evaluation. See R.E. Johnson, C.C. Rosen, and P.E. Levy, "Getting to the Core of Core Self-Evaluation: A Review and Recommendations," *Journal of Organizational Behavior* 29 (2008): 391-413; C.-H. Chang et al., "Core Self-Evaluations: A Review and Evaluation of the Literature," *Journal of Management* 38 (2012): 81-128; R.E. Johnson et al., "Getting to the Core of Locus of Control: Is It an Evaluation of the Self or the Environment?" *Journal of Applied Psychology* 100 (2015): 1568-78.

24. W.B. Swann Jr., C. Chang-Schneider, and K.L. McClarty, "Do People's Self-Views Matter?: Self-Concept and Self-Esteem in Everyday Life," *American Psychologist* 62, no. 2 (2007): 84-94; J.L. Pierce, D.G. Gardner, and C. Crowley, "Organization-Based Self-Esteem and Well-Being: Empirical Examination of a Spillover Effect," *European Journal of Work and Organizational Psychology* 25, no. 2 (2016): 181-99.

25. "Fake It 'til You Make It?; Understanding Employee Job Confidence and Know-How" (Toronto: docebo, December 2018); H. Chapman, "Less than 2 in 5 Teachers Feel Confident in Their Role," *Tes Magazine*, January 25, 2022; "4 In 10 U.S. Workers Considering A Job Change In The Second Half Of 2022," Press Release (Menlo Park, Calif.: Robert Half, June 15, 2022); "2022 Federal Employee Viewpoint Survey" (Washington, DC: United States Federal Government, Office of Personnel Management, November 2022); S. Bloznalis, "Human Workplace Index: Diversity, Equity, and Inclusion Efforts in the New Year," *Human Workplace Index* (blog), January 4, 2023.

26. A. Bandura, *Self-Efficacy: The Exercise of Control* (New York: W. H. Freeman, 1997); J.B. Vancouver and J.D. Purl, "A Computational Model of Self-Efficacy's Various Effects on Performance: Moving the Debate Forward," *Journal of Applied Psychology* 102 (2017): 599-616.

27. However, general self-efficacy may have more than one dimension and might vary across cultures. See: G. Villegas Barahona et al., "Seven Methods to Determine the Dimensionality of Tests: Application to the General Self-Efficacy Scale in Twenty-Six Countries," *Psicothema*, no. 4 (2018): 442-48; G. Zeng et al., "Evaluating the Psychometric Properties and Factor Structure of the General Self-Efficacy Scale in China," *Current Psychology* 41, no. 6 (2022): 3970-80.

28. J.B. Rotter, "Generalized Expectancies for Internal versus External Control of Reinforcement," *Psychological Monographs* 80, no. 1 (1966): 1-28; B.M. Galvin et al., "Changing the Focus of Locus (of Control): A Targeted Review of the Locus of Control Literature and Agenda for Future Research," *Journal of Organizational Behavior* 39, no. 7 (2018): 820-33; D. Niessen et al., "The Internal-External Locus of Control Short Scale-4 (IE-4): A Comprehensive Validation of the English-Language Adaptation," *PLoS ONE* 17, no. 7 (2022): e0271289.

29. T.W.H. Ng, K.L. Sorensen, and L.T. Eby, "Locus of Control at Work: A Meta-Analysis," *Journal of Organizational Behavior* 27 (2006): 1057-87; Q. Wang, N.A. Bowling, and K.J. Eschleman, "A Meta-Analytic Examination of Work and General Locus of Control," *Journal of Applied Psychology* 95, no. 4 (2010): 761-68.

30. G.J. Leonardelli, C.L. Pickett, and M.B. Brewer, "Optimal Distinctiveness Theory: A Framework for Social Identity, Social Cognition, and Intergroup Relations," in *Advances in Experimental Social Psychology*, ed. M.P. Zanna and J.M. Olson (San Diego, CA: Academic Press, 2010), 63-113; M. Ormiston, "Explaining the Link between Objective and Perceived Differences in Groups: The Role of the Belonging and Distinctiveness Motives," *Journal of Applied Psychology* 101, no. 2 (2016): 222-36; J.D. Way et al., "Predicting Perceptions of Team Process Using Optimal Distinctiveness Theory," *Small Group Research* 53, no. 3 (2022): 464-89. One recent paper suggests that personal and social identities are not dichotomous. See: B.W. Walker, "A Dynamic Reframing of the Social/Personal Identity Dichotomy," *Organizational Psychology Review* 12, no. 1 (2022): 73-104.

31. We describe relational self-concept as a form of social identity because such connections are inherently social and the dyads are typically members of a collective entity. For example, an employee has a relationship identity with their boss, but this is connected to a social identity with the team or department. However, recent discussion suggests that relational self-concept also may be part of personal identity or a separate form of self-concept. See B.E. Ashforth, B.S. Schinoff, and K.M. Rogers, "'I Identify with Her,' 'I Identify with Him': Unpacking the Dynamics of Personal Identification in Organizations," *Academy of Management Review* 41, no. 1 (2016): 28-60.

32. C. Sedikides and A.P. Gregg, "Portraits of the Self," in *The Sage Handbook of Social Psychology*, ed. M.A. Hogg and J. Cooper (London: Sage, 2003), 110–38; S.A. Haslam and N. Ellemers, "Identity Processes in Organizations," in *Handbook of Identity Theory and Research*, ed. J.S. Schwartz, K. Luyckx, and L.V. Vignoles (New York: Springer, 2011), 715–44; M.A. Hogg and M.J. Rinella, "Social Identities and Shared Realities," *Current Opinion in Psychology*, 23 (October 2018): 6–10.

33. M.R. Edwards, "Organizational Identification: A Conceptual and Operational Review," *International Journal of Management Reviews* 7, no. 4 (2005): 207–30; E.S. Lee, T.Y. Park, and B. Koo, "Identifying Organizational Identification as a Basis for Attitudes and Behaviors: A Meta-Analytic Review," *Psychological Bulletin* 141, no. 5 (2015): 1049–80.

34. M.B. Brewer, "The Social Self: On Being the Same and Different at the Same Time," *Personality and Social Psychology Bulletin* 17, no. 5 (1991): 475–82; R. Imhoff and H.-P. Erb, "What Motivates Nonconformity? Uniqueness Seeking Blocks Majority Influence," *Personality and Social Psychology Bulletin* 35, no. 3 (2009): 309–20; K.R. Morrison and S.C. Wheeler, "Nonconformity Defines the Self: The Role of Minority Opinion Status in Self-Concept Clarity," *Personality and Social Psychology Bulletin* 36, no. 3 (2010): 297–308; J.D. Way et al., "Predicting Perceptions of Team Process Using Optimal Distinctiveness Theory," *Small Group Research* 53, no. 3 (2022): 464–89.

35. See, for example: L. Ramarajan, "Past, Present and Future Research on Multiple Identities: Toward an Intrapersonal Network Approach," *The Academy of Management Annals* 8 (2014): 589–659; D.L. Ferris, R.E. Johnson, and C. Sedikides, eds., *The Self at Work: Fundamental Theory and Research* (New York: Routledge/Taylor & Francis Group, 2018).

36. E.I. Knudsen, "Fundamental Components of Attention," *Annual Review of Neuroscience* 30, no. 1 (2007): 57–78. For an evolutionary psychology perspective of selective attention and organization, see L. Cosmides and J. Tooby, "Evolutionary Psychology: New Perspectives on Cognition and Motivation," *Annual Review of Psychology* 64, no. 1 (2013): 201–29.

37. A. Bechara and A.R. Damasio, "The Somatic Marker Hypothesis: A Neural Theory of Economic Decision," *Games and Economic Behavior* 52 (2005): 336–72; T.S. Saunders and M.J. Buehner, "The Gut Chooses Faster Than the Mind: A Latency Advantage of Affective over Cognitive Decisions," *Quarterly Journal of Experimental Psychology* 66 (2012): 381–88; R. Smith and R.D. Lane, "The Neural Basis of One's Own Conscious and Unconscious Emotional States," *Neuroscience & Biobehavioral Reviews* 57 (2015): 1–29.

38. Plato, *The Republic*, trans. D. Lee (Harmondsworth: Penguin, 1955). For the importance of emotions on memory, see: I. Xenakis, A. Arnellos, and J. Darzentas, "The Functional Role of Emotions in Aesthetic Judgment," *New Ideas in Psychology* 30 (2012): 212–26; S. Sheldon and J. Donahue, "More Than a Feeling: Emotional Cues Impact the Access and Experience of Autobiographical Memories," *Memory & Cognition* 45 (2017): 731–44; H.J. Bowen, S.M. Kark, and E.A. Kensinger, "NEVER Forget: Negative Emotional Valence Enhances Recapitulation," *Psychonomic Bulletin & Review* 25 (2018): 870–91.

39. D.J. Simons and C.F. Chabris, "Gorillas in Our Midst: Sustained Inattentional Blindness for Dynamic Events," *Perception* 28 (1999): 1059–74.

40. R.S. Nickerson, "Confirmation Bias: A Ubiquitous Phenomenon in Many Guises," *Review of General Psychology* 2, no. 2 (1998): 175–220; A. Gilbey and S. Hill, "Confirmation Bias in General Aviation Lost Procedures," *Applied Cognitive Psychology* 26, no. 5 (2012): 785–95; A.M. Scherer, P.D. Windschitl, and A.R. Smith, "Hope to Be Right: Biased Information Seeking Following Arbitrary and Informed Predictions," *Journal of Experimental Social Psychology* 49, no. 1 (2013): 106–12.

41. C. Wastell et al., "Identifying Hypothesis Confirmation Behaviors in a Simulated Murder Investigation: Implications for Practice," *Journal of Investigative Psychology and Offender Profiling* 9, no. 2 (2012): 184–98; D.K. Rossmo, "Case Rethinking: A Protocol for Reviewing Criminal Investigations," *Police Practice and Research* 17, no. 3 (2016): 212–28.

42. Earl Derr Biggars, the author of the Charlie Chan novels, is sometimes cited as the source of this quotation. However, this statement is found only in the 1935 film *Charlie Chan in Egypt*, which is based on Biggars' character. It does not appear in any Charlie Chan novels.

43. C.N. Macrae and G.V. Bodenhausen, "Social Cognition: Thinking Categorically about Others," *Annual Review of Psychology* 51 (2000): 93–120; K.A. Quinn and H.E.S. Rosenthal, "Categorizing Others and the Self: How Social Memory Structures Guide Social Perception and Behavior," *Learning and Motivation* 43, no. 4 (2012): 247–58; L.T. Phillips, M. Weisbuch, and N. Ambady, "People Perception: Social Vision of Groups and Consequences for Organizing and Interacting," *Research in Organizational Behavior* 34 (2014): 101–27; B.D. Langhe and P. Fernbach, "The Dangers of Categorical Thinking: We're Hardwired to Sort Information into Buckets—and That Can Hamper Our Ability to Make Good Decisions," *Harvard Business Review* 97, no. 5 (2019): 80–92.

44. J.L. Brooks, "Traditional and New Principles of Perceptual Grouping," in *The Oxford Handbook of Perceptual Organization*, ed. J. Wagemans (Oxford University Press, 2015), 57–87; L. Papeo and E. Abassi, "Seeing Social Events: The Visual Specialization for Dyadic Human–Human Interactions," *Journal of Experimental Psychology: Human Perception and Performance* 45, no. 7 (2019): 877–88. Proximity is mostly studied in visual perception (Gestalt), but recent studies are discovering the social dynamics of proximity categorization.

45. A. Roets et al., "The Motivated Gatekeeper of Our Minds: New Directions in Need for Closure Theory and Research," in *Advances in Experimental Social Psychology*, ed. M.O. James and P.Z. Mark (San Diego, CA: Academic Press, 2015), 221–83; S. Suetens, C.B. Galbo-Jørgensen, and J.-R. Tyran, "Predicting Lotto Numbers: A Natural Experiment on the Gambler's Fallacy and the Hot-Hand Fallacy," *Journal of the European Economic Association* 14, no. 3 (2016): 584–607; Q. Kong et al., "Judgment Error in Lottery Play: When the Hot Hand Meets the Gambler's Fallacy," *Management Science* 66, no. 2 (2020): 844–62; R.M. Stetzka and S. Winter, "How Rational Is Gambling?," *Journal of Economic Surveys* 37, no. 4 (2023): 1432–1488.

46. J. Willis and A. Todorov, "First Impressions: Making Up Your Mind after a 100-Ms Exposure to a Face," *Psychological Science* 17 (2006): 592–98; D. Kahneman, *Thinking Fast and Slow* (New York: Farrar, Strauss and Giroux, 2011); A. Todorov, *Face Value: The Irresistible Influence of First Impressions* (Princeton, NJ: Princeton University Press, 2017).

47. P.M. Senge, *The Fifth Discipline: The Art and Practice of the Learning Organization* (New York: Doubleday Currency, 1990), Chap. 10; T.J. Chermack, "Mental Models in Decision Making and Implications for Human Resource Development," *Advances in Developing Human Resources* 5, no. 4 (2003): 408–22; P.N. Johnson-Laird, "Mental Models and Deductive Reasoning," in *Reasoning: Studies of Human Inference and Its Foundations*, ed. J.E. Adler and L.J. Rips (Cambridge: Cambridge University Press, 2008); S. Ross and N. Allen, "Examining the Convergent Validity of Shared Mental Model Measures," *Behavior Research Methods* 44, no. 4 (2012): 1052–62.

48. G.W. Allport, *The Nature of Prejudice* (Reading, MA: Addison-Wesley, 1954); J.C. Brigham, "Ethnic Stereotypes," *Psychological Bulletin* 76, no. 1 (1971): 15–38; D.J. Schneider, *The Psychology of Stereotyping* (New York: Guilford, 2004); S. Kanahara, "A Review of the Definitions of Stereotype and a Proposal for a Progressional Model," *Individual Differences Research* 4, no. 5 (2006): 306–21.

49. L. Jussim, J.T. Crawford, and R.S. Rubinstein, "Stereotype (in)Accuracy in Perceptions of Groups and Individuals," *Current Directions in Psychological Science* 24, no. 6 (2015): 490–97; P. Bordalo et al., "Stereotypes," *The Quarterly Journal of Economics* 131, no. 4 (2016): 1753–94.

50. C.N. Macrae, A.B. Milne, and G.V. Bodenhausen, "Stereotypes as Energy-Saving Devices: A Peek inside the Cognitive Toolbox," *Journal of Personality and Social Psychology* 66 (1994): 37–47; J.W. Sherman et al., "Stereotype Efficiency Reconsidered: Encoding Flexibility under Cognitive Load," *Journal of Personality and Social Psychology* 75 (1998): 589–606; C.K. Soderberg et al., "The Effects of Psychological Distance on Abstraction: Two Meta-Analyses," *Psychological Bulletin* 141 (2015): 525–48.

51. J.C. Turner and S.A. Haslam, "Social Identity, Organizations, and Leadership," in *Groups at Work: Theory and Research*, ed. M.E. Turner (Mahwah, NJ: Erlbaum, 2001), 25–65; J. Jetten, R. Spears, and T. Postmes, "Intergroup Distinctiveness and Differentiation: A Meta-Analytic Integration," *Journal of Personality and Social Psychology* 86, no. 6 (2004): 862–79; M.A. Hogg et al., "The Social Identity Perspective: Intergroup Relations, Self-Conception, and Small Groups," *Small Group Research* 35, no. 3 (2004): 246–76; K. Hugenberg and D.F. Sacco, "Social Categorization and Stereotyping: How Social Categorization Biases Person Perception and Face Memory," *Social and Personality Psychology Compass* 2, no. 2 (2008): 1052–72.

52. N. Halevy, G. Bornstein, and L. Sagiv, "'In-Group Love' and 'Out-Group Hate' as Motives for Individual Participation in Intergroup Conflict: A New Game Paradigm," *Psychological Science* 19, no. 4 (2008): 405–11; T. Yamagishi and N. Mifune, "Social Exchange and Solidarity: In-Group Love or Out-Group Hate?," *Evolution and Human Behavior* 30, no. 4 (2009): 229–37; N. Halevy, O. Weisel, and G. Bornstein, "'In-Group Love' and 'Out-Group Hate' in Repeated Interaction between Groups," *Journal of Behavioral Decision Making* 25, no. 2 (2012): 188–95; M. Parker and R. Janoff-Bulman, "Lessons from Morality-Based Social Identity: The Power of Outgroup 'Hate,' Not Just Ingroup 'Love,'" *Social Justice Research* 26, no. 1 (2013): 81–96.

53. C.R. Pennington et al., "Twenty Years of Stereotype Threat Research: A Review of Psychological Mediators," *PLoS ONE* 11, no. 1 (2016): e0146487; D.J. Wu, J. Park, and N. Dasgupta, "The Influence of Male Faces on Stereotype Activation among Women in STEM: An ERP Investigation," *Biological Psychology* 156 (2020): 107948; R.G. Swab et al., "Stereotype Threat Theory in Organizational Research: Constructive Analysis and Future Research Agenda," *Group & Organization Management* 47, no. 3 (2022): 530–70.

54. C.A. Moss-Racusin et al., "Science Faculty's Subtle Gender Biases Favor Male Students," *Proceedings of the National Academy of Sciences* 109, no. 41 (2012): 16474–79. Several studies conducted earlier and subsequently have similarly reported unintentional bias in job and research grant applications. For example, see: H.O. Witteman et al., "Are Gender Gaps Due to Evaluations of the Applicant or the Science? A Natural Experiment at a National Funding Agency," *The Lancet* 393, no. 10171 (February 9, 2019): 531–40; A.A. Eaton et al., "How Gender and Race Stereotypes Impact the Advancement of Scholars in STEM: Professors' Biased Evaluations of Physics and Biology Post-Doctoral Candidates," *Sex Roles* 82, no. 3/4 (2020): 127–41.

55. S.T. Fiske, "Stereotyping, Prejudice, and Discrimination," in *Handbook of Social Psychology*, ed. D.T. Gilbert, S.T. Fiske, and G. Lindzey (New York: McGraw Hill, 1998): 357–411; M. Hewstone, M. Rubin, and H. Willis, "Intergroup Bias," *Annual Review of Psychology* 53 (2002): 575–604; C. Stangor, "The Study of Stereotyping, Prejudice, and Discrimination within Social Psychology: A Quick History of Theory and Research," in *Handbook of Prejudice, Stereotyping, and Discrimination*, ed. T.D. Nelson (New York: Psychology Press, 2016), 1–22.

56. M.D. Burns, M.J. Monteith, and L.R. Parker, "Training Away Bias: The Differential Effects of Counterstereotype Training and Self-Regulation on Stereotype Activation and Application," *Journal of Experimental Social Psychology* 73 (2017): 97–110; I.R. Johnson, B.M. Kopp, and R.E. Petty, "Just Say No! (and Mean It): Meaningful Negation as a Tool to Modify Automatic Racial Attitudes," *Group Processes & Intergroup Relations* 21, no. 1 (2018): 88–110; G.B. Humiston and E.J. Wamsley, "Unlearning Implicit Social Biases during Sleep: A Failure to Replicate," *PLoS ONE* 14, no. 1 (2019): e0211416.

57. A.M. Rivers et al., "On the Roles of Stereotype Activation and Application in Diminishing Implicit Bias," *Personality and Social Psychology Bulletin* 46 (2020): 349–64.

58. H.H. Kelley, *Attribution in Social Interaction* (Morristown, NJ: General Learning Press, 1971); B.F. Malle, "Attribution Theories: How People Make Sense of Behavior," in *Theories of Social Psychology*, ed. D. Chadee (Chichester: Blackwell, 2011), 72–95. This "internal–external" or "person–situation" perspective of the attribution process differs somewhat from the original "intentional–unintentional" perspective, which says that we try to understand the deliberate or accidental/involuntary reasons why people engage in behaviors, as well as the reasons for behavior. Some writers suggest the original perspective is more useful. See B.F. Malle, "Time to Give Up the Dogmas of Attribution: An Alternative Theory of Behavior Explanation," in *Advances in Experimental Social Psychology*, vol. 44, ed. K.M. Olson and M.P. Zanna (San Diego: Elsevier Academic, 2011), 297–352.

59. Some OB books state that high consistency predicts internal attribution and low consistency predicts external attribution. These sources describe low consistency as a one-off deviation from the past. That description seems to differ from the attribution literature and research, which defines consistency as the degree that the person's responses vary across time and settings (i.e., reliability). In fact, Kelley's seminal writing on attribution theory only discusses high consistency, not low consistency. Kelley and Michela state: "The basic point is that a person trusts his reactions to a stimulus (i.e. attributes them to objective properties of the stimulus) when they are consistent (over time and modality) and distinctive from those to other stimuli." Van Overwalle states: "High consensus information resulted in stimulus dispositions and low distinctiveness information lead to person dispositions; and, as predicted, consistency information often increased these ratings." DiVitto and McArthur state: "causal attributions to the target of a response are facilitated by high consensus, high distinctiveness, or high consistency, whereas low consensus, low distinctiveness, or high consistency information facilitate causal attributions to the agent." See: L.A. McArthur, "The How and What of Why: Some Determinants and Consequences of Causal Attribution," *Journal of Personality & Social Psychology* 22 (1970): 171–93; B. Divitto and L.Z. McArthur, "Developmental Differences in the Use of Distinctiveness, Consensus and Consistency Information for Making Causal Attributions," *Developmental Psychology* 14, no. 5 (1978): 474–82; H.H. Kelley and J.L. Michela, "Attribution Theory and Research," *Annual Review of Psychology* 31 (1980): 457–501; F. van Overwalle, "Dispositional Attributions Require the Joint Application of the Methods of Difference and Agreement," *Personality and Social Psychology Bulletin* 23, no. 9 (1997): 974–80.

60. However, attribution alone does not explain how people determine causation and assign blame. See S.A. Sloman and D. Lagnado, "Causality in Thought," *Annual Review of Psychology* 66, no. 1 (2015): 223–47; M.D. Alicke et al., "Causal Conceptions in Social Explanation and Moral Evaluation: A Historical Tour," *Perspectives on Psychological Science* 10, no. 6 (2015): 790–812; J.E. Mroz and J.A. Allen, "To Excuse or Not to Excuse: Effect of Explanation Type and Provision on Reactions to a Workplace Behavioral Transgression," *Journal of Business and Psychology* 35, no. 2 (2020): 187–201; P. Catellani et al., "How Expert Witnesses' Counterfactuals Influence Causal and Responsibility Attributions of Mock Jurors and Expert Judges," *Applied Cognitive Psychology* 35, no. 1 (2021): 3–17.

61. J.M. Crant and T.S. Bateman, "Assignment of Credit and Blame for Performance Outcomes," *Academy of Management Journal* 36 (1993): 7–27; B. Weiner, "Intrapersonal and Interpersonal Theories of Motivation from an Attributional Perspective," *Educational Psychology Review* 12 (2000): 1–14; N. Bacon and P. Blyton, "Worker Responses to Teamworking: Exploring Employee Attributions of Managerial Motives," *International Journal of Human Resource Management* 16, no. 2 (2005): 238–55.

62. D.T. Miller and M. Ross, "Self-Serving Biases in the Attribution of Causality: Fact or Fiction?," *Psychological Bulletin* 82, no. 2 (1975): 213–25; J. Shepperd, W. Malone, and K. Sweeny, "Exploring Causes of the Self-Serving Bias," *Social and Personality Psychology Compass* 2, no. 2 (2008): 895–908; M.S. Allen et al., "Systematic Review and Meta-Analysis of Self-Serving Attribution Biases in the Competitive Context of Organized Sport," *Personality and Social Psychology Bulletin* 46, no. 7 (2020): 1027–43.

63. E.W.K. Tsang, "Self-Serving Attributions in Corporate Annual Reports: A Replicated Study," *Journal of Management Studies* 39, no. 1 (2002): 51–65; J. Lammers and P. Burgmer, "Power Increases the Self-Serving Bias in the Attribution of Collective Successes and Failures," *European Journal of Social Psychology* 49, no. 5 (2019): 1087–95; L. Laidroo, "Are Annual Report Graphs Being Used for Making Performance Attributions?," *International Journal of Business Communication* 56, no. 4 (2019): 476–504; D. Lehmberg and C. Tangpong, "Do Top Management Performance Attribution Patterns Matter to Subsequent Organizational Outcomes? A Two-Country Study of Attribution in Economic Crisis," *Journal of Management & Organization* 26, no. 5 (2020): 736–55; A. Melis and S. Aresu, "Analyst Following, Country's Financial Development, and the Selective Use of Graphical Information in Corporate Annual Reports," *International Journal of Business Communication* 59, no. 4 (2022): 459–84.

64. D.T. Gilbert and P.S. Malone, "The Correspondence Bias," *Psychological Bulletin* 117, no. 1 (1995): 21–38.

65. B.F. Malle, "The Actor–Observer Asymmetry in Attribution: A (Surprising) Meta-Analysis," *Psychological Bulletin* 132 (2006): 895–919; C.W. Bauman and L.J. Skitka, "Making Attributions for Behaviors: The Prevalence of Correspondence Bias in the General Population," *Basic and Applied Social Psychology* 32 (2010): 101–17; D.O. Goto et al., "Cultural Differences in Sensitivity to Social Context: Detecting Affective Incongruity Using the N400," *Social Neuroscience* 8 (2013): 63–74; T. Scopelliti et al., "Individual Differences in Correspondence Bias: Measurement, Consequences, and Correction of Biased Interpersonal Attributions," *Management Science* 64 (2017): 1879–910.

66. Similar models are presented in D. Eden, "Self-Fulfilling Prophecy as a Management Tool: Harnessing Pygmalion," *Academy of Management Review* 9 (1984): 64–73; R.H.G. Field and D.A. Van Seters, "Management by Expectations (MBE): The Power of Positive Prophecy," *Journal of General Management* 14 (1988): 19–33; D.O. Trouilloud et al., "The Influence of Teacher Expectations on Student Achievement in Physical Education Classes: Pygmalion Revisited," *European Journal of Social Psychology* 32 (2002): 591–607.

67. P. Whiteley, T. Sy, and S.K. Johnson, "Leaders' Conceptions of Followers: Implications for Naturally Occurring Pygmalion Effects," *Leadership Quarterly* 23, no. 5 (2012): 822–34; J. Weaver, J.F. Moses, and M. Snyder, "Self-Fulfilling Prophecies in Ability Settings," *Journal of Social Psychology* 156, no. 2 (2016): 179–89.

68. D. Eden, "Interpersonal Expectations in Organizations," in *Interpersonal Expectations: Theory, Research, and Applications*, ed. P.D. Blanck (Cambridge: Cambridge University Press, 1993), 154–78.

69. D. Eden, "Pygmalion Goes to Boot Camp: Expectancy, Leadership, and Trainee Performance," *Journal of Applied Psychology* 67 (1982): 194–99; B.J. Avolio et al., "A Meta-Analytic Review of Leadership Impact Research: Experimental and Quasi-Experimental Studies," *The Leadership Quarterly* 20, no. 5 (2009): 764–84; P. Whiteley, T. Sy, and S.K. Johnson, "Leaders' Conceptions of Followers: Implications for Naturally Occurring Pygmalion Effects," *Leadership Quarterly* 23, no. 5 (2012): 822–34.

70. S. Madon, L. Jussim, and J. Eccles, "In Search of the Powerful Self-Fulfilling Prophecy," *Journal of Personality and Social Psychology* 72 (1997): 791–809; A.E. Smith, L. Jussim, and J. Eccles, "Do Self-Fulfilling Prophecies Accumulate, Dissipate, or Remain Stable over Time?," *Journal of Personality and Social Psychology* 77 (1999): 548–65; S. Madon et al., "Self-Fulfilling Prophecies: The Synergistic Accumulative Effect of Parents' Beliefs on Children's Drinking Behavior," *Psychological Science* 15 (2005): 837–45.

71. J. Hoffman, "Doctors' Delicate Balance in Keeping Hope Alive," *New York Times*, December 24, 2005, A1, A14; K. Blakely et al., "Optimistic Honesty: Understanding Surgeon and Patient Perspectives on Hopeful Communication in Pancreatic Cancer Care," *HPB* 19 (2017): 611–19.

72. W.H. Cooper, "Ubiquitous Halo," *Psychological Bulletin* 90 (1981): 218–44; P. Rosenzweig, *The Halo Effect . . . and the Eight Other Business Delusions That Deceive Managers* (New York: Free Press, 2007); J.W. Keeley et al., "Investigating Halo and Ceiling Effects in Student Evaluations of Instruction," *Educational and Psychological Measurement* 73, no. 3 (2013): 440–57.

73. B. Mullen et al., "The False Consensus Effect: A Meta-Analysis of 115 Hypothesis Tests," *Journal of Experimental Social Psychology* 21, no. 3 (1985): 262–83; F.J. Flynn and S.S. Wiltermuth, "Who's with Me? False Consensus, Brokerage, and Ethical Decision Making in Organizations," *Academy of Management Journal* 53, no. 5 (2010): 1074–89; B. Roth and A. Voskort, "Stereotypes and False Consensus: How Financial Professionals Predict Risk Preferences," *Journal of Economic Behavior & Organization* 107, Part B (2014): 553–65.

74. D.D. Steiner and J.S. Rain, "Immediate and Delayed Primacy and Recency Effects in Performance Evaluation," *Journal of Applied Psychology* 74 (1989): 136–42; A. Guirall-Contreras, J.A. Gonzalo-Angulo, and W. Rodgers, "Information Content and Recency Effect of the Audit Report in Loan Rating Decisions," *Accounting & Finance* 47, no. 2 (2007): 285–304; P. Henne et al., "Counterfactual Thinking and Recency Effects in Causal Judgment," *Cognition* 212 (July 2021): 104708.

75. E.A. Lind, L. Kray, and L. Thompson, "Primacy Effects in Justice Judgments: Testing Predictions from Fairness Heuristic Theory," *Organizational Behavior and Human Decision Processes* 85 (2001): 189–210; T. Mann and M. Ferguson, "Can We Undo Our First Impressions? The Role of Reinterpretation in Reversing

Implicit Evaluations," *Journal of Personality & Social Psychology* 108, no. 6 (2015): 823–49; T.C. Mann and M.J. Ferguson, "Reversing Implicit First Impressions through Reinterpretation after a Two-Day Delay," *Journal of Experimental Social Psychology* 68 (2017): 122–27.

76. "Survey: One or Two Resume Mistakes Enough for Majority of Managers to Pass on a Job Candidate," Press Release (Menlo Park, Calif.: Accountemps, May 15, 2014); "Make No Mistake–It's Vital," *CareerOne Career Advice* (blog), May 14, 2018; "Employers Share Their Most Outrageous Resume Mistakes and Instant Deal Breakers in a New CareerBuilder Study," News Release (Chicago and Atlanta: CareerBuilder, August 24, 2018); Mateja, "19 Real Resume & CV Mistakes That Make An Impact (Research)," *OfficeNeedle* (blog), April 1, 2021; B. Turczynski, "Common Cover Letter Mistakes: Biggest Blunders to Avoid," *ResumeLab* (blog), September 2, 2021; "Resumania®: Avoid These Easy-to-Make Resume Mistakes," *Robert Half* (blog), November 12, 2021.

77. K. Bezrukova, K.A. Jehn, and C.S. Spell, "Reviewing Diversity Training: Where We Have Been and Where We Should Go," *Academy of Management Learning & Education* 11, no. 2 (2012): 207–27; S.M. Shepherd, "Cultural Awareness Workshops: Limitations and Practical Consequences," *BMC Medical Education* 19, no. 1 (2019): 14; E.M. Krockow, "The Halo Effect: What It Is and How to Beat It," *Psychology Today*, October 8, 2021.

78. D. Eden et al., "Implanting Pygmalion Leadership Style through Workshop Training," *The Leadership Quarterly* 11, no. 2 (June 2000): 171–210; B. Gawronski et al., "When 'Just Say No' Is Not Enough: Affirmation versus Negation Training and the Reduction of Automatic Stereotype Activation," *Journal of Experimental Social Psychology* 44 (2008): 370–77; M.M. Duguid and M.C. Thomas-Hunt, "Condoning Stereotyping? How Awareness of Stereotyping Prevalence Impacts Expression of Stereotypes," *Journal of Applied Psychology* 100, no. 2 (2015): 343–59; F. Dobbin and A. Kalev, "Why Diversity Programs Fail," *Harvard Business Review* 94, no. 7/8 (2016): 52–60; L.M. Leslie, "Diversity Initiative Effectiveness: A Typological Theory of Unintended Consequences," *Academy of Management Review* 44, no. 3 (2019): 538–63.

79. T.W. Costello and S.S. Zalkind, *Psychology in Administration: A Research Orientation* (Englewood Cliffs, NJ: Prentice Hall, 1963), 45–46; J.M. Kouzes and B.Z. Posner, *The Leadership Challenge*, 4th ed. (San Francisco, CA: Jossey-Bass, 2007), Chap. 3.

80. A.G. Greenwald et al., "Understanding and Using the Implicit Association Test: III. Meta-Analysis of Predictive Validity," *Journal of Personality and Social Psychology* 97, no. 1 (2009): 17–41; M.C. Wilson and K. Scior, "Attitudes Towards Individuals with Disabilities as Measured by the Implicit Association Test: A Literature Review," *Research in Developmental Disabilities* 35, no. 2 (2014): 294–321; B.A. Nosek et al., "Understanding and Using the Brief Implicit Association Test: Recommended Scoring Procedures," *PLoS ONE* 9, no. 12 (2014): e110938; B. Schiller et al., "Clocking the Social Mind by Identifying Mental Processes in the IAT with Electrical Neuroimaging," *Proceedings of the National Academy of Sciences* 113, no. 10 (2016): 2786–91.

81. J. Luft, *Of Human Interaction* (Palo Alto, CA: National Press, 1969). For a variation of this model, see J. Hall, "Communication Revisited," *California Management Review* 15 (1973): 56–67. For recent discussion of the Johari blind spot, see A.-M.B. Gallrein et al., "You Spy with Your Little Eye: People Are 'Blind' to Some of the Ways in Which They Are Consensually Seen by Others," *Journal of Research in Personality* 47, no. 5 (2013): 464–71; A.-M.B. Gallrein et al., "I Still Cannot See It—A Replication of Blind Spots in Self-Perception," *Journal of Research in Personality* 60 (2016): 1–7.

82. S. Vazire and M.R. Mehl, "Knowing Me, Knowing You: The Accuracy and Unique Predictive Validity of Self-Ratings and Other-Ratings of Daily Behavior," *Journal of Personality and Social Psychology* 95, no. 5 (2008): 1202–16; D. Leising, A.-M.B. Gallrein, and M. Dufner, "Judging the Behavior of People We Know: Objective Assessment, Confirmation of Preexisting Views, or Both?" *Personality and Social Psychology Bulletin* 40 (2014): 153–63. However, too much self-disclosure may have unintended negative consequences for individuals in team settings. See K.R. Gibson, D. Harari, and J.C. Marr, "When Sharing Hurts: How and Why Self-Disclosing Weakness Undermines the Task-Oriented Relationships of Higher Status Disclosers," *Organizational Behavior and Human Decision Processes* 144 (2018): 25–43.

83. N. Hagiwara et al., "A Call for Grounding Implicit Bias Training in Clinical and Translational Frameworks," *Lancet* 395, no. 10234 (May 2, 2020): 1457–60.

84. I.R. Johnson, B.M. Kopp, and R.E. Petty, "Just Say No! (and Mean It): Meaningful Negation as a Tool to Modify Automatic Racial Attitudes," *Group Processes & Intergroup Relations* 21, no. 1 (2018): 88–110; G.B. Humiston and E.J. Wamsley, "Unlearning Implicit Social Biases during Sleep: A Failure to Replicate," *PLoS ONE* 14, no. 1 (2019): e0211416.

85. J.D. Vorauer, "Completing the Implicit Association Test Reduces Positive Intergroup Interaction Behavior," *Psychological Science* 23 (2012): 1168–75.

86. T.F. Pettigrew and L.R. Tropp, "A Meta-Analytic Test of Intergroup Contact Theory," *Journal of Personality and Social Psychology* 90 (2006): 751–83; S.C. Wright, A. Mazziotta, and L.R. Tropp, "Contact and Intergroup Conflict: New Ideas for the Road Ahead," *Journal of Peace Psychology* 23 (2017): 317–27; J.F. Dovidio et al., "Reducing Intergroup Bias through Intergroup Contact: Twenty Years of Progress and Future Directions," *Group Processes & Intergroup Relations* 20 (2017): 606–20.

87. The contact hypothesis was first introduced in G.W. Allport, *The Nature of Prejudice* (Reading, MA: Addison-Wesley, 1954), Chap. 16. For recent discussion on how to implement intergroup contact, see: S. Paolini et al., "Intergroup Contact Research in the 21st Century: Lessons Learned and Forward Progress If We Remain Open," *Journal of Social Issues* 77, no. 1 (2021): 11–37; J. Harwood, "Modes of Intergroup Contact: If and How to Interact with the Outgroup," *Journal of Social Issues* 77, no. 1 (2021): 154–70; M.S. Choi and S.E. Jarrott, "Application of Intergroup Contact Theory to Managing Age-Diverse Teams," *Journal of Intergenerational Relationships* 19, no. 3 (2021): 377–91.

88. C.K. Soderberg et al., "The Effects of Psychological Distance on Abstraction: Two Meta-Analyses," *Psychological Bulletin* 141, no. 3 (2015): 525–48; J. Boin et al., "The Generalization of Intergroup Contact Effects: Emerging Research, Policy Relevance, and Future Directions," *Journal of Social Issues* 77, no. 1 (2021): 105–31.

89. The meaning of empathy is a never-ending debate. Our definition tries to capture the most widely accepted view, but carefully avoids two dimensions found in a couple of definitions. First, our definition doesn't explicitly refer to emotional contagion, which is automatic whereas empathy is a conscious ability. Second, we avoid "empathetic concern," which is empirically a distinct concept and implies a distancing from the target person. J. Zaki, "Empathy: A Motivated Account," *Psychological Bulletin* 140, no. 6 (2014): 1608–47; B.M.P. Cuff et al., "Empathy: A Review of the Concept," *Emotion Review* 8, no. 2 (2016): 144–53; J.A. Hall, R. Schwartz, and F. Duong, "How Do Laypeople Define Empathy?," *The Journal of Social Psychology* 161, no. 1 (2021): 5–24.

90. M. Tarrant, R. Calitri, and D. Weston, "Social Identification Structures the Effects of Perspective Taking," *Psychological Science* 23, no. 9 (2012): 973–78; J.L. Skorinko and S.A. Sinclair, "Perspective Taking Can Increase Stereotyping: The Role of Apparent Stereotype Confirmation," *Journal of Experimental Social Psychology* 49, no. 1 (2013): 10–18.

4 Workplace Emotions, Attitudes, and Stress

fizkes/Shutterstock

Learning Objectives

After reading this chapter, you should be able to:

LO4-1 Explain how emotions and cognition (conscious reasoning) influence attitudes and behavior.

LO4-2 Describe emotional labor and discuss strategies for displaying expected emotions at work.

LO4-3 Define emotional intelligence and discuss its importance in the workplace.

LO4-4 Explain how job satisfaction and dissatisfaction affect work behavior, including job performance and customer service.

LO4-5 Summarize the three types of organizational commitment, and discuss strategies to increase affective commitment.

LO4-6 Discuss the dynamics (stressors, stress processes, stress outcomes) of work-related stress, and identify five ways to manage work-related stress.

The staff at Piedmont Spine Specialists perform serious work diagnosing and repairing the causes of musculoskeletal pain. But this Duke University medical group in North Carolina also knows the value of having some fun, such as lunch socials, staff art events which are voted on by patients, wrapping up coworkers to look like a mummy at Halloween, and every day practical jokes (furry fake mice near the coffee creamer). "There is this side to working that you really need to have that moment where you're taking a breather to have fun, smile, laugh for a minute before you get back to the serious stuff," says Latrisha Smith, a financial care counselor at the Piedmont clinic.

Fun at work? It sounds like an oxymoron. But to help employees offset the daily stresses of work and to attract new talent, companies are finding creative ways to generate positive emotions in the workplace. At Geotab, which develops world-leading telematics for commercial fleet vehicles, employees celebrate National Hispanic Heritage Month with a special "make your own burrito" luncheon, enjoy outings such as go-kart track racing, and hold cookie bake-off competitions. "Most of all, we're a team, and the best teams always make time for a bit of fun," declares Geotab's culture book.

Studies report that fun at work can be a powerful way to improve employee attitudes and well-being as well as strengthen team bonding and corporate culture. But companies that try to crank up the fun meter often find the opposite result. Employees may be offended or feel disempowered by silly activities created by management or a few staff. Some types of fun aren't fun at all to specific groups of people.

"We are still finding ways for employees to be themselves and connect with each other," acknowledges Michael LaVista, CEO of Caxy, a software development and technology-enablement consulting agency in Chicago. "We don't have it completely figured out, but we've gotten a lot better. We live a lot in Slack, and we've done a lot with GIF challenges and non-work-related channels about cats, video games and more."

Fun at work often comes naturally through humorous moments during meetings or work breaks. "We've overhauled our all-agency internal meetings to put fun and silly-business back center-stage," explains an executive at the Australian operations of advertising, marketing, and public relations agency Ogilvy. "Shared laughter goes a long way in making everyone feel connected."[1]

Piedmont Spine Specialists, Geotab, Caxy, Ogilvy, and a legion of other companies around the world recognize that emotions and attitudes make a difference in individual behavior and well-being, as well as in the organization's performance and customer service. Over the past two decades, the field of organizational behavior has experienced a sea change in thinking about workplace emotions, so this chapter begins by introducing the concept and explaining why researchers are so eager to discover how emotions influence attitudes and behavior. Next, we consider the dynamics of emotional labor, followed by the popular topic of emotional intelligence. The specific work attitudes of job satisfaction and organizational commitment are then discussed, including their association with various employee behaviors and work performance. The final section looks at work-related stress, including the stress experience, four prominent stressors, individual differences in stress, and ways to combat excessive stress.

LO4-1 Explain how emotions and cognition (conscious reasoning) influence attitudes and behavior.

EMOTIONS IN THE WORKPLACE

Emotions influence almost everything we do in the workplace. This is a strong statement, and one that was rarely expressed by organizational behavior experts a few decades ago. Most OB theories still assume that a person's thoughts and actions are governed primarily or exclusively by logical thinking (called *cognitions*).[2] Yet groundbreaking neuroscience discoveries have revealed that our perceptions, attitudes, decisions, and behavior are influenced by emotions as well as cognition.[3] Emotions often occur before cognitive processes and, consequently, influence the latter. By ignoring emotionality, many theories have overlooked a large piece of the puzzle about human behavior in the workplace.

Emotions are physiological, behavioral, and psychological episodes experienced toward an object, person, or event that create a state of readiness.[4] These "episodes" are very brief events, some lasting less than a second. However, we usually experience emotions over several minutes or longer because they occur in waves as we continue to think about the source of the emotion. Emotions are directed toward someone or something. For example, we experience joy, fear, anger, and other emotional episodes toward tasks, customers, or a phone app we are using. This differs from *moods,* which tend to be longer-term background emotional states that are no longer associated with specific events or people.

Emotions are experiences. They represent changes in our physiological state (e.g., blood pressure, heart rate), psychological state (e.g., thought process), and behavior (e.g., facial expression).[5] Most emotional reactions are subtle; they occur without our awareness. This is an important point because the topic of emotions often conjures up images of people "getting emotional." In reality, most emotions are fleeting, usually nonconscious events that influence our conscious thinking and behavior.[6] Finally, emotions put us in a state of readiness. When we get worried, for example, our heart rate and blood pressure increase to make our body better prepared to engage in fight or flight. Strong emotions trigger our conscious awareness of a threat or opportunity in the external environment. The "state of readiness" generated by emotions is the engine of our motivation, which we discuss more fully in Chapter 5.[7]

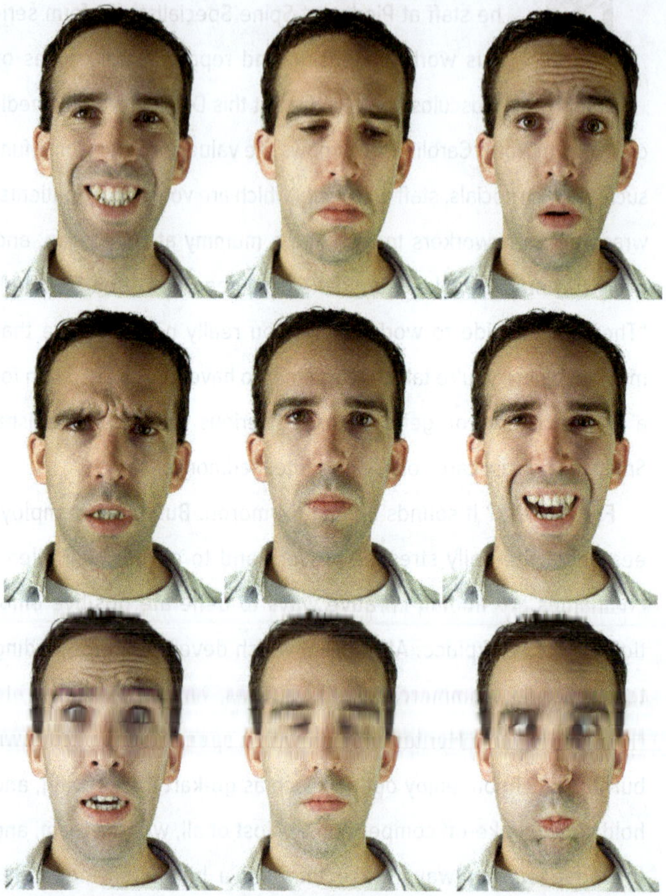

Emotions are physiological, behavioral, and psychological episodes experienced toward an object, person, or event that create a state of readiness.
Richard Nelson/Cutcaster

Don't let us forget that the small emotions are the great captains of our lives, and that we obey them without knowing it.[8]

—Vincent Van Gogh (late 1800s Dutch painter)

Types of Emotions

People experience many emotions and various combinations of emotions, but all of them have two common features, illustrated in Exhibit 4.1.[9] One feature is that emotions vary in their level of activation. By definition, emotions put us in a state of readiness and, as mentioned, are the primary source of a person's motivation. Some emotional experiences, such as when we are suddenly surprised, are strong enough to consciously motivate us to act without careful thought. Most emotional experiences are more subtle, but even they activate enough to make us more aware of our environment.

The second feature is that all emotions evaluate the situation as positive or negative, good or bad, helpful or harmful, and so forth. In other words, all emotions have an associated valence (called *core affect*) signaling that the perceived object or event should be approached or avoided. Negative emotions tend to generate stronger levels of activation than do positive emotions.[10] Fear and anger, for instance, are more intense experiences than are joy and delight, so they have a stronger effect on

emotions Physiological, behavioral, and psychological episodes experienced toward an object, person, or event that create a state of readiness

attitudes The cluster of beliefs, assessed feelings, and behavioral intentions toward a person, object, or event (called an *attitude object*)

Exhibit 4.1 Circumplex Model of Emotions

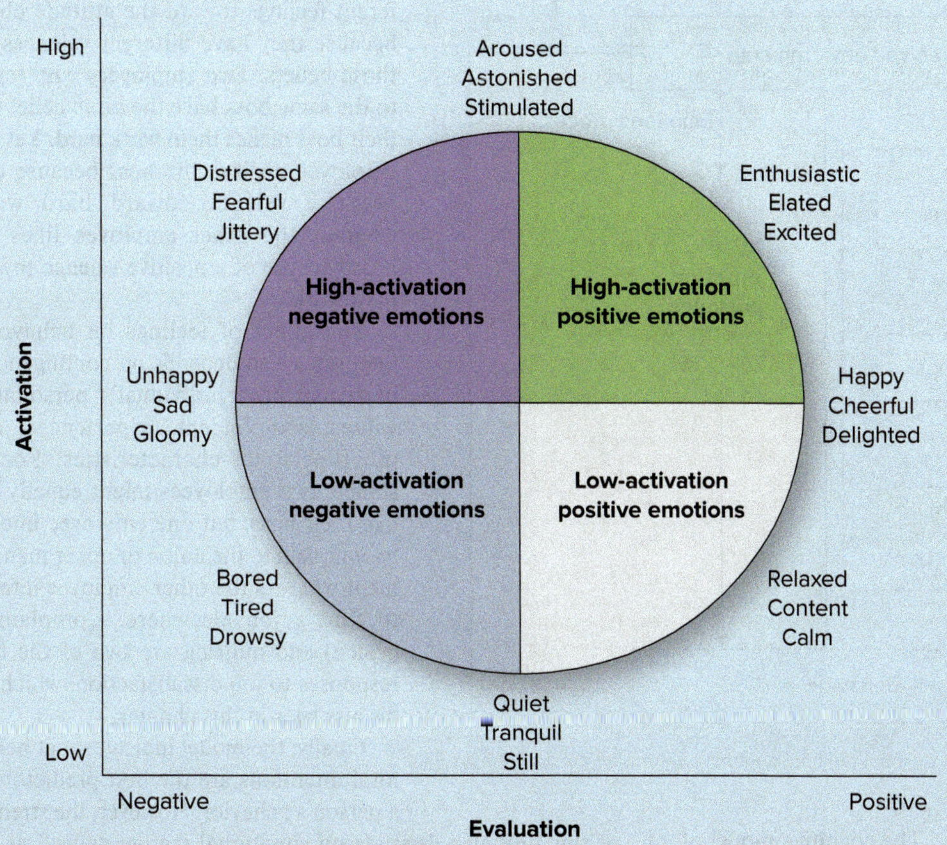

Sources: Adapted from J.A. Russell, "Core Affect and the Psychological Construction of Emotion," *Psychological Review* 110, no. 1 (2003): 145–72; M. Yik, J.A. Russell, and J.H. Steiger, "A 12-Point Circumplex Structure of Core Affect," *Emotion* 11, no. 4 (2011): 705–31.

our actions. This valence asymmetry likely occurs because negative emotions protect us from harm and are therefore more critical for our survival.

Emotions, Attitudes, and Behavior

To understand how emotions influence our thoughts and behavior in the workplace, we first need to know about attitudes. **Attitudes** represent the cluster of beliefs, assessed feelings, and behavioral intentions toward a person, object, or event (called an *attitude object*).[11] Attitudes are *judgments,* whereas emotions are *experiences.* In other words, attitudes involve evaluations of an attitude object, whereas emotions operate as events that we experience, usually without our awareness. Attitudes might occasionally be nonconscious, but more often we are aware of and actively think about them. Another distinction is that we experience most emotions very briefly, whereas our attitude toward someone or something is more stable over time.[12]

Until recently, experts believed that attitudes could be understood just by the three cognitive components illustrated on the left side of Exhibit 4.2: beliefs, feelings, and behavioral intentions. Now evidence suggests that a parallel emotional process is also at work, shown on the right side of the exhibit.[13] Using attitude toward mergers as an example, let's look more closely at this model, beginning with the traditional cognitive perspective of attitudes.

- *Beliefs.* These are your perceptions about the attitude object—what you believe to be true.[14] For example, you might believe that mergers reduce job security for employees in the combined firms, or that mergers increase the company's competitiveness in this era of globalization. These beliefs are perceived facts that you acquire from experience and other forms of learning. Each of these beliefs also has a valence; that is, you have a positive or negative feeling about each belief (e.g., less job security is bad).
- *Feelings.* This element represents your conscious positive or negative evaluations of the attitude object. Some people think mergers are good; others think they are bad. Your positive or negative opinion of mergers represents your assessed feelings. According to the traditional cognitive perspective of attitudes (left side of the model), feelings are calculated from your beliefs about mergers and the associated feelings about those beliefs. Consider the example of your attitude toward mergers. If you believe that mergers typically have negative outcomes such as layoffs and organizational politics, then you will form negative feelings toward mergers in general or about a specific planned merger in your organization.
- *Behavioral intentions.* This third element represents your planned effort to engage in a particular behavior regarding the attitude object.[15] Upon hearing that the company will merge with another organization, you might become motivated to look for a job elsewhere or possibly to complain to management about the merger decision. Your feelings toward mergers influence your behavioral intentions, and which actions you choose depends on your past experience, personality, and social norms of appropriate behavior.

Exhibit 4.2 Model of Emotions, Attitudes, and Behavior

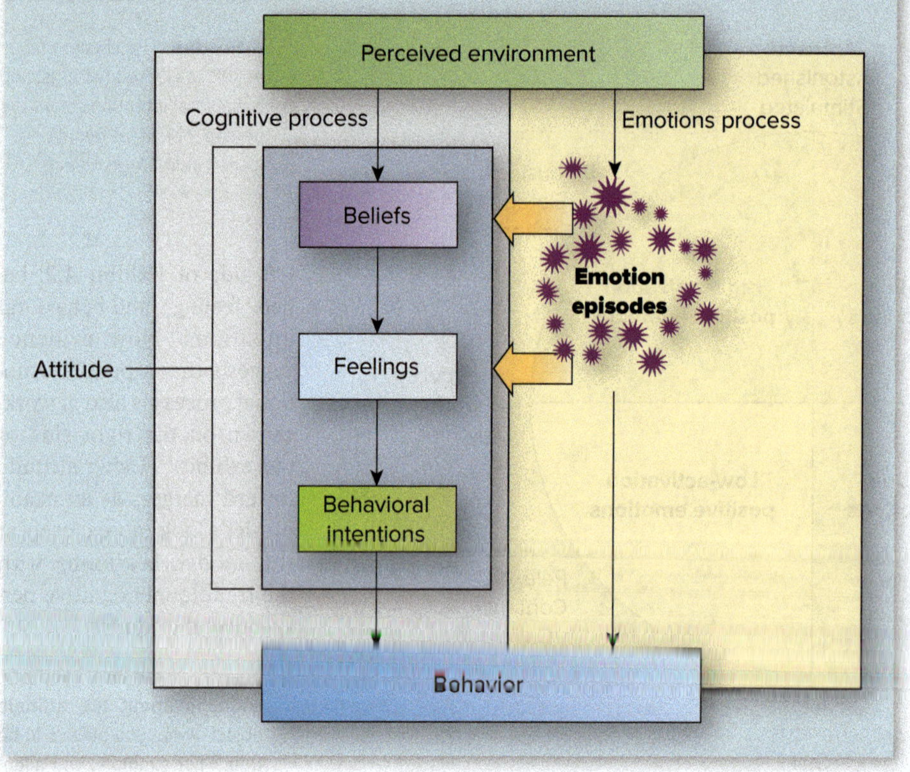

begin with the beliefs–feelings link. People with the same beliefs might form quite different feelings toward the attitude object because they have different valences for those beliefs. Two employees who report to the same boss have the same belief that their boss makes them work hard. Yet one employee dislikes the boss because of a negative valence toward hard work, whereas the other employee likes the boss because of a positive valence toward hard work.

The effect of feelings on behavioral intentions also depends on contingencies, particularly an individual's personality, values, self-concept, experiences, and other personal characteristics. For instance, two employees might equally dislike their boss, but one employee intends to complain to the union or upper management whereas the other employee intends to find a job elsewhere. Complaining (voice) and quitting are two of the four responses to job dissatisfaction, which we discuss later in this chapter.

Finally, the model indicates that behavioral intentions are the best predictors of a person's behavior. However, the strength

Attitude–Behavior Contingencies The cognitive model of attitudes (beliefs–feelings–intentions) gives the impression that we can predict behavior from each element of the individual's attitude. This is potentially true, but several contingencies at each stage in the model usually weaken that predictability. Let's

of this link also depends on situational factors as well as the person's ability and role perceptions (see the MARS model in Chapter 1). For example, two people might intend to quit because they dislike their boss, but only one does so because the other employee can't find a job elsewhere.

Several contingencies at each stage in the cognitive model of attitudes weaken the ability to predict behavior from beliefs, feelings, and behavioral intentions.
ImageFlow/Shutterstock

How Emotions Influence Attitudes and Behavior

To some extent, the cognitive model describes how attitudes are formed and changed, but emotions also have a central role in this process.[16] The right side of Exhibit 4.2 illustrates this process, which (like the cognitive process) also begins with perceptions of the world around us. Our brain tags incoming sensory information with emotional markers based on a quick and imprecise evaluation of whether that information supports or threatens our innate drives. These markers are not calculated feelings; they are automatic and nonconscious emotional responses based on very thin slices of sensory information.[17] The experienced emotions then influence our feelings about the attitude object.

Consider once again the scenario in which your employer intends to merge with a competitor. You might experience worry, nervousness, or relief upon learning that your company intends to complete that merger. The fuzzy dots on the right side of Exhibit 4.2 depict the numerous emotional episodes you experience upon hearing the merger announcement, subsequently thinking about

> While consciously evaluating whether something is good or bad, your brain generates emotions with positive or negative valences, which sway your conscious evaluation.

the merger, discussing the merger with coworkers, and so forth. These emotions are transmitted to your brain's cognitive centers, where they are logically analyzed along with other information about the attitude object.[18] So, while you are consciously evaluating whether the merger is good or bad, your brain is also generating emotions with positive or negative valences, and those emotional signals sway your conscious evaluation. In fact, we often deliberately "listen in" on our emotions to help us consciously decide whether to support or oppose something (see Chapter 6 on emotions and decision making).[19]

The influence of both cognitive reasoning and emotions on attitudes is most apparent when they disagree with each other. People occasionally experience this mental tug-of-war, sensing that something isn't right even though they can't think of any logical reason to be concerned. This internal conflict or ambivalence indicates that the person's logical analysis of the situation (left side of Exhibit 4.2) generates feelings that differ from the emotional response (right side of Exhibit 4.2).[20] Should we pay attention to our emotions or our logical analysis? This question is not easy to answer, but some studies indicate that logical analysis should play a central role in most decisions. Although executives are known to make quick decisions based on their gut feelings (emotional response), their best decisions tend to occur after logically assessing the possible choices.[21] Therefore, we should pay attention to both the cognitive and emotional sides of the attitude model, and hope they agree with each other most of the time!

Generating Positive Emotions at Work This chapter began by describing a few organizations that generate positive emotions at work in various ways. Google is famous for its in-house coffee bars, gourmet cafeterias, conversation areas that look like vintage subway cars, personal development courses, game rooms, free haircuts, and slides to descend to the floor below. Zoom Video Communications has an entire team—called the happiness crew—at each location dedicated to maintaining a positive and engaging workplace. "If you get an offer to work at Zoom, take it," advises a Zoom employee in Atlanta, Georgia. "Zoom takes employee happiness seriously and people genuinely love the company."[22]

Some critics of fun-oriented workplace events argue that the organization's main focus should be to create positive emotions through the job itself as well as through natural everyday occurrences such as polite customers and supportive

OB THEORY TO PRACTICE

Short List of Fun Events for the Workplace[23]

Interesting work, supportive coworkers, a healthy work environment, and good pay are some of the well-established ways to make employees happier at work. But companies also introduce events that potentially inject more positive emotions. Here are some of the more interesting (and apparently effective) fun strategies:

- Office races—individual and team races down hallways with tricycles, wheeled chairs, or scooters. At some fun-oriented businesses, employees start these races without formal planning.
- Peer learning classes on nonwork skills—from music lessons to printmaking, employees enjoy learning something different during lunch, after hours, or on special learning days.
- Attending sports games—baseball, hockey, and many other sporting events are great to watch and share the enthusiasm with coworkers.
- Nature hikes—a noncompetitive walk in the woods with coworkers through terrain that most can handle is a healthy break from office stress and builds positive relations with coworkers.
- Go-kart and bumper car races—these competitive activities rev up excitement for most employees without being dangerous (the vehicles are designed for anyone over 12 years old). For those with a more aggressive bent, there are also paintball and Nerf battles.

g-stockstudio/Shutterstock

cognitive dissonance An emotional experience caused by a perception that our beliefs, feelings, and behavior are incongruent with one another

emotional labor The effort, planning, and control needed to express organizationally desired emotions during interpersonal transactions

coworkers. These are, indeed, important sources of positive emotions. Even so, most people perform work that produces some negative emotions, and research has found that humor and fun at work—whether natural or contrived—can potentially counteract the negative experiences.[24] Overall, emotions shape employee attitudes and, as we will discuss later, those attitudes influence various forms of work-related behavior.

One last comment about Exhibit 4.2: Notice the arrow from the emotional episodes to behavior. It indicates that emotions directly influence a person's behavior without conscious thought. This occurs when we jump suddenly if someone sneaks up on us. It also occurs in everyday situations because even low-intensity emotions automatically change our facial expressions. These actions are not carefully thought out. They are automatic emotional responses that are learned or hardwired by heredity for particular situations.[25]

Cognitive Dissonance

Imagine that you have just signed a contract for new digital whiteboards to be installed throughout the company's meeting rooms. The deal was expensive but, after consulting with several staff, you decided that the technology would be valuable in this digital age. Yet, you felt ambivalence and a twinge of regret soon after signing the contract. This emotional experience is **cognitive dissonance**, which occurs when people perceive that their beliefs, feelings, and behavior are incongruent with one another.[26] The inconsistency among these three attitude components generates emotions (such as feeling ambivalence and regret) that motivate people to create more consistency by changing one or more of them.

Why did you experience cognitive dissonance after purchasing the digital whiteboards?[27] Perhaps you remembered that some staff wanted flexibility, whereas the whiteboards require special markers and computer software. Or maybe you feel an increasing awareness that the high cost of digital whiteboards versus traditional whiteboards is inconsistent with your personal values and your company's culture of thriftiness. Generally, dissonance occurs because your attitude (it's good to be cost conscious) is incongruous with your behavior (buying expensive whiteboards). Most people like to think of themselves—and be viewed by others—as rational and logical. Cognitive dissonance occurs when our behavior and beliefs conflict, which is not so rational.

How do we reduce cognitive dissonance?[28] Reversing the behavior might work, but most behaviors can't be undone. It would be too expensive to remove the digital whiteboards after they have been installed. In any event, dissonance would still exist because you and your coworkers already know that you made this purchase and did so willingly.

More often, people reduce cognitive dissonance by changing their beliefs and feelings. One dissonance-reducing strategy is to amplify or discover additional positive features of their selected alternative (e.g., the digital whiteboards can change handwriting into typed text). A second strategy is to amplify or discover additional problems or weaknesses with the alternatives that weren't chosen (e.g., traditional boards are poor projection screens).

A third strategy is more indirect; rather than try to ignore the high price of the digital whiteboards, you reduce dissonance by emphasizing how your other decisions have been frugal. This framing compensates for your expensive digital whiteboard fling and thereby maintains your self-concept as a thrifty decision maker. Each of these mental acrobatics maintains some degree of consistency between the person's behavior (buying expensive digital whiteboards) and attitudes (it's good to be thrifty).

Emotions and Personality

Throughout this section, we have implied that emotional experiences are triggered by workplace experiences. This is mostly true, but emotions are also partly determined, amplified, or suppressed by an individual's personality.[29] People with higher emotional stability and extraverted personalities (see Chapter 2) tend to experience more positive emotions. Those with higher neuroticism (lower emotional stability) and introverted personalities tend to experience more negative emotions. Although these personality traits have some effect, studies have found that the actual situation in which people work has a noticeably stronger influence on their attitudes and behavior.[30]

LO4-2 Describe emotional labor and discuss strategies for displaying expected emotions at work.

MANAGING EMOTIONS AT WORK

Employees are expected to manage their emotions in the workplace. They must conceal their frustration when serving an irritating customer, display compassion to an ill patient, and hide their boredom in a long meeting with other executives. These are all forms of **emotional labor**—the effort, planning, and control needed to express organizationally desired emotions during interpersonal transactions.[31]

McGraw Hill connect

SELF-ASSESSMENT 4.1: What Is Your Emotional Personality?

> Emotional labor requires considerable mental effort and can be stressful when employees must display emotions that are quite different from the emotions they actually experience at that moment.

Almost everyone is expected to abide by *display rules.* These norms or explicit rules require employees to display behaviors representing specific emotions and to hide observable evidence of other emotions. Emotional labor demands are higher in jobs requiring a variety of emotions (e.g., anger as well as joy) and more intense emotions (e.g., showing delight rather than smiling weakly), as well as in jobs where interaction with clients is frequent and longer. Emotional labor also increases when employees must precisely rather than casually abide by the display rules.[32] This work requirement is most common in service industries, where employees have frequent face-to-face interaction with clients.

Employees sometimes need to show emotions that are quite different from—sometimes opposite to—the emotions they actually experience at that moment. For instance, they must display patience and positive feelings toward a customer who they actually dislike. This incongruence requires considerable mental effort and can be very stressful. Emotional labor may also require employees to act contrary to their self-concept, which can lead to psychological separation from self as well as job dissatisfaction.[33]

Emotional Display Norms across Cultures

Norms about displaying or hiding your true emotions vary considerably across cultures.[34] One large global study reports that norms in several countries in Asia and Africa strongly discourage emotional expression. People in those cultures are expected to be subdued, have relatively monotonic voice intonation, and avoid physical movement and touching that display emotions. In contrast, several Latin and Middle Eastern cultures allow or encourage more vivid display of emotions and expect people to act more consistently with their true emotions. In these cultures, people are expected to reveal their true thoughts and feelings, be dramatic in their conversational tones, and be animated in their use of nonverbal behaviors. For example, 81 percent of Ethiopians and 74 percent of Japanese agreed that it is considered unprofessional to express emotions overtly in their culture, whereas 43 percent of Americans, 33 percent of Italians, and only 19 percent of Spaniards, Cubans, and Egyptians agreed with this statement.[35] When required to suppress their true emotions at work, employees from cultures that tolerate or encourage emotional expression experience more stress and lower life satisfaction compared to coworkers from cultures that discourage emotional expression.

Strategies for Displaying Expected Emotions

Emotional labor is ultimately about displaying expected emotions through facial expressions and other forms of behavior. Two general approaches to emotional labor are (1) pretending to have the expected emotions by consciously trying to display behaviors depicting those emotions and (2) actively changing our perceptions and situation so they naturally produce the expected emotions and associated behaviors.

The first approach—consciously pretending to display the expected emotions—is known as *surface acting.* We do surface acting when trying to show interest in a client's lengthy explanation even though we are actually weary from hearing it. We act out the verbal and nonverbal behaviors that symbolize the expected emotions, even though our actual emotions are quite different.[36]

A genuine emotion automatically activates a complex set of facial muscles and body positions, all of which are difficult to replicate when pretending to have this emotion (surface acting).
RapidEye/Getty Images

Surface acting is usually a poor strategy for emotional labor. It requires considerable mental effort that is often stressful and alienating.[37] Surface acting also tends to display insincere emotions. A genuine emotion automatically activates a complex set of facial muscles and body positions, all of which are difficult to replicate when pretending to have this emotion. Also, while trying to display desired emotions through surface acting, our true emotions reveal themselves as subtle gestures, usually without our awareness. The result of surface acting is that observers recognize the fake emotions, which undermines the social exchange.[38]

OB THEORY TO PRACTICE

Strategies for Regulating Emotions (Deep Acting)

Strategy	Description	Example
Change the situation	Move out of or into work settings that produce or avoid specific emotions.	• Temporarily leave a work area that makes us feel lethargic. • Keep away from a particular client who is deeply irritating.
Modify the situation	Modify the current setting to create or avoid specific emotions.	• Switch from a task that is aggravating to one that is more enjoyable. • Shift a conversation away from an awkward or sensitive topic (e.g., politics) to a less emotionally laden topic.
Suppress or amplify emotions	Consciously block out thoughts that produce dysfunctional emotions or more actively think about things that produce expected emotions.	• Maintain an impersonal relationship with patients (avoid becoming emotionally attached to their plight).
Shift attention	Change the focus of one's attention.	• Switch to an engaging and enjoyable work activity that takes your mind off something that caused negative emotions earlier that day.
Reframe the situation	Cognitively reevaluate a particular event so it generates desired emotions.	• Rather than viewing a client presentation as a failure, reframe the event as a learning moment that had a low probability of success.

Regulating Emotions through Deep Acting The second approach—called *deep acting*—involves displaying the expected emotions by actually experiencing them (rather than faking them). In other words, deep acting involves actually producing the emotions that are expected in a particular situation, whereas surface acting does not attempt to experience the expected emotion.[39]

There are five main strategies for regulating our emotions.[40] One approach is to change the situation, such as moving out of or into work settings that affect our emotions: for example, avoiding a place or person that we expect would create undesirable emotions. A second tactic, modifying the existing situation, occurs when we remain in the same physical location, but adapt that environment so it alters our emotional state (e.g., changing tasks or altering physical arrangements in the work area). The third strategy, suppressing or amplifying emotions, involves consciously trying to block out dysfunctional emotions or to increase the intensity of expected emotions.[41] An example of suppressing emotions is trying to stop thinking about events that bother us or, at least, psychologically distance ourselves from those events.

The fourth emotion regulation strategy also blocks unwanted emotions, but we do this specifically by redirecting our focus of attention. This occurs when we actively do things to take our mind off a past or future event and the undesirable emotions that thought creates. Finally, reframing the situation is a cognitive reevaluation of a particular event that generates more appropriate emotions. Flight attendants apply reframing when they define an incident with an unruly passenger as a test of their customer service skill. These interactions are challenging accomplishments rather than dreaded chores.[42]

All five emotion regulation strategies generate deep acting, but reframing the situation and shifting attention are likely the most common. Changing and modifying the situation can be applied when employees work alone, but seldom in social settings, such as when attending a client meeting and interacting with an upset passenger. Suppressing or amplifying emotions produce deep acting, but these cognitive activities can be difficult for most of us. No matter which strategy is applied to manage emotions, emotion regulation requires emotional intelligence, which we discuss next.

LO4-3 Define emotional intelligence and discuss its importance in the workplace.

EMOTIONAL INTELLIGENCE

Emotional intelligence (EI) is a set of *abilities* that enable us to recognize and regulate our own emotions as well as the emotions of other people. This definition refers to the four main dimensions shown in Exhibit 4.3.[43]

- *Awareness of our own emotions.* This is the ability to perceive and understand the meaning of our own emotions. People with higher emotional intelligence have better awareness of their emotions and are better able to make sense of them. They can eavesdrop on their emotional responses to specific situations and use this awareness as conscious information.[44]

Exhibit 4.3 Dimensions of Emotional Intelligence

Abilities	Yourself	Others
Recognition of emotions	**Awareness of own emotions**	**Awareness of others' emotions**
Regulation of emotions	**Management of own emotions**	**Management of others' emotions**

Sources: Variations of these dimensions are found in: D. Goleman, R. Boyatzis, and A. McKee, *Primal Leadership* (Boston: Harvard Business School Press, 2002), Chap. 3; P.J. Jordan and S.A. Lawrence, "Emotional Intelligence in Teams: Development and Initial Validation of the Short Version of the Workgroup Emotional Intelligence Profile (WEIP-S)," *Journal of Management & Organization* 15 (2009): 452–69; K.A. Pekaar et al., "Dynamic Self- and Other-Focused Emotional Intelligence: A Theoretical Framework and Research Agenda," *Journal of Research in Personality* 86 (2020): 103958.

Mc Graw Hill connect

SELF-ASSESSMENT 4.2: How Well Do You Recognize and Regulate Emotions?

- *Management of our own emotions.* Everyone manages their own emotions to some extent. We suppress disruptive impulses and try not to feel angry or frustrated when events go against us. We try to feel joy and happiness toward others on such occasions. We re-energize ourselves to break out of mid-day lethargy. More generally, management of our own emotions involves deep acting and the associated emotion regulation practices described earlier.
- *Awareness of others' emotions.* This is the ability to perceive and understand the emotions of other people.[45] It relates to *empathy*—the ability to understand another person's situation or viewpoint (perspective taking), be sensitive to their thoughts and feelings, and experience their emotions (see Chapter 3). Awareness of others' emotions also includes being organizationally aware, such as sensing office politics and the presence of informal social networks.
- *Management of others' emotions.* This dimension of EI includes consoling people who feel sad, emotionally inspiring team members to complete a class project on time, getting strangers to feel comfortable working with you, and dissipating coworker stress and other dysfunctional emotions that they experience.

emotional intelligence (EI) A set of abilities to perceive and express emotion, assimilate emotion in thought, understand and reason with emotion, and regulate emotion in oneself and others

The four dimensions of emotional intelligence form a foundational hierarchy.[46] Awareness of your own emotions is the base level of that foundation because you need awareness to engage in the higher levels of emotional intelligence. You can't manage your own emotions if you don't know what they are. Managing other people's emotions is the highest level of EI because this ability requires awareness of your own and others' emotions. To diffuse an angry conflict between two employees, for example, you need to understand the emotions they are experiencing, understand the emotions you are experiencing, and manage your own emotions (and display emotions) so you can manage the conflict situation effectively.

Emotional Intelligence Outcomes and Development

Employees need emotional intelligence to work effectively because most jobs involve social interaction with coworkers or external stakeholders.[47] Studies suggest that people with high EI are more effective team members, perform better in jobs requiring emotional labor, make better decisions involving other people, and maintain a more positive mindset for creative work. EI also is associated with effective leadership

Importance of Emotional Intelligence in the Workplace[48]

17% of 750 executives from Europe, United States, India, and China say their organization conducts emotional intelligence training for nonsupervisory employees.

92% of 800 American and Canadian employees surveyed believe they have strong emotional intelligence.

22% of 860 UK and Australian managers surveyed say too little emphasis is put on emotional intelligence by employers during the hiring process.

74% of 750 executives from Europe, United States, India, and China believe that emotional intelligence will become a "must-have" skill for all employees.

61% of 800 American and Canadian employees surveyed admit they've let emotions get the better of them at work.

(Photo): Jack Hollingsworth/Blend Images LLC

job satisfaction A person's evaluation of their job and work context

exit-voice-loyalty-neglect (EVLN) model The four ways, as indicated in the name, that employees respond to job dissatisfaction

because leaders engage in emotional labor (e.g., showing patience to employees even when they might feel frustrated) and actively regulate the emotions of others (e.g., helping staff members feel optimism after they have lost an important contract). However, emotional intelligence does not improve some forms of performance, such as tasks that require minimal social interaction.[49]

Given the potential value of emotional intelligence, it's not surprising that some organizations try to measure this ability in job applicants. Several organizations also have training programs to improve employees' emotional intelligence.[50] These programs usually teach participants about the concept, test their EI when the program begins, and provide ongoing feedback about how well they understand and manage others' emotions.

Indian Railways tested and then coached a large number of managers to improve their self-awareness, empathy, and management of emotions. Several police departments have emotional intelligence programs, so law enforcement officers are better able to de-escalate conflict situations and manage their own emotions when approaching others (and thereby avoid escalating the conflict). Fidelity offers its employees training in emotional intelligence along with other soft skills and technical education. "I personally believe that the top advisors over the next decade or two will actually be those that have the greatest EQ (emotional intelligence) rather than IQ," says the president of Fidelity Institutional. "It's going to really be those who can modify behavior and coach and sell and be empathetic."[52] Emotional intelligence also increases with age; it is part of the process called maturity.

OB THEORY TO PRACTICE

Police Empathy and De-escalation through Emotional Intelligence Training[51]

Emotional intelligence training is becoming an important component of officer development in law enforcement agencies across the United States. Several police departments in Massachusetts have a multiday program that includes EI testing, experiential exercises, and learning about the neuroscience of emotion and empathy. "It is very valuable training, from deescalation to simple community engagement," says Wellesley Police Chief Jack Pilecki.

Police officers in Ohio participate in the RITE program, which includes recognizing and regulating emotions. "We want officers to recognize what their emotions are before they get out of their car and engage with the public," says Linda Webb, who co-created the program. "If I get out of a patrol car and I'm mad or I'm angry, that engagement with a public member is not going to be good." The emotional intelligence principles that Webb now teaches saved her from life-threatening incidents during her 35-year career as a law enforcement officer and detective in Florida.

LO4-4 Explain how job satisfaction and dissatisfaction affect work behavior, including job performance and customer service.

JOB SATISFACTION

So far, this chapter has introduced the model of emotions and attitudes, as well as emotional intelligence, which is the means by which we manage emotions in the workplace. We now turn our attention to two specific attitudes: job satisfaction and organizational commitment. Both have a substantial influence on behavior in the workplace. And although distinct concepts, they are highly correlated with each other and are the core foundations of the individual's "overall job attitude."[53]

Job satisfaction is defined as a person's evaluation of their job and work context.[54] It is an *appraisal* of the perceived job characteristics, work environment, and emotional experiences at work. Satisfied employees have a favorable evaluation of their jobs, based on their observations and emotional experiences. Job satisfaction is best viewed as a collection of attitudes about different aspects of the job and work context. You might like your coworkers but are less satisfied with your work schedule, for instance.

How satisfied are employees at work? The answer depends on the person, the workplace, and the country. Global surveys, such as the one shown in Exhibit 4.4, estimate that job satisfaction is currently highest in India, Mexico, Turkey, and the United States. The lowest levels of overall job satisfaction have recently been recorded in Japan, Hong Kong, and Singapore.

Can we conclude from these surveys that most employees in India, Mexico, Turkey, and the United States are happy at work? Possibly, but their overall job satisfaction probably isn't as high as these statistics suggest. One problem is that surveys often use a single direct question, such as "How satisfied are you with your job?" Many dissatisfied employees are reluctant to reveal their feelings in a direct question because this is tantamount to admitting that they made a poor job choice and are not enjoying a large part of their life. The inflated results are evident in the fact that employees tend to report less satisfaction when asked about specific aspects of their work. Furthermore, studies report that many employees plan to look for work within the next year or would leave their current employer if the right opportunity came along.[55]

A second problem is that cultural values make it difficult to compare job satisfaction across countries. People in Japan tend to subdue their emotions in public, and there is evidence that they also avoid extreme survey ratings such as "very satisfied." A

Exhibit 4.4 Job Satisfaction in Selected Countries[56]

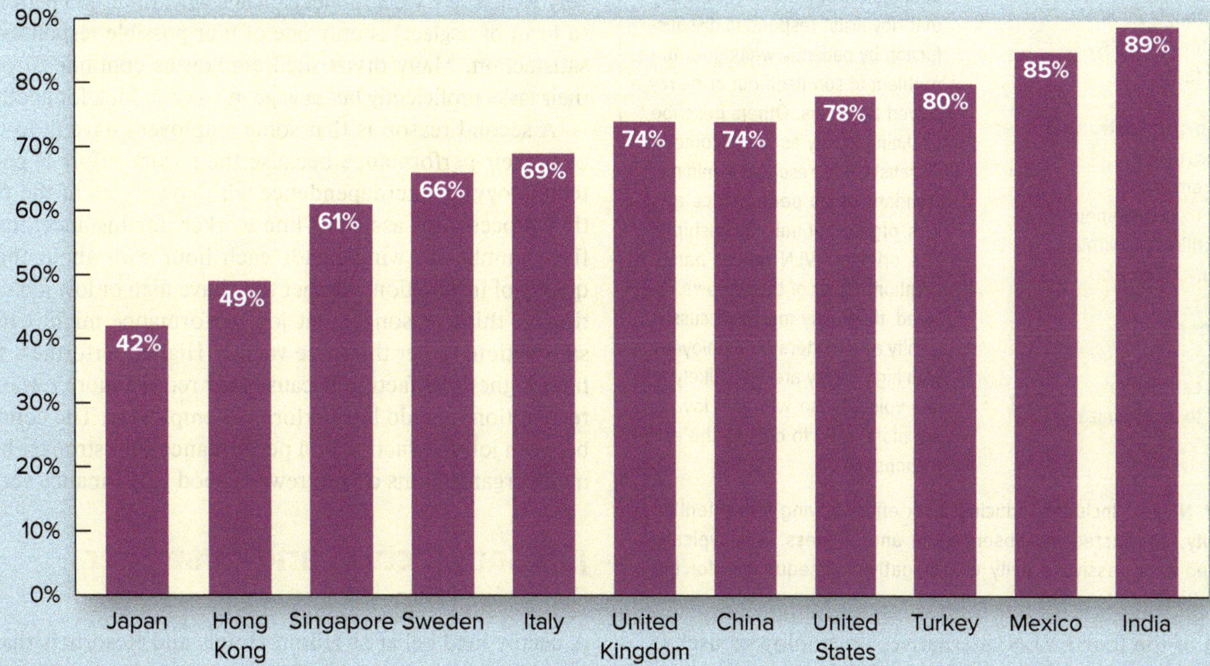

Percentage of employees in each country who said they are, in general, satisfied or very satisfied working for their current employer. Survey data were collected in 2019 for Randstad Holdings NV, with a minimum of 400 employees in each country. This exhibit shows results from selected countries across the full range of 34 countries studied.

third problem is that job satisfaction changes with economic conditions. Employees with the highest job satisfaction in current surveys tend to be in countries where the economies are chugging along quite well.[57]

Job Satisfaction and Work Behavior

Job satisfaction influences task performance, organizational citizenship, employee turnover, and other individual behaviors described in Chapter 1.[58] A useful template is the **exit–voice–loyalty–neglect (EVLN) model**. As the name suggests, the EVLN model identifies four ways that employees respond to dissatisfaction:[59]

- *Exit.* Exit includes leaving the organization, transferring to another work unit, or at least trying to get away from the dissatisfying situation. The traditional theory is that job dissatisfaction builds over time and eventually becomes strong enough that the employee is motivated to search for better work opportunities elsewhere. This is likely true to some extent, but it is more likely that specific "shock events" quickly energize employees to think about and engage in exit behavior. For example, the emotional reaction you experience to an unfair management decision or a conflict episode with a coworker motivates you to look at job ads and speak to friends about job opportunities where they work. This begins the process of visualizing yourself working at another company and psychologically withdrawing from your current employer.[60]
- *Voice.* Voice is any attempt to change, rather than escape from, the dissatisfying situation. Voice can be a constructive response, such as recommending ways for management to improve the situation, or it can be more confrontational, such as complaining about the problem, filing formal grievances, or mounting a coalition to oppose a decision.[61] In the extreme, some employees might engage in counterproductive behaviors to get attention and force changes in the organization.

Voice is any attempt to change, rather than escape from, the dissatisfying situation, such as providing recommendations, complaining about the problem, mounting opposition through a coalition, or filing a formal grievance.
fizkes/Getty Images

service profit chain model A theory explaining how employees' job satisfaction influences company profitability indirectly through service quality, customer loyalty, and related factors

affective organizational commitment An individual's emotional attachment to, involvement in, and identification with an organization

continuance commitment An individual's calculative attachment to an organization

- *Loyalty.* EVLN research has discussed "loyalty" in various and debatable ways. Some writers say that "loyalists" respond to dissatisfaction by patiently waiting for the problem to sort itself out or be resolved by others. Others describe declining loyalty as an outcome of dissatisfaction, resulting in minimal standard of job performance and less organizational citizenship.[62] The original EVLN model barely mentions either of these views. Instead, the theory mostly discusses loyalty as a moderator. Employees with high loyalty are more likely to use voice; those with low loyalty are more likely to choose the exit response.[63]
- *Neglect.* Neglect includes reducing work effort, paying less attention to quality, and increasing absenteeism and lateness. It is typically described as a passive activity with negative consequences for the organization.

Which of the four EVLN alternatives do employees use? It depends on the person and the situation.[64] Voice is preferred by employees with higher extraversion and conscientiousness, likely because these personality factors relate to a person's assertiveness, dutifulness, and outgoing nature. Past experience also influences which EVLN action is applied. Dissatisfied employees are more likely to engage in exit or neglect if they have previously been unsuccessful with voice. Loyalty, as it was intended in the original exit-voice-loyalty model, is another important factor. Specifically, employees are more likely to quit when they have low loyalty to the company, and they are more likely to engage in voice when they have high loyalty.

> It just seems common sense to me that if you start with a happy, well-motivated workforce, you're much more likely to have happy customers.[69]
>
> —Sir Richard Branson, founder of Virgin Group

An employee's response to dissatisfaction also depends on the situation. Employees are less likely to use the exit option when there are few alternative job prospects, for example. Dissatisfied employees are more likely to use voice than the other options when they are aware that other employees are dependent on them and when organizational leaders encourage employees to discuss their concerns.[65]

Job Satisfaction and Performance

Are happy workers more productive workers? Yes, over the past two decades, studies have fairly consistently reported a positive association between job satisfaction and task performance. However, this positive association is somewhat suppressed, for a few reasons.[66] One reason why the satisfaction-performance relationship isn't even stronger is that general attitudes (such as job satisfaction) don't predict specific behaviors such as task performance very well. The EVLN model explains why; lower job performance (a form of neglect) is only one of four possible responses to dissatisfaction. Many dissatisfied employees continue to perform their tasks proficiently but engage in voice or look for another job.

A second reason is that some employees have little control over their performance because their work effort is paced by technology or interdependence with coworkers in the production process. An assembly-line worker, for instance, installs a fixed number of windshields each hour with about the same quality of installation whether they have high or low job satisfaction. A third reason is that job performance might cause job satisfaction, rather than vice versa.[67] Higher performers tend to have higher satisfaction because they receive more rewards and recognition than do low-performing employees. The connection between job satisfaction and performance isn't stronger because many organizations do not reward good performance very well.

Job Satisfaction and Customer Satisfaction

A deeply held belief at Hilton Hotels and Resorts is that great customer service results from positive employee attitudes. Hilton has become one of the best big companies to work for in America and is among the top 25 workplaces in the world. "Our mission is to be the most hospitable company in the world, and you can't do that without great people, and you can't get great people without being a great workplace," says Matt Schuyler, Hilton's chief brand officer.[68]

Research supports Hilton's philosophy. In fact, studies estimate that job satisfaction has a stronger effect on customer service than on overall performance. The effect of job satisfaction on customer service and company profits is detailed in the **service profit chain model**, diagrammed in Exhibit 4.5. This model shows that job satisfaction has a positive effect on customer service, which has a flow-on benefit for stockholder financial returns.[70]

The service profit chain model process begins with workplace practices that increase or decrease job satisfaction. Job satisfaction then influences whether employees stay (employee retention) as well as their motivation and behavior on the job. Retention, motivation, and behavior affect service quality, which influences the customer's satisfaction, perceived value of the service, and tendency to recommend the service to others (referrals). These customer activities influence the company's profitability and growth. The service profit chain model has strong research support. However, the benefits of job satisfaction take time to flow through to the organization's bottom line.

Exhibit 4.5 Service Profit Chain Model

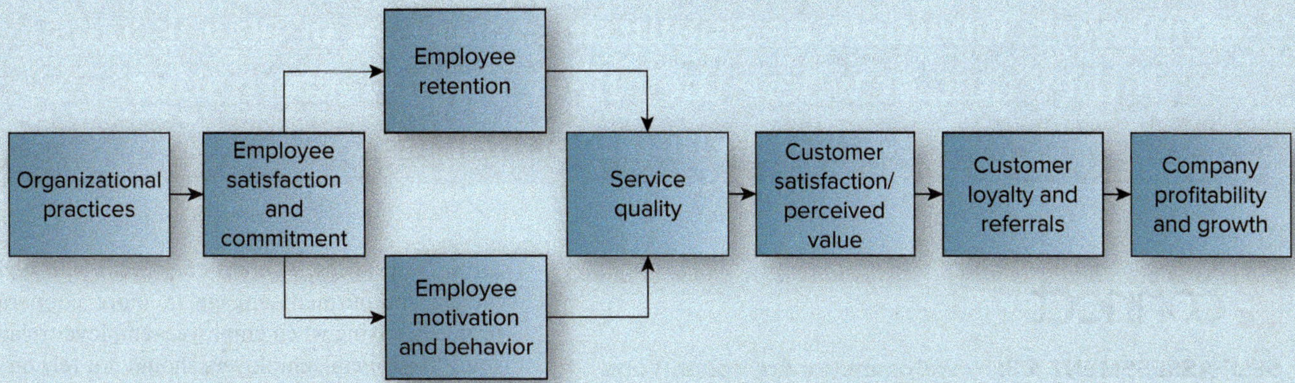

Sources: This model is based on J.I. Heskett, W.E. Sasser, and L.A. Schlesinger, *The Service Profit Chain* (New York: Free Press, 1997); A.J. Rucci, S.P. Kirn, and R.T. Quinn, "The Employee-Customer-Profit Chain at Sears," *Harvard Business Review* 76 (1998): 83–97; S.P. Brown and S.K. Lam, "A Meta-Analysis of Relationships Linking Employee Satisfaction to Customer Responses," *Journal of Retailing* 84 (2008): 243–55.

Service profit chain research provides two key explanations why satisfied employees tend to produce happier and more loyal customers.[71] One explanation is that job satisfaction tends to put employees in a more positive mood, and people in a good mood more naturally and frequently display friendliness and positive emotions. When employees have good feelings, their display of positive emotions "rubs off" on most customers, so customers feel happier and consequently form a positive evaluation of the service experience (i.e., higher service quality). The effect is also mutual–happy customers make employees happier–which can lead to a virtuous cycle of positive emotions in the service experience.

The second explanation is that satisfied employees are less likely to quit their jobs, so they have more work experience (i.e., better knowledge and skills) to serve clients. Lower turnover also enables customers to have the same employees serve them on different occasions, so there is more consistent service. Some evidence indicates that customers build their loyalty to specific employees, not to the organization, so keeping employee turnover low tends to build customer loyalty.

Job Satisfaction and Business Ethics

Along with its significant effect on employee behavior, job satisfaction is an ethical issue that influences the organization's reputation in the community. People spend a large portion of their time working in organizations, and many societies now expect companies to provide work environments that are safe and enjoyable. Indeed, employees in several countries closely monitor ratings of the best companies to work for, an indication that employee satisfaction is a virtue worth considerable goodwill to employers. The importance of this reputation is apparent when an organization has low job satisfaction. The company typically tries to hide this fact, and when morale problems become public, corporate leaders are usually quick to take steps to improve the situation.

LO4-5 Summarize the three types of organizational commitment, and discuss strategies to increase affective commitment.

ORGANIZATIONAL COMMITMENT

Organizational commitment–specifically **affective organizational commitment**–represents the other half (with job satisfaction) of what some experts call "overall job attitude." Affective commitment is the employee's emotional attachment to, involvement in, and identification with an organization. It is a psychological bond whereby an individual chooses to be dedicated to and responsible for the organization. Furthermore, affective commitment is intrinsically motivated because it originates from alignment with the employee's self-concept and values rather than from external forces.[72]

Affective commitment differs from **continuance commitment**, which is a calculative attachment to the organization. Continuance commitment develops in situations where employees would incur significant financial or social costs if they left the organization (e.g., "I hate this place but can't afford to quit!").[73] This happens when quitting forfeits a large deferred financial bonus or risks weakening social bonds with friends at work. Continuance commitment also occurs when people have limited alternative employment opportunities (e.g., "I dislike working here but there are no other jobs available"). In each situation, continuance commitment is motivation to remain with and participate in the organization due to external factors, whereas the motivation of affective commitment originates internally from the person's identity, bond, and psychological attachment to the organization.

> **Continuance commitment develops in situations where employees would incur significant financial or social costs if they quit, or where they have limited alternative employment opportunities.**

connect

SELF-ASSESSMENT 4.3: How Committed Are You to Your School?

Affective and continuance commitment have a third sibling, called *normative commitment*, which refers to a felt obligation or moral duty to the organization.[74] Felt obligation applies the **norm of reciprocity**—a natural human motivation to support, contribute, and otherwise "pay back" the organization because it has invested in and supported the employee (see Chapter 9). The sense of moral duty is the motivation to remain with and contribute to the organization because it is the right thing to do as a member of the organization. Normative commitment receives less attention because it overlaps somewhat with affective commitment and its meaning is somewhat ambiguous.

Consequences of Affective and Continuance Commitment

Affective commitment can be a significant competitive advantage.[75] Employees with a strong psychological bond to the organization are less likely to quit their jobs and be absent from work. They also have higher work motivation and organizational citizenship, as well as somewhat higher job performance. Affective commitment also improves customer satisfaction because long-tenure employees have better knowledge of work practices and because clients like to do business with the same employees. One concern is that employees with very high affective commitment tend to have high conformity, which results in lower creativity. Another problem is that employees with very high commitment are more motivated to engage in illegal activity in defense of the organization. However, most companies suffer from too little rather than too much affective commitment.

In contrast to the benefits of affective commitment, employees with high levels of continuance commitment tend to have *lower* performance and are *less* likely to engage in organizational citizenship behaviors. Furthermore, unionized employees with high continuance commitment are more likely to use formal grievances, whereas employees with high affective commitment engage in more cooperative problem solving when employee–employer relations sour.[76] In general, employers should not rely on continuance commitment to retain staff. Instead, they should focus on winning employees' hearts through affective commitment.

Building Organizational Commitment

There are almost as many ways to build and maintain affective commitment as there are topics in this textbook, but here are the most frequently mentioned strategies in the literature:

- *Justice and support.* Affective commitment is higher in organizations that support organizational justice, which we discuss in the next chapter. Similarly, organizations that support employee well-being tend to cultivate higher levels of loyalty in return.[77]
- *Shared values.* The definition of affective commitment refers to a person's identification with the organization, and that identification is highest when

Organizational comprehension is a necessary prerequisite to affective commitment because it is difficult to identify with or feel loyal to something that you don't know very well.
Mykola Kravchenko/123RF

employees believe their values are congruent with the organization's dominant values. Employees also experience more positive emotions when their personal values are aligned with corporate values and actions, and these positive emotions increase their motivation to stay with the organization.[78]

norm of reciprocity A felt obligation and social expectation of helping or otherwise giving something of value to someone who has already helped or given something of value to you

trust Positive expectations one person has toward another person or group in situations involving risk

stress An adaptive response to a situation that is perceived as challenging or threatening to the person's well-being

- *Trust.* **Trust** refers to positive expectations one person has toward another person in situations involving risk.[79] Trust means putting faith in others. It is also a reciprocal activity: To receive trust, you must demonstrate trust. Employees identify with and feel obliged to work for an organization only when they trust its leaders. This explains why layoffs are one of the greatest blows to affective commitment. By reducing job security, companies reduce the trust employees have in their employer and the employment relationship.[80]
- *Organizational comprehension.* Organizational comprehension refers to how well employees understand the organization, including its strategic direction, social dynamics, and physical layout.[81] This awareness is a necessary prerequisite to affective commitment because it is difficult to identify with or feel loyal to something that you don't know very well. Furthermore, lack of information produces uncertainty, and the resulting stress can distance employees from that source of uncertainty (i.e., the organization). The practical implication here is to ensure that employees develop a reasonably clear and complete mental model of the organization. This occurs by giving staff information and opportunities to keep up to date about organizational events, to interact with coworkers, to discover what goes on in different parts of the organization, and to learn about the organization's history and future plans.[82]
- *Employee involvement.* Employee involvement increases affective commitment by strengthening the employee's psychological ownership and social identity with the organization.[83] Employees have a sense of being part of the organization when they participate in decisions that guide the organization's future (see Chapter 6). Participation also builds loyalty because it demonstrates the company's trust in its employees.

LO4-6 Discuss the dynamics (stressors, stress processes, stress outcomes) of work-related stress, and identify five ways to manage work-related stress.

WORK-RELATED STRESS AND ITS MANAGEMENT

When asked if they often feel stressed by their work, most employees these days will answer with an emphatic Yes! Not only do most people understand the concept; they seem to have plenty of personal experience with it. **Stress** is most often described as an adaptive response to a situation that is perceived as challenging or threatening to the person's well-being.[84] It is a physiological and psychological condition that prepares us to adapt to hostile or noxious environmental conditions. One school of thought suggests that stress is a negative evaluation of the external environment. However, critics of this cognitive appraisal perspective point out that stress is more accurately described as an emotional experience, which may occur before or after a conscious evaluation of the situation.[85]

Whether stress is a complex emotion or a cognitive evaluation of the environment, it has become a pervasive experience in the daily lives of most people. Stress is typically described as a negative experience. This is known as *distress*—the degree of physiological, psychological, and behavioral deviation from healthy functioning. However, a lower level or different form of stress—called *eustress*—is a necessary part of life because it activates and motivates people to achieve goals, change their environments, and succeed in life's challenges.[86] Our focus here is on the causes and management of distress because it has become a chronic problem in organizations.

Stress in the Workplace[87]

41% of 127,000 adults interviewed across 122 countries say they had experienced significant stress the previous day.

24% of a very large survey of Canadian adults (18–64 years) say that most days in their life are quite a bit or extremely stressful.

5% of 1,815 British employees say workplace stress makes them more productive.

47% of 594,974 National Health Service employees in the UK say they felt unwell as a result of work-related stress over the previous year (40% said this in the year before the pandemic began).

84% of 11,922 adults 18–65 years in 15 countries say they are stressed (14% of those 18–24 years old say their stress is unmanageable).

(Photo): Donskarpo/Getty Images

General Adaptation Syndrome

In the 1930s, Hans Selye (often described as the "father" of stress research) first documented the stress

SELF-ASSESSMENT 4.4: How Stressed Are You?

experience, called the **general adaptation syndrome**. Selye determined that people have a fairly consistent and automatic physiological response to stressful situations, which helps them cope with environmental demands.[88]

The general adaptation syndrome consists of the three stages shown in Exhibit 4.6. The *alarm reaction* stage occurs when a threat or challenge activates the physiological stress responses that we described a few paragraphs ago. The individual's energy level and coping effectiveness decrease in response to the initial shock. The second stage, *resistance,* activates various biochemical, psychological, and behavioral mechanisms that give the individual more energy and engage coping mechanisms to overcome or remove the source of stress. People have a limited resistance capacity, and if the source of stress persists, the individual will eventually move into the third stage, *exhaustion*. Most of us are able to remove the source of stress or remove ourselves from that source before becoming too exhausted. However, people who frequently reach exhaustion have an increased risk of long-term physiological and psychological damage.[89]

Consequences of Distress

Stress takes its toll on the human body.[90] Many people experience tension headaches, muscle pain, and related problems mainly due to muscle contractions from the stress response. High stress levels also contribute to cardiovascular disease, including heart attacks and strokes, and may be associated with some forms of cancer. Stress also causes job dissatisfaction, moodiness, depression, and lower organizational commitment. Furthermore, various behavioral outcomes have been linked to high or persistent stress, including lower job performance, poor decision making, and increased workplace accidents and aggressive behavior. Most people react to stress through "fight or flight," so, as a form of flight, increased absenteeism is another outcome of stress.[91]

Stressors: The Causes of Stress

Stressors include any environmental conditions that place a physical or emotional demand on a person.[92] Four of the most common work-related stressors are organizational constraints, interpersonal conflict, work overload, and low task control.[93]

Organizational Constraints Organizational constraints are collectively one of the most pervasive causes of workplace stress.[94] This stressor includes lack of equipment, supplies, budget funding, coworker support, information, and other resources necessary to complete the required work. Most employees experience stress because these constraints interfere with task performance, which indirectly threatens their rewards, status, and job security. Organizational constraints are situational factors, which is one of the four direct predictors of individual behavior and performance (see the MARS model in Chapter 1). It is the only direct influence on individual performance that is beyond the employee's immediate control. This lack of control is a powerful stressor because it threatens the individual's fundamental drive to influence their external environment.

Interpersonal Conflict As we will learn in Chapter 10, dysfunctional conflict can easily flair up and, left unchecked, escalate to a level that produces considerable stress. In organizational settings, most interpersonal conflict is caused by structural sources such as ambiguous rules, different interpersonal beliefs and values, and conflicting goals between employees or departments. However, conflict-induced stress is further amplified when the parties attack each other's personal attributes (intelligence, experience, etc.) rather than focus on the logic and factual foundation of the arguments presented. Also, one form of interpersonal conflict that has become an increasing concern is workplace harassment, including workplace bullying, sexual harassment, and other forms of incivility and mistreatment by coworkers, managers, or customers.[95]

Work Overload Work overload is a common workplace stressor. Employees are under pressure to complete more work with more effort than they can provide within the allotted time.[96]

Exhibit 4.6 General Adaptation Syndrome

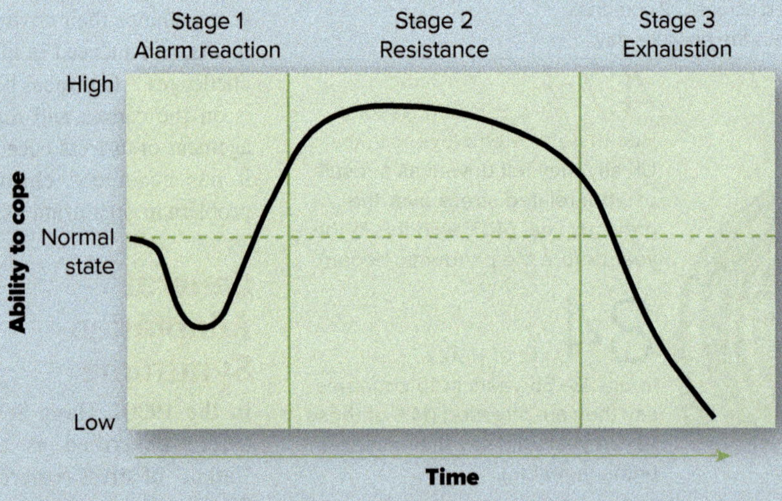

Source: Adapted from H. Selye, *The Stress of Life* (New York: McGraw Hill, 1956).

general adaptation syndrome A model of the stress experience, consisting of three stages: alarm reaction, resistance, and exhaustion

stressors Any environmental conditions that place a physical or emotional demand on a person

Work overload is a common workplace stressor because employees are under pressure to complete more work with more effort than they can provide within the allotted time.
Antonio Guillem/Shutterstock

Technology and globalization contribute to work overload because they tether employees to their job for more hours of the day. People increasingly work with coworkers in distant time zones, and their communication habits of being constantly "on" make it difficult to separate work from personal life. Some employees amplify their work overload by adopting an "ideal worker norm" in which they expect themselves and others to work longer hours.[97]

Low Task Control, High Responsibility Workplace stress is higher when employees lack control over how and when they perform their tasks as well as the pace of work activity. Work is potentially more stressful when it is paced by a machine, it involves monitoring equipment, or the work schedule is controlled by someone else. Low task control is a stressor because employees face high workloads without the ability to adjust the pace of the load to their own energy, attention span, and other resources. Furthermore, the degree to which low task control is a stressor increases with the burden of responsibility the employee must carry.[98] Assembly-line workers have low task control, but they experience fairly low stress if their level of responsibility is also low. In contrast, sports coaches are under immense pressure to win games (high responsibility), yet they have little control over what happens on the playing field (low task control).

Individual Differences in Stress

Employees exposed to the same stressor often experience different degrees of stress. One reason is the employee's physical health. Regular exercise and a healthy lifestyle produce a larger store of energy to cope with stress. A second reason is that people use different strategies to cope with the stressor.[99] Some try to remove the stressor or to minimize its presence. Others seek out support from coworkers and friends or try to reframe the stressor in a more positive light. Some coping strategies work better for specific stressors and some are better across all stressors.[100] Those who tend to rely on a less effective coping mechanism in a particular situation would experience more stress in response to that situation.

Personality is a third reason why people experience different levels of stress when faced with the same stressor.[101] Individuals with low neuroticism (high emotional stability) usually have lower stress levels because, by definition, they are less prone to anxiety, depression, and other negative emotions. Extraverts also tend to experience lower stress than do introverts, likely

Mc Graw Hill connect

SELF-ASSESSMENT 4.5: Are You a Workaholic?

> **Employees have divergent stress responses to the same stressor because of their unique coping strategies, personality traits, and physical health.**

work–life integration The degree that people are effectively engaged in their various work and nonwork roles and have a low degree of role conflict across those life domains

because extraversion includes a degree of positive thinking and extraverts interact with others, which can be an effective coping mechanism in many situations. Those with a positive self-concept—high self-esteem, self-efficacy, and internal locus of control (see Chapter 3)—feel more confident and in control when faced with a stressor. In other words, they tend to have a stronger sense of optimism.[102] Stress also tends to be higher among those who suffer from *workaholism.* Workaholics have an uncontrollable work motivation, constantly think about work, and have low work enjoyment.[103]

Managing Work-Related Stress

Many people deny the existence of their stress until its serious outcomes become apparent. This avoidance strategy amplifies the stress, because the failure to cope with stress becomes another stressor on top of the one that created the stress in the first place. To prevent this vicious cycle, employers and employees need to apply one or more stress management strategies: remove the stressor, withdraw from the stressor, change stress perceptions, control stress consequences, and receive social support.[104]

Remove the Stressor There are many ways to remove the stressor, but some of the more common actions involve assigning employees to jobs that match their skills and preferences, reducing excessive workplace noise, having a complaint system that takes corrective action against harassment, and giving employees more control over the work process. Another important way that companies can remove stressors is through **work–life integration** initiatives (see Chapter 1). For example, personal leave benefits, such as parental leave, temporarily offer employees paid nonwork time to manage special circumstances. Remote work potentially improves work–life integration by reducing or eliminating commuting time and increasing flexibility to perform nonwork obligations (such as picking up the kids from school).[105]

Withdraw from the Stressor Removing the stressor may be the ideal solution, but it isn't feasible in every situation. An alternative strategy is to permanently or temporarily remove employees from the stressor. Permanent withdrawal occurs when employees are transferred to jobs that are more compatible with their abilities and values. Temporarily withdrawing from stressors is the most frequent way that employees manage stress. Vacations and holidays are important opportunities for employees to recover from stress and reenergize for future challenges.[106] Many firms also provide innovative ways for employees to withdraw from stressful work throughout the day such as game rooms, ice-cream cart breaks, nap rooms, and cafeterias that include live music.

Change Stress Perceptions How much stress employees experience depends on how they perceive the stressor.[107] Consequently, another way to manage stress is by coaching employees to improve their self-concept, personal goal setting, and self-reinforcement practices. Job challenges are perceived as less threatening when employees develop these self-views and self-management activities. In addition, research suggests that some forms of humor can improve optimism and create positive emotions by reducing the psychological burden of a stressful situation.[108]

Control Stress Consequences Keeping physically fit and maintaining a healthy lifestyle are effective stress management strategies because they control stress consequences. Good physical fitness reduces the adverse physiological consequences of

OB THEORY TO PRACTICE

Reducing Stress through Forest Bathing/Therapy[109]

"Forest bathing" is one of the many events that technology consulting firm Capco offers its employees in Toronto, Canada, to improve their mental health. Nissan, TDK-Lambda, and other companies in Japan also encourage employees to reduce stress by taking these strolls in the woods.

At Chungbuk University Hospital in South Korea, employees took 20-minute forest walks three times each week. After three weeks, participants reported significantly lower stress and less negative moods. This is consistent with two recent comprehensive reviews, which concluded that spending time in a forest environment significantly reduces stress, depression, anxiety, and negative emotions.

Health care professionals in the United States, Canada, Scotland, and other countries are now formally prescribing nature walks (typically 20-minutes per walk, two hours per week) to help relieve stress and other negative emotions.

StockPhotosArt/Shutterstock

stress by helping employees moderate their breathing and heart rate, muscle tension, and stomach acidity. The key variable here is physical fitness, not exercise. Exercise leads to physical fitness, but research suggests that exercise does not reduce stress symptoms among people who are not yet physically fit.[110] Various forms of meditation reduce anxiety and other symptoms of stress, but their effect on blood pressure and other physiological symptoms is minimal.[111] Some firms educate employees about the benefits of better nutrition and fitness, regular sleep, and other good health habits. Employers also offer *employee assistance programs (EAPs)*—counseling services that help employees resolve financial, marital, or work-related troubles.

Receive Social Support Social support occurs when coworkers, supervisors, family members, friends, and others provide emotional and/or informational support to buffer an individual's stress experience. Social support potentially improves the person's optimism and self-confidence because support makes people feel valued and worthy. Social support also provides information to help the person interpret, comprehend, and possibly remove the stressor. For instance, to reduce a new employee's stress, coworkers could describe ways to handle difficult customers. Seeking social support is called a "tend and befriend" response to stress, and research suggests that women often take this route rather than the "fight-or-flight" response mentioned earlier.[112]

Mc Graw Hill connect

SELF-ASSESSMENT 4.6: How Do You Cope with Stressful Situations?

Study Checklist

Connect® is available for *M: Organizational Behavior*. Additional resources include:

✓ Exercises:

- **Case Analysis:** Apply concepts within the context of a real-world situation.
- **Click and Drag:** Helps make the connection between theory and application through matching, ranking, or grouping activities.
- **Video Case:** See management in action through interactive videos.
- **Self-Assessment:** Designed to promote student self-awareness and reflection, these research-based surveys contain detailed feedback for students.
- **Application-Based Activities:** These highly interactive, application- and analysis-based exercises allow students to take on specific roles to complete management related tasks within a real-world context.

✓ **SmartBook 2.0™**—Smartbook 2.0 is an adaptive learning solution that provides personalized learning to individual student needs, continually adapts to pinpoint knowledge gaps and focuses learning on concepts requiring additional study. It fosters more productive learning, takes the guesswork out of what to study, and helps students better prepare for class.

Notes

1. C. Pash and M. Obeid, "The Benefits Flowing to Agency Staff to Fight Lockdown Fatigue," *AdNews* (Australia), September 15, 2021; A.Z. Liran, "Having Fun In The Hybrid Workplace," LinkedIn, April 24, 2022; J. Frederick, "Forward Together: Incorporating Fun in the Workplace," *Duke Today*, November 14, 2022; O. Arnold, "5 Fast-Growing Chicago Companies Investing In Employee Well-Being," *Built In Chicago*, February 14, 2023. Some fun activities describes at Geotab are described on the firm's Facebook and Instagram pages.
2. Emotions are also cognitive processes. However, we use the narrow definition of *cognition* as a well-used label referring only to reasoning processes. Also, this and other chapters emphasize that emotional and cognitive processes are intertwined. For recent discussion of this in neuroscience, see L. Pessoa, "Understanding Emotion with Brain Networks," *Current Opinion in Behavioral Sciences*, 19 (2018): 19–25.
3. For discussion of emotions in marketing, economics, and sociology, see W. Kalkhoff, S.R. Thye, and J. Pollock, "Developments in Neurosociology," *Sociology Compass* 10 (2016): 242–58; H. Lin and O. Vartanian, "A Neuroeconomic Framework for Creative Cognition," *Perspectives on Psychological Science* 13 (2018): 655–77; W.M. Lim, "Demystifying Neuromarketing," *Journal of Business Research* 91 (2018): 205–20; A. Konovalov and I. Krajbich, "Over a Decade of Neuroeconomics: What Have We Learned?" *Organizational Research Methods* 22 (2019): 148–73.
4. Although definitions of *emotion* vary, the definition stated here seems to be the most widely accepted. See, for example, N.H. Frijda, "Varieties of Affect: Emotions and Episodes, Moods, and Sentiments," in *The Nature of Emotion: Fundamental Questions*, ed. P. Ekman and R.J. Davidson (New York: Oxford University Press,

1994), 59–67; G. Van Kleef, H. van den Berg, and M. Heerdink, "The Persuasive Power of Emotions: Effects of Emotional Expressions on Attitude Formation and Change," *Journal of Applied Psychology* 100 (2015): 1124–42; A. Scarantino, "The Philosophy of Emotions and Its Impact on Affective Science," in *Handbook of Emotions*, ed. L.F. Barrett, M. Lewis, and J.M. Haviland-Jones, 4th ed. (New York: Guilford Press, 2016), 3–47; R. Smith and R.D. Lane, "Unconscious Emotion: A Cognitive Neuroscientific Perspective," *Neuroscience & Biobehavioral Reviews* 69 (2016): 216–38; M. Résibois et al., "The Relation between Rumination and Temporal Features of Emotion Intensity," *Cognition and Emotion* 32 (2018): 259–74; L.F. Barrett and A.B. Satpute, "Historical Pitfalls and New Directions in the Neuroscience of Emotion," *Neuroscience Letters*, 693 (2019): 9–18.

5. R. Reisenzein, M. Studtmann, and G. Horstmann, "Coherence between Emotion and Facial Expression: Evidence from Laboratory Experiments," *Emotion Review* 5, no. 1 (2013): 16–23; M.D. Lieberman, "Boo! The Consciousness Problem in Emotion," *Cognition and Emotion* 33, no. 1 (2019): 24–30.
6. R.B. Zajonc, "Emotions," in *Handbook of Social Psychology*, ed. D.T. Gilbert, S.T. Fiske, and L. Gardner (New York: Oxford University Press, 1998), 591–634; P. Winkielman, "Bob Zajonc and the Unconscious Emotion," *Emotion Review* 2, no. 4 (2010): 353–62; K.R. Scherer and A. Moors, "The Emotion Process: Event Appraisal and Component Differentiation," *Annual Review of Psychology* 70 (2019): 719–45.
7. A.R. Damasio, *The Feeling of What Happens: Body and Emotion in the Making of Consciousness* (New York: Harcourt Brace, 1999), 286; B.Q. Ford and J.J. Gross, "Emotion Regulation: Why Beliefs Matter," *Canadian Psychology* 59 (2018): 1–14; K.C. Berridge, "Evolving Concepts of Emotion and Motivation," *Frontiers in Psychology* 9 (Sept. 7, 2018): 01646.
8. V. van Gogh, T. van Gogh, and I. Stone, *Dear Theo: The Autobiography* (New York: Doubleday, 1937; repr., 1995), 441. This quotation originally appeared in a letter sent by Vincent van Gogh to his brother Théo in 1889.
9. R.J. Larson, E. Diener, and R.E. Lucas, "Emotion: Models, Measures, and Differences," in *Emotions in the Workplace*, ed. R.G. Lord, R.J. Klimoski, and R. Kanfer (San Francisco: Jossey-Bass, 2002), 64–113; L.F. Barrett et al., "The Experience of Emotion," *Annual Review of Psychology* 58, no. 1 (2007): 373–403; M. Yik, J.A. Russell, and J.H. Steiger, "A 12-Point Circumplex Structure of Core Affect," *Emotion* 11, no. 4 (2011): 705–31.
10. R.F. Baumeister, E. Bratslavsky, and C. Finkenauer, "Bad Is Stronger Than Good," *Review of General Psychology* 5, no. 4 (2001): 323–70; A. Vaish, T. Grossmann, and A. Woodward, "Not All Emotions Are Created Equal: The Negativity Bias in Social-Emotional Development," *Psychological Bulletin* 134, no. 3 (2008): 383–403; R.H. Fazio et al., "Positive versus Negative Valence: Asymmetries in Attitude Formation and Generalization as Fundamental Individual Differences," in *Advances in Experimental Social Psychology*, vol. 51, ed. J.M. Olson and M.P. Zanna (Waltham, MA: Academic Press, 2015), 97–140; K. Bebbington et al., "The Sky Is Falling: Evidence of a Negativity Bias in the Social Transmission of Information," *Evolution and Human Behavior* 38, no. 1 (2017): 92–101.
11. A.P. Brief, *Attitudes in and around Organizations* (Thousand Oaks, CA: Sage, 1998); A.H. Eagly and S. Chaiken, "The Advantages of an Inclusive Definition of Attitude," *Social Cognition* 25, no. 5 (2007): 582–602; G. Bohner and N. Dickel, "Attitudes and Attitude Change," *Annual Review of Psychology* 62, no. 1 (2011): 391–417; R.S. Dalal, "Job Attitudes: Cognition and Affect," in *Handbook of Psychology: Industrial and Organizational Psychology*, ed. N.W. Schmidt, S. Highhouse, and I.B. Weiner, 2nd ed., vol. 12 (New York: Wiley, 2013), 341–66.
12. Neuroscience has a slightly more complicated distinction between conscious "feeling a feeling" and nonconscious "feeling." See A.R. Damasio, *The Feeling of What Happens: Body and Emotion in the Making of Consciousness* (New York: Harcourt Brace, 1999); F. Hansen, "Distinguishing between Feelings and Emotions in Understanding Communication Effects," *Journal of Business Research* 58, no. 10 (2005): 1426–36; T. Bosse, C.M. Jonker, and J. Treur, "Formalisation of Damasio's Theory of Emotion, Feeling and Core Consciousness," *Consciousness and Cognition* 17, no. 1 (2008): 94–113.
13. W.A. Cunningham and P.D. Zelazo, "Attitudes and Evaluations: A Social Cognitive Neuroscience Perspective," *TRENDS in Cognitive Sciences* 11, no. 3 (2007): 97–104; M.D. Lieberman, "Social Cognitive Neuroscience: A Review of Core Processes," *Annual Review of Psychology* 58, no. 1 (2007): 259–89; M. Fenton-O'Creevy et al., "Thinking, Feeling and Deciding: The Influence of Emotions on the Decision Making and Performance of Traders," *Journal of Organizational Behavior* 32 (2011): 1044–61. The dual emotion–cognition processes are likely the same as the implicit–explicit attitude processes reported by several scholars, as well as tacit knowledge structures. See W.J. Becker and R. Cropanzano, "Organizational Neuroscience: The Promise and Prospects of an Emerging Discipline," *Journal of Organizational Behavior* 31, no. 7 (2010): 1055–59; D. Kahneman, *Thinking Fast and Slow* (New York: Farrar, Straus and Giroux, 2011).
14. D. Albarracin, M.S. Chan, and D. Jiang, "Attitudes and Attitude Change: Social and Personality Considerations About Specific and General Patterns of Behavior," in *The Oxford Handbook of Personality and Social Psychology*, ed. K. Deaux and M. Snyder, 2nd ed. (New York: Oxford University Press, 2018), 439–64.
15. P. Sheeran and T.L. Webb, "The Intention–Behavior Gap," *Social and Personality Psychology Compass* 10, no. 9 (2016): 503–18.
16. H.M. Weiss and R. Cropanzano, "Affective Events Theory: A Theoretical Discussion of the Structure, Causes and Consequences of Affective Experiences at Work," *Research in Organizational Behavior* 18 (1996): 1–74; A. Bechara et al., "Deciding Advantageously before Knowing the Advantageous Strategy," *Science* 275, no. 5304 (1997): 1293–95; B. Russell and J. Eisenberg, "The Role of Cognition and Attitude in Driving Behavior: Elaborating on Affective Events Theory," in *Experiencing and Managing Emotions in the Workplace*, ed. N.M. Ashkanasy, C.E.J. Hartel, and W.J. Zerbe (Bingley: Emerald Group, 2012), 203–24.
17. J.A. Bargh and M.J. Ferguson, "Beyond Behaviorism: On the Automaticity of Higher Mental Processes," *Psychological Bulletin* 126, no. 6 (2000): 925–45; P. Winkielman and K.C. Berridge, "Unconscious Emotion," *Current Directions in Psychological Science* 13, no. 3 (2004): 120–23; A. Moors, "Automaticity: Componential, Causal, and Mechanistic Explanations," *Annual Review of Psychology* 67, no. 1 (2016): 263–87.
18. A.R. Damasio, *Descartes' Error: Emotion, Reason, and the Human Brain* (New York: Putnam Sons, 1994); P. Ekman, "Basic Emotions," in *Handbook of Cognition and Emotion*, ed. T. Dalgleish and M. Power (San Francisco: Jossey-Bass, 1999), 45–60; A.R. Damasio, *The Feeling of What Happens: Body and Emotion in the Making of Consciousness* (New York: Harcourt Brace and Company, 1999); J.E. LeDoux, "Emotion Circuits in the Brain," *Annual Review of Neuroscience* 23 (2000): 155–84; R. Smith and R.D. Lane, "The Neural Basis of One's Own Conscious and Unconscious Emotional States," *Neuroscience & Biobehavioral Reviews* 57 (2015): 1–29.
19. M.T. Pham, "The Logic of Feeling," *Journal of Consumer Psychology* 14, no. 4 (2004): 360–69; N. Schwarz, "Feelings-as-Information Theory," in *Handbook of Theories of Social Psychology*, ed. P. Van Lange, A. Kruglanski, and E.T. Higgins (London: Sage, 2012), 289–308.

20. We have described likely the most common form of emotion–attitude conflict and ambivalence, but other forms exist. See: A.I. Snyder and Z.L. Tormala, "Valence Asymmetries in Attitude Ambivalence," *Journal of Personality and Social Psychology* 112 (2017): 555–76; I.K. Schneider and N. Schwarz, "Mixed Feelings: The Case of Ambivalence," *Current Opinion in Behavioral Sciences, Mixed Emotions*, 15 (2017): 39–45; N.B. Rothman and S. Melwani, "Feeling Mixed, Ambivalent, and in Flux: The Social Functions of Emotional Complexity for Leaders," *Academy of Management Review* 42 (2017): 259–82.

21. P.C. Nutt, *Why Decisions Fail* (San Francisco, CA: Berrett-Koehler, 2002); S. Finkelstein, *Why Smart Executives Fail* (New York: Viking, 2003); P.C. Nutt, "Search During Decision Making," *European Journal of Operational Research* 160 (2005): 851–76.

22. B. Nordlo, "Why Zoom Video Communications Built a Team Dedicated to Happiness," *Built In Colorado* (blog), July 27, 2018, https://www.builtincolorado.com/2018/07/27/spotlight-working-at-zoom-video-communications-culture; Globe Newswire, "Zoom Is a Glassdoor Employees' Choice Award Winner, Honored as a Top Workplace Again," News Release (San Jose, CA: Zoom Video Communications, December 4, 2018). The quotation was retrieved from an employee comment submitted to Glassdoor on June 24, 2019.

23. M. Kohrman, "10 Ways to Make Your Office More Fun," *Fast Company*, July 23, 2013; J. Ball, "80 Unique & Quirky Corporate Event Ideas," *Friday Funnies* (Sutton Coldfield: Coburg Banks, May 19, 2016), https://www.coburgbanks.co.uk/blog/friday-funnies/corporate-event-ideas/ (accessed June 23, 2017); "39 Insanely Fun Team Building Activities for Work ('Trust Falls' Not Included)," *SnackNation* (blog) (Los Angeles: SnackNation, August 29, 2016), http://www.snacknation.com/blog/team-building-activities-for-work/ (accessed June 23, 2017).

24. J. Mesmer-Magnus, D.J. Glew, and C. Viswesvaran, "A Meta-Analysis of Positive Humor in the Workplace," *Journal of Managerial Psychology* 27, no. 2 (2012): 155–90; C. Robert and S.P. da Motta Veiga, "Conversational Humor and Job Satisfaction at Work: Exploring the Role of Humor Production, Appreciation, and Positive Affect," *Humor* 30, no. 4 (2017): 417–38; J.W. Michel, M.J. Tews, and D.G. Allen, "Fun in the Workplace: A Review and Expanded Theoretical Perspective," *Human Resource Management Review* 29, no. 1 (2019): 98–110.

25. R.W. Levenson et al., "Emotion," in *Handbook of Psychophysiology*, ed. G.G. Berntson, J.T. Cacioppo, and L.G. Tassinary, 4th ed., Cambridge Handbooks in Psychology (Cambridge: Cambridge University Press, 2016), 444–64; T.T.A. Höfling et al., "Read My Face: Automatic Facial Coding Versus Psychophysiological Indicators of Emotional Valence and Arousal," *Frontiers in Psychology* 11 (2020): 01388.

26. L. Festinger, *A Theory of Cognitive Dissonance* (Evanston, IL: Row, Peterson, 1957); J. Cooper, *Cognitive Dissonance: Fifty Years of a Classic Theory* (London: Sage, 2007); J. Hagège et al., "Suggestion of Self-(in)Coherence Modulates Cognitive Dissonance," *PLoS ONE* 13, no. 8 (August 30, 2018): e0202204, https://doi.org/10.1371/journal.pone.0202204.

27. This example focuses on cognitive dissonance due to counter-attitudinal behaviors. Two lesser known causes are free choice and effort/behavior commitment. See: A.S. Hinojosa et al., "A Review of Cognitive Dissonance Theory in Management Research: Opportunities for Further Development," *Journal of Management* 43, no. 1 (2017): 170–99.

28. G.R. Salancik, "Commitment and the Control of Organizational Behavior and Belief," in *New Directions in Organizational Behavior*, ed. B.M. Staw and G.R. Salancik (Chicago: St. Clair, 1977), 1–54; A. McGrath, "Dealing with Dissonance: A Review of Cognitive Dissonance Reduction," *Social and Personality Psychology Compass* 11, no. 12 (2017): e12362.

29. T.W.H. Ng and K.L. Sorensen, "Dispositional Affectivity and Work-Related Outcomes: A Meta-Analysis," *Journal of Applied Social Psychology* 39, no. 6 (2009): 1255–87; S. Nelis et al., "Trait Affectivity and Response Styles to Positive Affect: Negative Affectivity Relates to Dampening and Positive Affectivity Relates to Enhancing," *Personality and Individual Differences* 96 (2016): 148–54.

30. J. Schaubroeck, D.C. Ganster, and B. Kemmerer, "Does Trait Affect Promote Job Attitude Stability?" *Journal of Organizational Behavior* 17 (1996): 191–96; C. Dormann and D. Zapf, "Job Satisfaction: A Meta-Analysis of Stabilities," *Journal of Organizational Behavior* 22 (2001): 483–504; A.C. Keller and N.K. Semmer, "Changes in Situational and Dispositional Factors as Predictors of Job Satisfaction," *Journal of Vocational Behavior* 83, no. 1 (2013): 88–98.

31. A.S. Wharton, "The Sociology of Emotional Labor," *Annual Review of Sociology* 35 (2009): 147–65; H. Wang, N.C. Hall, and J.L. Taxer, "Antecedents and Consequences of Teachers' Emotional Labor: A Systematic Review and Meta-Analytic Investigation," *Educational Psychology Review* 31, no. 3 (2019): 663–98; A.A. Grandey and G.M. Sayre, "Emotional Labor: Regulating Emotions for a Wage," *Current Directions in Psychological Science* 28 (2019): 131–37.

32. J.A. Morris and D.C. Feldman, "The Dimensions, Antecedents, and Consequences of Emotional Labor," *Academy of Management Review* 21 (1996): 986–1010; J. Li, B.F. Canziani, and C. Barbieri, "Emotional Labor in Hospitality: Positive Affective Displays in Service Encounters," *Tourism and Hospitality Research* 18, no. 2 (2018): 242–53.

33. A.A. Grandey and R.C. Melloy, "The State of the Heart: Emotional Labor as Emotion Regulation Reviewed and Revised," *Journal of Occupational Health Psychology* 22 (2017): 407–22; H. Wang, N.C. Hall, and J.L. Taxer, "Antecedents and Consequences of Teachers' Emotional Labor: A Systematic Review and Meta-Analytic Investigation," *Educational Psychology Review* 31 (2019): 663–98.

34. D. Matsumoto, S.H. Yoo, and J. Fontaine, "Mapping Expressive Differences around the World," *Journal of Cross-Cultural Psychology* 39, no. 1 (2008): 55–74; B.Q. Ford and I.B. Mauss, "Culture and Emotion Regulation," *Current Opinion in Psychology* 3 (2015): 1–5; B. Mesquita, M. Boiger, and J. De Leersnyder, "Doing Emotions: The Role of Culture in Everyday Emotions," *European Review of Social Psychology* 28, no. 1 (2017): 95–133; D. Matsumoto and H.C. Hwang, "Culture and Emotion: Integrating Biological Universality with Cultural Specificity," in *The Handbook of Culture and Psychology*, 2nd ed. (New York: Oxford University Press, 2019), 361–98.

35. F. Trompenaars and C. Hampden-Turner, *Riding the Waves of Culture*, 2nd ed. (New York: McGraw Hill, 1998), Chap. 6. This major survey is two decades old, but recent studies report similar emotional display rules in the cultures reported by Trompenaars and Hampden-Turner. For example, see: Ю. Менджерицкая, М. Ханзен, and Х. Хорц, "Правила выражения эмоций преподавателями российских и немецких университетов (The Rules of Emotional Display in Lecturers of Russian and German Universities)," *Российский психологический журнал* 12 (2015): 54–77; H.C. Hwang et al., "Self-Reported Expression and Experience of Triumph across Four Countries," *Motivation and Emotion* 40 (2016): 731–39.

36. D.P. Bhave and T.M. Glomb, "The Role of Occupational Emotional Labor Requirements on the Surface Acting–Job Satisfaction Relationship," *Journal of Management* 42, no. 3 (2016): 722–41; T. Huyghebaert et al., "Investigating the Longitudinal Effects of Surface Acting on Managers' Functioning through Psychological Needs," *Journal of Occupational Health Psychology* 23, no. 2 (2018): 207–22; D. Zapf et al., "Emotion Work: A Work Psychology Perspective," *Annual Review of Organizational Psychology and Organizational Behavior* 8 (2021): 139–72.

37. A.A. Grandey and R.C. Melloy, "The State of the Heart: Emotional Labor as Emotion Regulation Reviewed and Revised," *Journal of Occupational Health Psychology* 22 (2017): 407–22. However, recent evidence suggests that deep acting can also be stressful because it requires cognitive effort. Also, faking negative emotions may be less stressful than faking positive emotions. Another recent study concluded that both surface and deep acting are effortful activities, so both produce emotional exhaustion. See F. Cheung, V.M.C. Lun, and M.W.-L. Cheung, "Emotional Labor and Occupational Well-Being: Latent Profile Transition Analysis Approach," *Frontiers in Psychology* 9 (July 3, 2018): 01084; A.C. Lennard, B.A. Scott, and R.E. Johnson, "Turning Frowns (and Smiles) Upside Down: A Multilevel Examination of Surface Acting Positive and Negative Emotions on Well-Being," *Journal of Applied Psychology* 104 (2019): 1164–80.

38. S. Côté, I. Hideg, and G.A. van Kleef, "The Consequences of Faking Anger in Negotiations," *Journal of Experimental Social Psychology* 49 (2013): 453–63; Y. Zhan, M. Wang, and J. Shi, "Interpersonal Process of Emotional Labor: The Role of Negative and Positive Customer Treatment," *Personnel Psychology* 69 (2016): 525–57; K. Picard, M. Cossette, and D. Morin, "Service with a Smile: A Source of Emotional Exhaustion or Performance Incentive in Call-Centre Employees," *Canadian Journal of Administrative Sciences* 35 (2018): 214–27.

39. J.D. Kammeyer-Mueller et al., "A Meta-Analytic Structural Model of Dispositonal Affectivity and Emotional Labor," *Personnel Psychology* 66 (2013): 47–90; R.H. Humphrey, B.E. Ashforth, and J.M. Diefendorff, "The Bright Side of Emotional Labor," *Journal of Organizational Behavior* 36 (2015): 749–69. Deep acting is considered an adaptation of method acting used by professional actors.

40. J.J. Gross, "Emotion Regulation: Current Status and Future Prospects," *Psychological Inquiry* 26 (2015): 1–26; J.M. Diefendorff et al., "Emotion Regulation in the Context of Customer Mistreatment and Felt Affect: An Event-Based Profile Approach," *Journal of Applied Psychology* 104 (2019): 965–83; J. Yih et al., "Better Together: A Unified Perspective on Appraisal and Emotion Regulation," *Cognition and Emotion* 33 (2019): 41–47.

41. Y. Kivity and J.D. Huppert, "Emotion Regulation in Social Anxiety: A Systematic Investigation and Meta-Analysis Using Self-Report, Subjective, and Event-Related Potentials Measures," *Cognition and Emotion* 33 (2019): 213–30.

42. R. Brockman et al., "Emotion Regulation Strategies in Daily Life: Mindfulness, Cognitive Reappraisal and Emotion Suppression," *Cognitive Behaviour Therapy* 46, no. 2 (2017): 91–113.

43. This model is an ability-based adaptation of the original mixed model by Goleman et al. Most recent models and measures of emotional intelligence have also adopted a similar four-quadrant model. These studies have adopted a "trait" approach to EI measurement, which might be more accurately described as a self-perceived EI ability approach. See D. Goleman, R. Boyatzis, and A. McKee, *Primal Leadership* (Boston: Harvard Business School Press, 2002), Chap. 3; R.P. Tett and K.E. Fox, "Confirmatory Factor Structure of Trait Emotional Intelligence in Student and Worker Samples," *Personality and Individual Differences* 41 (2006): 1155–68; D.L. Joseph and D.A. Newman, "Emotional Intelligence: An Integrative Meta-Analysis and Cascading Model," *Journal of Applied Psychology* 95 (2010): 54–78; X. Wei, Y. Liu, and N. Allen, "Measuring Team Emotional Intelligence: A Multimethod Comparison," *Group Dynamics: Theory, Research, & Practice* 20 (2016): 34–50; K.A. Pekaar et al., "Self- and Other-Focused Emotional Intelligence: Development and Validation of the Rotterdam Emotional Intelligence Scale (REIS)," *Personality and Individual Differences* 120 (2018): 222–33.

44. H.A. Elfenbein and N. Ambady, "Predicting Workplace Outcomes from the Ability to Eavesdrop on Feelings," *Journal of Applied Psychology* 87 (2002): 963–71; T. Quarto et al., "Association between Ability Emotional Intelligence and Left Insula during Social Judgment of Facial Emotions," *PLoS ONE* 11, no. 2 (2016): e0148621.

45. For neurological evidence that people with higher EI have higher sensitivity to others' emotions, see W.D.S. Killgore et al., "Emotional Intelligence Correlates with Functional Responses to Dynamic Changes in Facial Trustworthiness," *Social Neuroscience* 8, (2013): 334–46.

46. The hierarchical nature of the four EI dimensions is discussed by Goleman, but it is more explicit in the Salovey and Mayer model. See D.R. Caruso and P. Salovey, *The Emotionally Intelligent Manager* (San Francisco: Jossey-Bass, 2004). Aspects of this hierarchy are also incorporated in recent studies. For example, see: K.A. Pekaar et al., "Managing Own and Others' Emotions: A Weekly Diary Study on the Enactment of Emotional Intelligence," *Journal of Vocational Behavior* 109 (2018): 137–51.

47. S. Côté, "Emotional Intelligence in Organizations," *Annual Review of Organizational Psychology and Organizational Behavior* 1 (2014): 459–88; M. Parke, M.-G. Seo, and E. Sherf, "Regulating and Facilitating: The Role of Emotional Intelligence in Maintaining and Using Positive Affect for Creativity," *Journal of Applied Psychology* 100 (2015): 917–34; D. Delpechitre and L. Beeler, "Faking It: Salesperson Emotional Intelligence's Influence on Emotional Labor Strategies and Customer Outcomes," *Journal of Business & Industrial Marketing* 33 (2017): 53–71; C. Miao, R.H. Humphrey, and S. Qian, "Emotional Intelligence and Authentic Leadership: A Meta-Analysis," *Leadership & Organization Development Journal* 39 (2018): 679–90.

48. "Why You Need Emotional Intelligence at Work," News Release (Toronto: OfficeTeam, February 22, 2017); "Emotional Intelligence Undervalued by One in Four Firms," News Release (London: Robert Half, August 16, 2018); "Survey Shows Lack of Emphasis Put on EQ during Hiring Process for One in Five Australian Companies," News Release (Sydney: Robert Half, March 12, 2019); C. Crummeneri et al., "Emotional Intelligence–The Essential Skillset for the Age of AI" (Paris: Capgemini Research Institute, November 2019).

49. D. Joseph et al., "Why Does Self-Reported Emotional Intelligence Predict Job Performance? A Meta-Analytic Investigation of Mixed EI," *Journal of Applied Psychology* 100 (2015): 298–342; P. Checa and P. Fernández-Berrocal, "Cognitive Control and Emotional Intelligence: Effect of the Emotional Content of the Task. Brief Reports," *Frontiers in Psychology* 10 (2019): 0195.

50. S. Hodzic et al., "How Efficient Are Emotional Intelligence Trainings: A Meta-Analysis," *Emotion Review* 10 (2018): 138–48; I. Kotsou et al., "Improving Emotional Intelligence: A Systematic Review of Existing Work and Future Challenges," *Emotion Review* 11, no. 2 (2019): 151–65.

51. E. Richter, "Police from around Ohio Train in Middletown on Handling Emotions, Racial Intelligence," *Journal-News (Butler County, Ohio)*, July 22, 2020; M. Gabrilska, "Lunenburg, Sudbury and Wellesley Police Take Part in Empathy Training Program," News Release (Boston: Massachusetts Municipal Association, August 9, 2021); M. Kuhlman, "Ohio State Legislators Eye Emotional-Intelligence Training for Police," *Cleveland Scene*, September 15, 2021; O. Magny and N. Todak, "Emotional Intelligence in Policing: A State-of-the-Art Review," *Policing: An International Journal* 44, no. 6 (2021): 957-69.

52. P. Risan, P.-E. Binder, and R.J. Milne, "Emotional Intelligence in Police Interviews—Approach, Training and the Usefulness of the Concept," *Journal of Forensic Psychology Practice* 16, no. 5 (2016): 410-24; "Railways Plans to Improve Senior Leaders' EQ," *Mint (India)*, November 16, 2018; "To Improve Service, Railways to Give Emotional Intelligence Training to Its Officers," *India Today*, December 17, 2018; D.W. Brin, "The 4 Tiers of Value Advisors Provide to Clients," *ThinkAdvisor* (blog), October 25, 2022.

53. D.A. Harrison, D.A. Newman, and P.L. Roth, "How Important Are Job Attitudes? Meta-Analytic Comparisons of Integrative Behavioral Outcomes and Time Sequences," *Academy of Management Journal* 49, no. 2 (2006): 305-25; H. Le et al., "The Problem of Empirical Redundancy of Constructs in Organizational Research: An Empirical Investigation," *Organizational Behavior and Human Decision Processes* 112, no. 2 (2010): 112-25; M. Credé, "Attitudes: Satisfaction, Commitment and Involvement," in *The SAGE Handbook of Industrial, Work & Organizational Psychology (Organizational Psychology)*, vol. 2, ed. D.S. Ones et al., 2nd ed. (London: SAGE, 2018), 3-24; H.M. Woznyj et al., "Job Attitudes: A Meta-Analytic Review and an Agenda for Future Research," *Journal of Organizational Behavior* 43, no. 5 (2022): 946-64.

54. E.A. Locke, "The Nature and Causes of Job Satisfaction," in *Handbook of Industrial and Organizational Psychology*, ed. M. Dunnette (Chicago: Rand McNally, 1976), 1297-350; H.M. Weiss, "Deconstructing Job Satisfaction: Separating Evaluations, Beliefs and Affective Experiences," *Human Resource Management Review*, no. 12 (2002): 173-94; M. Credé, "Attitudes: Satisfaction, Commitment and Involvement," in *The SAGE Handbook of Industrial, Work & Organizational Psychology (Organizational Psychology)*, vol. 2, ed. D.S. Ones et al., 2nd ed. (London: SAGE, 2018), 3-24. Some definitions still include emotion as an element of job satisfaction, whereas the definition presented in this book views emotion as a cause of job satisfaction. Also, this definition views job satisfaction as a "collection of attitudes," not several "facets" of job satisfaction.

55. For example, see Randstad's work mobility index across countries. "Randstad Workmonitor Q4 2019" (Amsterdam: Randstad Holding NV, December 2019).

56. "Randstad Workmonitor Q4 2019" (Amsterdam: Randstad Holding NV, December 2019). Survey data were collected from 34 countries with a minimum of 400 interviews per country of adults working 24 hours or more per week as employees. Respondents were asked, "How satisfied are you in general about working with your current employer?" This exhibit shows results from selected countries across the full range of results.

57. The problems with measuring attitudes and values across cultures are discussed in L. Saari and T.A. Judge, "Employee Attitudes and Job Satisfaction," *Human Resource Management* 43, no. 4 (2004): 395-407; A.K. Uskul et al., "How Successful You Have Been in Life Depends on the Response Scale Used: The Role of Cultural Mindsets in Pragmatic Inferences Drawn from Question Format," *Social Cognition* 31, no. 2 (2013): 222-36.

58. For a review of the various job satisfaction outcome theories, see R.S. Dalal, "Job Attitudes: Cognition and Affect," in *Handbook of Psychology, Second Edition*, ed. I.B. Weiner (New York: John Wiley & Sons, 2013), 341-66.

59. D. Farrell, "Exit, Voice, Loyalty, and Neglect as Responses to Job Dissatisfaction: A Multidimensional Scaling Study," *Academy of Management Journal* 26, no. 4 (1983): 596-607; M.J. Withey and W.H. Cooper, "Predicting Exit, Voice, Loyalty, and Neglect," *Administrative Science Quarterly*, no. 34 (1989): 521-39; A.B. Whitford and S.-Y. Lee, "Exit, Voice, and Loyalty with Multiple Exit Options: Evidence from the US Federal Workforce," *Journal of Public Administration Research and Theory* 25, no. 2 (2015): 373-98. For a critique and explanation of historical errors in the EVLN model, see S.L. McShane, "Reconstructing the Meaning and Dimensionality of Voice in the Exit-Voice-Loyalty-Neglect Model" (paper presented at the Voice and Loyalty Symposium, Annual Conference of the Administrative Sciences Association of Canada, Organizational Behaviour Division, Halifax, 2008).

60. K. Morrell, J. Loan-Clarke, and A. Wilkinson, "The Role of Shocks in Employee Turnover," *British Journal of Management* 15 (2004): 335-49; M. Zhang, D.D. Fried, and R.W. Griffeth, "A Review of Job Embeddedness: Conceptual, Measurement Issues, and Directions for Future Research," *Human Resource Management Review* 22 (2012): 220-31; P.W. Hom et al., "One Hundred Years of Employee Turnover Theory and Research," *Journal of Applied Psychology* 102 (2017): 530-45; A.L. Rubenstein et al., "Surveying the Forest: A Meta-Analysis, Moderator Investigation, and Future-Oriented Discussion of the Antecedents of Voluntary Employee Turnover," *Personnel Psychology* 71 (2018): 23-65.

61. M.R. Bashshur and B. Oc, "When Voice Matters: A Multilevel Review of the Impact of Voice in Organizations," *Journal of Management* 41, no. 5 (2015): 1530-54; P.K. Mowbray, A. Wilkinson, and H.H.M. Tse, "An Integrative Review of Employee Voice: Identifying a Common Conceptualization and Research Agenda," *International Journal of Management Reviews* 17, no. 3 (2015): 382-400. One recent EVLN study concluded that the EVLN model should include multiple types of voice (e.g., neutral versus aggressive). See: A. Sabino, F. Nogueira, and F. Cesário, "An Extension to the EVLN Model: The Role of Employees' Silence," *Management Research: Journal of the Iberoamerican Academy of Management* 17, no. 3 (2019): 266-82.

62. D. Farrell, "Exit, Voice, Loyalty, and Neglect as Responses to Job Dissatisfaction: A Multidimensional Scaling Study," *Academy of Management Journal* 26, no. 4 (1983): 596-607; C.E. Rusbult et al., "Impact of Exchange Variables on Exit, Voice, Loyalty, and Neglect: An Integrative Model of Responses to Declining Job Satisfaction," *Academy of Management Journal* 31, no. 3 (1988): 599-627; M.N. Akhtar, M. Bal, and L. Long, "Exit, Voice, Loyalty, and Neglect Reactions to Frequency of Change, and Impact of Change: A Sensemaking Perspective through the Lens of Psychological Contract," *Employee Relations* 38, no. 4 (2016): 536-62; J. Lee and A.L. Varon, "Employee Exit, Voice, Loyalty, and Neglect in Response to Dissatisfying Organizational Situations: It Depends on Supervisory Relationship Quality," *International Journal of Business Communication* 57, no. 1 (2020): 30-51.

63. A.O. Hirschman, *Exit, Voice, and Loyalty: Responses to Decline in Firms, Organizations, and States* (Cambridge, MA: Harvard University Press, 1970); P. John, "Finding Exits and Voices: Albert Hirschman's Contribution to the Study of Public Services," *International Public Management Journal* 20, no. 3 (2017): 512-29. Hirschman does mention the "loyalist" view, but even that very brief passage on one page refers to a continuum from passively waiting to active voice ("Many of these 'loyalists' will actively participate in actions designed to change A's policies and practices, but some may simply refuse to exit and suffer in silence, confident that things will soon get better," p. 38). Almost all of Hirschman's discussion about loyalty (including an entire chapter on loyalty, Chap. 7) takes the view that loyalty is a moderator variable for the exit versus voice alternatives.

64. M.J. Withey and I.R. Gellatly, "Situational and Dispositional Determinants of Exit, Voice, Loyalty and Neglect," *Proceedings of the Administrative Sciences Association of Canada, Organizational Behaviour Division*, 1998; R.D. Zimmerman et al., "Who Withdraws? Psychological Individual Differences and Employee Withdrawal Behaviors," *Journal of Applied Psychology* 101 (2016): 498–519; É. Lapointe and C. Vandenberghe, "Examination of the Relationships between Servant Leadership, Organizational Commitment, and Voice and Antisocial Behaviors," *Journal of Business Ethics* 148, (2018): 99–115; M. Zare and C. Flinchbaugh, "Voice, Creativity, and Big Five Personality Traits: A Meta-Analysis," *Human Performance* 32 (2019): 30–51.

65. V.V. Venkataramani and S. Tangirala, "When and Why Do Central Employees Speak Up? An Examination of Mediating and Moderating Variables," *Journal of Applied Psychology* 95 (2010): 582–91; M. Weiss et al., "We Can Do It! Inclusive Leader Language Promotes Voice Behavior in Multi-Professional Teams," *The Leadership Quarterly* 29 (2018): 389–402; I. Hussain et al., "The Voice Bystander Effect: How Information Redundancy Inhibits Employee Voice," *Academy of Management Journal* 62 (2019): 828–49.

66. D.J. Schleicher, J.D. Watt, and G.J. Greguras, "Reexamining the Job Satisfaction-Performance Relationship: The Complexity of Attitudes," *Journal of Applied Psychology* 89 (2004): 165–77; D.A. Harrison, D.A. Newman, and P.L. Roth, "How Important Are Job Attitudes? Meta-Analytic Comparisons of Integrative Behavioral Outcomes and Time Sequences," *Academy of Management Journal* 49 (2006): 305–25; N.A. Bowling et al., "Situational Strength as a Moderator of the Relationship Between Job Satisfaction and Job Performance: A Meta-Analytic Examination," *Journal of Business and Psychology* 30 (2015): 89–104; T.A. Judge et al., "Job Attitudes, Job Satisfaction, and Job Affect: A Century of Continuity and of Change," *Journal of Applied Psychology* 102 (2017): 356–74; P. Warr and K. Nielsen, "Wellbeing and Work Performance," in *Handbook of Well-Being,* ed. E. Diener, S. Oishi, and L. Tay (Salt Lake City, UT: DEF Publishers, 2018); J. Peiró et al., "The Happy-Productive Worker Model and Beyond: Patterns of Wellbeing and Performance at Work," *International Journal of Environmental Research and Public Health* 16 (2019): 479.

67. However, panel studies suggest that satisfaction has a stronger effect on performance than the other way around. For a summary, see C.D. Fisher, "Happiness at Work," *International Journal of Management Reviews* 12, no. 4 (2010): 384–412.

68. O. Staley, "Hilton Hotels' Newest Upgrades Are Strictly for Staff," *Quartz at Work*, April 2, 2018; "Hilton Named #1 Best Big Company to Work For, #3 Best Company to Work For in the U.S.," Press Release (Hilton Hotels & Resorts, April 12, 2021); "Hilton Ranked #3 Workplace in the World," Press Release (Hilton Hotels & Resorts, October 19, 2021).

69. "The Greatest Briton in Management and Leadership," *Personnel Today* (2003): 20.

70. J.I. Heskett, W.E. Sasser, and L.A. Schlesinger, *The Service Profit Chain* (New York: Free Press, 1997); Y. Hong et al., "Missing Link in the Service Profit Chain: A Meta-Analytic Review of the Antecedents, Consequences, and Moderators of Service Climate," *Journal of Applied Psychology* 98, no. 2 (2013): 237–67; D. Solnet, R. Ford, and C. Moyle, "What Matters Most in the Service-Profit Chain? An Empirical Test in a Restaurant Company," *International Journal of Contemporary Hospitality Management* 30, no. 1 (2018): 260–85; J. Hogreve, A. Iseke, and K. Derfuss, "The Service-Profit Chain: Reflections, Revisions, and Reimaginations," *Journal of Service Research* 25, no. 3 (2022): 460–77.

71. Z. Wang et al., "Effects of Employees' Positive Affective Displays on Customer Loyalty Intentions: An Emotions-as-Social-Information Perspective," *Academy of Management Journal* 60, no. 1 (2017): 109–29; H. Weijun et al., "Study of E-Smile Service Influence on Customers' Satisfaction in Social Business Context," *The Journal of Supercomputing* 76, no. 5 (2020): 3673–88; J.H. Son, J.H. Kim, and G.J. Kim, "Does Employee Satisfaction Influence Customer Satisfaction? Assessing Coffee Shops through the Service Profit Chain Model," *International Journal of Hospitality Management* 94 (2021): 102866.

72. R.T. Mowday, L.W. Porter, and R.M. Steers, *Employee Organization Linkages: The Psychology of Commitment, Absenteeism, and Turnover* (New York: Academic Press, 1982); J.P. Meyer, "Organizational Commitment," *International Review of Industrial and Organizational Psychology* 12 (1997): 175–228. For a somewhat different view of affective commitment, see: H.J. Klein and H.M. Park, "Commitment as a Unidimensional Construct," in *Handbook of Employee Commitment*, ed. J.P. Meyer (Cheltenham: Edward Elgar, 2016), 15–27.

73. M. Taing et al., "The Multidimensional Nature of Continuance Commitment: Commitment Owing to Economic Exchanges versus Lack of Employment Alternatives," *Journal of Business and Psychology* 26 (2011): 269–84; C. Vandenberghe and A. Panaccio, "Perceived Sacrifice and Few Alternatives Commitments: The Motivational Underpinnings of Continuance Commitment's Subdimensions," *Journal of Vocational Behavior* 81 (2012): 59–72; S. Jaros and R.A. Culpepper, "An Analysis of Meyer and Allen's Continuance Commitment Construct," *Journal of Management & Organization* 20 (2014): 79–99.

74. J.P. Meyer and N.M. Parfyonova, "Normative Commitment in the Workplace: A Theoretical Analysis and Re-Conceptualization," *Human Resource Management Review* 20 (2010): 283–94; S. Jaros, "A Critique of Normative Commitment in Management Research," *Management Research Review* 40 (2017): 517–37.

75. J.P. Meyer et al., "Affective, Continuance, and Normative Commitment to the Organization: A Meta-Analysis of Antecedents, Correlates, and Consequences," *Journal of Vocational Behavior* 61 (2002): 20–52; M. Riketta, "Attitudinal Organizational Commitment and Job Performance: A Meta-Analysis," *Journal of Organizational Behavior* 23 (2002): 257–66; J.C. Wombacher and J. Felfe, "Dual Commitment in the Organization: Effects of the Interplay of Team and Organizational Commitment on Employee Citizenship Behavior, Efficacy Beliefs, and Turnover Intentions," *Journal of Vocational Behavior* 102 (2017): 1–14; D. Charbonneau and V.M. Wood, "Antecedents and Outcomes of Unit Cohesion and Affective Commitment to the Army," *Military Psychology* 30, no. 1 (2018): 43–53; Q. Wang, Q.(D.) Weng, and Y. Jiang, "When Does Affective Organizational Commitment Lead to Job Performance?: Integration of Resource Perspective," *Journal of Career Development* 47, no. 4 (2020): 380–93.

76. J.P. Meyer et al., "Organizational Commitment and Job Performance: It's the Nature of the Commitment That Counts," *Journal of Applied Psychology* 74 (1989): 152–56; H. Gill et al., "Affective and Continuance Commitment and Their Relations with Deviant Workplace Behaviors in Korea," *Asia Pacific Journal of Management* 28 (2011): 595–607. The negative effect on performance might depend on the type of continuance commitment. See M. Taing et al., "The Multidimensional Nature of Continuance Commitment: Commitment Owing to Economic Exchanges versus Lack of Employment Alternatives," *Journal of Business and Psychology* 26 (2011): 269–84.

77. K.Y. Kim, R. Eisenberger, and K. Baik, "Perceived Organizational Support and Affective Organizational Commitment: Moderating Influence of Perceived Organizational Competence," *Journal of Organizational Behavior* 37 (2016): 558–83; J.N. Kurtessis et al., "Perceived Organizational Support: A Meta-Analytic

Evaluation of Organizational Support Theory," *Journal of Management* 43 (2017): 1854–84; D. Charbonneau and V.M. Wood, "Antecedents and Outcomes of Unit Cohesion and Affective Commitment to the Army," *Military Psychology* 30, no. 1 (2018): 43–53.

78. A.L. Kristof-Brown, R.D. Zimmerman, and E.C. Johnson, "Consequences of Individuals' Fit at Work: A Meta-Analysis of Person-Job, Person-Organization, Person-Group, and Person-Supervisor Fit," *Personnel Psychology* 58 (2005): 281–342; M.E. Bergman et al., "An Event-Based Perspective on the Development of Commitment," *Human Resource Management Review* 23 (2013): 148–60; O.A.U. Byza et al., "When Leaders and Followers Match: The Impact of Objective Value Congruence, Value Extremity, and Empowerment on Employee Commitment and Job Satisfaction," *Journal of Business Ethics* 158 (2019): 1097–112.

79. D.M. Rousseau et al., "Not So Different after All: A Cross-Discipline View of Trust," *Academy of Management Review* 23 (1998): 393–404; D. Balliet and P.A.M. Van Lange, "Trust, Conflict, and Cooperation: A Meta-Analysis," *Psychological Bulletin* 139, no. 5 (2013): 1090–112; P.C. Bauer, "Clearing the Jungle: Conceptualising Trust and Trustworthiness," in *Trust Matters: Cross-Disciplinary Essays*, ed. R.B. de Freitas and S.L. Iacono (Oxford: Hart Publishing, 2021), 17–34.

80. D.K. Datta et al., "Causes and Effects of Employee Downsizing: A Review and Synthesis," *Journal of Management* 36, no. 1 (2010): 281–348; R. van Dick, F. Drzensky, and M. Heinz, "Goodbye or Identify: Detrimental Effects of Downsizing on Identification and Survivor Performance," *Frontiers in Psychology* 7 (2016): 00771.

81. C. Leighton and S.L. McShane, "Being 'in the Know': Introducing Organisational Comprehension and Its Nomological Net" (paper presented at the ANZAM Annual Conference, Brisbane, Australia, August 8, 2016). For similar concepts on information acquisition, see: P. Bordia et al., "Uncertainty during Organizational Change: Types, Consequences, and Management Strategies," *Journal of Business and Psychology* 18, no. 4 (2004): 507–32; H.D. Cooper-Thomas and N. Anderson, "Organizational Socialization: A Field Study into Socialization Success and Rate," *International Journal of Selection and Assessment* 13, no. 2 (2005): 116–28; T.N. Bauer, "Newcomer Adjustment during Organizational Socialization: A Meta-Analytic Review of Antecedents, Outcomes, and Methods," *Journal of Applied Psychology* 92, no. 3 (2007): 707–21; R. Bommaraju et al., "The Impact of Mergers and Acquisitions on the Sales Force," *Journal of Marketing Research* 55, no. 2 (2018): 254–64.

82. T.S. Heffner and J.R. Rentsch, "Organizational Commitment and Social Interaction: A Multiple Constituencies Approach," *Journal of Vocational Behavior* 59 (2001): 471–90.

83. T.-S. Han, H.-H. Chiang, and A. Chang, "Employee Participation in Decision Making, Psychological Ownership and Knowledge Sharing: Mediating Role of Organizational Commitment in Taiwanese High-Tech Organizations," *International Journal of Human Resource Management* 21 (2010): 2218–33; D. Gallie et al., "The Implications of Direct Participation for Organisational Commitment, Job Satisfaction and Affective Psychological Well-Being: A Longitudinal Analysis," *Industrial Relations Journal* 48 (2017): 174–91.

84. J.C. Quick et al., *Preventive Stress Management in Organizations* (Washington, DC: American Psychological Association, 1997), 3–4; A.L. Dougall and A. Baum, "Stress, Coping, and Immune Function," in *Handbook of Psychology*, ed. M. Gallagher and R.J. Nelson (Hoboken, NJ: John Wiley & Sons, Inc., 2003), 441–55. For the various definitions and perspectives of stress, see T.A. Day, "Defining Stress as a Prelude to Mapping Its Neurocircuitry: No Help from Allostasis," *Progress in Neuro-Psychopharmacology and Biological Psychiatry* 29 (2005): 1195–200; D.C. Ganster and C.C. Rosen, "Work Stress and Employee Health: A Multidisciplinary Review," *Journal of Management* 39 (2013): 1085–122.

85. The cognitive appraisal view is described in R.S. Lazarus, *Stress and Emotion: A New Synthesis* (New York: Springer Publishing, 2006). In contrast, recent neuroscience studies and reviews indicate a dissociation between a person's subjective feeling of stress and their autonomic physiological responses (i.e., release of stress hormones into the blood stream). In other words, people respond physiologically to stressful situations even when they do not consciously feel stressed. See J. Campbell and U. Ehlert, "Acute Psychosocial Stress: Does the Emotional Stress Response Correspond with Physiological Responses?" *Psychoneuroendocrinology* 37 (2012): 1111–34; N. Ali et al., "Suppressing the Endocrine and Autonomic Stress Systems Does Not Impact the Emotional Stress Experience after Psychosocial Stress," *Psychoneuroendocrinology* 78 (2017): 125–30.

86. M.G. González-Morales and P. Neves, "When Stressors Make You Work: Mechanisms Linking Challenge Stressors to Performance," *Work & Stress* 29, no. 3 (2015): 213–29; M.B. Hargrove, W.S. Becker, and D.F. Hargrove, "The HRD Eustress Model: Generating Positive Stress with Challenging Work," *Human Resource Development Review* 14, no. 3 (2015): 279–98.

87. Statistics Canada, "Perceived Life Stress, by Age Group," Health Characteristics, Annual Estimates (Ottawa: Statistics Canada, June 26, 2018), https://doi.org/10.25318/1310009601-eng; "Worried Workers: Korn Ferry Survey Finds Professionals Are More Stressed Out at Work Today Than 5 Years Ago," News Release (Los Angeles: Korn Ferry, November 8, 2018); "2019 CIGNA 360 Well-Being Survey: Well and Beyond" (Bloomfield, CT: CIGNA, March 26, 2019); "2019 Global Emotions Report" (Washington, DC: Gallup, April 18, 2019); "NHS Staff Survey 2019: National Results Briefing" (London: National Health Service, February 2020).

88. H. Selye, *Stress without Distress* (Philadelphia: J.B. Lippincott, 1974); S.L. Buckner et al., "The General Adaptation Syndrome: Potential Misapplications to Resistance Exercise," *Journal of Science and Medicine in Sport* 20 (2017): 1015–17; A.J. Cunanan et al., "The General Adaptation Syndrome: A Foundation for the Concept of Periodization," *Sports Medicine* 48 (2018): 787–97.

89. K. Hasselberg et al., "Self-Reported Stressors among Patients with Exhaustion Disorder: An Exploratory Study of Patient Records," *BMC Psychiatry* 14 (2014): 1–10; I.H. Jonsdottir et al., "Working Memory and Attention Are Still Impaired after Three Years in Patients with Stress-Related Exhaustion," *Scandinavian Journal of Psychology* 58 (2017): 504–9; I. Savic, A. Perski, and W. Osika, "MRI Shows That Exhaustion Syndrome Due to Chronic Occupational Stress Is Associated with Partially Reversible Cerebral Changes," *Cerebral Cortex* 28 (2018): 894–906.

90. D.C. Ganster and C.C. Rosen, "Work Stress and Employee Health: A Multidisciplinary Review," *Journal of Management* 39 (2013): 1085–122; J. Goh, J. Pfeffer, and S.A. Zenios, "The Relationship between Workplace Stressors and Mortality and Health Costs in the United States," *Management Science* 62 (2016): 608–28; C. Johansen et al., "Stress and Cancer," in *The Handbook of Stress and Health*, ed. C.L. Cooper and J.C. Quick (Chicester, UK: John Wiley & Sons, Ltd, 2017), 125–34.

91. M. Lauzier, S. Melancon, and K. Cote, "The Effect of Stress Seen on Absenteeism and Presenteeism Behavior: The Mediating Role of Health," *Canadian Journal of Behavioural Science* 49 (2017): 221–30; B. Schmidt et al., "A Comparison of Job Stress Models: Associations with Employee Well-Being, Absenteeism, Presenteeism, and Resulting Costs," *Journal of Occupational and Environmental Medicine* 61 (2019): 535–44.

92. C.L. Cooper and J. Marshall, "Occupational Sources of Stress: A Review of the Literature Relating to Coronary Heart Disease and Mental Ill Health," in *From Stress to Wellbeing Volume 1: The Theory and Research on Occupational Stress and Wellbeing*, ed. C.L. Cooper (London: Palgrave Macmillan UK, 2013), 3–23.

93. C.C. Rosen et al., "Occupational Stressors and Job Performance: An Updated Review and Recommendations," in *New Developments in Theoretical and Conceptual Approaches to Job Stress, Research in Occupational Stress and Well-Being* (Emerald Group Publishing Limited, 2010), 1–60; A.E. Nixon et al., "Can Work Make You Sick? A Meta-Analysis of the Relationships between Job Stressors and Physical Symptoms," *Work & Stress* 25, no. 1 (2011): 1–22.

94. A.E. Nixon et al., "Can Work Make You Sick? A Meta-Analysis of the Relationships between Job Stressors and Physical Symptoms," *Work & Stress* 25, no. 1 (2011): 1–22; S. Pindek and P.E. Spector, "Organizational Constraints: A Meta-Analysis of a Major Stressor," *Work & Stress* 30, no. 1 (2016): 7–25.

95. P. McDonald, "Workplace Sexual Harassment 30 Years On: A Review of the Literature," *International Journal of Management Reviews* 14, no. 1 (2012): 1–17; B. Verkuil, S. Atasayi, and M.L. Molendijk, "Workplace Bullying and Mental Health: A Meta-Analysis on Cross-Sectional and Longitudinal Data," *PLOS ONE* 10, no. 8 (2015): e0135225; J.D. Mackey et al., "Abusive Supervision: A Meta-Analysis and Empirical Review," *Journal of Management* 43, no. 6 (2017): 1940–65.

96. N.A. Bowling et al., "A Meta-Analytic Examination of the Potential Correlates and Consequences of Workload," *Work & Stress* 29, no. 2 (2015): 95–113.

97. R. Drago, D. Black, and M. Wooden, "The Persistence of Long Work Hours," Melbourne Institute Working Paper Series, Melbourne Institute of Applied Economic and Social Research, University of Melbourne, August 2005; L. Golden, "A Brief History of Long Work Time and the Contemporary Sources of Overwork," *Journal of Business Ethics* 84, no. S2 (2009): 217–27; M. Tarafdar, E.B. Pullins, and T.S. Ragu-Nathan, "Technostress: Negative Effect on Performance and Possible Mitigations," *Information Systems Journal* 25, no. 2 (2015): 103–32; E. Reid, "Embracing, Passing, Revealing, and the Ideal Worker Image: How People Navigate Expected and Experienced Professional Identities," *Organization Science* 26, no. 4 (2015): 997–1017; Project: Time Off, *The Work Martyr's Cautionary Tale: How the Millennial Experience Will Define America's Vacation Culture* (Washington, DC: Project: Time Off, August 17, 2016).

98. R. Karasek and T. Theorell, *Healthy Work: Stress, Productivity, and the Reconstruction of Working Life* (New York: Basic Books, 1990); M. Lavigne-Robichaud et al., "Job Strain and the Prevalence of Uncontrolled Hypertension among White-Collar Workers," *Hypertension Research* 42 (2019): 1616–23.

99. M.K. Holton, A.E. Barry, and J.D. Chaney, "Employee Stress Management: An Examination of Adaptive and Maladaptive Coping Strategies on Employee Health," *Work* 53 (2016): 299–305.

100. S. Folkman and J.T. Moskowitz, "Coping: Pitfalls and Promise," *Annual Review of Psychology* 55 (2004): 745–74; C.A. Thompson et al., "On the Importance of Coping: A Model and New Directions for Research on Work and Family," *Research in Occupational Stress and Well-Being* 6 (2007): 73–113; K. Stanisławski, "The Coping Circumplex Model: An Integrative Model of the Structure of Coping with Stress," *Frontiers in Psychology* 10 (2019): 0694.

101. P. Steel, J. Schmidt, and J. Shultz, "Refining the Relationship between Personality and Subjective Well-Being," *Psychological Bulletin* 134, no. 1 (2008): 138–61; G. Alarcon, K.J. Eschleman, and N.A. Bowling, "Relationships between Personality Variables and Burnout: A Meta-Analysis," *Work & Stress* 23, no. 3 (2009): 244–63; T.R. Schneider et al., "The Influence of Neuroticism, Extraversion and Openness on Stress Responses," *Stress and Health: Journal of the International Society for the Investigation of Stress* 28, no. 2 (2012): 102–10; Y. Xin et al., "The Relationship between Personality and the Response to Acute Psychological Stress," *Scientific Reports* 7, no. 1 (2017): 16906.

102. E.M. Kleiman et al., "Optimism and Well-Being: A Prospective Multi-Method and Multi-Dimensional Examination of Optimism as a Resilience Factor Following the Occurrence of Stressful Life Events," *Cognition and Emotion* 31, no. 2 (2017): 269–83; D. Saleh, N. Camart, and L. Romo, "Predictors of Stress in College Students," *Frontiers in Psychology* 8 (January 25, 2017): 19; F. Sabouripour et al., "Mediating Role of Self-Efficacy in the Relationship between Optimism, Psychological Well-Being, and Resilience among Iranian Students," *Frontiers in Psychology* 12 (April 15, 2021): 675645.

103. M.A. Clark et al., "All Work and No Play? A Meta-Analytic Examination of the Correlates and Outcomes of Workaholism," *Journal of Management* 42, no. 7 (2016): 1836–73; M. Morkevičiūtė, A. Endriulaitienė, and M.S. Poškus, "Understanding the Etiology of Workaholism: The Results of the Systematic Review and Meta-Analysis," *Journal of Workplace Behavioral Health* 36, no. 4 (2021): 351–72.

104. This list is based on various reviews, but stress management interventions have been organized in several ways. See, for example, J.H. Ruotsalainen et al., "Preventing Occupational Stress in Healthcare Workers," *Cochrane Database of Systematic Reviews* 2015, no. 4 (2015): CD002892; L.E. Tetrick and C.J. Winslow, "Workplace Stress Management Interventions and Health Promotion," *Annual Review of Organizational Psychology and Organizational Behavior* 2 (2015): 583–603; M. Savic et al., "How Do Nurses Cope with Shift Work? A Qualitative Analysis of Open-Ended Responses from a Survey of Nurses," *International Journal of Environmental Research and Public Health* 16, no. 20 (2019): 03821.

105. E.E. Kossek and R.J. Thompson, "Workplace Flexibility: Integrating Employer and Employee Perspectives to Close the Research–Practice Implementation Gap," in *The Oxford Handbook of Work and Family*, ed. T.D. Allen and L.T. Eby (New York: Oxford University Press, 2016), 255–70; M.J. Sirgy and D.-J. Lee, "Work-Life Balance: An Integrative Review," *Applied Research in Quality of Life* 13 (2018): 229–54; M. Charalampous et al., "Systematically Reviewing Remote E-Workers' Well-Being at Work: A Multidimensional Approach," *European Journal of Work and Organizational Psychology* 28, no. 1 (2019): 51–73; T.A. Beauregard, K.A. Basile, and E. Canonico, "Telework: Outcomes and Facilitators for Employees," in *The Cambridge Handbook of Technology and Employee Behavior*, ed. R.N. Landers (Cambridge: Cambridge University Press, 2019), 511–43.

106. C. Fritz et al., "Happy, Healthy, and Productive: The Role of Detachment from Work during Nonwork Time," *Journal of Applied Psychology* 95, no. 5 (2010): 977–83.

107. M. Tuckey et al., "Hindrances Are Not Threats: Advancing the Multidimensionality of Work Stress," *Journal of Occupational Health Psychology* 20, no. 2 (2015): 131–47.

108. M.H. Abel, "Humor, Stress, and Coping Strategies," *Humor: International Journal of Humor Research* 15 (2002): 365–81; K. Ebner et al., "Coaching as Stress-Management Intervention: The Mediating Role of Self-Efficacy in a Framework of Self-Management and Coping," *International Journal of Stress Management* 25 (2018): 209–33.

109. S.-J. Han and K. Chang-Duck, "Effects of Healing Forest Walks for Short Breaks on Mood State, Quality of Life, and Stress Reduction of University Hospital Workers," *Journal of People, Plants, and Environment* 21, no. 5 (2018): 423–31; J. Mock, "Why Doctors Are Prescribing Nature Walks," *Time*, April 27, 2022; P.-S. Yeon et al., "Effect of Forest Therapy on Depression and Anxiety: A Systematic Review and Meta-Analysis," *International Journal of Environmental Research and Public Health* 18, no. 23 (2021): 12685; M. Stier-Jarmer et al., "The Psychological and Physical Effects of Forests on Human Health: A Systematic Review of Systematic Reviews and Meta-Analyses," *International Journal of Environmental Research and Public Health* 18, no. 4 (2021): 1770; "Capco Recognized as One of Greater Toronto's Top Employers (2023)," *Canada's Top 100,* December 8, 2022; J. Austin, "PaRx: A Prescription for Nature," *Brandon Sun (Manitoba)*, December 27, 2022.

110. O. Kettunen et al., "Greater Levels of Cardiorespiratory and Muscular Fitness Are Associated with Low Stress and High Mental Resources in Normal but Not Overweight Men," *BMC Public Health* 16, no. 1 (2016): 788; M. Gerber et al., "Fitness Moderates the Relationship between Stress and Cardiovascular Risk Factors," *Medicine & Science in Sports & Exercise* 48, no. 11 (2016): 2075–81.

111. H.O. Dickinson et al., "Relaxation Therapies for the Management of Primary Hypertension in Adults: A Cochrane Review," *Journal of Human Hypertension* 22, no. 12 (2008): 809–20; O.L. Siu, "Stress Management Techniques in the Workplace," in *Routledge Companion to Wellbeing at Work*, ed. C.L. Cooper and M.P. Leiter (New York: Routledge: 2017), 284–97.

112. C. Viswesvaran, J.I. Sanchez, and J. Fisher, "The Role of Social Support in the Process of Work Stress: A Meta-Analysis," *Journal of Vocational Behavior* 54, no. 2 (1999): 314–34; S.E. Taylor et al., "Biobehavioral Responses to Stress in Females: Tend-and-Befriend, Not Fight-or-Flight," *Psychological Review* 107, no. 3 (2000): 411–29; T.A. Beehr, N.A. Bowling, and M.M. Bennett, "Occupational Stress and Failures of Social Support: When Helping Hurts," *Journal of Occupational Health Psychology* 15, no. 1 (2010): 45–59; B.A. Scott et al., "A Daily Investigation of the Role of Manager Empathy on Employee Well-Being," *Organizational Behavior and Human Decision Processes* 113, no. 2 (2010): 127–40; S.Y. Shin and S.G. Lee, "Effects of Hospital Workers? Friendship Networks on Job Stress," *PLoS ONE* 11, no. 2 (2016): e0149428.

5 Employee Motivation

StudioByTheSea/Shutterstock

Learning Objectives

After reading this chapter, you should be able to:

LO5-1 Define motivation and explain how drives and emotions influence employee motivation.

LO5-2 Explain through four-drive theory the process of human motivation, and summarize Maslow's needs hierarchy, intrinsic and extrinsic motivation, and learned needs theory.

LO5-3 Outline the expectancy theory model, and prescribe how to improve employee motivation through the elements of this model.

LO5-4 Describe organizational behavior modification (OB Mod) and social cognitive theory, and explain their relevance to employee motivation.

LO5-5 Discuss the characteristics of effective goal setting and feedback.

LO5-6 Explain how equity theory, procedural justice, and interactional justice influence employee motivation.

LO5-7 List the advantages and disadvantages of job specialization and explain how to improve employee motivation through job design.

Motivating employees through an ownership culture has been an important ingredient in KKR's success. For instance, the private equity firm introduced deferred stock ownership for permanent employees after it acquired a large stake in Ingersoll Rand. Over the next several years, employee engagement (motivation) scores skyrocketed at the industrial flow products manufacturer from the 20th to 90th percentile and employee turnover dropped from 20 percent annually to less than 3 percent. KKR has reported similar results at C.H.I. Overhead Doors, Insight Global, Capital Safety, and several other firms over the past decade.

Pete Stavros, KKR's co-chief of Americas Private Equity, advises that financial rewards alone won't motivate employees very much or create an ownership culture. "You have to treat employees like owners. Set goals and talk about progress often. Share information transparently. Ensure there is a strong understanding of stock and its potential value," says Stavros.

An ownership culture has also been an important foundation for employee motivation at CGI Inc. Although it is one the world's largest IT and business consulting services firms, CGI refers to its 88,000 employees as "members" because 85 percent of them own a piece of the business through a stock purchase plan. They also share in the company's success through a companywide profit-sharing plan. Along with the financial rewards, CGI nurtures an ownership culture by investing in employee development and involving employees in company decisions.

"In my experience, I can affirm that making us members rather than employees is one of the catalysts of CGI's success over the years," says CGI Information Technology Service Delivery Manager Rocio Pospisil. "Participating in the share purchase plan encourages members to work towards a common goal in developing the company. It is motivating to feel part of the company vision and mission, to take pride in CGI's success, and share the results of a well implemented strategy."[1]

motivation The forces within a person that affect the direction, intensity, and persistence of effort for voluntary behavior

Corporate leaders around the world are discovering that motivating employees is not as simple as handing out paychecks. It involves understanding fundamental human drives and individual differences in needs derived from those drives, providing autonomy and competence, maintaining organizational justice in the allocation of work obligations and rewards, and guiding employees expectancies about the outcomes of effort toward various work-related goals.

We begin this chapter by defining motivation and explaining how drives and emotions are the prime movers of employee motivation. Four-drive theory is then presented to explain how drives and emotions produce goal-directed needs and motivational effort. Three other needs-based theories are also briefly introduced. Next, expectancy theory is described, including the practical implications of this popular cognitive decision model of employee motivation. Organizational behavior modification and social cognitive theory are then introduced and linked to expectancy theory. Next, we consider theory and practices related to the important motivation topics of goal setting and feedback, as well as organizational justice. The final section of this chapter examines the effect of job design on employee motivation and performance.

LO5-1 Define motivation and explain how drives and emotions influence employee motivation.

EMPLOYEE MOTIVATION, DRIVES, AND NEEDS

Employee motivation should be on anyone's short list of the most important topics in organizational behavior. Why? Because motivation is one of the four elements of the MARS model, meaning that it is critical to understanding human behavior and performance (see Chapter 1). Even when people are able to perform the work (A), understand their role responsibilities (R), and work in a situation that supports their work objectives (S), they won't get the job done without sufficient motivation (M) to achieve those tasks.

Motivation is defined as the forces within a person that affect the direction, intensity, and persistence of their effort for voluntary behavior.[2] *Direction* refers to what people are focused on achieving; in other words, the goal or outcome toward which they steer their effort. *Intensity* is the amount of physical, cognitive, and emotional energy expended at a given moment to

Motivated employees exert varying levels of effort (intensity), for varying lengths of time (persistence), toward various goals (direction).
K-PHOTOS/Alamy Stock Photo

achieve a task or other objective. *Persistence,* the third element of motivation, refers to how long people sustain their effort as they move toward their goal. In short, motivated employees exert varying levels of effort (intensity), for varying lengths of time (persistence), toward various goals (direction).

When executives discuss employee motivation these days, they are just as likely to use the phrase *employee engagement.* Employee engagement is an individual's emotional and cognitive (logical) motivation, particularly a focused, intense, persistent, and purposive effort toward work-related goals.[3] It is associated with self-efficacy—the belief that you have the ability, role clarity, and resources to get the job done (see Chapter 3). Employee engagement also includes a high level of absorption in the work—the experience of focusing intensely on the task with limited awareness of events beyond that work.

Employee Drives and Needs

To build a more engaged and motivated workforce, we first need to understand where motivation begins, that is, the motivational "forces" or "prime movers" of employee behavior.[4] Our starting point is **drives** (also called *primary needs*), which we define as hardwired characteristics of the brain that attempt to keep us in balance by correcting deficiencies. Neuroscience (brain) research has highlighted the central role of emotions in this process. Specifically, drives produce emotions that energize us to act on our environment.[5] There is no agreed-upon list of human drives, but research has consistently identified several, such as the drive to have social interaction, to develop our competence, to comprehend our surroundings, and to defend ourselves against physiological and psychological harm.[6]

Drives are universal and innate, which means that everyone has them and they exist from birth. Drives are the starting point of motivation because they generate emotions that, as we learned in Chapter 4, put people in a state of readiness to act on their environment. Cognition (logical thinking) also plays an important role in motivation, but emotions are the real sources of energy in human behavior.[7] In fact, both words (*emotion* and *motivation*) originate from the same Latin word, *movere,* which means "to move."

Exhibit 5.1 illustrates how drives and emotions translate into felt needs and behavior. Drives, and the emotions generated by these drives, form human needs. We define **needs** as goal-directed forces that people experience. They are the motivational forces of emotions channeled toward particular goals to correct deficiencies or imbalances. In other words, needs are the emotions we eventually become consciously aware of. For example, you sense a need to interact with people after being alone for a while, or to do something challenging after performing tedious activities.

Consider the following example: You arrive at work to discover a stranger sitting at your desk. This situation produces emotions (worry, curiosity) that motivate you to act. These emotions are generated from drives, such as the drive to defend and drive to comprehend. When strong enough, these emotions motivate you to do something about this situation, such as finding out who that person is and possibly seeking reassurance from coworkers about your job security. In this case, you have a need to make sense of what is going on (comprehend), to feel secure, and possibly to correct a sense of personal violation (defend).

> **It is the paradox of Intelligence that it directs forces or energies without being itself a force or energy.[8]**
>
> —William McDougall, early 20th-century motivation scholar

drives Hardwired characteristics of the brain that correct deficiencies or maintain an internal equilibrium by producing emotions to energize individuals

needs Goal-directed forces that people experience

four-drive theory A motivation theory based on the innate drives to acquire, bond, comprehend, and defend that incorporates both emotions and rationality

Exhibit 5.1 Drives, Needs, and Behavior

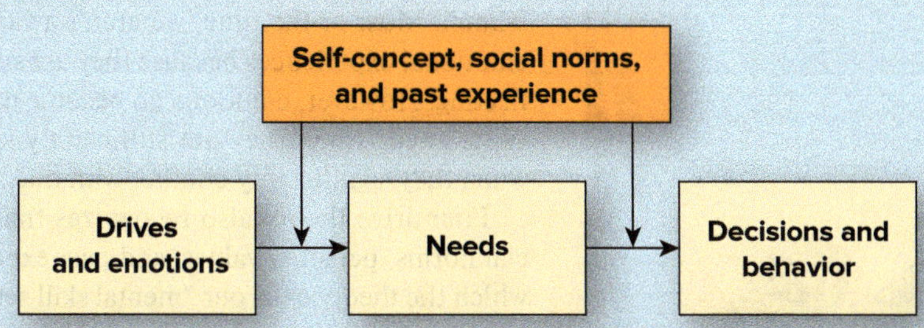

Notice that your emotional reactions to seeing the stranger sitting at your desk represent the forces that move you, and that your logical thinking plays an active role in channeling those emotions toward specific goals and behaviors.

Individual Differences in Needs

Everyone has the same drives; they are hardwired in us through evolution. However, people develop different intensities of needs in a particular situation. Exhibit 5.1 explains why this difference occurs. The left side of the model shows that the individual's self-concept (as well as personality and values), social norms, and past experience amplify or suppress emotions, thereby resulting in stronger or weaker needs.[9] For example, people who define themselves as very sociable typically experience a stronger need for social interaction if they have been alone for a while, whereas people who view themselves as less sociable would experience a less intense need to be with others over that time. These individual differences can be "learned" to some extent through socialization and reinforcement. We will discuss learned needs in the next section of this chapter.

Individual differences–including self-concept, social norms, and past experience–regulate the motivation process in a second way. They influence what goals and behaviors are motivated by the felt emotions, as the right side of Exhibit 5.1 illustrates. Consider the earlier example of the stranger sitting at your desk. You probably wouldn't walk up to that person and demand that they leave; such blunt behavior is contrary to social norms in most cultures. Employees who view themselves as forthright might approach the stranger directly, whereas those who have a different personality and self-view are more likely to first gather information from coworkers before approaching the individual. In summary, your drives (to comprehend, to defend, to bond, etc.) and resulting emotions energize you to act, and your self-concept, social norms, and past experience direct that energy toward goal-directed behavior.

Exhibit 5.1 provides a useful template for understanding how drives and emotions are the prime sources of employee motivation and how individual characteristics (self-concept, experience, social norms) influence goal-directed behavior. We will refer to elements of this drive theory of motivation when we discuss four-drive theory, expectancy theory, equity theory, and other concepts in this chapter. The next section describes theories that explain the dynamics of drives and needs.

LO5-2 Explain through four-drive theory the process of human motivation, and summarize Maslow's needs hierarchy, intrinsic and extrinsic motivation, and learned needs theory.

DRIVE-BASED MOTIVATION THEORIES

Four-Drive Theory

The process through which drives, emotions, and needs influence motivation is most effectively explained by **four-drive theory**. This theory states that emotions are the source of human motivation and that these emotions are generated through four drives:[10]

- *Drive to acquire.* This is the drive to seek, take, control, and retain objects and personal experiences. It produces several needs, including achievement, competence, status, and self-esteem.[11] The drive to acquire also motivates competition.
- *Drive to bond.* This drive produces the need for belonging and affiliation.[12] It explains why our self-concept is partly defined by associations with social groups (see Chapter 3). The drive to bond motivates people to cooperate and, consequently, is essential for organizations and societies.
- *Drive to comprehend.* We are inherently curious and need to make sense of our environment and ourselves.[13] When observing something that is inconsistent with or beyond our current knowledge, we experience a tension that motivates us to close that information gap. The drive to comprehend motivates curiosity as well as the broader need to reach our knowledge potential.
- *Drive to defend.* This is the drive to protect ourselves physically, psychologically, and socially. Probably the first drive to develop in human beings, it creates a fight-or-flight response when we are confronted with threats to our physical safety, our possessions, our self-concept, our values, and the well-being of people around us.[14]

Four-drive theory states that emotions are the source of human motivation and that these emotions are generated through the drive to acquire, bond, comprehend, and defend.
gradyreese/Getty Images

Four-drive theory proposes that the four drives determine which emotions are tagged to incoming stimuli. Most of the time, we aren't aware of our emotional experiences because they are subtle and fleeting. However, emotions do become conscious experiences when they are sufficiently strong or when they significantly conflict with one another.

Four-drive theory also recognizes that our social norms, personal values, and past experience—which the theory calls our "mental skill set"—guide our motivational energy and reduce the felt need (see Exhibit 5.2). In other words, our mental skill set chooses courses of action that are acceptable to society, consistent with our own moral compass, and have a high probability of achieving the goal of fulfilling our felt needs.[16]

Practical Implications of Four-Drive Theory

Four-drive theory recommends that jobs and workplaces should provide a balanced opportunity for employees to fulfill the four drives.[17] There are really two recommendations here. The first is that the best workplaces help employees fulfill all four drives. Employees continually seek fulfillment of their innate drives, so successful companies provide sufficient rewards, learning opportunities, social interaction, and so forth for all employees.

The second recommendation is that fulfillment of the four drives must be kept in balance; that is, organizations shouldn't give employees too much or too little opportunity to fulfill each drive. The reason for this advice is that the four drives counterbalance each other. The drive to bond, which motivates mutual support and cohesion, counterbalances the drive to acquire, which motivates competitiveness. An organization that fuels the drive to

All drives are hardwired in our brains and exist in all human beings. They are also independent of one another; there is no hierarchy of drives. Four-drive theory also claims that no fundamental drives are excluded from the model. Another key feature is that three of the four drives are proactive—we regularly try to fulfill them. Therefore, need "fulfillment" is brief and ongoing. Only the drive to defend is reactive—it is triggered by threat.

How Drives Influence Motivation and Behavior Recall from Chapter 3 that the stimuli received through our senses are quickly and nonconsciously tagged with emotional markers.[15]

Exhibit 5.2 Four-Drive Theory of Motivation

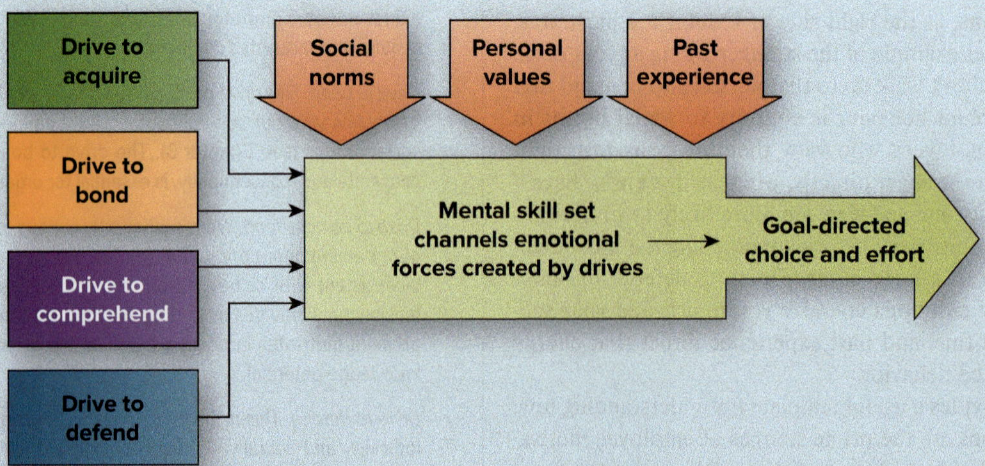

Source: Based on information in P.R. Lawrence and N. Nohria, *Driven: How Human Nature Shapes Our Choices* (San Francisco: Jossey-Bass, 2002).

acquire without encouraging the drive to bond may eventually suffer from organizational politics, dysfunctional conflict, and insufficient collaboration.[18] The drive to comprehend, which motivates investigation of the unknown, counterbalances the drive to defend, which motivates avoidance of the unknown. Change and novelty in the workplace will feed the drive to comprehend, but too much of it will trigger the drive to defend to such an extent that employees become territorial and resistant to change.

Maslow's Needs Hierarchy Theory

Mention needs and drives to most people and they will probably refer to **Maslow's needs hierarchy theory**, which was developed by psychologist Abraham Maslow in the 1940s.[19] Maslow condensed and organized the dozens of previously studied drives (which he called primary needs) into five basic categories, organized in a hierarchy from lowest to highest: *physiological* (need for food, air, water, shelter, etc.), *safety* (need for security and stability), *belongingness/love* (need for interaction with and affection from others), *esteem* (need for self-esteem and social esteem/status), and *self-actualization* (need for self-fulfillment, realization of one's potential).[20] Along with these five categories, Maslow identified the need to know and the need for aesthetic beauty as two innate drives that do not fit within the hierarchy.

Maslow's theory states that we are motivated simultaneously by several needs, but the strongest motivation comes from the lowest unsatisfied need. When satisfied, the next higher need in the hierarchy becomes the strongest motivator and remains so even if never satisfied. The exception to this need fulfillment process is self-actualization, which is an ongoing need that is never fulfilled. Thus, while the bottom four groups are *deficiency needs* because they become activated when unfulfilled, self-actualization is known as a *growth need* because it continues to develop even when temporarily satiated.

Maslow's needs hierarchy theory may be well known, but it was rejected long ago by research studies.[21] The main flaw is that not everyone has the same needs hierarchy. Some people place social status at the top of their personal hierarchy whereas others view personal development and growth above social relations or status. This variation occurs because employee needs are strongly influenced by self-concept, personal values, and personality.[22] People have different hierarchies of values, so they also have parallel differences in their needs hierarchies. Furthermore, a person's values hierarchy can change over time, so their needs hierarchy also changes over time.[23]

Although Maslow's needs hierarchy has been rejected by scientific analysis, we briefly described this theory because Maslow improved our understanding of motivation in a few ways.[24] Specifically, he emphasized that needs should be studied together (holistically), not separately from one another. He recognized that motivation can be shaped by human thoughts (humanistic), not just from instincts. And Maslow's focus on self actualization and growth needs introduced a more positive view of motivation, whereas previous motivation theories focused on need deficiencies such as hunger.

Maslow's needs hierarchy theory A motivation theory of needs arranged in a hierarchy, whereby people are motivated to fulfill a higher need as a lower one becomes gratified

intrinsic motivation Motivation that occurs when people are fulfilling their needs for competence and autonomy by engaging in the activity itself, rather than from an externally controlled outcome of that activity

extrinsic motivation Motivation that occurs when people want to engage in an activity for instrumental reasons, that is, to receive something that is beyond their personal control

Intrinsic and Extrinsic Motivation

By extolling the importance of self-actualization, Maslow launched an entirely new way of thinking about human motivation. People experience self-actualization by applying their skills and knowledge, observing how their talents achieve meaningful results, and experiencing personal growth through learning.

These are the conditions for **intrinsic motivation**, which is motivation that occurs when people are fulfilling their needs for competence and autonomy by engaging in the activity itself, rather than from an externally controlled outcome of that activity.[25] Intrinsically motivated employees apply their talents toward a meaningful task and experience progress or success in that task.[26] They feel competent when applying their skills and observing positive, meaningful outcomes from that effort. They feel autonomous when their motivation is self-initiated rather than controlled from an external source.

Intrinsic motivation contrasts with **extrinsic motivation**, which is motivation that occurs when

Mc Graw Hill connect

SELF-ASSESSMENT 5.1: How Strong Are Your Growth Needs?

> Intrinsic motivation occurs when people are fulfilling their needs for competence and autonomy by engaging in the activity itself.

people want to engage in an activity for instrumental reasons, that is, to receive something that is beyond their personal control. This involves directing one's effort toward a reward controlled by others that indirectly fulfills a need. Extrinsic motivators exist throughout organizations, such as pay incentives, recognition awards, and frequent reminders from the boss about work deadlines. Extrinsic motivation also occurs indirectly, such as when we are motivated to complete our part of a team project partly due to our concerns about how team members will react if we submit it late or with inferior quality.

Pay incentives, recognition awards, and frequent reminders from the boss about work deadlines are extrinsic motivators because the outcomes are controlled by others and are not need fulfillment in themselves.
Peshkova/Shutterstock

Does Extrinsic Motivation Undermine Intrinsic Motivation?

There are two contrasting hypotheses about how extrinsic and intrinsic motivation work together.[27] One hypothesis is that someone performing an intrinsically motivating job becomes even more motivated by also receiving an extrinsic source of motivation for that work. The extrinsic motivator energizes the employee more than the intrinsic motivator alone. The opposing hypothesis states that introducing extrinsic sources of motivation will reduce the amount of intrinsic motivation. For example, employees who were energized from the work itself will experience loss of that intrinsic motivation when they receive extrinsic rewards, such as a performance bonus. The explanation is that introducing extrinsic motivators diminishes the employee's feeling of autonomy, which is a key source of intrinsic motivation.

Which hypothesis is correct? So far, the research evidence is mixed. Extrinsic motivators may reduce existing intrinsic motivation to some extent and under some conditions, but the effect is often minimal. Extrinsic rewards do not undermine intrinsic motivation when they are unexpected (e.g., a surprise bonus), when they have low value relative to the intrinsic motivator, and when they are not contingent on specific behavior (such as receiving a fixed salary). Even so, when employees are intrinsically motivated, employers should be careful about the potential unintended effect of undermining that motivation with performance bonuses and other sources of extrinsic motivation.[28]

Learned Needs Theory

In the previous section of this chapter, we explained that needs are shaped, amplified, or suppressed through self-concept, social norms, and past experience. Maslow noted this when he observed that individual differences influence the strength of higher-order needs, such as the need to belong. Psychologist David McClelland further investigated the idea that a person's needs can be strengthened or weakened through reinforcement, learning, and social conditions. He examined three "learned" needs: achievement, affiliation, and power.[29]

- People with a high **need for achievement (nAch)** choose moderately challenging tasks, desire unambiguous feedback and recognition for their success, and prefer working alone rather than in teams. Except as a source of feedback, money is a weak motivator for people with high nAch, whereas it can be a strong motivator for those with low nAch.[30]
- People with a high **need for affiliation (nAff)** seek approval from others, want to conform to others' wishes and expectations, and avoid conflict and confrontation. High nAff employees generally work well in jobs responsible for cultivating long-term relations, but their strong need for approval makes them less effective at allocating scarce resources and making other decisions that potentially generate conflict.[31]
- People with a high **need for power (nPow)** want to exercise control over others, are highly involved in team decisions, rely on persuasion, and are concerned about maintaining their leadership position. There are two types of nPow.[32] The need for *personalized power* occurs when individuals enjoy their power for its own sake, use it to advance personal interests, and wear their power as a status symbol. The need for *socialized power* exists when individuals desire power as a means to help others.

McClelland developed interventions that attempt to amplify or suppress needs through reinforcement, learning, and social conditions. One program increased achievement motivation by having participants write achievement-oriented stories, practice achievement-oriented behaviors in business games, and meet frequently with other trainees to maintain their newfound achievement motivation. These interventions programs prime participants to focus on goals associated with the primed need, thereby amplifying their need for achievement, affiliation, or power. They may also change, at least temporarily, how individuals viewed themselves (their self-concept) in terms of the learned needs.[33]

Mc Graw Hill connect

SELF-ASSESSMENT 5.2: How Strong Are Your Learned Needs?

LO5-3 Outline the expectancy theory model, and prescribe how to improve employee motivation through the elements of this model.

EXPECTANCY THEORY OF MOTIVATION

The theories described so far mainly explain *what motivates us*—the prime movers of employee motivation—but they don't tell us *what we are motivated to do.* Four-drive theory recognizes that social norms, personal values, and past experience direct our effort, but it doesn't offer any detail about what goals we choose or where our effort is directed under various circumstances.

Expectancy theory offers a more detailed understanding of the logical decisions employees make when directing their effort toward specific behavior. The theory states that people are rational decision makers who are motivated to choose goals that are expected to result in the most favorable outcomes. Specifically, individuals direct their effort toward goals based on the perceived probability of accomplishing them, the perceived probability that an accomplished goal will lead to specific outcomes, and the expected satisfaction (positive or negative valences) of those outcomes.[34] The theory consists of three distinct components, as illustrated in Exhibit 5.3: effort-to-performance (E-to-P) expectancy, performance-to-outcome (P-to-O) expectancy, and outcome valences. Employee motivation is influenced by all three components of this model. If any component weakens, motivation weakens.[35]

- *E-to-P expectancy.* This is the individual's perception that their effort will result in a specific level of performance. In some situations, employees may believe that they can unquestionably accomplish the task (a probability of 1.0). In other situations, they expect that even their highest level of effort will not result in the desired performance level (a probability of 0.0). In most cases, the E-to-P expectancy falls somewhere between these two extremes.
- *P-to-O expectancy.* This is the perceived probability that a specific behavior or performance level will lead to a particular outcome. In extreme cases, employees may believe that accomplishing a particular task (performance) will definitely result in a specific outcome (a probability of 1.0), or they may believe that successful performance will have no effect on this outcome occurring (a probability of 0.0). More often, the P-to-O expectancy falls somewhere between these two extremes.
- *Outcome valences.* A *valence* is the individual's anticipated satisfaction or dissatisfaction with an outcome.[36] It ranges from negative to positive. (The actual range doesn't matter; it may be from −1 to +1 or from −100 to +100.) Outcomes have a positive valence when they are consistent with our values and satisfy our needs; they have a negative valence when they oppose our values and inhibit need fulfillment.

Expectancy Theory in Practice

One of the appealing characteristics of expectancy theory is that it provides clear guidelines for increasing employee motivation, at least extrinsic motivation.[37] Several practical applications of expectancy theory are described below.

Exhibit 5.3 Expectancy Theory of Motivation

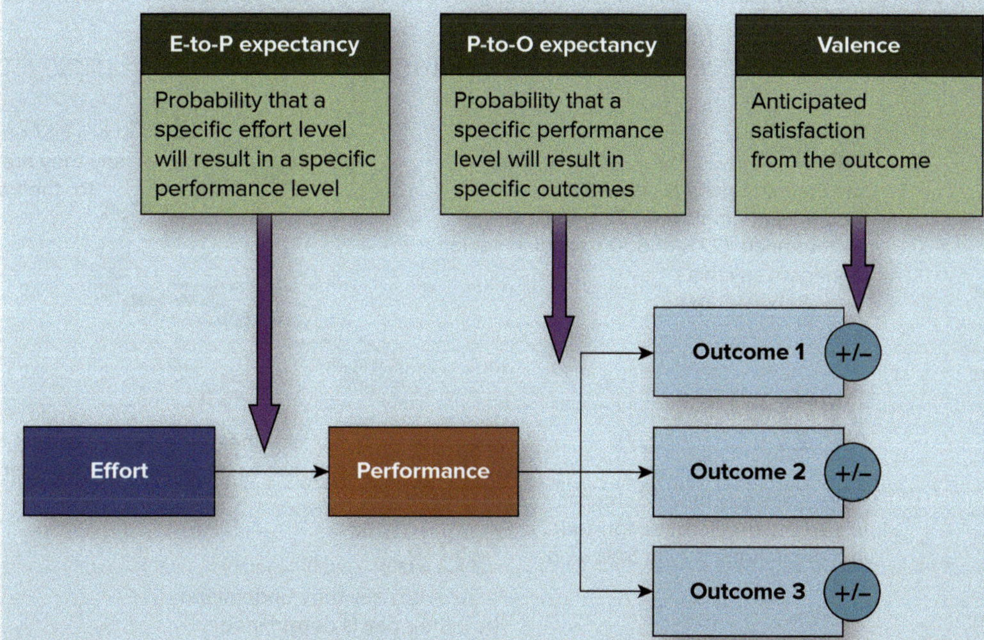

need for achievement (nAch) A learned need in which people want to accomplish reasonably challenging goals and desire unambiguous feedback and recognition for their success

need for affiliation (nAff) A learned need in which people seek approval from others, conform to their wishes and expectations, and avoid conflict and confrontation

need for power (nPow) A learned need in which people want to control their environment, including people and material resources, to benefit either themselves (personalized power) or others (socialized power)

expectancy theory A motivation theory based on the idea that work effort is directed toward behaviors that people believe will lead to desired outcomes

organizational behavior modification (OB Mod) A theory that explains employee behavior in terms of the antecedent conditions and consequences of that behavior

Increasing E-to-P Expectancies

E-to-P expectancies are influenced by the individual's belief that they can successfully complete the task. Some companies increase this can-do attitude by assuring employees that they have the required abilities and resources as well as clear role perceptions to reach the desired levels of performance. An important part of this process involves matching employee abilities to job requirements and clearly communicating the tasks required for the job. Similarly, E-to-P expectancies are learned, so behavior modeling and supportive feedback typically strengthen the individual's belief that they are able to perform the task.

Increasing P-to-O Expectancies The most obvious ways to improve P-to-O expectancies are to measure employee performance accurately and distribute more valued rewards to those with higher job performance. P-to-O expectancies are perceptions, so employees also need to believe that higher performance will result in higher rewards. Furthermore, they need to know how that connection occurs, so leaders should use examples, anecdotes, and public ceremonies to illustrate when behavior has been rewarded.

Increasing Outcome Valences One size does not fit all when motivating and rewarding people. The valence of a reward varies from one person to the next because each person has different need priorities. One solution is to individualize rewards by allowing employees to choose the rewards of greatest value to them. When this isn't possible, companies should find a reward that everyone values to some degree. Finally, we need to watch out for countervalent outcomes. If a company offers individual performance bonuses, for example, it should beware of team norms that discourage employees from working above a minimum standard. These norms and associated peer pressure are countervalent outcomes to the bonus.

OB THEORY TO PRACTICE

Putting Expectancy Theory into Practice

Increasing E → P expectancies

- Select people with the required skills and knowledge.
- Provide required training and clarify job requirements.
- Provide sufficient time and resources.
- Assign simpler or fewer tasks until employees can master them.
- Provide examples of similar employees who have successfully performed the task.
- Provide coaching to employees who lack self-confidence.

Increasing P → O expectancies

- Measure job performance accurately.
- Clearly explain the outcomes that will result from successful performance.
- Describe how the employee's rewards were based on past performance.
- Provide examples of other employees whose good performance has resulted in higher rewards.

Increasing outcome valences

- Distribute rewards that employees value.
- Individualize rewards.
- Minimize the presence of countervalent outcomes.

Overall, expectancy theory is a useful model that explains how people rationally figure out the best direction, intensity, and persistence of effort. It has been tested in a variety of

Performance-to-Outcome Expectancy: A Weak Link in Employee Motivation[38]

43% of 2,800 US senior managers say their company is very effective at recognizing employees for good performance. (27% of 600 Canadian senior managers say this.)

21% of 1,347 employed Americans say they are never recognized for their efforts.

25% of 1,347 employed Americans say their employer asks how they would like to be recognized for their efforts.

42% of 557,778 US federal government employees say that differences in performance are recognized in a meaningful way in their work unit.

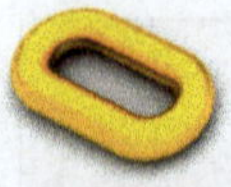

38% of 3,200 American employees say they understand how their pay is determined.

(Photo): alxpin/iStock/Getty Images

situations and predicts employee motivation in different cultures.[39] One limitation, however, is that expectancy theory assumes people are perfectly rational decision makers; in reality, human decisions are not perfectly rational (see Chapter 6). A second concern is that the theory mainly explains extrinsic motivation, whereas applying the model's features to intrinsic motivation is more difficult (although not impossible). Third, expectancy theory ignores emotions as a source of motivation. The valence element of expectancy theory captures some of this emotional process, but only peripherally.[40] Fourth, E-to-P and P-to-O expectancies are critical components of expectancy theory, yet the theory doesn't explain how employees develop these expectancies. Two theories that provide this explanation are organizational behavior modification and social cognitive theory, which we describe next.

LO5-4 Describe organizational behavior modification (OB Mod) and social cognitive theory, and explain their relevance to employee motivation.

ORGANIZATIONAL BEHAVIOR MODIFICATION AND SOCIAL COGNITIVE THEORY

Expectancy theory states that motivation is determined by employee beliefs about expected performance and outcomes. But how do employees learn these expectancy beliefs? For example, how do they form the impression that one level of task performance is more likely than another performance level to produce a pay increase, promotion, or other outcomes? Two theories—organizational behavior modification (OB Mod) and social cognitive theory—complement expectancy theory by explaining how people *learn* what to expect from their actions, which is how people develop the expectancies that affect motivation.

Organizational Behavior Modification

For most of the first half of the 1900s, the dominant paradigm about managing individual behavior was *behaviorism,* which argues that a good theory should rely exclusively on behavior and the environment and ignore nonobservable cognitions and emotions.[41] Although behaviorists don't deny the existence of human thoughts and attitudes, they dismiss them as unobservable and, therefore, irrelevant to scientific study. A variation of this paradigm, called **organizational behavior modification (OB Mod)**, eventually entered organizational studies of motivation and learning.[42]

A-B-Cs of OB Mod The core elements of OB Mod are depicted in the A-B-C model shown in Exhibit 5.4. Essentially, OB Mod attempts to change behavior (B) by managing its antecedents (A) and consequences (C).[43] *Consequences* are events following a particular behavior that influence its future occurrence. Consequences include receiving words of thanks from coworkers after assisting them, receiving preferred work schedules after being with the company longer than the average employee, and finding useful information on your smartphone after checking for new messages. Consequences also include no outcome at all, such as when no one says anything to you about how well you have been serving customers.

Exhibit 5.4 A-B-Cs of Organizational Behavior Modification

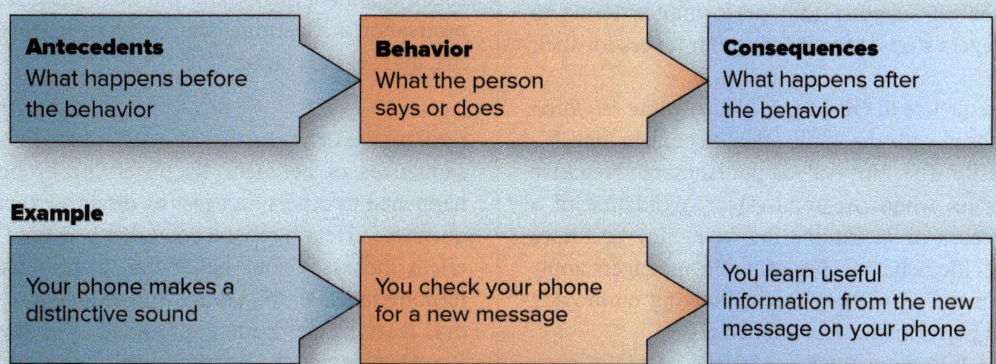

Sources: Adapted from T.K. Connellan, *How to Improve Human Performance* (New York: Harper & Row, 1978), 50; F. Luthans and R. Kreitner, *Organizational Behavior Modification and Beyond* (Glenview, IL: Scott, Foresman, 1985), 85–88.

social cognitive theory A theory that explains how learning and motivation occur by observing and modeling others as well as by anticipating the consequences of our behavior

self-reinforcement Reinforcement that occurs when an employee has control over a reinforcer but doesn't "take" it until completing a self-set goal

goal A cognitive representation of a desired end state that a person is committed to attain

> In most situations, positive reinforcement should follow desired behaviors and extinction (do nothing) should follow undesirable behaviors.

Antecedents are events preceding the behavior, informing employees that a particular action will produce specific consequences. An antecedent could be a sound from your mobile (cell) phone signaling that a text message has arrived. Or it could be your supervisor's request to complete a specific task by tomorrow. Notice that antecedents do not cause behavior. The sound from your phone doesn't cause you to open the text message. Rather, the sound (antecedent) is a cue signaling that if you look at your phone messages (behavior), you will find a new message with potentially useful information (consequence).

Contingencies and Schedules of Reinforcement OB Mod identifies four types of consequences, called the *contingencies of reinforcement.*[44] *Positive reinforcement* occurs when the introduction of a consequence increases or maintains the frequency or future probability of a specific behavior. Receiving praise from coworkers is an example of positive reinforcement because the praise usually maintains or increases your likelihood of helping them in future. *Punishment* occurs when a consequence decreases the frequency or future probability of a specific behavior. Most of us would consider being demoted or criticized by our coworkers as forms of punishment. A third type of consequence is *extinction.* Extinction occurs when the target behavior decreases because no consequence follows it. For instance, research suggests that performance tends to decline when managers stop congratulating employees for their good work.[45]

The fourth consequence in OB Mod, called *negative reinforcement,* is often confused with the application of punishment. It's actually the opposite—the removal of punishment. Negative reinforcement occurs when the removal or avoidance of a consequence increases or maintains the frequency or future probability of a specific behavior. For example, managers apply negative reinforcement when they *stop* criticizing employees whose substandard performance has improved.

Which of these four consequences works best? In most situations, positive reinforcement should follow desired behaviors (but not necessarily after every occurrence), and extinction (do nothing) should follow undesirable behaviors. Positive reinforcement is preferred because focusing on the positive rather than negative aspects of life tends to improve organizational success and individual well-being.[46] In contrast, punishment and negative reinforcement generate negative emotions and attitudes toward the person (e.g., supervisor) and organization who initiated and later removed the punishment. However, punishment (dismissal, suspension, demotion, etc.) may be necessary for extreme behaviors, such as deliberately hurting a coworker or stealing inventory. Indeed, research suggests that, under some conditions, punishment maintains a sense of fairness among those affected by or aware of the employee's indiscretion.[47]

Along with the four consequences, OB Mod considers the frequency and timing of these reinforcers (called the *schedules of reinforcement*).[48] The most effective reinforcement schedule for learning new tasks is *continuous reinforcement*—providing positive reinforcement after every occurrence of the desired behavior. For motivating skilled employees, the most effective reinforcement schedule tends to be the *variable ratio schedule*—providing positive reinforcement after a varying number of times. Salespeople experience variable ratio reinforcement because they make a successful sale (positive reinforcement) after a varying number of client calls. The variable ratio schedule makes behavior highly resistant to extinction because the reinforcer is never expected at a particular time or after a fixed number of behaviors.

Social Cognitive Theory

Social cognitive theory states that much learning occurs by observing and modeling others as well as by anticipating the consequences of our behavior.[49] There are several pieces to social cognitive theory, but the three most relevant to employee motivation are learning behavior consequences, behavior modeling, and self-regulation.

Learning Behavior Consequences People learn the consequences of behavior by observing or hearing about what happened to others, not just by directly experiencing the consequences.[50] Hearing that a coworker was fired for being rude to a client increases your belief that rude behavior will result in termination of employment. In the language of expectancy theory, learning behavior consequences changes an individual's P-to-O expectancy. Furthermore, people logically anticipate consequences in related situations. For instance, the story about the fired employee might also strengthen your P-to-O

People learn the consequences of behavior by observing or hearing about what happened to others, not just by directly experiencing the consequences.
BulentBARIS/Getty Images

expectancy that being rude toward coworkers and suppliers (not just clients) will get you fired.

Behavior Modeling Along with observing others, people learn by imitating and practicing their behaviors.[51] Modeling the behavior of others gives learners direct sensory experience, which helps them to acquire knowledge and skills, such as the subtle person-machine interaction while driving a vehicle. Behavior modeling also increases E to P expectancy because people develop a stronger self-efficacy (see Chapter 3) after observing others and performing the task successfully themselves. Self-efficacy particularly improves when observers are similar to the model in age, experience, gender, and related characteristics.

Self-Regulation An important feature of social cognitive theory is that human beings set goals and engage in other forms of intentional, purposive action.[52] They establish their own short- and long-term objectives, choose their own standards of achievement, work out a plan of action, consider backup alternatives, and have the forethought to anticipate the consequences of their goal-directed behavior. Furthermore, people self-regulate by engaging in **self-reinforcement**; they reward and punish themselves for exceeding or falling short of their self-set goals. For example, you might have a goal of completing the rest of this chapter, after which you reward yourself by going for a relaxing walk. The work break at a nearby park is a form of self-induced positive reinforcement for completing this reading assignment.

OB Mod and social cognitive theory explain how people learn probabilities of successful performance (E-to-P expectancies) as well as probabilities of various outcomes from that performance (P-to-O expectancies). As such, these theories explain motivation through their relationship with expectancy theory of motivation, described earlier. Elements of these theories also help us to understand other motivation processes. For instance, self-regulation is the cornerstone of motivation through goal setting and feedback, which we discuss next.

Social cognitive theory states that people self-regulate through self-reinforcement; they reward and punish themselves for exceeding or falling short of their self-set goals.
Tim Teebken/Getty Images

LO5-5 Discuss the characteristics of effective goal setting and feedback.

GOAL SETTING AND FEEDBACK

Key performance indicators, task objectives, stretch targets, job duties. No matter what they are called, goals figure prominently in everyone's job. A **goal** is a cognitive representation of a desired end state that a person is committed to attain.[53] Goals motivate people by clarifying role perceptions and, consequently, the direction of effort. Goals also amplify the intensity and persistence of effort because they make it easier to judge how much energy is required to reach them. However, the motivational potential of goals depends on how well they are stated.[54] Rather than just trying to "do your best," effective goals have several

strengths-based coaching An approach to coaching and feedback that focuses on building and leveraging the employee's strengths rather than trying to correct his or her weaknesses

characteristics identified in the popular acronym SMARTER: specific, measurable, achievable, relevant, time-framed, exciting, and reviewed.[55]

OB THEORY TO PRACTICE

The SMARTER Approach to Goal Setting

S*pecific.* Goals lead to better performance when they are specific. Specific goals state what needs to be accomplished; how it should be accomplished; and where, when, and with whom it should be accomplished. Specific goals clarify performance expectations, so employees can direct their effort more efficiently and reliably.

M*easurable.* Goals need to be measurable because motivation occurs when people have some indication of their progress toward and achievement of those goals. This measurement ideally includes how much (quantity), how well (quality), and at what cost the goal was achieved. However, some types of employee performance are difficult to measure, and those non-measurable tasks might be neglected in companies preoccupied with quantifiable outcomes.[56]

A*chievable.* One of the trickiest aspects of goal setting is developing goals that are sufficiently but not overly challenging.[57] Easier goals motivate employees to perform well below their potential. Yet goals that are too challenging may also lead to substandard effort if employees believe there is a low probability of accomplishing them (i.e., low E-to-P expectancy). Studies also have found that very difficult goals increase the probability that employees will engage in unethical behavior to achieve them.[58]

R*elevant.* Goals need to be relevant to the job and within the individual's control. For example, a goal to reduce waste materials won't motivate employees who have negligible control over waste in the production process.

T*ime-framed.* Goals need a due date. They should specify when the objective should be completed or when it will be assessed for comparison against a standard.

E*xciting.* Goals tend to be more effective when employees are committed to them, not just compliant. Challenging goals tend to be more exciting for most (but not all) employees because growth need fulfillment is stronger when difficult goals are achieved. Goal commitment also increases when employees are involved in goal setting.[59]

R*eviewed.* The motivational value of goal setting depends on employees receiving feedback about reaching those goals.[60] Effective feedback requires measurement, which we discussed earlier in this list, but it also includes reflecting or discussing with others your goal progress and accomplishment. Reviewing goal progress and accomplishment helps employees redirect their effort. It is also a potential source of recognition that fulfills growth needs.

SELF-ASSESSMENT 5.3: What Is Your Goal Orientation?

Characteristics of Effective Feedback

Feedback—information that lets us know whether we have achieved the goal or are properly directing our effort toward it—is an essential partner with goal setting. Feedback contributes to motivation and performance by clarifying role perceptions, improving employee skills and knowledge, and strengthening self-efficacy.[61]

Effective feedback has many of the same characteristics as effective goal setting (see Exhibit 5.5).[62] It should be *specific* and *relevant*—that is, the information should refer to specific metrics (e.g., sales increased by 5 percent last month) and to the individual's behavior or outcomes within their control. Feedback also should be *timely*—available soon after the behavior or results occur. Feedback also needs to be *credible;* that is, the person providing the feedback should have complete and accurate information about the employee's performance, is reliable at recalling that information, is unbiased in communicating and applying the feedback to decisions (such as performance ratings), and describes the feedback in a supportive and empathetic manner.

Finally, effective feedback is *sufficiently frequent.* "Sufficiently" means that the feedback is provided more often for employees learning new tasks and less often for employees who already know how to perform those tasks. It also means that feedback is provided in a time frame proportional to how long it takes to complete the task (i.e., the job cycle). Less frequent feedback usually occurs in jobs with a long cycle time (e.g., executives and scientists) because indicators of goal progress and accomplishment in these jobs are less frequent than in jobs with a short cycle time (e.g., grocery store cashiers).

Feedback through Strengths-Based Coaching **Strengths-based coaching** (also known as *appreciative coaching*) is a positive approach to coaching and feedback that focuses on building and leveraging the employee's strengths rather than their weaknesses.[63] In strengths-based coaching, employees describe areas of work where they excel or demonstrate potential. The coach guides this discussion by asking exploratory questions that help employees discover ways to build on these strengths. Situational barriers, as well as strategies to overcome those barriers, are identified to further support the employee's potential.

Strengths-based coaching might not be best in all situations, but it is associated with higher employee motivation, satisfaction, self-efficacy, and relations with management.[64] One reason is that people are more receptive to information about their strengths than they are to information about their flaws. In fact, for more than three decades scholars have warned that traditional problem-focused feedback leads to employee defensiveness and potentially lower self-efficacy, which can result in reduced (rather than increased) employee performance.[65] Strengths-based coaching also makes sense because personality becomes quite stable in the early stages of a person's career,

EXHIBIT 5.5 Characteristics of Effective Feedback

Feedback Characteristic	Description	Example
Specific	Information refers to identifiable behaviors and (when possible) measurable outcomes	"Inventory shrinkage (theft, damage) fell to 1% of inventory over the previous three months."
Relevant	Information should relate to behaviors and outcomes within the individual's or team's control	"You have submitted the monthly budget reports without error and on time every month over the past year, one of the few district managers to do so" (where district managers have few situational barriers to submitting the reports accurately or on schedule).
Timely	Information should be available soon after the behavior or results occur	"Two of our customers noted this week that you were unable to answer their questions about how the new widget model differs from the previous model."
Credible	Information source should: • Have complete and accurate information • Recall information reliably • Be unbiased in communicating and applying the feedback • Describe the feedback in a supportive and empathetic manner	Supervisor has good knowledge of the employee's job duties, regularly observes them performing the work, and offers constructive feedback with optimism and sensitivity on how the employee can perform specific tasks better.
Sufficiently frequent	Information is provided: • More often for those learning new tasks • According to the job cycle's frequency	Supervisor meets twice monthly with every experienced production employee and at least twice weekly with every new employee to discuss their individual safety behavior and output (where task cycle times are usually less than one hour).

which limits their flexibility regarding interests, preferences, and abilities.[66] Consequently, employees become less motivated and less able to improve themselves in areas where they previously lacked interest or skill.

Sources of Feedback

Feedback can originate from nonsocial or social sources. Nonsocial sources provide feedback without someone communicating that information. Corporate intranets allow many executives to receive feedback instantaneously on their computer or other digital device, usually in the form of graphic output on an executive dashboard.

Some companies set up *multisource (360-degree) feedback,* which, as the name implies, is information about an employee's performance collected from a full circle of people, including subordinates, peers, supervisors, and customers. Multisource feedback tends to provide more complete and accurate information than feedback from a supervisor alone. It is particularly useful when the supervisor is unable to observe the employee's behavior or performance in every situation. Lower-level employees also feel a greater sense of fairness when they are able to provide upward feedback about their boss's performance.[67] However, multisource feedback can be expensive and time-consuming. It may also be biased by coworkers avoiding interpersonal conflict. Multisource feedback also tends to be ambiguous because several observers have different perspectives of the employee's behavior.

The preferred feedback source depends on the purpose of the information and the emotional effect of positive versus negative feedback.[68] Feedback from nonsocial sources, such as digital images or feedback directly from the job, is better when employees

Feedback from nonsocial sources is better than from social sources when employees need to learn about goal progress and accomplishment.
fizkes/123RF

distributive justice An ethical principle stating that appropriate decision criteria should be applied to calculate how various benefits and burdens are distributed

procedural justice The perception that appropriate procedural rules have been applied throughout the decision process

interactional justice The perception that appropriate rules have been applied in the way the people involved are treated throughout the decision process

equity theory A theory explaining how people develop perceptions of fairness in the distribution and exchange of resources

need to learn about goal progress and accomplishment. This is because information from nonsocial sources is considered more accurate and less damaging to self-esteem (when the feedback is negative) than information from social sources. In contrast, social sources tend to delay or exclude some negative information, as well as distort the bad news in a positive way. Employees should receive some positive feedback from social sources. It feels better to have coworkers say that you are performing the job well than to discover this from data on an impersonal digital dashboard.

Evaluating Goal Setting and Feedback

Goal setting (in partnership with feedback) is generally a highly effective practice for employee motivation and performance.[69] Putting goal setting into practice can be challenging, however.[70] It tends to focus employees on a narrow subset of measurable performance indicators while ignoring aspects of job performance that are difficult to measure. Another concern is that very difficult goals may motivate some people to engage in unethical behavior to achieve those targets. Difficult goals are also stressful, which can undermine overall job performance.

Yet another problem is that goal setting tends to interfere with the learning process in new, complex jobs. Therefore, setting performance goals may be effective for employees who are already experienced in a job but should be avoided for those who are in an intensive learning process. A final issue is that when goal achievement is tied to financial rewards, many employees are motivated to set easy goals (while making the boss think they are difficult) so that they have a higher probability of receiving the bonus or pay increase. As a former Ford Motor Company CEO once quipped: "At Ford, we hire very smart people. They quickly learn how to make relatively easy goals look difficult!"[72]

LO5-6 Explain how equity theory, procedural justice, and interactional justice influence employee motivation.

ORGANIZATIONAL JUSTICE

Treating employees fairly is both morally correct and good for employee motivation, loyalty, and well-being. Yet feelings of injustice are regular occurrences in the workplace. To minimize these incidents, we need to first understand the three most common types of justice (there are others): distributive, procedural, and interactional justice. All three refer to the perception that appropriate formal or informal rules have been applied to the situation. People have a sense of fairness when they believe those rules are being followed.[73]

- **Distributive justice** refers to the perception that appropriate decision criteria (rules) have been applied to calculate how various benefits and burdens are distributed. These criteria—such as effort, need, or membership—determine how much each person should receive, such as higher pay, more tedious tasks, better workspace, and so forth.
- **Procedural justice** is the perception that appropriate procedural rules have been applied throughout the decision process. Procedural justice tends to be higher, for example, when the decision maker demonstrates neutrality (no favoritism), allows everyone involved to have their say, and allows an appeal of the decision.
- **Interactional justice** is the perception that appropriate rules have been applied in the way employees are treated throughout the decision process. For example, employees have a greater sense of interactional justice when the decision maker is polite toward the potential beneficiaries and is honest and candid in providing information about the decision.

Distributive Justice and Equity Theory

At its most basic level, employment in any organization is an exchange relationship; we provide our time, skills, and behavior in exchange for pay, fulfilling work, skill development opportunities, and other desired outcomes. What is considered "fair" in this exchange relationship depends on what criteria we use to determine distributive justice in various situations.[74] An *equality principle* states that everyone in the group should receive the same outcomes, such as when all employees receive subsidized meals in the company cafeteria. The *need principle* says that those with the greatest need should receive more outcomes than others with less need. This occurs, for instance, when employees get paid time off to recover from illness. The *equity principle* states that the benefits people receive should be in proportion to what they contribute to

> Not everything that can be counted counts, and not everything that counts can be counted.[71]
>
> —William Bruce Cameron, sociologist

Exhibit 5.6 Equity Theory Model

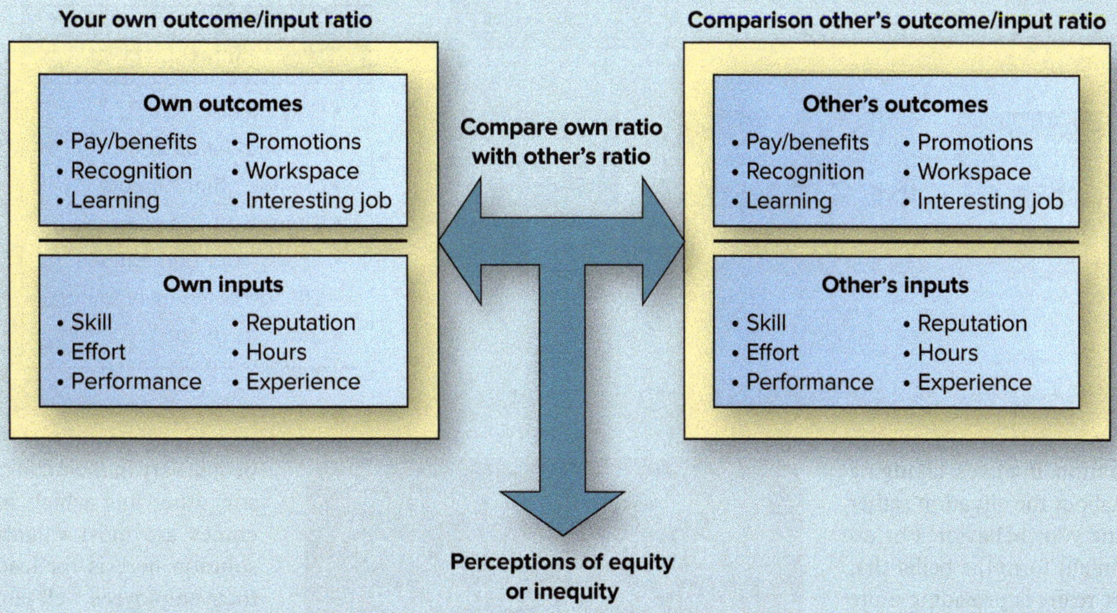

the organization. The equity principle relates to the most common set of distributive justice rules in organizational settings, so let's look at equity-based distributive justice in more detail.

Equity-based fairness is explained by **equity theory**, which says that employees determine whether a decision is equitable by comparing their own outcome/input ratio to the outcome/input ratio of another person or group.[75] As Exhibit 5.6 illustrates, the *outcome/input ratio* is the value of the outcomes you receive divided by the value of the inputs you provide in the exchange relationship. Inputs include such things as skill, effort, reputation, performance, experience, and hours worked. Outcomes are what employees receive from the organization, such as pay, promotions, recognition, interesting jobs, and opportunities to improve one's skills and knowledge.

A central feature of equity theory is that individuals determine fairness in terms of a *comparison other*.[76] The comparison other might be another person or group of people who perform the same work (same job) or who work in other jobs (e.g., comparing your pay with your boss's pay). The comparison other might even be one or more people in other organizations. Some research suggests that employees frequently collect information on several referents to form a "generalized" comparison other. For the most part, however, the comparison other varies from one person and situation to the next and is not easily identifiable.

The comparison of our own outcome/input ratio with the ratio of someone else results in perceptions of equity, underreward inequity, or overreward inequity. In the equity condition, people believe that their outcome/input ratio is similar to the ratio of the comparison other. In the underreward inequity situation, people believe their outcome/input ratio is lower than the comparison other's ratio. In the overreward inequity condition, people believe their outcome/input ratio is higher than the comparison other's ratio.

Inequity and Employee Motivation How do perceptions of equity or inequity affect employee motivation? The answer is illustrated in Exhibit 5.7. When people believe they are under- or overrewarded, they experience negative emotions (called *inequity tension*).[77] As we have pointed out throughout this chapter, emotions are the engines of motivation. In the case of inequity, people are motivated to reduce the emotional tension. They tend to have a strong emotional response when the situation seems to be unfair, and this emotion nags them until they take steps to correct the perceived inequity.

There are several ways to try to reduce the inequity tension.[78] Let's consider each of these in the context of underreward inequity. One action is to reduce your inputs so the outcome/input ratio is similar to that of the higher-paid coworker. Some employees do this by working more slowly, offering fewer suggestions, and engaging in less organizational citizenship behavior. A second action is to increase your outcomes. Some people who think they are underpaid ask for a pay raise. Others make unauthorized use of company resources. A third behavioral response is to increase the comparison other's inputs. You might subtly ask the better-paid coworker to do a larger share of the work, for instance. A fourth action is to reduce the comparison other's outcomes. This might occur by ensuring that the coworker gets less desirable jobs or working conditions. Another action, although uncommon, is to ask the company to reduce the coworker's pay so it is the same as yours.

Exhibit 5.7 Motivational Effects of Inequity Perceptions

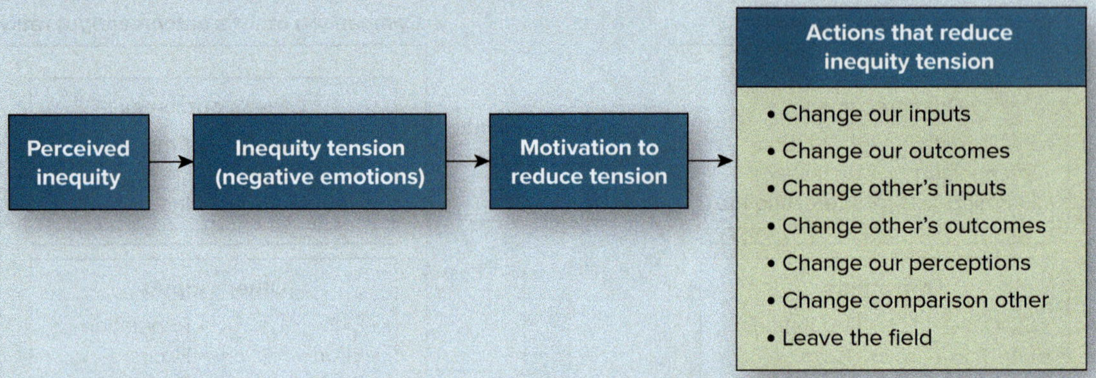

A fifth action involves changing your beliefs about the situation rather than changing your behavior. For example, you might form the belief that the coworker really is providing more inputs (e.g., working longer hours) for that higher pay. Alternatively, you might change your perceived valence of some outcomes. Rather than viewing a coworker's work-related travel as a desirable perk, you now perceive most of that travel as an undesirable nuisance. A sixth action to reduce the inequity tension is to change the comparison other. Instead of comparing yourself with the higher-paid coworker, you might increasingly compare with a friend or neighbor who works in a similar job. Finally, if the inequity tension is strong enough and can't be reduced through other actions, you might leave the field. This occurs by moving to another department, joining another company, or keeping away from the work site where the overpaid coworker is located.

> I was underpaid for the first half of my life. I don't mind being overpaid for the second half.[79]
>
> —Pierre Burton, journalist and popular history author

People who feel overreward inequity would reverse these actions. Some overrewarded employees reduce their feelings of inequity by working harder; others encourage the underrewarded coworker to work at a more leisurely pace. A common reaction, however, is that the overrewarded employee changes their perceptions to justify the more favorable outcomes, such as believing the assigned work is more difficult or their skills are more valuable than the lower-paid coworker's skills.

Evaluating Equity Theory Equity theory is quite successful at understanding (usually in hindsight) why people feel unfairly rewarded.[80] However, it is more difficult to use as a practical tool for preventing inequity in the future. The main problem is that people vary in their choice of comparison other and which inputs or outcomes are most valuable. The best solution here is for leaders to know their employees well enough to minimize the risk of inequity feelings. Open communication is also key, so employees can advise decision makers when they believe reward allocations are unfair. A second problem is that equity theory accounts for only some of our feelings of fairness in the workplace. Procedural and interactional justice can be just as important as distributive justice.

Procedural and Interactional Justice

Procedural justice is the perception that appropriate rules are applied in the procedures used throughout the course of deciding how to distribute workplace benefits and burdens. *Interactional justice* is the perception that appropriate rules are applied in the way the people involved are treated throughout that decision process.[81] Exhibit 5.8 lists the main rules that people consider when determining procedural and interactional justice.

There are several ways to maintain procedural justice.[82] Decision makers must be perceived as unbiased, without self-interest in the results, and not blinded by narrow doctrines. Their allocation decisions need to be based on as much relevant and accurate information as possible. Those decisions also need to be timely and take into account the positions and circumstances of the diverse groups affected by the outcomes. Another factor to consider in procedural justice is whether the decision criteria and decision procedures are compatible with ethical principles. For example, gathering accurate information might not be fair if it involves closely monitoring employees or violating their individual privacy. The decision criteria used to allocate benefits as well as the procedural justice rules need to be applied consistently to everyone (equality) and over time (stability).

Another important condition for procedural justice is that employees are given "voice" in the

McGraw Hill connect
SELF-ASSESSMENT 5.4: How Sensitive Are You to Inequities?

EXHIBIT 5.8 Procedural and interactional Justice Rules

Procedural Justice Rules	Interactional Justice Rules
• Decision makers are not biased by self-interest or restrictive doctrines. • Allocation decisions are based on a full complement of accurate information. • Decision makers consider the interests of all groups affected by the outcomes. • Decisions and procedures are compatible with ethical principles. • Decision criteria and procedures are applied consistently across persons and over time. • Employees have the opportunity to present their evidence and opinions to decision makers (voice). • Questionable decisions and procedures can be appealed and overturned.	• Employees are treated in a polite manner. • Employees are treated with respect. • Employees receive thorough and well-justified explanations about the decision. • Employees receive honest, candid, and timely information about the decision.

Sources: Based on information in: G.S. Leventhal, "What Should Be Done with Equity Theory? New Approaches to the Study of Fairness in Social Relationships," in *Social Exchange*, ed. K.J. Gergen, M.S. Greenberg, and R.H. Willis (Boston: Springer US, 1980), 27–55; J.A. Colquitt and J.B. Rodell, "Measuring Justice and Fairness," in *The Oxford Handbook of Justice in the Workplace*, ed. R.S. Cropanzano and M.L. Ambrose (New York: Oxford University Press, 2015), 187–202.

An important condition for procedural justice is that employees are given "voice" in the process—they have the opportunity to present their evidence and opinions.
fizkes/Shutterstock

process—they have the opportunity to present their evidence and opinions to decision makers. Voice improves the quality of information applied to the decision. It also provides a value-expressive function; employees tend to feel better after having an opportunity to speak their mind. Lastly, employees should have a right to appeal the decision (so it is reviewed and possibly overturned) if they believe there were errors in how resources were distributed or flaws in the procedures leading to that decision.

Interactional justice also depends on a set of rules that people believe are being applied to the situation.[83] Two of these rules—treating people with politeness and with respect—support the feeling of fairness in the interpersonal relationship. Abusive supervision is a clear example of violation of these interactional justice rules because employees are treated rudely and their self-worth is attacked.[84] To generate a sense of fairness regarding the information provided, employees should receive thorough and well justified explanations about the decision, and honest, candid, and timely information about the decision. For instance, people are more likely to feel that a decision is unfair if decision makers refuse to explain how the decision was made, or if they seem evasive in their explanation.

Consequences of Procedural and Interactional Injustice

Employees who believe procedural or interactional justice rules have been violated experience negative emotions, such as anger, frustration, insult, resentment, and shame.[85] Procedural or interactional injustice often results in less work effort (and performance), fewer organizational citizenship behaviors, less cooperation with coworkers, increased involvement in union activities, and higher turnover. Victims of procedural and interactional injustice sometimes retaliate to restore their self-esteem, reinstate their status and power in the relationship, and to educate the perpetrator of the injustice.[86] A related outcome is increased aggression toward the decision maker (e.g., supervisor) and sometimes toward coworkers who are seemingly treated more favorably. Procedural or interactional injustice can also lead to more extreme dysfunctional behaviors, such as theft, sabotage, and violence.

LO5-7 List the advantages and disadvantages of job specialization and explain how to improve employee motivation through job design.

JOB DESIGN

How do you build a better job? That question has challenged organizational behavior experts, psychologists, engineers, and economists for a few centuries. Some jobs have very few tasks and usually require very little skill. Other jobs are immensely complex and require years of experience and learning to master them. From one extreme to the other, jobs have different effects on work efficiency and employee motivation. The ideal, at least from

job specialization The result of a division of labor, in which work is subdivided into separate jobs assigned to different people

the organization's perspective, is to find the right combination so that work is performed efficiently but employees are engaged and satisfied.[87] Job design—the process of assigning tasks to a job, including the interdependency of those tasks with other jobs—tries to balance these potentially competing effects of efficiency and motivation. To understand this issue more fully, we'll begin by describing early job design efforts aimed at increasing work efficiency through job specialization.

Job Design and Work Efficiency

By any measure, supermarket cashiers have highly repetitive work. One consulting firm estimated that cashiers should be able to scan each item in an average of 4.6 seconds. Cashiers at five British supermarket chains took between 1.75 and 3.25 seconds to scan each item from a standardized list of 20 products. Along with scanning, cashiers process the payment, move the divider stick, and (in some stores) bag the checked groceries.[88]

Supermarket cashier jobs have high job specialization; with a very short cycle time; it takes about four seconds to scan each grocery item before the task is repeated with the next item.
Antenna/Getty Images

Supermarket cashiers perform jobs with a high degree of **job specialization**. Job specialization occurs when the work required to serve a customer—or provide any other product or service—is subdivided into separate jobs assigned to different people. For instance, supermarkets have separate jobs for checking out customers, stocking shelves, preparing fresh foods, and so forth. Except in the smallest family grocery stores, one person would not perform all of these tasks as part of one job. Each resulting job includes a narrow subset of tasks, usually completed in a short cycle time. *Cycle time* is the time required to complete the task before starting over with another item or client. Supermarket cashiers have a cycle time of about four seconds to scan each item before they repeat the activity with the next item. They also have a cycle time for serving each customer, which works out to somewhere between 20 and 40 times per hour in busy stores.

Why would companies divide work into such tiny bits? The simple answer is that job specialization potentially improves work efficiency. It does so in four ways:

- *Fewer skills and less knowledge to learn.* Employees can master specialized jobs more quickly because there are fewer physical and cognitive skills and knowledge to learn and therefore less time required to become proficient in the job.
- *More frequent practice.* More specialized jobs typically have shorter cycle times. Shorter task cycles give employees more frequent practice with the task, so jobs are mastered more quickly.
- *Less attention residue from changing tasks.* Employees experience "attention residue" after they change from one type of task to another. Their cognitive attention lingers on the previous type of work, which slows down performance on the new task. Specialized jobs have fewer and less varied tasks, so there is less changeover and, consequently, less attention residue and productivity loss.[89]
- *Better person–job matching.* Job specialization tends to increase work efficiency by enabling employers to more precisely match employees with specific aptitudes, skills, knowledge, interests, and other characteristics to the jobs for which these talents are best suited.[90]

The benefits of job specialization were noted more than 2,300 years ago by the Chinese philosopher Mencius and the Greek philosopher Plato. Scottish economist Adam Smith wrote 250 years ago about the advantages of job specialization. Smith described a small factory where 10 pin makers collectively produced as many as 48,000 pins per day because they performed specialized tasks. One person straightened the metal, another cut it, another sharpened one end of the cut piece, yet another added a white tip to the other end, and so forth. By comparison, Smith suggested that if each of these 10 people working alone produced entire pins, they would collectively manufacture no more than 20 pins per day.[91]

Scientific Management

One of the strongest advocates of job specialization was Frederick Winslow Taylor, an American industrial engineer who

scientific management The practice of systematically partitioning work into its smallest elements and standardizing tasks to achieve maximum efficiency

job characteristics model A job design model that relates the motivational properties of jobs to specific personal and organizational consequences of those properties

skill variety The extent to which employees must use different skills and talents to perform tasks within their jobs

task identity The degree to which a job requires completion of a whole or an identifiable piece of work

task significance The degree to which a job has a substantial impact on the organization and/or larger society

introduced the principles of **scientific management** in the early 1900s.[92] Scientific management consists of a toolkit of activities. Some of these interventions–employee selection, training, goal setting, and work incentives–are common today but were rare until Taylor popularized them. However, scientific management is mainly associated with high levels of job specialization and standardization of tasks to achieve maximum efficiency.

Taylor recommended that the most effective companies should have detailed procedures and work practices developed by engineers, enforced by supervisors, and executed by employees. Even supervisory tasks should be divided among different people (operations, inspection, discipline). Although the accuracy of Taylor's evidence is suspect, scientific management practices do improve work efficiency in many situations. These productivity gains are partly due to training, goal setting, and work incentives, but job specialization quickly became popular in its own right.

Problems with Job Specialization

Frederick Winslow Taylor and his contemporaries focused on how job specialization reduces labor "waste" by improving the mechanical efficiency of work (i.e., skills matching, faster learning, less switchover time). Yet they didn't seem to notice how this extreme job specialization adversely affects employee attitudes and motivation. Some jobs–such as scanning grocery items–are so specialized and repetitive that they become tedious, socially isolating, and cognitively dysfunctional. Specialized jobs with very short cycle times often produce higher employee turnover and absenteeism. Companies sometimes have to pay higher wages to attract job applicants to this dissatisfying, narrowly defined work.[93]

Job specialization affects work quality, but in two opposing ways. On the positive side, employees in specialized short-cycle jobs tend to produce higher quality output because, as we mentioned earlier, they master their work faster compared to people in jobs with more complex or varied tasks. This higher proficiency explains why specialist lawyers tend to provide better quality service than do generalist lawyers.[94]

However, job specialization also has two negative effects on work quality. First, many jobs (such as supermarket cashiers) are specialized to the point that they are highly repetitive and monotonous. This type of work tends to reduce attentiveness and motivation, both of which undermine output quality. Second, by performing a tiny piece of the overall product or service, employees in specialized jobs have difficulty striving for better quality or even noticing flaws with the work unit's overall production process.

Job Design and Work Motivation

Frederick Winslow Taylor may have overlooked the motivational effect of job characteristics, but it is now the central focus of many job design initiatives. The motivational potential of the job itself is the focus of the **job characteristics model**, shown in Exhibit 5.9. The model identifies five core job dimensions that produce three psychological states. Employees who experience these psychological states tend to have higher levels of intrinsic motivation, work performance (quality and efficiency), and job satisfaction with the work itself.[95]

Core Job Characteristics The five job characteristics are skill variety, task identity, task significance, autonomy, and job feedback:

- *Skill variety.* **Skill variety** refers to the use of different skills and talents to perform tasks within a job. For example, sales clerks who normally only serve customers might be assigned the additional duties of stocking inventory and changing storefront displays.
- *Task identity.* **Task identity** is the degree to which a job requires completion of a whole or identifiable piece of work, such as assembling an entire broadband modem rather than just soldering in the circuitry.
- *Task significance.* **Task significance** is the degree to which the job affects the organization and/or larger society. This job characteristic is most strongly felt when employees regularly and directly see how their work affects customers or others in society. As an example, when chefs in one study were able to directly observe the customers who ordered food (and vice versa), they felt more appreciated and, consequently,

> Job specialization has opposing effects on work quality: quality may improve because short-cycle tasks are mastered sooner, yet quality worsens because these repetitive and monotonous tasks reduce attentiveness and motivation.

Exhibit 5.9 The Job Characteristics Model

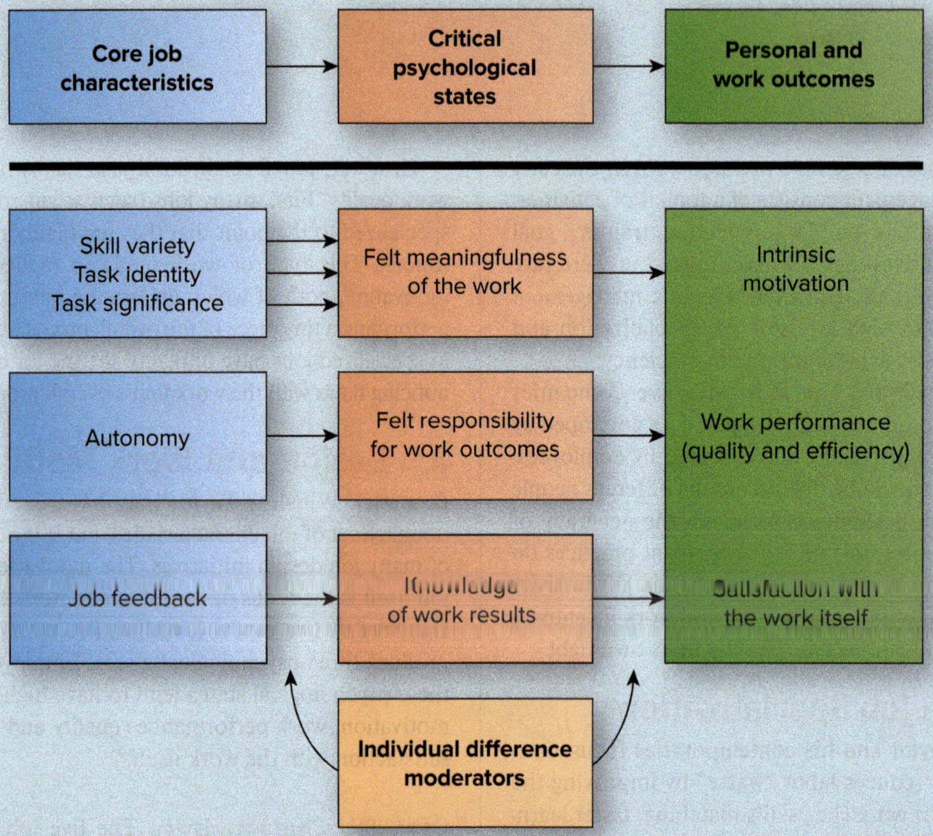

Sources: J.R. Hackman and E.E. Lawler, "Employee Reactions to Job Characteristics," *Journal of Applied Psychology* 55, no. 3 (1971): 259–86; J.R. Hackman and G.R. Oldham, "The Job Diagnostic Survey: An Instrument for the Diagnosis of Jobs and the Evaluation of Job Redesign Projects" (New Haven, CT: Department of Administrative Sciences, Yale University, May 1974); J.R. Hackman and G.R. Oldham, "Motivation through the Design of Work: Test of a Theory," *Organizational Behavior and Human Performance* 16, no. 2 (1976): 250–79; J.R. Hackman and G. Oldham, *Work Redesign* (Reading, MA: Addison-Wesley, 1980).

exerted more effort and felt more satisfied with their job. "When [the customers] can see us [make their food], they appreciate it, and I appreciate that. It makes me want to improve," says a cook who participated in the study.[96]

- *Autonomy.* As we discussed earlier in this chapter, autonomy is a key contributor to intrinsic motivation. In jobs with high levels of autonomy, employees make their own decisions rather than rely on detailed instructions from supervisors or procedure manuals. These jobs provide freedom, independence, and discretion in scheduling the work and determining the procedures to be used to complete the work.[97]
- *Job feedback.* Job feedback is the degree to which employees can tell how well they are doing from direct sensory information from the job itself. Airline pilots can tell how well they land their aircraft, and road crews can see how well they have prepared the roadbed and laid the asphalt.

Critical Psychological States The five core job characteristics affect employee motivation, performance, and satisfaction through three critical psychological states, shown in Exhibit 5.9. Skill variety, task identity, and task significance directly contribute to the job's *felt meaningfulness of the work*—the belief that one's work is worthwhile or important. Autonomy directly contributes to *felt responsibility for work outcomes*—a sense of being personally accountable for the work outcomes. The third critical psychological state is *knowledge of work results*—an awareness of the work outcomes based on information from the job itself.

Individual Differences Job design doesn't increase work motivation, performance, or satisfaction for everyone in every situation. Employees must have the required skills and knowledge to master the more challenging work. Otherwise, job design

Reality Check on the Motivational Potential of Jobs[98]

72% of 557,778 US federal government employees say their work gives them a feeling of personal accomplishment.

67% of 4,500 office workers in the U.S., U.K., France, Germany, India, and Singapore say they are constantly doing the same tasks over and over again (low skill variety).

39% of 637 Australian employees say they want to work for an organization that gives them more job autonomy.

16% of 308 Australian managers say employees in their organization have control (autonomy) over how, when, and where they do their job. (47% say these are dictated to employees by established policies).

15% of 1,021 US employees say they are living their purpose in day-to-day work (85% of executives and upper management say this).

(Photo): Samuel Borges Photography/Shutterstock

tends to increase stress and reduce job performance. The original model also states that employees will be motivated only when they have a high *growth need strength* (the need for personal growth and development–similar to self-actualization).[99] However, research findings have been mixed, suggesting that employees might be motivated by the job no matter how they score on growth needs.[100]

Social and Information Processing Job Characteristics

The job characteristics model overlooks two clusters of job features: social characteristics and information processing demands.[101] Two *social job characteristics* are:

- *Social interaction requirements.* This is the extent to which the job requires employees to interact with coworkers, clients, suppliers, and other stakeholders. Jobs with high social interaction requirements tend to be more motivating because employees need greater use of emotion regulation skills (see Chapter 4). Social interaction also increases the complexity of the work due to the person's interdependence with these other people (see *task interdependence* in Chapter 7).
- *Social feedback.* A second social characteristic of the job is feedback from others. Jobs that include feedback from people may be just as motivating as jobs that provide feedback from the task itself. Feedback from others may be communicated explicitly through conversation or more subtly through nonverbal cues.

task variability The degree to which job duties are nonroutine and unpredictable; employees perform diverse tasks from one day to the next because they are faced with unfamiliar and unexpected issues

Information processing demands represent the other category of job characteristics excluded from the job characteristics model.[102] The two information processing demands are:

- **Task variability.** This information processing demand refers to how predictable the job duties are from one day to the next. Task variability increases employee motivation because employees in these jobs have nonroutine work patterns; they perform different types of tasks from one day to the next, and don't know which tasks are required until that time. Jobs with low task variability, on the other hand, are less motivating because the work is repetitive; employees perform similar tasks using similar skills in the same way every day.

> Jobs with high social interaction requirements tend to be more motivating because the employee's interdependence with others increases task complexity and requires greater use of emotion regulation skills.

task analyzability The degree to which job duties allow the application of established procedures and rules to guide decisions and behavior (high analyzability); employee creativity and judgment are necessary to perform jobs with low task analyzability

job enlargement The practice of increasing the number and variety of related tasks assigned to a job

job enrichment The practice of giving employees more responsibility for scheduling, coordinating, and planning their own work

- **Task analyzability.** This information processing demand refers to how much the job can be performed using known procedures and rules. Jobs with high task analyzability have low information processing demand because job incumbents rely on established guidelines for most decisions and actions. Consequently, employees are less motivated when performing jobs with high task analyzability. Jobs with low task analyzability, on the other hand, have higher motivational potential because employees need to rely on their creativity and judgment to determine the best courses of action for most tasks. The novel or complex work activities in low task analyzability jobs make it difficult to create fixed procedures and rules.

Task variability and task analyzability will be discussed again in Chapter 7 on task structures for teams and in Chapter 12 on contingencies for designing organizational structures.

Job Design Practices That Motivate

Three main strategies can increase the motivational potential of jobs: frequent job rotation, job enlargement, and job enrichment.

Frequent Job Rotation Frequent job rotation involves moving employees through two or more jobs each day. For example, many grocery stores reduce the repetitiveness of checkout work by moving cashiers to other jobs during the work shift. This rotation differs from career development transfers, which involves transferring employees once or twice each year to different jobs. One benefit of frequent job rotation is that it potentially reduces the risk of repetitive strain and heavy lifting injuries. A second benefit is that employees learn how to perform multiple jobs. When employees are trained to perform multiple jobs, companies can more easily fill positions during vacations and other absences.

Third, employees who perform multiple jobs within a production or service process develop a clearer picture of that process and ways to improve product quality. In other words, job rotation seems to reverse the performance quality problem that we discussed earlier for job specialization. The fourth potential benefit of frequent job rotation is that employees use a wider variety of skills throughout the workday—their daily work has more skill variety—which potentially improves their motivation and satisfaction.[103]

Job Enlargement **Job enlargement** is the practice of increasing the number and variety of related tasks assigned to a job held by an employee. This might involve combining two or more complete jobs into one or just adding one or two more tasks to an existing job. Either way, job enlargement offers the same benefits as job rotation because adding more and varied tasks gives employees more skill variety and reduces the risk of repetitive strain injuries.[104]

Putting employees in direct contact with clients increases task significance because employees more easily see how their work affects those clients.
Spiderstock/Getty Images

Job Enrichment **Job enrichment** occurs when employees are given more responsibility for scheduling, coordinating, and planning their own work.[105] It relates to all aspects of the job characteristics model, but it is particularly about autonomy and its psychological outcome of felt responsibility for work outcomes. Job enrichment potentially increases job satisfaction and work motivation, and reduces absenteeism and turnover. Productivity typically improves when task identity and job feedback increase. Product and service quality also tend to improve because job enrichment increases the jobholder's felt responsibility and sense of ownership over the product or service.[106]

One way to increase job enrichment is by combining highly interdependent tasks into one job. This *natural grouping* approach occurs in the video journalist job because it naturally groups tasks together to complete an entire product (i.e., a news story). By forming natural work units, jobholders have stronger feelings of responsibility for an identifiable body of work. They feel a sense of ownership and, therefore, tend to deliver higher quality work output. Forming natural work units increases task identity and task significance because employees perform a complete product or service and can more readily see how their work affects others.

A second job enrichment strategy, called *establishing client relationships,* involves putting employees in direct contact with their clients rather than using another job group or the supervisor as the liaison between the employee and the customer. Establishing client relationships increases task significance because employees more easily see how their work affects those clients. By being directly responsible for specific clients, employees also have more information and can make better decisions affecting those clients.[107]

Study Checklist

Connect® is available for *M: Organizational Behavior.* Additional resources include:

✓ Exercises:

- **Case Analysis:** Apply concepts within the context of a real-world situation.
- **Click and Drag:** Helps make the connection between theory and application through matching, ranking, or grouping activities.
- **Video Case:** See management in action through interactive videos.
- **Self-Assessment:** Designed to promote student self-awareness and reflection, these research-based surveys contain detailed feedback for students.
- **Application-Based Activities:** These highly interactive, application- and analysis-based exercises allow students to take on specific roles to complete management related tasks within a real-world context.

✓ **SmartBook 2.0™**—Smartbook 2.0 is an adaptive learning solution that provides personalized learning to individual student needs, continually adapts to pinpoint knowledge gaps and focuses learning on concepts requiring additional study. It fosters more productive learning, takes the guesswork out of what to study, and helps students better prepare for class.

Notes

1. "The Power of Ownership at CGI," *CGI Australia: Careers* (article), March 2021; "Why CGI Members Love Our Share Purchase Plan," *CGI UK: Careers* (article), May 2021; B. Sutherland, "KKR Wins by Treating Workers More Like Owners," *Washington Post*, May 31, 2022; P. Stavros, "Greater Employee Ownership Can Make Work Fairer," *Financial Times*, July 31, 2022; C. Mendoza, "Employee Ownership Programmes: How Do They Affect Returns for LPs?," *Private Equity International* (blog), September 30, 2022; "CGI Fiscal 2022 Results," Annual Report (Montreal: CGI Inc, December 2022).
2. C.C. Pinder, *Work Motivation in Organizational Behavior* (Upper Saddle River, NJ: Prentice Hall, 1998); A.M. Schmidt, J.W. Beck, and J.Z. Gillespie, "Motivation: Industrial and Organizational Psychology," in *Handbook of Psychology*, 2nd ed., ed. Schmidt, Neil and Highouse, S., vol. 12 (John Wiley & Sons, Inc., 2012), 311-40.
3. W.H. Macey and B. Schneider, "The Meaning of Employee Engagement," *Industrial and Organizational Psychology* 1 (2008): 3-30; A.M. Saks and J.A. Gruman, "What Do We Really Know about Employee Engagement?" *Human Resource Development Quarterly* 25, no. 2 (2014): 155-82; J.L. Whittington et al., *Enhancing Employee Engagement: An Evidence-Based Approach* (New York: Palgrave Macmillan, 2017), Chap. 1.
4. The confusing array of definitions about drives and needs has been the subject of criticism for a half century. See, for example, R.S. Peters, "Motives and Motivation," *Philosophy* 31 (1956): 117-30; H. Cantril, "Sentio, Ergo Sum: 'Motivation' Reconsidered," *Journal of Psychology* 65 (1967): 91-107; G.R. Salancik and J. Pfeffer, "An Examination of Need-Satisfaction Models of Job Attitudes," *Administrative Science Quarterly* 22 (1977): 427-56. For a recent effort to condense 162 human "motives" into a small set, see J.R. Talevich et al., "Toward a Comprehensive Taxonomy of Human Motives," *PLoS ONE* 12, no. 2 (2017): e0172279.
5. D.W. Pfaff, *Drive: Neurobiological and Molecular Mechanisms of Sexual Motivation* (Cambridge, MA: MIT Press, 1999); A. Blasi, "Emotions and Moral Motivation," *Journal for the Theory of Social Behaviour* 29 (1999): 1-19; K.C. Berridge, "Motivation Concepts in Behavioral Neuroscience," *Physiology & Behavior* 81 (2004): 179-209; D. Scheffer and H. Heckhausen, "Trait Theories of Motivation," in *Motivation and Action*, ed. J. Heckhausen and H. Heckhausen (Cham: Springer International Publishing, 2018), 67-112. We distinguish drives from emotions, but future research may find that the two concepts are not so different as is stated here. Woodworth is credited with either coining or popularizing the term *drives* in the context of human motivation. His classic book is certainly the first source to discuss the concept in detail. See R.S. Woodworth, *Dynamic Psychology* (New York: Columbia University Press, 1918).
6. P.R. Lawrence and N. Nohria, *Driven: How Human Nature Shapes Our Choices* (San Francisco: Jossey-Bass, 2002); N. Nohria, B. Groysberg, and L.-E. Lee, "Employee Motivation: A Powerful New Model," *Harvard Business Review* (2008): 78-84; P. Lawrence and M. Pirson, "Economistic and Humanistic Narratives of Leadership in the Age of Globality: Toward a Renewed Darwinian Theory of Leadership," *Journal of Business Ethics* 128, no. 2 (2015): 383-394.
7. S.G. Barsade and D.E. Gibson, "Why Does Affect Matter in Organizations?" *Academy of Management Perspectives* 21 (2007): 36-59; K.C. Berridge, "Evolving Concepts of Emotion and Motivation," *Frontiers in Psychology* 9 (2018); E. Harmon-Jones, "On Motivational Influences, Moving beyond Valence, and Integrating Dimensional and Discrete Views of Emotion," *Cognition and Emotion* 33 (2019): 101-8.
8. W. McDougall, *Outline of Psychology* (New York: Charles Scribner's Sons, 1923), 440 fn#1.
9. B. Monin, D.A. Pizarro, and J.S. Beer, "Deciding Versus Reacting: Conceptions of Moral Judgment and the Reason-Affect Debate," *Review of General Psychology* 11 (2007): 99-111; S.H. Schwartz et al., "Refining the Theory of Basic Individual Values," *Journal of Personality and Social Psychology* 103 (2012): 663-88; M. Driver, "Motivation and Identity: A Psychoanalytic Perspective on the Turn to Identity in Motivation Research," *Human Relations* 70 (2017): 617-37.
10. P.R. Lawrence and N. Nohria, *Driven: How Human Nature Shapes Our Choices* (San Francisco: Jossey-Bass, 2002); N. Nohria, B. Groysberg, and L.-E. Lee, "Employee Motivation: A Powerful New Model," *Harvard Business Review* (2008): 78-84; P. Lawrence and M. Pirson, "Economistic and Humanistic Narratives of Leadership in the Age of Globality: Toward a Renewed Darwinian Theory of Leadership," *Journal of Business Ethics* 128 (2015): 383-94.

11. The drive to acquire is likely associated with research on getting ahead, desire for competence, the selfish gene, and desire for social distinction. See R.H. Frank, *Choosing the Right Pond: Human Behavior and the Quest for Status* (New York: Oxford University Press, 1985); R. Dawkins, *The Selfish Gene*, 30th Anniversary Ed. (Oxford, UK: Oxford University Press, 2006); M.R. Leary, "Motivational and Emotional Aspects of the Self," *Annual Review of Psychology* 58, no. 1 (2007): 317–44; F. Martela and T.J.J. Riekki, "Autonomy, Competence, Relatedness, and Beneficence: A Multicultural Comparison of the Four Pathways to Meaningful Work," *Frontiers in Psychology* 9 (2018): 1157.

12. R.E. Baumeister and M.R. Leary, "The Need to Belong: Desire for Interpersonal Attachments as a Fundamental Human Motivation," *Psychological Bulletin* 117 (1995): 497–529.

13. G. Loewenstein, "The Psychology of Curiosity: A Review and Reinterpretation," *Psychological Bulletin* 116 (1994): 75–98; J. Litman, "Curiosity and the Pleasures of Learning: Wanting and Liking New Information," *Cognition and Emotion* 19 (2005): 793–814; C. Kidd and B.Y. Hayden, "The Psychology and Neuroscience of Curiosity," *Neuron* 88 (2015): 449–60.

14. N. Nohria, B. Groysberg, and L.-E. Lee, "Employee Motivation: A Powerful New Model," *Harvard Business Review*, August 2008, 78–84; F. Beyer et al., "Hit or Run: Exploring Aggressive and Avoidant Reactions to Interpersonal Provocation Using a Novel Fight-or-Escape Paradigm (FOE)," *Frontiers in Behavioral Neuroscience* 11 (2017): 00190.

15. A.R. Damasio, *Descartes' Error: Emotion, Reason, and the Human Brain* (New York: Putnam's Sons, 1994); J.E. LeDoux, "Emotion Circuits in the Brain," *Annual Review of Neuroscience* 23 (2000): 155–84; M. Reimann and A. Bechara, "The Somatic Marker Framework as a Neurological Theory of Decision-Making: Review, Conceptual Comparisons, and Future Neuroeconomics Research," *Journal of Economic Psychology* 31, no. 5 (2010): 767–76; P. Winkielman, K. Berridge, and S. Sher, "Emotion, Consciousness, and Social Behavior," in *The Oxford Handbook of Social Neuroscience*, ed. J. Decety and J.T. Cacioppo (Oxford University Press, 2011), 195–211; T. Poppa and A. Bechara, "The Somatic Marker Hypothesis: Revisiting the Role of the 'Body-Loop' in Decision-Making," *Current Opinion in Behavioral Sciences* 19 (2018): 61–66.

16. P.R. Lawrence and N. Nohria, *Driven: How Human Nature Shapes Our Choices* (San Francisco: Jossey-Bass, 2002), 145–47; R.F. Baumeister, E.J. Masicampo, and K.D. Vohs, "Do Conscious Thoughts Cause Behavior?" *Annual Review of Psychology* 62, no. 1 (2011): 331–61.

17. P.R. Lawrence and N. Nohria, *Driven: How Human Nature Shapes Our Choices* (San Francisco: Jossey-Bass, 2002), Chap. 11.

18. For recent discussion on the benefits and risks of work practices that encourage employee competition, see: A. Sapegina and A. Weibel, "The Good, the Not So Bad and the Ugly of Competitive Human Resource Practices: A Multidisciplinary Conceptual Framework," *Group & Organization Management* 42 (2017): 707–47.

19. A.H. Maslow, "A Theory of Human Motivation," *Psychological Review* 50 (1943): 370–96; A.H. Maslow, *Motivation and Personality* (New York: Harper & Row, 1954).

20. Maslow did not diagram his theory as a pyramid. He does not even mention pyramids in his writing on human motivation. Instead, Maslow mostly repeats the term *hierarchy* in describing how human needs (drives) are organized relative to each other. The earliest description of human needs as a pyramid is likely from Chapter 2 ("The Pyramid of Man's Needs") of a 1960 book on conflict by F. Alexander Magoun, a professor of human relations at MIT. Magoun's chapter discusses Maslow's needs hierarchy theory. A recent review also points to a step model of Maslow's model in Keith Davis's human relations book and of a pyramid model in a 1960 article by Charles McDermid. See F.A. Magoun, *Cooperation and Conflict in Industry* (New York: Harper, 1960), 20–31; T. Bridgman, S. Cummings, and J. Ballard, "Who Built Maslow's Pyramid? A History of the Creation of Management Studies' Most Famous Symbol and Its Implications for Management Education," *Academy of Management Learning & Education* 18 (2019): 81–98.

21. D.T. Hall and K.E. Nougaim, "An Examination of Maslow's Need Hierarchy in an Organizational Setting," *Organizational Behavior and Human Performance* 3, no. 1 (1968): 12; M.A. Wahba and L.G. Bridwell, "Maslow Reconsidered: A Review of Research on the Need Hierarchy Theory," *Organizational Behavior and Human Performance* 15 (1976): 212–40; E.L. Betz, "Two Tests of Maslow's Theory of Need Fulfillment," *Journal of Vocational Behavior* 24, no. 2 (1984): 204–20; P.A. Corning, "Biological Adaptation in Human Societies: A 'Basic Needs' Approach," *Journal of Bioeconomics* 2, no. 1 (2000): 41–86. For a recent proposed revision of the model, see D.T. Kenrick et al., "Renovating the Pyramid of Needs: Contemporary Extensions Built upon Ancient Foundations," *Perspectives on Psychological Science* 5, no. 3 (2010): 292–314.

22. Maslow did acknowledge that the needs hierarchy has a different ordering for some people, but he described these as relatively rare exceptions. See: A.H. Maslow, "A Theory of Human Motivation," *Psychological Review* 50 (1943): 386–88. For discussion of personal values hierarchies and motivation, see: L. Sagiv and S.H. Schwartz, "Personal Values across Cultures," *Annual Review of Psychology* 73, no. 1 (2022): 517–46.

23. J. Jin and J. Rounds, "Stability and Change in Work Values: A Meta-Analysis of Longitudinal Studies," *Journal of Vocational Behavior* 80 (2012): 326–39; L.M. Taciano, M. Petar, and G.S. Chris, "Values Stability and Change in Adulthood: A 3-Year Longitudinal Study of Rank-Order Stability and Mean-Level Differences," *Personality and Social Psychology Bulletin* 42 (2016): 572–88; C.M. Lechner et al., "The Development of Work Values during the Transition to Adulthood: A Two-Country Study," *Journal of Vocational Behavior* 99 (2017): 52–65.

24. K. Dye, A.J. Mills, and T.G. Weatherbee, "Maslow: Man Interrupted–Reading Management Theory in Context," *Management Decision* 43, no. 10 (2005): 1375–95; S. Kesebir, J. Graham, and S. Oishi, "A Theory of Human Needs Should Be Human-Centered, Not Animal-Centered," *Perspectives on Psychological Science* 5 (2010): 315–19; C. Peterson and N. Park, "What Happened to Self-Actualization?," *Perspectives on Psychological Science* 5, no. 3 (2010): 320–22; J.A. Krems, D.T. Kenrick, and R. Neel, "Individual Perceptions of Self-Actualization: What Functional Motives Are Linked to Fulfilling One's Full Potential?," *Personality and Social Psychology Bulletin* 43, no. 9 (2017): 1337–52.

25. M. Gagné and E.L. Deci, "Self-Determination Theory and Work Motivation," *Journal of Organizational Behavior* 26, no. 4 (2005): 331–62; C.P. Cerasoli, J.M. Nicklin, and M.T. Ford, "Intrinsic Motivation and Extrinsic Incentives Jointly Predict Performance: A 40-Year Meta-Analysis," *Psychological Bulletin* 140, no. 4 (2014): 980–1008.

26. M. Gagné and D. Bhave, "Autonomy in the Workplace: An Essential Ingredient to Employee Engagement and Well-Being in Every Culture," in *Human Autonomy in Cross-Cultural Context*, ed. V.I. Chirkov, R.M. Ryan and K.M. Sheldon, *Cross-Cultural Advancements in Positive Psychology* (Dordrecht, Netherlands: Springer Netherlands, 2011), 163–87; E.L. Deci and M.R. Ryan, "The Importance of Universal Psychological Needs for Understanding Motivation in the Workplace," in

The Oxford Handbook of Work Engagement, Motivation, and Self-Determination Theory, ed. M. Gagne (New York: Oxford University Press, 2014), 13–32. For neuroscience research on intrinsic motivation (particularly need for competence), see W. Lee and J. Reeve, "Identifying the Neural Substrates of Intrinsic Motivation during Task Performance," *Cognitive, Affective, & Behavioral Neuroscience* 17, no. 5 (2017): 939–53; S.I. Di Domenico and R.M. Ryan, "The Emerging Neuroscience of Intrinsic Motivation: A New Frontier in Self-Determination Research," *Frontiers in Human Neuroscience* 11 (2017): 00145.

27. C.P. Cerasoli, J.M. Nicklin, and M.T. Ford, "Intrinsic Motivation and Extrinsic Incentives Jointly Predict Performance: A 40-Year Meta-Analysis," *Psychological Bulletin* 140, no. 4 (2014): 980–1008; Y. Garbers and U. Konradt, "The Effect of Financial Incentives on Performance: A Quantitative Review of Individual and Team-Based Financial Incentives," *Journal of Occupational and Organizational Psychology* 87, no. 1 (2014): 102–37.
28. J. Schroeder and A. Fishbach, "How to Motivate Yourself and Others? Intended and Unintended Consequences," *Research in Organizational Behavior* 35 (2015): 123–41.
29. D.C. McClelland, *The Achieving Society* (New York: Van Nostrand Reinhold, 1961); D. McClelland and D. Burnham, "Power Is Great Motivator," *Harvard Business Review* 54, no. 2 (1976): 100–10; M.G. Köllner and O.C. Schultheiss, "Meta-Analytic Evidence of Low Convergence between Implicit and Explicit Measures of the Needs for Achievement, Affiliation, and Power," *Frontiers in Psychology* 5 (2014), https://doi.org/10.3389/fpsyg.2014.00826.
30. D.C. McClelland, *The Achieving Society* (New York: Van Nostrand Reinhold, 1961).
31. S. Leroy et al., "Synchrony Preference: Why Some People Go with the Flow and Some Don't," *Personnel Psychology* 68, no. 4 (2015): 759–809; M.H. Do and A. Minbashian, "A Meta-Analytic Examination of the Effects of the Agentic and Affiliative Aspects of Extraversion on Leadership Outcomes," *Leadership Quarterly* 25, no. 5 (2014): 1040–53, https://doi.org/10.1016/j.leaqua.2014.04.004; B. Steinmann et al., "Implicit Motives and Leadership Performance Revisited: What Constitutes the Leadership Motive Pattern?," *Motivation and Emotion* 39, no. 2 (2015): 167–74, https://doi.org/10.1007/s11031-014-9458-6; B. Steinmann, S.K. Ötting, and G.W. Maier, "Need for Affiliation as a Motivational Add-On for Leadership Behaviors and Managerial Success," *Frontiers in Psychology* 7 (2016), https://doi.org/10.3389/fpsyg.2016.01972.
32. J.C. Magee and C.A. Langner, "How Personalized and Socialized Power Motivation Facilitate Antisocial and Prosocial Decision-Making," *Journal of Research in Personality* 42, no. 6 (2008): 1547–59; D. Rus, D. van Knippenberg, and B. Wisse, "Leader Self-Definition and Leader Self-Serving Behavior," *Leadership Quarterly* 21, no. 3 (2010): 509–29; C. Case and J. Maner, "Divide and Conquer: When and Why Leaders Undermine the Cohesive Fabric of Their Group," *Journal of Personality and Social Psychology* 107, no. 6 (2014): 1033–50.
33. D. Miron and D.C. McClelland, "The Impact of Achievement Motivation Training on Small Business," *California Management Review* 21 (1979): 13–28; M.J. Hoffarth, "From Achievement to Power: David C. McClelland, McBer & Company, and the Business of the Thematic Apperception Test (TAT), 1962–1985," *Journal of the History of the Behavioral Sciences* 56, no. 3 (2020): 153–68; X. Chen et al., "An Enumerative Review and a Meta-Analysis of Primed Goal Effects on Organizational Behavior," *Applied Psychology* 70, no. 1 (2021): 216–53.
34. Expectancies and valences have a long history in motivation and decision making, dating back to the earliest writing on the economics of utilitarianism. See, for example, W.S. Jevons, *The Theory of Political Economy* (London: MacMillan, 1871), Chaps. 2 and 3. For recent discussion in organizational behavior, see S. Sun, J.B. Vancouver, and J.M. Weinhardt, "Goal Choices and Planning: Distinct Expectancy and Value Effects in Two Goal Processes," *Organizational Behavior and Human Decision Processes* 125 (2014): 220–33.
35. Expectancy theory of motivation in work settings originated in V.H. Vroom, *Work and Motivation* (New York: Wiley, 1964). The version of expectancy theory presented here was developed by Edward Lawler. Lawler's model provides a clearer presentation of the model's three components. P-to-O expectancy is similar to "instrumentality" in Vroom's original expectancy theory model. The difference is that instrumentality is a correlation whereas P-to-O expectancy is a probability. See J.P. Campbell et al., *Managerial Behavior, Performance, and Effectiveness* (New York: McGraw Hill, 1970); E.E. Lawler III, *Motivation in Work Organizations* (Monterey, CA: Brooks-Cole, 1973); D.A. Nadler and E.E. Lawler, "Motivation: A Diagnostic Approach," in *Perspectives on Behavior in Organizations*, ed. J.R. Hackman, E.E. Lawler III, and L.W. Porter (New York: McGraw Hill, 1983), 67–78.
36. The earliest economic theorists argued that valence is the positive or negative emotion that the decision maker anticipates from an outcome. See: S.L. McShane, "Organisational Decision-Making," in *Contemporary Issues in Management and Organisational Behaviour*, ed. P. Murray, D. Poole, and G. Jones (Sydney: Cengage Learning Australia, 2006), 136–65. The connection between valence and emotion is supported by recent neuroscience studies. See: A. Bechara and A.R. Damasio, "The Somatic Marker Hypothesis: A Neural Theory of Economic Decision," *Games and Economic Behavior* 52 (2005): 336–72; J. Bartol and S. Linquist, "How Do Somatic Markers Feature in Decision Making?," *Emotion Review* 7 (2014): 81–89; J.S. Lerner et al., "Emotion and Decision Making," *Annual Review of Psychology* 66 (2015): 799–823.
37. D.A. Nadler and E.E. Lawler, "Motivation: A Diagnostic Approach," in *Perspectives on Behavior in Organizations,* ed. J.R. Hackman, E.E. Lawler III, and L.W. Porter (New York: McGraw Hill, 1983), 70–73.
38. "Survey: 43 Percent of Companies Are Getting Employee Recognition Right," Press Release (Menlo Park, Calif.: OfficeTeam, April 16, 2019); "Survey: Only 27 Per Cent of Companies in Canada Are Acing Employee Recognition" (Toronto: OfficeTeam, April 16, 2019); Office of Personnel Management, "2022 Federal Employee Viewpoint Survey" (Washington, DC: United States Government, November 2022); "New National Survey from Eagle Hill Consulting Finds Employee Recognition Programs Are Lacking" (Arlington, VA: Eagle Hill Consulting, November 10, 2022); "Gartner HR Research Finds Only 32% of Employees Believe Their Pay Is Fair," Press Release (Stamford, CT: Gartner, November 28, 2022).
39. For recent applications of expectancy in diverse settings, see: E. Shweiki et al., "Applying Expectancy Theory to Residency Training: Proposing Opportunities to Understand Resident Motivation and Enhance Residency Training," *Advances in Medical Education and Practice* 6 (2015): 339–46; K.N. Bauer et al., "Re-Examination of Motivation in Learning Contexts: Meta-Analytically Investigating the Role Type of Motivation Plays in the Prediction of Key Training Outcomes," *Journal of Business and Psychology* 31 (2016): 33–50; R. Meymandpour and P. Pawar, "Study of Expectancy Motivation in IT Developers," *Telecom Business Review* 11 (2018): 6–11; E. Osafo, A. Paros, and R.M. Yawson, "Valence–Instrumentality–Expectancy Model of Motivation as an Alternative Model for Examining Ethical Leadership Behaviors," *SAGE Open* 11, no. 2 (2021): 21582440211021896; H.T.W. Frankort and A. Avgoustaki, "Beyond Reward Expectancy: How Do Periodic Incentive Payments Influence the Temporal Dynamics of Performance?," *Journal of Management* 48, no. 7 (2022): 2075–2107.

40. This limitation was acknowledged by Victor Vroom, who had introduced expectancy theory in his 1964 book. See G.P. Latham, *Work Motivation: History, Theory, Research, and Practice* (Thousand Oaks, CA: Sage, 2007), 47–48.

41. J.B. Watson, *Behavior: An Introduction to Comparative Psychology* (New York: Henry Holt, 1914).

42. B.F. Skinner, *About Behaviorism* (New York: Knopf, 1974); J. Komaki, T. Coombs, and S. Schepman, "Motivational Implications of Reinforcement Theory," in *Motivation and Leadership at Work*, ed. R.M. Steers, L.W. Porter, and G.A. Bigley (New York: McGraw Hill, 1996), 34–52; R.G. Miltenberger, *Behavior Modification: Principles and Procedures* (Pacific Grove, CA: Brooks/Cole, 1997).

43. T.K. Connellan, *How to Improve Human Performance* (New York: Harper & Row, 1978), 48–57; F. Luthans and R. Kreitner, *Organizational Behavior Modification and Beyond* (Glenview, IL: Scott, Foresman, 1985), 85–88.

44. B.F. Skinner, *Science and Human Behavior* (New York: Free Press, 1965); R.G. Miltenberger, *Behavior Modification: Principles and Procedures* (Pacific Grove, CA: Brooks/Cole, 1997), Chaps. 4–6.

45. T.R. Hinkin and C.A. Schriesheim, "If You Don't Hear from Me You Know You Are Doing Fine," *Cornell Hotel & Restaurant Administration Quarterly* 45, no. 4 (2004): 362–72; T.R. Hinkin and C.A. Schriesheim, "An Examination of 'Nonleadership': From Laissez-Faire Leadership to Leader Reward Omission and Punishment Omission," *Journal of Applied Psychology* 93, no. 6 (2008): 1234–48.

46. K. Cameron et al., "Effects of Positive Practices on Organizational Effectiveness," *Journal of Applied Behavioral Science* 47 (2011): 266–308; F. Luthans and C.M. Youssef-Morgan, "Psychological Capital: An Evidence-Based Positive Approach," *Annual Review of Organizational Psychology and Organizational Behavior* 4 (2017): 339–66; A.B. Bakker and M. van Woerkom, "Strengths Use in Organizations: A Positive Approach of Occupational Health," *Canadian Psychology* 59 (2018): 38–46.

47. L.K. Trevino, "The Social Effects of Punishment in Organizations: A Justice Perspective," *Academy of Management Review* 17 (1992): 647–76; L. Wang and J.K. Murnighan, "The Dynamics of Punishment and Trust," *Journal of Applied Psychology* 102 (2017): 1385–1402; L. Wang et al., "Does Anger Expression Help or Harm Leader Effectiveness? The Role of Competence-Based versus Integrity-Based Violations and Abusive Supervision," *Academy of Management Journal* 61 (2018): 1050–72.

48. G.P. Latham and V.L. Huber, "Schedules of Reinforcement: Lessons from the Past and Issues for the Future," *Journal of Organizational Behavior Management* 12 (1992): 125–49; B.A. Williams, "Challenges to Timing-Based Theories of Operant Behavior," *Behavioural Processes* 62 (2003): 115–23.

49. A. Bandura, *Social Foundations of Thought and Action: A Social Cognitive Theory* (Englewood Cliffs, NJ: Prentice Hall, 1986); A. Bandura, "Social Cognitive Theory of Self-Regulation," *Organizational Behavior and Human Decision Processes* 50, no. 2 (1991): 248–87; A. Bandura, "Social Cognitive Theory: An Agentic Perspective," *Annual Review of Psychology* 52, no. 1 (2001): 1–26.

50. M.E. Schnake, "Vicarious Punishment in a Work Setting," *Journal of Applied Psychology* 71 (1986): 343–45; L.K. Trevino, "The Social Effects of Punishment in Organizations: A Justice Perspective," *Academy of Management Review* 17 (1992): 647–76; J. Malouff et al., "Effects of Vicarious Punishment: A Meta-Analysis," *Journal of General Psychology* 136, no. 3 (2009): 271–86.

51. A. Pescuric and W.C. Byham, "The New Look of Behavior Modeling," *Training & Development* 50 (1996): 24–30; P.J. Taylor, D.F. Russ-Eft, and D.W.L. Chan, "A Meta-Analytic Review of Behavior Modeling Training," *Journal of Applied Psychology* 90, no. 4 (2005): 692–709; C.G. Myers and D.S. DeRue, "Agency in Vicarious Learning at Work," in *Autonomous Learning in the Workplace*, ed. J.E. Ellingson and R.A. Noe (New York: Routledge, 2017), 15–37.

52. A. Bandura, "Self-Reinforcement: Theoretical and Methodological Considerations," *Behaviorism* 4 (1976): 135–55; J.B. Vancouver and D.V. Day, "Industrial and Organization Research on Self-Regulation: From Constructs to Applications," *Applied Psychology: An International Journal* 54, no. 2 (2005): 155–85; A. Neal, T. Ballard, and J.B. Vancouver, "Dynamic Self-Regulation and Multiple-Goal Pursuit," *Annual Review of Organizational Psychology and Organizational Behavior* 4, no. 1 (2017): 401–23.

53. M. Milyavskaya and K.M. Werner, "Goal Pursuit: Current State of Affairs and Directions for Future Research," *Canadian Psychology* 59 (May 2018): 163–75.

54. E.A. Locke and G.P. Latham, *A Theory of Goal Setting and Task Performance* (Englewood Cliffs, NJ: Prentice Hall, 1990); G. Latham, G. Seijts, and J. Slocum, "The Goal Setting and Goal Orientation Labyrinth: Effective Ways for Increasing Employee Performance," *Organizational Dynamics* 45, no. 4 (2016): 271–77.

55. The SMARTER goal-setting model is an extension of the earlier SMART model. SMARTER apparently originated from British sports psychology writing around the mid-1990s, such as: P. Butler, *Performance Profiling* (Leeds, UK: The National Coaching Foundation, 1996), 36. There are several variations of the SMARTER goal-setting model; "achievable" is sometimes "acceptable," "reviewed" is sometimes "recorded," and "exciting" is sometimes "ethical." For a summary of variations of meanings within the SMARTER acronym, see: G. Brown, C. Leonard, and M. Arthur-Kelly, "Writing SMARTER Goals for Professional Learning and Improving Classroom Practices," *Reflective Practice* 17, no. 5 (2016): 621–35.

56. The value and limitations of measurement are discussed in J.M. Henshaw, *Does Measurement Measure Up? How Numbers Reveal and Conceal the Truth* (Baltimore, MD: Johns Hopkins Press, 2006).

57. A.C. Crossley, C. Cooper, and T. Wernsing, "Making Things Happen through Challenging Goals: Leader Proactivity, Trust, and Business-Unit Performance," *Journal of Applied Psychology* 98, no. 3 (2013): 540–49; A. Kruglanski et al., "The Rocky Road from Attitudes to Behaviors: Charting the Goal Systemic Course of Actions," *Psychological Review* 122, no. 4 (2015): 598–620; K.M. Roose and W.L. Williams, "An Evaluation of the Effects of Very Difficult Goals," *Journal of Organizational Behavior Management* 38, no. 1 (2018): 18–48.

58. Z. Zhang and M. Jia, "How Can Companies Decrease the Disruptive Effects of Stretch Goals? The Moderating Role of Interpersonal–and Informational–Justice Climates," *Human Relations* 66, no. 7 (2013): 993–1020; L.D. Ordóñez and D.T. Welsh, "Immoral Goals: How Goal Setting May Lead to Unethical Behavior," *Current Opinion in Psychology* 6 (2015): 93–96.

59. E.A. Locke and G.P. Latham, *A Theory of Goal Setting and Task Performance* (Englewood Cliffs, NJ: Prentice Hall, 1990), Chaps. 6 and 7; H. Klein, J.T. Cooper, and C.A. Monahan, "Goal Commitment," in *New Developments in Goal Setting and Task Performance*, ed. E.A. Locke and G.P. Latham (London: Taylor and Francis, 2012), 65–89.

60. G.P. Latham and C.C. Pinder, "Work Motivation Theory and Research at the Dawn of the Twenty-First Century," *Annual Review of Psychology* 56 (2005): 485–516; S.J. Ashford and K.E.M. Stobbelier, "Feedback, Goal Setting, and Task Performance Revisited," in *New Developments in Goal Setting and Task Performance*, ed. E.A. Locke and G.P. Latham (New York: Routledge, 2013), 51–64.

61. G.P. Latham, *Work Motivation: History, Theory, Research, and Practice* (Thousand Oaks, CA: Sage, 2007), 198–203; A. Baker et al., "Feedback and Organizations: Feedback Is Good, Feedback-Friendly Culture Is Better," *Canadian Psychology* 54, no. 4 (2013): 260–68.

62. F. Anseel et al., "How Are We Doing after 30 Years? A Meta-Analytic Review of the Antecedents and Outcomes of Feedback-Seeking Behavior," *Journal of Management* 41 (2015): 318–48; M. London, *The Power of Feedback: Giving, Seeking, and Using Feedback for Performance Improvement* (New York: Routledge, 2015); J. Lechermeier and M. Fassnacht, "How Do Performance Feedback Characteristics Influence Recipients' Reactions? A State-of-the-Art Review on Feedback Source, Timing, and Valence Effects," *Management Review Quarterly* 68, no. 2 (2018): 145–93.

63. M. Buckingham, *Go Put Your Strengths to Work* (New York: Free Press, 2007); H. Aguinis, R.K. Gottfredson, and H. Joo, "Delivering Effective Performance Feedback: The Strengths-Based Approach," *Business Horizons* 55, no. 2 (2012): 105–11; A.B. Bakker and M. van Woerkom, "Strengths Use in Organizations: A Positive Approach of Occupational Health," *Canadian Psychology* 59, no. 1 (2018): 38–46; H.F. Grammer et al., "Positive Performance Reviews Using Strengths-Based Goal Setting," in *Positive Organizational Psychology Interventions: Design and Evaluation* (Hoboken, NJ: Wiley-Blackwell, 2021), 65–106.

64. M. van Woerkom and B. Kroon, "The Effect of Strengths-Based Performance Appraisal on Perceived Supervisor Support and the Motivation to Improve Performance," *Frontiers in Psychology* 11 (2020), 1883; M.J. Peláez, C. Coo, and M. Salanova, "Facilitating Work Engagement and Performance through Strengths-Based Micro-Coaching: A Controlled Trial Study," *Journal of Happiness Studies* 21, no. 4 (2020): 1265–84; C.K. Wijekuruppu, A. Coetzer, and P. Susomrith, "The Prospective Applicability of the Strengths-Based Approach to Managing and Developing Employees in Small Businesses," *Journal of Organizational Effectiveness: People and Performance* 8, no. 3 (2021): 323–46.

65. H.H. Meyer, "A Solution to the Performance Appraisal Feedback Enigma," *Academy of Management Executive* 5, no. 1 (1991): 68–76; M. Alam and P. Singh, "Performance Feedback Interviews as Affective Events: An Exploration of the Impact of Emotion Regulation of Negative Performance Feedback on Supervisor–Employee Dyads," *Human Resource Management Review* 31, no. 2 (2021): 100740; L. Xing, J. (James) Sun, and D. Jepsen, "Feeling Shame in the Workplace: Examining Negative Feedback as an Antecedent and Performance and Well-Being as Consequences," *Journal of Organizational Behavior* 42, no. 9 (2021): 1244–60.

66. A. Terracciano, P.T. Costa, and R.R. McCrae, "Personality Plasticity after Age 30," *Personality and Social Psychology Bulletin* 32 (2006): 999–1009; R. Mõttus et al., "Within-Trait Heterogeneity in Age Group Differences in Personality Domains and Facets: Implications for the Development and Coherence of Personality Traits," *PLoS ONE* 10, no. 3 (2015): e0119667; L.H. Schultz et al., "Vocational Interests across 20 Years of Adulthood: Stability, Change, and the Role of Work Experiences," *Journal of Research in Personality* 71 (2017): 46–56.

67. J.W. Smither, M. London, and R.R. Reilly, "Does Performance Improve Following Multisource Feedback? A Theoretical Model, Meta-Analysis, and Review of Empirical Findings," *Personnel Psychology* 58, no. 1 (2005): 33–66; L.E. Atwater, J.F. Brett, and A.C. Charles, "Multisource Feedback: Lessons Learned and Implications for Practice," *Human Resource Management* 46, no. 2 (2007): 285-307; M.C. Campion, E.D. Campion, and M.A. Campion, "Improvements in Performance Management through the Use of 360 Feedback," *Industrial and Organizational Psychology* 8, no. 1 (2015): 85-93.

68. S.J. Ashford and G.B. Northcraft, "Conveying More (or Less) Than We Realize: The Role of Impression Management in Feedback Seeking," *Organizational Behavior and Human Decision Processes* 53 (1992): 310–34; J. Peterburs et al., "Look Who's Judging—Feedback Source Modulates Brain Activation to Performance Feedback in Social Anxiety," *NeuroImage* 133 (2016): 430–37; J. Lechermeier and M. Fassnacht, "How Do Performance Feedback Characteristics Influence Recipients' Reactions? A State-of-the-Art Review on Feedback Source, Timing, and Valence Effects," *Management Review Quarterly* 68, no. 2 (2018): 145–93; L. Xing, J. Sun, and D. Jepsen, "Feeling Shame in the Workplace: Examining Negative Feedback as an Antecedent and Performance and Well-Being as Consequences," *Journal of Organizational Behavior* 42, no. 9 (2021): 1244–60.

69. J.B. Miner, "The Rated Importance, Scientific Validity, and Practical Usefulness of Organizational Behavior Theories: A Quantitative Review," *Academy of Management Learning and Education* 2 (2003): 250–68; D. McEwan et al., "The Effectiveness of Multi-Component Goal Setting Interventions for Changing Physical Activity Behaviour: A Systematic Review and Meta-Analysis," *Health Psychology Review* 10, no. 1 (2016): 67–88; T. Epton, S. Currie, and C.J. Armitage, "Unique Effects of Setting Goals on Behavior Change: Systematic Review and Meta-Analysis," *Journal of Consulting and Clinical Psychology* 85 (2017): 1182–98.

70. P.M. Wright, "Goal Setting and Monetary Incentives: Motivational Tools That Can Work Too Well," *Compensation and Benefits Review* 26 (1994): 41–49; S. Kerr and D. LePelley, "Stretch Goals: Risks, Possibilities, and Best Practices," in *New Developments in Goal Setting and Task Performance*, ed. E.A. Locke and G.P. Latham (London: Taylor and Francis, 2012), 21–32; L.D. Ordóñez and D.T. Welsh, "Immoral Goals: How Goal Setting May Lead to Unethical Behavior," *Current Opinion in Psychology* 6 (2015): 93–96.

71. W.B. Cameron, *Informal Sociology: A Casual Introduction to Sociological Thinking* (Random House, 1963), 13; "Not Everything That Counts Can Be Counted—Quote Investigator," May 26, 2010, https://quoteinvestigator.com/2010/05/26/everything-counts-einstein/.

72. G.P. Latham, *Work Motivation: History, Theory, Research, and Practice* (Thousand Oaks, CA: Sage, 2007), 188.

73. The most widely studied types in organizational behavior are distributive, procedural, and interactional justice, the latter of which includes two subsets (informational and interpersonal). However, other writers have identified completely different typologies, such as legalistic, retributive, and restorative justice. See, for example, G.D. Paul and L.L. Putnam, "Emergent Paradigms of Organizational Justice," in *Transforming Conflict through Communication in Personal, Family, and Working Relationships*, ed. P.M. Kellett and T. Matyók, Peace and Conflict Studies (Lanham: Lexington Books, 2016), 271–92. For a detailed discussion and critique of the development of the justice domain, see D.E. Rupp et al., "A Critical Analysis of the Conceptualization and Measurement of Organizational Justice: Is It Time for Reassessment?" *Academy of Management Annals* 11, no. 2 (2017): 919–59.

74. M. Deutsch, "Equity, Equality, and Need: What Determines Which Value Will Be Used as the Basis of Distributive Justice?," *Journal of Social Issues* 31, no. 3 (1975): 137–49; D.A. Morand and K.K. Merriman, "Equality Theory as a Counterbalance to Equity Theory in Human Resource Management," *Journal of Business Ethics* 111, no. 1 (2012): 133–44; T. Reeskens and W. van Oorschot, "Equity, Equality, or Need? A Study of Popular Preferences for Welfare Redistribution Principles across 24 European Countries," *Journal of European Public Policy* 20, no. 8 (2013): 1174–95.

75. J.S. Adams, "Toward an Understanding of Inequity," *Journal of Abnormal and Social Psychology* 67 (1963): 422–36; P.H. Siegel, M. Schraeder, and R. Morrison, "A Taxonomy of Equity Factors," *Journal of Applied Social Psychology* 38, no. 1 (2008): 61–75; R. Cropanzana, D.E. Bowen, and S.W. Gilliland, "The Management of Organizational Justice," *Academy of Management Perspectives* 21, no. 4 (2007): 34–48; D.E. Rupp et al., "A Critical Analysis of the Conceptualization and Measurement of Organizational Justice: Is It Time for Reassessment?," *Academy of Management Annals* 11, no. 2 (2017): 919–59.

76. T.P. Summers and A.S. DeNisi, "In Search of Adams' Other: Reexamination of Referents Used in the Evaluation of Pay," *Human Relations* 43 (1990): 497–511; C.T. Kulik and M.L. Ambrose, "Personal and Situational Determinants of Referent Choice," *Academy of Management Review* 17 (1992): 212–37; J. Koopman et al., "My Coworkers Are Treated More Fairly than Me! A Self-Regulatory Perspective on Justice Social Comparisons," *Academy of Management Journal* 63, no. 3 (2020): 857–80.

77. The emotive dynamics of feelings of inequity are studied in A.W. Cappelen et al., "Equity Theory and Fair Inequality: A Neuroeconomic Study," *Proceedings of the National Academy of Sciences* 111, no. 43 (2014): 15368–72.

78. Y. Cohen-Charash and P.E. Spector, "The Role of Justice in Organizations: A Meta-Analysis," *Organizational Behavior and Human Decision Processes* 86 (2001): 278–321; B. Walker and R.T. Hamilton, "Employee–Employer Grievances: A Review," *International Journal of Management Reviews* 13, no. 1 (2011): 40–58; R. Cropanzana and C. Moliner, "Hazards of Justice: Egocentric Bias, Moral Judgments, and Revenge-Seeking," in *Deviant and Criminal Behavior in the Workplace*, ed. S.M. Elias (New York: New York University Press, 2013), 155–77; B.C. Holtz and C.M. Harold, "Interpersonal Justice and Deviance: The Moderating Effects of Interpersonal Justice Values and Justice Orientation," *Journal of Management* 39, no. 2 (2013): 339–65; C.L. Wilkin and C.E. Connelly, "Green with Envy and Nerves of Steel: Moderated Mediation between Distributive Justice and Theft," *Personality and Individual Differences* 72 (2015): 160–64.

79. Canadian Press, "Pierre Berton, Canadian Cultural Icon, Enjoyed Long and Colourful Career," *Times Colonist* (Victoria, BC), November 30, 2004.

80. J. Fizel, A.C. Krautman, and L. Hadley, "Equity and Arbitration in Major League Baseball," *Managerial and Decision Economics* 23, no. 7 (2002): 427–35; M. Ezzamel and R. Watson, "Pay Comparability across and within UK Boards: An Empirical Analysis of the Cash Pay Awards to CEOs and Other Board Members," *Journal of Management Studies* 39, no. 2 (2002): 207–32.

81. D.R. Bobocel and L. Gosse, "Procedural Justice: A Historical Review and Critical Analysis," in *Oxford Handbook of Justice in the Workplace*, ed. R.S. Cropanzano and M.L. Ambrose (New York: Oxford University Press, 2015), 51–88; R.J. Bies, "Interactional Justice: Looking Backward, Looking Forward," in *The Oxford Handbook of Justice in the Workplace*, ed. R. Cropanzano and M.L. Ambrose, Oxford Library of Psychology (New York: Oxford University Press, 2015), 89–107.

82. G.S. Leventhal, "What Should Be Done with Equity Theory?," in *Social Exchange: Advances in Theory and Research*, ed. K.J. Gergen, M.S. Greenberg, and R.H. Willis (Boston, MA: Springer US, 1980), 27–55; M.K. Lee et al., "Procedural Justice in Algorithmic Fairness: Leveraging Transparency and Outcome Control for Fair Algorithmic Mediation," *Proceedings of the ACM on Human-Computer Interaction* 3, no. CSCW (2019): 182; R. Outlaw et al., "How Fair versus How Long: An Integrative Theory-Based Examination of Procedural Justice and Procedural Timeliness," *Personnel Psychology* 72, no. 3 (2019): 361–91.

83. R.J. Bies, "Interactional Justice: Looking Backward, Looking Forward," in *The Oxford Handbook of Justice in the Workplace*, ed. R. Cropanzano and M.L. Ambrose, Oxford Library of Psychology (New York: Oxford University Press, 2015), 89–107; R. Cropanzano, J.F. Kirk, and M. Fortin, "How Do We Know When We Are Treated Fairly? Justice Rules and Fairness Judgments," *Research in Personnel and Human Resources Management* 33 (2015): 279–350.

84. J.S. Michel, K. Newness, and K. Duniewicz, "How Abusive Supervision Affects Workplace Deviance: A Moderated-Mediation Examination of Aggressiveness and Work-Related Negative Affect," *Journal of Business and Psychology* 31 (2016): 1–22; J.K. Oh and C.I.C. Farh, "An Emotional Process Theory of How Subordinates Appraise, Experience, and Respond to Abusive Supervision over Time," *Academy of Management Review* 42 (2017): 207–32.

85. D.T. Miller, "Disrespect and the Experience of Injustice," *Annual Review of Psychology* 52 (2001): 527–53; R. Vermunt and H. Steensma, "Procedural Justice," in *Handbook of Social Justice Theory and Research*, ed. C. Sabbagh and M. Schmitt (New York, NY: Springer New York, 2016), 219–36; K.A. DeCelles and K. Aquino, "Dark Knights: When and Why an Employee Becomes a Workplace Vigilante," *Academy of Management Review* 45, no. 3 (2020): 528–48.

86. J. Le Roy, M. Bastounis, and J.M. -Poussard, "Interactional Justice and Counterproductive Work Behaviors: The Mediating Role of Negative Emotions," *Social Behavior and Personality* 40, no. 8 (2012): 1341–55; J.C. Jackson, V.K. Choi, and M.J. Gelfand, "Revenge: A Multilevel Review and Synthesis," *Annual Review of Psychology* 70, no. 1 (2019): 319–45.

87. M.A. Campion et al., "Work Redesign: Eight Obstacles and Opportunities," *Human Resource Management* 44, no. 4 (2005): 367–90; S.-J. Cullinane et al., "Job Design under Lean Manufacturing and Its Impact on Employee Outcomes," *Organizational Psychology Review* 3, no. 1 (2013): 41–61.

88. A. Shinnar et al., "Survey of Ergonomic Features of Supermarket Cash Registers," *International Journal of Industrial Ergonomics* 34, no. 6 (2004): 535–41; V. O'Connell, "Stores Count Seconds to Trim Labor Costs," *The Wall Street Journal*, November 13, 2008; A. Kihlstedt and G.M. Hägg, "Checkout Cashier Work and Counter Design–Video Movement Analysis, Musculoskeletal Disorders and Customer Interaction," *International Journal of Industrial Ergonomics* 41, no. 3 (2011): 201–07; "One Checkout Item Every Three Seconds," *Mail Online* (London), July 8, 2012. Average scanning times vary considerably with the scanning technology, product standardization, and ergonomic design of the cashier station.

89. S. Leroy, "Why Is It So Hard to Do My Work? The Challenge of Attention Residue When Switching between Work Tasks," *Organizational Behavior and Human Decision Processes* 109 (2009): 168–81; S. Leroy and T.M. Glomb, "Tasks Interrupted: How Anticipating Time Pressure on Resumption of an Interrupted Task Causes Attention Residue and Low Performance on Interrupting Tasks and How a 'Ready-to-Resume' Plan Mitigates the Effects," *Organization Science* 29 (2018): 380–97.

90. H. Fayol, *General and Industrial Management*, trans. C. Storrs (London: Pitman, 1949); E.E. Lawler III, *Motivation in Work Organizations* (Monterey, CA: Brooks/Cole, 1973), Chap. 7; M.A. Campion, "Ability Requirement Implications of Job Design: An Interdisciplinary Perspective," *Personnel Psychology* 42 (1989): 1–24.

91. A. Smith, *An Inquiry into the Nature and Causes of the Wealth of Nations*, 1st ed., 2 vols. (London: W. Strahan and T. Cadell, 1776), pp. 6–7. Although Smith's general premise is true in most cases, the estimates he provided were speculated, not empirically tested. He even suggested that the 10 pin makers couldn't complete one pin per day, but he also stipulated that is "without any of them having been educated to this peculiar business."

92. F.W. Taylor, *The Principles of Scientific Management* (New York: Harper & Row, 1911); R. Kanigel, *The One Best Way: Frederick Winslow Taylor and the Enigma of Efficiency* (New York: Viking, 1997); M. Derksen, "Turning Men into Machines? Scientific Management, Industrial Psychology, and the 'Human Factor,'" *Journal of the History of the Behavioral Sciences* 50, no. 2 (2014): 148–65.

93. W.F. Dowling, "Job Redesign on the Assembly Line: Farewell to Blue-Collar Blues?" *Organizational Dynamics* (1973): 51–67; J.A. Häusser et al., "Experimental Evidence for the Effects of Task Repetitiveness on Mental Strain and Objective Work Performance," *Journal of Organizational Behavior* 35 (2014): 705–21; E.A.J. van Hooft and M.L.M. van Hooff, "The State of Boredom: Frustrating or Depressing?," *Motivation and Emotion* 42 (2018): 931–46; W. Han et al., "Assessing the Brain 'on the Line': An Ecologically-Valid Assessment of the Impact of Repetitive Assembly Line Work on Hemodynamic Response and Fine Motor Control Using FNIRS," *Brain and Cognition* 136 (2019): 103613, https://doi.org/10.1016/j.bandc.2019.103613.

94. R. Moorhead, "Lawyer Specialization—Managing the Professional Paradox," *Law & Policy* 32, no. 2 (2010): 226–59.

95. J.R. Hackman and E.E. Lawler, "Employee Reactions to Job Characteristics," *Journal of Applied Psychology* 55, no. 3 (1971): 259–86; J.R. Hackman and G.R. Oldham, "The Job Diagnostic Survey: An Instrument for the Diagnosis of Jobs and the Evaluation of Job Redesign Projects" (New Haven, CT: Department of Administrative Sciences, Yale University, May 1974); J.R. Hackman and G.R. Oldham, "Motivation through the Design of Work: Test of a Theory," *Organizational Behavior and Human Performance* 16, no. 2 (1976): 250–79; J.R. Hackman and G. Oldham, *Work Redesign* (Reading, MA: Addison-Wesley, 1980).

96. R.W. Buell, T. Kim, and C.-J. Tsay, "Creating Reciprocal Value through Operational Transparency," *Management Science* 63 (2017): 1673–95; R.W. Buell, "Operational Transparency," *Harvard Business Review* 97 (March–April 2019): 102–13.

97. M. Gagné and D. Bhave, "Autonomy in the Workplace: An Essential Ingredient to Employee Engagement and Well-Being in Every Culture," in *Human Autonomy in Cross-Cultural Context,* ed. V.I. Chirkov, R.M. Ryan, and K.M. Sheldon, *Cross-Cultural Advancements in Positive Psychology* (Springer: Netherlands, 2011), 163–87.

98. N. Dhingra et al., "Help Your Employees Find Purpose—or Watch Them Leave," *McKinsey & Company: Organization Practice*, April 2021; "Study Finds Global Office Workers Crushed by Repetitive Tasks," Press Release (New York: UiPath, May 20, 2021); "Autonomy to the People" (Chatswood NSW: Access Group, October 2021); "Powering Profits and Prosperity" (Chatswood NSW: Access Group, August 2022); "2022 Federal Employee Viewpoint Survey" (Washington, DC: United States Federal Government, Office of Personnel Management, November 2022).

99. Maslow introduced or popularized the notion of "growth" to human motivation, and his writing suggests that it is the same as self-actualization. However, a few others suggest that "growth need strength" in the Hackman/Oldham model is a permanent (trait) characteristic. See A.H. Maslow, *Motivation and Personality* (New York: Harper & Row, 1954); J.B. Miner, *Organizational Behavior: Integrated Theory Development and the Role of the Unconscious*, vol. 6 (Armonk, NY: M.E. Sharpe, 2011), 32–33.

100. R.B. Tiegs, L.E. Tetrick, and Y. Fried, "Growth Need Strength and Context Satisfactions as Moderators of the Relations of the Job Characteristics Model," *Journal of Management* 18, no. 3 (1992): 575–93; J.E. Champoux, "A Multivariate Test of the Job Characteristics Theory of Work Motivation," *Journal of Organizational Behavior* 12, no. 5 (1991): 431–46.

101. An early version of the job characteristics model included social interaction but was later excluded. The authors of that work now recommend including social interaction. G.R. Oldham and J.R. Hackman, "Not What It Was and Not What It Will Be: The Future of Job Design Research," *Journal of Organizational Behavior* 31, no. 2-3 (2010): 463–79. See also: S.E. Humphrey, J.D. Nahrgang, and F.P. Morgeson, "Integrating Motivational, Social, and Contextual Work Design Features: A Meta-Analytic Summary and Theoretical Extension of the Work Design Literature," *Journal of Applied Psychology* 92, no. 5 (2007): 1332–56.

102. C. Perrow, "A Framework for the Comparative Analysis of Organizations," *American Sociological Review* 32 (1967): 194–208; R.L. Daft and N.B. Macintosh, "A Tentative Exploration into the Amount and Equivocality of Information Processing in Organizational Work Units," *Administrative Science Quarterly* 26 (1981): 207–24. Job analyzability and variability are embedded in "job complexity," but the latter is a much broader concept that has suffered from many diverse interpretations. See P. Liu and Z. Li, "Task Complexity: A Review and Conceptualization Framework," *International Journal of Industrial Ergonomics* 42 (2012): 553–68; S.Y. Sung, A. Antefelt, and J.N. Choi, "Dual Effects of Job Complexity on Proactive and Responsive Creativity: Moderating Role of Employee Ambiguity Tolerance," *Group & Organization Management* 42 (2017): 388–418.

103. M.M. Coşgel and T.J. Miceli, "Job Rotation: Cost, Benefits, and Stylized Facts," *Journal of Institutional and Theoretical Economics* 155 (1999): 301–20; D. Rissén et al., "Psychophysiological Stress Reactions, Trapezius Muscle Activity, and Neck and Shoulder Pain among Female Cashiers before and after Introduction of Job Rotation," *Work & Stress* 16, no. 2 (2002): 127–37; S. Gallagher et al., "Job Rotation as a Technique for the Control of MSDs: A Fatigue Failure Perspective," *Proceedings of the Human Factors and Ergonomics Society Annual Meeting* 61 (September 1, 2017): 993–94; R.S. Padula et al., "Job Rotation Designed to Prevent Musculoskeletal Disorders and Control Risk in Manufacturing Industries: A Systematic Review," *Applied Ergonomics* 58 (2017): 386–97.

104. M.D. Kilbridge, "Reduced Costs through Job Enlargement: A Case," *The Journal of Business* 33, no. 4 (1960): 357–62; L.E. Davis, "The Design of Jobs," *Industrial Relations* 6, no. 1 (1966): 21–45; W.E. Reif and P.P. Schoderbek, "Job Enlargement: Antidote to Apathy," *Human Resource Management* 5, no. 1 (1966): 16–23. Recent job enlargement studies are mainly between-person correlational analyses, whereas early research more richly studied temporal attitude and behavioral changes from job enlargement interventions. Some recent studies that investigate job enlargement include: J.A. Häusser et al., "Experimental Evidence for the Effects of Task Repetitiveness on Mental Strain and Objective Work Performance," *Journal of Organizational Behavior* 35, no. 5 (2014): 705–21; F. Fraccaroli et al., "Who Benefits from More Tasks? Older versus Younger Workers," *Journal of Managerial Psychology* 29, no. 5 (2014): 508–23; D. Berdicchia, G. Masino, and F. Nicolli, "Job Enlargement, Job Crafting and the Moderating Role of Self-Competence," *Journal of Managerial Psychology* 31, no. 2 (2016): 318–30.

105. J.R. Hackman et al., "A New Strategy for Job Enrichment," *California Management Review* 17, no. 4 (1975): 57–71; R.W. Griffin, *Task Design: An Integrative Approach* (Glenview, IL: Scott Foresman, 1982).

106. J.R. Hackman and G. Oldham, *Work Redesign* (Reading, MA: Addison-Wesley, 1980), 137–38.

107. J.R. Hackman and G. Oldham, *Work Redesign* (Reading, MA: Addison-Wesley, 1980), 137–38.

6 Decision Making and Creativity

Aviator Fortuner/Shutterstock

Learning Objectives

After reading this chapter, you should be able to:

LO6-1 Describe the elements of rational choice decision making.

LO6-2 Explain why people deviate from rational choice decision making when identifying problems and opportunities.

LO6-3 Explain why people deviate from rational choice decision making when searching for, appraising, and choosing alternatives.

LO6-4 Discuss how emotions and intuition relate to decision making.

LO6-5 Explain how decision makers bias the evaluation of decision outcomes, and identify ways to minimize those decision evaluation problems.

LO6-6 Outline the creative process, and identify employee characteristics, workplace conditions, and specific activities that support creativity.

LO6-7 Summarize the benefits of employee involvement and discuss five contingencies that affect the optimal level of employee involvement.

The Ullrich Water Treatment Plant (WTP) in Austin, Texas, receives untreated water from the Lower Colorado River and converts it to drinkable water through disinfection and clarification processes that remove suspended matter (clay, silt, organisms, organic matter). Employees monitor several large water basins for turbidity (cloudiness) and other indicators of water quality.

Ullrich WTP employees were busy in early February due to problems with faulty equipment as well as preparation for unusually cold weather the next day. When the three night shift technicians arrived at 7:00 p.m., four basins and two centrifuges were "online" and operating mostly within normal range. The day shift crew provided the night crew with verbal and written information about ongoing issues and required actions.

Basin #6, which the day shift brought online that afternoon, measured increasing turbidity throughout the evening and exceeded recommended levels by 10:00 p.m. The night shift lead technician assumed the problem was a broken line feeding ferric sulfate into the basin because some of those lines froze the previous winter. Ferric sulfate is a critical ingredient to reduce turbidity in the water treatment process. From 10:00 p.m. through to 4:00 a.m., all three technicians repeatedly searched for a line break that may have prevented ferric sulfate from mixing with the water in Basin #6. No break was ever found.

Turbidity in Basin #6 increased throughout the night. Turbid water from that basin flowed into the later stage filters, most of which became clogged by the suspended matter. The water then entered the final stage clear wells, contaminating the drinking quality water stored there. When the day shift crew arrived at 7:00 a.m., they contacted management and immediately shut down Basin #6. Less than an hour later, Austin residents were advised to boil their water over the next three days.

decision making The conscious process of making choices among alternatives with the intention of moving toward some desired state of affairs

Several decision errors led to the "Boil Water Notice" at the Ullrich WTP. But one error that stood out was poor problem identification; the night shift crew spent most of their time trying to solve the wrong problem. "The night shift misdiagnosed what was going on" explains Austin Water operations manager Stephanie Sue. "They were searching for a ferric sulfate leak that did not exist and they did not determine quickly enough what was going on and what was causing that elevated turbidity."

What actually caused very high turbidity in Basin #6? The day crew had brought that basin online and was "seeding" it with previously coagulated matter—a standard practice that enables suspended particles in the untreated water to coagulate and settle out of the water more efficiently. The day crew had notified the night crew to turn off the seeding valve that evening, but the night crew either didn't hear (or read) that message or soon forgot about it. At 4:00 a.m., the night crew discovered and immediately closed the open valve that was spewing coagulated matter into Basin #6, but they incorrectly assumed downstream water contamination had been avoided.[1]

The Ullrich Water Treatment Plant and all other organizations depend on employees to foresee and correctly identify problems or opportunities, to consider the full range of alternatives, to pick the best alternative based on several relevant factors, and to execute and evaluate those decisions effectively and objectively. Decision making is not only a critical management skill; it is also a core activity for all staff members directly in their jobs and through employee involvement.

This chapter examines each of these themes. It begins by describing the rational choice view of decision making. Next, the human limitations of rational choice—we call it imperfect rationality—are discussed in the context of how human beings actually make decisions. We also examine the emerging view that decisions consist of a complex interaction of logic and emotion. The latter part of this chapter focuses on two topics that intertwine with decision making: creativity and employee involvement.

LO6-1 Describe the elements of rational choice decision making.

RATIONAL CHOICE DECISION MAKING

Decision making is the process of making choices among alternatives with the intention of moving toward some desired state of affairs.[2] How can we make effective decisions in organizations? This chapter answers this question by describing different ways of thinking about decision making and by examining several issues at each stage of the decision-making process. We begin this journey by discussing the earliest

> **I am not a product of my circumstances. I am a product of my decisions.**[3]
>
> —Stephen R. Covey, author and educator

perspective—**rational choice decision making**—which is the process of using pure logic and all available information about all alternatives to choose the alternative with the highest value. Choices with the highest value might have the highest expected profitability, customer satisfaction, employee well-being, or some combination of these outcomes.

For most of written history, Western societies have characterized pure rationality as an ideal state of decision making.[4] The rational choice view was extolled 2,500 years ago when Plato and his contemporaries in ancient Greece raised logical debate and reasoning to a fine art. About 400 years ago, Descartes and other European philosophers argued that the ability to make logical decisions is one of the most important accomplishments of human beings. In the 1700s, Scottish philosophers refined the notion that the best choice is the one that offers the greatest expected satisfaction. As we shall discover, these views of rational choice decision making are flawed, but this approach provides a useful foundation to understand this topic.

Rational choice decisions often involve complex calculations of data using a formula that points to the best choice. Basically,

Rational choice decision making selects the best alternative by calculating the probabilities that various outcomes will occur from the choices and the expected satisfaction (valences) from each of those outcomes.
ESB Professional/Shutterstock

this formula determines the best alternative by considering the probabilities that various outcomes will occur from the choices along with the expected satisfaction (valences) from each of those outcomes.[5] We have already described expected utility calculations (i.e., using probabilities and valences) in organizational behavior theories presented earlier in this book, notably the attitude model in Chapter 4 and expectancy theory of motivation in Chapter 5.

To illustrate the rational choice calculation, consider the example in Exhibit 6.1.[6] Suppose that you need to choose a new supplier of a specific raw material used in the company's products. From experience, you estimate that the preferred supplier should provide a high-quality product (+9) with low prices (+6) and ontime delivery (+4).[7] The numbers, which are on a plus or minus 10 point scale in this example, indicate each outcome's valence—that is, its expected satisfaction or importance. You estimate that supplier A has excellent on-time delivery (about 90 percent probability of exceeding the company's expectations), an 80 percent likelihood of offering low prices, and a 70 percent probability of providing a product with exceptional quality. Supplier B has a 90 percent chance of providing very high product quality but a lower likelihood of on-time delivery (60 percent) and of offering low prices (40 percent).

Which of these two suppliers should be selected? A rational choice decision maker would choose Supplier A because that company would produce the highest expected satisfaction. This composite valence is calculated by multiplying the valence of each outcome by the probability of that outcome occurring, then adding those results across all three outcomes. The supplier with the higher score is the better choice, given available information. This is a highly simplified illustration because a truly rational choice decision would examine all potential suppliers and all possible outcomes. The key point from this example is that all rational decisions rely primarily on two types of information: (1) the probability that each outcome will occur and (2) the valence or expected satisfaction of each outcome.

Rational Choice Decision Process

Calculating the best alternative is at the heart of rational choice decision making, but it goes hand-in-hand with the systematic decision process illustrated in Exhibit 6.2.[8] The first step is to identify the problem or recognize an opportunity. A *problem* is a deviation between the current and the desired situation—the gap between "what is" and "what ought to be." This deviation is a symptom of more fundamental causes that need to be corrected. The "ought to be" refers to goals or performance expectations, which later help to evaluate the success of the selected choice.[9]

rational choice decision making The process of using pure logic and all available information about all alternatives to choose the alternative with the highest value

Exhibit 6.1 Rational Choice Decision-Making Example

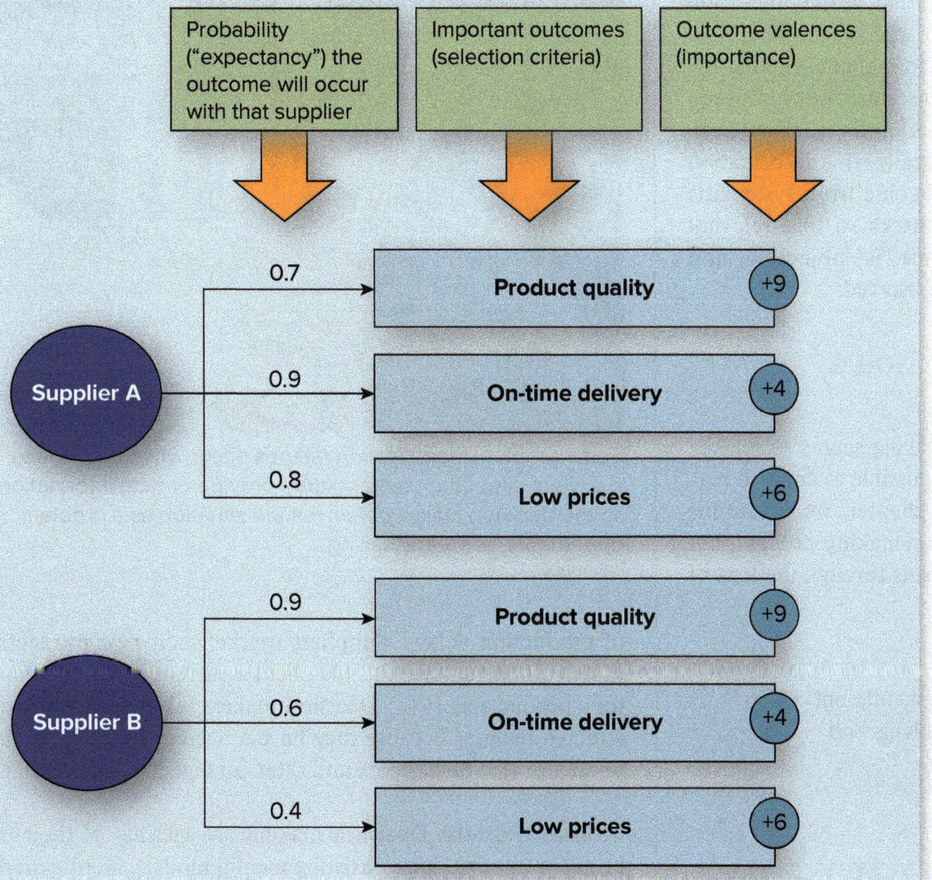

Exhibit 6.2 Rational Choice Decision Process

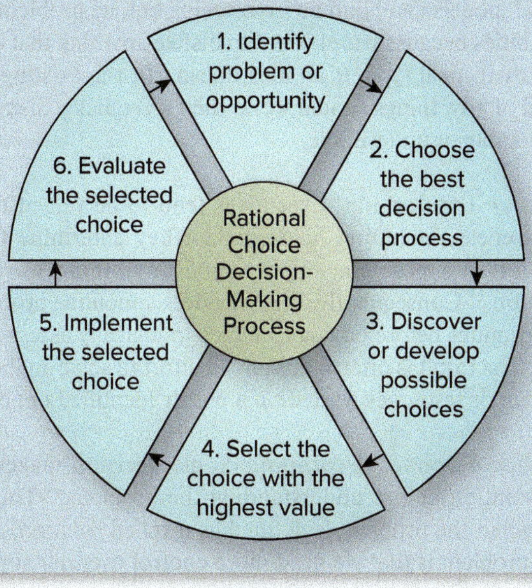

For instance, if a customer contact center's goal is to answer incoming client calls within 30 seconds, the problem is the gap between that goal and the actual time the contact center takes to answer most client calls. An *opportunity* is a deviation between current expectations and a potentially better situation that was not previously expected. In other words, an opportunity exists when decision makers discover that some choices may produce better results than current goals or expectations.

The second step involves choosing the best decision process. This is really a meta-decision—deciding how to decide—because it refers to choosing among the different approaches and processes to make the decision.[10] One meta-decision is whether to solve the problem alone or involve others in the process. We'll examine the contingencies of employee involvement in decision making in the last section of this chapter. A second meta-decision is whether the problem is routine or novel. Routine problems are *programmed decisions* because the decision maker would have ready-made alternatives or even solutions learned from the earlier encounters with that problem. In contrast, new or unique problems are *nonprogrammed decisions* because they require the decision maker to work through all steps in the decision model. These are just two factors to consider when deciding how to decide.

The third step in the rational choice decision-making process is to identify and/or develop a list of possible choices. This usually begins by searching for ready-made solutions, such as practices that have worked well on similar problems. If none of the existing solutions is acceptable, then decision makers need to design a custom-made solution or modify an existing one.

The fourth step is to select the best choice by applying the rational choice calculation we described in Exhibit 6.1. To choose the alternative with the greatest expected satisfaction, the decision maker must have information about all possible alternatives and their outcomes. That condition is usually impossible, but the rational choice view of decision making assumes it can be accomplished without any effort or challenges.

The fifth step in the rational choice decision-making process is to implement the selected alternative. The rational

mental models Visual and relational images that we develop in our mind to describe, explain, and predict the world around us

bounded rationality The view that people are bounded in their decision-making capabilities, including access to limited information, limited information processing, and tendency toward satisficing rather than maximizing when making choices

choice view has little to say about this step because it assumes that implementation occurs with ease. The final step is to evaluate whether the gap has narrowed between "what is" and "what ought to be." Ideally, this information should come from systematic benchmarks so that relevant feedback is objective and easily observed.

Problems with Rational Choice Decision Making

The rational choice view of decision making seems so logical, yet there are several reasons why it is impossible to apply in reality. Over the next few sections of this chapter, we reexamine each step in the rational choice decision-making process, but with more detail about what really happens through the lens of "imperfect rationality."

LO6-2 Explain why people deviate from rational choice decision making when identifying problems and opportunities.

IDENTIFYING PROBLEMS AND OPPORTUNITIES

Physicists Albert Einstein and Leopold Infeld once wrote: "The formulation of a problem is far more often essential than its solution, which may be merely a matter of mathematical or experimental skill."[11] In other words, problem identification is not just the first step in decision making; it is arguably the most important step. But problems and opportunities are not clearly labeled as such. Instead, they are conclusions that we form from ambiguous and conflicting information.[12]

Problems with Problem Identification

This chapter's opening vignette about the Ullrich Water Treatment Plant in Austin, Texas, illustrates how poor problem identification and trying to solve the wrong problem can have costly consequences. Only by forming an accurate understanding of the problem can we move toward a meaningful solution. Unfortunately, the problem identification stage is, itself, filled with problems. Here are five of the most widely recognized concerns.

Stakeholder Framing Stakeholders provide or hide information in ways that makes the decision maker perceive the situation as a problem, opportunity, or steady sailing.[13] Employees point to external factors rather than their own faults as the cause

Some problem identification failures occur when employees, suppliers, and other stakeholders provide or hide information, so the decision maker perceives the situation as a problem, opportunity, or steady sailing.
lmtmphoto/123RF

of production delays. Suppliers market their new products as unique opportunities and the client's current use of a competitor's products as risky. Decision makers fall prey to these constructed realities because they have a need to simplify the daily bombardment of complex and often ambiguous information.

Mental Models Decision makers are victims of their own problem framing due to existing mental models. **Mental models** are knowledge structures that we develop in our minds to describe, explain, and predict the world around us.[14] These visual or relational images of the external world fill in information that we don't immediately see, which satisfies our need to comprehend and navigate the surrounding environment (see Chapter 3). Many mental images are also images of ideal conditions—they represent models of how things should be. Unfortunately, these mental models can blind us from seeing unique problems or opportunities because people tend to dislike anything that deviates from their ideal type. If an idea doesn't fit the existing mental model of how things should work, then it is quickly dismissed as unworkable or undesirable.

Decisive Leadership Executives tend to be valued for their decisiveness, including how quickly they determine that the situation is a problem, opportunity, or nothing worth their attention.[15] Consequently, many leaders announce problems or opportunities before having a chance to logically assess the situation. The result is often a misguided effort to solve an ill-defined problem or resources wasted on a poorly identified opportunity.

Solution-Focused Problems Some decision makers jump to a solution before understanding the problem.[16] This is evident when the problem is defined as a veiled solution, such as: "The problem is that we need more control over our suppliers."

> **I suppose it is tempting, if the only tool you have is a hammer, to treat everything as if it were a nail.[17]**
>
> —Abraham Maslow, psychologist and scholar

This statement isn't a description of the problem; it is a rephrased statement of a solution to a problem that has little or no diagnosis.

Decision makers fall into the solution-focused problem trap because they have been reinforced by past successes with that solution. When new problems arise, the solution that worked well in the past quickly comes to mind before the actual problem is understood. A second reason is that decision makers are comforted by closure to problems, so they nonconsciously embed a solution in their problem definition. A third explanation is that solution-focused problem identification is decisive decision making; the problem and solution are wrapped up together. Unfortunately, this decisiveness often wastes resources solving the wrong problem.

Perceptual Defense Under some conditions, decision makers either fail to recognize or quickly forget information that threatens the situation. The tendency to engage in perceptual defense (or its variation, called repressive coping) is a coping mechanism. It is more likely to occur in decision makers with higher trait anxiety (high neuroticism) and when they have limited options to solve the problem.[18]

Identifying Problems and Opportunities More Effectively

Recognizing problems and opportunities will always be a challenge, but one way to improve the process is by becoming aware of the five problem identification biases just described. For example, by recognizing that mental models restrict a person's perspective of the world, decision makers are more motivated to consider other perspectives of reality. Along with increasing their awareness of problem identification flaws, leaders require considerable willpower to resist the temptation of looking decisive when a more thoughtful examination of the situation is warranted.

A third way to improve problem identification is to create a norm of "divine discontent." Decision makers with this mindset are never satisfied with current conditions, no matter how successful that situation may be, so they more actively search for problems and opportunities.[19] Fourth, problem identification errors can be minimized by discussing the situation with other people, particularly those with different experiences and backgrounds. It is much easier to discover blind spots in problem identification when listening to how others perceive the situation. Opportunities also become apparent when outsiders explore this information from their different mental models.

OB THEORY TO PRACTICE

Identifying Problems and Opportunities More Effectively

- Be aware of the problem identification biases.
- Resist the temptation to look decisive.
- Have an aversion to complacency (practice divine discontent).
- Discuss the situation with others.

LO6-3 Explain why people deviate from rational choice decision making when searching for, appraising, and choosing alternatives.

SEARCHING FOR, EVALUATING, AND CHOOSING ALTERNATIVES

The rational choice view of decision making assumes that decision makers rely on logic to evaluate and choose alternatives. It also assumes that they have well-articulated and agreed-upon organizational goals, that they efficiently and simultaneously process facts about all alternatives and the consequences of those alternatives, and that they choose the alternative with the most favorable outcomes.

Nobel Prize–winning organizational scholar Herbert Simon questioned these assumptions a half century ago. He argued that people engage in **bounded rationality** because they process limited and imperfect information, and they rarely try to select the best choice.[20] Bounded rationality is the most widely known theory questioning the rational choice view, but it is not alone. Other *imperfect rationality* theories identify flaws in how people form preferences, how they short-circuit the decision-making process, and how their choices are distorted by faulty heuristics and other perceptual biases.[21] Overall, as Exhibit 6.3 illustrates, organizational behavior theories identify several ways that human decision making differs from rational choice assumptions. Let's look at these differences in terms of goals, information processing, and maximization.

Exhibit 6.3 Rational Choice Assumptions versus Organizational Behavior Findings about Choosing Alternatives

Rational choice assumptions	Observations from organizational behavior
Goals are clear, compatible, and agreed upon.	Goals are ambiguous, are in conflict, and lack full support.
Decision makers can calculate all alternatives and their outcomes.	Decision makers have limited information-processing abilities.
Decision makers evaluate all alternatives simultaneously.	Decision makers evaluate alternatives sequentially.
Decision makers use absolute standards to evaluate alternatives.	Decision makers evaluate alternatives against an implicit favorite.
Decision makers use factual information to choose alternatives.	Decision makers process perceptually distorted information.
Decision makers choose the alternative with the highest payoff.	Decision makers choose the alternative that is good enough (satisficing).

Problems with Goals

Goals are a critical component of all decisions because they establish "what ought to be" and, therefore, provide a standard against which each alternative is evaluated. The rational choice view assumes that organizational goals are clear and agreed on, yet in reality they are often ambiguous or in conflict with each other.[22] Ambiguous goals make it difficult to know if a particular choice has greater value to the organization. For example, "satisfy customer needs" may refer to providing efficient service, a variety of services, more personalized service, and other possibilities. Conflicting goals also create havoc with rational decision making. When goals conflict, decision makers need to determine which goal gets priority. Unfortunately, they rarely have a guide map to determine which goals take precedence.

Problems with Information Processing

The rational choice approach assumes that decision makers assess all alternatives and all of their features and outcomes simultaneously using unbiased estimates of valences and outcome probabilities (illustrated earlier in Exhibit 6.1). In reality, people sequentially (not all at the same time) appraise only a few alternatives and only a handful of characteristics.[23] For example, there are hundreds of mobile/cell phone models on the market and dozens of features to consider in each model, yet phone purchasers typically pay attention to a small subset of phones and a handful of characteristics or expected outcomes of those products.

Furthermore, purchasers rarely line up their limited range of alternatives at the same time to select the best phone. Instead, they typically assess alternatives sequentially using an

> **Some problems are so complex that you have to be highly intelligent and well-informed just to be undecided about them.[24]**
>
> —Laurence J. Peter, educational scholar and author

implicit favourite
An alternative that the decision maker implicitly (usually nonconsciously) prefers and uses repeatedly as a comparison against other alternatives

confirmation bias
The process of screening out information that is contrary to our decisions, beliefs, values, and assumptions, while more readily accepting confirming information

anchoring and adjustment heuristic
A natural tendency for people to be influenced by an initial anchor point such that they do not sufficiently move away from that point as new information is provided

availability heuristic
A natural tendency to assign higher probabilities to objects or events that are easier to recall from memory, even though ease of recall is also affected by nonprobability factors (e.g., emotional response, recent events)

representativeness heuristic A natural tendency to evaluate probabilities of events or objects by the degree to which they resemble (are representative of) other events or objects rather than on objective probability information

implicit favorite. An implicit favorite is an alternative that the decision maker implicitly prefers and uses repeatedly as a comparison against other alternatives. The preferred alternative is called "implicit" because decision makers don't explicitly choose it and often aren't even aware of their favoritism.[25]

Why do decision makers follow a sequential appraisal process using an implicit favorite? One reason is that all alternatives are rarely available at the same time.[26] It is impossible to collect information about every type of phone on the same day, so the most favorable phone found early in your search becomes the implicit favorite when considering phones that you investigate later. Second, human beings have a natural preference for comparing two choices rather than systematically assessing many alternatives simultaneously.[27] An implicit favorite assists this process by serving as an anchor comparator for assessing the other choices. A third reason is that people are cognitive misers. They minimize mental effort by quickly forming a preferred alternative (their implicit favorite) and then looking mainly for evidence that supports the preferred choice. In other words, they engage in **confirmation bias** (see Chapter 3).[28]

The fourth reason why we compare alternatives sequentially against an implicit favorite is the human need for cognitive consistency and coherence. People want to think and act logically, so they try to align their emotional preference (implicit favorite) with the logical choice. This occurs through sequential analysis of alternatives by subtly changing valences and probabilities. Specifically, decision makers nonconsciously ignore or underweight positive features of the alternatives relative to the implicit favorite, and they change the importance of factors to support the favorite. Suppose that the camera on another phone brand gets more positive reviews than the camera on the phone you prefer (your implicit favorite). Chances are, you nonconsciously make camera quality less important (at least while making the decision) and discount the accuracy of the reviews about camera quality. Ultimately, you distort valences (importance of camera quality) and probabilities (likelihood that the other phone's camera is superior) so your implicit favorite remains the rational best choice.[29]

Decision makers have an implicit favorite because of their need to form preferences quickly, compare options, and maintain consistency between their decision and attitudes.
Mirexon/Shutterstock

Biased Decision Heuristics The cornerstone of rational choice decision making is to calculate the alternative with the highest expected satisfaction. However, psychologists Amos Tversky and Daniel Kahneman discovered that human beings have built-in *decision heuristics* that automatically distort those calculations. Three of the most widely studied heuristic biases are anchoring and adjustment, availability, and representativeness:[30]

- **Anchoring and adjustment heuristic.** This heuristic states that we are influenced by an initial anchor point and do not sufficiently move away from that point as new information is provided.[31] The anchor point might be an initial offer price, initial opinion of someone, or initial estimated probability that something will occur. This bias is associated with the problem we described a few paragraphs ago, namely that human beings tend to compare alternatives rather than assess them purely against objective criteria. Therefore, if someone requests a high initial price for a car we want to buy, we naturally compare—and thereby anchor—our alternative offer against that high initial price.
- **Availability heuristic.** The availability heuristic is the tendency to estimate the probability of something occurring by how easily we can recall that event. Unfortunately, how easily we recall something is due to several factors, not just how often it occurs (probability).[32] For instance, recent events and emotional events (such as earthquakes and shark attacks) are more easily remembered, so we tend to overestimate how likely or frequently they occur.
- **Representativeness heuristic.** This heuristic states that we pay more attention to whether something resembles (is representative of) something else and less attention to more objective statistics about its probability.[33] In other words, our decisions tend to rely more on stereotypes (see Chapter 3) and less on objective statistical probabilities. Suppose that 80 percent of the students in a sociology course are sociology majors, but the remaining 20 percent are computer science students taking the course as an interdepartmental elective. Statistically, there is a 20 percent chance that any classmate is from computer science, yet we tend to believe a student is from computer science if they look and act like a stereotype of a computer science student.

satisficing Selecting an alternative that is satisfactory or "good enough," rather than the alternative with the highest value (maximization)

intuition The ability to know when a problem or opportunity exists and to select the best course of action without conscious reasoning

Problems with Maximization

One of the main assumptions of rational choice decision making is that people are both motivated and able to identify and select the best alternative (maximization). In reality, decision makers usually engage in **satisficing**—they choose the first alternative that exceeds an acceptable standard for their needs and preferences.[34] In short, they choose an alternative that is "good enough."

Satisficing is usually necessary because choosing the absolutely best choice (maximization) requires complete and perfect information. This is impossible because information is imperfect, costly, or can't be found at all when the decision is made. Even if decision makers could receive complete and perfect information, they wouldn't have the time or cognitive capacity to digest and analyze the mammoth amount of complex data. For example, it is difficult to choose the best possible mobile/cell phone because of the large number of choices, the many features to consider for each choice, the numerous consequences of each choice (time to first breakdown, system update limits, etc.), and the ambiguous information about those features and outcomes. Given this overwhelming complexity, maximization leads to a spiral of endless trade-offs among the various choices, which can actually result in worse decisions and less satisfied decision makers.[35]

> When faced with a large number of alternatives, people often opt for the least cognitive draining decision strategy: They don't make any decision at all!

Studies report that people like to have choices, but deciding from among dozens of alternatives and many outcomes for each alternative is cognitively and emotionally draining. Consequently, decision makers satisfice as a way to minimize cognitive effort.[36] They also reduce cognitive effort by discarding a large selection of alternatives using easily identifiable factors (color, size, etc.) and by assessing them using only a handful of possible outcomes (selection criteria).

People who face a large number of alternatives often opt for a decision strategy that is even less cognitively challenging than satisficing: They don't make any decision at all! And those who do choose one of the many options tend to be less satisfied with their decision than those who choose from a few alternatives. In one study, for example, grocery store customers saw one of two jam-tasting booths. Thirty percent of consumers who visited the booth displaying six types of jam purchased one of those products. In contrast, only 3 percent of customers who saw the booth displaying 24 types of jam made a purchase. The larger number of choices discouraged them from making any decision. Other studies revealed similar results in decisions about chocolates, pens, vacation packages, mobile phones, and pension plan investment options.[37]

Individuals don't always experience decision paralysis when faced with a large number of alternatives.[38] Decision makers choose more easily when they are familiar or have expertise with the products and are reasonably clear about what they are looking for (criteria clarity). It is also easier to select among many alternatives that vary widely (very good to very bad features, taste, appearance, etc.), particularly when those characteristics are systematically organized rather than presented randomly. For example, a financial advisor could easily choose a preferred investment fund from hundreds of funds, even more so when the advisor knows which fund characteristics are most important, when those funds have widely varying characteristics (performance, volatility, etc.), and when information about the different funds is well organized.

Evaluating Opportunities

Opportunities are just as important as problems, but the process of acting on an opportunity differs from the process of solving a problem. Decision makers seldom evaluate several alternatives when they find an opportunity; after all, the opportunity is the solution, so why look for others! An opportunity is usually experienced as an exciting and rare revelation, so decision makers tend to have an emotional attachment to the opportunity. Unfortunately, this emotional preference motivates decision makers to apply the opportunity and short-circuit any detailed assessment of its likely benefits. Furthermore, studies indicate that decision makers tend to personalize an opportunity (i.e., it belongs to them) rather than remain impartial evaluators of the opportunity. This ownership mindset makes impersonal analysis of the opportunity even more difficult.[39]

LO6-4 Discuss how emotions and intuition relate to decision making.

EMOTIONS AND INTUITION IN DECISION MAKING

Emotions and Making Choices

The previous sections of this chapter explained why people are far from perfect at rational decision making. However, Herbert Simon and other scholars who studied imperfect rationality neglected to mention another problem: the rational choice model completely ignores the effect of emotions in human decision making. Just as both the rational and emotional brain centers alert us to problems, they also influence our choice of alternatives.[40] Emotions affect the evaluation of alternatives in three ways: (1) they form early preferences, (2) they influence the decision appraisal process, and (3) they serve as information when making choices.

Emotions Form Early Preferences The emotional marker process described earlier in this book (Chapters 3, 4, and 5) shapes our preferences for alternatives before we consciously evaluate them. Our brain very quickly attaches specific emotions to information about each alternative, and our preferred alternative is strongly influenced by those initial emotional markers.[41] Of course, logical analysis also influences which alternative we choose, but it requires strong logical evidence to change our initial preferences (initial emotional markers). Yet even logical analysis depends on emotions to sway our decision. Specifically, neuroscientific evidence indicates that information produced from logical analysis is tagged with emotional markers, and it is those emotional markers, not logical analysis, that motivate us to choose or avoid a particular alternative. In other words, emotions, not rational logic, energize us to make the preferred choice. In fact, people with damaged emotion brain centers have difficulty making decisions.

Emotions Influence the Decision Evaluation Process Moods and specific emotions influence the *process* of evaluating alternatives.[42] For instance, we pay more attention to details when in a negative mood, possibly because a negative mood signals that there is something wrong that requires attention. When in a positive mood, on the other hand, we pay less attention to details and rely on a more programmed decision routine. This phenomenon explains why executive teams are often less vigilant about competitors and other environmental threats after they have experienced successful events.[43] Research also suggests that when angry, decision makers rely on stereotypes and other shortcuts to speed up the choice process. Anger also makes them more optimistic about the success of risky alternatives, whereas the emotion of fear tends to make them less optimistic. Overall, emotions shape *how* we evaluate information, not just which alternative we select.

Emotions Serve as Information When We Evaluate Alternatives The third way that emotions influence the evaluation of alternatives is through a process called "emotions as information." This refers to the idea that we listen in on our emotions to acquire guidance when making choices.[44] The emotions-as-information effect is similar to having a temporary improvement in emotional intelligence. Most emotional experiences remain below the level of conscious awareness, but people actively try to be more sensitive to these subtle emotions when making a decision.

When buying a new car, for example, you not only logically evaluate each vehicle's features; you also try to gauge your emotions when visualizing what it would be like to own each of the cars on your list of choices. Even when you have information about each vehicle (purchase price, fuel efficiency, maintenance costs, resale value, etc.), you are swayed by your emotional reaction and actively try to sense those emotional responses when thinking about the decision. Everyone pays attention to their emotions to some degree when choosing alternatives. This phenomenon ties directly into our next topic, intuition.

Decision makers tend to pay more attention to details when in a negative mood, and are less vigilant about external threats when in a positive mood.
fizkes/Shutterstock

Intuition and Making Choices

Do you get a gut feeling when something isn't quite right? Or perhaps a different emotional experience occurs when you sense an opportunity? These emotional events potentially (but not necessarily) indicate your **intuition**–the ability to know when a problem or opportunity exists and to select the best course of action without conscious reasoning.[45] Some people pay more attention to their gut feelings, whereas others are more comfortable with decisions based on logic and data analysis. However, intuition and logical analysis are not opposites and never completely replace each other. Both are always present in human decision making.[46]

Intuition is both an emotional experience and a rapid nonconscious analytic process. The gut feelings we experience are emotional signals that have enough intensity to make us consciously aware of them. These signals warn us of impending danger or motivate us to take advantage of an opportunity. Some intuition also directs us to preferred choices relative to other alternatives in the situation.

Mc Graw Hill connect

SELF-ASSESSMENT 6.1: What Is Your Preferred Decision-Making Style?

> All gut feelings are emotional signals, but those emotional signals are intuition only when based on well-grounded mental models developed through relevant experience.

All gut feelings are emotional signals, but not all emotional signals are intuition. Emotional signals are valid intuition when they rely on mental models that reasonably and accurately depict the situation where we sense the problem or opportunity. Intuition involves rapidly comparing our observations with these "templates of the mind." Positive or negative emotions are produced, depending on how well that situation fits our mental model.[47] For example, when chess masters quickly scan a chessboard, they experience emotional signals that the chess configuration poses an opportunity or threat. These emotional signals motivate closer observation to logically confirm the situation and to act on it. Thus, intuition signals that a problem or opportunity exists long before conscious rational analysis has occurred.

However, not all emotional signals are intuition because they are not always based on well-grounded mental models. Instead, we sometimes compare the current situation to more remote templates, which may or may not be relevant. A new employee might feel confident about relations with a supplier, whereas an experienced employee senses potential problems. The difference is that the new employee relies on poorly developed or more remote templates from other experiences that might not fit this situation. Thus, the extent to which our gut feelings in a situation represent intuition depends on our level of experience in that setting. The key message here is that some emotional signals are not intuition, so gut feelings alone shouldn't guide our decisions.

So far, we have described intuition as an emotional experience (gut feeling) and a process in which we compare the current situation with well-established templates of the mind. Intuition also relies on *action scripts* that speed up our response to pattern matches or mismatches.[48] Action scripts are programmed decisions; they shorten the decision-making process by jumping from problem identification to selection of a solution. Action scripts are also generic, so we need to consciously adapt them to the specific situation.

Making Choices More Effectively

It is very difficult to get around the human limitations of making choices, but a few strategies can minimize these problems. One important discovery is that decisions tend to have a higher failure rate when leaders are decisive rather than contemplative about the available options. Of course, decisions can also be ineffective when leaders procrastinate in decision making, but research indicates that a lack of logical evaluation of alternatives is a greater concern. This recommendation does not suggest that we ignore intuition; rather, it suggests that we use it in combination with careful analysis of relevant information. By systematically assessing alternatives against relevant factors, decision makers minimize the implicit favorite and satisficing problems that occur when they rely on general, subjective judgments.[49]

Another recommendation is to revisit important problems and opportunities at another time so information is reviewed when decision makers are in different moods and have allowed time for their initial emotions to subside. For example, if you sense that your team is feeling too confident when making an important decision, you might have the committee revisit

Intuition versus Data Analysis: Crunch Your Hunch[50]

63% of 1,048 U.S. senior managers do not believe their companies are analytics-driven.

80% of 509 senior business leaders from small, medium, and large Australian businesses say they have experienced negative consequences from organizational decisions made using gut feeling rather than evidence.

48% of 9,000 employees across 9 countries say they defer to a 'gut feeling' rather than data-driven insights when making decisions (67% of top level executives say this versus 41% of junior managers).

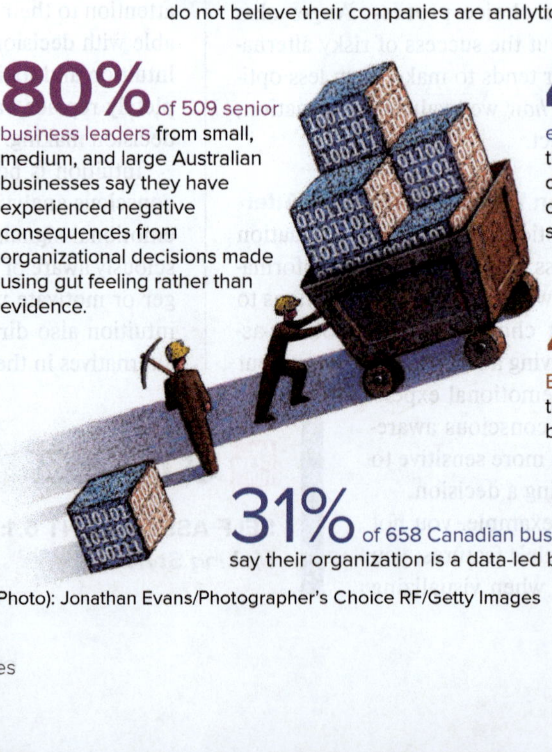

46% of 3,750 US and European knowledge workers believe that business decisions are made based on data.

31% of 658 Canadian business decision-makers say their organization is a data-led business.

(Photo): Jonathan Evans/Photographer's Choice RF/Getty Images

OB THEORY TO PRACTICE

Making Choices More Effectively

- Be more contemplative than decisive for complex problems.
- Use intuition only in combination with logical analysis.
- Revisit decisions that were made when feeling overly positive and confident.
- Practice scenario planning.

the decision a few days later when its members are thinking more critically.

A related strategy is **scenario planning**, which is a disciplined method for imagining possible futures.[51] It typically involves thinking about what would happen if a significant environmental condition changed and what the organization should do to anticipate and react to such an outcome. Scenario planning is a useful vehicle for choosing the best solutions under possible scenarios long before they occur, because alternative courses of action are evaluated without the pressure and emotions that occur during real emergencies.

LO6-5 Explain how decision makers bias the evaluation of decision outcomes, and identify ways to minimize those decision evaluation problems.

IMPLEMENTING AND EVALUATING DECISIONS

Implementing Decisions

Implementing decisions is often skipped over in most writing about decision making. Yet leading business writers emphasize that execution—translating decisions into action—is one of the most important and challenging tasks in the decision-making process.[52] Implementing decisions is mainly about organizational change, which we discuss in Chapter 14, but also relates to motivation (Chapter 5), influence processes (Chapter 9), leadership (Chapter 11), and several other topics throughout this book.

Evaluating Decisions

Contrary to the rational choice view, decision makers aren't completely honest with themselves when evaluating the effectiveness of their decisions. Earlier in this chapter, we explained that decision makers engage in *confirmation bias* to support their implicit favorite and to maintain consistency in their preference and decision. This bias continues long after the decision has been made; during the evaluation stage it is also known as *postdecisional justification*.[53] Decision makers ignore or underemphasize negative outcomes of the alternative they selected and overemphasize new information about its positive features. Postdecisional justification gives people an excessively optimistic evaluation of their decisions, but only until they receive very clear and undeniable information to the contrary.

scenario planning A systematic process of thinking about alternative futures and what the organization should do to anticipate and react to those environments

escalation of commitment The tendency to repeat an apparently bad decision or allocate more resources to a failing course of action

self-enhancement A person's inherent motivation to have a positive self-concept (and to have others perceive them favorably), such as being competent, attractive, lucky, ethical, and important

Escalation of Commitment

Another reason why decision makers don't evaluate their decisions very well is due to **escalation of commitment**—the tendency to repeat an apparently bad decision or allocate more resources to a failing course of action.[54] Why are decision makers led deeper and deeper into failing projects? Several explanations have been identified and discussed over the years, but the four main influences are self-justification effect, self-enhancement effect, prospect theory effect, and sunk costs effect.

Self-Justification Effect People try to convey a positive public image of themselves. In decision making, this self-justification typically involves appearing to be rational and competent. Decision makers are therefore motivated to demonstrate that their choices will be successful, which includes continuing to support a decision even when it is not having the desired outcomes. In contrast, pulling the plug symbolizes the project's failure and the decision maker's incompetence. This self-justification effect is particularly evident when decision makers are personally identified with the project, have staked their reputations to some extent on the project's success, and have low self-esteem.[55]

Self-Enhancement Effect People have a natural tendency to feel good about themselves—to feel luckier, more competent, and more successful than average—regarding things that are important to them (see Chapter 3).[56] This **self-enhancement** supports a positive self-concept, but it also increases the risk of escalation of commitment. When presented with evidence that a project is in trouble, self-enhancement biases our interpretation of the information as a temporary aberration from an otherwise positive trend line. And when we eventually realize that the project isn't going as well as planned, we continue to invest in the project because our self-enhancement overestimates our probability of rescuing the project. Self-justification and self-enhancement often occur together, but they are different mechanisms. Self-justification is a deliberate attempt to maintain a favorable public image, whereas self-enhancement nonconsciously distorts our perceptions so problems are recognized later and our probabilities of success are biased so we continue to invest in the losing project.[57]

Escalation of commitment occurs partly because people are motivated to invest resources in projects with high sunk costs (large amounts already spent), whereas they should consider only the additional investment's expected future gains.
Pogonici/Shutterstock

Prospect Theory Effect **Prospect theory effect** is the tendency to experience stronger negative emotions when losing something of value than positive emotions when gaining something of equal value. This is also known as *loss aversion* because we have a stronger motivation to avoid losses than to risk receiving equally valuable gains. The stronger negative valence of a potential loss motivates escalation of commitment because stopping a project is a certain loss which typically evokes more negative emotions than the uncertainty of success associated with continuing to fund the project. Given the choice, decision makers choose escalation of commitment, which is the less painful option at the time.[58]

Sunk Costs Effect People inherently feel motivated to invest more resources in projects that have high sunk costs—the value of resources already invested in the decision.[59] This contrasts with the rational choice view, which states that investing resources should be determined by expected future gains and risk of the new investment, not by the size of earlier resources invested in the project. A variation of sunk costs is time investment. Time is a resource, so the more time decision makers have devoted to a project, the more motivated they are to continue investing in that project. Finally, sunk costs can take the form of closing costs, that is, the financial or nonfinancial penalties associated with shutting down a project. As with other forms of sunk costs, the higher the closing costs, the more motivated decision makers are to engage in escalation of commitment.

Escalation of commitment is usually framed as poor decision making, but adding more resources to a failing project may be beneficial under some circumstances.[60] Indeed, many breakthroughs have occurred because of the decision maker's persistence and optimism. Continuing with a losing project may be prudent when the cost overruns are small relative to the project cost, the benefits of success are high, and the rewards of a successful project are received quickly. Some experts also suggest that throwing more money into a failing project is sometimes a logical attempt to further understand an ambiguous situation. By adding more resources, the decision maker gains new information about the project's development, which provides more feedback about the project's future success. This strategy is particularly common where the project has high closing costs.

Evaluating Decision Outcomes More Effectively

There are several ways to evaluate decisions with less bias.[61] Self-justification effect is minimized by ensuring that the people who made the original decision are not the same people who later evaluate that decision. A second strategy is to publicly establish a preset level at which the decision is abandoned or reevaluated. This action forces the decision maker to abandon the investment if its value falls or cost overruns increase too much, although determining the best stop loss point can be difficult.

Third, decision evaluators should seek out factual and social feedback about the project. Even the strongest escalation and confirmation bias effects collapse when the decision maker is faced with systematic and clear feedback about the project's failings. In addition, decision evaluators can become aware of problems earlier by seeking ongoing feedback from several (preferably impartial) people.

OB THEORY TO PRACTICE

Evaluating Decision Outcomes More Effectively

- *Separate the decision maker from the decision evaluator.* Ensure that the decision evaluators are not the same people who made the decision.
- *Create a stop-loss.* Publicly establish a preset level at which the decision is abandoned or reevaluated.
- *Seek out factual and social feedback.* Develop accessible sources of systematic and clear evidence about the project's development and setbacks, and receive ongoing feedback about the project from several (preferably impartial) people.
- *Change the decision evaluator's mindset.* Apply interventions that refocus decision evaluator's away from the negative emotions of past financial losses and toward the positive emotions of future growth opportunities.

Finally, recent evidence suggests that decision evaluators are less likely to engage in escalation of commitment if they change their mindset away from the negative consequences of project failure and focus more on future opportunities to grow the business.

LO6-6 Outline the creative process, and identify employee characteristics, workplace conditions, and specific activities that support creativity.

CREATIVITY

The entire decision-making process depends to some degree on **creativity**—the development of original ideas that make a socially recognized contribution.[62] Creativity enables us to imagine opportunities, such as discovering new products or services, or recognizing problems that are not easily apparent from traditional perspectives. It helps us to develop and choose alternatives by visualizing the future in different ways and figuring out how each option might be useful or a liability in those scenarios.

The Creative Process

How does creativity occur? That question has puzzled experts for centuries and has fascinated scientists who saw how creative thinking contributed to their own important discoveries. Notably, more than a century ago, German physicist Hermann von Helmholtz gave a public talk describing the process that led to his innovations (energy physics, instruments for examining eyes, and many others). A few decades later, London School of Economics professor Graham Wallas built on Helmholtz's ideas to construct the four-stage model shown in Exhibit 6.4.[63] To this day, this model is considered the most elegant representation of the creative process.

The first stage is *preparation*—the process of investigating the problem or opportunity. Preparation involves developing a clear understanding of what you are trying to achieve through a novel solution and then actively studying information seemingly related to the topic. It is a process of developing knowledge and possibly skills about the topic. The second stage, called *incubation,* is the period of reflective thought. We put the problem aside, but our mind is still working on it in the background.[64] The important condition here is to maintain a low-level awareness by frequently revisiting the problem.

Incubation assists **divergent thinking**—reframing the problem in a unique way and generating different approaches to the issue. Divergent thinking breaks us away from existing mental models so that we can apply concepts or processes from completely different areas of life. This contrasts with *convergent thinking,* which involves calculating the conventionally accepted "right answer" to a logical problem.

Illumination (also called *insight*), the third stage of creativity, refers to the experience of suddenly becoming aware of a unique idea.[65] This stage begins with a "fringe" awareness before the idea fully enters our consciousness. Illumination is often visually

prospect theory effect An innate tendency to feel stronger negative emotions from losing a particular amount than positive emotions from gaining an equal amount

creativity The development of original ideas that make a socially recognized contribution

divergent thinking Reframing a problem in a unique way and generating different approaches to the issue

connect

SELF-ASSESSMENT 6.2: How Well Do You Engage in Divergent Thinking?

Exhibit 6.4 The Creative Process Model

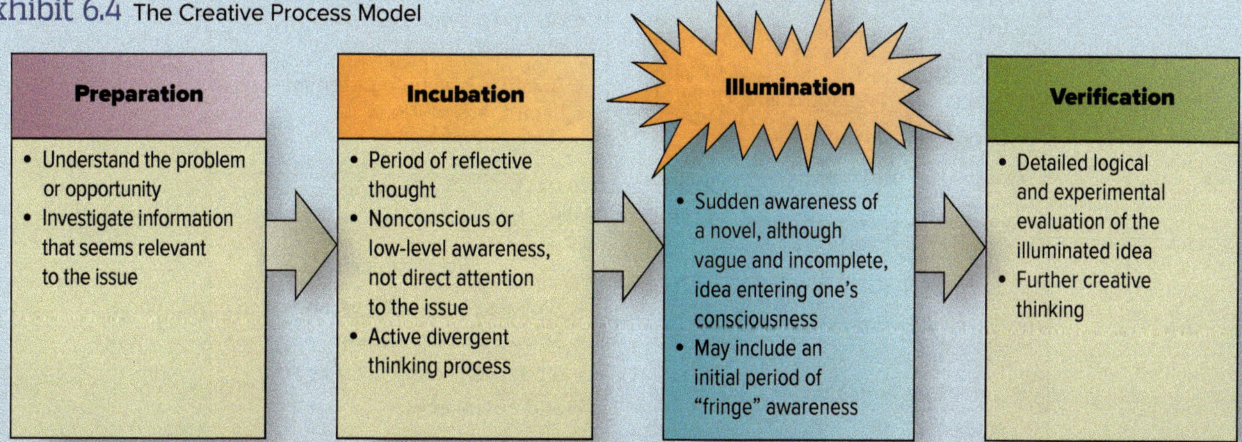

Source: Based on G. Wallas, *The Art of Thought* (London: Jonathan Cape, 1926), Chap. 4.

depicted as a lightbulb, but a better image would be a flash of light or perhaps a briefly flickering candle—these bits of inspiration are fleeting and can be quickly lost if not documented. For this reason, many creative people keep a journal or notebook nearby so they can jot down their ideas before they disappear. Also, flickering ideas don't keep a particular schedule; they might come to you at any time of day or night.

Illumination presents ideas that are usually vague, roughly drawn, and untested. Therefore, the essential final stage of creativity is *verification,* whereby we flesh out the illuminated ideas and subject them to detailed experimentation and evaluation. Although verification is labeled the final stage of creativity, it is really the beginning of a long process of further creative decision making toward development of an innovative product or service.

Characteristics of Creative People

Everyone is creative, but some people have a higher potential for creativity. Four of the main characteristics that give individuals more creative potential are intelligence, persistence, knowledge and experience, and a cluster of personality traits and values representing independent imagination (see Exhibit 6.5).

- *Cognitive and practical intelligence.* People with higher creative potential have above-average intelligence to synthesize information, analyze possibilities, and apply their ideas.[66] They recognize the significance of small bits of information and are able to connect them in ways that few others can imagine. They also have *practical intelligence*—the capacity to evaluate the potential usefulness of their ideas.
- *Persistence.* Creative people have persistence, which is based on a high need for achievement, a strong motivation from the task itself, and a moderate or higher self-esteem. Persistence is vital because people need this motivation to continue working on and investing in a project in spite of failures and advice from others to quit. In fact, human beings have a general tendency to dismiss or criticize new ideas, so creative people need persistence to withstand these negative social forces.[67]
- *Knowledge and experience.* Creative people require a foundation of knowledge and experience to discover or acquire new knowledge.[68] However, this expertise is a double-edged sword. As people acquire specific knowledge and experience, their mental models about that topic tend to become more rigid. They are less adaptable to new information or rules about that knowledge domain. Some writers suggest that expertise also increases "mindless behavior" because it reduces the tendency to question why things happen.[69] To overcome the limitations of expertise, some corporate leaders like to hire people from other industries and with different expertise.
- *Independent imagination.* Creative people possess a cluster of personality traits and values that support an independent imagination: high openness to experience, moderately low need for affiliation, and strong values around self-direction and stimulation.[70] Openness to experience is a Big Five personality dimension representing the extent to which a person is imaginative, curious, sensitive, open-minded, and original (see Chapter 2). Creative people have a moderately low need for affiliation so they are less embarrassed when making mistakes. Self-direction includes the values of creativity and independent thought; stimulation includes the values of excitement and challenge. Together, these values form openness to change—representing the motivation to pursue innovative ways of solving problems (see Chapter 2).

connect

SELF-ASSESSMENT 6.3: Do You Have a Creative Personality?

Exhibit 6.5 Characteristics of Creative People

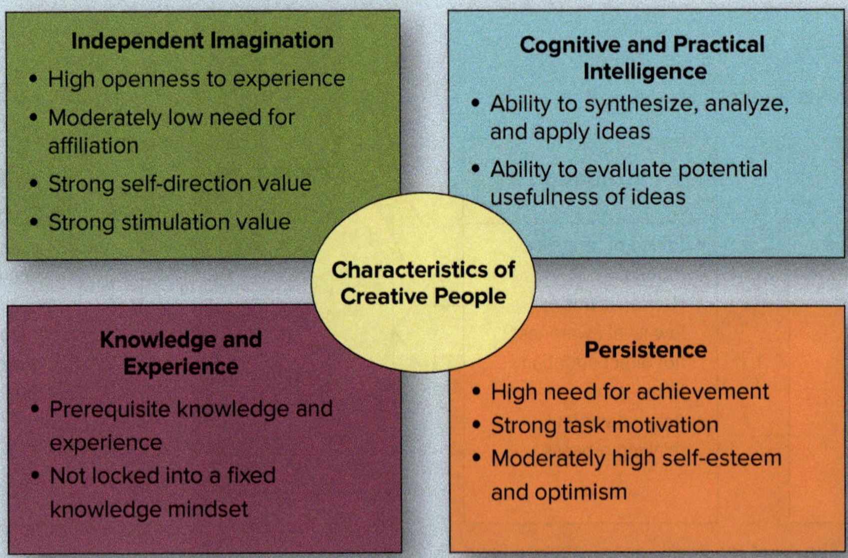

Organizational Conditions Supporting Creativity

Intelligence, persistence, expertise, and independent imagination represent a person's creative potential, but the extent to which these characteristics produce more creative output depends on how well the work environment supports the creative process.[71] Several job and workplace characteristics have been identified in the literature, and different combinations of situations can equally support creativity; there isn't one best work environment.

One of the most important conditions for creativity is a **learning orientation.**[72] A learning orientation is a set of collective beliefs and norms that encourage employees to question past practices, to learn new ideas, to experiment putting ideas into practice, and to view mistakes as part of the learning process. Job enrichment is a second contributor to creativity. Employees tend to be more creative when they believe their work benefits the organization and/or larger society (i.e., task significance) and that they have the freedom to pursue novel ideas without bureaucratic delays (i.e., autonomy).[73] Creativity is about changing things, and change is possible only when employees have autonomy and the authority to experiment.

learning orientation A set of beliefs and norms in which people are encouraged to question past practices, learn new ideas, experiment putting ideas into practice, and view mistakes as part of the learning process

Along with a learning orientation and enriched jobs, creativity blossoms through open communication (enabling employees to share ideas and information) and sufficient resources. Organizations also nurture creativity by providing a comfortable degree of job security, which explains why creativity suffers during times of downsizing and corporate restructuring.[75] Some companies also support creativity by designing nontraditional workspaces, such as a unique building design or unconventional office areas.[76]

Leadership is another important influence on creativity.[77] Creativity is more likely to thrive when leaders communicate an appealing vision of the future and encourage employees to experiment with new ways to achieve that vision (see *transformational leadership* in Chapter 11). Coworker support and teamwork can also improve creativity, but studies also suggest that competition among coworkers and teams improves creativity under some conditions. Another issue is how much pressure should be exerted on employees to produce creative ideas. Extreme time pressures are well-known creativity inhibitors, but lack of pressure doesn't seem to produce the highest creativity, either.

The Creativity Challenge[74]

59% of 1,973 managers in Brazil, Germany, India, Singapore, the United Kingdom, and the United States say that to succeed over the next three years, their organization needs employees with creative thinking personal attributes.

60% of 52,195 workers in 44 countries say they can be creative in their job.

56% of 557,778 US federal government employees say that management in their department encourages innovation.

64% of 6,000 workers in seven European countries say they would enjoy their work more if they had more time for creative tasks.

46% of 3,500 employees agree that their organization encourages creative thinking.

(Photo): ImageFlow/Shutterstock

design thinking A human-centered, solution-focused creative process that applies both intuition and analytical thinking to clarify problems and generate innovative solutions

Activities That Encourage Creativity

We have described two cornerstones of creativity in organizations: employing people with strong creative potential and providing a work environment that supports creativity. The third cornerstone consists of activities that stimulate more creative thinking in employees. Four types of creativity-building activities are: redefine the problem, associative play, cross-pollination, and design thinking.

Redefine the Problem Redefining the problem is a potentially powerful way to unleash creative thinking. One approach is to revisit projects that have been set aside. After a period of neglect, these projects might be seen in new ways.[78] You can also see the problem from different perspectives by asking coworkers unfamiliar with the issue to explore the problem. You state the objectives and give some facts and then let the other person ask questions to further understand the situation. By verbalizing the problem, listening to questions, and hearing what others think, you are more likely to form new perspectives on the issue.[79]

Associative Play Associative play literally involves playing games or being challenged in unusual ways.[80] One form of associative play is to engage in playful activities, particularly with unusual twists to the traditional equipment or rules. Creative thinking emerges naturally from these playful activities and then carries over to work-related problem solving. A second variation is challenging participants to create something new with a specific purpose (e.g., cleaning cutlery) using existing unrelated products (e.g., blow dryer and electric toothbrush). These activities exercise the mind to break out of traditional mental models about existing products and services.

A third variation of associative play, called *morphological analysis,* involves systematically investigating all combinations of characteristics of a product, service, or event, and then looking at the feasibility of each combination.[82] This exercise encourages people to carefully examine combinations that initially seem nonsensical. For instance, employees at a dairy company might look at all combinations of yogurt-based products by considering the contents (fruit, low fat, etc.), occasion (breakfast, dessert, etc.), target group (children, older adults, etc.), size, and packaging. A novel, yet commercially successful, innovation may emerge from the resulting list.

Cross-Pollination Cross-pollination occurs when people from different areas of the organization exchange ideas or when new people are brought into an existing team.[83] This may occur by arranging formal social gatherings, bringing new people with divergent backgrounds into an existing team, or encouraging happenstance interactions with people from other work areas. A few firms encourage cross-pollination by moving employees every few months to another location with coworkers who are only acquaintances. Cross-pollination highlights the fact that

OB THEORY TO PRACTICE

Supporting Creative Thinking at Ubisoft[81]

Creativity is the lifeblood of video game development. This is evident at French game developer Ubisoft, which has instilled a culture of empowering every studio as an ecosystem of creativity. "Yves [Guillemot, Ubisoft's cofounder] enables us and empowers us, the studio teams, to be creative and to pursue our dreams," says Darryl Long, Ubisoft's managing director in Singapore and the Philippines.

At Ubisoft, creativity is typically a social process. Long explains that new ideas emerge from the involvement of employees at all levels, as well as from game users and other stakeholders. "When there are decisions we need to make, we make sure to get as many people involved in that decision as possible, to do collaborative problem-solving and decision-making to leverage that experience from outside of Ubisoft."

Long also stimulates creative thinking through specific team-based activities, such as Studio Game Jam. "We will let people form teams, get together for a few days to build their own really quick indie (independent) game, and then we'll celebrate those games at the studio during our meetings." Another initiative is Open Innovation, which encourages individuals to pitch their game idea to others. "Nearly half of this year's pitch ideas came from junior and mid-level employees," Long observes.

These activities spark new ideas, but Long emphasizes that another important ingredient for creativity is workplace diversity and inclusion. "What diversity brings is it sparks creativity, that challenge, that different ways of thinking, coming together in new ways," says Long. "If we're not innovating, if we're not pushing the boundaries, then we're just going to get left behind and that's where diversity actually makes such a huge contribution."

bazava/123RF

Exhibit 6.6 Four Rules of Design Thinking

Design Thinking Rule	Description
Human Rule	• Involve several people so the issue and possible solutions are viewed from several angles. • Include clients and end users to enable an iterative process of problem identification and solution development.
Ambiguity Rule	• Preserve ambiguity rather than seek clarity too quickly. • Question and refine the stated problem. • Develop more than one solution to the problem.
Re-design Rule	• Review past solutions to understand how those inventions tried to satisfy human needs. • Use foresight tools to imagine better solutions for the future.
Tangible Rule	• Build several low-cost prototypes to test ideas. • Don't analyze alternatives at a purely conceptual level. • Tolerate failure; embrace a learning orientation.

Source: Based on information in C. Meinel and L. Leifer, "Introduction—Design Thinking Is Mainly about Building Innovators," in *Design Thinking Research: Building Innovators*, ed. H. Plattner, C. Meinel, and L. Leifer (Cham, Switzerland: Springer International, 2015), 1–11.

creativity rarely occurs alone. Some creative people may be individualistic, but most creative ideas are generated through teams and informal social interaction.

Design Thinking **Design thinking** is a human-centered, solution-focused creative process that applies both intuition and analytical thinking to clarify problems and generate innovative solutions. It is a framework with four sets of practices to improve creativity and development of new products and services (see Exhibit 6.6).[84]

The Human Rule emphasizes the need for collaboration and empathy with several stakeholders who bring diverse knowledge and experiences so the issue and its possible solutions are viewed from several angles. The Ambiguity Rule identifies the need to continually question possible solutions and to avoid defining the problem too early in the process. The Re-design Rule highlights the need to understand and learn from past solutions as well as to notice trends that might guide possible future possibilities. The Tangible Rule encourages design thinkers to spend more time trying out ideas with low-cost prototypes, rather than analyzing those ideas at a purely conceptual level. These prototypes are made quickly and frequently along the journey to the final result.

LO6-7 Summarize the benefits of employee involvement and discuss five contingencies that affect the optimal level of employee involvement.

EMPLOYEE INVOLVEMENT IN DECISION MAKING

Employee involvement refers to activities in which employees participate in and influence decisions about their jobs, work units, or organization.[85] This participation is more than just giving workers a voice in decisions; it exists when they actually influence decisions to some degree. There are several levels of employee involvement.[86] A low level of involvement occurs when employees are individually asked for specific information but the problem is not described to them. Somewhat higher involvement occurs when the problem is described and employees are asked individually or collectively for information relating to that problem.

Moving further up the involvement scale, the problem is described to employees, who are collectively given responsibility

> **Tell me and I will forget; show me and I will remember; involve me and I will understand.[87]**
>
> —Variation of a proverb by Chinese Confucian philosopher Xun Kuang

for developing recommendations. However, the decision maker is not bound to accept those recommendations. At the highest level of involvement, the entire decision-making process is handed over to employees. They identify the problem, discover alternative solutions, choose the best alternative, and implement that choice. The original decision maker serves only as a facilitator to guide the team's decision process and keep everyone on track.

Exhibit 6.7 Model of Employee Involvement in Decision Making

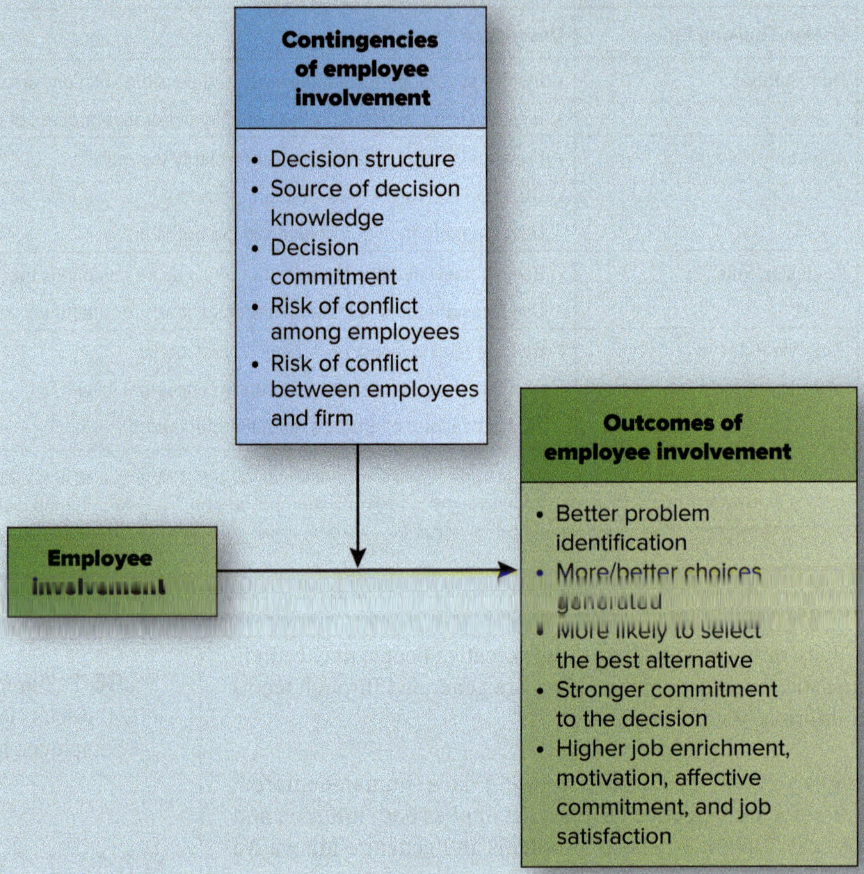

Benefits of Employee Involvement

Employee involvement offers enormous benefits to organizations and employees alike, particularly when the level and type of participation is aligned with the situation.[88] In fact, it may be difficult for any company to function effectively or retain employees without some degree of employee participation in decisions outside their daily work activities. Exhibit 6.7 identifies five main outcomes of employee involvement.

First, employee involvement improves the identification of problems and opportunities. Employees are usually the first to know when the organization's activities are misaligned with customer or community expectations, or with the supply of input resources. Employee involvement provides a conduit to alert executives to those problems. Second, employee involvement can potentially improve the number and quality of solutions generated. People working together tend to create a synergy that produces more and better solutions than the same people working alone.

A third benefit is that, under specific conditions, employee involvement improves the appraisal of alternatives. This process brings out more diverse perspectives, tests ideas, and provides more valuable knowledge, all of which help select the best alternative.[89] As the Marquis de Condorcet stated more than two centuries ago, the alternative selected by the team's majority is more likely to be correct than is the alternative selected by any team member individually.[90]

A fourth benefit is that involvement tends to strengthen employee commitment to the decision. Rather than viewing themselves as agents of someone else's decision, those who participate in a decision feel personally responsible for its success. This explains why some degree of involvement is usually valuable during organizational change; employees are more motivated to implement the decision and less likely to resist changes resulting from the decision.[91] Finally, employee involvement potentially increases

Employee involvement potentially improves problem identification, the number and quality of solutions generated, the appraisal of alternatives, employee commitment to implementing the decision, and employee motivation and satisfaction with the job.
Stockbroker/123RF

skill variety, feelings of autonomy, and task identity, all of which increase job enrichment, employee motivation, and job satisfaction. Similarly, involvement is associated with higher levels of affective commitment to the organization, not just to the decision.[92]

Contingencies of Employee Involvement

If employee involvement is so wonderful, why don't leaders leave all decisions to employees? The answer is that the optimal level of employee involvement depends on the situation. The employee involvement model shown earlier in Exhibit 6.7 lists five contingencies: decision structure, source of decision knowledge, decision commitment, risk of conflict among employees, and risk of conflict between employees and the organization.[93]

- *Decision structure.* At the beginning of this chapter, we described how some decisions are programmed whereas others are nonprogrammed. Programmed decisions are less likely to need employee involvement because the solutions are already worked out from past incidents. In other words, the benefits of employee involvement increase with the novelty and complexity of the problem or opportunity.
- *Source of decision knowledge.* Subordinates should be involved in some level of decision making when the leader lacks sufficient knowledge and subordinates have additional information to improve decision quality. In many cases, employees are closer to customers and production activities, so they often know where the company can save money, improve product or service quality, and realize opportunities. This is particularly true for complex decisions where employees are more likely to possess relevant information.
- *Decision commitment.* Participation tends to improve employee commitment to the decision. If employees are unlikely to accept a decision made without their involvement, some level of participation is usually necessary.
- *Risk of conflict among employees.* The degree of involvement depends on whether employees will agree with one another on the preferred solution. If conflict is likely to occur, low or moderate involvement is advisable because employees are unlikely to reach a consensus regarding the preferred decision.
- *Risk of conflict between employees and the organization.* A higher level of involvement is possible when employee goals and norms are congruent with the organization's goals. When employee preferences and choices are likely to conflict with the organization's success and survival, only a low level of involvement should occur.

Employee involvement is an important component of the decision-making process. To make the best decisions, we need to involve people who have valuable information and who will be more motivated to implement the decision. Employee involvement is a formative stage of team dynamics, so it carries many of the benefits and challenges of working in teams. The next chapter provides a closer look at team dynamics, including processes for making decisions in teams.

Study Checklist

Connect® is available for *M: Organizational Behavior.* Additional resources include:

✓ Exercises:

- **Case Analysis:** Apply concepts within the context of a real-world situation.
- **Click and Drag:** Helps make the connection between theory and application through matching, ranking, or grouping activities.
- **Video Case:** See management in action through interactive videos.
- **Self-Assessment:** Designed to promote student self-awareness and reflection, these research-based surveys contain detailed feedback for students.
- **Application-Based Activities:** These highly interactive, application- and analysis-based exercises allow students to take on specific roles to complete management related tasks within a real-world context.

✓ **SmartBook 2.0™**—Smartbook 2.0 is an adaptive learning solution that provides personalized learning to individual student needs, continually adapts to pinpoint knowledge gaps and focuses learning on concepts requiring additional study. It fosters more productive learning, takes the guesswork out of what to study, and helps students better prepare for class.

Notes

1. S. Hampton and T. Tatum, "February 2022 Boil Water Notice Investigation Reports" (Austin, TX: City of Austin, March 29, 2022); M. Torre, "Austin Water: February Boil Notice Result of Poor Judgment, Bad Communication," *CBS Austin*, March 31, 2022. As with many organizational calamities, other problems and decision errors contributed to Austin's boil water notice. For example, the superintendent advised crews to keep the basins operating so the line feeding another chemical (lime) would not freeze again. The night crew assumed that shutting down Basin #6 was contrary to those orders, so they didn't contact management to request that action.
2. F.A. Shull Jr., A.L. Delbecq, and L.L. Cummings, *Organizational Decision Making* (New York: McGraw Hill, 1970), 31.

3. S.R. Covey, *The Wisdom and Teachings of Stephen R. Covey* (New York: Free Press, 2012).

4. Harvard Business School, *Decision Making: 5 Steps to Better Results* (Cambridge, MA: Harvard Business School Press 2006), Chap. 1; D. Baltzly, "Stoicism" (*Stanford Encyclopedia of Philosophy*, 2008); I. Pownall, *Effective Management Decision Making* (Holstebro, DK: Ventus Publishing, 2012), Chap. 1; C.P. Webel, *The Politics of Rationality: Reason through Occidental History* (New York: Routledge, 2014), Chaps. 1 and 3.

5. J.G. March and H.A. Simon, *Organizations* (New York: Wiley, 1958); K. Manktelow, *Thinking and Reasoning: An Introduction to the Psychology of Reason, Judgment and Decision Making* (Hoboken, NJ: Taylor & Francis, 2012), Chap. 8; S.B.M. Yoo and B.Y. Hayden, "Economic Choice as an Untangling of Options into Actions," *Neuron* 99, no. 3 (2018): 434–47; F. Lieder and T.L. Griffiths, "Strategy Selection as Rational Metareasoning," *Psychological Review* 124 (2017): 762–94; R.G. O'Connell et al., "Bridging Neural and Computational Viewpoints on Perceptual Decision-Making," *Trends in Neurosciences* 41 (2018): 838–52.

6. The expected utility model of rational choice, which we describe here, is the foundational theory of rational choice decision making. See, for example: A. Tversky and D. Kahneman, "The Framing of Decisions and the Psychology of Choice," *Science* 211 (January 30, 1981): 453–58. It differs from a version of game theory whereby the "outcomes" are alternatives, so the probabilities must add up to 1.0. For example, if there is a 30 percent probability that your company will choose supplier A, then there is necessarily a 70 percent chance that the company will choose supplier B (if those are the only choices). In contrast, the expected utility model calculates each alternative's composite valence from a set of criteria (outcomes) associated with all alternatives. These probabilities do not add up to 1.0 because they refer to entities that are not perfectly correlated (e.g., both suppliers might have a high probability of offering low prices). The expected utility model more closely depicts decision making situations and how people (imperfectly) make rational choice decisions among multiple alternatives.

7. These criteria are commonly used in supplier selection modeling. See, for example, H. Karimi and A. Rezaeinia, "Supplier Selection Using Revised Multi-Segment Goal Programming Model," *International Journal of Advanced Manufacturing Technology* 70, no. 5/8 (2014): 1227–34.

8. This model is adapted from several sources, including H.A. Simon, *The New Science of Management Decision* (New York: Harper & Row, 1960); H. Mintzberg, D. Raisinghani, and A. Théorét, "The Structure of 'Unstructured' Decision Processes," *Administrative Science Quarterly* 21 (1976): 246–75; W.C. Wedley and R.H.G. Field, "A Predecision Support System," *Academy of Management Review* 9 (1984): 696–703.

9. P.F. Drucker, *The Practice of Management* (New York: Harper & Brothers, 1954), 353–57; B.M. Bass, *Organizational Decision Making* (Homewood, IL: Irwin, 1983), Chap. 3; H.E. Posen et al., "Renewing Research on Problemistic Search—A Review and Research Agenda," *Academy of Management Annals* 12, no. 1 (2018): 208–51.

10. J.G. March and H.A. Simon, *Organizations* (New York: John Wiley & Sons, 1958), Chap. 7; L.R. Beach and T.R. Mitchell, "A Contingency Model for the Selection of Decision Strategies," *Academy of Management Review* 3 (1978): 439–49; I.L. Janis, *Crucial Decisions* (New York: Free Press, 1989), 35–37; W. Zhongtuo, "Meta-Decision Making: Concepts and Paradigm," *Systematic Practice and Action Research* 13, no. 1 (2000): 111–15; Y.-L. Boureau, P. Sokol-Hessner, and N.D. Daw, "Deciding How To Decide: Self-Control and Meta-Decision Making," *Trends in Cognitive Sciences* 19, no. 11 (2015): 700–10; F. Lieder and T.L. Griffiths, "Strategy Selection as Rational Metareasoning," *Psychological Review* 124, no. 6 (2017): 762–94.

11. A. Einstein and L. Infeld, *The Evolution of Physics* (Cambridge, UK: Cambridge University Press, 1938), 92. This statement is likely the true origin of what other writers claim Einstein said: when asked how he would save the world in one hour, Einstein replied that he would spend the first 55 minutes defining the problem and the last 5 minutes solving it. The importance of problem finding above other steps is also discussed in: H. Mintzberg, D. Raisinghani, and A. Théorêt, "The Structure of 'Unstructured' Decision Processes," *Administrative Science Quarterly* 21, no. 2 (1976): 246–75; H.E. Posen et al., "Renewing Research on Problemistic Search—A Review and Research Agenda," *Academy of Management Annals* 12, no. 1 (2018): 208–51.

12. M.A. Roberto, *Know What You Don't Know: How Great Leaders Prevent Problems before They Happen* (Saddle River, NJ: Wharton School Publishing, 2009); M. Meckler and K. Boal, "Decision Errors, Organizational Iatrogenesis, and Errors of the Seventh Kind," *Academy of Management Perspectives* 34, no. 2 (2020): 266–84.

13. P.C. Nutt, "Framing Strategic Decisions," *Organization Science* 9, no. 2 (1998): 195–216; S. Kaplan, "Framing Contests: Strategy Making Under Uncertainty," *Organization Science* 19, no. 5 (2008): 729–52; J.P. Cornelissen and M.D. Werner, "Putting Framing in Perspective: A Review of Framing and Frame Analysis across the Management and Organizational Literature," *Academy of Management Annals* 8, no. 1 (2014): 181–235.

14. M.S. Gary and R.E. Wood, "Mental Models, Decision Rules, and Performance Heterogeneity," *Strategic Management Journal* 32 (2011): 569–94; D. Martignoni, A. Menon, and N. Siggelkow, "Consequences of Misspecified Mental Models: Contrasting Effects and the Role of Cognitive Fit," *Strategic Management Journal* 37, no. 13 (2016): 2545–68.

15. P.C. Nutt, *Why Decisions Fail* (San Francisco: Berrett-Koehler, 2002); S. Finkelstein, *Why Smart Executives Fail* (New York: Viking, 2003); G. Bhardwaj et al., "Alleviating the Plunging-In Bias, Elevating Strategic Problem-Solving," *Academy of Management Learning & Education* 17, no. 3 (2018): 279–301.

16. N.P. Repenning, D. Kieffer, and T. Astor, "The Most Underrated Skill in Management," *MIT Sloan Management Review* 58, no. 3 (2017): 39–48; G. Bhardwaj et al., "Alleviating the Plunging-In Bias, Elevating Strategic Problem-Solving," *Academy of Management Learning & Education* 17 (2018): 279–301.

17. A.H. Maslow, *The Psychology of Science: A Reconnaissance* (Chapel Hill, NC: Maurice Bassett Publishing, 2002).

18. L.B. Myers, "The Importance of the Repressive Coping Style: Findings from 30 Years of Research," *Anxiety, Stress & Coping* 23, no. 1 (2010): 3–17; C. MacLeod, "Anxiety-Linked Attentional Bias: Backward Glances and Future Glimpses," *Cognition and Emotion* 33, no. 1 (2019): 139–45; J. Weinberger and V. Stoycheva, *The Unconscious: Theory, Research, and Clinical Implications* (Guilford Publications, 2020), Chap. 5.

19. Various sources suggest that the phrase "divine discontent" may have originated with unspecified writing by either of the poets John Milton (1608–1674) or Alexander Pope (1688–1744). Alternatively, it may have been inspired later based on John Stuart Mill's famous quotation in *Utilitarianism* (1863): "It is better to be a human being dissatisfied than a pig satisfied; better to be Socrates dissatisfied than a fool satisfied." Divine discontent became a particularly popular phrase for a couple of decades from the 1890s. It appeared in various books (e.g., Robert Bury, *The Symposium of Plato*, 1909, xlii) as well as in articles in a wide array of magazines and newspapers, including *The Athenaeum Journal* (1896), *Punch Magazine* (1894), *Edinburgh Review* (1900), and frequently in *The Independent* (New York).

20. H.A. Simon, *Administrative Behavior*, 2nd ed. (New York: Free Press, 1957); H.A. Simon, "Rational Decision Making in Business Organizations," *American Economic Review* 69, no. 4 (1979): 493–513; M. Cristofaro, "Herbert Simon's Bounded Rationality: Its Historical Evolution in Management and Cross-Fertilizing Contribution," *Journal of Management History* 23, no. 2 (2017): 170–90; R. Viale, "Why Bounded Rationality?," in *Routledge Handbook of Bounded Rationality*, ed. R. Viale (London: Routledge, 2021), 1–53.

21. Here are a few of the prominent studies among the dozens that demonstrate imperfect rationality in decision making: E. Witte, N. Joost, and A.L. Thimm, "Field Research On Complex Decision-Making Processes–The Phase Theorem," *International Studies of Management & Organization* 2 (1972): 156–82; H. Mintzberg, D. Raisinghani, and A. Théorêt, "The Structure of 'Unstructured' Decision Processes," *Administrative Science Quarterly* 21 (1976): 246–75; T. Gilovich, D. Griffin, and D. Kahneman, *Heuristics and Biases: The Psychology of Intuitive Judgment* (Cambridge: Cambridge University Press, 2002); S. Finkelstein, *Why Smart Executives Fail: And What You Can Learn from Their Mistakes* (New York: Penguin, 2004).

22. M.D. Cohen, J.G. March, and J.P. Olsen, "A Garbage Can Model of Organizational Choice," *Administrative Science Quarterly* 17, no. 1 (1972): 1–25; R.A. Ferrer, E. Orehek, and L.S. Padgett, "Goal Conflict when Making Decisions for Others," *Journal of Experimental Social Psychology* 78 (2018): 93–103.

23. H.A. Simon, *Administrative Behavior*, 2nd ed. (New York: Free Press, 1957), xxv, 80–84.

24. L.J. Peter, *Peter's Almanac* (New York: Morrow, 1982).

25. Current researchers refer to implicit favorite as "predecision information distortion" and the "coherence effect," but these theories are essentially implicit favorite bias. P.O. Soelberg, "Unprogrammed Decision Making," *Industrial Management Review* 8 (1967): 19–29; K.H. Ehrhart and J.C. Ziegert, "Why Are Individuals Attracted to Organizations?" *Journal of Management* 31, no. 6 (2005): 901–19; J.E. Russo, "The Predecisional Distortion of Information," in *Neuroeconomics, Judgment, and Decision Making*, ed. E.A. Wilhelms and V.F. Reyna, *Frontiers of Cognitive Psychology* (New York: Psychology Press, 2015), 91–110.

26. S. Sacchi and M. Burigo, "Strategies in the Information Search Process: Interaction among Task Structure, Knowledge, and Source," *Journal of General Psychology* 135, no. 3 (2008): 252–70.

27. Milton Rokeach famously stated, "Life is ipsative, because decisions in everyday life are inherently and phenomenologically ipsative decisions." *Ipsative* is a process of comparing (usually two) things side-by-side. M. Rokeach, "Inducing Changes and Stability in Belief Systems and Personality Structures," *Journal of Social Issues* 41, no. 1 (1985): 153–71.

28. R.S. Nickerson, "Confirmation Bias: A Ubiquitous Phenomenon in Many Guises," *Review of General Psychology* 2, no. 2 (1998): 175–220; O. Svenson, I. Salo, and T. Lindholm, "Post-Decision Consolidation and Distortion of Facts," *Judgment and Decision Making* 4, no. 5 (2009): 397–407; A.M. Scherer, P.D. Windschitl, and A.R. Smith, "Hope to Be Right: Biased Information Seeking Following Arbitrary and Informed Predictions," *Journal of Experimental Social Psychology* 49, no. 1 (2013): 106–12.

29. A.L. Brownstein, "Biased Predecision Processing," *Psychological Bulletin* 129, no. 4 (2003): 545–68; M. Nurek, O. Kostopoulou, and Y. Hagmayer, "Predecisional Information Distortion in Physicians' Diagnostic Judgments: Strengthening a Leading Hypothesis or Weakening Its Competitor?" *Judgment and Decision Making* 9, no. 6 (2014): 572–85; D. Simon, D. Stenstrom, and S. Read, "The Coherence Effect: Blending Cold and Hot Cognitions," *Journal of Personality & Social Psychology* 109, no. 3 (2015): 369–94; M.L. DeKay, "Predecisional Information Distortion and the Self-Fulfilling Prophecy of Early Preferences in Choice," *Current Directions in Psychological Science* 24, no. 5 (2015): 405–11.

30. T. Gilovich, D. Griffin, and D. Kahneman, *Heuristics and Biases: The Psychology of Intuitive Judgment* (Cambridge: Cambridge University Press, 2002); D. Kahneman, "Maps of Bounded Rationality: Psychology for Behavioral Economics," *American Economic Review* 93 (2003): 1449–75; J.S. Blumenthal-Barby and H. Krieger, "Cognitive Biases and Heuristics in Medical Decision Making: A Critical Review Using a Systematic Search Strategy," *Medical Decision Making* 35 (2015): 539–57; M. Richie and S.A. Josephson, "Quantifying Heuristic Bias: Anchoring, Availability, and Representativeness," *Teaching and Learning in Medicine* 30 (2018): 67–75.

31. A. Tversky and D. Kahneman, "Judgment under Uncertainty: Heuristics and Biases," *Science* 185, no. 4157 (1974): 1124–31; I. Ritov, "Anchoring in Simulated Competitive Market Negotiation," *Organizational Behavior and Human Decision Processes* 67, no. 1 (1996): 16; J.D. Jasper and S.D. Christman, "A Neuropsychological Dimension for Anchoring Effects," *Journal of Behavioral Decision Making* 18 (2005): 343–69; M.H. Jung, H. Perfecto, and L.D. Nelson, "Anchoring in Payment: Evaluating a Judgmental Heuristic in Field Experimental Settings," *Journal of Marketing Research* 53, no. 3 (2016): 354–68.

32. A. Tversky and D. Kahneman, "Availability: A Heuristic for Judging Frequency and Probability," *Cognitive Psychology* 5 (1973): 207–32; A. Kudryavtsev, "The Availability Heuristic and Reversals Following Large Stock Price Changes," *Journal of Behavioral Finance* 19, no. 2 (2018): 159–76.

33. D. Kahneman and A. Tversky, "Subjective Probability: A Judgment of Representativeness," *Cognitive Psychology* 3, no. 3 (1972): 430–54; D. Kahneman, *Thinking Fast and Slow* (New York: Farrar, Strauss, Giroux, 2011), Chap. 14; S.S. Kulkarni et al., "Defining the Representativeness Heuristic in Trauma Triage: A Retrospective Observational Cohort Study," *PLoS ONE* 14, no. 2 (February 8, 2019): e0212201.

34. H.A. Simon, "Rational Choice and the Structure of Environments," *Psychological Review* 63 (1956): 129–38; B. Schwartz, "On the Meaning and Measurement of Maximization," *Judgment and Decision Making* 11, no. 2 (2016): 126–46.

35. K. Jain, J.N. Bearden, and A. Filipowicz, "Do Maximizers Predict Better Than Satisficers?," *Journal of Behavioral Decision Making* 26, no. 1 (2013): 41–50; W. Mao, "When One Desires Too Much of a Good Thing: The Compromise Effect under Maximizing Tendencies," *Journal of Consumer Psychology* 26, no. 1 (2016): 66–80.

36. S. Botti and S.S. Iyengar, "The Dark Side of Choice: When Choice Impairs Social Welfare," *Journal of Public Policy and Marketing* 25, no. 1 (2006): 24–38; K.D. Vohs et al., "Making Choices Impairs Subsequent Self-Control: A Limited-Resource Account of Decision Making, Self-Regulation, and Active Initiative," *Journal of Personality and Social Psychology* 94, no. 5 (2008): 883–98.

37. S. Iyengar, *The Art of Choosing* (New York: Hachette, 2010), 177–95; A. Chernev, U. Böckenholt, and J. Goodman, "Choice Overload: A Conceptual Review and Meta-Analysis," *Journal of Consumer Psychology* 25, no. 2 (2015): 333–58.

38. R. Greifeneder, B. Scheibehenne, and N. Kleber, "Less May Be More When Choosing Is Difficult: Choice Complexity and Too Much Choice," *Acta Psychologica* 133, no. 1 (2010): 45–50; A. Chernev, U. Böckenholt, and J. Goodman, "Choice Overload: A Conceptual Review and Meta-Analysis," *Journal of Consumer Psychology* 25, no. 2 (2015): 333–58; N.T. Thai and U. Yuksel, "Too Many Destinations to Visit: Tourists' Dilemma?," *Annals of Tourism Research* 62 (January 2017): 38–53; A. Mayol and C. Staropoli, "Giving Consumers Too Many Choices: A False Good Idea? A Lab Experiment on Water and Electricity Tariffs," *European Journal of Law and Economics* 51, no. 2 (2021): 383–410; R. Misuraca et al., "How Much Choice Is 'Good Enough'?: Moderators of Information and Choice Overload," in *Routledge Handbook of Bounded Rationality*, ed. R. Viale (London: Routledge, 2021), 637–49.

39. P.C. Nutt, "Search During Decision Making," *European Journal of Operational Research* 160 (2005): 851–76; M.S. Wood, A. McKelvie, and J.M. Haynie, "Making It Personal: Opportunity Individuation and the Shaping of Opportunity Beliefs," *Journal of Business Venturing* 29 (2014): 252–72; Y. Chandra, "A Time-Based Process Model of International Entrepreneurial Opportunity Evaluation," *Journal of International Business Studies* 48 (2017): 423–51.

40. P. Winkielman et al., "Affective Influence on Judgments and Decisions: Moving Towards Core Mechanisms," *Review of General Psychology* 11, no. 2 (2007): 179–92; J.S. Lerner et al., "Emotion and Decision Making," *Annual Review of Psychology* 66, no. 1 (2015): 799–823; G. Loewenstein, T. O'Donoghue, and S. Bhatia, "Modeling the Interplay between Affect and Deliberation," *Decision* 2, no. 2 (2015): 55–81; T. Poppa and A. Bechara, "The Somatic Marker Hypothesis: Revisiting the Role of the 'Body-Loop' in Decision-Making," *Current Opinion in Behavioral Sciences*, 19 (2018): 61–66; C.A. Trujillo, "The Complementary Role of Affect-Based and Cognitive Heuristics to Make Decisions under Conditions of Ambivalence and Complexity," *PLoS ONE* 13, no. 11 (November 9, 2018): e0206724.

41. A. Bechara and A.R. Damasio, "The Somatic Marker Hypothesis: A Neural Theory of Economic Decision," *Games and Economic Behavior* 52, no. 2 (2005): 336–72; T.S. Saunders and M.J. Buehner, "The Gut Chooses Faster Than the Mind: A Latency Advantage of Affective over Cognitive Decisions," *Quarterly Journal of Experimental Psychology* 66, no. 2 (2013): 381–88; A. Moors, "Automaticity: Componential, Causal, and Mechanistic Explanations," *Annual Review of Psychology* 67, no. 1 (2016): 263–87; T. Poppa and A. Bechara, "The Somatic Marker Hypothesis: Revisiting the Role of the 'Body-Loop' in Decision-Making," *Current Opinion in Behavioral Sciences* 19 (2018): 61–66.

42. J.P. Forgas and J.M. George, "Affective Influences on Judgments and Behavior in Organizations: An Information Processing Perspective," *Organizational Behavior and Human Decision Processes* 86 (2001): 3–34; J.P. Forgas and A.S. Koch, "Mood Effects on Cognition," in *Handbook of Cognition and Emotion*, ed. M.D. Robinson, E.R. Watkins, and E. Harmon-Jones (New York: Guilford, 2013), 231–51; J.M. George and E. Dane, "Affect, Emotion, and Decision Making," *Organizational Behavior and Human Decision Processes* 136 (2016): 47–55; A. Prinz, V. Bergmann, and J. Wittwer, "Happy but Overconfident: Positive Affect Leads to Inaccurate Metacomprehension," *Cognition and Emotion* 33, no. 3 (2019): 606–15; K.M. Hengen and G.W. Alpers, "Stress Makes the Difference: Social Stress and Social Anxiety in Decision-Making Under Uncertainty," *Frontiers in Psychology* 12 (February 22, 2021): 578293.

43. D. Miller, *The Icarus Paradox* (New York: HarperBusiness, 1990); D. Miller, "What Happens after Success: The Perils of Excellence," *Journal of Management Studies* 31, no. 3 (1994): 325–68; A.C. Amason and A.C. Mooney, "The Icarus Paradox Revisited: How Strong Performance Sows the Seeds of Dysfunction in Future Strategic Decision-Making," *Strategic Organization* 6, no. 4 (2008): 407–34.

44. M.T. Pham, "The Logic of Feeling," *Journal of Consumer Psychology* 14 (2004): 360–69; N. Schwarz, "Feelings-as-Information Theory," in *Handbook of Theories of Social Psychology*, ed. P. Van Lange, A. Kruglanski, and E.T. Higgins (London: Sage, 2012), 289–308; A.I. Tiba, "Feelings-as-Embodied Information: Studying the Role of Feelings as Images in Emotional Disorders," *Frontiers in Psychology* 9 (2018): 00186.

45. O. Behling and N.L. Eckel, "Making Sense out of Intuition," *Academy of Management Executive* 5 (1991): 46–54; R.M. Hogarth, "Intuition: A Challenge for Psychological Research on Decision Making," *Psychological Inquiry* 21, no. 4 (2010): 338–53; S. Epstein, "Demystifying Intuition: What It Is, What It Does, and How It Does It," *Psychological Inquiry* 21, no. 4 (2010): 295–312; G.P. Hodgkinson and E. Sadler-Smith, "The Dynamics of Intuition and Analysis in Managerial and Organizational Decision Making," *Academy of Management Perspectives* 32, no. 4 (2018): 473–92.

46. L. Sjöberg, "Intuitive vs. Analytical Decision Making: Which Is Preferred?" *Scandinavian Journal of Management* 19 (2003): 17–29; K. Hamilton, S.-I. Shih, and S. Mohammed, "The Development and Validation of the Rational and Intuitive Decision Styles Scale," *Journal of Personality Assessment* 98 (2016): 523–35; Y. Wang et al., "Meta-Analytic Investigations of the Relation Between Intuition and Analysis," *Journal of Behavioral Decision Making* 30 (2017): 15–25.

47. W.G. Chase and H.A. Simon, "Perception in Chess," *Cognitive Psychology* 4, no. 1 (1973): 55–81; G. Klein, *Intuition at Work* (New York: Currency/Doubleday, 2003); E. Dane, K.W. Rockmann, and M.G. Pratt, "When Should I Trust My Gut? Linking Domain Expertise to Intuitive Decision-Making Effectiveness," *Organizational Behavior and Human Decision Processes* 119, no. 2 (2012): 187–94; A. Linhares and D.M. Chada, "What Is the Nature of the Mind's Pattern-Recognition Process?" *New Ideas in Psychology* 31, no. 2 (2013): 108–21.

48. G. Klein, *Intuition at Work* (New York: Currency/Doubleday, 2003), 12–13, 16–17; G. Kefalidou, D. Golightly, and S. Sharples, "Identifying Rail Asset Maintenance Processes: A Human-Centric and Sensemaking Approach," *Cognition, Technology & Work* 20, no. 1 (2018): 73–92.

49. P.C. Nutt, "Search During Decision Making," *European Journal of Operational Research* 160 (2005): 851–76; P.C. Nutt, "Investigating the Success of Decision Making Processes," *Journal of Management Studies* 45, no. 2 (2008): 425–55; S.A. Kreindler, "Planning without Action and Action without Planning? Examining a Regional Health System's Efforts to Improve Patient Flow, 1998–2013," *The International Journal of Health Planning and Management* 33, no. 1 (2018): e333–43.

50. D. Kiron, K. Prentice, and R. B. Ferguson, *The Analytics Mandate* (Cambridge, MA: MIT Sloan Management Review and SAS Institute, May 12, 2014); "PwC's Data and Analytics Survey 2016 Big Decisions" (London: PricewaterhouseCoopers, 2016); "PitchBook Survey Finds Only 38% of Venture Capital Investors Currently Use Data to Source and Evaluate All Investments Opportunities," News release (Seattle: Pitchbook, February 14, 2019); "Study Shows Many Senior Managers Distrust Big Data," news release (New Zealand: Massey University, April 12, 2019).

51. T.J. Chermack, *Scenario Planning in Organizations* (San Francisco: Berrett-Koehler, 2011); G. Bowman, "The Practice of Scenario Planning: An Analysis of Inter- and Intra-Organizational Strategizing," *British Journal of Management* 27, no. 1 (2016): 77–96; J.J. Oliver and E. Parrett, "Managing Uncertainty: Harnessing the Power of Scenario Planning," *Strategic Direction* 33, no. 1 (2016): 5–6; R. Vecchiato, "Scenario Planning, Cognition, and Strategic Investment Decisions in a Turbulent Environment," *Long Range Planning* 52, no. 5 (2019): 101865.

52. J. Pfeffer and R.I. Sutton, "Knowing 'What' to Do Is Not Enough: Turning Knowledge into Action," *California Management Review* 42, no. 1 (1999): 83–108; R. Charan, C. Burke, and L. Bossidy, *Execution: The Discipline of Getting Things Done* (New York: Crown Business, 2002); S.A. Kreindler, "What If Implementation Is Not the Problem? Exploring the Missing Links between Knowledge and Action," *The International Journal of Health Planning and Management* 31, no. 2 (2016): 208–26.

53. C.A. O'Reilly and D.F. Caldwell, "The Commitment and Job Tenure of New Employees: Some Evidence of Postdecisional Justification," *Administrative Science Quarterly* 26, no. 4 (1981): 597–616. Postdecisional justification is the flip side of postdecisional dissonance. For example, see S.W.S. Lee and N. Schwarz, "Washing Away Postdecisional Dissonance," *Science* 328, no. 5979 (2010): 709.

54. B.M. Staw and J. Ross, "Behavior in Escalation Situations: Antecedents, Prototypes, and Solutions," *Research in Organizational Behavior* 9 (1987): 39–78; D.J. Sleesman et al., "Cleaning up the Big Muddy: A Meta-Analytic Review of the Determinants of Escalation of Commitment," *Academy of Management Journal* 55 (2012): 541–62; D.J. Sleesman et al., "Putting Escalation of Commitment in Context: A Multilevel Review and Analysis," *Academy of Management Annals* 12 (2018): 178–207.

55. B.M. Staw, "Knee-Deep in the Big Muddy: A Study of Escalating Commitment to a Chosen Course of Action," *Organizational Behavior and Human Performance* 16 (1976): 27–44; D. Steinkühler, M.D. Mahlendorf, and M. Brettel, "How Self-Justification Indirectly Drives Escalation of Commitment–A Motivational Perspective," *Schmalenbach Business Review: ZFBF* 66 (2014): 191–222; E.A. Lofquist and R. Lines, "Keeping Promises: A Process Study of Escalating Commitment Leading to Organizational Change Collapse," *The Journal of Applied Behavioral Science* 53 (2017): 417–45.

56. S. Loughnan et al., "Universal Biases in Self-Perception: Better and More Human Than Average," *British Journal of Social Psychology* 49 (2010): 627–36; D.L. Ferris and C. Sedikides, "Self-Enhancement in Organizations," in *The Self at Work: Fundamental Theory and Research*, ed. D.L. Ferris, R.E. Johnson, and C. Sedikides (New York: Routledge, 2018), 91–118.

57. M. Keil, G. Depledge, and A. Rai, "Escalation: The Role of Problem Recognition and Cognitive Bias," *Decision Sciences* 38, no. 3 (2007): 391–421; R. Ronay et al., "Pride before the Fall: (Over)Confidence Predicts Escalation of Public Commitment," *Journal of Experimental Social Psychology* 69 (2017): 13–22.

58. G. Whyte, "Escalating Commitment in Individual and Group Decision Making: A Prospect Theory Approach," *Organizational Behavior and Human Decision Processes* 54 (1993): 430–55; D. Kahneman and J. Renshon, "Hawkish Biases," in *American Foreign Policy and the Politics of Fear: Threat Inflation since 9/11*, ed. T. Thrall and J. Cramer (New York: Routledge, 2009), 79–96.

59. D.J. Sleesman et al., "Cleaning up the Big Muddy: A Meta-Analytic Review of the Determinants of Escalation of Commitment," *Academy of Management Journal* 55 (2012): 541–62; B.M. Sweis et al., "Sensitivity to 'Sunk Costs' in Mice, Rats, and Humans," *Science* 361, no. 6398 (July 13, 2018): 178–81.

60. J.D. Bragger et al., "When Success Breeds Failure: History, Hysteresis, and Delayed Exit Decisions," *Journal of Applied Psychology* 88, no. 1 (2003): 6–14; H. Drummond, "Escalation of Commitment: When to Stay the Course?," *The Academy of Management Perspectives* 28, no. 4 (2014): 430–46.

61. I. Simonson and B.M. Staw, "De-Escalation Strategies: A Comparison of Techniques for Reducing Commitment to Losing Courses of Action," *Journal of Applied Psychology* 77 (1992): 419–26; M. Keil and D. Robey, "Turning around Troubled Software Projects: An Exploratory Study of the Deescalation of Commitment to Failing Courses of Action," *Journal of Management Information Systems* 15 (1999): 63–87; D.C. Molden and C.M. Hui, "Promoting De-Escalation of Commitment: A Regulatory-Focus Perspective on Sunk Costs," *Psychological Science* 22 (2011): 8–12; A.C. Hafenbrack, Z. Kinias, and S.G. Barsade, "Debiasing the Mind through Meditation: Mindfulness and the Sunk-Cost Bias," *Psychological Science* 25 (2014): 369–76; K.R. Sarangee et al., "De-Escalation Mechanisms in High-Technology Product Innovation," *Journal of Product Innovation Management* 31 (2014): 1023–38; D.V. Chulkov and J.M. Barron, "Turnover in Top Management and De-Escalation of Commitment," *Applied Economics* 51 (2019): 2534–51.

62. M.I. Stein, "Creativity and Culture," *Journal of Psychology* 36 (1953): 311–22; M.A. Runco and G.J. Jaeger, "The Standard Definition of Creativity," *Creativity Research Journal* 24, no. 1 (2012): 92–96.

63. G. Wallas, *The Art of Thought* (London: Jonathan Cape, 1926). For recent applications of Wallas's classic model, see T. Kristensen, "The Physical Context of Creativity," *Creativity and Innovation Management* 13, no. 2 (2004): 89–96; U.E. Haner, "Spaces for Creativity and Innovation in Two Established Organizations," *Creativity and Innovation Management* 14, no. 3 (2005): 288–98.

64. R.S. Nickerson, "Enhancing Creativity," in *Handbook of Creativity*, ed. R.J. Sternberg (New York: Cambridge University Press, 1999), 392–430. There are varied subprocesses within incubation and illumination, such as serendipitous insights, disciplined imagination, and hunches. See: M.A. Mithani and I. Kocoglu, "Idea Generation in Abductive Thinking: Not One but Three Approaches," *Academy of Management Review* (October 20, 2021, in press.

65. R.J. Sternberg and J.E. Davidson, *The Nature of Insight* (Cambridge, MA: MIT Press, 1995); W. Shen et al., "Feeling the Insight: Uncovering Somatic Markers of the 'Aha' Experience," *Applied Psychophysiology and Biofeedback* September 19, 2017, https://doi.org/10.1007/s10484-017-9381-1.

66. R.J. Sternberg and L.A. O'Hara, "Creativity and Intelligence," in *Handbook of Creativity*, ed. R.J. Sternberg (New York: Cambridge University Press, 1999), 251–72; S. Taggar, "Individual Creativity and Group Ability to Utilize Individual Creative Resources: A Multilevel Model," *Academy of Management Journal* 45 (2002): 315–30; R.J. Sternberg, "Successful Intelligence: A Model for Testing Intelligence beyond IQ Tests," *European Journal of Education and Psychology* 8, no. 2 (2015): 76–84.

67. G.J. Feist, "The Influence of Personality on Artistic and Scientific Creativity," in *Handbook of Creativity*, ed. R.J. Sternberg (New York: Cambridge University Press, 1999), 273–96; T. Åsterbro, S.A. Jeffrey, and G.K. Adomdza, "Inventor Perseverance after Being Told to Quit: The Role of Cognitive Biases," *Journal of Behavioral Decision Making* 20 (2007): 253–72; J.S. Mueller, S. Melwani, and J.A. Goncalo, "The Bias against Creativity: Why People Desire but Reject Creative Ideas," *Psychological Science* 23, no. 1 (2012): 13–17.

68. R.W. Weisberg, "Creativity and Knowledge: A Challenge to Theories," in *Handbook of Creativity*, ed. R.J. Sternberg (New York: Cambridge University Press, 1999), 226–50.

69. R.I. Sutton, *Weird Ideas That Work* (New York: Free Press, 2002), 53–54, 121; E. Dane, "Reconsidering the Trade-Off between Expertise and Flexibility: A Cognitive Entrenchment Perspective," *Academy of Management Review* 35, no. 4 (2010): 579–603.

70. G.J. Feist, "The Influence of Personality on Artistic and Scientific Creativity," in *Handbook of Creativity*, ed. R.J. Sternberg (New York: Cambridge University Press, 1999), 273–96; C.E. Shalley, J. Zhou, and G.R. Oldham, "The Effects of Personal and Contextual Characteristics on Creativity: Where Should We Go from Here?," *Journal of Management* 30, no. 6 (2004): 933–58; S.J. Dollinger, K.K. Urban, and T.A. James, "Creativity and Openness to Experience: Validation of Two Creative Product Measures," *Creativity Research Journal* 16, no. 1 (2004): 35–47; T.S. Schweizer, "The Psychology of Novelty-Seeking, Creativity and Innovation: Neurocognitive Aspects within a Work-Psychological Perspective," *Creativity and Innovation Management* 15, no. 2 (2006): 164–72; S. Acar and M.A. Runco, "Creative Abilities: Divergent Thinking," in *Handbook of Organizational Creativity*, ed. M. Mumford (Waltham, MA: Academic Press, 2012), 115–39.

71. C.E. Shalley, J. Zhou, and G.R. Oldham, "The Effects of Personal and Contextual Characteristics on Creativity: Where Should We Go from Here?" *Journal of Management* 30, no. 6 (2004): 933–58; S.T. Hunter, K.E. Bedell, and M.D. Mumford, "Climate for Creativity: A Quantitative Review," *Creativity Research Journal* 19, no. 1 (2007): 69–90; N. Anderson, K. Potočnik, and J. Zhou, "Innovation and Creativity in Organizations: A State-of-the-Science Review, Prospective Commentary, and Guiding Framework," *Journal of Management* 40, no. 5 (2014): 1297–1333.

72. Learning orientation has multiple meanings. This definition and discussion refers to the marketing-based concept associated with organizational learning. It differs from "learning goal orientation." See, for example: W.E. Baker and J.M. Sinkula, "The Synergistic Effect of Market Orientation and Learning Orientation on Organizational Performance," *Journal of the Academy of Marketing Science* 27 (1999): 411–27; O. Pesämaa et al., "How a Learning Orientation Affects Drivers of Innovativeness and Performance in Service Delivery," *Journal of Engineering and Technology Management* 30 (2013): 169–87; J.C. Real, J.L. Roldán, and A. Leal, "From Entrepreneurial Orientation and Learning Orientation to Business Performance: Analysing the Mediating Role of Organizational Learning and the Moderating Effects of Organizational Size," *British Journal of Management* 25 (2014): 186–208.

73. A. Cummings and G.R. Oldham, "Enhancing Creativity: Managing Work Contexts for the High Potential Employee," *California Management Review* 40 (Fall 1997): 22–38; F. Coelho and M. Augusto, "Job Characteristics and the Creativity of Frontline Service Employees," *Journal of Service Research* 13 (2010): 426–38; G. Hirst et al., "How Does Bureaucracy Impact Individual Creativity? A Cross-Level Investigation of Team Contextual Influences on Goal Orientation–Creativity Relationships," *Academy of Management Journal* 54 (2011): 624–41; W. Zhang et al., "Exploring the Effects of Job Autonomy on Engagement and Creativity: The Moderating Role of Performance Pressure and Learning Goal Orientation," *Journal of Business and Psychology* 32 (2017): 235–51.

74. "Curiosity@Work Report - 2021" (Cary, NC: SAS Institute, November 2021); "PwC's Global Workforce Hopes and Fears Survey 2022" (London: PricewaterhouseCoopers, May 24, 2022); "Gartner Survey Shows 49% of HR Leaders Named Innovating For Success As One Of Their Top Three Priorities," Press Release (London: Gartner, September 16, 2022); "Employers Face 'Creativity' Challenge, Not Worker Apathy," Press Release (London: Ricoh Europe, October 27, 2022); "2022 Federal Employee Viewpoint Survey" (Washington, DC: United States Federal Government, Office of Personnel Management, November 2022).

75. T.M. Amabile and R. Conti, "Changes in the Work Environment for Creativity during Downsizing," *Academy of Management Journal* 42 (1999): 630–40; L. Jiang, "Job Insecurity and Creativity: The Buffering Effect of Self-Affirmation and Work-Affirmation," *Journal of Applied Social Psychology* 48, no. 7 (2018): 388–97.

76. K. Thoring, P. Desmet, and P. Badke-Schaub, "Creative Environments for Design Education and Practice: A Typology of Creative Spaces," *Design Studies* 56 (2018): 54–83; A.J. Blomberg and T.J. Kallio, "A Review of the Physical Context of Creativity: A Three-Dimensional Framework for Investigating the Physical Context of Creativity," *International Journal of Management Reviews* 24, no. 3 (2022): 433–51.

77. C.E. Shalley, J. Zhou, and G.R. Oldham, "The Effects of Personal and Contextual Characteristics on Creativity: Where Should We Go from Here?," *Journal of Management* 30 (2004): 933–58; S. Powell, "The Management and Consumption of Organisational Creativity," *Journal of Consumer Marketing* 25 (2008): 158–66; D.J. Hughes et al., "Leadership, Creativity, and Innovation: A Critical Review and Practical Recommendations," *Leadership Quarterly* 29 (2018): 549–69.

78. A. Hiam, "Obstacles to Creativity—and How You Can Remove Them," *Futurist* 32 (1998): 30–34.

79. M.A. West, *Developing Creativity in Organizations* (Leicester, UK: BPS Books, 1997), 33–35.

80. S. Brown, *Play: How It Shapes the Brain, Opens the Imagination, and Invigorates the Soul* (New York: Avery, 2009); C. Mainemelis and D.D. Dionysiou, "Play, Flow, and Timelessness," in *The Oxford Handbook of Creativity, Innovation, and Entrepreneurship*, ed. C. Shalley, M. Hitt, and J. Zhou (New York: Oxford University Press, 2015), 121–40; C.A. Petelczyc et al., "Play at Work: An Integrative Review and Agenda for Future Research," *Journal of Management* 44 (2018): 161–90.

81. Y. Maguid, "How Ubisoft Winnipeg's Managing Director Is Building a New Studio," *Ubisoft Latest News* (blog), January 11, 2019; D. Long, "Ubisoft Winnipeg: Building a Culture of Innovation and Technology from the Ground Up," *LinkedIn Pulse* (blog), January 17, 2019; "Ep 27: Justsaying with Darryl Long – Diversity In The Gaming Industry," YouTube, June 13, 2022; B. Spurlin, "How the Skull and Bones Studio Is Building a Culture of Creativity," *Ubisoft Latest News* (blog), July 9, 2022.

82. T. Ritchey, *Wicked Problems—Social Messes: Decision Support Modelling with Morphological Analysis, Risk, Governance and Society* (Berlin: Springer-Verlag, 2011); S. Seidenstricker and C. Linder, "A Morphological Analysis-Based Creativity Approach to Identify and Develop Ideas for BMI: A Case Study of a High-Tech Manufacturing Company," *International Journal of Entrepreneurship and Innovation Management* 18, no. 5/6 (2014): 409–24.

83. A. Hargadon and R.I. Sutton, "Building an Innovation Factory," *Harvard Business Review* 78 (2000): 157–66; T. Kelley, *The Art of Innovation* (New York: Currency Doubleday, 2001), 158–62; P.F. Skilton and K.J. Dooley, "The Effects of Repeat Collaboration on Creative Abrasion," *Academy of Management Review* 35, no. 1 (2010): 118–34.

84. E. Köppen and C. Meinel, "Empathy via Design Thinking: Creation of Sense and Knowledge," in *Design Thinking Research: Building Innovators*, ed. H. Plattner, C. Meinel, and L. Leifer (Cham, Switzerland: Springer International, 2015), 15–28; K.D. Elsbach and I. Stigliani, "Design Thinking and Organizational Culture: A Review and Framework for Future Research," *Journal of Management* 44, no. 6 (2018): 2274–2306, https://doi.org/10.1177/0149206317744252.

85. C.D. Zatzick and R.D. Iverson, "Putting Employee Involvement in Context: A Cross-Level Model Examining Job Satisfaction and Absenteeism in High-Involvement Work Systems," *The International Journal of Human Resource Management* 22 (2011): 3462–76; R. Markey and K. Townsend, "Contemporary Trends in Employee Involvement and Participation," *Journal of Industrial Relations* 55 (2013): 475–87; M. Marchington, "Analysing the Forces Shaping Employee Involvement and Participation (EIP) at Organisation Level in Liberal Market Economies (LMEs)," *Human Resource Management Journal* 25 (2015): 1–18.

86. V.H. Vroom and A.G. Jago, *The New Leadership: Managing Participation in Organizations* (Englewood Cliffs, NJ: Prentice Hill, 1988); A. Wilkinson et al., "Conceptualizing Employee Participation in Organizations," in *The Oxford Handbook of Participation in Organizations*, ed. A. Wilkinson et al., vol. 1 (Oxford, UK: Oxford University Press, 2010), Chap. 1; J.S. Abildgaard et al., "Forms of Participation: The Development and Application of a Conceptual Model of Participation in Work Environment Interventions," *Economic and Industrial Democracy* 41, no. 3 (2020): 746-69.

87. This quotation has a long and convoluted history. It has been attributed (incorrectly) to Benjamin Franklin and to Native Americans. The quotation stated here was popular in education during the 1960s and is cited in the 1975 source below. However, this quotation is almost certainly an adaptation of writing by Chinese Confucian philosopher Xun Kuang (circa 250 BC). A simplified version of his original statement is: "I hear and I forget; I see and I remember; I do and I understand." R.E. Keeton, "Tell Me, Show Me, Involve Me," *Learning and the Law* 2 (1975): 16-21, 64-65.

88. The benefits of employee involvement have been discussed for more than a half century, such as: C. Argyris, *Personality and Organization* (New York: Harper & Row, 1957); D. McGregor, *The Human Side of Enterprise* (New York: McGraw Hill, 1960); R. Likert, *New Patterns of Management* (New York: McGraw Hill, 1961). Recent studies have observed that the benefits of involvement depend on the form of involvement and employee characteristics. For example, see: K. Hutter, B.A. Nketia, and J. Füller, "Falling Short with Participation—Different Effects of Ideation, Commenting, and Evaluating Behavior on Open Strategizing," *Long Range Planning* 50, no. 3 (2017): 355-70; Y. Zhou, X. Fan, and J. Son, "How and When Matter: Exploring the Interaction Effects of High-Performance Work Systems, Employee Participation, and Human Capital on Organizational Innovation," *Human Resource Management* 58, no. 3 (2019): 253-68.

89. M.R. Bashshur, "When Voice Matters: A Multilevel Review of the Impact of Voice in Organizations," *Journal of Management* 41 (2015): 1530-54; F.A. Guzman and A. Espejo, "Introducing Changes at Work: How Voice Behavior Relates to Management Innovation," *Journal of Organizational Behavior* 40, no. 1 (2019): 73-90; Y. Zhou, X. Fan, and J. Son, "How and When Matter: Exploring the Interaction Effects of High-performance Work Systems, Employee Participation, and Human Capital on Organizational Innovation," *Human Resource Management* 58, no. 3 (2019): 253-68; M. del C. Triana et al., "The Relationship Between Team Deep-Level Diversity and Team Performance: A Meta-Analysis of the Main Effect, Moderators, and Mediating Mechanisms," *Journal of Management Studies* 58, no. 8 (2021): 2137-79.

90. D. Berend and J. Paroush, "When Is Condorcet's Jury Theorem Valid?" *Social Choice and Welfare* 15, no. 4 (1998): 481-88.

91. K.T. Dirks, L.L. Cummings, and J.L. Pierce, "Psychological Ownership in Organizations: Conditions under Which Individuals Promote and Resist Change," *Research in Organizational Change and Development*, no. 9 (1996): 1-23; R. Markey, J. McIvor, and C.F. Wright, "Employee Participation and Carbon Emissions Reduction in Australian Workplaces," *The International Journal of Human Resource Management* 27, no. 2 (2016): 173-91; F.A. Guzman and A. Espejo, "Introducing Changes at Work: How Voice Behavior Relates to Management Innovation," *Journal of Organizational Behavior* 40, no. 1 (2019): 73-90.

92. Y. Zhu et al., "Employee Participation and the Influence on Job Satisfaction of the 'New Generation' of Chinese Employees," *The International Journal of Human Resource Management* 26, no. 19 (2015): 2395-2411; M. Valverde-Moreno, M. Torres-Jimenez, and A.M. Lucia-Casademunt, "Participative Decision-Making amongst Employees in a Cross-Cultural Employment Setting: Evidence from 31 European Countries," *European Journal of Training and Development* 45, no. 1 (2020): 14-35.

93. V.H. Vroom and A.G. Jago, *The New Leadership: Managing Participation in Organizations* (Englewood Cliffs, NJ: Prentice Hall, 1988); N. Lührs et al., "How Participatory Should Environmental Governance Be? Testing the Applicability of the Vroom-Yetton-Jago Model in Public Environmental Decision-Making," *Environmental Management* 61, no. 2 (2018): 249-62.

PART 3

7 Team Dynamics

Zamrznuti tonovi/Shutterstock

Learning Objectives

After reading this chapter, you should be able to:

LO7-1 Define teams and informal groups, and explain why employees join informal groups.

LO7-2 Discuss the benefits and limitations of teams.

LO7-3 Outline the team effectiveness model and discuss how task characteristics, team size, and team composition influence team effectiveness.

LO7-4 Discuss how the six team processes—team development, norms, roles, cohesion, trust, and mental models—influence team effectiveness.

LO7-5 Identify the features of self-directed teams (SDTs), and discuss ways to support the success of SDTs.

LO7-6 Contrast remote teams with traditional teams in organizations, and discuss ways to support the success of remote teams.

LO7-7 Identify four constraints on team decision making and discuss ways to improve decision making and creativity in teams.

team(s) Groups of two or more people who interact with and influence one another, are mutually accountable for achieving common goals associated with organizational objectives, and perceive themselves as a social entity within an organization

Advokatfirmaet Thommessen AS is one of the oldest (since 1856), largest, and top-rated commercial law firms in Norway. It is also one of the industry's leading advocates for teamwork. "Teamwork and new forms of collaboration have helped us establish an innovation culture," says the company, which has 300 employees, including 240 lawyers, at its offices in Oslo, Bergen, and London.

"An advantage of working at Thommessen is that we work in teams," explains partner Ylva B. Gjesdahl Petersen. "Well-composed teams whose members complement each other enable everyone to have a life outside their professional commitments, also during hectic periods."

Thommessen's team-oriented culture is evident in its new Oslo offices, which have an "activity-based landscape specifically designed to encourage teamwork." The building has dozens of project rooms where legal teams can meet face-to-face or in hybrid arrangements. The company's digital project management tools also support efficient team-based work and have reduced emails by 40 percent. "These premises are specifically designed to encourage teamwork, knowledge transfer and innovation—which we believe are key to creating the law firm of the future," says Managing Partner Sverre Tyrhaug.[1]

Law firms and other professional services organizations increasingly depend on teamwork rather than individuals working alone to effectively serve clients and perform other complex tasks. Why are teams becoming so important, and how can organizations improve team effectiveness? We find the answers to these and other questions in this chapter on team dynamics. This chapter begins by defining teams, examining the advantages and limitations of teams in organizations, and explaining why people join informal groups in organizational settings. A large segment of this chapter examines a model of team effectiveness, which includes team and organizational environment, team design, and team processes. We then turn our attention to two specific types of teams: self-directed teams and remote teams. The final section of this chapter looks at the challenges and strategies for improving team decision making.

LO7-1 Define teams and informal groups, and explain why employees join informal groups.

TEAMS AND INFORMAL GROUPS

Teams are groups of two or more people who interact with and influence one another, are mutually accountable for achieving common goals associated with organizational objectives, and perceive themselves as a social entity within an organization.[2] This definition has a few important components worth repeating. First, all teams exist to fulfill some purpose, such as providing legal advice and litigation, repairing electric power lines, designing a new educational program, or making an important executive decision.

Second, team members are held together by their interdependence and need for collaboration to achieve common goals. All teams require some form of communication so that members can coordinate, share information, and develop a common mindset regarding their purpose and objectives. Third, team members influence one another, although some members may be more influential than others regarding the team's goals and activities. Finally, a team exists when its members perceive themselves to be a team. They feel connected to one another through a common interest or purpose.

There are many types of teams in organizations, and each type can be distinguished by three characteristics: team permanence, skill diversity, and authority dispersion (see Exhibit 7.1).[3] *Team permanence* refers to how long that type of team usually exists. Accounting, marketing, and other departments are usually long-lasting structures, so these teams have high permanence. In contrast, task forces and project teams usually have low permanence because most are formed temporarily to solve a problem, realize an opportunity, or design a product or service.

A second distinguishing characteristic is the team's *skill diversity.* A team has high skill diversity when its members possess different skills and knowledge, whereas low diversity exists when team members have similar abilities and, therefore, are interchangeable. Most functional departments have low skill diversity because they organize employees around their common skill sets (e.g., people with accounting expertise are located in the accounting department). In contrast, team members in law firms have diverse subject expertise (corporate, estates, etc.) and jurisdictional expertise.

Authority dispersion, the third distinguishing characteristic of teams, refers to the degree that decision-making responsibility is distributed throughout the team (high dispersion) or is vested in one or a few members of the team (low dispersion). Departmental teams tend to have low authority dispersion because power is

Exhibit 7.1 Team Permanence, Skill Diversity, and Authority Dispersion for Selected Team Types

Team Type	Description	Typical Characteristics
Departmental teams	Teams that consist of employees who have similar or complementary skills and are located in the same unit of a functional structure; usually have minimal task interdependence because each person works with clients or with employees in other departments.	*Team permanence:* High—departments continue indefinitely. *Skill diversity:* Low to medium—departments are often organized around common skills (e.g., accounting staff located in the accounting department). *Authority dispersion:* Low—departmental power is usually concentrated in the departmental manager.
Self-directed teams	Teams whose members are organized around work processes that complete an entire piece of work requiring several interdependent tasks and have substantial autonomy over the execution of those tasks (i.e., they usually control inputs, flow, and outputs with little or no supervision).	*Team permanence:* High—teams are usually assigned indefinitely to a specific cluster of production or service activities. *Skill diversity:* Medium to high—members typically perform different tasks requiring diverse skill sets, but cross-training can somewhat reduce skill diversity. *Authority dispersion:* High—team members share power, usually with limited hierarchical authority.
Task force (project) teams	Cross-functional teams whose members are usually drawn from several disciplines to solve a specific problem, realize an opportunity, or design a product or service.	*Team permanence:* Low—teams typically disband on completion of a specific project. *Skill diversity:* Medium to high—members are typically drawn from several functional specializations associated with the complexity of the problem or opportunity. *Authority dispersion:* Medium—teams often have someone with formal authority (project leader), but members also have moderate power due to their expertise and functional representation.

concentrated to a large degree in a formal manager. Self-directed teams usually have high authority dispersion because the entire team makes key decisions and hierarchical authority is limited.

Informal Groups

This chapter mainly focuses on formal teams, but employees also belong to informal groups. All teams are groups, but many groups do not satisfy our definition of teams. Groups include people assembled together, whether or not they have any interdependence or organizational objective. The friends you meet for lunch are an *informal group,* but they wouldn't be called a team because they have little or no interdependence (each person could just as easily eat lunch alone) and no organizationally mandated purpose. Instead, an informal group exists primarily for the benefit of their members.

Why do informal groups exist? One reason is that human beings are social animals. Our drive to bond is hardwired through evolutionary development, creating a need to belong to informal groups.[4] This is evident by the fact that people invest considerable time and effort forming and maintaining social relationships without any special circumstances or ulterior motives. A second reason why people join informal groups is provided by social identity theory, which states that individuals partly define themselves by their group affiliations (see Chapter 3). Thus, we join groups—particularly those that are viewed favorably by others and have values similar to our own—because they shape and reinforce our self-concept.[5]

A third reason why informal groups exist is that they accomplish personal objectives that cannot be achieved by individuals working alone. For example, employees will sometimes congregate to support or oppose organizational changes because this collective effort has more power than individuals who try to

Informal groups exist in organizations because people have a drive to bond, define themselves partly by their social identity, need others to help accomplish nontask goals, and rely on social interaction to minimize stress.
Jetta Productions/Getty Images

bring about change alone (see Chapter 9 on coalitions). A fourth explanation for informal groups is that we are comforted by the mere presence of other people and are therefore motivated to be near them in stressful situations. When in danger, people congregate near one another even though doing so serves no protective purpose. Similarly, employees tend to mingle more often after hearing rumors that the company might be acquired by a competitor. As Chapter 4 explained, this social support minimizes stress by providing emotional and/or informational resources to buffer the stress experience.[6]

information and coordinate tasks, whereas these processes are slower and prone to more errors in traditional departments led by supervisors. Teams typically provide superior customer service because they offer clients a greater breadth of knowledge and expertise than do lone "stars."

social networks Social structures of individuals or social units that are connected to one another through one or more forms of interdependence

process losses Resources (including time and energy) expended toward team development and maintenance rather than the task

> **Talent wins games, but teamwork and intelligence win championships.[10]**
>
> —Michael Jordan, professional basketball player and sports executive

Informal Groups and Organizational Outcomes Informal groups are not created to serve corporate objectives, yet they have a profound influence on the organization and its employees. Informal groups potentially minimize employee stress because, as mentioned, group members provide emotional and informational social support. This stress-reducing capability of informal groups improves employee well-being, which potentially increases organizational effectiveness. Informal groups are also the backbone of **social networks**, which are important sources of trust building, information sharing, power, influence, and employee well-being in the workplace.[7] Chapter 9 explains how social networks are a source of influence in organizational settings. Employees with strong informal networks tend to have more power and influence because they receive better information and preferential treatment from others and their talent is more visible to key decision makers.

LO7-2 Discuss the benefits and limitations of teams.

BENEFITS AND LIMITATIONS OF TEAMS

Why are teams important at Norwegian law firm Advokatfirmaet Thommessen and so many other organizations around the world? The answer to this question has a long history.[8] Early research on British coal mining in the 1940s, the Japanese economic miracle of the 1970s, and a huge number of investigations since then have revealed that *under the right conditions,* teams make better decisions, develop better products and services, and create a more engaged workforce than do employees working alone.[9] Similarly, team members can quickly share information and coordinate tasks, whereas these processes are slower and prone to more errors in traditional departments led by supervisors. Teams typically provide superior customer service because they offer clients a greater breadth of knowledge and expertise than do lone "stars."

Teams are also potentially more productive because, in many situations, their members exert more effort than when working alone.[11] Teamwork motivates in three ways. First, employees have a drive to bond, which motivates them to fulfill their team's goals. This felt obligation is particularly strong when the employee's social identity is connected to the team. Second, employees have high accountability to fellow team members, who monitor performance more closely than a traditional supervisor. This accountability is particularly strong when the team's performance is limited by the worst performer, such as on an assembly line. Third, each team member creates a moving performance standard for the others. When a few employees complete tasks faster, other team members recognize that they could (and should) work faster as well. This benchmark effect also motivates because employees are often apprehensive that their performance will be compared to others' performance.

The Limitations of Teams

Teams are potentially very productive, but they are not always as effective as individuals working alone.[12] The main problem is that teams have additional costs called **process losses**—resources (including time and energy) expended on team development and maintenance rather than on performing the task.[13] Team members need time and effort to develop mutual understanding of their goals, determine the best strategy for accomplishing those goals, negotiate their specific roles, agree on informal rules of conduct, and resolve their disagreements. An employee working alone on a project does not have these internal misunderstandings, divergent viewpoints, disagreements, or coordination problems (at least, not nearly as much as with other people). Teams may be necessary when the work is so complex that it requires knowledge and skills from several people. But when the work can be performed by one person, process losses can make a team much less effective than an individual working alone.

> If I could solve all the problems myself, I would.[14]
>
> —Thomas Edison, inventor, when asked why he needed a team of 21 assistants

OB THEORY TO PRACTICE

What Organizations Say about Teamwork[15]

Company	What They Say about Teamwork
Airbus	"We are One / Team Work!—The complexity of our work also means that we rely on team work ...there are no 'one-person' jobs, but collaborative efforts. This value of unitedness helps create an environment where everyone feels connected, enabling a collective intelligence."
Nike	"At the heart of Nike, you'll find our people ... it's never just one person's effort to reach our goals—we do it as a team. Nike brings together people from diverse backgrounds with a wide range of skill sets, mindsets and assets—and together, we make the impossible possible."
National Aeronautics and Space Administration	"NASA's most powerful tool for achieving mission success is a multidisciplinary team of diverse competent people across all NASA Centers. Our approach to teamwork is based on a philosophy that each team member brings unique experience and important expertise to project issues."
PC Electric (Austria)	"Team spirit is the most essential, as well as the most promising element within our (PCE) family. We promote the feeling of togetherness and the motivation of everyone. Only the different, complementary skills of the individual team members lead to the goal. Then a team is also a family and feels like one."

Process losses tend to increase with the team's diversity and size.[16] A diverse team has a range of beliefs and values, which can slow development toward a high-performance unit. Conflicts about the team's purpose, roles, and coordination routines are more likely to flare up and take longer to resolve. Larger teams have higher process losses because understanding, agreeing with, and synchronizing work with many people is more difficult than with a few people. Larger teams also require more time for each member to be meaningfully involved in the team's decisions.

Process losses are also amplified, at least temporarily, when adding new members to an existing team. The new team members consume time and effort figuring out how to work well with coworkers. Performance also suffers among current team members while their attention is partially diverted from task performance to accommodating and integrating newcomers. The software industry even has a name for the problems of adding people to a team: *Brooks's law* says that adding more people to a late software project only makes it later![17]

Social Loafing The process losses just described mainly refer to coordination challenges, but teams also suffer from motivational process losses. The best-known motivational process loss is **social loafing**, which occurs when people exert less effort (and usually perform at a lower level) in teams than when working alone.[18]

Social loafing is more pervasive under several conditions.[19] It is more likely to occur when individual performance is hidden or difficult to distinguish from the performance of other team members. Individual performance is less visible in larger rather than smaller teams. It is also hidden when the team produces a single output (e.g., solving a client's problem) rather than

Social loafing is more likely to occur when individual performance is hidden or difficult to distinguish from the performance of other team members.
Westend61/Getty Images

separate outputs for each team member (e.g., each member reviews several accounting reports per day). Second, social loafing is more common when the work is boring or the team's overall task has low task significance (see Chapter 5). Third, social loafing is more prevalent among team members with low conscientiousness and low agreeableness personality traits as well as low collectivist values.

Fourth, social loafing is more widespread when employees aren't motivated to help the team achieve its goals. This situation occurs when individual members have low social identity with the team. Motivation is also lower when employees believe other team members aren't pulling their weight. In other words, social loafing is a way to maintain perceived fairness by contributing the same effort as others seem to be providing. Employees also exert less effort when they believe they have little control over the team's success. This perception is more likely to occur when the team is large (their contribution has minimal effect on the team's performance) and when the team is dependent on other members who have known performance problems.

OB THEORY TO PRACTICE

Minimizing Social Loafing[20]

- *Form smaller teams*—Splitting the team into several smaller groups reduces social loafing because each person's performance becomes more noticeable and important for team performance. A smaller group also potentially increases individual commitment to and identity with the team.
- *Measure individual performance*—Social loafing is minimized when each member's contribution is measured. This is possible when each member can perform parallel tasks, such as serving different customers. But measuring individual performance is difficult when the team produces a single output, such as solving one client's problem.
- *Specialize tasks*—It is easier to measure individual performance when each team member performs a different work activity. For example, rather than pooling their effort for all incoming customer inquiries, each customer service representative might be permanently assigned to clients for specific region.
- *Increase job enrichment*—Social loafing is minimized when each team member's job is high motivating, such as when the work has high task significance or is sufficiently varied and challenging rather than boring.
- *Increase mindfulness of team obligations*—Social loafing can be minimized by alerting team members to this problem and asking them to declare their commitment to the team's performance objectives.
- *Select motivated, team-oriented employees*—Employees are less susceptible to social loafing when they are self-motivated, identify with the team, have at least moderate conscientiousness and agreeableness personality traits, and have a fairly high collectivist value orientation.

social loafing The problem that occurs when people exert less effort (and usually perform at a lower level) when working in teams than when working alone

Overall, teams can be very powerful forces for competitive advantage, or they can be much more trouble than they are worth. To understand when teams are better than individuals working alone, we need to more closely examine the conditions that make teams effective or ineffective. The next few sections of this chapter discuss the model of team effectiveness.

LO7-3 Outline the team effectiveness model and discuss how task characteristics, team size, and team composition influence team effectiveness.

A MODEL OF TEAM EFFECTIVENESS

Why are some teams effective while others fail? To answer this question, we first need to clarify the meaning of team effectiveness, which has three key components.[21] First, teams exist to serve some organizational purpose, so effectiveness is partly measured by the achievement of that objective. Second, a team's effectiveness relies on the satisfaction and well-being of its members. People join groups to fulfill their personal needs, so effectiveness is partly measured by this need fulfillment. Third, team effectiveness includes the ability and motivation of team members to remain together long enough to accomplish the assigned goals. Even temporary teams have been known to fall apart either behaviorally (people refuse to join or stay with the team) or cognitively (members become emotionally disengaged from the team).

Researchers have developed several models over the years to identify the features, conditions, and processes that make some teams more effective than others.[22] Exhibit 7.2 integrates the main components of these team effectiveness models. This exhibit is a meta-model because each component (team norms, team cohesion, etc.) includes its own set of theories to explain how that component operates. Over the next two sections, we discuss theories for each part of this model.

The organizational and team environment refers to the context surrounding the team, such as its physical work space and organizational leadership. Team design refers to variables that, for the most part, are assigned to the team when it is created and altered throughout its existence. The number of people assigned to the team (team size) and the personal attributes these members bring to the team (team composition) are elements of team design, for example. Team processes are the cognitive and emotional dynamics of the team that continually change with its development. These processes center around the team's development and the associated variables of team norms, roles, cohesion, trust, and shared/complementary mental models.[23]

Exhibit 7.2 Team Effectiveness Model

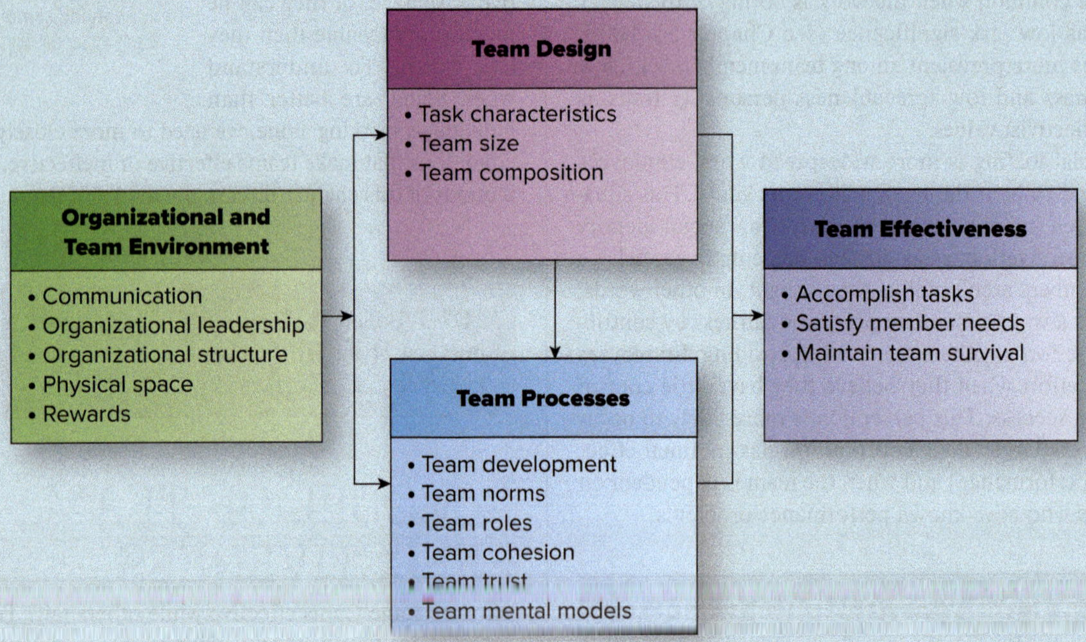

Organizational and Team Environment

The organizational and team environment represents all conditions beyond the team's boundaries that influence its effectiveness. The environment is typically viewed as a resource pool that either supports or inhibits the team's ability to function and achieve its objectives.[24] Teams thrive where the physical workspace encourages collaborative interaction, information systems support team coordination, organizational leaders instill a culture of teamwork, and the reward system reinforces collaboration rather than competition among team members. Team effectiveness also benefits from an organizational structure that clusters work activities within the team and creates fairly distinct boundaries between the team and other work units.[25]

TEAM DESIGN ELEMENTS

Even when operating a team-friendly environment, the team's effectiveness will fall short of its potential if the task characteristics, team size, and team composition are poorly designed.

Task Characteristics

Teams are more effective than individuals in specific types of tasks.[26] They are better for work that is too complex for any individual to perform, such as launching the business in a new market, developing a digital operating system, or constructing a bridge. Complex work requires skills and knowledge beyond one person's abilities. Teams are particularly well suited for complex work that can be divided into more specialized roles, and where the people in those specialized roles are able to coordinate with one another.

Task complexity demands teamwork, but teams also function better when the work is well structured and predictable rather than ambiguous and unpredictable. Team members on an automobile assembly line have well-structured and predictable tasks. They perform the same set of work activities each day (low *task variability*—see Chapter 5)—and the work is predictable enough for well-established procedures (high *task analyzability*). The main benefit of well-structured tasks is that it is easier to coordinate the work among several people.

Task complexity demands teamwork, but teams perform better when the work is well structured rather than ambiguous and unpredictable.
Kristy-Anne Glubish/Design Pics

In contrast, ambiguous and unpredictable tasks are more difficult to coordinate among team members, which leads to higher process losses and errors. Fortunately, teams can still perform these less-structured and less predictable tasks reasonably well when members are experienced in well-defined broader roles. During surgery, for example, medical team members know generally what to expect of one another even when unique problems arise.[27]

Task Interdependence Another task-related influence on team effectiveness is **task interdependence**—the extent to which team members must share materials, information, or expertise to perform their jobs.[28] Apart from complete independence, there are three levels of task interdependence, as illustrated in Exhibit 7.3.[29] The lowest level, called *pooled interdependence,* occurs when an employee or work unit shares machinery, technical support, financial support, or other common (pooled) resources, but otherwise operates independently from other employees or work units. A higher level of interdependence occurs when the output of one person or work unit becomes the direct input for another person or unit. This *sequential interdependence* typically occurs on an assembly line because each team member's output is forwarded to the next person on the line for further assembly of the product or service.

Reciprocal interdependence, in which work output is exchanged back and forth among individuals or work units, produces the highest level of interdependence. People who develop a new product or service would typically have reciprocal interdependence because their decisions affect others involved in the design process. Any decision made by the design engineers would influence the work of the manufacturing engineers and purchasing specialists, and vice versa.

task interdependence
The extent to which team members must share materials, information, or expertise in order to perform their jobs

As a rule, the higher the level of task interdependence, the greater the need to organize people into teams rather than have them work alone.[30] A team structure is much more important for employees with reciprocal interdependence than for those with only pooled interdependence. Higher task interdependence usually requires more intense coordination, and team structures enable better interpersonal communication than when employees work independently from one another or in different departments. High task interdependence also motivates most people to be part of the team and to coordinate with one another.

However, this rule has one important condition: employees with high interdependence should be formed into teams *only* when they have the same task goals, such as serving the same clients or collectively assembling the same product. In contrast, a team structure may lead to dysfunctional conflict when each member has unique goals (such as serving different clients) even though these employees are dependent on one another to achieve those distinct goals. Under these conditions, the company should try to reduce the level of interdependence or rely on supervision as a buffer or mediator among employees.

Team Size

Teams need to be large enough to provide the necessary abilities and viewpoints to perform the assigned work, yet small enough to maintain efficient coordination and meaningful involvement of each member.[31] The ideal team size varies with the type of team, the tasks it is expected to perform, and the available forms of coordination (see Chapter 12). Smaller teams (say, a half-dozen members) operate more effectively than larger teams because they have less process loss (easier coordination, less conflict, less time to make decisions, etc.). Members of smaller teams also tend to feel more motivated because they have more influence on the group's norms and goals and feel more responsible for its successes and failures. Also, members of smaller teams get to know one another better, which improves mutual trust as well as perceived assistance and psychological support from those team members.[32]

Should a team have dozens of members if the task is highly complex? The answer is that a group this large probably isn't a team, even if management calls it one. A team exists when its members

Exhibit 7.3 Levels of Task Interdependence

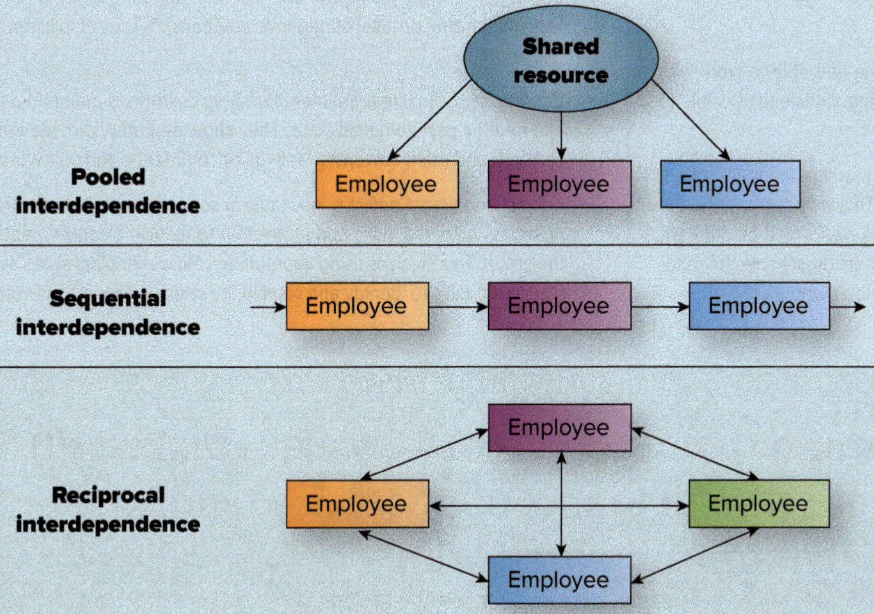

interact and influence one another, are mutually accountable for achieving common goals associated with organizational objectives, and perceive themselves as a social entity within an organization. It is very difficult for everyone in a large work unit to influence one another and perceive themselves as members of the same team. Instead, such complex projects usually consist of a *multi-team system*—several teams that coordinate more formally together as a large work unit.

Team Composition

Team effectiveness depends on the qualities of the people who are assigned to those teams.[33] To begin with, a team's performance depends on how well its members engage in *taskwork*—that is, perform task-related behaviors toward the achievement of the team's objectives. Taskwork requires team members who are highly motivated, possess the required abilities, and have clear role perceptions about how and when to perform the assigned work (see the MARS model in Chapter 1).

But effective teams need more than just individuals who perform their own jobs well. They also need members who are motivated, able, and have clear role perceptions about engaging in *teamwork* behaviors.[34] Teamwork behaviors maintain the team's existence and functioning. In other words, the best performing teams have members who are effective at performing their tasks and also effective at supporting the team's dynamics.

Exhibit 7.4 Five Cs of Effective Team Member Behavior

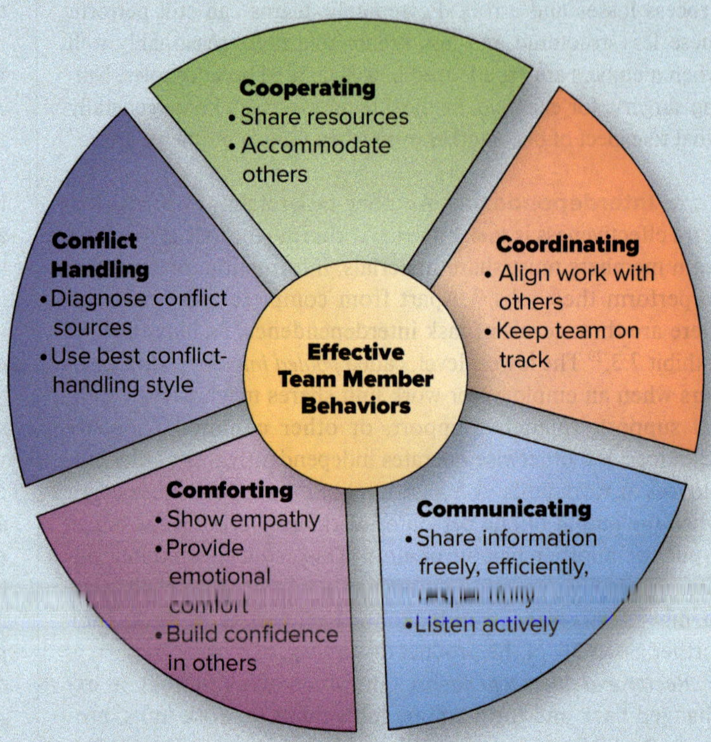

Sources: Based on information in V. Rousseau, C. Aubé, and A. Savoie, "Teamwork Behaviors: A Review and an Integration of Frameworks," *Small Group Research* 37, no. 5 (2006): 540–70; M.L. Loughry, M.W. Ohland, and D.D. Moore, "Development of a Theory-Based Assessment of Team Member Effectiveness," *Educational and Psychological Measurement* 67, no. 3 (2007): 505–24; E. Salas et al., "Understanding and Improving Teamwork in Organizations: A Scientifically Based Practical Guide," *Human Resource Management* 54, no. 4 (2015): 599–622.

The most frequently mentioned teamwork behaviors are depicted in the "Five Cs" model illustrated in Exhibit 7.4. Coordinating, communicating, and cooperating are mainly about supporting team members on their task, whereas comforting and conflict resolving primarily maintain healthy psychological and interpersonal dynamics in the team.[35]

- *Cooperating.* Effective team members are willing and able to work with others. This includes sharing resources and being sufficiently flexible to accommodate the needs of other team members.
- *Coordinating.* Effective team members actively manage the team's work so it is performed efficiently and harmoniously. This includes keeping the team on track and helping to integrate the work performed by different members. To effectively coordinate, team members must know the other team members' work to some extent, not just their own.
- *Communicating.* Effective team members transmit information frequently, efficiently (using the best channel and language), and respectfully (minimizing arousal of negative emotions).[36] They also listen actively to coworkers.
- *Comforting.* Effective team members help coworkers maintain a positive and healthy psychological state. They show empathy, provide emotional comfort, and build coworker feelings of confidence and self-worth.
- *Conflict handling.* Conflict is inevitable in social settings, but effective team members have the skills and motivation to resolve disagreements within the group. This involves using appropriate conflict-handling styles as well as diagnostic skills to identify and resolve the structural sources of conflict.

Along with performing their individual jobs well (taskwork), members of successful teams support the team's dynamics (teamwork).

Teamwork Behaviors in College Graduates and Coworkers[37]

73% of 157 American employers say that recent college graduates are proficient in teamwork skills.

94% of 15,860 bachelor's degree students at U.S. colleges and universities consider themselves proficient in teamwork.

81% of 25,000 employees in 1,000 companies globally believe they have the right people on their team.

32% of 2,000 UK workers say they are hiding their teamwork skill because it is not part of their job.

57% of 200 American and Canadian IT decision makers say that cross-team collaboration is one of the top skills they have had to learn (2nd highest skill after cybersecurity solutions).

(Photo): solarseven/Shutterstock

Team Diversity Diversity, another aspect of team composition, has both advantages and challenges for team effectiveness.[38] One advantage of diverse teams is that people from dissimilar backgrounds tend to see a problem or opportunity from different angles. Members of diverse teams have more varied personal mental models, which increases their likelihood of identifying viable solutions to difficult problems. A second advantage is that diverse team members have a broader pool of technical abilities to serve clients or design new products.

Third, diverse teams often provide better representation of the team's constituents, such as other departments or clients from similarly diverse backgrounds. This representation not only brings different viewpoints to the decision, but it also gives stakeholders a belief that they have a voice in the team's decision process. As we learned in Chapter 5, voice is an important ingredient in procedural justice, so stakeholders are more likely to believe the team's decision is fair when the team mirrors the surface or deep-level diversity of its constituents.

Team diversity also presents a number of challenges.[39] The team development process tends to be slower in teams with high degrees of surface or deep-level diversity. This occurs because team members take longer to reach agreement on team goals, operational procedures, team roles, and informal norms. In some situations, members of diverse teams also take longer to build trust with one another. As a result, the team development process is often slower in heterogeneous than in homogeneous teams.

A related challenge is that diverse teams are susceptible to "faultlines"—hypothetical dividing lines that may split a team into subgroups along sex, ethnic, professional, or other dimensions. These faultlines undermine team effectiveness by reducing the motivation to communicate and coordinate with teammates on the other side of the hypothetical divisions. In contrast, members of homogeneous teams experience higher satisfaction, less conflict, and better interpersonal relations.

Mc Graw Hill connect

SELF-ASSESSMENT 7.1: Are You a Team Player?

OB THEORY TO PRACTICE

Diverse Teams Improve Investment Advice and Research[40]

Investment advisory firms depend increasingly on diverse teams because no individual has sufficient expertise to provide complex investment services. Derek Neldner, CEO and group head of RBC Capital Markets, gives this example: "If you are going to offer serious coverage to a health care client, you need an analyst who can talk authoritatively on medical devices, an expert on pharmaceuticals, one on biotech, and so on."

The shift from individual stars to high-performing teams whose members have diverse backgrounds and expertise is evident at Merrill Lynch Wealth Management (Merrill). A dozen years ago, most of the company's 15,000 financial advisors worked alone with their clients. Today, more than three-quarters of Merrill's advisors work in teams. "It's exceedingly rare that a single individual could deliver everything a client needs today," says Merrill President Andy Sieg. "When you look at what clients need—comprehensive advice across their financial lives—it very quickly becomes obvious that the only way to deliver that is through a team."

Investment firms are also discovering that diverse analyst teams are more effective than individuals working alone. One recent study found that 70 percent of investment analyst research reports are now completed by teams rather than individuals. More important, reports prepared by teams have significantly more accurate earnings forecasts than do reports written by individual analysts. Furthermore, earnings forecast accuracy increases with the team's diversity (educational background, sex, and level of experience).

LO7-4 Discuss how the six team processes—team development, norms, roles, cohesion, trust, and mental models—influence team effectiveness.

TEAM PROCESSES

Team processes comprise the third set of elements in the team effectiveness model. These include team development, norms, roles, cohesion, trust, and team mental models. Team processes are the cognitive and emotional dynamics of the team that continually change (develop, deteriorate, and transform in other ways). In other words, this section looks at the continuously evolving collective abilities, beliefs, expectations, and feelings of the team as well as how those team dynamics influence team effectiveness.[41]

Team Development

Team development is at the heart of team processes because the other dynamics shaping norms, roles, cohesion, trust, and mental models—are embedded in team development. Team members resolve several issues and pass through several stages of development before emerging as an effective work unit. They need to get to know and trust one another, understand and agree on their respective roles, discover appropriate and inappropriate behaviors (norms), develop mutual understanding of the team's objectives and their coordination in that process (team mental models), and develop a strong bond with the team and its members (cohesion).

A popular model that captures most team development activities is illustrated in Exhibit 7.5.[42] The diagram shows teams moving systematically from one stage to the next, while the dashed lines indicate that teams might—and often do—fall back to an earlier stage of development as new members join or other conditions disrupt the team's maturity. *Forming* is a period of testing and orientation in which members learn about one another and evaluate the benefits and costs of continued membership. People tend to be polite, will defer to authority, and try to find out what is expected of them and how they will fit into the team. *Storming* is depicted by interpersonal conflict as members become more proactive, compete for various team roles, and try to establish norms of appropriate behavior and performance standards.

During the *norming* stage, the team develops its first real sense of cohesion as roles are established, a consensus forms around group objectives, and members align their team mental

Exhibit 7.5 Stages of Team Development

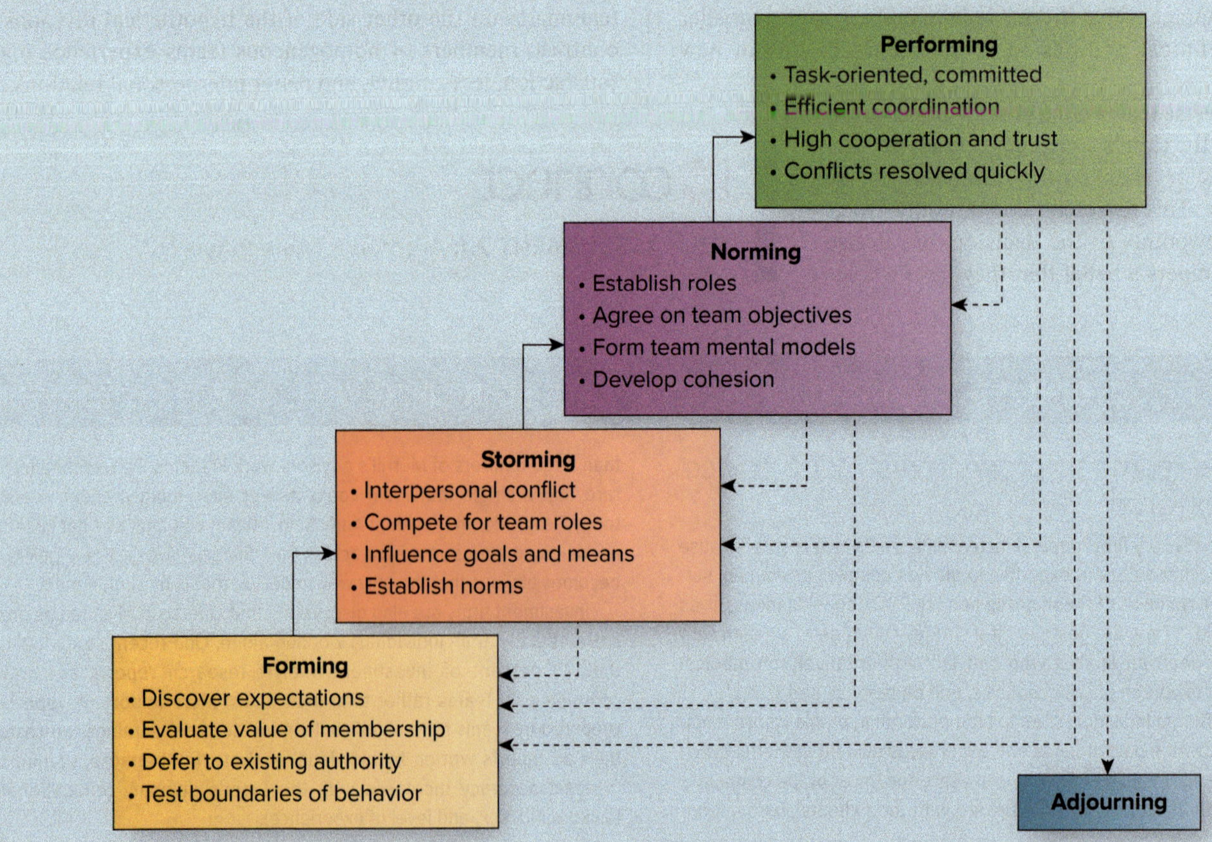

models. By the *performing* stage, team members have learned to efficiently coordinate and resolve conflicts. They are highly co-operative, have a high level of trust in one another, partly define themselves by their membership in that team, and have functional shared mental models of group objectives and work processes. Finally, the *adjourning* stage occurs when the team is about to disband. Team members shift their attention away from task orientation to a relationship focus.

This model depicts team development fairly well because it identifies and incorporates all of the other team processes. It recognizes that team members become cohesive, develop norms to guide behavior, adopt roles, form team mental models, and develop trust in one another. However, the model is not a perfect representation of team development.[43] It does not show that some teams remain in a particular stage longer than others and does not explain why teams sometimes regress back to earlier stages of development. Perhaps most important, this model does not explain the intricacies of how norms, cohesion, mental models, and other team dynamics evolve (sometimes rapidly, sometimes slowly) over time. Fortunately, these team processes are explained by separate theories. The remainder of this section describes each of these, beginning with team norms.

Team Norms

Norms are the informal rules and shared expectations that groups establish to regulate the behavior of their members. Norms apply only to behavior, not to private thoughts or feelings. Furthermore, norms exist only for behaviors that are important to the team.[44] The team development model in Exhibit 7.5 suggests that team norms develop during the storming stage, likely because conflict often occurs when members try to reach agreement on what behavior is expected or forbidden. However, it is more accurate to say that norms begin as soon as the team forms and that some norms continue to change over the team's lifespan.

norms The informal rules and shared expectations that groups establish to regulate the behavior of their members

Team norms improve predictability and conflict-avoidance in coworker relations; they also improve social order and coordination among team members.
Larry Williams/Getty Images

Teams develop norms for a few reasons.[45] First, most norms develop when members associate these behaviors with the team's performance or the well-being of its members. The perceived value of norms motivates members to enact them as well as influence others to do the same. Some norms originate from a critical incident; for instance, a norm of wearing safety glasses emerges after a team member is seriously hurt from not wearing them. Other norms are brought into the team due to experiences that some members have had in previous teams.

Second, team norms develop because they improve predictability and conflict-avoidance in coworker relations. Newcomers, for instance, try to fit in with the group by actively discovering and behaving consistently with the team's norms. Third, teams develop norms to routinize behavior with minimal cognitive effort, which improves social order and coordination among team members. This explains why norms often develop regarding seemingly minor issues, such as where people sit in meetings.

An important feature of team norms is that they are enforced.[46] Coworkers display their displeasure if we are absent from work too often or don't have our part of a project completed on time. Norms are also directly reinforced through praise from high-status members and easier access to valued resources. These forms of peer pressure and reinforcement can occur even when team members work remotely from one another. But team members often conform to prevailing norms without direct reinforcement or punishment because they identify with the group and want to align their behavior with the team's expectations. The more closely the person's social identity is connected to the group, the more the individual is motivated to obey the team's norms.[47]

Developing and Changing Team Norms One of the best ways to establish desired norms in new teams is to select team members whose values and past behavior are compatible with those norms. An associated practice is for the leader to clearly state and justify specific norms when the team is formed. As an example, if organizational leaders want their teams to have strong safety norms, they should hire people who already value safety and clearly state the importance of safety during one of the team's first meetings.

For existing teams, research indicates that leaders have the capacity to remove dysfunctional norms by cautioning team members against these behaviors. They can also introduce desired norms through ongoing coaching of team members.[48] Another suggestion that is sometimes effective is to introduce team-based rewards that reinforce desired norms and counteract dysfunctional norms. Finally, if dysfunctional norms are deeply ingrained and the previous solutions don't work, it may be necessary to disband the group and form a new team whose members have more appropriate norms.

OB THEORY TO PRACTICE

Managing Norms in New and Established Teams

For New Teams

- Select team members whose values and past behavior are compatible with the desired norms.
- Clearly state desired norms to incoming team members.

For Established Teams

- Remove dysfunctional norms by cautioning team members against these behaviors.
- Introduce desired norms through ongoing coaching of team members.
- Introduce team-based rewards that reinforce desired norms and counteract dysfunctional norms.
- If the above actions fail: Disband the group and form a new team whose members have more appropriate norms.

Team Roles

An inherent part of the team development process is assigning and maintaining team roles. A **role** is a set of behaviors that people are expected to perform because they hold specific formal or informal positions in a team and organization.[49] Roles are similar to norms in the sense that they both establish and reinforce expected patterns of behavior. However, most norms apply to all team members, whereas a role typically applies to one or a few specific team members.

Some team roles are formally assigned to individuals when the team is created (as part of team design in the team effectiveness model). For example, most teams have a formal leader, and that person is expected to help clarify task responsibilities, ensure that everyone has an opportunity to present their views in meetings, and so forth. However, some roles are adopted informally as the team develops. Informal roles are shared, but many are eventually associated with specific team members through subtle positioning and negotiation. In many cases, employees are attracted to roles that suit their personality and values. In other cases, team members encourage specific coworkers to take on selected roles.

Several lists of team roles have been proposed over the years.[50] One recent model identifies six role categories: organizer, doer, challenger, innovator, team builder, and connector. More broadly, most team roles focus on either task performance (taskwork) or team maintenance (teamwork). Taskwork roles might include coordinating the team, providing constructive critique of the team's plans, and motivating team members when effort is lagging. Teamwork roles might include providing emotional support when the team is frustrated, maintaining harmony among team members, and creating opportunities for social interaction among team members.

Team Cohesion

Team cohesion is the degree of attraction people feel toward the team and their motivation to remain members. A team has high cohesion when its members are attracted to the team, take ownership of the team's success, make the team part of their self-concept, are committed to the team's goals or tasks, and collectively feel a sense of team pride.[51] Thus, team cohesion is an emotional experience, not just a calculation of whether to stay or leave the team.

Influences on Team Cohesion Six of the most important influences on team cohesion are described next. Some of these conditions strengthen the individual's identity with the team; others strengthen the individual's belief that team membership will fulfill personal needs.

- *Member similarity.* A well-established research finding is that we are attracted more to coworkers who are similar to us.[52] This similarity-attraction effect occurs because we assume that people are more trustworthy and more likely to accept us if they look and act like us. We also believe that these similar others will create fewer conflicts and violations of our expectations. Thus, teams have higher cohesion or become cohesive more quickly when members are similar to one another. In contrast, high cohesion is more difficult and takes longer to develop in teams with diverse members. This difficulty varies with the form of diversity, however.[53]
- *Team size.* Smaller teams tend to have more cohesion than larger teams. One reason is that it is easier for a few people to agree on goals and coordinate work activities. Another reason is that members have more influence in smaller teams, so they feel a greater sense of involvement and ownership in the team. However, small teams have less cohesion when they lack enough qualified members to perform the required tasks.
- *Member interaction.* Teams tend to have more cohesion when their members interact with one another fairly regularly. More frequent interaction occurs when team members perform highly interdependent tasks and work in the same physical area or at least communicate remotely through channels with high social presence.
- *Somewhat difficult entry.* Teams tend to have more cohesion when entry to the team is restricted. The more elite the team, the more prestige it confers on its members, and the more they tend to value their membership in the unit. At the same time, research suggests that severe initiations can weaken team cohesion because of the adverse effects of humiliation, even for those who successfully endure the initiation.[54]
- *Team success.* Team cohesion increases with the team's success because people are attracted to groups that fulfill their needs and goals.[55] Furthermore, individuals are more likely to identify with successful teams than with teams that often fail to achieve their goals.

McGraw Hill connect

SELF-ASSESSMENT 7.2: What Team Roles Do You Prefer?

Members of highly cohesive teams spend more time together, share information more frequently, and are more satisfied with one another.
Peopleimages/Getty Images

- *External competition and challenges.* Teams tend to have more cohesion when they face external competition or a challenging objective that is important to them. Employees value their membership on the team because of its ability to overcome the threat or competition and as a form of social support. However, cohesion can dissipate when external challenges overwhelm the team and threaten its success or viability.[56]

Consequences of Team Cohesion Teams with higher cohesion tend to perform better than those with lower cohesion.[57] In fact, the team's existence depends on some level of cohesion because it motivates team members to remain members and help the team achieve its objectives. Employees in highly cohesive teams spend more time together, share information more frequently, and are more satisfied with one another. They provide better social support in stressful situations and try to minimize dysfunctional conflict.[58] When conflict does arise, members of highly cohesive teams tend to resolve their differences swiftly and effectively.

The relationship between team cohesion and team performance depends on two conditions, however. First, team cohesion has less effect on team performance when the team has low task interdependence.[59] High cohesion motivates employees to coordinate and cooperate with other team members. But when the team members don't depend on one another to perform their jobs (i.e., low task interdependence), there are fewer events requiring cooperation and coordination.

Second, the effect of cohesion on team performance depends on whether the team's norms are aligned or conflict with organizational objectives.[60] As Exhibit 7.6 illustrates, teams with high cohesion perform better when their norms support the company's goals, whereas higher cohesion can potentially reduce team performance when norms are counterproductive. This effect occurs because cohesion motivates employees to perform at a level more consistent with team norms. If a team's norm tolerates or encourages absenteeism, employees will be more motivated to take unjustified sick leave. If the team's norm discourages absenteeism, employees are more motivated to avoid taking sick leave.

One last comment about team cohesion and performance: Earlier in this section we stated that team success (performance) causes cohesion, whereas we are now saying that team cohesion causes team performance. Both statements are correct. Teams with higher cohesion perform better, and teams with better performance become more cohesive. Which direction is stronger? A major review of past studies reported that in established teams (i.e., typical of teams in most organizations), cohesion affects team performance much more than team performance affects cohesion. Only lab experiments that studied short-lived student

role A set of behaviors that people are expected to perform because they hold specific formal or informal positions in a team and organization

team cohesion The degree of attraction people feel toward the team and their motivation to remain members

Exhibit 7.6 Effect of Team Cohesion on Task Performance

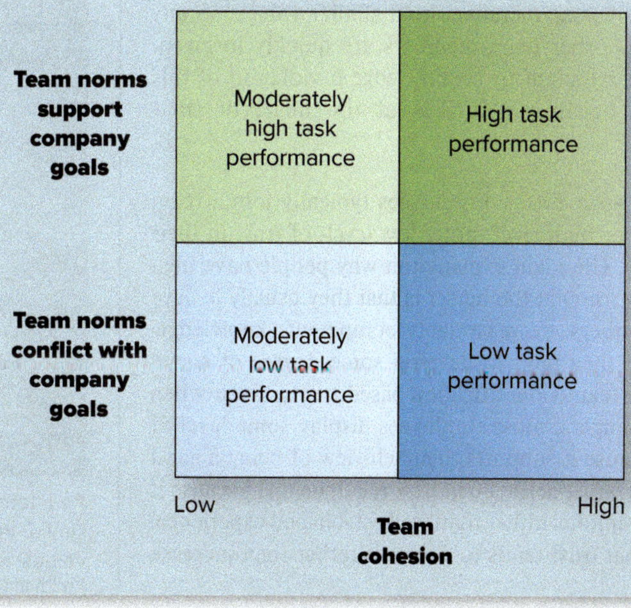

teams found that both directions were equal. Student teams typically begin with fairly low cohesion.[61]

Mc Graw Hill connect

SELF-ASSESSMENT 7.3: How Trusting Are You?

Team Trust

Any relationship—including the relationship among team members—depends on a certain degree of trust.[62] **Trust** refers to positive expectations one person has toward another person in situations involving risk (see Chapter 4). Trust is ultimately perceptual; we trust others on the basis of our beliefs about their ability, integrity, and benevolence. Trust is also emotional; we experience positive feelings toward those we trust.[63]

Trust is built on three foundations in a hierarchy from lowest to highest: calculus, knowledge, and identification.[64] *Calculus-based trust* represents a logical calculation that other team members will act appropriately because they face sanctions if their actions violate reasonable expectations.[65] It offers the lowest potential trust and is easily broken by a violation of expectations. *Knowledge-based trust* is based on the predictability of another team member's behavior. This predictability refers only to "positive expectations"—as the definition of trust states—because you would not trust someone who tends to engage in harmful or dysfunctional behavior. Knowledge-based trust includes our confidence in the other person's abilities (e.g., trusting a physician) as well as someone who acts consistently in their performance toward team goals.[66] Knowledge-based trust offers a higher potential level of trust and is more stable because it develops over time.

Identification-based trust is based on mutual understanding and an emotional bond among team members. It occurs when team members think, feel, and act like one another. High-performance teams exhibit this level of trust because they share the same values and mental models. Identification-based trust is potentially the strongest and most robust of all three types of trust.[67] The individual's self-concept is based partly on membership in the team whose members hold similar values, so any transgressions by other team members are quickly forgiven. People are more reluctant to acknowledge a violation of this high-level trust because it strikes at the heart of their self-concept.

Dynamics of Team Trust Employees typically join a team with a moderate or high level—not a low level—of trust in their new coworkers.[68] The main explanation why people have high trust (called *swift trust*) at the outset is that they usually believe fellow team members are reasonably competent (knowledge-based trust) and they tend to develop some degree of social identity with the team (identification-based trust). Even when working with strangers, most employees display some level of trust, if only because it supports their self-view of being a good person. However, trust is fragile in new relationships because it is based on assumptions rather than well-established experience. Studies report that trust tends to decrease rather than increase over time.[69]

Team Mental Models

Mental models are visual or relational images in our mind that we develop to describe, explain, and predict the world around us (see Chapter 3). Team mental models are cognitive images about the team's tasks, work process, relationship dynamics, and knowledge repository.[70] Team members have both shared and complementary mental models. As a team matures, its members form *shared mental models,* meaning that they develop similar images and expectations about the team's objectives, shared values, behavior norms, and work style, as well as a general picture of how each member participates in the work process.

Complementary mental models are cognitive images held by specific (rather than all) team members and are compatible with the mental models held by other team members. Each member has a unique mental picture of how the team operates because they have a unique background and are located in different parts of the work process than other team members. For example, an engineering team member would view customers somewhat differently from how the marketing person on that team views customers. In successful teams, each member's mental model operates in harmony with the unique mental models of other team members.

Shared and complementary mental models enable team members to establish effective coordinating routines.[71] In high-performing teams, each member develops habitual work

As a team matures, its members form shared mental models—similar images and expectations about the team's objectives, values, norms, and work style.
Art Phaneuf/Alamy Stock Photo

practices that coordinate almost automatically with the behaviors and expectations of other members. This alignment of mental images and predictions also supports the perception that the group is a functioning social entity with meaningful purpose and performance capabilities.

Team mental models also guide employees to where knowledge is located within the team.[72] Members of cross-functional teams, for instance, have diverse knowledge and skills (production, legal, marketing, technology, etc.) that are collectively applied to achieve the team's objectives. To make better decisions and serve clients well, team members often need to consult with coworkers who possesses specific skills and knowledge. This awareness of the team's diverse knowledge repository is therefore a vital feature of team mental models.

Improving Team Processes through Team Building

Teams require time to become cohesive, form productive norms, assign roles, build trust, and develop effective mental models. Team building consists of activities that attempt to speed up, improve, or repair these team development processes.[73]

Team development consists of the team processes we have described in this section, and several types of team building correspond to those processes. Some team-building interventions are task-focused. They clarify the team's performance goals, increase the team's motivation to accomplish these goals, and establish a mechanism for systematic feedback on the team's goal performance. A second type of team building attempts to improve the team's problem-solving skills.

A third team-building category clarifies and reconstructs the role and role expectations that each member has of the other team members. This type of intervention also develops shared and complementary mental models, such as how to interact with clients, maintain machinery, and engage in meetings.[74] A fourth—and likely the most popular—type of team building aims to improve interpersonal relations, such as building trust and becoming a more cohesive team.[75] Wilderness team activities, paintball wars, and obstacle-course challenges are intended to develop interpersonal relations among team members.

All four types of team building potentially accelerate, improve, or repair the team development process, but some interventions work better than others and in some situations more than others.[76] Goal setting tends to be the most successful, although role clarification and adventure programs (to improve interpersonal relations) are also effective to some extent. Interventions are also more successful when they focus on one rather than multiple team-building objectives.

However, many team-building activities are less successful.[77] One problem is that these activities are often applied as a general solution without adequately diagnosing the specific issues that need to be addressed to improve team effectiveness. Team building also tends to be applied as a one-shot jump start for a newly formed team, whereas it should be an ongoing process throughout the team's existence. Finally, we must remember that team building occurs on the job, not just on an obstacle course or in a national park. Organizations should encourage team members to reflect on their work experiences and to experiment with just-in-time learning for team development.

trust Positive expectations one person has toward another person or group in situations involving risk

mental models Visual and relational images that we develop in our mind to describe, explain, and predict the world around us

self-directed teams (SDTs) Cross-functional work groups that are organized around work processes, complete an entire piece of work requiring several interdependent tasks, and have substantial autonomy over the execution of those tasks

LO7-5 Identify the features of self-directed teams (SDTs), and discuss ways to support the success of SDTs.

SELF-DIRECTED AND REMOTE TEAMS

This chapter began by noting that there are many types of teams in organizations. This section highlights two increasingly important types of teams in the workplace: self-directed teams and remote teams.

Self-Directed Teams

Self-directed teams (SDTs) are cross-functional groups organized around work processes that complete an entire piece of work requiring several interdependent tasks and have

> Team-building interventions potentially accelerate, improve, or repair the team development process, but some interventions are more effective than others and in some situations more than others.

remote teams Teams whose members operate across space, time, and organizational boundaries and are linked through information technologies to achieve organizational tasks

substantial autonomy over the execution of those tasks.[78] This definition captures two distinct features of SDTs. First, these teams complete an entire piece of work requiring several interdependent tasks. Employees within the team perform jobs that are interdependently clustered together, whereas they have minimal interdependence or interaction with people outside the team. The result is a close-knit group of employees who depend on one another to accomplish the team's work objectives. The second distinctive feature of SDTs is that they have substantial autonomy over the execution of their tasks. In particular, these teams plan, organize, and control work activities with little or no direct involvement of a higher-level supervisor.

Success Factors for Self-Directed Teams Self-directed teams are found in several industries. For example, PepsiCo relies on autonomous cross-functional teams (called pods)—typically consisting of employees from engineering, data science, and business units—to build customer-facing and internal digital products and resources. Daimler, Bosch, Sun Life Financial, and many other organizations have organized many employees into cross-functional agile teams, which tend to match most characteristics of self-directed teams.[79]

LO7-6 Contrast remote teams with traditional teams in organizations, and discuss ways to support the success of remote teams.

Remote Teams

Chapter 1 described how *remote work*—performing organizational tasks from home or other sites away from the employer's physical premises—is now widely adopted in most organizations. Most employees work in teams for some or all of their tasks, so the increasing popularity of remote work has produced more remote teams.

Remote teams (also known as *distributed* or *virtual teams*) are teams whose members operate across space, time, and organizational boundaries and are linked through information technologies to achieve organizational tasks.[83] Remote teams differ from traditional teams in two ways: (1) One or more members work remotely at least some of the time rather than always being colocated (working in the same physical area as coworkers) and (2) due to their lack of colocation, members of remote teams depend on information technologies in addition to or instead of face-to-face interaction to communicate and coordinate their work effort.

> Self-directed teams should be responsible for an entire work process, so team members have high interdependence with one another and much lower interdependence with people outside the team.

The popularity of SDTs is consistent with research indicating that they potentially increase both productivity and job satisfaction.[80] However, this success depends on several factors.[81] SDTs should be responsible for an entire work process, such as making an entire product or providing a complete service. This structure creates high interdependence among team members and much lower interdependence with people outside the team.[82] SDTs should also have sufficient autonomy to organize and coordinate their work. Autonomy allows them to respond more quickly and effectively to the needs of clients and other stakeholders. It also increases intrinsic motivation among team members. Finally, SDTs are more successful when the work site and technology support coordination and communication among team members. Too often, management calls a group of employees a "team," yet the work layout, assembly-line structure, and other technologies isolate the employees from one another.

Teams vary in their degree of remoteness. Team remoteness increases with the geographic dispersion of team members, percentage of members who work apart (aren't colocated), and percentage of time that members work apart.[84] For example, a team has minimal remoteness when most of its members work in the same physical location most days and only one or two work from home occasionally. High remoteness exists when team members are spread around the world and few members have met the others face-to-face.

Remote teams multiplied rapidly during the COVID-19 pandemic, but they were gaining popularity in organizations many years earlier. One reason is that an increasing percentage of employees perform knowledge work (rather than physical production work), which enables them to do their job from almost anywhere. Second, information technologies have made it easier than ever to communicate and coordinate remotely with other knowledge workers.[85] A third reason is that organizations

OB THEORY TO PRACTICE

Hangouts and Bursts Support Shopify's Remote Teams[86]

Remote teams are the norm at Shopify. The leading e-commerce platform company has adopted a "work anywhere" policy, so its 10,000 employees in almost two dozen countries typically have hybrid or completely remote work arrangements.

Shopify relies on several practices to help remote team members work together effectively. "You may think that managing remote teams is hard, and it is, but there are real benefits that you can achieve by being open to remote employees and building a remote team," advises Lawrence Mandel, Shopify's vice president of engineering.

One practice is a virtual team hangout at the beginning of the day. These brief video gatherings are designed as social klatches, not as formal meetings. "The goal is to replicate those valuable 'water cooler' conversations where team bonding and informal brainstorming can spark new ideas, overcome challenges, and help you and your team develop a high-trust, dispersed culture," explains Shopify Senior Developer Advocate Liam Griffin.

Shopify recently introduced "bursts" as another practice to support remote teams. Shopify President Harley Finkelstein describes bursts as "curated moments where we bring people together for very intentional in-person gatherings." Teams gather at least twice a year, often at getaway locations, where they solve problems and team build. Bursts were created because these 2 to 3 day in-person events help remote team members form stronger bonds that so far can't be completely replicated online. "We do most of our work remotely. But that doesn't mean it's digital only. In fact, we still very much value real-life human connection," says Finkelstein.

Andrey_Popov/Shutterstock

increasingly recognize that their competitive advantage is *human capital*–the knowledge, skills, abilities, creativity, and other valued resources that employees bring to the organization. Leveraging human capital typically occurs through teams, many of which have degrees of remoteness because staff members are distributed across several cities and countries.

Success Factors for Remote Teams Remote teams face all the challenges of traditional teams, as well as the issues arising from time and distance. These challenges increase with the team's remoteness, particularly when it exists for only a short time.[87] Fortunately, OB research has identified the following strategies to minimize most remote team problems.[88] First, remote team members need to apply the effective team behaviors (five Cs) described earlier in this chapter. They also require good communication technology skills, self-management skills to motivate and guide their behavior without peers or bosses nearby, and emotional intelligence to decipher coworkers feelings from text messages and other limited communication channels.

Second, remote teams should have a toolkit of communication channels (messaging, online whiteboards, video conferencing, etc.) as well as the freedom to choose the channels that work best for them.[89] This recommendation may seem obvious, but unfortunately executives tend to impose technology on remote teams and expect team members to use the same communication technology throughout their work. In contrast, research suggests that communication channels gain and lose importance over time, depending on the task and level of trust.

Third, remote teams need plenty of structure, such as clear operational objectives, documented work processes, and agreed-on roles and responsibilities.[90] The final recommendation is that remote team members should meet face-to-face fairly early in the team development process. This idea may seem contradictory to the entire notion of remote teams, but so far, no technology has replaced face-to-face interaction for high-level bonding and mutual understanding.[91]

LO7-7 Identify four constraints on team decision making and discuss ways to improve decision making and creativity in teams.

TEAM DECISION MAKING

Self-directed teams, remote teams, and practically all other groups are expected to make decisions. Teams are potentially more effective than individuals at identifying problems, choosing alternatives, and evaluating their decisions. To leverage these benefits, however, we first need to understand the constraints on effective team decision making. Then, we look at specific ways to overcome these constraints as well as examine structures that improve creative decision making in teams.

Constraints on Team Decision Making

Anyone who has spent enough time in the workplace can recite several ways in which teams stumble in decision making. The

> **Creative ideas often sound bizarre or illogical when first presented, so evaluation apprehension tends to discourage employees from mentioning them in front of coworkers.**

four most common problems are time constraints, evaluation apprehension, pressure to conform, and overconfidence.

Time Constraints Committees keep minutes and waste hours. This age-old saying captures the fact that teams take longer than individuals to make decisions.[92] Teams consume time organizing, coordinating, and maintaining relationships (i.e., process losses). Team members require time to build rapport, agree on rules and norms of behavior in the decision process, and understand one another's ideas.

Another time-related constraint in most team structures is that only one person can speak at a time.[93] This problem, known as **production blocking**, undermines idea generation in a few ways. First, team members need to listen in on the conversation to find an opportune time to speak up, but this monitoring makes it difficult for them to concentrate on their own ideas. Second, ideas are fleeting, so the longer participants wait to speak, the more likely their flickering ideas will die out. Third, team members might remember their fleeting thoughts by concentrating on them, but this concentration reduces their ability to pay attention to the conversation. By ignoring what others are saying, team members miss other potentially good ideas.

Evaluation Apprehension Team members are often reluctant to mention ideas that seem silly because they believe (often correctly) that others in the decision-making group are silently evaluating them.[94] This **evaluation apprehension** is based on the individual's desire to create a favorable public image and need to protect self-esteem. It is most common in meetings attended by people with different levels of status or expertise or when members formally evaluate one another's performance throughout the year. Creative ideas often sound bizarre or illogical when first presented, so evaluation apprehension tends to discourage employees from mentioning them in front of coworkers.

Pressure to Conform Team cohesion motivates employees to conform to the team's norms. This control keeps the group organized around common goals, but it also may cause team members to suppress their dissenting opinions, particularly when a strong team norm is related to the issue. When someone does state a point of view that violates the majority opinion, other members might punish the violator or try to persuade them that the opinion is incorrect. Conformity also can be subtle. To some extent, we depend on the opinions that others hold to validate our own views. If coworkers don't agree with us, we begin to question our own opinions even without overt peer pressure.

> **Insanity in individuals is something rare—but in groups, parties, nations, and epochs, it is the rule.**[96]
>
> —Friedrich Nietzsche, 1800s German philosopher

Overconfidence (Inflated Team Efficacy) To some degree teams are more successful when their members have collective confidence in how well they work together and the likely success of their team effort. This **team efficacy** is similar to individual self-efficacy, which we discussed in Chapter 3. High-efficacy teams set more challenging goals and are more motivated to achieve them, both of which increase team performance.

Unfortunately, there is a curvilinear relationship between team efficacy and the quality of team decisions (as well as other forms of team performance). In other words, teams make worse decisions when they are overconfident as well as underconfident.[95] Overconfident teams are less vigilant when making decisions, partly because they have more positive than negative emotions and moods during these events. They also engage in less constructive debate and are less likely to seek out or accept information located outside the team, both of which undermine the quality of team decisions.

Why do teams become overconfident? The main reason is a team-level variation of self-enhancement (see Chapter 3). Team members have a natural motivation to believe that the team's capabilities are above average. Overconfidence is more common in highly cohesive teams because self-enhancement occurs for things that are important, and the team is important to people in a cohesive team. Overconfidence is also stronger when the team has external threats or competition because these adversaries generate "us versus them" differentiation. Team efficacy is further inflated by the mutually reinforcing beliefs of the team. We develop a clear and higher opinion of the team when other team members echo that opinion.

Improving Decision Making and Creativity in Teams

Team decision making is fraught with problems, but there are several ways to minimize these pitfalls. Checks and balances need to be in place to prevent the leader or other individuals from dominating the discussion. The team should also be large enough to possess the collective knowledge to resolve the problem, yet small enough that it doesn't consume too much time or restrict individual input. Team members should be confident in their decision making but also be wary about being overconfident. This calls for team norms that encourage critical thinking as well as team membership with sufficient diversity.

Another important ingredient for effective team decision making is an environment in which team members have psychological safety.[97] **Psychological safety** is a shared belief that engaging in interpersonal risk-taking will not have adverse consequences. This belief exists when employees are confident that they can constructively disagree with the majority, present weird ideas, or experiment with novel behaviors without fear that coworkers will belittle them or that the company will limit their career progress. Psychological safety requires team norms that encourage employees to respect and value one another, demonstrate interest in one another, be open-minded about and tolerant of coworkers' opinions, and show positive intentions toward one another. Showing positive intentions involves displaying positive emotions and nonthreatening behavior when discussing different points of view.

These recommendations improve most types of team-level decisions. OB studies have also identified four team structures that encourage creativity in a team setting: brainstorming, brainwriting, electronic brainstorming, and nominal group technique.

- **Brainstorming.** This team event encourages participants to think up many ideas for the ultimate objective of generating the most creative ideas.[98] The process consists of four rules: (1) Speak freely—the crazier the idea, the better, (2) don't criticize others or their ideas, (3) provide as many ideas as possible—the quality of ideas increases with the quantity of ideas, and (4) build on the ideas that others have presented. Brainstorming rules potentially increase divergent thinking and minimize evaluation apprehension, but field research indicates that these benefits require an experienced facilitator and confident employees who work in a collaborative learning orientation culture that prioritizes psychological safety.[99]
- **Brainwriting.** This is a variation of brainstorming that minimizes the problem of production blocking by removing conversation during idea generation.[100] There are many forms of brainwriting, but they all have the common feature that individuals write down their ideas rather than verbally describe them. In one version, participants write their ideas on cards and place them in the center of the table. At any time, participants can pick up one or more cards in the center to spark their thinking or further build (piggyback) on those ideas. The limited research on brainwriting suggests that it produces more and better quality ideas than brainstorming due to the lack of production blocking.
- **Electronic brainstorming.** This activity is similar to brainwriting but uses digital networks rather than handwritten cards to document and share ideas. After receiving the question or issue, participants type in their ideas using special digital software. The ideas are distributed anonymously to other participants, who are encouraged to piggyback on those ideas. Team members eventually vote electronically on the ideas presented. Electronic brainstorming can be quite effective at generating creative ideas with minimal production blocking, evaluation apprehension, or conformity problems.[101] Yet, this activity is seldom used because it tends to be too structured and technology-bound.

Brainstorming rules potentially increase divergent thinking and minimize evaluation apprehension, but field research indicates that these benefits require an experienced facilitator and confident employees who work in a collaborative learning orientation culture that prioritizes psychological safety.
fizkes/Shutterstock

production blocking A time constraint in team decision making due to the procedural requirement that only one person may speak at a time

evaluation apprehension Occurs when individuals are reluctant to mention ideas that seem silly because they believe that other team members are silently evaluating them

team efficacy The collective belief among team members in the team's capability to successfully complete a task

psychological safety A shared belief that it is safe to engage in interpersonal risk-taking; specifically, that presenting unusual ideas, constructively disagreeing with the majority, and experimenting with new work behaviors will not result in coworkers posing a threat to their self-concept, status, or career

brainstorming A freewheeling, face-to-face meeting where team members are encouraged to identify crazy ideas, build on the ideas that others have presented, generate as many ideas as possible (because quantity often leads to higher quality ideas), and are prohibited from evaluating or criticizing people or their ideas

brainwriting A variation of brainstorming whereby participants write (rather than speak about) and share their ideas

electronic brainstorming A form of brainwriting that relies on digital networks to anonymously submit and share creative ideas with others in the decision process

nominal group technique
A variation of brainwriting consisting of three stages in which participants (1) silently and independently document their ideas, (2) collectively describe these ideas to the other team members without critique, and then (3) silently and independently evaluate the ideas presented

- **Nominal group technique.** This is another variation of brainwriting, but it adds a verbal element to the process.[102] The problem is described, team members silently and independently write down as many solutions as they can, then they describe their solutions to the other team members, usually in a round-robin format. As with brainstorming, there is no criticism or debate, just clarification. Finally, participants silently and independently rank-order or vote on each proposed solution. Nominal group technique has been used in real-world decisions and tends to improve the quality of ideas generated. However, production blocking and evaluation apprehension still occur to some extent. Training improves this structured approach to team decision making.[103]

Study Checklist

Connect® is available for *M: Organizational Behavior.* Additional resources include:

✓ Exercises:

- **Case Analysis:** Apply concepts within the context of a real-world situation
- **Click and Drag:** Helps make the connection between theory and application through matching, ranking, or grouping activities.
- **Video Case:** See management in action through interactive videos.
- **Self-Assessment:** Designed to promote student self-awareness and reflection, these research-based surveys contain detailed feedback for students.
- **Application-Based Activities:** These highly interactive, application- and analysis-based exercises allow students to take on specific roles to complete management related tasks within a real-world context.

✓ **SmartBook 2.0®**—SmartBook 2.0 is an adaptive learning solution that provides personalized learning to individual student needs, continually adapts to pinpoint knowledge gaps and focuses learning on concepts requiring additional study. It fosters more productive learning, takes the guesswork out of what to study, and helps students better prepare for class.

©Natthawat Jamnapa/123RF

Notes

1. A Sneak Preview of Thommessen's New Oslo Premises," Thommessen Corporate News (blog), June 10, 2021; "Digital Services," Advokatfirmaet Thommessen AS, 2022; "Working at Thommessen," Advokatfirmaet Thommessen AS, accessed February 14, 2022.
2. M.E. Shaw, *Group Dynamics*, 3rd ed. (New York: McGraw Hill, 1981), 8; E. Sundstrom, "The Challenges of Supporting Work Team Effectiveness," in *Supporting Work Team Effectiveness,* ed. E. Sundstrom and Associates (San Francisco, CA: Jossey-Bass, 1999), 6–9; L.E. Benishek and E.H. Lazzara, "Teams in a New Era: Some Considerations and Implications," *Frontiers in Psychology* 10 (2019): 01006. Even though a distinct social entity, a team's boundaries (who is and who is not a member) may be fuzzier than previously assumed. See: M. Mortensen and M.R. Haas, "Perspective–Rethinking Teams: From Bounded Membership to Dynamic Participation," *Organization Science* 29 (2018): 341–55.
3. J.R. Hollenbeck, B. Beersma, and M.E. Schouten, "Beyond Team Types and Taxonomies: A Dimensional Scaling Conceptualization for Team Description," *Academy of Management Review* 37, no. 1 (2012): 82–106. This article uses the term *skill differentiation,* whereas we use *skill diversity* which is a more common label to describe variations among team members; skill differences represent a form of deep-level diversity. The original article also uses the label *authority differentiation,* whereas we believe that *authority dispersion* is more consistent with similar language on power in organizations, such as in decentralization of organizational structures.
4. J.R. Spoor and J.R. Kelly, "The Evolutionary Significance of Affect in Groups: Communication and Group Bonding," *Group Processes & Intergroup Relations* 7 (2004): 398–412; W.S. Jansen et al., "Inclusion: Conceptualization and Measurement," *European Journal of Social Psychology* 44 (2014): 370–85.
5. S.A. Haslam and N. Ellemers, "Identity Processes in Organizations," in *Handbook of Identity Theory and Research*, ed. J.S. Schwartz, K. Luyckx, and L.V. Vignoles (New York: Springer New York, 2011), 715–44; R. Spears, "Group Identities: The Social Identity Perspective," in *Handbook of Identity Theory and Research*, ed. S.J. Schwartz, K. Luyckx, and V.L. Vignoles (New York: Springer New York, 2011), 201–24; S.K. Kang and G.V. Bodenhausen, "Multiple Identities in Social Perception and Interaction: Challenges and Opportunities," *Annual Review of Psychology* 66 (2015): 547–74.
6. S. Cohen, "The Pittsburgh Common Cold Studies: Psychosocial Predictors of Susceptibility to Respiratory Infectious Illness," *International Journal of Behavioral Medicine* 12, no. 3 (2005): 123–31; S.Y. Shin and S.G. Lee, "Effects of Hospital Workers? Friendship Networks on Job Stress," *PLoS ONE* 11, no. 2 (2016): e0149428.

7. R. Cross and R.J. Thomas, *Driving Results through Social Networks: How Top Organizations Leverage Networks for Performance and Growth* (San Francisco: Jossey-Bass, 2009); R. McDermott and D. Archibald, "Harnessing Your Staff's Informal Networks," *Harvard Business Review* 88, no. 3 (2010): 82–89; J.R. Methot, E.H. Rosado-Solomon, and D.G. Allen, "The Network Architecture of Human Capital: A Relational Identity Perspective," *Academy of Management Review* 43 (2018): 723–48.

8. M. Moldaschl and W. Weber, "The 'Three Waves' of Industrial Group Work: Historical Reflections on Current Research on Group Work," *Human Relations* 51 (1998): 347–88. Several popular books in the 1980s encouraged teamwork, based on the Japanese economic miracle. These books include W. Ouchi, *Theory Z: How American Management Can Meet the Japanese Challenge* (Reading, MA: Addison-Wesley, 1981); R. T. Pascale and A. G. Athos, *Art of Japanese Management* (New York: Simon & Schuster, 1982).

9. C.R. Emery and L.D. Fredenhall, "The Effect of Teams on Firm Profitability and Customer Satisfaction," *Journal of Service Research* 4 (2002): 217–29; J.R. Hackman, *Collaborative Intelligence: Using Teams to Solve Hard Problems* (San Francisco: Berrett-Koehler Publishers, 2011); E. Salas, D.L. Reyes, and S.H. McDaniel, "The Science of Teamwork: Progress, Reflections, and the Road Ahead," *American Psychologist* 73 (2018): 593–600.

10. M. Jordan, *I Can't Accept Not Trying: Michael Jordan on the Pursuit of Excellence* (San Francisco: Harper, 1994), 24.

11. R.E. Baumeister and M.R. Leary, "The Need to Belong: Desire for Interpersonal Attachments as a Fundamental Human Motivation," *Psychological Bulletin* 117 (1995): 497–529; J.M. Feinberg and J.R. Aiello, "Social Facilitation: A Test of Competing Theories," *Journal of Applied Social Psychology* 36, no. 5 (2006): 1087–109; A.M. Grant, "Relational Job Design and the Motivation to Make a Prosocial Difference," *Academy of Management Review* 32, no. 2 (2007): 393–417; N.L. Kerr and D.H. Seok, "'. . . with a Little Help from My Friends': Friendship, Effort Norms, and Group Motivation Gain," *Journal of Managerial Psychology* 26, no. 3 (2011): 205–18; D. Herbst and A. Mas, "Peer Effects on Worker Output in the Laboratory Generalize to the Field," *Science* 350, no. 6260 (2015): 545–49.

12. E.A. Locke et al., "The Importance of the Individual in an Age of Groupism," in *Groups at Work: Theory and Research*, ed. M.E. Turner (Mahwah, NJ: Erlbaum, 2001), 501–28; N.J. Allen and T.D. Hecht, "The 'Romance of Teams': Toward an Understanding of Its Psychological Underpinnings and Implications," *Journal of Occupational and Organizational Psychology* 77 (2004): 439–61; A. Almaatouq et al., "Task Complexity Moderates Group Synergy," *Proceedings of the National Academy of Sciences* 118, no. 36 (2021): e2101062118.

13. I.D. Steiner, *Group Process and Productivity* (New York: Academic Press, 1972); S. Coyle, K. Conboy, and T. Acton, "Group Process Losses in Agile Software Development Decision Making," *International Journal of Intelligent Information Technologies* 9, no. 2 (2013): 38–53; K. Srikanth, S. Harvey, and R. Peterson, "A Dynamic Perspective on Diverse Teams: Moving from the Dual-Process Model to a Dynamic Coordination-Based Model of Diverse Team Performance," *Academy of Management Annals* 10 (2016): 453–93.

14. The origin of this quotation remains unknown. The earliest publication of this quotation that we could find is in *Madison (WI) Magazine* 43 (2001): 62.

15. "Values - We Are One -Teamwork," Airbus, October 28, 2021, https://www.airbus.com/en/newsroom/news/2019-04-values-we-are-one-teamwork; "NASA Strategic Plan for Diversity, Equity, Inclusion, and Accessibility" (Washington, DC: National Aeronautics and Space Administration (NASA), March 2022); "Nike Careers-Teams," Nike, accessed March 2, 2023, https://jobs.nike.com/teams; "Philosophy & Guiding Values," PC Electric Gesellschaft m.b.H., accessed March 2, 2023, https://www.pcelectric.at/en/company/pc-electric-gesellschaft-m-b-h/philosophy-guiding-values.html.

16. G.K. Stahl et al., "Unraveling the Effects of Cultural Diversity in Teams: A Meta-Analysis of Research on Multicultural Work Groups," *Journal of International Business Studies* 41 (2010): 690–709; M.W. McCarter and R.M. Sheremeta, "You Can't Put Old Wine in New Bottles: The Effect of Newcomers on Coordination in Groups," *PLoS ONE* 8, no. 1 (2013): e55058.

17. F.P. Brooks, ed. *The Mythical Man-Month: Essays on Software Engineering*, Second ed. (Reading, MA: Addison-Wesley, 1995); B.R. Staats, K.L. Milkman, and C.R. Fox, "The Team Scaling Fallacy: Underestimating the Declining Efficiency of Larger Teams," *Organizational Behavior and Human Decision Processes* 118, no. 2 (2012): 132–42; T. van Balen and M. Tarakci, "Never Change a Winning Team?" SSRN Scholarly Paper (Rochester, NY: Social Science Research Network, May 4, 2017).

18. S.J. Karau and K.D. Williams, "Social Loafing: A Meta-Analytic Review and Theoretical Integration," *Journal of Personality and Social Psychology* 65 (1993): 681–706; R.C. Liden et al., "Social Loafing: A Field Investigation," *Journal of Management* 30 (2004): 285–304; A. Simms and T. Nichols, "Social Loafing: A Review of the Literature," *Journal of Management Policy & Practice* 15, no. 1 (2014): 58–67.

19. B. Latane, K. Williams, and S. Harkins, "Many Hands Make Light the Work: The Causes and Consequences of Social Loafing," *Journal of Personality & Social Psychology* 37 (1979): 822–32; U.-C. Klehe and N. Anderson, "The Moderating Influence of Personality and Culture on Social Loafing in Typical versus Maximum Performance Situations," *International Journal of Selection and Assessment* 15 (2007): 250–62; R.B. Lount and S.L. Wilk, "Working Harder or Hardly Working? Posting Performance Eliminates Social Loafing and Promotes Social Laboring in Workgroups," *Management Science* 60 (2014): 1098–106; M.C. Schippers, "Social Loafing Tendencies and Team Performance: The Compensating Effect of Agreeableness and Conscientiousness," *Academy of Management Learning & Education* 13 (2014): 62–81; B. Meyer, C.C. Schermuly, and S. Kauffeld, "That's Not My Place: The Interacting Effects of Faultlines, Subgroup Size, and Social Competence on Social Loafing Behaviour in Work Groups," *European Journal of Work and Organizational Psychology* 25 (2016): 31–49.

20. C. Lam, "The Role of Communication and Cohesion in Reducing Social Loafing in Group Projects," *Business and Professional Communication Quarterly* 78 (2015): 454–75; S.H. Czyż et al., "Participation in Team Sports Can Eliminate the Effect of Social Loafing," *Perceptual and Motor Skills* 123 (2016): 754–68; V. Peñarroja, V. Orengo, and A. Zornoza, "Reducing Perceived Social Loafing in Virtual Teams: The Effect of Team Feedback with Guided Reflexivity," *Journal of Applied Social Psychology* 47 (2017): 424–35; I. Fronza and X. Wang, "Towards an Approach to Prevent Social Loafing in Software Development Teams," in *11th ACM/IEEE International Symposium on Empirical Software Engineering and Measurement (Esem 2017)* (New York: IEEE, 2017), 241–46; A.A. Curcio and M.A. Lynch, "Addressing Social Loafing on Faculty Committees," *Journal of Legal Education* 67 (2017): 242–62.

21. E. Sundstrom, K.P. De Meuse, and D. Futrell, "Work Teams: Applications and Effectiveness," *American Psychologist, Organizational Psychology*, 45, no. 2 (1990): 120–33; J.R. Hackman et al., "Team Effectiveness in Theory and in Practice," in *Industrial and Organizational Psychology: Linking Theory with Practice*, ed. C.L.

Cooper and E.A. Locke (Oxford, UK: Blackwell, 2000), 109–29. Recent literature has focused mainly on the first two functions, but team survival is also an important outcome. See J.E. Mathieu et al., "Embracing Complexity: Reviewing the Past Decade of Team Effectiveness Research," *Annual Review of Organizational Psychology and Organizational Behavior* 6 (2019): 17–46.

22. P.S. Goodman, E.C. Ravlin, and L. Argote, "Current Thinking About Groups: Setting the Stage for New Ideas," in *Designing Effective Work Groups*, ed. P.S. Goodman and Associates (San Francisco: Jossey-Bass, 1986); M.A. West, C.S. Borrill, and K.L. Unsworth, "Team Effectiveness in Organizations," *International Review of Industrial and Organizational Psychology* 13 (1998): 1–48; M.A. Marks, J.E. Mathieu, and S.J. Zaccaro, "A Temporally Based Framework and Taxonomy of Team Processes," *Academy of Management Review* 26, no. 3 (2001): 356–76; E. Salas, D.L. Reyes, and S.H. McDaniel, "The Science of Teamwork: Progress, Reflections, and the Road Ahead.," *American Psychologist* 73, no. 4 (2018): 593–600; J.E. Mathieu et al., "Embracing Complexity: Reviewing the Past Decade of Team Effectiveness Research," *Annual Review of Organizational Psychology and Organizational Behavior* 6, no. 1 (2019): 17–46.

23. McGrath recommended that team models and studies should focus on team processes rather than the snapshot "series of states" that emerge from those processes. He explained that the processes generating team states are logically more important for understanding team dynamics. Unfortunately, recent writers on teams have neglected that advice. See J.E. McGrath, "Studying Groups at Work: Ten Critical Needs for Theory and Practice," in *Designing Effective Work Groups*, ed. P.S. Goodman and Associates (San Francisco: Jossey-Bass, 1986), 362–92.

24. M. Kouchaki et al., "The Treatment of the Relationship between Groups and Their Environments: A Review and Critical Examination of Common Assumptions in Research," *Group & Organization Management* 37, no. 2 (2012): 171–203; T. Driskell, E. Salas, and J.E. Driskell, "Teams in Extreme Environments: Alterations in Team Development and Teamwork," *Human Resource Management Review* 28, no. 4 (2018): 434–49.

25. E. Sundstrom, "The Challenges of Supporting Work Team Effectiveness," in *Supporting Work Team Effectiveness,* ed. E. Sundstrom and Associates (San Francisco, CA: Jossey-Bass, 1999), 6–9; G.L. Stewart, "A Meta-Analytic Review of Relationships between Team Design Features and Team Performance," Journal of Management 32, no. 1 (2006): 29–54; J.E. Mathieu, L. D'Innocenzo, and M.R. Kukenberge, "Contextual Issues in Project Performance: A Multilevel Perspective," in *The Psychology and Management of Project Teams: An Interdisciplinary Perspective*, ed. B. Hobbs, E.K. Kelloway, and F. Chiocchio (New York: Oxford University Press, 2015), 101–36; F. Schölmerich, C.C. Schermuly, and J. Deller, "How Leaders' Diversity Beliefs Alter the Impact of Faultlines on Team Functioning," *Small Group Research* 47, no. 2 (2016): 177–206; S.A. Conroy and N. Gupta, "Team Pay-for-Performance: The Devil is in the Details," *Group & Organization Management* [illegible]

26. J.E. Mathieu et al., "Embracing Complexity: Reviewing the Past Decade of Team Effectiveness Research," *Annual Review of Organizational Psychology and Organizational Behavior* 6 (2019): 17–46.

27. M.A. Campion, E.M. Papper, and G.J. Medsker, "Relations between Work Team Characteristics and Effectiveness: A Replication and Extension," *Personnel Psychology* 49 (1996): 429–52; N. Sivasubramaniam, S.J. Liebowitz, and C.L. Lackman, "Determinants of New Product Development Team Performance: A Meta-Analytic Review," *Journal of Product Innovation Management* 29, no. 5 (2012): 803–20; M.A. Valentine and A.C. Edmondson, "Team Scaffolds: How Mesolevel Structures Enable Role-Based Coordination in Temporary Groups," *Organization Science* 26, no. 2 (2015): 405–22.

28. G. Van der Vegt and E. Van de Vliert, "Intragroup Interdependence and Effectiveness: Review and Proposed Directions for Theory and Practice," *Journal of Managerial Psychology* 17, no. 1/2 (2002): 50–67; J. Lyubovnikova et al., "24-Karat or Fool's Gold? Consequences of Real Team and Co-Acting Group Membership in Healthcare Organizations," *European Journal of Work and Organizational Psychology* 24, no. 6 (2015): 929–50; S. H. Courtright et al., "Structural Interdependence in Teams: An Integrative Framework and Meta-Analysis," *Journal of Applied Psychology* 100, no. 6 (2015): 1825–46.

29. J.D. Thompson, *Organizations in Action* (New York: McGraw Hill, 1967), 54–55; F.M. Barbibi and G. Masino, *J.D. Thompson's Organizations in Action 50th Anniversary: A Reflection* (Bologna. Italy: TAO Digital Library, 2017), Chap. 1. A slight variation of Thompson's model is also applied to understand interdependence in multi-team systems. See: R. Rico et al., "Structural Influences upon Coordination and Performance in Multiteam Systems," *Human Resource Management Review* 28 (2018): 332–46.

30. J.D. Thompson, *Organizations in Action* (New York: McGraw Hill, 1967), 55–59.

31. J.R. Hackman, *Leading Teams: Setting the Stage for Great Performances* (Boston: Harvard Business Review Press, 2002), 116–22; C. Aube, V. Rousseau, and S. Tremblay, "Team Size and Quality of Group Experience: The More the Merrier?, *Group Dynamics: Theory Research and Practice* 15, no. 4 (2011): 357–75; J.S. Mueller, "Why Individuals in Larger Teams Perform Worse," *Organizational Behavior and Human Decision Processes* 117, no. 1 (2012): 111–24; Y.-N. Lee, J.P. Walsh, and J. Wang, "Creativity in Scientific Teams: Unpacking Novelty and Impact," *Research Policy* 44, no. 3 (2015): 684–97.

32. J.S. Mueller, "Why Individuals in Larger Teams Perform Worse," *Organizational Behavior and Human Decision Processes* 117, no. 1 (2012): 111–24.

33. J.E. Mathieu et al., "A Review and Integration of Team Composition Models: Moving toward a Dynamic and Temporal Framework," *Journal of Management* 40, no. 1 (2014): 130–60; N.J. Allen and T. O'Neill, "Team Composition and Performance: Considering the Project-Team Challenge," in *The Psychology and Management of Project Teams: An Interdisciplinary Perspective*, ed. B. Hobbs, E.K. Kelloway, and F. Chiocchio (New York: Oxford University Press, 2015), 301–28.

34. Taskwork and teamwork have varied definitions in the literature (e.g., behaviors versus competencies; individual- versus team-level phenomena). Our definition, which refers to individual-level behaviors focused on task performance versus team maintenance, is similar to the conceptualizations by Eduardo Salas and his colleagues, as well as to Lewin's seminal ideas about locomotion versus maintenance in groups. See, for example, J.E. Driskell, E. Salas, and T. Driskell, "Foundations of Teamwork and Collaboration," *American Psychologist* 73, no. 4 (2018): 334–48; E. Salas et al., "Can Teamwork Promote Safety in Organizations?" *Annual Review of Organizational Psychology and Organizational Behavior* 7 (2020): 283–313.

35. F.P. Morgeson, M.H. Reider, and M.A. Campion, "Selecting Individuals in Team Settings: The Importance of Social Skills, Personality Characteristics, and Teamwork Knowledge," *Personnel Psychology* 58, no. 3 (2005): 583–611; V. Rousseau, C. Aubé, and A. Savoie, "Teamwork Behaviors: A Review and an Integration of Frameworks," *Small Group Research* 37, no. 5 (2006): 540–70; M.L. Loughry, M.W. Ohland, and D.D. Moore, "Development of a Theory-Based Assessment of Team Member Effectiveness," *Educational and Psychological Measurement* 67, no. 3 (2007): 505–24; E. Salas et al., "Understanding and Improving Teamwork in Organizations: A Scientifically Based Practical Guide," *Human Resource Management* 54, no. 4 (2015): 599–622.

36. S.L. Marlow et al., "Does Team Communication Represent a One-Size-Fits-All Approach?: A Meta-Analysis of Team Communication and Performance," *Organizational Behavior and Human Decision Processes* 144 (2018): 145–70; M.J.W. McLarnon et al., "Global Virtual Team Communication, Coordination, and Performance across Three Peer Feedback Strategies," *Canadian Journal of Behavioural Science* 51 (2019): 207–18.

37. "The 2019 Employee Engagement Report" (Seattle: TINYpulse, February 21, 2019); "Your Employees Miss Their Printers More Than Happy Hours," Press Release (Palo Alto, CA: HP Development Company, June 21, 2022); J. Urquhart, "Third of Workers Hiding 'Secret Skills' from Employers, Professional Body Says," *People Management*, June 21, 2022; M. Collins, "Recruiters and Students Have Differing Perceptions of New Grad Proficiency in Competencies," *National Association of Colleges and Employers* (blog), October 24, 2022.

38. D. van Knippenberg, C.K.W. De Dreu, and A.C. Homan, "Work Group Diversity and Group Performance: An Integrative Model and Research Agenda," *Journal of Applied Psychology* 89, no. 6 (2004): 1008–22; L.M. Shore et al., "Inclusion and Diversity in Work Groups: A Review and Model for Future Research," *Journal of Management* 37, no. 4 (2011): 1262–89; J. Wang et al., "Team Creativity/Innovation in Culturally Diverse Teams: A Meta-Analysis," *Journal of Organizational Behavior* 40, no. 6 (2019): 693–708; M. del C. Triana et al., "The Relationship Between Team Deep-Level Diversity and Team Performance: A Meta-Analysis of the Main Effect, Moderators, and Mediating Mechanisms," *Journal of Management Studies* 58, no. 8 (2021): 2137–79.

39. D.C. Lau and J.K. Murnighan, "Interactions within Groups and Subgroups: The Effects of Demographic Faultlines," *Academy of Management Journal* 48, no. 4 (2005): 645–59; S.T. Bell et al., "Getting Specific about Demographic Diversity Variable and Team Performance Relationships: A Meta-Analysis," *Journal of Management* 37, no. 3 (2011): 709–43; S.M.B. Thatcher and P.C. Patel, "Group Faultlines: A Review, Integration, and Guide to Future Research," *Journal of Management* 38, no. 4 (2012): 969–1009; P. Choudhury and M.R. Haas, "Scope versus Speed: Team Diversity, Leader Experience, and Patenting Outcomes for Firms," *Strategic Management Journal* 39, no. 4 (2018): 977–1002; E. Seo, H. Kang, and J. Song, "Blending Talents for Innovation: Team Composition for Cross-Border R&D Collaboration within Multinational Corporations," *Journal of International Business Studies* 51, no. 5 (2020): 851–85.

40. S. Garmhausen, "Why Teams Dominate at the Top Financial Advisors," *Barron's*, April 19, 2019; A. Willis, "Why RBC Is Becoming the New England Patriots of Bay Street," *Globe & Mail*, April 24, 2019; "Canada's Best Investment Bank 2019: RBC Capital Markets," *Euromoney*, July 10, 2019; B. Fang and O.-K. Hope, "Analyst Teams," *Review of Accounting Studies* 26, no. 2 (2021): 425–67.

41. This book applies the widely held definition of *team processes,* namely causal changes within teams. Team development, norms, cohesion, and trust are some of these team processes. A few team models describe *team processes* as a team's actions contributing to the organization's transformation of inputs to outputs (see open systems in Chapter 1). But these behaviors are team outcomes, not processes, at the team level of analysis. Most team effectiveness models adopt our meaning of *team processes.* For example, see: J.S. Christian et al., "Team Adaptation in Context: An Integrated Conceptual Model and Meta-Analytic Review," *Organizational Behavior and Human Decision Processes* 140 (2017): 62–89; M.L. Shuffler et al., "Developing, Sustaining, and Maximizing Team Effectiveness: An Integrative, Dynamic Perspective of Team Development Interventions," *Academy of Management Annals* 12, no. 2 (2018): 688–724; H. Roh et al., "Opening the Black Box: A Meta-Analytic Examination of the Effects of Top Management Team Diversity on Emergent Team Processes and Multilevel Contextual Influence," *Group & Organization Management* 44, no. 1 (2019): 112–64.

42. B.W. Tuckman and M.A.C. Jensen, "Stages of Small-Group Development Revisited," *Group and Organization Studies* 2 (1977): 419–42; B.W. Tuckman, "Developmental Sequence in Small Groups," *Group Facilitation* (2001): 66–81; D.A. Bonebright, "40 Years of Storming: A Historical Review of Tuckman's Model of Small Group Development," *Human Resource Development International* 13, no. 1 (2010): 111–20.

43. D.A. Bonebright, "40 Years of Storming: A Historical Review of Tuckman's Model of Small Group Development," *Human Resource Development International* 13, no. 1 (2010): 111–20; C.F. Peralta et al., "Team Development: Definition, Measurement and Relationships with Team Effectiveness," *Human Performance* 31, no. 2 (2018): 97–124; B. Fyhn, V. Schei, and T.E. Sverdrup, "Taking the Emergent in Team Emergent States Seriously: A Review and Preview," *Human Resource Management Review* 33, no. 1 (2023): 100928.

44. D.C. Feldman, "The Development and Enforcement of Group Norms," *Academy of Management Review* 9 (1984): 47–53; E. Fehr and U. Fischbacher, "Social Norms and Human Cooperation," *Trends in Cognitive Sciences* 8, no. 4 (2004): 185–90; B.A. De Jong, K.M. Bijlsma-Frankema, and L.B. Cardinal, "Stronger Than the Sum of Its Parts? The Performance Implications of Peer Control Combinations in Teams," *Organization Science* 25 (2014): 1703–21.

45. K. Bettenhausen and J.K. Murnighan, "The Emergence of Norms in Competitive Decision-Making Groups," *Administrative Science Quarterly* 30, no. 3 (1985): 350-72; K.D. Opp, "How Do Norms Emerge? An Outline of a Theory," *Mind & Society* 2, no. 1 (2001): 101–28; J.M. Nolan, "Social Norms and Their Enforcement," in *The Oxford Handbook of Social Influence*, ed. S.G. Harkins, K.D. Williams, and J. Burger (New York: Oxford University Press, 2015); A. Diekmann and W. Przepiorka, "'Take One for the Team!' Individual Heterogeneity and the Emergence of Latent Norms in a Volunteer's Dilemma," *Social Forces* 94 (2016): 1309–33.

46. J.M. Nolan, "Social Norms and Their Enforcement," in *The Oxford Handbook of Social Influence*, ed. S.G. Harkins, K.D. Williams, and J. Burger (New York: Oxford University Press, 2015); B. Manata, "The Structural Effects of Team Density and Normative Standards on Team Member Performance," *Human Communication Research* 45 (2019): 309–33.

47. N. Ellemers and F. Rink, "Identity in Work Groups: The Beneficial and Detrimental Consequences of Multiple Identities and Group Norms for Collaboration and Group Performance," *Advances in Group Processes* 22 (2005): 1–41. For research on norm development and reinforcement in virtual teams, see K. Moser and C. Axtell, "The Role of Norms in Virtual Work: A Review and Agenda for Future Research," *Journal of Personnel Psychology* 12 (2013): 1–6.

48. S. Taggar and R. Ellis, "The Role of Leaders in Shaping Formal Team Norms," *Leadership Quarterly* 18, no. 2 (2007): 105–20; B.A. De Jong, K.M. Bijlsma-Frankema, and L.B. Cardinal, "Stronger Than the Sum of Its Parts? The Performance Implications of Peer Control Combinations in Teams," *Organization Science* 25, no. 6 (2014): 1703–21; A. Lieberman, K.E. Duke, and O. Amir, "How Incentive Framing Can Harness the Power of Social Norms," *Organizational Behavior and Human Decision Processes* 151 (2019): 118–31.

49. A.P. Hare, "Types of Roles in Small Groups: A Bit of History and a Current Perspective," *Small Group Research* 25 (1994): 443–48; A. Aritzeta, S. Swailes, and B. Senior, "Belbin's Team Role Model: Development, Validity and Applications for Team Building," *Journal of Management Studies* 44, no. 1 (2007): 96–118;

N. Lehmann-Willenbrock, S.J. Beck, and S. Kauffeld, "Emergent Team Roles in Organizational Meetings: Identifying Communication Patterns via Cluster Analysis," *Communication Studies* 67, no. 1 (2016): 37–57.

50. A.P. Hare, "Types of Roles in Small Groups: A Bit of History and a Current Perspective," *Small Group Research* 25 (1994): 443–48; A. Aritzeta, S. Swailes, and B. Senior, "Belbin's Team Role Model: Development, Validity and Applications for Team Building," *Journal of Management Studies* 44, no. 1 (2007): 96–118; J.E. Mathieu et al., "Team Role Experience and Orientation: A Measure and Tests of Construct Validity," *Group & Organization Management* 40 (2015): 6–34; N. Lehmann-Willenbrock, S.J. Beck, and S. Kauffeld, "Emergent Team Roles in Organizational Meetings: Identifying Communication Patterns Via Cluster Analysis," *Communication Studies* 67 (2016): 37–57; T. Driskell et al., "Team Roles: A Review and Integration," *Small Group Research* 48 (2017): 482–511.

51. D.J. Beal et al., "Cohesion and Performance in Groups: A Meta-Analytic Clarification of Construct Relations," *Journal of Applied Psychology* 88, no. 6 (2003): 989–1004. The definition of *social cohesion* is still being debated, such as its level of analysis. see: S. Drescher, G. Burlingame, and A. Fuhriman, "Cohesion: An Odyssey in Empirical Understanding," *Small Group Research* 43, no. 6 (2012): 662–89; X. Fonseca, S. Lukosch, and F. Brazier, "Social Cohesion Revisited: A New Definition and How to Characterize It," *Innovation: The European Journal of Social Science Research* 32, no. 2 (2019): 231–53.

52. R.M. Montoya, R.S. Horton, and J. Kirchner, "Is Actual Similarity Necessary for Attraction? A Meta-Analysis of Actual and Perceived Similarity," *Journal of Social and Personal Relationships* 25, no. 6 (2008): 889–922; S.T. Bell and S.G. Brown, "Selecting and Composing Cohesive Teams," in *Research on Managing Groups and Teams*, ed. E. Salas, W.B. Vessey, and A.X. Estrada, vol. 17 (Emerald Group Publishing Limited, 2015), 181–209.

53. D. van Knippenberg, C.K.W. De Dreu, and A.C. Homan, "Work Group Diversity and Group Performance: An Integrative Model and Research Agenda," *Journal of Applied Psychology* 89, no. 6 (2004): 1008–22; K.A. Jehn, G.B. Northcraft, and M.A. Neale, "Why Differences Make a Difference: A Field Study of Diversity, Conflict, and Performance in Workgroups," *Administrative Science Quarterly* 44, no. 4 (1999): 741–63. For evidence that diversity/similarity does not always influence cohesion, see S.S. Webber and L.M. Donahue, "Impact of Highly and Less Job-Related Diversity on Work Group Cohesion and Performance: A Meta-Analysis," *Journal of Management* 27, no. 2 (2001): 141–62.

54. E. Aronson and J. Mills, "The Effects of Severity of Initiation on Liking for a Group," *Journal of Abnormal and Social Psychology* 59 (1959): 177–81; J.E. Hautaluoma and R.S. Enge, "Early Socialization into a Work Group: Severity of Initiations Revisited," *Journal of Social Behavior & Personality* 6 (1991): 725–48.

55. B. Mullen and C. Copper, "The Relation between Group Cohesiveness and Performance: An Integration," *Psychological Bulletin* 115 (1994): 210–27; [illegible] and D.O. Egleston, "Norming and Performing: Using Microworlds to Understand the Relationship between Team Cohesiveness and Performance," *Journal of Applied Social Psychology* 38, no. 10 (2008): 2574–93; R. Wageman et al., *Senior Leadership Teams* (Boston: Harvard Business School Press, 2008): 69–70.

56. M. Rempel and R.J. Fisher, "Perceived Threat, Cohesion, and Group Problem Solving in Intergroup Conflict," *International Journal of Conflict Management* 8 (1997): 216–34; M.E. Turner and T. Horvitz, "The Dilemma of Threat: Group Effectiveness and Ineffectiveness under Adversity," in *Groups at Work: Theory and Research*, ed. M.E. Turner (Mahwah, NJ: Erlbaum, 2001), 445–70.

57. A.V. Carron et al., "Cohesion and Performance in Sport: A Meta-Analysis," *Journal of Sport and Exercise Psychology* 24 (2002): 168–88; D.J. Beal et al., "Cohesion and Performance in Groups: A Meta-Analytic Clarification of Construct Relations," *Journal of Applied Psychology* 88, no. 6 (2003): 989–1004; L.A. DeChurch and J.R. Mesmer-Magnus, "The Cognitive Underpinnings of Effective Teamwork: A Meta-Analysis," *Journal of Applied Psychology* 95, no. 1 (2010): 32–53; S.M. Gully, D.J. Devine, and D.J. Whitney, "A Meta-Analysis of Cohesion and Performance: Effects of Level of Analysis and Task Interdependence," *Small Group Research* 43, no. 6 (2012): 702–25.

58. W. Piper et al., "Cohesion as a Basic Bond in Groups," *Human Relations* 36 (1983): 93–108; S.Y. Shin and S.G. Lee, "Effects of Hospital Workers? Friendship Networks on Job Stress," *PLoS ONE* 11, no. 2 (2016): e0149428.

59. S.M. Gully, D.J. Devine, and D.J. Whitney, "A Meta-Analysis of Cohesion and Performance: Effects of Level of Analysis and Task Interdependence," *Small Group Research* 43, no. 6 (2012): 702–25.

60. C. Langfred, "Is Group Cohesiveness a Double-Edged Sword? An Investigation of the Effects of Cohesiveness on Performance," *Small Group Research* 29 (1998): 124–43; K.L. Gammage, A.V. Carron, and P.A. Estabrooks, "Team Cohesion and Individual Productivity: The Influence of the Norm for Productivity and the Identifiability of Individual Effort," *Small Group Research* 32 (2001): 3–18. Concerns about existing research on cohesion–performance are discussed in M. Casey-Campbell and M.L. Martens, "Sticking It All Together: A Critical Assessment of the Group Cohesion–Performance Literature," *International Journal of Management Reviews* 11, no. 2 (2009): 223–46.

61. J. Mathieu et al., "Modeling Reciprocal Team Cohesion-Performance Relationships, as Impacted by Shared Leadership and Members' Competence," *Journal of Applied Psychology* 100, no. 3 (2015): 713–34.

62. D.M. Rousseau et al., "Not So Different after All: A Cross-Discipline View of Trust," *Academy of Management Review* 23 (1998): 393–404; I. Yang, "What Makes an Effective Team? The Role of Trust (Dis)Confirmation in Team Development," *European Management Journal* 32 (2014): 858–69; A.C. Costa, C.A. Fulmer, and N.R. Anderson, "Trust in Work Teams: An Integrative Review, Multilevel Model, and Future Directions," *Journal of Organizational Behavior* 39 (2018): 169–84.

63. D.J. McAllister, "Affect- and Cognition-Based Trust as Foundations for Interpersonal Cooperation in Organizations," *Academy of Management Journal* 38, no. 1 (1995): 24–59; M. Williams, "In Whom We Trust: Group Membership as an Affective Context for Trust Development," *Academy of Management Review* 26, no. 3 (2001): 377–96; M. Pirson and D. Malhotra, "Foundations of Organizational Trust: What Matters to Different Stakeholders?" *Organization Science* 22, no. 4 (2011): 1087–104.

64. R.J. Lewicki, E.C. Tomlinson, and N. Gillespie, "Models of Interpersonal Trust Development: Theoretical Approaches, Empirical Evidence, and Future Directions," *Journal of Management* 32, no. 6 (2006): 991–1022.

65. R.J. Lewicki, E.C. Tomlinson, and N. Gillespie, "Models of Interpersonal Trust Development: Theoretical Approaches, Empirical Evidence, and Future Directions," *Journal of Management* 32 (2006): 991–1022; N. Zhao et al., "The Impact of Traditionality/Modernity on Identification- and Calculus-Based Trust," *International Journal of Psychology* 54 (2019): 237–46.

66. E.M. Whitener et al., "Managers as Initiators of Trust: An Exchange Relationship Framework for Understanding Managerial Trustworthy Behavior," *Academy of Management Review* 23 (1998): 513–30; T. Simons et al., "How Leader Alignment of Words and Deeds Affects Followers: A Meta-Analysis of Behavioral Integrity Research," *Journal of Business Ethics* 132 (2015): 831–44.

67. H. Akrout and M.F. Diallo, "Fundamental Transformations of Trust and Its Drivers: A Multi-Stage Approach of Business-to-Business Relationships," *Industrial Marketing Management* 66 (2017): 159–71; A.C. Costa, C.A. Fulmer, and N.R. Anderson, "Trust in Work Teams: An Integrative Review, Multilevel Model, and Future Directions," *Journal of Organizational Behavior* 39 (2018): 169–84.

68. C.B. Crisp and S.L. Jarvenpaa, "Swift Trust in Global Virtual Teams: Trusting Beliefs and Normative Actions," *Journal of Personnel Psychology* 12 (2013): 45–56; O. Schilke and L. Huang, "Worthy of Swift Trust? How Brief Interpersonal Contact Affects Trust Accuracy," *Journal of Applied Psychology* 103 (2018): 1181–97.

69. K.T. Dirks and D.L. Ferrin, "The Role of Trust in Organizations," *Organization Science* 12 (2004): 450–67; I. Yang, "What Makes an Effective Team? The Role of Trust (Dis)Confirmation in Team Development," *European Management Journal* 32 (2014): 858–69.

70. L.A. DeChurch and J.R. Mesmer-Magnus, "The Cognitive Underpinnings of Effective Teamwork: A Meta-Analysis," *Journal of Applied Psychology* 95 (2010): 32–53; C. Aubé, V. Rousseau, and S. Tremblay, "Perceived Shared Understanding in Teams: The Motivational Effect of Being 'on the Same Page,'" *British Journal of Psychology* 106 (2015): 468–86; J.M. Schmidtke and A. Cummings, "The Effects of Virtualness on Teamwork Behavioral Components: The Role of Shared Mental Models," *Human Resource Management Review* 27 (2017): 660–77.

71. R. Rico, M. Sánchez-Manzanares, and C. Gibson, "Team Implicit Coordination Processes: A Team Knowledge-Based Approach," *Academy of Management Review* 33 (2008): 163–84; J.C. Gorman, "Team Coordination and Dynamics: Two Central Issues," *Current Directions in Psychological Science* 23 (2014): 355–60; J. Schmutz et al., "Effective Coordination in Medical Emergency Teams: The Moderating Role of Task Type," *European Journal of Work and Organizational Psychology* 24 (2015): 761–76.

72. L. Argote, B.L. Aven, and J. Kush, "The Effects of Communication Networks and Turnover on Transactive Memory and Group Performance," *Organization Science* 29 (2018): 191–206.

73. C.A. Beatty and B.A. Barker, *Building Smart Teams: Roadmap to High Performance* (Thousand Oaks, CA: Sage, 2004); W.G. Dyer, J.H. Dyer, and W.G. Dyer, *Team Building: Proven Strategies for Improving Team Performance*, 5th ed. (San Francisco: Jossey-Bass, 2013); M.R. Beauchamp, D. McEwan, and K.J. Waldhauser, "Team Building: Conceptual, Methodological, and Applied Considerations," *Current Opinion in Psychology*, 16 (2017): 114–17; C.N. Lacerenza et al., "Team Development Interventions: Evidence-Based Approaches for Improving Teamwork," *American Psychologist* 73 (2018): 517–31.

74. J. Langan-Fox and J. Anglim, "Mental Models, Team Mental Models, and Performance: Process, Development, and Future Directions," *Human Factors and Ergonomics in Manufacturing* 14 (2004): 331–52; J.E. Mathieu et al., "Scaling the Quality of Teammates' Mental Models: Equifinality and Normative Comparisons," *Journal of Organizational Behavior* 26 (2005): 37–56.

75. D.R. Seibold and R.A. Meyers, "Interventions in Groups: Methods for Facilitating Team Development," in *Research Methods for Studying Groups and Teams: A Guide to Approaches, Tools, and Technologies*, ed. A. Hollingshead and M.S. Poole (New York: Routledge, 2012), 418–41; A. Hämmelmann and R. van Dick, "Building the Team: Effect on the Individual—An Evaluation of Team Building Interventions (Entwickeln Im Team—Effekte Für Den Einzelnen: Eine Evaluation Von Teamentwicklungsmaßnahmen)," *Gruppendynamik und Organisationsberatung* 44, no. 2 (2013): 221–38.

76. L.J. Martin, A.V. Carron, and S.M. Burke, "Team Building Interventions in Sport: A Meta-Analysis," *Sport & Exercise Psychology Journal* 5, no. 2 (2009): 3–18; C. Klein et al., "Does Team Building Work?" *Small Group Research* 40, no. 2 (2009): 181–222; I. Nadler, P.M. Sanderson, and H.G. Liley, "The Accuracy of Clinical Assessments as a Measure for Teamwork Effectiveness," *Simulation in Healthcare* 6, no. 5 (2011): 260–68; Y.J. Yi, "Effects of Team-Building on Communication and Teamwork among Nursing Students," *International Nursing Review* 63, no. 1 (2016): 33–40; C.N. Lacerenza et al., "Team Development Interventions: Evidence-Based Approaches for Improving Teamwork," *American Psychologist* 73 (2018): 517–31.

77. R.W. Woodman and J.J. Sherwood, "The Role of Team Development in Organizational Effectiveness: A Critical Review," *Psychological Bulletin* 88 (1980): 166–86; C.J. Miller et al., "A Systematic Review of Team-Building Interventions in Non-Acute Healthcare Settings," *BMC Health Services Research* 18, no. 1 (2018): 146.

78. S.A. Mohrman, S.G. Cohen, and A.M. Mohrman Jr., *Designing Team-Based Organizations: New Forms for Knowledge Work* (San Francisco: Jossey-Bass, 1995), 39–40; D.E. Yeatts and C. Hyten, *High-Performing Self-Managed Work Teams: A Comparison of Theory and Practice* (Thousand Oaks, CA: Sage, 1998); E.E. Lawler, *Organizing for High Performance* (San Francisco: Jossey-Bass, 2001); R.J. Torraco, "Work Design Theory: A Review and Critique with Implications for Human Resource Development," *Human Resource Development Quarterly* 16, no. 1 (2005): 85–109.

79. R. Deiser, "Part 5: Agility in Practice: The Swarm Organization at Daimler," *The Digital Transformation People* (blog), May 7, 2019; A. Howard, "Scrum@Scale at Bosch: Embracing Agility," *Scrum@Scale Case Study* (blog), September 2, 2020; E. Shein, "Cross-Functional Teams: The New IT Imperative," *CIO*, December 14, 2021.

80. A. Krause and H. Dunckel, "Work Design and Customer Satisfaction: Effects of the Implementation of Semi-Autonomous Group Work on Customer Satisfaction Considering Employee Satisfaction and Group Performance (translated abstract)," *Zeitschrift für Arbeits-und Organisationspsychologie* 47, no. 4 (2003): 182–93; G.L. Stewart, S.H. Courtright, and M.R. Barrick, "Peer-Based Control in Self-Managing Teams: Linking Rational and Normative Influence with Individual and Group Performance," *Journal of Applied Psychology* 97 (2012): 435–47; E.E.M. Maurits et al., "Home-Care Nursing Staff in Self-Directed Teams Are More Satisfied with Their Job and Feel They Have More Autonomy over Patient Care: A Nationwide Survey," *Journal of Advanced Nursing* 73 (2017): 2430–40.

81. J.L. Cordery et al., "The Impact of Autonomy and Task Uncertainty on Team Performance: A Longitudinal Field Study," *Journal of Organizational Behavior* 31 (2010): 240–58; N.C. Magpili and P. Pazos, "Self-Managing Team Performance: A Systematic Review of Multilevel Input Factors," *Small Group Research* 49 (2018): 3–33; M. Renkema, T. Bondarouk, and A. Bos-Nehles, "Transformation to Self-Managing Teams: Lessons Learned: A Look at Current Trends and Data," *Strategic HR Review* 17 (2018): 81–84.

82. E. Ulich and W.G. Weber, "Dimensions, Criteria, and Evaluation of Work Group Autonomy," in *Handbook of Work Group Psychology*, ed. M.A. West (Chichester, UK: Wiley, 1996), 247–82.

83. J. Lipnack and J. Stamps, *Virtual Teams: People Working across Boundaries with Technology* (New York: Wiley, 2001); J.H. Dulebohn and J.E. Hoch, "Virtual Teams in Organizations," *Human Resource Management Review* 27 (2017): 569–74. Some suggest that remote teams differ slightly from distributed teams, where the latter have no physical base location. However, we group them together because they overlap in terms of OB concepts and practices.

84. L. Schweitzer and L. Duxbury, "Conceptualizing and Measuring the Virtuality of Teams," *Information Systems Journal* 20, no. 3 (2010): 267–95; M.K. Foster et al., "Rethinking Virtuality and Its Impact on Teams," *Small Group Research* 46, no. 3 (2015): 267–99; J.M. Schaubroeck and A. Yu, "When Does Virtuality Help or Hinder Teams? Core Team Characteristics as Contingency Factors," *Human Resource Management Review* 27 (2017): 635–47.

85. L.L. Gilson et al., "Virtual Teams Research: 10 Years, 10 Themes, and 10 Opportunities," *Journal of Management* 41, no. 5 (2015): 1313–37.

86. L. Mandel, "Lessons from Leading a Remote Engineering Team," *Shopify Engineering* (blog), July 25, 2019; I. Dzhambazova, "Succeeding as a Remote Company: Lessons from Shopify," *Boundless* (blog), April 10, 2020; M. Elliot, "Scoop Our Strategies: Shopify's Remote Work Systems," *Shopify Partners* (blog), April 22, 2020; P. Wahba, "Shopify Believes Office Life No Longer Provides Competitive Edge," *Fortune*, May 20, 2022.

87. A. Ortiz de Guinea, J. Webster, and D.S. Staples, "A Meta-Analysis of the Consequences of Virtualness on Team Functioning," *Information & Management* 49, no. 6 (2012): 301–08; S. Morrison-Smith and J. Ruiz, "Challenges and Barriers in Virtual Teams: A Literature Review," *SN Applied Sciences* 2, no. 6 (2020): 1096; S.A. Newman and R.C. Ford, "Five Steps to Leading Your Team in the Virtual COVID-19 Workplace," *Organizational Dynamics* 50, no. 1 (2021): 100802.

88. L.L. Martins and M.C. Schilpzand, "Global Virtual Teams: Key Developments, Research Gaps, and Future Directions," *Research in Personnel and Human Resources Management* 30 (2011): 1–72; S. Krumm et al., "What Does It Take to Be a Virtual Team Player? The Knowledge, Skills, Abilities, and Other Characteristics Required in Virtual Teams," *Human Performance* 29, no. 2 (2016): 123–42; J.L. Gibbs, A. Sivunen, and M. Boyraz, "Investigating the Impacts of Team Type and Design on Virtual Team Processes," *Human Resource Management Review* 27 (2017): 590–603.

89. S.L. Marlow, C.N. Lacerenza, and E. Salas, "Communication in Virtual Teams: A Conceptual Framework and Research Agenda," *Human Resource Management Review* 27 (2017): 575–89; S.L. Marlow et al., "Does Team Communication Represent a One-Size-Fits-All Approach?: A Meta-Analysis of Team Communication and Performance," *Organizational Behavior and Human Decision Processes* 144 ([illegible]): [illegible]; L. Handke et al., "Teams, Time, and Technology: Variations of Media Use Over Project Phases," *Small Group Research* 50 (2019): 266–305; M. Hartner-Tiefenthaler et al., "Development and Validation of a Scale to Measure Team Communication Behaviors," *Frontiers in Psychology* 13 (December 8, 2022): 961732.

90. G.G. Harwood, "Design Principles for Successful Virtual Teams," in *The Handbook of High-Performance Virtual Teams: A Toolkit for Collaborating across Boundaries*, ed. J. Nemiro and M.M. Beyerlein (San Francisco: Jossey-Bass, 2008), 59–84; R. Haines, "Group Development in Virtual Teams: An Experimental Reexamination," *Computers in Human Behavior* 39 (2014): 213–22.

91. L. Dubé and D. Robey, "Surviving the Paradoxes of Virtual Teamwork," *Information Systems Journal* 19, no. 1 (2009): 3–30.

92. V.H. Vroom and A.G. Jago, *The New Leadership* (Englewood Cliffs, NJ: Prentice Hall, 1988), 28–29.

93. M. Diehl and W. Stroebe, "Productivity Loss in Idea-Generating Groups: Tracking Down the Blocking Effects," *Journal of Personality and Social Psychology* 61 (1991): 392–403; W. Stroebe, B.A. Nijstad, and E.F. Rietzschel, "Beyond Productivity Loss in Brainstorming Groups: The Evolution of a Question," in *Advances in Experimental Social Psychology*, ed. [illegible] (Academic Press, [illegible]), [illegible]; [illegible] Henningsen and [illegible] Henningsen, "Generating Ideas about the Uses of Brainstorming: Reconsidering the Losses and Gains of Brainstorming Groups Relative to Nominal Groups," *Southern Communication Journal* 78 (2013): 42–55.

94. P. Bordia, B.E. Irmer, and D. Abusah, "Differences in Sharing Knowledge Interpersonally and via Databases: The Role of Evaluation Apprehension and Perceived Benefits," *European Journal of Work and Organizational Psychology* 15, no. 3 (2006): 262–80; L. McGrath, "When Pairing Reduces Scaring: The Effect of Dyadic Ideation on Evaluation Apprehension," *International Journal of Innovation Management* 19, no. 04 (2015): 1550039.

95. D. Miller, *The Icarus Paradox: How Exceptional Companies Bring about Their Own Downfall* (New York: HarperBusiness, 1990); G. Whyte, "Recasting Janis's Groupthink Model: The Key Role of Collective Efficacy in Decision Fiascoes," *Organizational Behavior and Human Decision Processes* 73, no. 2–3 (1998): 185–209; K. Tasa and G. Whyte, "Collective Efficacy and Vigilant Problem Solving in Group Decision Making: A Non-Linear Model," *Organizational Behavior and Human Decision Processes* 96, no. 2 (2005): 119–29; T.L. Rapp et al., "The Role of Team Goal Monitoring in the Curvilinear Relationship between Team Efficacy and Team Performance," *Journal of Applied Psychology* 99 (2014): 976–87; W.-W. Park, M.S. Kim, and S.M. Gully, "Effect of Cohesion on the Curvilinear Relationship between Team Efficacy and Performance," *Small Group Research* 48 (2017): 455–81.

96. F.W. Nietzsche, *Beyond Good and Evil: Prelude to a Philosophy of the Future*, trans. H. Zimmern (London: G. Allen & Unwin, 1906), Chap. 4, statement 156.

97. A.C. Edmondson and Z. Lei, "Psychological Safety: The History, Renaissance, and Future of an Interpersonal Construct," *Annual Review of Organizational Psychology and Organizational Behavior* 1 (2014): 23–43; A. Newman, R. Donohue, and N. Eva, "Psychological Safety: A Systematic Review of the Literature," *Human Resource Management Review* 27 (2017): 521–35.

98. The term *brainstorm* dates back to a 1907 New York murder case during which an alienist (psychiatrist) gave expert testimony that the accused's temporary insanity was a "brainstorm." By the mid-1920s, the meaning of a brainstorm had shifted markedly to a state of creative thinking. Advertising executive Alex Osborn (the *O* in BBDO, a global advertising agency) first described the brainstorming process in the little-known 1942 booklet *How to Think Up* (p. 29). Osborn gave a fuller description of the brainstorming process in his popular 1948 (*Your Creative Power*) and 1953 (*Applied Imagination*) books. See A. F. Osborn, *How to Think Up* (New York: McGraw Hill, 1942), Chap. 4; A. F. Osborn, *Your Creative Power* (New York: Scribner's Sons, 1948); A. F. Osborn, *Applied Imagination* (New York: Scribner's Sons, 1953).

99. R.I. Sutton and A. Hargadon, "Brainstorming Groups in Context: Effectiveness in a Product Design Firm," *Administrative Science Quarterly* 41 (1996): 685–718; T. Kelley, *The Art of Innovation* (New York: Currency Doubleday, 2001); J.M. Levine et al., "Group Brainstorming: When Regulatory Nonfit Enhances Performance," *Group Processes & Intergroup Relations* 19, no. 2 (2016): 257–71; K.J. Levine, K.B. Heuett, and K.M. Reno, "Re-Operationalizing Established Groups in Brainstorming: Validating Osborn's Claims," *The Journal of Creative Behavior* 51, no. 3 (2017): 252–62; P.B. Paulus and J.B. Kenworthy, "Effective Brainstorming," in *The Oxford Handbook of Group Creativity and Innovation*, ed. P.B. Paulus and B.A. Nijstad (New York: Oxford University Press, 2019), 287–306.

100. P.A. Heslin, "Better Than Brainstorming? Potential Contextual Boundary Conditions to Brainwriting for Idea Generation in Organizations," *Journal of Occupational and Organizational Psychology* 82, no. 1 (2009): 129–45; N. Michinov, "Is Electronic Brainstorming or Brainwriting the Best Way to Improve Creative Performance in Groups? An Overlooked Comparison of Two Idea-Generation Techniques," *Journal of Applied Social Psychology* 42 (2012): E222–E243; M. Litcanu et al., "Brain-Writing Vs. Brainstorming Case Study For Power Engineering Education," *Procedia - Social and Behavioral Sciences* 191 (2015): 387–90.

101. R.B. Gallupe, L.M. Bastianutti, and W.H. Cooper, "Unblocking Brainstorms," *Journal of Applied Psychology* 76 (1991): 137–42; W.H. Cooper et al., "Some Liberating Effects of Anonymous Electronic Brainstorming," *Small Group Research* 29, no. 2 (1998): 147–78; J. Baruah and P.B. Paulus, "The Role of Time and Category Relatedness in Electronic Brainstorming," *Small Group Research* 47 (2016): 333–42; H. Al-Samarraie and S. Hurmuzan, "A Review of Brainstorming Techniques in Higher Education," *Thinking Skills and Creativity* 27 (2018): 78–91.

102. A.L. Delbecq, A.H. Van de Ven, and D.H. Gustafson, *Group Techniques for Program Planning: A Guide to Nominal Group and Delphi Processes* (Middleton, WI: Green Briar Press, 1986).

103. S. Frankel, "NGT + MDS: An Adaptation of the Nominal Group Technique for Ill-Structured Problems," *Journal of Applied Behavioral Science* 23 (1987): 543–51; H. Barki and A. Pinsonneault, "Small Group Brainstorming and Idea Quality: Is Electronic Brainstorming the Most Effective Approach?" *Small Group Research* 32, no. 2 (2001): 158–205; P.P. Lago et al., "Structuring Group Decision Making in a Web-Based Environment by Using the Nominal Group Technique," *Computers & Industrial Engineering* 52, no. 2 (2007): 277–95; D.M. Spencer, "Facilitating Public Participation in Tourism Planning on American Indian Reservations: A Case Study Involving the Nominal Group Technique," *Tourism Management* 31, no. 5 (2011): 684–90.

8 Communicating in Teams and Organizations

Learning Objectives

After reading this chapter, you should be able to:

LO8-1 Explain why communication is important in organizations and discuss four influences on effective communication encoding and decoding.

LO8-2 Compare and contrast the advantages and disadvantages of digital written communication channels, other verbal communication channels, and nonverbal communication.

LO8-3 Discuss the relevance of synchronicity, social presence, social acceptance, and media richness when choosing the preferred communication channel.

LO8-4 Discuss various barriers (noise) to effective communication, including cross-cultural and male-female differences in communication.

LO8-5 Explain how to get your message across more effectively and summarize the elements of active listening.

LO8-6 Summarize effective communication strategies in organizational hierarchies, and review the role and relevance of the organizational grapevine.

communication The process by which information is transmitted and understood between two or more people

CBI Health, Canada's largest provider of home care services, faced a major challenge. It wanted its 13,000 health care professionals and support staff across 250 locations to become a more unified organization with improved communication and a stronger corporate culture. Most staff identified with the clinic where they worked rather than with the overall organization. They also communicated mainly with coworkers within the clinic, which deprived people at other CBI Health locations of valuable knowledge and insights.

CBI Health's solution was to install an enterprise communication platform (in this case, Microsoft Teams). The technology exceeded expectations. Clinicians soon formed cross-Canada connections through text-based themed channels. CBI Health professionals regionally and nationally now discuss new techniques in "best practice days" video workshops, which are recorded as a resource in the company's digital library. The communication platform has also strengthened CBI Health's culture and staff perspective. "Before, our people felt that they worked for a clinic. Now, they work for an organization that gives them access to a rich palette of personal development and support resources," says CBI Health CEO Jon Hantho.[1]

We are experiencing the most significant and disruptive transformation of organizational communication in our lifetimes. Team channels, workflow and planners, video meetings, private chat, document repositories, and other methods barely existed a dozen years ago. As CBI Health discovered, digital communication offers significant potential for information sharing and social bonding. Equally important, employees use these emerging communication channels in their private lives and expect to have them available at work.

Communication refers to the process by which information is transmitted and *understood* between two or more people. We emphasize the word *understood* because communication is effective when the receiver accurately deciphers the sender's message. This chapter begins by discussing the importance of effective communication, outlining the communication process model, and discussing factors that improve communication coding and decoding. Next, we identify types of communication channels, including digital messaging and social media, followed by factors to consider when choosing the most appropriate communication channel. The chapter then examines ways to improve interpersonal communication. The latter part of this chapter looks at communication in organizational hierarchies and offers insight about the pervasive organizational grapevine.

LO8-1 Explain why communication is important in organizations and discuss four influences on effective communication encoding and decoding.

THE IMPORTANCE OF COMMUNICATION

Effective communication is vital to all organizations, so much so that no company could exist without it. The reason? Recall from Chapter 1 that organizations are defined as groups of people who work interdependently toward some purpose. People work interdependently only when they can communicate with one another. Organizations rely on a variety of coordinating mechanisms (see Chapter 12), but frequent, timely, and accurate communication remains the primary means through which employees and work units effectively synchronize their work.[2]

Along with its importance for coordinating work, communication is vital for effective decision making. Imagine the challenge of selecting the best alternative without any information about the decision context, the alternatives available, the likely outcomes of those options, or the extent to which the decision is achieving its objectives. Communication brings this information

> **An organization comes into being when there are persons able to communicate with each other.[3]**
>
> —Chester Barnard, pioneering OB scholar and telecommunications CEO

Effective communication is vital to all organizations because it is the primary means through which employees and work units synchronize their work.
Iam Anupong/Getty Images

from the external environment into the organization and distributes it so employees can solve problems and discover opportunities. For example, airline cockpit crews make much better decisions–and thereby cause far fewer accidents–when the captain encourages the crew to openly share information.[4]

A third function of communication is to change behavior.[5] When conveying information to others, we are often trying to alter their beliefs, feelings, and ultimately their actions. This influence process might be passive, such as by merely describing the situation more clearly and fully, or it might be a deliberate attempt to change someone's thoughts and emotions. We discuss the topic of persuasion later in this chapter.

A fourth function of communication is to support employee well-being.[6] Communication minimizes stress by conveying knowledge that helps employees better manage their work setting more effectively. For instance, research shows that new employees adjust much better to the organization when coworkers communicate subtle nuggets of wisdom, such as how to complete work procedures correctly, find useful resources, handle difficult customers, and avoid office politics.[7] Communication also minimizes stress emotionally; talking with others can be a soothing balm during difficult times. In essence, people have an inherent drive to bond, to validate their self-worth, and to maintain their social identity. Communication is the means through which these drives and needs are fulfilled.

A MODEL OF COMMUNICATION

The model presented in Exhibit 8.1 provides a useful "conduit" metaphor for thinking about the communication process.[8] According to this model, communication flows through one or more channels (also called *media*) between the sender and receiver. The sender forms a message and encodes it into words, gestures, voice intonations, and other symbols or signs. Next, the encoded message is transmitted to the intended receiver through

Exhibit 8.1 The Communication Process Model

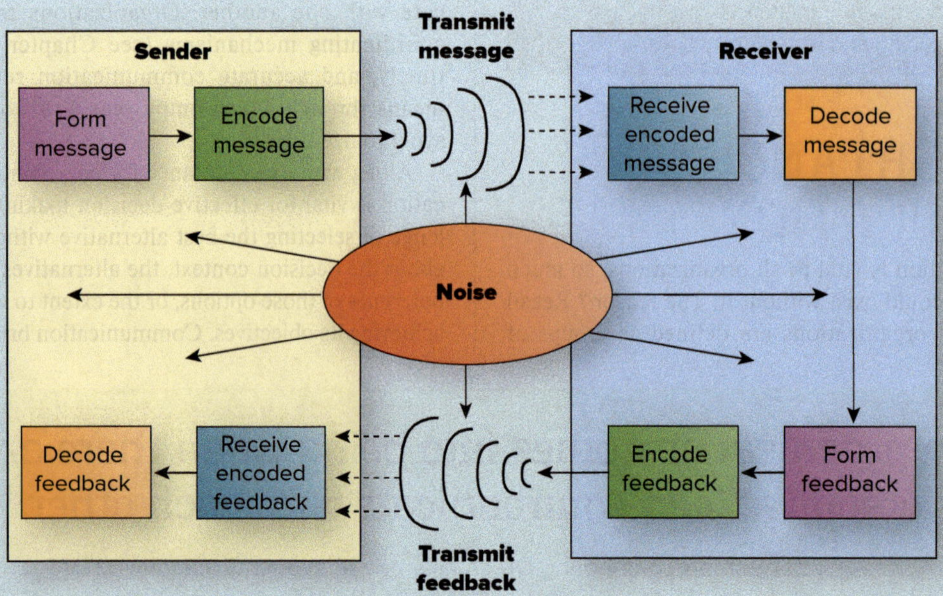

voice, text, nonverbal cues, or other channels. The receiver senses and decodes the incoming message into something meaningful. Ideally, the decoded meaning is what the sender had intended.

In most situations, the sender looks for evidence that the other person has received and understood the transmitted message. This feedback may involve the receiver repeating the message back to the sender or demonstrating awareness of the message indirectly through the receiver's subsequent actions. Notice that feedback repeats the communication process. Intended feedback is encoded, transmitted, received, and decoded from the receiver to the sender of the original message.

This model recognizes that communication is not a free-flowing conduit. Instead, the transmission of meaning from one person to another is hampered by *noise*—the psychological, social, and structural barriers that distort and obscure the sender's intended message. If any part of the communication process is distorted or broken, the sender and receiver will not have a common understanding of the message.

Influences on Effective Encoding and Decoding

According to the communication process model, effective communication depends on the sender's and receiver's ability, motivation, role clarity, and situational support (i.e., MARS model, see Chapter 1) to efficiently and accurately encode and decode information. Four main factors influence the effectiveness of this encoding-decoding process.[9]

- *Similar codebooks.* The sender and receiver encode and decode more effectively when they have similar "codebooks," which are dictionaries of symbols, language, gestures, idioms, and other tools used to convey information. With similar codebooks, the communication participants assign the same or similar meaning to the transmitted symbols and signs. Communication efficiency also improves because there is less need for redundancy (repeating the message in different ways) and less need for confirmation feedback ("So, you are saying that ... ?").
- *Sender's coding experience.* The encoding–decoding process improves with the sender's experience at transmitting a message. The more frequently the sender transmits a specific message, particularly to a similar audience, the more the sender learns which words, symbols, voice intonations, and other features transmit the message more clearly and persuasively to others.
- *Communication channel motivation and ability.* The encoding–decoding process is better when the sender and receiver are skilled and motivated to use the selected communication channel(s). Some people are better at face-to-face conversations, whereas others are more skilled at writing and receiving detailed reports. Even when the sender and receiver are able to communicate using a particular channel, they might misunderstand each other when one or both of them dislike using that channel and, consequently, lack the effort to communicate effectively.[10]
- *Shared mental models of the communication context.* A sender and receiver with shared mental models of the communication context have similar images and expectations regarding the communication context. These shared mental models potentially increase the accuracy of the message content and reduce the need for communication about that context.[11] For example, it is easier for two people to discuss events that occur in a national electricity market control center if both of them have detailed mental models of that control center. Notice that shared mental models of the communication context differs from a shared codebook. Codebooks are symbols used to convey message content, whereas mental models are knowledge structures of the communication topic setting.

With similar codebooks, the sender and receiver assign similar meaning to the transmitted symbols and signs, so there is less need for redundancy or confirmation feedback.
Jorg Greuel/Getty Images

OB THEORY TO PRACTICE

Encoding and Decoding More Effectively

The message is more likely to be received and understood when

- Both sender and receiver possess similar "codebooks" of symbols, language, gestures, and so on.
- The sender has experience encoding the specific message to a specific audience.
- Both sender and receiver have the ability and motivation to use the selected communication channel(s).
- Both sender and receiver have shared mental models of the communication context.

LO8-2 Compare and contrast the advantages and disadvantages of digital written communication channels, other verbal communication channels, and nonverbal communication.

COMMUNICATION CHANNELS

A central feature of the communication model is the channel or medium through which information is transmitted. There are two main types of channels: verbal and nonverbal. The distinction is that *verbal communication* uses words, so it includes both spoken and written channels. Spoken communication, particularly face-to-face interaction, tends to be better than written methods for transmitting emotions and persuading the receiver. This is because conversations are usually accompanied by a nonverbal channel as well as a paralanguage dimension, such as voice intonations, loudness, and silence. Also, most face-to-face spoken communication has the advantage of transmitting immediate feedback from the receiver, so the sender can adjust the message accordingly.

Written communication is more appropriate for recording, presenting, and retrieving technical details. Employees tend to have a higher comprehension of content when they receive it in writing rather than in a spoken conversation. Traditionally, written communication has been much slower than spoken communication at transmitting messages, but text chats and other digital channels have significantly improved written communication efficiency.

Nonverbal Communication

Nonverbal communication is any type of communication that does not use words.[12] It includes facial gestures, voice intonation, physical distance, and even silence. Images, diagrams, and other wordless documents are also categorized as nonverbal communication.

Nonverbal communication is helpful where noise or physical distance prevent effective verbal exchanges, and the need for immediate feedback precludes written communication. But even in quiet face-to-face meetings, nonverbal communication is immensely important for most information exchanges. In fact, in traditional face-to-face conversations, more information tends to be transmitted nonverbally than verbally. Rather like a parallel conversation, nonverbal cues are subtle signals that amplify the verbal message, add emotional meaning to the message, and influence the relationship between the parties. For example, nonverbal communication reinforces the person's interest in the verbal conversation and signals relative status in the relationship.[13]

Unfortunately, we often transmit messages nonverbally without being aware of this communication. To illustrate, Exhibit 8.2 identifies the top eight nonverbal behaviors of job interviewers that job applicants find disconcerting and uncomfortable. Job interviewers are usually unaware that their body language is conveying wrong messages, yet this nonverbal miscommunication deters candidates from accepting a job offer.

Nonverbal communication is less rule-bound than verbal communication. We receive considerable formal training on how to understand and transmit spoken words but very little on how to understand and use the nonverbal signals that accompany those words. Consequently, nonverbal cues are generally more ambiguous and susceptible to misinterpretation. Not all nonverbal communication is ambiguous, however. Some facial expressions (such as smiling) are hardwired and universal, thereby providing somewhat more reliable means of communicating across cultures.

Exhibit 8.2 Body Language Miscommunication by Job Interviewers[14]

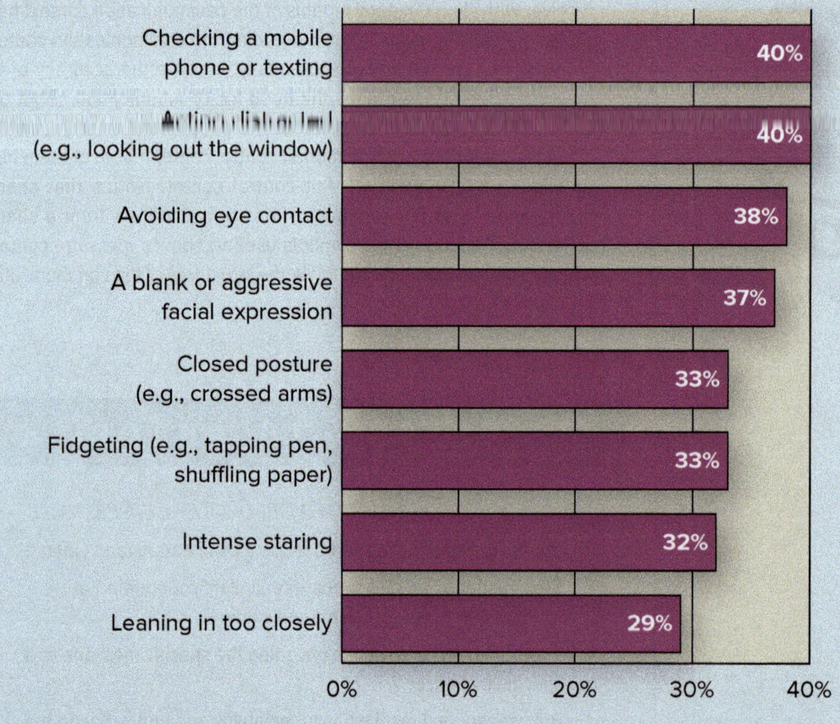

Note: Percentage of 1,000 UK employees surveyed who identified each of these nonverbal behaviors as off-putting body language mistakes by job interviewers during hiring interviews.

> **The most important thing in communication is hearing what isn't said.[15]**
>
> —Peter Drucker, scholar, consultant, "father" of management theory

The other difference between nonverbal and verbal communication is that the latter is typically intentional and conscious, whereas most nonverbal communication is automatic and nonconscious. We normally plan the words we say or write, but we rarely plan every blink, smile, or other gesture during a conversation. Indeed, as we just mentioned, many of these facial expressions communicate the same meaning across cultures because they are hardwired, nonconscious responses to human emotions. For example, pleasant emotions cause the brain center to widen the mouth, whereas negative emotions produce constricted facial expressions (squinting eyes, pursed lips, etc.).

Emotional Contagion One of the most fascinating aspects of nonverbal communication is **emotional contagion,** which is the automatic process of "catching" or sharing another person's emotions by mimicking that person's facial expressions and other nonverbal behavior. Technically, human beings have brain receptors that cause them to mirror what they observe. In other words, to some degree our brain causes us to act as though we are the person we are watching.[16]

Consider what happens when you see a book suddenly fall from a shelf onto a coworker's head. Chances are, you wince and put your hand on your own head as if you had been hit by the falling book. Similarly, while listening to someone describe a positive event, you tend to smile and exhibit other emotional displays of happiness. While some of our nonverbal communication is planned, emotional contagion represents nonconscious behavior—we automatically mimic and synchronize our nonverbal behaviors with other people.[17]

Emotional contagion influences communication and social relationships in three ways.[18] First, mimicry provides continuous feedback, communicating that we understand and empathize with the sender. To consider the significance of this, imagine employees remaining expressionless after watching a book fall on a coworker's head! The lack of parallel behavior conveys an absence of understanding or caring. A second function is that we have a stronger emotional experience by mimicking the nonverbal behaviors relating to the event that someone is describing to us. If a coworker is angry with a client, our tendency to frown and show anger while listening helps us to experience that emotion more fully.

The third function of emotional contagion is to fulfill the drive to bond that we mentioned earlier in this chapter and introduced in Chapter 5. Emotional contagion generates a communal experience because those participating in the communication event witness others sharing the same emotions that they feel. This strengthens relations among team members as well as between leaders and followers by providing evidence of their similarity.

emotional contagion
The nonconscious process of "catching" or sharing another person's emotions by mimicking that person's facial expressions and other nonverbal behavior

Digital Verbal Communication

Team channels, collaborative whiteboards, video meetings, workflows, private chat, and other digital communication channels barely existed in the workplace a dozen years ago, whereas many organizations now embed them in enterprise communication platforms. Email has dominated the corporate landscape, but it is rapidly waning for internal discussions. Generation Z employees—those born after 1996—have always preferred digital text messaging rather than email in the workplace.[19]

Exhibit 8.3 shows estimated digital communication usage among knowledge workers in the United States in recent years.[20] A decade ago, almost 75 percent of work-related digital communication time involved preparing, reading, and sending email. Today, digital text messages have approximately equal time usage as emails. This transition accelerated as the COVID-19 pandemic triggered a massive shift to digital communication platforms (Slack, Teams, Workplace, etc.) that rely on text-based team channels and private chat rather than email. In many organizations today, email is used mostly for external correspondence. For instance, one small annual survey of knowledge workers recently reported that email and digital text channels each represent about 30 percent of communication with coworkers, whereas email represents 62 percent and digital texting is only 11 percent of communication with clients.[21]

Video chats and meetings now represent a larger percentage of time in workplace digital communication than a decade ago. This channel's usage increased slowly a few years ago, but soared during the pandemic as a replacement for face-to-face meetings. Zoom meeting minutes increased 3,000 percent, and Zoom's business customers increased tenfold during the pandemic. Voice-only communication was on a downward trend earlier in the past decade and remains low today. Other digital communication methods (calendars, whiteboards, project management tools) have increased only slightly, possibly because they are less time intensive.

Exhibit 8.3 Use of Digital Communication Channels[22]

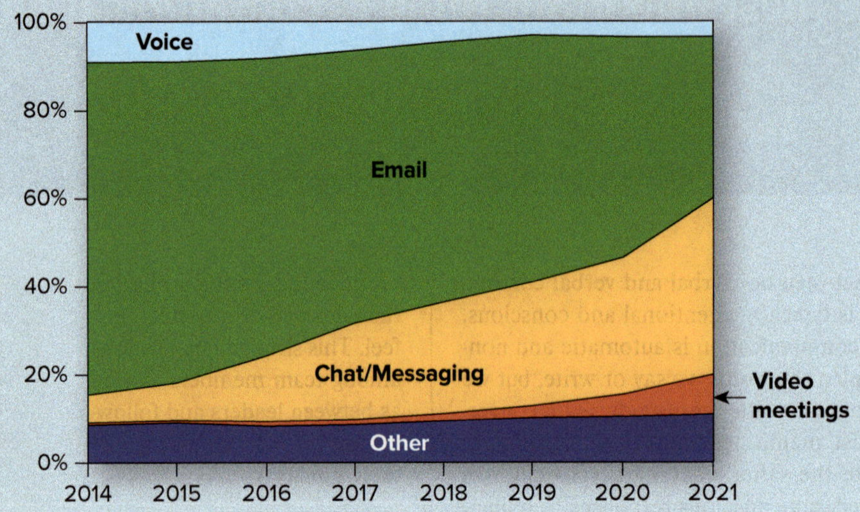

As you can see, the COVID-19 pandemic significantly shifted digital communication patterns in organizations. However, two other factors also influenced these changes beginning a few years before the pandemic. One of these is generational differences in communication preferences. Younger employees grew up in the era of mobile (cell) phones, so text messaging and other emerging digital text-based communication channels are already embedded in their lives. The other reason is that Slack, Microsoft Teams, Workplace, and other enterprise-grade communication platforms became available throughout the past decade. In fact, many of these products didn't exist in 2014! Enterprise communication platforms mainly rely on team channels (threads of text messages) and chat, not email, as the core communication channels.

Benefits of Digital Written Communication Team channel messages, private chat, and emails are the first choice for coordinating work and transmitting well-defined information. They can be written, edited, appended, and transmitted quickly to many people. Most messages can be sent and received at different times (they are asynchronous), so coordination is less important for message transmission. Furthermore, digital communication platforms and email software include search engines, which makes these channels convenient filing cabinets.[23]

Communication patterns changed significantly when email entered the workplace, and these changes will likely continue as other digital written channels become more popular. Specifically, digital written communication reduces face-to-face interactions and traditional phone calls but increases communication with people further up the hierarchy.[24] Digital channels also reduce social and organizational status differences between sender and receiver, mainly because they provide fewer cues of these differences than is evident in face-to-face interaction. However, status differences still exist to some extent, such as when managers reply less quickly and with shorter messages.[25]

Problems with Digital Written Communication

Digital written channels dominate organizational communication, but they have several limitations. Here are the top four complaints.

- *Faulty communication of emotions.* People consistently and significantly overestimate the degree to which they understand the emotional meaning of digital messages. The problem is that we rely on facial expressions and other nonverbal cues to interpret the emotional meaning of words, whereas digital text-based communication lacks this parallel channel.

> Text messages are almost as common as emails at work because younger employees prefer this channel and it is a central component of enterprise communication platforms.

People consistently and significantly overestimate the degree to which they understand the emotional meaning of digital messages.
ESB Professional/Shutterstock

Expressive language ("Wonderful to hear from you!") and emojis provide some substitution for the lack of nonverbal channels, but they also have limitations and flaws.[26]

- *Less politeness and respectfulness.* Digital messages are often less diplomatic than written letters and visual interactions. This cyberbullying tendency occurs because digital media are more impersonal (less social presence) than most other communication channels, which reduces the sender's empathy and sensitivity when crafting the message. A second reason is that digital messages can be written and transmitted before the sender's emotions subside. Receivers are also partly to blame because, on average, they infer a less respectful interpretation of the digital message than was intended by the sender.[27]
- *Inefficient for ambiguous, complex, and novel situations.* Digital messages are incredibly efficient for well-defined situations, such as giving basic instructions for a routine activity or arranging a video meeting. But in ambiguous, complex, and novel situations, digital written communication lacks the ability to transmit large volumes of information with rapid feedback. In other words, when the issue gets messy, stop texting or emailing and start talking, preferably face-to-face.
- *Contributes to information overload.* Digital messages contribute to information overload.[28] More than 330 billion business and consumer emails are sent and received every day. As for text messages, 100 billion are sent through WhatsApp every day; Slack reports that its users post 300,000 messages every second in team channels and private chats.[29] One of the most frequently mentioned drawbacks with enterprise communication platforms is the overwhelming number of messages created in team channels.

Social Media in the Workplace

Not long ago, most organizational communication pushed messages one-way from the content creator (sender) to the audience. For instance, memos, corporate intranet web pages, policy guidelines, paper-based company magazines, and video clips transmitted from the CEO provide little or no opportunity for recipients to respond, append, revise, or make any other collaborative contribution to the original message. Even email tends to be a one-way exchange, such as when the CEO emails corporate news to employees.

social media Digital communication channels that enable people to collaborate in the creation and exchange of user-generated content

Today, workplace communication has shifted toward social media. **Social media** refers to digital communication channels that enable people to collaborate in the creation and exchange of user-generated content. User-generated content exists when audience members (users) are partly or completely responsible for the creation or amendment of the content.[30] Social media are called "social" because user-generated content creation is a reciprocally interactive social process.

Most social media activity within organizations initially occurred through Facebook, Twitter, and other public platforms, often without the company's formal approval. These public platforms are mostly being replaced by enterprise communication platforms (Microsoft Teams, Slack, Workplace, etc.), all of which rely heavily on structured channels for team messages and private text messaging. They also include shared file space, collaborative document editing, media sharing, team video calls, and shared task scheduling. Almost all of these forms of communication are social media.

This chapter began by describing how CBI Health benefited from the introduction of an enterprise communication platform, which resulted in improved information sharing, team collaboration, social bonding, and identification with the organization. These functions and benefits are largely due to the social media characteristics of these platforms.[31]

Digital Nonverbal Communication

Digital text messages alone do not replace face-to-face communication, partly because they lack an inherent nonverbal channel. Consequently, users are supplementing their written content by manually inserting various forms of digital nonverbal communication, particularly emoticons, emojis, and animated GIFs.[32] Emoticons are keyboard symbols or letters combined to look like a face or object. More common today are emojis—small images depicting faces, animals, or objects, which are intended to have conceptual and emotional meaning.

GIFs are short video clips, often depicting a person's (or animal's) emotional response, such as cheering, showing frustration, or working quickly. These are typically visually engaging by being humorous or having sudden action. Most are symbolic representations of how the sender would act if they were in-person with the message recipient.[33]

Emoji Benefits and Risks in Workplace Communication

Emojis serve three main functions to improve digital written communication.[34] First, they transmit rich emotional meaning that is either too subtle or ambiguous in text-only messages. Research indicates that emoji faces generate similar emotional responses as in-person faces. Most emojis have a positive valence, so they tend to produce more positive than negative emotions in the interpersonal exchange. In one recent large global survey, more than half of emoji users said they were more comfortable expressing emotions through emojis in text messages than in phone and in-person conversations.

synchronicity The extent to which the channel requires or allows both sender and receiver to be actively involved in the conversation at the same time (synchronous) or at different times (asynchronous)

social presence The extent to which a communication channel creates psychological closeness to others, awareness of their humanness, and appreciation of the interpersonal relationship

A second benefit of emojis is that they symbolize ideas or objects, thereby strengthening or clarifying the meaning of the written text. Studies have found that viewers interpret the meaning of emojis more quickly than they interpret the text message. Some messages are sent only with emojis, conveying both a message and an emotion. A third function of emojis is to improve interpersonal relations. In many settings, recipients tend to feel a closer social presence when the message includes positive emojis. These images also symbolize personal characteristics of the sender, such as being thoughtful, humorous, or cool.

In spite of these benefits, emojis should be used cautiously in workplace communication.[35] One problem is that some coworkers disapprove of emoji-laden messages in some or all work settings. Senders who include a standard emoji in a basic descriptive text message (such as instructions about a meeting) may be viewed as less professional, less motivated, and less committed. Emojis are also considered less useful and less appropriate when sent to people in socially distant rather than close relationships, as well as to people in higher status positions.

Even when both parties approve of emojis in the workplace, there is a good chance that they have different codebooks to interpret those images. Studies report that most people misinterpret the meaning of many of the 10 most popular emojis. There are more than 3,600 registered emojis and multitudes more on some message apps and platforms, so misinterpretations are common. Most emoji users believe these nonverbal icons are ideal for communicating across languages and cultures, yet emoji misinterpretations are even more likely across cultures. For example, a waving hand means a friendly goodbye or hello in many countries. But in China, this symbol usually means that we aren't friends anymore, either in a teasing or serious tone.

OB THEORY TO PRACTICE

Benefits and Risks of Emojis in Workplace Communication

Emojis serve three useful functions in workplace communication:

- Emojis usually transmit rich emotional meaning that tends to be too subtle or ambiguous in text-only messages.
- Emojis symbolize ideas or objects, thereby strengthening or clarifying the meaning of the written text.
- Emojis improve interpersonal relations by symbolizing the sender's personal characteristics and thereby generating more social presence.

Risks of using emojis in workplace communication:

- Social acceptance of emojis at work varies with demographic groups, sender–receiver status differences, and message content.
- Even the most popular emojis are misinterpreted by recipients (i.e., sender and receivers have different emoji codebooks).
- Emojis are even more likely to be misinterpreted when communicating with people in other cultures.

LO8-3 Discuss the relevance of synchronicity, social presence, social acceptance, and media richness when choosing the preferred communication channel.

CHOOSING THE BEST COMMUNICATION CHANNEL

Employees have more communication channels to choose from than ever before, ranging from colocated and digital forms of face-to-face interaction to a multitude of ways to transmit written messages. Which communication channel is most appropriate in a particular situation? There are many factors to consider, but the four most important are summarized in Exhibit 8.4 and described in this section.

Synchronicity

Communication channels vary in their **synchronicity**, that is, the extent to which they require or allow both sender and receiver to be actively involved in the conversation at the same time.[36] Face-to-face conversations are almost always synchronous, whereas most digital text communication can occur with each party participating at different times (asynchronous). Team channel messages can be asynchronous, but some text-based chat interactions are so responsive that they become synchronous conversations. Synchronous communication is preferred when the information is required quickly (high immediacy) or where the issue is complex and therefore requires the parties to address several related decisions. Asynchronous communication is better when the issue is simple, the issue has low time urgency, getting both parties together at the same time is costly, and/or the receiver would benefit from time to reflect on the message before responding.

Social Presence

Social presence refers to how much the communication channel creates psychological closeness to others, awareness that there is another human being (or several others) in the conversation, and appreciation of the interpersonal relationship.[37]

Exhibit 8.4 Factors in Choosing the Best Communication Channel

Channel Choice Factor	Description	Depends on . . .
Synchronicity	The channel requires or allows the sender and receiver to communicate with each other at the same time (synchronous) or at different times (asynchronous).	• Time urgency (immediacy) • Complexity of the topic • Cost of both parties communicating at the same time • Whether receiver should have time to reflect before responding
Social presence	The channel creates psychological closeness to others, awareness of their humanness, and appreciation of the interpersonal relationship.	• Need to empathize with others • Need to influence others
Social acceptance	The channel is approved and supported by others (receiver, team, organization, or society).	• Organizational, team, and cultural norms • Each party's preferences and skills with the channel • Symbolic meaning of the channel
Media richness	The channel has high data-carrying capacity—the volume and variety of information that can be transmitted during a specific time.	• Situation is nonroutine • Situation is ambiguous

Face-to-face interactions almost always have the highest social presence, whereas low social presence would typically occur when uploading a document that anyone in the organization can retrieve. Social presence is usually stronger in synchronous communication because the receiver immediately responds to our messages, which increase the sense of connectedness with that person. Although social presence is affected mostly by specific channel characteristics, message content also plays a role. For example, social presence is higher when the sender's message style is casual rather than formal and when the message describes personal information about the sender.

A communication channel is valued for its social presence effect when the purpose of the dialogue is to understand and empathize with the other person or group. People are also more willing to listen and help others when there is a degree of interpersonal relationship or feeling of human connectedness. Therefore, channels with high social presence are better when the sender wants to influence the receiver.[38]

OB THEORY TO PRACTICE

Canceling Meetings and Going Async[39]

Shopify employees returned from their December holiday break to discover that the e-commerce technology giant had canceled all scheduled video and face-to-face meetings over the next two weeks (involving three or more coworkers, not clients). Also, the company now prohibits meetings on Wednesdays and allows large meetings only on Thursdays. Shopifolks (employees) now need to communicate more through asynchronous channels than through synchronous meetings.

Workplace communication has changed rapidly over the past decade, and companies are still learning which channels are the most effective for employees to get work done. Shopify and many other companies are concluding that less synchronous and more asynchronous communication would improve productivity, reduce "Zoom fatigue," and involve more employees across multiple time zones.

Several firms are weaning employees off of synchronous meetings through "Async Weeks," during which meetings are completely prohibited. Employee feedback from Salesforce's first Async Week was so positive that the software company has since arranged several more of them. "When you can't jump in a meeting or on a video call to sort something out, you start getting creative with communication," notes Salesforce Marketing Vice President Renata Bertram. "And once you start getting comfortable with those options, you're better equipped to know when a meeting is necessary and when it really isn't."

NicoElNino/Shutterstock

media richness A medium's data-carrying capacity—that is, the volume and variety of information that can be transmitted during a specific time

A communication channel is valued for its social presence effect when the purpose of the dialogue is to understand and empathize with the other person or group.
Larry Williams/LWA/Blend Images LLC

Social Acceptance

Social acceptance refers to how well the communication medium is approved and supported by coworkers, teams, the organization, and society.[40] One social acceptance factor is the norms held by others involved in the communication event. Norms explain why face-to-face meetings are daily events among staff in some firms, whereas text messaging is the medium of choice in other organizations. National culture also influences preferences for specific communication channels.[41] For instance, emojis populate more business emails and text messages in China than in the United States, likely because people in China prefer conveying emotions indirectly rather than directly (in words) and because they value the complex, ambiguous, and cute symbolism of emojis.[42]

A second social acceptance factor is the sender's and receiver's preferences for specific communication channels.[43] You may have noticed that some coworkers ignore (or rarely check) voicemail, yet they quickly respond to text messages. These preferences are due to the individual's personality, values, experience, and previous success with some channels more than others.

A third social acceptance factor is the symbolic meaning of a channel.[44] Many years ago, communications scholar Marshall McLuhan wrote: "The medium is the message." This famous statement has multiple meanings, including the notion that an emerging communication channel (medium) shapes society. However, the statement also refers to the notion that the channel selected communicates a message beyond the content sent through that channel. Some communication channels are viewed as impersonal whereas others are more personal; some are considered professional whereas others are casual; some are seen as "cool" whereas others are old-fashioned. For instance, phone calls and other synchronous communication channels convey a greater sense of urgency than do text messages and other asynchronous channels.

Media Richness

Media richness refers to the communication channel's data-carrying capacity—the volume and variety of information that can be transmitted during a specific time.[45] Exhibit 8.5 illustrates various communication channels arranged in a hierarchy of richness, with face-to-face interaction at the top and lean data-only reports at the bottom. A communication channel has high richness when it is able to convey multiple cues (such as both verbal and nonverbal information), allows timely feedback from receiver to sender, allows the sender to customize the message to the receiver, and makes use of complex symbols (such as words and phrases with multiple meanings).

Face-to-face communication has very high media richness because it allows us to communicate both verbally and nonverbally at the same time, to get feedback almost immediately from the receiver, to quickly adjust our message and style, and to use complex language such as metaphors and idioms (e.g., "spilling the beans"). For example, many hospital teams have brief stand-up daily huddles during which participants share information and expectations about the day's work.[46] Rich media tend to be synchronous and have high social presence.

Rich media are better than lean media when the communication situation is nonroutine and ambiguous.[47] Under these conditions, the sender and receiver need to transmit a large volume of information with immediate feedback so they can understand the situation and agree on the best way to coordinate. Lean media work well in routine situations because the sender and receiver have shared mental models to understand the situation and determine how to coordinate their work. Using a rich medium—such as holding a special meeting—when the situation is routine and clear would be a waste of time.

Exceptions to the Media Richness Theory Research generally supports media richness theory for traditional channels (face-to-face, written memos, etc.). However, the model doesn't fit reality nearly as well when digital communication channels are studied.[48] Three factors seem to explain why digital channels may have more media richness than media richness theory proposes:

- *Ability to multicommunicate.* It is usually difficult (as well as rude) to communicate face-to-face with someone while transmitting messages to another person using another channel. Most digital communication channels, on the other hand, require less social etiquette and attention, so employees can easily engage in two or more communication events

Exhibit 8.5 Media Richness Hierarchy

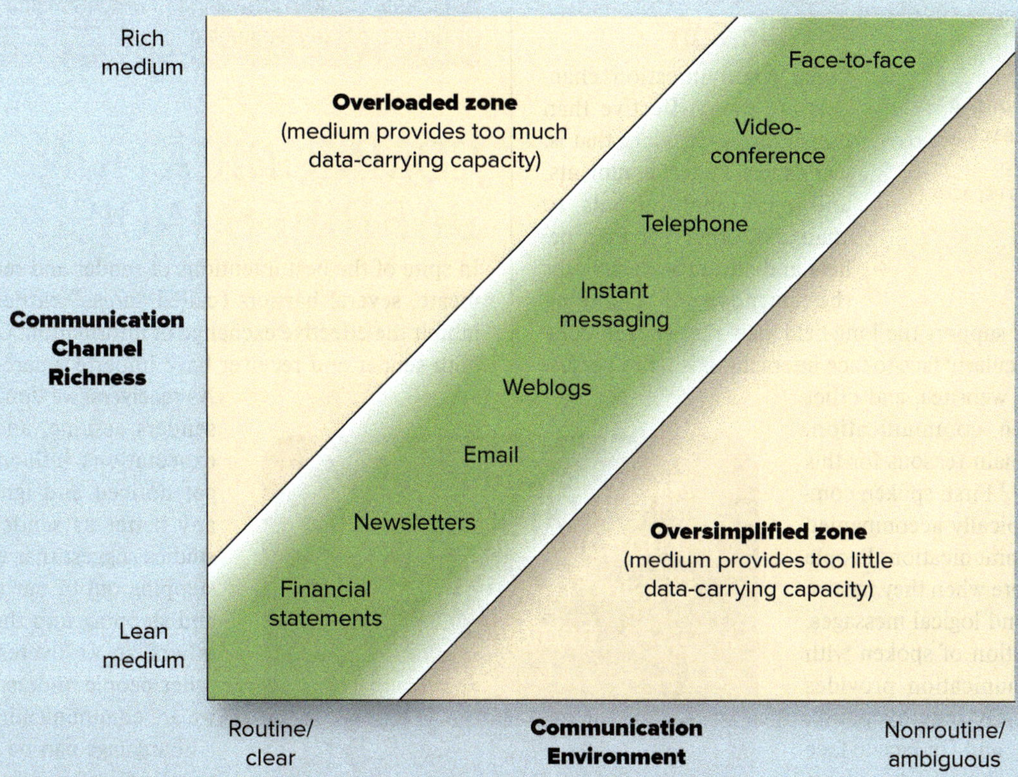

Sources: Based on R.L. Daft and R.H. Lengel, "Information Richness: A New Approach to Managerial Behavior and Organization Design," *Research in Organizational Behavior* 6 (1984): 199; R.H. Lengel and R.L. Daft, "The Selection of Communication Media as an Executive Skill," *Academy of Management Executive* 2, no. 3 (August 1988): 226.

at the same time. In other words, they can multicommunicate.[49] For example, people routinely scan web pages while talking to someone on the phone. Research consistently finds that people multitask less efficiently than they assume,[50] but the volume of information transmitted simultaneously through two digital communication channels is sometimes greater than through one high media richness channel.

- *Communication proficiency.* Earlier in this chapter we explained that communication effectiveness is partially determined by the sender's ability and motivation to use the selected communication channel. People with higher proficiency can "push" more information through the channel. Experienced mobile/cell phone users, for instance, can whip through messages in a flash, whereas new users struggle to type and search through these text transmissions. In contrast, the ability to communicate through casual conversation and other natural channels is less varied, because most of us develop good levels of proficiency throughout life and possibly through hardwired evolutionary development.[51]
- *Social presence effects.* Channels with high media richness, such as face-to-face conversations, tend to have more social presence. This improves empathy, but it also sensitizes both parties to their relative status and self-presentation, which can distort or divert attention away from the message.[52] During a personal meeting with the company's CEO, you might concentrate more on your image than on what the executive is saying to you. In other words, the benefits of high media richness channels may be offset by more social presence distractions, whereas lean media have much less social presence to distract or distort the transmitted information.

Digital channels have more media richness than the theory predicts possibly because there is considerable variation in the proficiency with which people can "push" information through these types of channels.
ra2studio/Shutterstock

persuasion The use of facts, logical arguments, and emotional appeals to change another person's beliefs and attitudes, usually for the purpose of changing the person's behavior

information overload A condition in which the volume of information received exceeds the person's capacity to process it

Communication Channels and Persuasion

Some communication channels are more effective than others for **persuasion**; that is, using facts, logical arguments, and emotional appeals to change another person's beliefs and attitudes, usually for the purpose of changing behavior. Studies support the long-held view that spoken communication, particularly face-to-face interaction, is more persuasive than emails, websites, and other forms of written communication. There are three main reasons for this persuasive effect.[53] First, spoken communication is typically accompanied by nonverbal communication. People are persuaded more when they receive both emotional and logical messages, and the combination of spoken with nonverbal communication provides this dual punch. A lengthy pause, raised voice tone, and (in face-to-face interaction) animated hand gestures can amplify the emotional tone of the message, thereby signaling the vitality of the issue.

A second reason why conversations are more persuasive is that spoken communication offers the sender high-quality immediate feedback about whether the receiver understands and accepts the message (i.e., is being persuaded). This feedback allows the sender to adjust the content and emotional tone of the message more quickly than with written communication. A third reason is that people are persuaded more under conditions of high social presence than low social presence. Listeners have higher motivation to pay attention and consider the sender's ideas in face-to-face conversations (high social presence). In contrast, persuasive communication through a website, text message, and other low social presence channels are less effective due to the higher degree of anonymity and psychological distance from the persuader.

Although spoken communication tends to be more persuasive, written communication also can persuade others to some extent. Written messages have the advantage of presenting more technical detail than can occur through conversation. This factual information is valuable when the issue is important to the receiver. Also, people experience a moderate degree of social presence in written communication with friends and coworkers, so written messages can be persuasive when sent and received with close associates. Furthermore, emojis and animated gifs provide some degree of parallel nonverbal communication, which increases persuasiveness by amplifying the emotional dimension of the written message.

LO8-4 Discuss various barriers (noise) to effective communication, including cross-cultural and male-female differences in communication.

COMMUNICATION BARRIERS (NOISE)

In spite of the best intentions of sender and receiver to communicate, several barriers (called "noise" earlier in Exhibit 8.1) inhibit the effective exchange of information. One barrier is that both sender and receiver have imperfect perceptual processes. As receivers, we don't listen as well as senders assume, and our needs and expectations influence what signals get noticed and ignored. We aren't any better as senders, either. Some studies suggest that we have difficulty stepping out of our own perspectives and stepping into the perspectives of others, so we overestimate how well other people understand the message we are communicating.[54]

> The greatest barrier to communication is the illusion that it has been achieved.[55]
>
> —adapted from William H. Whyte (journalist and sociologist)

Language can be a huge source of communication noise because sender and receiver seldom have identical codebooks. They might struggle to communicate in a language that neither of them has mastered, or they might come from cultures that assign different meanings for specific words and phrases. The English language (among others) also has built-in ambiguities that cause misunderstandings. Consider the phrase "Can you close the door?" You might assume the sender is asking whether shutting the door is permitted. However, the question might be asking whether you are physically able to shut the door, or possibly whether the door is designed such that it can be shut. In fact, this question might not be a question at all; the person could be politely *telling* you to shut the door.[56]

The ambiguity of language isn't always dysfunctional noise, however.[57] At times, leaders purposively use obscure language to reflect the ambiguity of the topic or to avoid unwanted emotional responses produced from more specific words. They might use metaphors to represent an abstract vision of the company's future, or use obtuse phrases such as "rightsizing" and "restructuring" to obscure the underlying message that people would be fired or laid off. Studies report that effective communicators also use more abstract words and symbols when addressing diverse or socially distant audiences, because abstraction increases the likelihood that the message is understood across a broader range of listeners.

Jargon—specialized words and phrases for specific occupations or groups—potentially improves communication efficiency. However, it is a source of communication noise when transmitted to people who do not possess the jargon codebook. This problem was apparent in one recent study that reported physicians used more than two dozen jargon terms, on average, during consultations with parents of children with sleep disorders.[58] Another source of noise in the communication process is the tendency to filter messages. Filtering may involve deleting or delaying negative information or using less harsh words so the message sounds more favorable.[59]

Information Overload

Information overload occurs whenever the job's information load exceeds the individual's capacity to get through it.[60] Employees have an *information processing capacity*—the amount of information that they are able to process in a fixed unit of time. Concurrently, jobs have a varying *information load*—the amount of information to be processed per unit of time. Information overload creates noise in the communication system because information gets overlooked or misinterpreted when people can't process it fast enough. The result is poorer-quality decisions as well as higher stress.[61]

Information overload problems can be minimized by increasing our information processing capacity, reducing the job's information load, or through a combination of both. Employees can temporarily increase their information processing capacity by reading faster, scanning through documents more efficiently, managing their time use (less wasted time), removing distractions that slow information processing speed, and working longer hours. However, working beyond one's natural capacity is not sustainable for the long term.

Information load can be reduced by buffering, omitting, and summarizing. Buffering involves having incoming communication filtered, usually by an assistant. Omitting occurs when we decide to overlook messages, such as using software rules to redirect emails to folders that we rarely look at. Summarizing involves digesting a condensed version of the complete communication, such as reading an executive summary rather than the full report.

Information overload occurs whenever the job's information load exceeds the individual's capacity to get through it.
alphaspirit/Shutterstock

OB THEORY TO PRACTICE

Minimizing Information Overload

Increase information processing capacity by:

- Learning to read faster.
- Scanning through documents more efficiently.
- Removing distractions that slow information-processing speed.
- Working longer hours (when overload is temporary).

Reduce information load by:

- Buffering—have incoming messages filtered by an assistant (human or automated).
- Omitting—have nonessential messages discarded or redirected somewhere that you might (or might not) view later.
- Summarizing—view only the executive summary or other condensed version of the complete communication.

CROSS-CULTURAL AND MALE-FEMALE COMMUNICATION

Globalization and increasing cultural diversity have created more cross-cultural communication issues in the workplace.[62] As mentioned in the previous section, language differences can be a significant source of noise in the communication process. Words are easily misunderstood in verbal communication when those involved have a limited vocabulary (such as when two executives need to communicate in a language that neither of them uses regularly). Even when both are fluent, the sender's accent might distort the usual sound of some words.

Voice intonation is another cross-cultural communication barrier. How loudly, deeply, and quickly people speak varies across cultures, and these voice intonations send secondary messages that have different meaning in each society. Words are also assigned somewhat different meaning across cultures. For example, KPMG staff from the United Kingdom sometimes referred to another person's suggestions as "interesting." They had to clarify to their German colleagues that "interesting" might not be complimenting the idea.[63]

Another cross-cultural dimension of communication is how people interpret conversational gaps (silence) and overlaps. Silence is revered in Japan because it symbolizes respect, indicates that the listener is thoughtfully contemplating what has just been said, and is a way of avoiding overt conflict.[64] Consequently, the informal communication practice in Japan and a few other countries is to let the other person finish speaking and sometimes wait a few seconds before saying anything. In contrast, most people in the United States and similar cultures avoid silence and interpret those incidents as a sign of disagreement. Conversational overlaps are considered rude in Japan, whereas people from Brazil and France are more likely to interpret interruptions and overlaps as evidence of the person's interest and involvement in the conversation. Meetings in countries that expect overlapping conversations can seem like a chaotic cacophony to those from other cultures.

Nonverbal Differences across Cultures

Nonverbal communication represents another potential area for misunderstanding across cultures. Many nonconscious or involuntary nonverbal cues (such as smiling) have the same meaning around the world, but deliberate gestures often have different interpretations. For example, most of us shake our head from side to side to say, "No," but a variation of head shaking means "I understand" to many people in India. Filipinos raise their eyebrows to give an affirmative answer, yet Arabs interpret this expression (along with clicking one's tongue) as a negative response. Most Americans maintain eye contact with the speaker to show interest and respect, whereas some Indigenous Americans learn at an early age to show respect by looking down when an older or more senior person is talking to them.[65]

Male-Female Differences in Communication

Males and females have similar communication practices, but there are subtle distinctions that can occasionally lead to misunderstanding and conflict (see Exhibit 8.6).[66] One distinction is that males are more likely than females to view conversations as negotiations of relative status and power. They assert their power by directly giving advice to others (e.g., "You should do the following") and using combative language. There is also evidence that males dominate the talk time in conversations with females, as well as interrupt more and adjust their speaking style less than do females.

Males tend to engage in more "report talk," in which the primary function of the conversation is impersonal and efficient information exchange. However, females often engage in more "rapport talk"—verbal and nonverbal communication that builds relationships by showing egalitarian, empathetic support, and engagement with the other person.[67] They also subdue their power in the relationship through more deferential communication, including modifiers ("It might be a good idea ... "), disclaimers ("I'm not certain, but ... "), and tag questions ("This works, doesn't it?").

Females tend to make more use of indirect requests ("Do you think you should ..."), apologize more often, and seek advice from others more quickly than do males. Males also use these speech patterns to some extent, but females use them more frequently as well as across communication channels (conversations, text messages, etc.). Research also reports that females are more sensitive than males to nonverbal cues in face-to-face meetings. Together, these conditions can create communication conflicts. Females who describe problems get frustrated that males offer advice rather than rapport, whereas males become frustrated because they can't understand why females don't appreciate their advice.

Exhibit 8.6 Male-Female Differences in Communication

	When Males Communicate	When Females Communicate	
	1. Report talk—give advice, assert power 2. Give advice directly 3. Dominant conversation style 4. Apologize less often 5. Less sensitive to nonverbal cues	1. Rapport talk—relationship building 2. Give advice indirectly 3. Flexible conversation style 4. Apologize more often 5. More sensitive to nonverbal cues	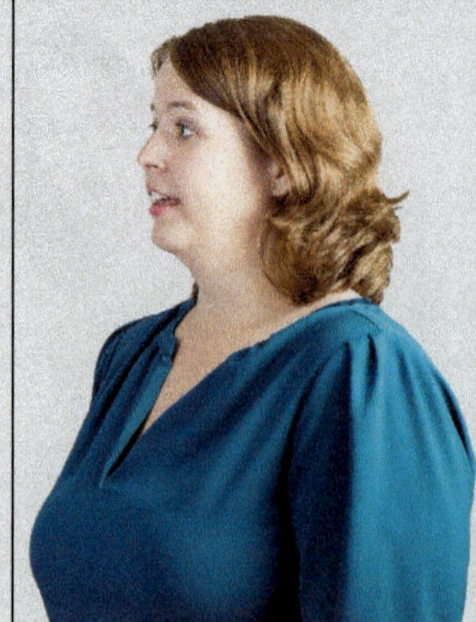

(Photos): Brittany Herbert/McGraw Hill

LO8-5 Explain how to get your message across more effectively and summarize the elements of active listening.

IMPROVING INTERPERSONAL COMMUNICATION

Effective interpersonal communication depends on the sender's ability to get the message across and the receiver's performance as an active listener. In this section, we outline these two essential features of effective interpersonal communication.

Getting Your Message Across

This chapter began with the statement that effective communication occurs when the other person receives and understands the message. This is more difficult to accomplish than most people believe. To get your message across to the other person, you first need to empathize with the receiver, such as being sensitive to words that may be ambiguous or trigger the wrong emotional response. Second, you should repeat the message, such as by rephrasing the key points a couple of times. Third, your message competes with other messages and noise, so find a time when the receiver is less likely to be distracted by these other matters. Finally, focus on the problem, not the person, if you have negative information to convey. People stop listening when the information attacks their self-concept. Also, suggest things the listener can do to improve, rather than pointing to them as the problem.

Active Listening

Active listening is a process of mindfully sensing the sender's signals, evaluating them accurately, and responding appropriately. These three components of active listening–sensing, evaluating, and responding–represent the listener's side of the communication model described at the beginning of this chapter. Listeners receive the sender's signals, decode them as intended, and provide appropriate and timely feedback to the sender (see Exhibit 8.7). Active listeners constantly cycle through sensing, evaluating, and responding during the conversation and engage in various activities to improve these processes.[68]

- *Sensing.* Sensing is the process of receiving signals from the sender and paying attention to them. Active listeners improve sensing in three ways. First, they postpone evaluation by not forming an opinion until the speaker has finished. Second, they avoid interrupting the speaker's conversation. Third, they remain motivated to listen to the speaker.
- *Evaluating.* This component of listening includes understanding the message meaning, evaluating the message, and remembering the message. To improve their evaluation of the conversation, active listeners empathize with the speaker—they try to understand and be sensitive to the speaker's feelings, thoughts, and situation. Evaluation also improves by organizing the speaker's ideas during the communication episode.
- *Responding.* This third component of listening involves providing feedback to the sender, which motivates and directs the speaker's communication. Active listeners accomplish this by maintaining sufficient eye contact and sending back channel signals (e.g., "I see"), both of which show interest. They also respond by clarifying the message—rephrasing the speaker's ideas at appropriate breaks ("So you're saying that ... ?").

Mc Graw Hill connect

SELF-ASSESSMENT 8.1: Are You an Active Listener?

Exhibit 8.7 Active Listening Process and Strategies

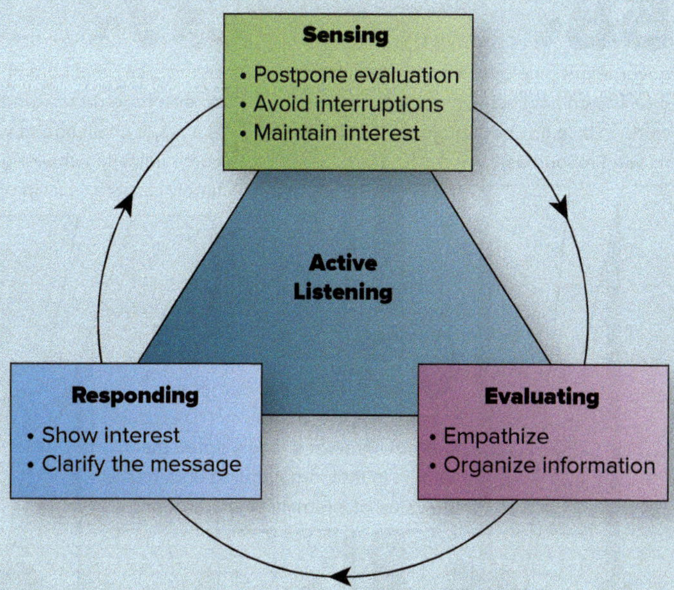

> **Nature gave us one tongue, but two ears, so we may listen twice as much as we speak.[69]**
>
> —Epictetus, Greek philosopher

LO8-6 Summarize effective communication strategies in organizational hierarchies, and review the role and relevance of the organizational grapevine.

IMPROVING COMMUNICATION THROUGHOUT THE HIERARCHY

So far, we have looked at micro-level issues in the communication process, namely, sending and receiving information between two employees or among team members. But in this era where knowledge is a competitive advantage, corporate leaders also need to maintain an open flow of communication up, down, and across the entire organization. In this section, we discuss three organization-wide communication strategies: workspace design, digitally based communication, and direct communication with top management.

Workspace Design

The location and design of hallways, offices, cubicles, and communal areas (cafeterias, elevators) all influence which people we speak to as well as the frequency of that communication.[70] Many organizations have shifted from cubicles to open spaces in the hope that the increased line-of-sight to coworkers will improve information sharing. However, open-space arrangements potentially undermine employee productivity due to noise, distractions, and loss of privacy.

Another workspace strategy is to enable employees to collaborate in team spaces. These aren't necessarily open-plan offices. Some cloister team members into an area separate from other teams. Others have more semi-private individual spaces. However, the work area consists of small breakout spaces, happenstance cubbyholes along hallways, and larger conference rooms where teams can frequently congregate. "We're moving even more to a team-based space approach

The Quality of Direct Communication with Management[71]

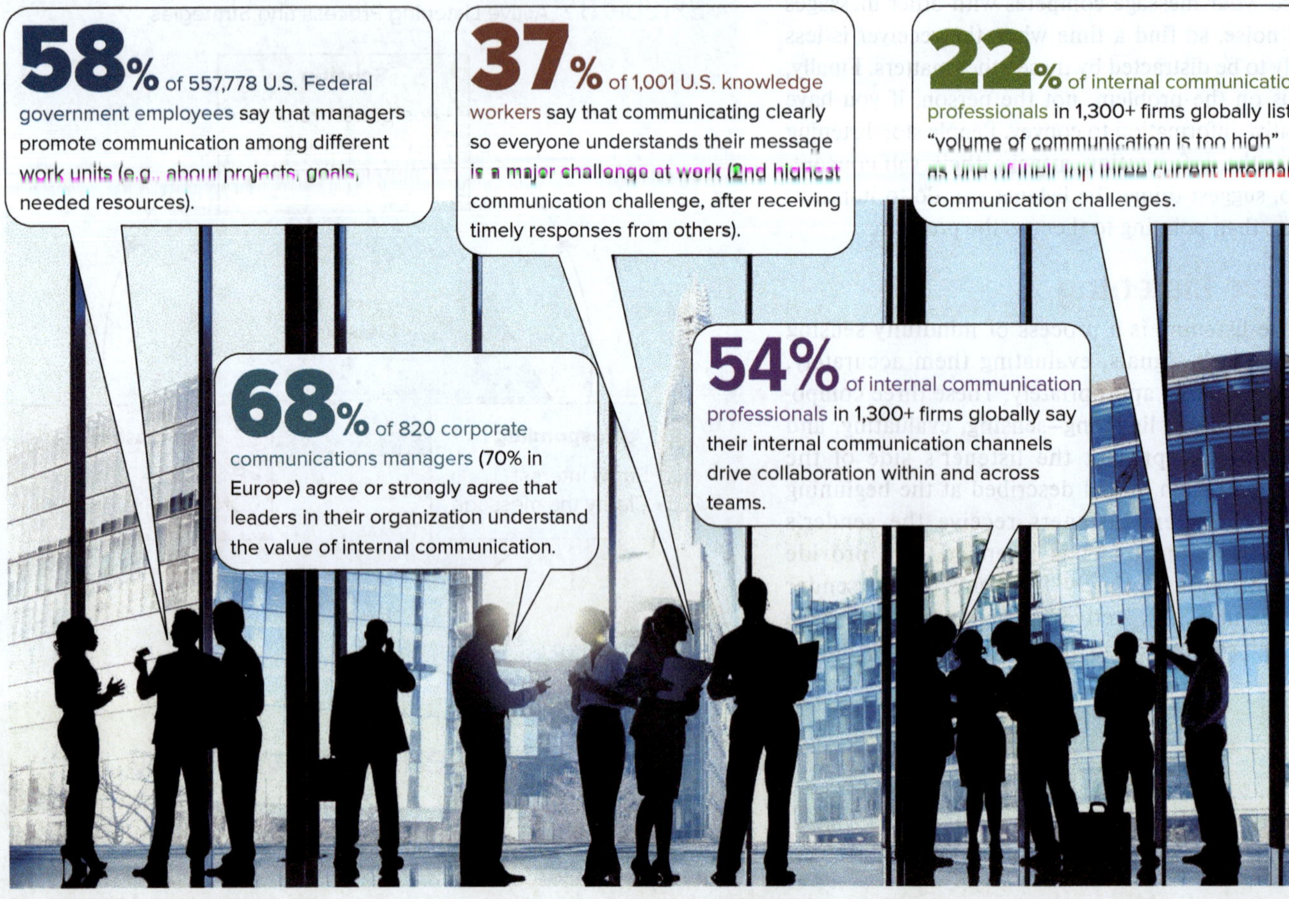

(Photos): Rawpixel.com/Shutterstock

management by wandering around (MBWA) A communication practice in which executives get out of their offices and learn from others in the organization through face-to-face dialogue

grapevine An unstructured and informal communication network founded on social relationships rather than organizational charts or job descriptions

where we're giving the employees a variety of spaces to use," says Michael Ford, Microsoft's vice president of global real estate and security.[72]

Digitally Based Organizational Communication

For decades, employees received official company news through hard-copy newsletters and magazines. Some firms still use these communication devices, but the traditional company magazine has almost completely been replaced by intranet web pages or PDF format files.

Even so, employees are increasingly skeptical of information that has been screened and packaged exclusively by management. Companies are adapting to this skepticism by introducing social media channels through the emerging enterprise communication platforms described earlier in this chapter. Along with enabling task-focused message threads, these systems allow users to generate blogs, shared notices, and other news-oriented sites, most of which also allow feedback comments from readers within the organization. In many instances, company magazines have been replaced by real-time text messages directly from employees where the events occur.[73]

Direct Communication with Top Management

Effective organizational communication includes regular interaction directly between senior executives and employees further down the hierarchy. One form of direct communication is through town hall meetings, where executives brief a large gathering of staff on the company's current strategy and results. Although the communication is mostly from executives to employees, town hall meetings are more personal and credible than video or written channels. Also, these events usually provide some opportunity for employees to ask questions. Another strategy is for senior executives to hold roundtable forums with a small representation of employees, mainly to hear their opinions on various issues.

A less formal approach to direct communication is **management by wandering around (MBWA).** Coined by people at Hewlett-Packard several decades ago, this is the practice in which senior executives get out of their offices and chat with employees on a regular basis.[74] These direct conversations help executives acquire a deeper meaning and quicker understanding of internal organizational problems because less information is filtered out. In addition, casual discussion with executives potentially increases employee empathy regarding decisions made further up the corporate hierarchy.

COMMUNICATING THROUGH THE GRAPEVINE

Organizational leaders may try their best to quickly communicate breaking news to employees through emails, text messages, and other direct formal channels, but employees still rely to some extent on the corporate **grapevine.** The grapevine is an unstructured and informal network founded on social relationships rather than organizational charts or job descriptions. What do employees think about the grapevine? Surveys have found that almost all employees use the grapevine, but very few of them prefer this source of information. In one survey, only one-third of employees believe grapevine information is credible. In other words, employees turn to the grapevine when they have few other options.[75]

Grapevine Characteristics

Research conducted several decades ago reported that the grapevine transmits information very rapidly in all directions throughout the organization. The typical pattern is a cluster chain, whereby a few people actively transmit information to many others. The grapevine works through informal social networks, so it is more active where employees have similar backgrounds and are able to communicate easily. Many rumors seem to have at least a kernel of truth, possibly because they are transmitted through media-rich communication channels (e.g., face-to-face) and employees are motivated to communicate effectively. Nevertheless, the grapevine distorts information by deleting fine details and exaggerating key points of the story.[76]

Some of these characteristics might still be true, but the grapevine has almost certainly changed as text messaging, email,

> "The grapevine works through informal social networks, so it is more active where employees have similar backgrounds and are able to communicate easily."

and social media practices have replaced the traditional water cooler as sources of gossip. For example, several Facebook sites are unofficially themed around specific companies, allowing employees and customers to vent their complaints about the organization. Along with altering the speed and network of corporate grapevines, the Internet has expanded these networks around the globe, not just around the next cubicle.[77]

Grapevine Benefits and Limitations

Should the grapevine be encouraged, tolerated, or quashed? The difficulty in answering this question is that the grapevine has both benefits and limitations.[78] One benefit, as was mentioned earlier, is that employees rely on the grapevine when information is not available through formal channels. It is also the main conduit through which organizational stories and other symbols of the organization's culture are communicated. A third benefit of the grapevine is that this social interaction relieves anxiety. This explains why rumor mills are most active during times of uncertainty.[79] Finally, the grapevine is associated with the drive to bond. Being a recipient of gossip is a sign of inclusion, according to evolutionary psychologists. Trying to quash the grapevine is, in some respects, an attempt to undermine the natural human drive for social interaction.[80]

Although the grapevine offers these benefits, it is not a preferred communication medium. Grapevine information is sometimes so distorted that it escalates rather than reduces employee anxiety. Furthermore, employees develop more negative attitudes toward the organization when management is slower than the grapevine in communicating information. What should corporate leaders do with the grapevine? They should listen to the grapevine as a signal of employee anxiety, then correct the cause of this anxiety. They also need to advise employees when the grapevine transmits blatant errors and fabrications. Most important, the company needs to view the grapevine as a competitor and meet this challenge by directly informing employees of news before it spreads throughout the grapevine.

Study Checklist

Connect® is available for *M: Organizational Behavior.* Additional resources include:

✓ Exercises:

- **Case Analysis:** Apply concepts within the context of a real-world situation.
- **Click and Drag:** Helps make the connection between theory and application through matching, ranking, or grouping activities.
- **Video Case:** See management in action through interactive videos.
- **Self-Assessment:** Designed to promote student self-awareness and reflection, these research-based surveys contain detailed feedback for students.
- **Application-Based Activities:** These highly interactive, application- and analysis-based exercises allow students to take on specific roles to complete management related tasks within a real-world context.

✓ **SmartBook 2.0™**—Smartbook 2.0 is an adaptive learning solution that provides personalized learning to individual student needs, continually adapts to pinpoint knowledge gaps and focuses learning on concepts requiring additional study. It fosters more productive learning, takes the guesswork out of what to study, and helps students better prepare for class.

©Natthawat Jamnapa/123RF

Notes

1. L. Carroll. "Pandemic Fast-Tracks the Use of Teams," *Canadian Health Technology*, June 30, 2020; L. Agrba, "How CBI Health Helped Create a Unified Culture–and Stave off Employee Burnout," *The Globe and Mail*, September 16, 2022.

2. A.H. Van de Ven, A.L. Delbecq, and R. Koenig Jr., "Determinants of Coordination Modes within Organizations," *American Sociological Review* 41, no. 2 (1976): 322–38; R. Foy et al., "Meta-Analysis: Effect of Interactive Communication between Collaborating Primary Care Physicians and Specialists," *Annals of Internal Medicine* 152, no. 4 (2010): 247–58; R. Rico et al., "Structural Influences upon Coordination and Performance in Multiteam Systems," *Human Resource Management Review* 28, no. 4 (2018): 332–46; J.L. Claggett and E. Karahanna, "Unpacking the Structure of Coordination Mechanisms and the Role of Relational Coordination in an Era of Digitally Mediated Work Processes," *Academy of Management Review* 43, no. 4 (2018): 704–22.

3. C. Barnard, *The Functions of the Executive* (Cambridge, MA: Harvard University Press, 1938), 82. Barnard's entire statement also refers to the other features of organizations that we describe in Chapter 1, namely, that (1) people are willing to contribute their effort to the organization and (2) they have a common purpose.

4. J. O'Toole and W. Bennis, "What's Needed Next: A Culture of Candor," *Harvard Business Review* 87, no. 6 (2009): 54–61.

5. W.J.L. Elving, "The Role of Communication in Organisational Change," *Corporate Communications* 10, no. 2 (2005): 129–38; S. Muthusamy, "Power of Positive Words: Communication, Cognition, and Organizational Transformation," *Journal of Organizational Change Management* 32, no. 1 (2019): 103–22; C. Schulz-Knappe, T. Koch, and J. Beckert, "The Importance of Communicating Change: Identifying Predictors for Support and Resistance toward Organizational Change Processes," *Corporate Communications: An International Journal* 24, no. 4 (2019): 670–85.

6. R.E. Baumeister and M.R. Leary, "The Need to Belong: Desire for Interpersonal Attachments as a Fundamental Human Motivation," *Psychological Bulletin* 117 (1995): 497–529; K.H. Greenaway et al., "Social Identities Promote Well-Being because They Satisfy Global Psychological Needs," *European Journal of Social Psychology* 46 (2016): 294–307; N. Steverink et al., "The Associations of Different Social Needs with Psychological Strengths and Subjective Well-Being: An Empirical Investigation Based on Social Production Function Theory," *Journal of Happiness Studies* 21 (2020): 799–824.

7. A.M. Saks, K.L. Uggerslev, and N.E. Fassina, "Socialization Tactics and Newcomer Adjustment: A Meta-Analytic Review and Test of a Model," *Journal of Vocational Behavior* 70, no. 3 (2007): 413–46; M. Wang et al., "Context, Socialization, and Newcomer Learning," *Organizational Psychology Review* 5, no. 1 (2015): 3–25; A.M. Saks and J.A. Gruman, "How Do You Socialize Newcomers during a Pandemic?," *Industrial and Organizational Psychology* 14, no. 1-2 (2021): 217–20.

8. C.E. Shannon and W. Weaver, *The Mathematical Theory of Communication* (Urbana: University of Illinois Press, 1949); R.M. Krauss and S.R. Fussell, "Social Psychological Models of Interpersonal Communication," in *Social Psychology: Handbook of Basic Principles*, ed. E.T. Higgins and A. Kruglanski (New York: Guilford Press, 1996), 655–701.

9. J.R. Carlson and R.W. Zmud, "Channel Expansion Theory and the Experiential Nature of Media Richness Perceptions," *Academy of Management Journal* 42 (1999): 153–70; S.C. D'Urso and S.A. Rains, "Examining the Scope of Channel Expansion: A Test of Channel Expansion Theory with New and Traditional Communication Media," *Management Communication Quarterly* 21, no. 4 (2008): 486–507; R.S. Burt and S. Wang, "Bridge Supervision: Correlates of a Boss on the Far Side of a Structural Hole," *Academy of Management Journal* 65, no. 6 (2022): 1835–63.

10. Y. van den Boer et al., "Towards a Model of Source and Channel Choices in Business-to-Government Service Interactions: A Structural Equation Modeling Approach," *Government Information Quarterly* 34 (2017): 434–56; R. McColl and M. Michelotti, "Sorry, Could You Repeat the Question? Exploring Video-Interview Recruitment Practice in HRM," *Human Resource Management Journal* 29 (2019): 637–56.

11. A.A. Niler et al., "Conditioning Team Cognition: A Meta-Analysis," *Organizational Psychology Review* 11, no. 2 (2021): 144–74; R. Müller and C.H. Antoni, "Effects of ICT Shared Mental Models on Team Processes and Outcomes," *Small Group Research* 53, no. 2 (2022): 307–35.

12. S. Bonaccio et al., "Nonverbal Behavior and Communication in the Workplace: A Review and an Agenda for Research," *Journal of Management* 42 (2016): 1044–74; J.A. Hall, T.G. Horgan, and N.A. Murphy, "Nonverbal Communication," *Annual Review of Psychology* 70 (2019): 271–94. Some writers suggest that the interaction of words with nonword symbols makes it difficult to distinguish verbal from nonverbal by the presence or absence of words.

13. S.D. Farley et al., "Nonverbal Reactions to Conversational Interruption: A Test of Complementarity Theory and the Status/Gender Parallel," *Journal of Nonverbal Behavior* 34, no. 4 (2010): 193–206; D.R. Carney, "The Nonverbal Expression of Power, Status, and Dominance," *Current Opinion in Psychology* 33 (2020): 256–64.

14. Based on information in: "The Ultimate Guide to Using Body Language in Business," *Lenstore-Lifestyle and Vision* (blog), January 11, 2022.

15. J. Champy, *What I Learned from Peter Drucker* (Boston: New Word City, 2010), Chap. 4.

16. W.J. Becker and R. Cropanzano, "Organizational Neuroscience: The Promise and Prospects of an Emerging Discipline," *Journal of Organizational Behavior* 31 (2010): 1055–59; S.G. Barsade, C.G.V. Coutifaris, and J. Pillemer, "Emotional Contagion in Organizational Life," *Research in Organizational Behavior* 38 (2018): 137–51.

17. M. Sonnby-Borgstrom, P. Jonsson, and O. Svensson, "Emotional Empathy as Related to Mimicry Reactions at Different Levels of Information Processing," *Journal of Nonverbal Behavior* 27 (2003): 3–23; V. Vijayalakshmi and S. Bhattacharyya, "Emotional Contagion and Its Relevance to Individual Behavior and Organizational Processes: A Position Paper," *Journal of Business and Psychology* 27 (2012): 363–74. However, emotional contagion is not universally automatic. It may depend on social relations between the parties. See M. Wróbel and K.K. Imbir, "Broadening the Perspective on Emotional Contagion and Emotional Mimicry: The Correction Hypothesis," *Perspectives on Psychological Science* 14 (2019): 437–51.

18. T.L. Chartrand and J.L. Lakin, "The Antecedents and Consequences of Human Behavioral Mimicry," *Annual Review of Psychology* 64 (2013): 285–308; E. Prochazkova and M.E. Kret, "Connecting Minds and Sharing Emotions through Mimicry: A Neurocognitive Model of Emotional Contagion," *Neuroscience & Biobehavioral Reviews* 80 (2017): 99–114.

19. "Communication Barriers in the Modern Workplace" (London: The Economist Intelligence Unit, March 2018); L. Wright and N. McCullough, "New Survey Explores the Changing Landscape of Teamwork," *Microsoft 365 Blog* (blog), April 19, 2018; "Email Statistics Report, 2021-2026—Executive Summary" (Palo Alto, CA: The Radicati Group, November 2022).

20. Although this exhibit likely reflects actual changes, there are no known large-scale data on digital communication usage in the workplace. In this exhibit, 2014 to 2019 data are from 12,000 RescueTime app users. Data points are January of each year. On average, users actively focused on their screens for 5.5 hours each work day. The data shown here represent the 18 percent (about one hour) of total active screen time spent communicating. The data for 2020 and 2021 extrapolate from the earlier data, guided by macro-level statistics on user counts and corporate adoptions of Microsoft Teams, Slack, and Zoom, as well as global email activity. Small surveys (e.g., communication activities surveyed by project.co) support these extrapolations.

21. "Communication Statistics 2023" (Sefton, UK: Project.co, January 19, 2023).

22. 2014–2019 data are from 12,000 RescueTime app users, calculated from information in R. Molla, "The Productivity Pit: How Slack Is Ruining Work," *Vox*, May 1, 2019. These data represent the 18 percent (about one hour) of total active screen time spent engaging in communication activity. The data for 2020 and 2021 extrapolate from the earlier data, guided by macro-level statistics on user counts and corporate adoptions of Microsoft Teams, Slack, and Zoom, as well as global

email activity. Small-scale surveys by project.co are consistent with the estimates shown here in digital workplace communication during these two years. See: D. Curry, "Microsoft Teams Revenue and Usage Statistics (2022)," *Business of Apps*, January 11, 2022; D. Curry, "Slack Revenue and Usage Statistics (2022)," *Business of Apps*, January 11, 2022; B. Dean, "Zoom User Stats: How Many People Use Zoom in 2022?" *Backlinko* (blog), January 6, 2022; M. Iqbal, "Zoom Revenue and Usage Statistics (2022)," *Business of Apps*, January 11, 2022; "Email Statistics Report, 2021-2026—Executive Summary" (Palo Alto, CA: The Radicati Group, November 2022); "Communication Statistics 2023" (Sefton, UK: Project.co, January 19, 2023).

23. Studies are now emerging on the observed benefits, user activity, and communication patterns in enterprise communication platforms. For example, see: V. Stray, N.B. Moe, and M. Noroozi, "Slack Me If You Can! Using Enterprise Social Networking Tools in Virtual Agile Teams," in *2019 ACM/IEEE 14th International Conference on Global Software Engineering (ICGSE)*, 2019, 111–21; R. Brisco, R.I. Whitfield, and H. Grierson, "A Novel Systematic Method to Evaluate Computer-Supported Collaborative Design Technologies," *Research in Engineering Design* 31, no. 1 (2020): 53–81; S.A. Ferguson et al., "Communication Patterns in Engineering Enterprise Social Networks: An Exploratory Analysis Using Short Text Topic Modelling," *Design Science* 8 (2022): e18.

24. W. Lucas, "Effects of E-mail on the Organization," *European Management Journal* 16 (1998): 18–30; D.A. Owens, M.A. Neale, and R.I. Sutton, "Technologies of Status Management Status Dynamics in E-Mail Communications," *Research on Managing Groups and Teams* 3 (2000): 205–30; G. de La Rupelle, C. Guthrie, and M. Kalika, "La relation entre l'intensité perçue d'utilisation de la messagerie électronique et la qualité de la relation hiérarchique," *Relations Industrielles* 70 (2015): 157–85; C.M. Brotheridge, D.J. Neufeld, and B. Dyck, "Communicating Virtually in a Global Organization," *Journal of Managerial Psychology* 30 (2015): 909–24.

25. N. Panteli, "Richness, Power Cues and Email Text," *Information & Management* 40 (2002): 75–86; C.T. Carr and C. Stefaniak, "Sent from My iPhone: The Medium and Message as Cues of Sender Professionalism in Mobile Telephony," *Journal of Applied Communication Research* 40 (2012): 403–24; D.C. DeAndrea, "Advancing Warranting Theory," *Communication Theory* 24 (2014): 186–204; C.M. Brotheridge, D.J. Neufeld, and B. Dyck, "Communicating Virtually in a Global Organization," *Journal of Managerial Psychology* 30 (2015): 909–24.

26. K. Byron, "Carrying Too Heavy a Load? The Communication and Miscommunication of Emotion by Email," *Academy of Management Review* 33 (2008): 309–27; M.A. Riordan and L.A. Trichtinger, "Overconfidence at the Keyboard: Confidence and Accuracy in Interpreting Affect in E-Mail Exchanges," *Human Communication Research* 43 (2017): 1–24; C. Laubert and J. Parlamis, "Are You Angry (Happy, Sad) or Aren't You? Emotion Detection Difficulty in Email Negotiation," *Group Decision and Negotiation* 28 (2019): 377–413.

27. K. Byron, "Carrying Too Heavy a Load? The Communication and Miscommunication of Emotion by Email," *Academy of Management Review* 33 (2008): 309–27; A. Sillars and T.E. Zorn, "Hypernegative Interpretation of Negatively Perceived Email at Work," *Management Communication Quarterly* 35, no. 2 (2021): 171–200; S. Farley, I. Coyne, and P. D'Cruz, "Cyberbullying at Work: Understanding the Influence of Technology," in *Concepts, Approaches and Methods*, ed. P. D'Cruz et al., vol. 1, Handbooks of Workplace Bullying, Emotional Abuse and Harassment (Singapore: Springer, 2021), 233–63.

28. N. Sobotta and M. Hummel, "A Capacity Perspective on E-Mail Overload: How E-Mail Use Contributes to Information Overload" (paper presented at the 2015 48th Hawaii International Conference on System Sciences, January 5-8, 2015), 692–701; S. Drössler et al., "Informationsüberflutung durch digitale Medien am Arbeitsplatz (Information overload by digital media at the workplace. Systematic review of qualitative studies)," *Zentralblatt für Arbeitsmedizin, Arbeitsschutz und Ergonomie (Central Journal for Occupational Medicine, Occupational Safety and Ergonomics)* 68 (2018): 77–88.

29. The estimated daily email messages is reported in: "Email Statistics Report, 2021-2026—Executive Summary" (Palo Alto, CA: The Radicati Group, November 2022). For information about the volume of mobile and platform messaging, see. D. Kent, "The State Of Workplace Messaging 2022: Microsoft Teams, Webex, & More," November 2, 2021; B. Dean, "WhatsApp 2022 User Statistics: How Many People Use WhatsApp?" *Backlinko* (blog), January 5, 2022. The daily number of SMS/MMS text messages in the United States alone is estimated at more than 2 trillion annually. P. Taylor, "Text Messages Sent in the U.S. 2021," *Statista*, January 18, 2023.

30. Social media definitions in the literature tend to be obtuse, varied, and in many cases, elusive. Our definition is based on two of the more widely cited sources: A.M. Kaplan and M. Haenlein, "Users of the World, Unite! The Challenges and Opportunities of Social Media," *Business Horizons* 53 (2010): 59–68; C.T. Carr and R.A. Hayes, "Social Media: Defining, Developing, and Divining," *Atlantic Journal of Communication* 23 (2015): 46–65.

31. G. Martin, E. Parry, and P. Flowers, "Do Social Media Enhance Constructive Employee Voice All of the Time or Just Some of the Time?" *Human Resource Management Journal* 25 (2015): 541–62; W. van Zoonen, J.W.M. Verhoeven, and R. Vliegenthart, "How Employees Use Twitter to Talk about Work: A Typology of Work-Related Tweets," *Computers in Human Behavior* 55, Part A (2016): 329–39; R. Brisco, R.I. Whitfield, and H. Grierson, "A Novel Systematic Method to Evaluate Computer-Supported Collaborative Design Technologies," *Research in Engineering Design* 31, no. 1 (2020): 53–81.

32. N. Aldunate and R. González-Ibáñez, "An Integrated Review of Emoticons in Computer-Mediated Communication," *Frontiers in Psychology* 7 (2017): 02061; Q. Bai et al., "A Systematic Review of Emoji: Current Research and Future Perspectives," *Frontiers in Psychology* 10 (2019): 02221.

33. J. Tolins and P. Samermit, "GIFs as Embodied Enactments in Text-Mediated Conversation," *Research on Language and Social Interaction* 49, no. 2 (2016): 75–91; J.A. Jiang, C. Fiesler, and J.R. Brubaker, "'The Perfect One': Understanding Communication Practices and Challenges with Animated GIFs," *Proceedings of the ACM on Human-Computer Interaction* 2, no. CSCW (2018): 80: 1–20; A. Wagener, "The Postdigital Emergence of Memes and GIFs: Meaning, Discourse, and Hypernarrative Creativity," *Postdigital Science and Education* 3, no. 3 (2021): 831–50.

34. Y. Tang and K. Hew, "Emoticon, Emoji, and Sticker Use in Computer-Mediated Communications: Understanding Its Communicative Function, Impact, User Behavior, and Motive," in *New Media for Educational Change*, ed. L. Deng, W.W.K. Ma, and C.W.R. Fong (Singapore: Springer Nature, 2018), 191–201; Q. Bai et al., "A Systematic Review of Emoji: Current Research and Future Perspectives," *Frontiers in Psychology* 10 (2019): 02221; C. Gantiva et al., "Cortical Processing of Human and Emoji Faces: An ERP Analysis," *Behaviour & Information Technology* 39, no. 8 (2020): 935–43; B. Fischer and C. Herbert, "Emoji as Affective Symbols: Affective Judgments of Emoji, Emoticons, and Human Faces Varying in Emotional Content," *Frontiers in Psychology* 12 (April 20, 2021): 645173.

35. E. Glikson, A. Cheshin, and G.A. van Kleef, "The Dark Side of a Smiley: Effects of Smiling Emoticons on Virtual First Impressions," *Social Psychological and Personality Science* 9, no. 5 (2018): 614–25; M. Prada et al., "Motives, Frequency and Attitudes toward Emoji and Emoticon Use," *Telematics and Informatics* 35, no. 7 (2018): 1925–34; S.C. Herring and A.R. Dainas, "Gender and Age Influences on Interpretation of Emoji Functions," *ACM Transactions on Social Computing*

3, no. 2 (2020): 1-26; M.A. Riordan and E. Glikson, "On the Hazards of the Technology Age: How Using Emojis Affects Perceptions of Leaders," *International Journal of Business Communication*, November 24, 2020, in press; Down To Earth Chinese, *These Emojis In China DON'T Mean This! DO NOT Use Them Incorrectly!*, YouTube, Learn Chinese, 2021; B.P. Cavalheiro et al., "Evaluating the Adequacy of Emoji Use in Positive and Negative Messages from Close and Distant Senders," *Cyberpsychology, Behavior, and Social Networking* 25, no. 3 (2022): 194-99.

36. A.R. Dennis, R.M. Fuller, and J.S. Valacich, "Media, Tasks, and Communication Processes: A Theory of Media Synchronicity," *MIS Quarterly* 32 (2008): 575-600; S. Taipale, "Synchronicity Matters: Defining the Characteristics of Digital Generations," *Information, Communication & Society* 19 (2016): 80-94; I. Geiger and C. Laubert, "Situational Strategic versus Personal Influences on Negotiation Medium Choice: Media Synchronicity Theory and Affect for Communication Channel," *International Journal of Conflict Management* 29 (2018): 398-423.

37. R.E. Rice, "Media Appropriateness: Using Social Presence Theory to Compare Traditional and New Organizational Media," *Human Communication Research* 19 (1993): 451-84; C.S. Oh, J.N. Bailenson, and G. Welch, "A Systematic Review of Social Presence: Definition, Antecedents, and Implications," *Frontiers in Robotics and AI* (October 15, 2018): 00114; A. Kumar and N. Epley, "It's Surprisingly Nice to Hear You: Misunderstanding the Impact of Communication Media Can Lead to Suboptimal Choices of How to Connect with Others," *Journal of Experimental Psychology: General* 150 (2021): 595-607.

38. N. Walter, K. Ortbach, and B. Niehaves, "Designing Electronic Feedback–Analyzing the Effects of Social Presence on Perceived Feedback Usefulness," *International Journal of Human-Computer Studies* 76 (2015): 1-11; S.C. Srivastava and S. Chandra, "Social Presence in Virtual World Collaboration: An Uncertainty Reduction Perspective Using a Mixed Methods Approach," *MIS Quarterly* 42 (2018): 779-803.

39. R. Bertram, "Our Marketing Team Gave up Meetings for a Week–Here's What Happened," *Salesforce Australia & NZ Blog* (blog), April 20, 2022; S. Bearne, "'Happier and More Fulfilled': How Some Companies Have Successfully Banned Meetings," *WorkLife*, April 27, 2022; L. Lee, "Can You Work without Meetings? Salesforce Tried for Another Week," *The 360 Blog from Salesforce* (blog), August 31, 2022; L. Soutar, "By Axing Meetings, Shopify Sets a Blueprint for Reducing Staff Burnout," *HR Grapevine*, January 4, 2023; T. Durrani, "Fewer Meetings and No More 'Pineapple on Pizza Debates': Shopify Changes Signal Company's Renewed Urgency," *The Globe and Mail*, January 6, 2023.

40. J. Fulk, "Social Construction of Communication Technology," *Academy of Management Journal* 36 (1993): 921-50; J.W. Turner et al., "Exploring the Dominant Media: How Does Media Use Reflect Organizational Norms and Affect Performance?" *Journal of Business Communication* 43 (2006): 220-50; J.B. Bayer, S.W. Campbell, and R. Ling, "Connection Cues: Activating the Norms and Habits of Social Connectedness," *Communication Theory* 26 (2016): 128-49.

41. Z. Lee and Y. Lee, "Emailing the Boss: Cultural Implications of Media Choice," *IEEE Transactions on Professional Communication* 52, no. 1 (2009): 61-74; D. Holtbrügge, A. Weldon, and H. Rogers, "Cultural Determinants of Email Communication Styles," *International Journal of Cross Cultural Management* 13, no. 1 (2013): 89-110.

42. "Emojis Gain Hearts, Business in Shy Chinese," *Xinhua News Agency*, August 18, 2016; J. D'Onfro, "13 Rules Regarding Proper Email Etiquette from around the World," *Mental Floss*, February 20, 2017; Z. Zhang, "WeChat's Exclusive Emojis Express Emotions Western Apps Cannot," *Quartz*, July 19, 2018; O. Surcouf, "Korean Apps Conquer Asia with Cute Emojis," *Asia Times*, March 16, 2019.

43. R.C. King, "Media Appropriateness: Effects of Experience on Communication Media Choice," *Decision Sciences* 28 (1997): 877-910; A. Oeldorf-Hirsch and K.L. Nowak, "There Is Something I Need to Tell You: Balancing Appropriateness and Efficiency in Modality Choice for Interpersonal Disclosures," *Communication Studies* 69 (2018): 125-41.

44. K.K. Stephens, A.K. Barrett, and M.J. Mahometa, "Organizational Communication in Emergencies: Using Multiple Channels and Sources to Combat Noise and Capture Attention," *Human Communication Research* 39 (2013): 230-51; J. Eden and A.E. Veksler, "Relational Maintenance in the Digital Age: Implicit Rules and Multiple Modalities," *Communication Quarterly* 64 (2016): 119-44. Marshall McLuhan's treatise on the medium is the message is found in: M. McLuhan, *Understanding Media: The Extensions of Man* (New York: McGraw Hill, 1964).

45. R.L. Daft and R.H. Lengel, "Information Richness: A New Approach to Managerial Behavior and Organization Design," *Research in Organizational Behavior* 6 (1984): 191-233; R.H. Lengel and R.L. Daft, "The Selection of Communication Media as an Executive Skill," *Academy of Management Executive* 2 (1988): 225-32.

46. H. Rodriguez et al., "Huddle Up! The Adoption and Use of Structured Team Communication for VA Medical Home Implementation," *Health Care Management Review* 40 (2015): 286-99; M. Harrison, "How a U.S. Health Care System Uses 15-Minute Huddles to Keep 23 Hospitals Aligned," *Harvard Business Review*, November 29, 2018.

47. R.E. Rice, "Task Analyzability, Use of New Media, and Effectiveness: A Multi-Site Exploration of Media Richness," *Organization Science* 3 (1992): 475-500; V.W. Kupritz and E. Cowell, "Productive Management Communication: Online and Face-to-Face," *Journal of Business Communication* 48 (2011): 54-82.

48. R.F. Otondo et al., "The Complexity of Richness: Media, Message, and Communication Outcomes," *Information & Management* 45, no. 1 (2008): 21-30.

49. N.L. Reinsch Jr., J.W. Turner, and C.H. Tinsley, "Multicommunicating: A Practice Whose Time Has Come?" *Academy of Management Review* 33 (2008): 391-403; A.F. Cameron and J. Webster, "Multicommunicating: Juggling Multiple Conversations in the Workplace," *Information Systems Research* 24 (2013): 352-71; N.L. Reinsch and J.W. Turner, "Multicommunicator Aspirational Stress, Suggestions for Teaching and Research, and Other Insights after 10 Years of Multicommunication Research," *Journal of Business and Technical Communication* 33 (2019): 141-71.

50. S. Xu, Z. Wang, and P. David, "Media Multitasking and Well-Being of University Students," *Computers in Human Behavior* 55, Part A (2016): 242-50; A.-F. Cameron et al., "Multicommunicating in Meetings: Effects of Locus, Topic Relatedness, and Meeting Medium," *Management Communication Quarterly* 32 (2018): 303-36.

51. J.R. Carlson and R.W. Zmud, "Channel Expansion Theory and the Experiential Nature of Media Richness Perceptions," *Academy of Management Journal* 42 (1999): 153-70; N. Kock, "Media Naturalness Theory: Human Evolution and Behaviour towards Electronic Communication Technologies," in *Applied Evolutionary Psychology*, ed. S.C. Roberts (Oxford, UK: Oxford University Press, 2012), 381-98; I. Blau, O. Weiser, and Y. Eshet-Alkalai, "How Do Medium Naturalness and Personality Traits Shape Academic Achievement and Perceived Learning? An Experimental Study of Face-to-Face and Synchronous E-Learning," *Research in Learning Technology* 25 (2017): 1974.

52. L.P. Robert and A.R. Dennis, "Paradox of Richness: A Cognitive Model of Media Choice," *IEEE Transactions on Professional Communication* 48 (2005): 10–21; C. Belletier et al., "Choking under Monitoring Pressure: Being Watched by the Experimenter Reduces Executive Attention," *Psychonomic Bulletin & Review* 22 (2015): 1410–16; C. Belletier, A. Normand, and P. Huguet, "Social-Facilitation-and-Impairment Effects: From Motivation to Cognition and the Social Brain," *Current Directions in Psychological Science* 28 (2019): 260–65.

53. E.V. Wilson, "Perceived Effectiveness of Interpersonal Persuasion Strategies in Computer-Mediated Communication," *Computers in Human Behavior* 19, no. 5 (2003): 537–52; K. Sassenberg, M. Boos, and S. Rabung, "Attitude Change in Face-to-Face and Computer-Mediated Communication: Private Self-Awareness as Mediator and Moderator," *European Journal of Social Psychology* 35 (2005): 361–74; P. Di Blasio and L. Milani, "Computer-Mediated Communication and Persuasion: Peripheral vs. Central Route to Opinion Shift," *Computers in Human Behavior* 24, no. 3 (2008): 798–815.

54. J.W. Bang and D. Rahnev, "Stimulus Expectation Alters Decision Criterion but Not Sensory Signal in Perceptual Decision Making," *Scientific Reports* 7, no. 1 (December 6, 2017): 1–12; M.M. Roghanizad and V.K. Bohns, "Ask in Person: You're Less Persuasive than You Think over Email," *Journal of Experimental Social Psychology* 69 (March 2017): 223–26; A. Tapal, Y. Yeshurun, and B. Eitam, "Relevance-Based Processing: Little Role for Task-Relevant Expectations," *Psychonomic Bulletin & Review* 26 (2019): 1426–32.

55. Most sources incorrectly attribute this famous quotation (usually with "accomplished" rather than "achieved") to the Irish playwright and social critic George Bernard Shaw. This specific statement was likely first uttered in the late 1950s by Joe Coffman, president of Tecnifax Corporation and an enthusiast of visual and interpersonal communication. Coffman almost certainly adapted it from the following passage in William H. Whyte's 1950 *Fortune* magazine article on communication, which became one of *Fortune*'s most-read articles: "The great enemy of communication, we find, is the illusion of it." Coffman's statement was originally published in a 1960 article summarizing a public health conference, during which one of the speakers credited Coffman as the originator of this quotation. See W.H. Whyte, "Is Anybody Listening," *Fortune*, September 1950, 77ff; "Web of Mutual Anticipations: Conference Report," *Public Health Reports* 75, no. 10 (1960): 927; D.M. Davis, *A Biased Biography: Mine* (Lincoln, NE: iUniverse, 2004); "The Biggest Problem in Communication Is the Illusion That It Has Taken Place," *Quote Investigator*, August 31, 2014, http://quoteinvestigator.com/2014/08/31/illusion/.

56. R.M. Krauss, "The Psychology of Verbal Communication," in *International Encyclopedia of the Social and Behavioral Sciences*, ed. N. Smelser and P. Baltes (London: Elsevier, 2002), 16161–65.

57. A.M. Carton, C. Murphy, and J.R. Clark, "A (Blurry) Vision of the Future: How Leader Rhetoric about Ultimate Goals Influences Performance," *Academy of Management Journal* 57 (2014): 1544–70; P.D. Joshi et al., "Communicating with Distant Others: The Functional Use of Abstraction," *Social Psychological and Personality Science* 7 (2016): 37–44. Ambiguous language by politicians also increases with the diversity of constituents. See C. Chapp et al., "Going Vague: Ambiguity and Avoidance in Online Political Messaging," *Social Science Computer Review* 37 (2019): 591–610.

58. A.R. Links et al., "Surgeon Use of Medical Jargon with Parents in the Outpatient Setting," *Patient Education and Counseling* 102 (2019): 1111–18.

59. C.E. Connelly et al., "Knowledge Hiding in Organizations," *Journal of Organizational Behavior* 33 (2012): 64–88; N. Garg, C. Kumar, and A. Ganguly, "Knowledge Hiding in Organization: A Comprehensive Literature Review and Future Research Agenda," *Knowledge and Process Management* 29, no. 1 (2022): 31–52.

60. P.G. Roetzel, "Information Overload in the Information Age: A Review of the Literature from Business Administration, Business Psychology, and Related Disciplines with a Bibliometric Approach and Framework Development," *Business Research* 12, no. 2 (2019): 479–522; D. Bawden and L. Robinson, "Information Overload: An Overview," in *Oxford Encyclopedia of Political Decision Making*, by D. Bawden and L. Robinson (Oxford, UK: Oxford University Press, 2021).

61. A. Edmunds and A. Morris, "The Problem of Information Overload in Business Organisations: A Review of the Literature," *International Journal of Information Management* 20 (2000): 17–28;C.-Y. Li, "Why Do Online Consumers Experience Information Overload? An Extension of Communication Theory," *Journal of Information Science* 43, no. 6 (2017): 835–51.

62. A.-W. Harzing, K. Köster, and U. Magner, "Babel in Business: The Language Barrier and Its Solutions in the HQ-Subsidiary Relationship," *Journal of World Business* 46 (2011): 279–87; N. Aichhorn and J. Puck, "Bridging the Language Gap in Multinational Companies: Language Strategies and the Notion of Company-Speak," *Journal of World Business* 52 (2017): 386–403; D.E. Welch and L.S. Welch, "Developing Multilingual Capacity: A Challenge for the Multinational Enterprise," *Journal of Management* 44 (2018): 854–69.

63. T. Craig, "Different Strokes," *Personnel Today*, November 24, 2008, 190.

64. D.C. Barnlund, *Communication Styles of Japanese and Americans: Images and Realities* (Belmont, CA: Wadsworth, 1988); H. Yamada, *American and Japanese Business Discourse: A Comparison of Interaction Styles* (Norwood, NJ: Ablex, 1992), Chap. 2; T. Hasegawa and W.B. Gudykunst, "Silence in Japan and the United States," *Journal of Cross-Cultural Psychology* 29 (1998): 668–84; M. Fujio, "Silence during Intercultural Communication: A Case Study," *Corporate Communications* 9 (2004): 331–39.

65. H. Blagg, "A Just Measure of Shame?" *British Journal of Criminology* 37 (1997): 481–501; R. E. Axtell, *Gestures: The Do's and Taboos of Body Language around the World*, rev. ed. (New York: Wiley, 1998); A. McCarthy et al., "Cultural Display Rules Drive Eye Gaze During Thinking," *Journal of Cross-Cultural Psychology* 37 (2006): 717–22; H. Akechi et al., "Attention to Eye Contact in the West and East: Autonomic Responses and Evaluative Ratings," *PLOS ONE* 8, no. 3 (March 13, 2013): e59312; H. Yamada, O.R. Kelm, and D.A. Victor, *The 7 Keys to Communicating in Japan: An Intercultural Approach* (Georgetown University Press, 2017), pp. 163–65.

66. D. Tannen, *You Just Don't Understand: Men and Women in Conversation* (New York: Ballantine Books, 1990); J.L. Locke, *Duels and Duets: Why Men and Women Talk So Differently* (Cambridge, UK: Cambridge University Press, 2011); M.R. Atai and F. Chahkandi, "Democracy in Computer-Mediated Communication: Gender, Communicative Style, and Amount of Participation in Professional Listservs," *Computers in Human Behavior* 28, no. 3 (2012): 881–88; A.B. Hancock and B.A. Rubin, "Influence of Communication Partner's Gender on Language," *Journal of Language and Social Psychology* 34, no. 1 (2015): 46–64.

67. A. Mulac et al., "'Uh-Huh. What's That All About?' Differing Interpretations of Conversational Backchannels and Questions as Sources of Miscommunication across Gender Boundaries," *Communication Research* 25 (1998): 641–68; N.M. Sussman and D.H. Tyson, "Sex and Power: Gender Differences in Computer-Mediated Interactions," *Computers in Human Behavior* 16 (2000): 381–94; C. Leaper and R.D. Robnett, "Women Are More Likely Than Men to Use Tentative Language, Aren't They? A Meta-Analysis Testing for Gender Differences and Moderators," *Psychology of Women Quarterly* 35, no. 1 (2011): 129–42.

68. L.B. Comer and T. Drollinger, "Active Empathetic Listening and Selling Success: A Conceptual Framework," *Journal of Personal Selling & Sales Management* 19 (1999): 15–29; T. Drollinger, L.B. Comer, and P.T. Warrington, "Development and Validation of the Active Empathetic Listening Scale," *Psychology and Marketing* 23, no. 2 (2006): 161–80; P. JungKun et al., "The Role of Listening in E-Contact Center Customer Relationship Management," *Journal of Services Marketing* 29, no. 1 (2015): 49–58.

69. This quotation is varied slightly from the original translations by E. Carter, *All the Works of Epictetus, Which Are Now Extant*, 3rd ed., vol. 2 (London: J. and F. Rivington, 1768), 333; T.W. Higginson, *The Works of Epictetus* (Boston: Little, Brown and Company, 1866), 428.

70. T.J. Allen, "Architecture and Communication among Product Development Engineers," *California Management Review* 49, no. 2 (2007): 23–41; J. Kim and R. de Dear, "Workspace Satisfaction: The Privacy-Communication Trade-Off in Open-Plan Offices," *Journal of Environmental Psychology* 36 (2013): 18–26; A. Seddigh et al., "The Association between Office Design and Performance on Demanding Cognitive Tasks," *Journal of Environmental Psychology* 42 (2015): 172–81; M. Yadav et al., "The Irrelevant Speech Effect in Multi-Talker Environments: Applications to Open-Plan Offices," *The Journal of the Acoustical Society of America* 143, no. 3 (2018): 1725.

71. "State of the Sector 2019: The Definitive Global Survey of the Internal Communication Profession" (London: Gatehouse, February 2019); "Dynamic Signal Study Finds U.S. Workforce Stressed and Ready to Quit, Compounding Concerns from Tight Labor Market and Possible Economic Downturn," news release (San Bruno, CA: Dynamic Signal, March 20, 2019); Office of Personnel Management, "2019 Federal Employee Viewpoint Survey" (Washington, DC: U.S. Government, October 2019); "Millennials Are Managers Now," *Zapier* (blog), March 10, 2020, https://zapier.com/blog/millennial-managers-report/; S.M. O'Keefe and J. Buono, "Crisis Communication: How Great Leaders Stop Rumors before They Start," *Gallup Workplace*, April 3, 2020.

72. "How to Reimagine Work Spaces for the Hybrid Era," *Microsoft Worklab* (blog), June 21, 2021.

73. C.J. Turco, "A New Era of Corporate Conversation," *MIT Sloan Management Review* 58, no. 1 (Fall 2016): 11–12; M. Ewing, L.R. Men, and J. O'Neil, "Using Social Media to Engage Employees: Insights from Internal Communication Managers," *International Journal of Strategic Communication* 13, no. 2 (2019): 110–32; C.A. Yue, L.R. Men, and M.A. Ferguson, "Examining the Effects of Internal Communication and Emotional Culture on Employees' Organizational Identification," *International Journal of Business Communication* 58, no. 2 (2021): 169–95.

74. W. Ouchi, *Theory Z* (New York: Avon Books, 1981), 176–77; T. Peters and R. Waterman, *In Search of Excellence* (New York: Harper and Row, 1982), 122.

75. R. Rousos, "Trust in Leaders Lacking at Utility," *The Ledger* (Lakeland, FL), July 29, 2003, B1; B. Whitworth and B. Riccomini, "Management Communication: Unlocking Higher Employee Performance," *Communication World*, March/April 2005, 18–21.

76. K. Davis, "Management Communication and the Grapevine," *Harvard Business Review* 31 (1953): 43–49; W.L. Davis and J.R. O'Connor, "Serial Transmission of Information: A Study of the Grapevine," *Journal of Applied Communication Research* 5 (1977): 61–72.

77. G. Dalziel, *Rumor and Communication in Asia in the Internet Age* (New York: Routledge, 2013); K.L. Robinson and P.D. Thelen, "What Makes the Grapevine So Effective? An Employee Perspective on Employee- Organization Communication and Peer-to-Peer Communication," *Public Relations Journal* 12, no. 2 (2018).

78. S.R. Clegg and A. van Iterson, "Dishing the Dirt: Gossiping in Organizations," *Culture and Organization* 15 (2009): 275–89; C. Mills, "Experiencing Gossip: The Foundations for a Theory of Embedded Organizational Gossip," *Group & Organization Management* 35 (2010): 213–40; T.J. Grosser et al., "Hearing It through the Grapevine: Positive and Negative Workplace Gossip," *Organizational Dynamics* 41 (2012): 52–61.

79. R.L. Rosnow, "Inside Rumor: A Personal Journey," *American Psychologist* 46 (1991): 484–96; P. Bordia et al., "Management Are Aliens! Rumors and Stress during Organizational Change," *Group & Organization Management* 31 (2006): 601–21; K. Smet et al., "The Explanatory Role of Rumours in the Reciprocal Relationship between Organizational Change Communication and Job Insecurity: A Within-Person Approach," *European Journal of Work and Organizational Psychology* 25 (2016): 631–44.

80. N. Nicholson, "Evolutionary Psychology: Toward a New View of Human Nature and Organizational Society," *Human Relations* 50 (1997): 1053–78; E.K. Foster, "Research on Gossip: Taxonomy, Methods, and Future Directions," *Review of General Psychology* 8, no. 2 (2004): 78–99; B. Beersma and G.A. Van Kleef, "Why People Gossip: An Empirical Analysis of Social Motives, Antecedents, and Consequences," *Journal of Applied Social Psychology* 42, no. 11 (2012): 2640–70.

9 Power and Influence in the Workplace

fizkes/Shutterstock

Learning Objectives

After reading this chapter, you should be able to:

LO9-1 Describe the dependence model of power and the five sources of power in organizations.

LO9-2 Discuss the four contingencies of power.

LO9-3 Explain how people and work units gain power through social networks.

LO9-4 Describe eight types of influence tactics, three consequences of influencing others, and three contingencies to consider when choosing an influence tactic.

LO9-5 Identify the organizational conditions and personal characteristics associated with organizational politics, as well as ways to minimize organizational politics.

power The capacity of a person, team, or organization to influence others

Managing up, also known as managing your boss, is a valuable process of gaining power and using influence for the benefit of the organization. Executives say it is a key factor in everyone's career success. "It's an important skill because you start to think of your relationship with your boss as a co-partnership," explains Mita Mallick, head of inclusion, equity, and impact at fintech company Carta. "You're both in it to be successful; neither of you will be successful without the other."

One aspect of managing up is understanding and adapting to your boss's preferences and style. "Get to know their communication preferences and adjust yours for greater understanding," advises Loren Margolis, CEO of Training & Leadership Success. "Know when to keep them in the loop and when to work independently."

Managing up requires several skills, including the ability to empathize and anticipate the other person's needs. "To manage up effectively requires understanding and having empathy for the challenges your manager faces and the realities of their role," observes Michelle Bennett, chief marketing officer for Niagara Institute.

An essential ingredient in managing your boss is helping them perform their job well by offering solutions, not just problems. "Here's a pro tip from me as a former dean and provost who has worked with many department chairs: For every problem you share with your dean, bring a couple of potential solutions as well," recommends Dartmouth College professor Carolyn Dever. "From the dean's perspective, this will be most welcome."

Managing up isn't just about adapting to the boss; it also involves setting boundaries and influencing how your boss interacts and supports you. "Whether a boss is new or seasoned, it's important to take the time to set goals, establish boundaries, and advocate for oneself," says Heidi Lynne Kurter, North American head of HR at Digital.ai.[1]

The fine art and science of upward influence (managing your boss) captures many of the themes in this chapter. It considers the individual's sources and contingencies of power, and how that power is applied to actually engage in upward influence. Everyone uses power and influence in organizations, whether they realize it or not.

This chapter unfolds as follows: First, we define power and present a model depicting the dynamics of power in organizational settings. The chapter then discusses the five bases of power. Next, we look at the contingencies necessary to translate those sources into meaningful power. Our attention then turns to social networks and how they provide power to members through social capital. The latter part of this chapter examines the various types of influence in organizational settings as well as the contingencies of effective influence strategies. The final section of this chapter looks at situations in which influence becomes organizational politics, as well as ways of minimizing political behavior.

LO9-1 Describe the dependence model of power and the five sources of power in organizations.

THE MEANING OF POWER

Power is the capacity of a person, team, or organization to influence others.[2] There are a few important features of this definition. First, power is not the act of changing someone's attitudes or behavior; it is only the *potential* to do so. People frequently have power they do not use; they might not even know they have power. Second, power is based on the target's *perception* that the power holder controls (i.e., possesses, has access to, or regulates) a valuable resource that can help to achieve the target person's goals.[3] An employee might have valuable expertise, yet this power base doesn't translate into actual power because others in the organization don't know about or understand the value of this expertise. However, power is not your own perception or feeling of power; it exists only when others believe you have power.

Third, power involves asymmetric (unequal) *dependence* of one party on another party.[4] This dependent relationship is illustrated in Exhibit 9.1. The line from Person B to the goal shows that they believe Person A controls a resource that can help or hinder Person B in achieving that goal. Person A—the dominant power holder in this illustration—might have power over Person B by controlling a desired job assignment, useful information, rewards, or even the privilege of being associated with Person A! For example, if you believe a coworker has expertise (the resource) that would substantially help you write a better report (your goal), then that coworker has some power over you because you value that expertise to achieve your goal. Whatever the resource is, Person B believes they are *dependent* on Person A (the power holder) to provide the resource so Person B can reach their goal.

Although dependence is a key element of power relationships, we use the phrase *asymmetric dependence* because the less

Exhibit 9.1 Dependence Model of Power

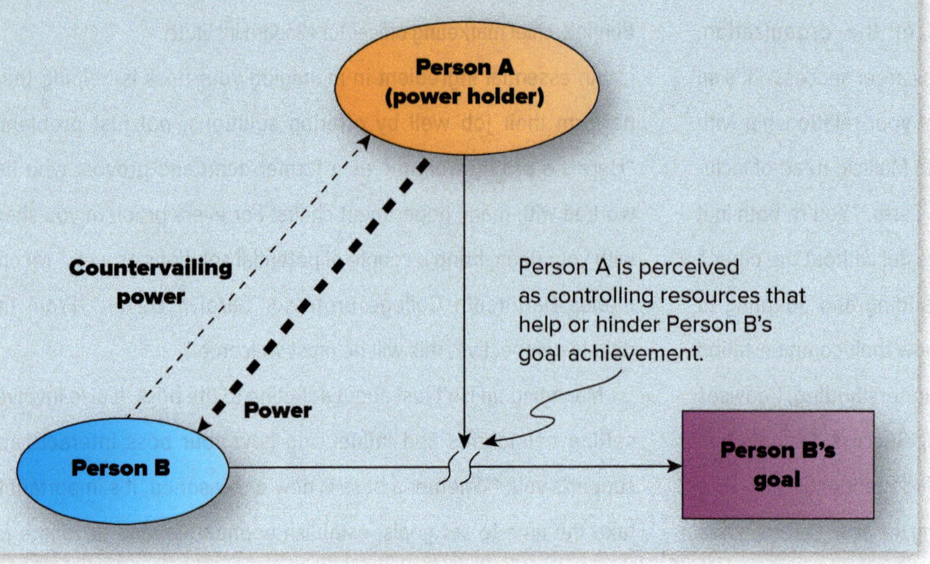

powerful party also has some power—called **countervailing power**—over the more powerful party. In Exhibit 9.1, Person A dominates the power relationship, but Person B has enough countervailing power to keep Person A in the exchange relationship and ensure that person uses their dominant power judiciously.

One other key feature of all power relationships is that they depend on some minimum level of trust. Trust indicates a level of expectation that the more powerful party will deliver the resource. For example, you trust your employer to give you a paycheck at the end of each pay period. Even those in extremely dependent situations will usually walk away from the relationship if they lack a minimum level of trust in the more powerful party.

Power involves asymmetric dependence of one party on another party because the less powerful party has countervailing power over the stronger power holder.
Kasper Ravlo/123RF

Let's look at this power dependence model in the employee–manager relationship. You depend on your boss to support your continued employment, satisfactory work arrangements, and other valued resources. At the same time, the manager depends on you to complete required tasks, to work effectively with others, and to engage in other behaviors that the manager values. Managers (and the companies they represent) typically have more power. Employees sometimes have more power than their bosses in the employment relationship, but usually they have lower countervailing power. Either way, the extent that your source of power (such as expertise) actually generates power depends on several factors, such as the employer's awareness of your source of power and how many other employees have that source of power. The employee–manager relationship also depends on sufficient trust in each other.

The dependence model reveals only the core features of power dynamics between people and work units in organizations. We also need to learn about the specific sources of power and contingencies that support or inhibit those power bases. As Exhibit 9.2 illustrates, power is derived from five sources: legitimate, reward, coercive, expert, and referent. The model also identifies four contingencies of power: the employee's or department's nonsubstitutability, centrality, visibility, and discretion. Over the next few sections of this chapter, we will discuss each of these sources and contingencies of power in the context of organizations.

SOURCES OF POWER IN ORGANIZATIONS

There are five main sources of power in human interactions.[5] Three of these—legitimate, reward, and coercive—originate mostly from the power holder's formal position or informal role. In other words, the person is granted these sources of power formally by the organization or informally by other people (coworkers, subordinates, etc.). Two other sources of power—expert and referent—originate mainly from the power holder's own characteristics; in other words, people carry these power bases around with them. However, even personal sources of power are not completely within the person because they depend on how others perceive them.

Legitimate Power

Legitimate power is an agreement among organizational members that people in certain roles can request a set of behaviors from others. This perceived right or obligation originates from formal job

countervailing power The capacity of a person, team, or organization to keep a more powerful person or group in the exchange relationship

legitimate power An agreement among organizational members that people in certain roles can request certain behaviors of others

norm of reciprocity A felt obligation and social expectation of helping or otherwise giving something of value to someone who has already helped or given something of value to you

Exhibit 9.2 Sources and Contingencies of Power

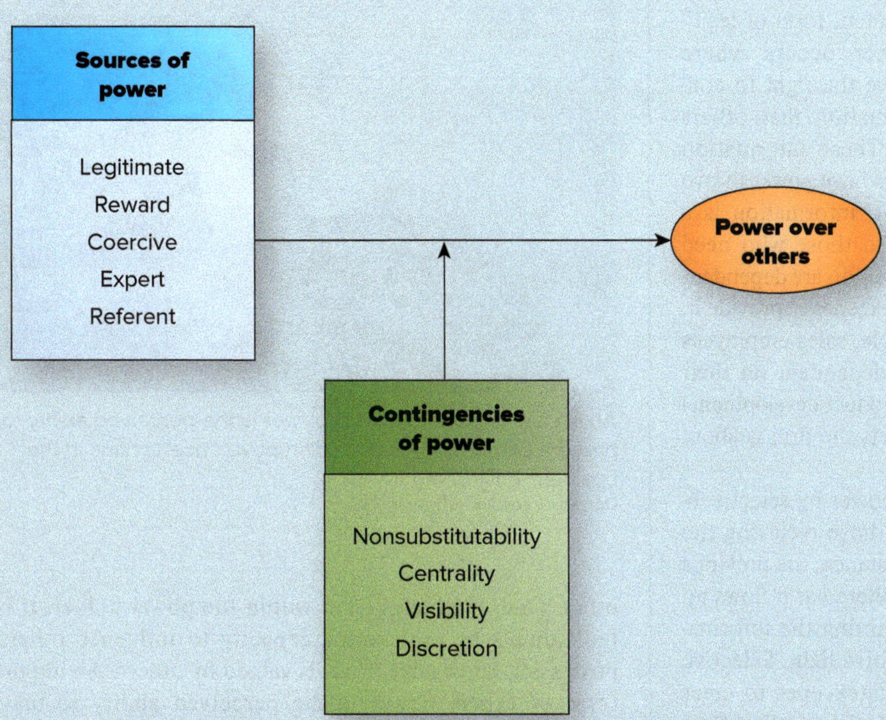

descriptions as well as informal rules of conduct. It is usually the most important source of power in organizational settings, particularly between employees and managers.[6] For example, managers have a legitimate right to tell employees what tasks to perform, whom to work with, what company resources they can use, and so forth. Employees comply with the boss's requests because they have agreed to do so from people in positions of higher authority. A person's motivation to follow directions occurs separately from the manager's ability to reward or punish employees.

Legitimate power has restrictions; it gives the power holder only the right to ask others to perform a limited domain of behaviors, known as the *zone of indifference.*[7] Although most employees accept the boss's right to deny them access to Facebook during company time, some might draw the line when the boss asks them to work several hours beyond the regular workday. They either overtly refuse to follow orders or engage in delaying and other evasive tactics.

Several factors influence the size of the zone of indifference and, consequently, the magnitude of legitimate power. Highly trusted power holders have a larger zone of indifference. Employees are more willing to abide by the requests of trusted leaders even when those requests are unusual or on the periphery of expected job duties. Some people are more obedient to authority due to their values and personality traits. Specifically, those who value conformity and tradition as well as have high power distance (i.e., they accept an unequal distribution of power) tend to give their bosses a larger zone of indifference. The organization's culture represents another influence on the willingness of employees to follow orders.[8]

Managers are not the only people with legitimate power in organizations. Employees also have legitimate power over their bosses and coworkers through legal and administrative rights as well as informal norms.[9] An organization might give employees the right to request information that is required for their job. Laws give employees the right to refuse to work in unsafe conditions. More subtle forms of legitimate power also exist, particularly the **norm of reciprocity.** This is a felt obligation and social expectation of helping or otherwise giving something of value to someone who has already helped or given something of value to you.[10] If a coworker previously helped you resolve a difficult problem with a client, that coworker has power because you feel an obligation to help the coworker on something of similar value in the future. The norm of reciprocity is a form of legitimate power because it is an informal rule of conduct that we are expected to follow.

Legitimate power gives the power holder only the right to ask others to perform a limited domain of behaviors, known as the *zone of indifference.*

referent power The capacity to influence others on the basis of an identification with and respect for the power holder

charisma A set of self-presentation characteristics and nonverbal communication behaviors (i.e., signaling) that generate interpersonal attraction and referent power over others as well as deference to the charismatic person

Legitimate Power through Information Control A particularly potent form of legitimate power occurs where people have the right to control information that others receive.[11] These information gatekeepers have power in two ways. First, information is a resource, so those who need that information are dependent on the gatekeeper to provide it. For example, sales employees might be dependent on their manager or other departments (marketing, product development) for information about details of new products the firm is about to launch.

Second, information gatekeepers gain power by selectively distributing information that frames how those receiving the information perceive the situation.[12] For instance, the previous chapter reported that information is often filtered as it flows up the hierarchy, which enables those transmitting the information to present the situation in a more positive light. Selective distribution of information enables the gatekeeper to steer recipients of that information toward one decision rather than another.

Reward Power

Reward power is derived from the person's ability to control the allocation of rewards valued by others and to remove negative sanctions (i.e., negative reinforcement). Managers have formal authority that gives them power over the distribution of organizational rewards such as pay, promotions, time off, vacation schedules, and work assignments. Employees have reward power over coworkers through organizational citizenship behaviors, such as lending work resources or coaching others. They also have reward power over their bosses through feedback they provide to the company about the boss's leadership.

Coercive Power

Coercive power is the ability to apply punishment. Managers usually have considerable coercive power, ranging from showing disapproval to firing employees. Employees also have coercive power, such as when coworkers use peer pressure to change another employee's behavior. In fact, one recent study found that hospital employees were more likely to follow prescribed hygienic activity (wash their hands) when faced with peer pressure than when the hospital rewarded this behavior with a large financial incentive.[13]

Expert Power

Legitimate, reward, and coercive power originate mostly from an organizational position or role.[14] Expert power, on the other hand, originates from within the power holder. It is an individual's or work unit's capacity to influence others by possessing knowledge or skills valued by others. An important form of expert power is the perceived ability to manage uncertainties in the business environment. Organizations are more effective when they operate in predictable environments, so they value people who can cope with turbulence in consumer trends, societal changes, unstable supply lines, and so forth. Expertise can help companies cope with uncertainty through prevention, forecasting, and absorption. These three coping strategies are arranged in a hierarchy of importance, with prevention being the most powerful:[15]

An important form of expert power is the perceived ability to prevent, forecast, or absorb disruptive uncertainties in the business environment.
Darren Greenwood/Design Pics

- *Prevention.* The most effective strategy is to prevent environmental changes from occurring. For example, financial experts acquire power by preventing the organization from experiencing a cash shortage or defaulting on loans.
- *Forecasting.* The second best strategy is to predict environmental changes or variations. In this respect, trendspotters and other marketing specialists gain power by predicting changes in consumer preferences so companies can adapt before the emerging environmental conditions occur.
- *Absorption.* People and work units also gain power by absorbing or neutralizing the impact of environmental shifts as they occur. An example is the ability of maintenance crews to come to the rescue when machines break down.

Referent Power

People have **referent power** when others identify with them, like them, or otherwise respect them. As with expert power, referent power originates within the power holder. It is mostly a function of the person's character and interpersonal skills. Referent power is associated with **charisma**. Experts have difficulty agreeing on the meaning of charisma. Some describe charisma as a special "gift" or trait within the charismatic person, whereas

> **Blind respect for authority is the greatest enemy of the truth.**[16]
>
> —Albert Einstein, theoretical physicist

others say it is mainly in the eyes of the beholder. Charisma may be best described as a set of self-presentation characteristics and nonverbal communication behaviors (i.e., signaling) that generate interpersonal attraction and referent power over others as well as deference to the charismatic person.[17]

Deference to Power

One of the most troubling observations about power in organizations is the human tendency to follow the guidance of people who are charismatic (i.e., have referent power) or claim to have legitimate or expert power. Deferential followers minimally evaluate the appropriateness of the requested behavior. They don't even investigate whether the power holder has legitimate authority to make the request or actually possesses the expertise they claim.[18]

Consider this recent example: Before the instructor of an undergraduate course arrived for class, two casually dressed people (a 29-year-old Black male and a 50-year-old White female) entered and set their belongings down at the front of the classroom. Without introduction, one of them said to the students: "I need you to put your cell phones in this box." One of them then walked around the classroom with a box to collect the students' phones. If any student questioned this task, they were authoritatively told, "It is important for you to follow instructions and put your phone in the box." The two also said (when asked) that they did not know where the instructor was at that time. Most students cherish their cell/mobile phones, yet an average of 85 percent of students across five small classes surrendered their phones to these strangers without receiving any explanation or assurance! Fortunately, these two people were confederates of the instructor and all phones were returned after the confederates had collected and counted them.[19]

This example was an experimental event in a classroom, but deference to power sometimes has tragic consequences. Not long ago, the Canadian justice system discovered that one of its "star" expert witnesses–a forensic child pathology expert–had provided inaccurate cause of death evaluations in at least 20 cases. A dozen of those cases resulted in wrongful or highly questionable criminal convictions. The pathologist's reputation as a renowned authority was the main reason why his often-weak evidence was accepted without question. "Experts in a courtroom–we give great deference to experts," admits a Canadian defense lawyer familiar with the situation.[20]

LO9-2 Discuss the four contingencies of power.

CONTINGENCIES AND CONSEQUENCES OF POWER

Contingencies of Power

Suppose that you have valuable expertise that can give the organization significant competitive advantage over rivals. Does this expertise mean that you are influential? Not necessarily. As was illustrated earlier in Exhibit 9.2, sources of power generate power only under some conditions. Four important contingencies of power are nonsubstitutability, centrality, visibility, and discretion.[21]

Nonsubstitutability Individuals and work units have more power when the resource they offer is nonsubstitutable.[22] If you have expertise that is valuable to the organization and that no other employee can provide, you would be more powerful than if several people in your company possess this valued knowledge. Conversely, power decreases as the number of alternative sources of the resource increases. Substitutability refers not only to other sources that offer the resource; it also refers to substitutions of the resource itself. You might be the only person with specialized knowledge about a topic, but that knowledge becomes substitutable if technology or documented procedures provide similar guidance.

Controlling access to the resource is one strategy to increase nonsubstitutability. Several professions leverage their expert power by restricting access to the profession and often to the educational programs that train people into that profession. Employees are also less substitutable when they operate special equipment that they personally modified or possess other knowledge that remains undocumented.

A second strategy is differentiating the resource from the alternatives. Consulting firms sometimes use this tactic. They take skills and knowledge that many competitors can also provide and wrap them into a package (with the latest buzz words, of course) so that it looks like a service that no one else can offer.

Nonsubstitutability through differentiation is a key ingredient for increasing your power in the workplace and labor market through your *personal brand.* Your public image and reputation should be authentic (who you really are and what you can deliver) and valuable to employers. But it also needs to be unique, which leverages the power of nonsubstitutability.

OB THEORY TO PRACTICE

The Power of Your Personal Brand[23]

Marketing experts and career advisors alike identify your personal brand as an important driver of career success. "Having your personal brand and perspective is now a calling card for traditional jobs," observes Raina Penchansky, CEO at Digital Brand Architects. Black Marketing CEO Chris J. Reed is equally emphatic: "The most important thing about your career is to actually have a personal brand."

An individual's personal brand is founded on their authentic talents, characteristics, and behaviors. "A personal brand is the combination of unique skills, experiences, and character traits that make you who you are," explains marketing and public relations executive Kelly Fletcher. Authenticity is critical because exaggeration typically fails, with long-term damage to one's reputation.

Your personal brand is a source of power in the marketplace, and that power increases with its nonsubstitutability—how much it differentiates you from others. "Your personal brand can often differentiate yourself in terms of how you go forward, how you succeed, how you raise investment, how you win clients," advises Chris Reed. William Arruda, founder of Reach Personal Branding, adds: "When competing with other similarly qualified job seekers, a unique, authentic personal brand will naturally set you apart and help you connect with your interviewers."

Visibility is another key ingredient for increasing the power of a personal brand. "Few people dispute the importance of visibility in a group, organization, or professional field," notes Brian H. Robb, chief marketing officer at real estate investment trust Reitum. "If your talents are unknown to others, they are less likely to consider you as a solution."

Overall, nurturing a personal brand is an ongoing process that needs to have specific characteristics. "Your personal brand should be relevant, authentic, values-driven, credibility-building, visible, unique, flattering, and consistent," says Kelly Fletcher.

Artem Furman/Shutterstock

Centrality Centrality refers to the power holder's importance based on the degree and nature of interdependence with others.[24] Centrality increases with the number of people dependent on you as well as how quickly and severely they are affected by that dependence. Think about your own centrality for a moment: If you decided not to show up for work or school tomorrow, how many people would have difficulty performing their jobs because of your absence? How soon after they arrive at work would these coworkers have to adjust their tasks and work schedule as a result of your absence? If you have high centrality, many people in the organization would be adversely affected by your absence, and they would be affected quickly.

Visibility Employees gain power when their talents remain in the forefront of the minds of their boss, coworkers, and others. In other words, power increases with visibility. This visibility can occur by taking on people-oriented jobs and projects that require frequent interaction with senior executives and coworkers elsewhere in the organization. Employees also gain visibility by being, quite literally, visible. Some people strategically locate themselves in more visible work areas, such as those closest to the boss or where other employees frequently pass by.

People often use public symbols as subtle (and not-so-subtle) cues to make their power sources known to others. Some display their educational diplomas and awards on office walls to remind visitors of their expertise. Medical professionals wear white coats with stethoscopes around their necks, which symbolize their legitimate and expert power in hospital settings. Some employees deliberately work more days in the office rather than remotely so their productively is more visible.

Discretion Another important contingency of power in organizations is the freedom to exercise judgment. This discretion involves making decisions without referring to a specific rule or receiving permission from someone else.[25] Employees have more power due to increased discretion when they are given more autonomy over their work (see Chapter 5). In contrast, an employee's discretion to apply their legitimate, reward, and coercive power is often curtailed by rules and vetoes from higher authorities.[26]

Middle managers currently feel powerless due to lack of discretion because they are sandwiched between employee expectations and senior executive demands in a post-pandemic world. A recent large global survey reported that 74 percent of managers say they lack discretion–they don't have the influence or resources–to do more to implement change for their employees. Middle managers are trying to minimize turnover at a time when employees are demanding higher wages and more hybrid work. Yet middle managers lack discretion because the executive team demands that managers keep a lid on spiraling wage bills and require employees to work full time in the office. Not surprisingly, the global survey found that 54 percent of managers believe their company's leadership is out of touch with employees.[27]

Consequences of Power

How does power affect the power holder? The answer depends to some extent on the type of power.[28] When people feel empowered (high self-determination, meaning, competence, and impact), they believe they have *power over themselves* and freedom from being influenced by others (power independence). Empowerment tends to increase motivation, job satisfaction, organizational commitment, and job performance. However, this feeling of being in control and free from others' authority also increases automatic rather than mindful thinking. In particular, people who feel powerful are more likely to rely on stereotypes, have difficulty empathizing, and generally have less accurate perceptions compared with people who have less power.[29]

The other type of power is one in which an individual has power *over others,* such as the legitimate, reward, and coercive power that managers have over employees in the workplace (power interdependence). In many situations, this type of power produces a sense of duty or responsibility for the people over whom the power holder has authority. Consequently, people who have power over others tend to be more mindful of their actions and engage in less stereotyping.

Power over oneself (independent power) and power over others (interdependent power) are not necessarily distinct from each other. As people are promoted into higher management positions they tend to have more of both. Therefore, the issue is more about how the power holder views their increasing power. Those who gain power (such as through promotions) relish their empowerment, and this power independence view produces the dysfunctional effects we described previously. Others feel increasingly responsible for stakeholders, and this power interdependence view tends to improve organizational outcomes.[30]

centrality A contingency of power pertaining to the degree and nature of interdependence between the power holder and others

social networks Social structures of individuals or social units that are connected to one another through one or more forms of interdependence

social capital The knowledge, opportunities, and other resources available to members of a social network, along with the mutual support, trust, reciprocity, and coordination that facilitate sharing of those resources

McGraw Hill connect

SELF-ASSESSMENT 9.1: Do You Have a Guanxi Orientation?

LO9-3 Explain how people and work units gain power through social networks.

THE POWER OF SOCIAL NETWORKS

"It's not what you know, but who you know that counts!" This often-heard statement reflects the idea that employees get ahead not just by developing their skills and knowledge, but by locating themselves within **social networks**—social structures of individuals or social units (e.g., departments, organizations) that are connected to one another through one or more forms of interdependence.[31] Some networks are held together due to common interests, such as employee resource groups that are organized around ethnicity, sexual orientations, ages, abilities, and other identities and interests. Other networks form around common status, expertise, kinship, or physical proximity. For instance, employees are more likely to form networks with coworkers who have common educational backgrounds and occupational interests.[32]

Social networks exist everywhere because people have a drive to bond. Cultural norms also seem to influence active network involvement. Social networking may be more of a central life activity in Asian cultures that emphasize *guanxi,* a Chinese term referring to an individual's network of social connections. Guanxi is an expressive activity because being part of a close-knit network of family and friends reinforces one's self-concept. It is also an instrumental activity for receiving favors and opportunities from others. Guanxi is sometimes so pervasive, however, that several experts warn it can undermine the organization's effectiveness.[33]

Social Capital and Sources of Power

Social networks generate power through **social capital**—the knowledge, opportunities, and other resources available to members of a social network as well as the mutual support, trust, reciprocity, and coordination that facilitate sharing of those resources.[34] Compared to nonmembers, members within a social network are more motivated and able to communicate, distribute, or otherwise provide resources within their power to others in that community.

Social networks potentially enhance and maintain the power of its members through three resources: information, visibility,

Social networks potentially enhance and maintain the power of its members through three resources: information, visibility, and referent power.
Helder Almeida/Shutterstock

and referent power. Probably the best-known resource is information from other network members, which improves the individual's expert power.[35] The goodwill of social capital opens communication pipelines among those within the network. Network members receive valuable knowledge more easily and more quickly from fellow network members than do people outside that network.[36] With better information access and timeliness, members have more power because their expertise is a scarce resource; it is not widely available to people outside the network.

Increased visibility is a second contributor to a person's power through social networks. When asked to recommend someone who has a particular expertise, other network members more readily think of you than of people outside the network. A third resource from social networks is increased referent power. People tend to gain referent power through networking because members of the network identify with or at least have greater trust in each other. Referent power is also apparent by the fact that reciprocity increases among network members as they become more embedded in the network.[37]

Social networks are often viewed as free spirits, yet they can be orchestrated to some extent through organizational structures and other practices.[38] Whether or not you try to manage social networks, you need to be aware of them. Indeed, employees gain power through their awareness of social networks throughout the organization and who is attached to those networks.[39]

Gaining Power through Social Networks

How do individuals (and teams and organizations) gain social capital from social networks? To answer this question, we need to consider the number, depth, variety, and centrality of connections that people have in their networks.

Strong Ties, Weak Ties, Many Ties The volume of information, opportunities, and other social capital that we receive from networks depends on strong ties, weak ties, and many ties. Strong ties are close-knit relationships, which are evident from how often we interact with specific people, how much we share resources with them, how much we experience psychological closeness to them, and whether we have multiple or single-purpose relationships with them (e.g., friend, coworker, sports partner). Strong ties are valuable because they offer resources more quickly and usually more plentifully than are available from weak ties (i.e., acquaintances). Strong ties also offer greater social support and greater cooperation for favors and assistance.[40]

Strong connections aren't necessarily the most valuable ties. Instead, having weak ties (i.e., being merely acquaintances) with people from diverse networks can be equally or more valuable than having only strong ties (i.e., having close friendships) with people in similar networks.[41] Why is this so? Strong ties—our close-knit circle of friends—tend to be similar to us and to one another. Consequently, they provide much of the same

Having weak ties (acquaintances) with people from diverse networks can be just as valuable as having strong ties (close friendships) with people in similar networks.
Brothers91/E+/Getty Images

information and other resources that we already have or that other strong ties provide.[42] Weak ties, on the other hand, are acquaintances who are different from us and therefore more likely to offer unique opportunities, connections, and other resources not available from our strong ties. Weak ties exist when we serve as a "bridge" across several unrelated networks.

The value of weak ties is most apparent in job hunting and career development.[43] People with diverse networks tend to be more successful job seekers because they have a wider net to catch new job opportunities. In contrast, people who belong to similar overlapping networks tend to receive fewer leads, many of which they already knew about. Careers are expanding across many organizations and industries. Therefore, you need to establish connections with people from a diverse range of industries, professions, and other spheres of life.

Finally, our power and social capital increase with many ties—the number of people connected to you in a social network. The more people you know, the more network resources are available to you. Generally, as your social network grows, you have less time and energy to maintain strong ties. However, some people have an amazing capacity to support relatively active and frequent connections to many people. Social media (Twitter, Facebook, LinkedIn, etc.) have further amplified this capacity to maintain numerous connections at a fairly strong level.[44]

Social Network Centrality Earlier in this chapter, we explained that centrality is an important contingency of power. This contingency also applies to social networks.[45] The more central a person (or team or organization) is located in the network, the more social capital and therefore more power they acquire. Centrality is your importance in that network.

Three factors determine your centrality in a social network. One factor is "betweenness," which literally refers to how much you are located between others in the network. In Exhibit 9.3,

structural hole An area between two or more dense social network areas that lacks network ties

Exhibit 9.3 Centrality in Social Networks

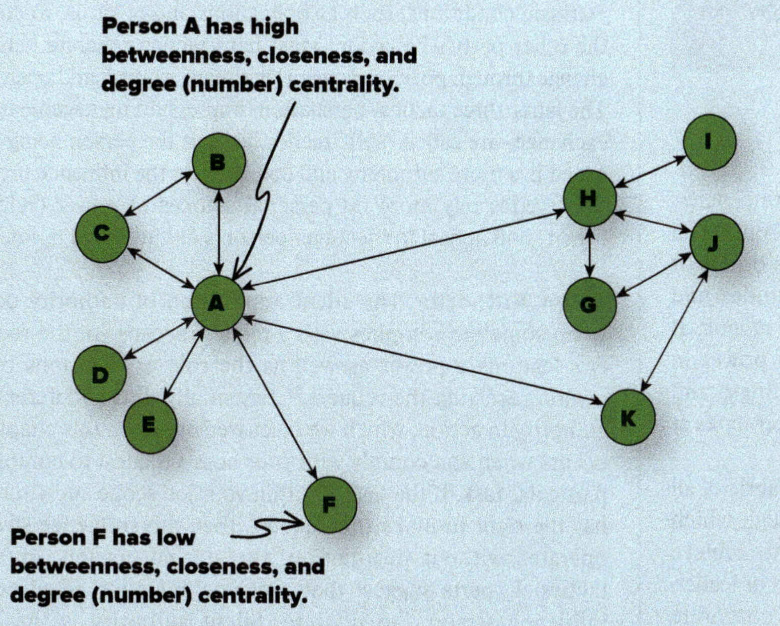

Person A has high betweenness centrality because that individual is a gatekeeper who controls the flow of information to and from many other people in the network. Person H has less betweenness, whereas Person F and several other network members in the diagram have no betweenness. The more betweenness you have, the more you control the distribution of information and other resources to people on either side of you.

A second factor in centrality is the number or percentage of connections you have to others in the network (called *degree centrality*). The network resources (information, favors, etc.) available to you increases with the number of people connected to you. The number of connections also increases centrality because you are more visible to other members of the network. Although being a member of a network gives you access to resources in that network, having a direct connection to more people within the network makes that resource sharing more fluid.

A third factor in centrality is the "closeness" of the relationship with others in the network. High closeness refers to strong ties. It is depicted by shorter, more direct, and more efficient paths or connections with others in the network. For example, Person A has fairly high closeness centrality because they have direct paths to most of the network. Also, many of these paths are short, which implies efficient and high-quality communication links. Your centrality increases with your closeness to other network members because they are affected more quickly and significantly by you.

One last observation is that Exhibit 9.3 illustrates two clusters of people in the network. The gap between these two clusters is called a **structural hole**.[46] Notice that Person A provides the main bridge across this structural hole (connecting to H and K in the other cluster). This bridging role gives Person A additional power in the network. By bridging this gap, Person A becomes a broker–someone who connects two independent networks and controls information flow between them. Research shows that the more brokering relationships you have, the more likely you are to get early promotions and higher pay.

The Dark Side of Social Networks Social networks occur naturally in all organizations, yet they can create a formidable barrier to those who are not actively connected to them.[47] Females are often excluded from social networks in male-dominated jobs and industries because people tend to network with others with similar characteristics and backgrounds. These gendered networks can be a liability because they limit referrals, knowledge, and other forms of career-enhancing resources that networks provide.

Today, many organizational leaders are fighting against the dark side of social networks by nurturing and consulting with employee resource groups. These voluntary employee-led groups provide support and education about diversity, equity, inclusion (DEI), and social issues, but they are also immensely valuable as informal social networks that have connections to the organization's senior decision makers.

OB THEORY TO PRACTICE

Franklin Women's Network Supports Networking and Inclusion[48]

A chance hallway encounter with Global Business Operations Vice President Amy Stauffer gave Engineering Manager Sukaynah Abu-Mulaweh the opportunity to learn and broaden her network at Fort Wayne manufacturer Franklin Electric. The two women worked in different areas of the company, yet they benefited from the regular meetings.

"As a new manager, Sukaynah wanted to form connections that would help her grow and learn about the business from someone who has worked in this industry for more than 20 years," says Stauffer. "Our ability to meet and connect took planning, but we both valued the discussions we had during those sessions."

During these conversations, Abu-Mulaweh and Stauffer discussed how to create a more formal network that would benefit all women at Franklin Electric. Over several months, a cross-departmental steering committee planned and launched the Franklin Women's Network (FWN).

Franklin Women's Network is an employee resource group designed to help women of Franklin Electric "connect, build alliances, and actively develop their careers." Networking figures prominently in the FWN's objectives. Specifically, it promotes "opportunities for networking and building professional relationships to share ideas and experiences while collaborating on projects throughout the organization."

LO9-4 Describe eight types of influence tactics, three consequences of influencing others, and three contingencies to consider when choosing an influence tactic.

INFLUENCING OTHERS

So far, this chapter has focused on the sources, contingencies, and consequences of power as well as power derived from social networks. But power is only the *capacity* to influence others. It represents the potential to change someone's attitudes and behavior. **Influence**, on the other hand, is *power in motion.* It applies one or more sources and contingencies of power in an attempt to alter another person's beliefs, feelings, and behavior.[49] Consequently, the remainder of this chapter looks at how people use power to influence others.

Influence tactics are woven throughout the social fabric of all organizations. Influence is an essential process through which people coordinate their efforts and act in concert to achieve organizational objectives. It is central to the definition of leadership. Influence operates down, across, and up the corporate hierarchy. Executives ensure that subordinates complete required tasks. Employees influence coworkers to help them with their job assignments.

Types of Influence Tactics

Organizational behavior researchers have devoted considerable attention to the various types of influence tactics found in organizational settings. They do not agree on a definitive list, but the most commonly discussed influence tactics are identified in Exhibit 9.4 and described in this section of the chapter.[50] The first five are known as "hard" influence tactics because the influencer applies extrinsic conditions, such as obligations and rewards, to control the other party's behavior. Most hard tactics generate behavior change through position power (legitimate, reward, and coercion). The latter three tactics–persuasion, impression management, and exchange–are called "soft" tactics because the person being influenced has more autonomy and control over the influence process. Soft tactics rely more on personal sources of power (referent, expert) and appeal to the target person's attitudes and needs.[51]

Silent Authority The silent application of authority occurs when someone complies with a request because of the requester's legitimate power as well as the role expectations of the person receiving the request.[52] Essentially, this is deference to authority in action, which we discussed earlier in this chapter. It occurs when you comply with your boss's request to complete a particular task. If the task is within your job scope and your boss has the right to make this request, then this influence strategy operates without negotiation, threats, persuasion, or other tactics. Experts suggest that every organization requires this influence strategy to operate. Silent authority is the most common form of influence in high power distance cultures.[53]

Assertiveness Assertiveness might be called "vocal authority" because it involves actively applying legitimate and coercive power to influence others. This includes persistently reminding the target of their obligations, frequently checking the target's work, confronting the target, and using threats of sanctions to force compliance. Workplace bullying is an extreme form of assertiveness because it involves explicit threats of punishment.

> **Nothing more enhances authority than silence.**[54]
>
> —Charles de Gaulle, former French president and military leader

Exhibit 9.4 Types of Influence Tactics in Organizations

Influence Tactic	Description
Silent authority	Influencing behavior through legitimate power without explicitly referring to that power base.
Assertiveness	Actively applying legitimate and coercive power by applying pressure or threats.
Information control	Explicitly manipulating someone else's access to information for the purpose of changing their attitudes and/or behavior.
Coalition formation	Forming a group that attempts to influence others by pooling the resources and power of its members.
Upward appeal	Relying symbolically or in reality on people with higher authority or expertise to support one's position.
Persuasion	Using logical arguments, factual evidence, and emotional appeals to convince people of the value of a request.
Impression management	Actively shaping, through self-presentation and other means, the perceptions and attitudes that others have of us. Includes ingratiation, which refers to the influencer's attempt to be more liked by the targeted person or group.
Exchange	Promising benefits or resources in exchange for the target person's compliance.

influence Any behavior that attempts to alter someone's attitudes or behavior

coalition A group that attempts to influence people outside the group by pooling the resources and power of its members

upward appeal A type of influence in which someone with higher authority or expertise is relied on in reality or symbolically to support the influencer's position

Dysfunctional Influence through Assertiveness[55]

19% of 1,215 adult Americans in the workforce say they have experienced workplace bullying within the past year. (An additional 20% experienced workplace bullying in previous years but not this past year.)

23% of 20,633 supervisors or managers in Malaysian Ministry of Health facilities (hospitals, etc.) admitted that they engage in workplace bullying.

32% of 2,179 United Kingdom workers say they have experienced workplace bullying disguised as banter (teasing remarks).

34% of 3,835 employees in 20 publicly funded higher education institutions in Ireland report that they have been bullied at work in the past three years.

25% of 2,204 year-old Japanese employees age 20 to 49 years old say they experienced "power harassment" (abuse of power) in the workplace (an additional 10% experienced other types of workplace harassment).

(Photo): Steve Luker/Getty Images

Information Control Earlier in this chapter we explained that people gain power when they have legitimate power or social network centrality to control how much and what type of information others receive. This power translates into influence when the power holder's selective distribution of information reframes how others perceive the situation and consequently alters their attitudes and/or behavior. For example, research has found that CEOs influence their board of directors by selectively feeding and withholding information.[56]

Coalition Formation When someone acting alone lacks sufficient power to influence others, they might be able to amplify that power by forming a **coalition** of people who support the proposed change.[57] A coalition is influential in three ways. First, it pools the power and resources of many people, so the coalition potentially has more influence than its members have if they operated alone. Second, the coalition's mere existence can influence others by symbolizing the legitimacy of the issue. In other words, a coalition creates a sense that the issue deserves attention because it has broad support. Third, a coalition increases the confidence and motivation of its members through social identity theory (see Chapter 3). This motivation occurs because a coalition consists of like-minded people, so its members identify with the group and feel more confident in supporting the coalition's mandate.[58]

Upward Appeal **Upward appeal** is a type of influence whereby someone with higher authority or expertise is relied on in reality or symbolically to support the influencer's position. It occurs when an employee says, "The boss likely agrees with me on this matter; let's find out!" Upward appeal also occurs when relying on the authority of the firm's policies or values. By reminding others that your request is consistent with the organization's overarching goals, you are implying support from senior executives without formally involving them.

Persuasion The influence tactics described so far are called "hard" influence tactics because the influencer attempts to control

> **Coalitions are influential by pooling the power and resources of many people, demonstrating broad support for the issue, and increasing the confidence and motivation of coalition members.**

persuasion The use of facts, logical arguments, and emotional appeals to change another person's beliefs and attitudes, usually for the purpose of changing the person's behavior

inoculation effect A persuasive communication strategy of warning listeners that others will try to influence them in the future and that they should be wary of the opponent's arguments

the other party's behavior through position power (legitimate, reward, and coercive). The three remaining categories—persuasion, impression management, and exchange–are "soft" influence strategies because the person being influenced has more autonomy and control over the influence process. The first of these, **persuasion**, involves the use of facts, logical arguments, and emotional appeals to change another person's beliefs and attitudes, usually for the purpose of changing their behavior. This is the most widely used and accepted influence strategy in organizations. It is a quality of effective leaders and, in many societies, a noble skill.

Persuasion tends to work best through communication channels with high social presence and media-richness, such as in face-to-face conversations.
Monkey Business Images/Shutterstock

The effectiveness of persuasion as an influence tactic depends on characteristics of the persuader, message content, communication channel, and the audience being persuaded (see Exhibit 9.5).[59] People are more persuasive when they are perceived to have expertise and credibility. Persuaders have more credibility when they do not seem to profit from the persuasion attempt, they acknowledge limitations with their position, and they note minor positive features of the alternative choices.

Several characteristics of message content increase your ability to persuade others, particularly when the issue is important to the audience.[60] The speaker's message is more persuasive when it acknowledges several points of view. This increases the speaker's credibility and avoids having the audience feel boxed in by the persuasion attempt. The message should also be limited to a few strong arguments, which are repeated a few times, but not too frequently. The message should use emotional appeals (such as graphically showing the unfortunate consequences of a bad decision), but only in combination with logical arguments and specific recommendations to overcome the threat. Finally, message content is more persuasive when the audience is warned about opposing arguments. This **inoculation effect** causes listeners to generate counterarguments to the anticipated persuasion attempts, which makes the opponent's subsequent persuasion attempts less effective.[61]

Exhibit 9.5 Elements of Persuasion

Persuasion Element	Characteristics of Effective Persuasion
Persuader characteristics	• Expertise • Credibility • No apparent profit motive • Appears somewhat neutral (acknowledges strengths of alternative choices)
Message content	• Multiple viewpoints (not exclusively supporting the preferred option) • Limited to a few strong arguments (not many arguments) • Repeats arguments, but not excessively • Uses emotional appeals in combination with logical arguments • Offers specific solutions to overcome the stated problems • Inoculation effect—audience warned of counterarguments that opponents will present
Communication channel	• Channels with high media-richness and social presence are usually more persuasive
Audience characteristics	Persuasion is *less* effective when the audience: • Has higher self-esteem • Has higher intelligence • Has a self-concept tied to an opposing position

Two other considerations when persuading people are the communication channel and characteristics of the audience. Generally, persuasion works best through communication channels with high social presence and media-richness, such as in face-to-face conversations (see Chapter 8). The human presence of face-to-face communication increases the persuader's credibility, and the richness of this channel provides faster feedback that the influence strategy is working. With respect to audience characteristics, it is more difficult to persuade people who have high self-esteem and intelligence, as well as a self-concept that is strongly tied to the opposing viewpoint.[62]

Impression Management The softest of the soft influence tactics is **impression management**—actively shaping the perceptions and attitudes that others have of us.[63] Impression management mostly occurs through self-presentation. Employees routinely engage in pleasant impression management behaviors to satisfy social norms, such as the way they dress and how they behave toward coworkers and customers. Some people also craft their public image to depict greater importance and expertise, which affects their influence under some circumstances. For this reason, impression management plays a significant role in an individual's personal brand—forming and displaying an accurate impression of that person's own distinctive, competitive advantage.[64]

One subcategory of impression management is *ingratiation,* which is any attempt to increase liking by, or perceived similarity to, some targeted person.[65] Ingratiation includes flattering your boss, demonstrating similar views as your boss (e.g., agreeing with the boss's suggestions), or asking your boss for advice. Ingratiation is one of the more effective influence tactics at boosting a person's career success. However, this is true only when the ingratiation occurs in moderation, the employee appears sincere when ingratiating the target, the ingratiation tactics are more complex (such as complimenting the target indirectly through another person), the ingratiation occurs in an organization that rewards cronyism, and the target person is naïve to ingratiation attempts or generally views them sincerely rather than as a political tactic. In other circumstances, people who engage in ingratiation are viewed by the target and coworkers as insincere and self-serving (i.e., the ingratiation is viewed as a form of organizational politics).[66]

Exchange Exchange activities involve the promise of benefits or resources in exchange for the target person's compliance with your request. Negotiation is an integral part of exchange influence activities. For instance, you might negotiate with your boss for a day off in return for working a less desirable shift at a future date. Exchange also includes applying the norm of reciprocity that we described earlier, such as reminding the target of past benefits or favors, with the expectation that the target will now make up for that debt. The norm of reciprocity also influences others in social networks. Active networkers build up "exchange credits" by helping colleagues in the short term for reciprocal benefits in the long term.

impression management
Actively shaping through self-presentation and other means the perceptions and attitudes that others have of us

Consequences and Contingencies of Influence Tactics

Faced with a variety of influence strategies, you are probably asking: Which ones are best? To answer this question, we first need to describe the three ways that people respond to influence: resistance, compliance, or commitment (see Exhibit 9.6).[67] *Resistance* occurs when individuals or work units oppose the behavior desired by the influencer. At the extreme, they refuse

connect

SELF-ASSESSMENT 9.2: What Is Your Approach to Influencing Coworkers?

Exhibit 9.6 Consequences of Hard and Soft Influence Tactics

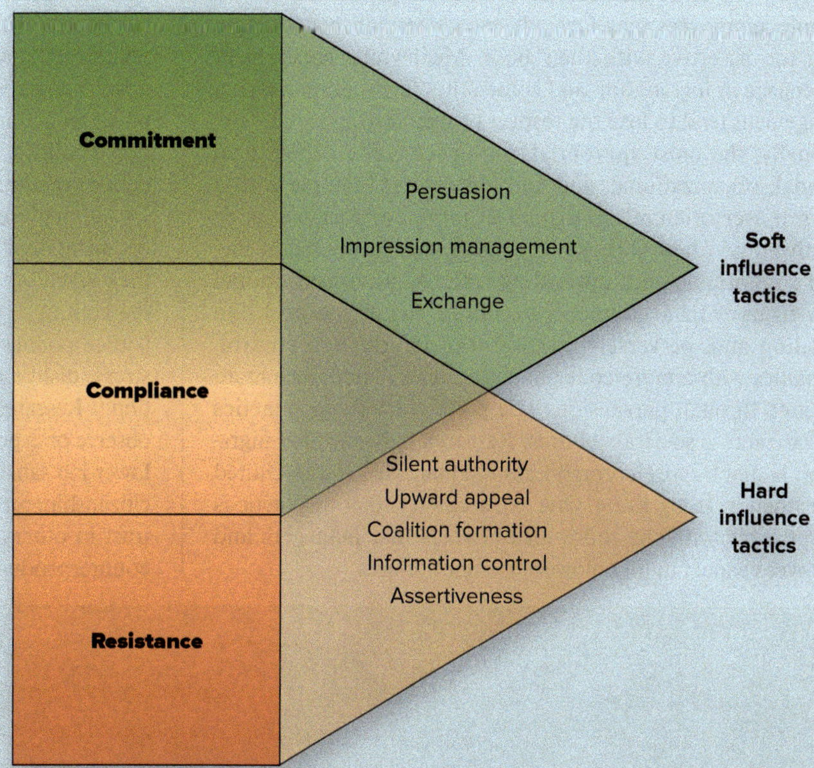

organizational politics Use of influence tactics for personal gain at the perceived expense of others and the organization

to engage in the behavior. However, there are degrees of resistance, such as when people do what the power holder has requested yet maintain their opposition by performing the tasks poorly or continuing to complain about the imposed work.

Compliance occurs when people are extrinsically motivated to implement the influencer's request (see Chapter 5). They perform the requested task for purely instrumental reasons. Compliance usually involves engaging in the behavior with no more effort than is required. Furthermore, compliance usually stops—employees no longer perform the requested behavior—when the extrinsic source of motivation is removed. The strongest outcome of influence is *commitment.* This occurs when people identify with the influencer's request and are highly motivated to implement it even when extrinsic sources of motivation are not present.

People usually react more favorably to soft tactics than to hard tactics. Soft influence tactics rely on personal sources of power (expert and referent power), which tend to build commitment to the influencer's request. In contrast, hard tactics rely on position power (legitimate, reward, and coercion), so they tend to produce compliance or, worse, resistance. Hard tactics also tend to undermine trust, which can hurt future relationships.

The most appropriate influence strategy depends on a few contingencies.[68] One obvious factor is the influencer's strongest sources of power. Those with expertise tend to have more influence using persuasion, whereas those with a strong legitimate power base may be more successful applying silent authority. A second contingency is whether the person being influenced is higher, lower, or at the same level in the organization. As an example, employees may face adverse career consequences by being too assertive with their boss. Meanwhile, supervisors who engage in ingratiation and some other forms of impression management tend to lose the respect of their staff.

Finally, the most appropriate influence tactic depends on personal, organizational, and cultural values.[69] People with a strong power orientation might feel more comfortable using assertiveness, whereas those who value conformity might feel more comfortable with upward appeals. At an organizational level, firms with a competitive culture encourage coalition formation and, perversely, more use of information control; companies with a more collegial culture likely encourage more influence through persuasion. The preferred influence tactics also vary across societal cultures. Research indicates that ingratiation is much more common among managers in the United States than in Hong Kong. One explanation is that this tactic is incompatible with the more distant roles that managers and employees expect in high power distance cultures.

LO9-5 Identify the organizational conditions and personal characteristics associated with organizational politics, as well as ways to minimize organizational politics.

ORGANIZATIONAL POLITICS

Organizational politics goes hand-in-hand with the topics of organizational power and influence. Unfortunately, the meaning of organizational politics is quite muddled. The most widely held view among scholars, which this book adopts, is that **organizational politics** is the use of influence tactics for personal gain at the perceived expense of others and the organization.[70] This definition recognizes that all political behaviors apply one or more influence tactics. However, influence activities are organizational politics only when the perpetrator is apparently motivated by self-interest and the action is likely to have an adverse effect on others and the organization. Organizational politics is necessarily a perceptual interpretation of events because it is very difficult to know the political actor's self-interest motives or awareness of how their actions affect others.

Some popular press writers (as well as a few scholars) claim that organizational politics can be beneficial.[71] These "positive politics" sources suggest that "politics is an essential skill in managers who wish to get things done" and that it is "an indispensable component of organizational life." The problem is that the "positive politics" writers seem to be claiming that all influence tactics are political tactics. For example, they define organizational politics as "power in action, using a range of techniques and tactics." Yet, as we stated in the previous section of this chapter, power in action defines *influence,* so it can't also define organizational politics. The "positive politics" writers have been unable to define organizational politics differently from existing concepts.

Although many employees admit to engaging in low levels of organizational politics to protect their work situation or advance their career, they do not claim it is good for the organization. On the contrary, surveys consistently report that employees identify "office politics" as one of the top reasons why they experience stress, dislike their workplace, and want to leave the organization.[72] Research studies similarly report that employees who either observe or experience organizational politics in the workplace have lower job satisfaction, organizational commitment, organizational citizenship, perceived organizational justice, task performance, and trust in others. They also experience higher work-related stress, counterproductive work behaviors, and intent to leave the

Keep your friends close and your enemies closer.[73]

—Attributed to Sun-Tzu, Chinese general, circa 500 BCE

dark triad A cluster of three socially undesirable (dark) personality traits: Machiavellianism, narcissism, and psychopathy

Office Politics by the Numbers[74]

83% of 520 human resources professionals in the United States and U.K. say that office politics is disrupting the workplace.

49% of 2,000 job seekers in South Africa say they occasionally had to deal with office politics and clashes.

44% of 1,002 Americans employed full-time in a business/corporate environment say office politics is the aspect of the job they dislike the most (highest percentage, followed by poor leadership).

37% of 1,815 British employees identify work-related office politics as the number one cause of work-related stress.

34% of 2,181 (mostly American) remote workers identify office politics and distractions as a major concern about returning to the office (third highest concern, after Covid-19 infection and less work flexibility).

(Photo): Schulte Productions/Getty Images

organization. And because political tactics serve individuals rather than organizations, they potentially divert resources away from the organization's effective functioning and may threaten its survival.[75]

Individual Differences in Organizational Politics

Some people are more likely than others to engage in organizational politics.[76] Employees with a strong need for personalized power seek power for its own sake and try to acquire more power. This contrasts with people with a strong need for socialized power; they seek power as an instrument to accomplish organizationally beneficial objectives.

Individuals with **dark triad** personality characteristics are also more likely to engage in organizational politics (see Chapter 2).[77] These people routinely engage in deceit and malevolently undermine others to maximize their own gains. They believe that using lies, manipulation, exploitation, and other undesirable influence tactics are acceptable ways to achieve their personal goals (*Machiavellianism*). They arrogantly exploit coworkers for personal aggrandizement and take pleasure in others' misfortune (*narcissism*). They are also selfish self-promoters who manipulate others and engage in antisocial, impulsive, and often fraudulent thrill-seeking behavior without feelings of remorse (*psychopathy*).

Minimizing Organizational Politics

Several conditions stimulate organizational politics, but these conditions also help us to identify countervailing strategies to minimize political behavior.[78] First, when budgets or other scarce resources are slashed, people rely on political tactics to safeguard their resources and maintain the status quo. Understandably, it is difficult to add resources, but sometimes this action is less costly than the consequences of organizational politics. Second, organizational politics is fueled by ambiguous, complex, or the complete absence of rules for allocating resources. Therefore, companies can suppress organizational politics by relying on clear resource allocation decision rules, and more generally by applying the distributive, procedural, and interactional justice principles described in Chapter 5.

Third, organizational change creates ambiguity and threatens the employee's power and other valued resources, which motivates some employees to engage in organizational politics. The recommendation for this is to apply the effective organizational change strategies that we describe in Chapter 14, particularly communication, learning, and involvement. Fourth, some firms nurture a culture that tolerates and possibly reinforces organizational politics. These organizations have reward systems that motivate self-serving behavior, and leaders who role-model dark triad personalities. Changing an organization's culture is difficult (see Chapter 13), but it is possible by introducing organizational systems (rewards, procedural justice principles, etc.) that discourage political behavior, attracting and hiring employees who eschew organizational politics, and installing leaders who role-model organizational citizenship rather than manipulative and exploitive behavior.

McGraw Hill connect

SELF-ASSESSMENT 9.3: How Politically Charged Is Your School?

OB THEORY TO PRACTICE

Strategies for Minimizing Organizational Politics

Organizational politics can be minimized:

- Provide sufficient resources so employees and work units do not rely on organizational politics to malevolently compete for resources.
- Establish clear resource allocation decision rules, and apply distributive, procedural, and interactional justice principles.
- During organizational change, rely on effective change strategies, including communication, learning, and involvement.
- Develop an organizational culture that eschews organizational politics by altering organizational systems, attracting and hiring aligned employees, and installing leaders who role-model organizational citizenship rather than manipulative and exploitive behavior.

Study Checklist

Connect® is available for *M: Organizational Behavior.* Additional resources include:

✓ Exercises:

- **Case Analysis:** Apply concepts within the context of a real-world situation.
- **Click and Drag:** Helps make the connection between theory and application through matching, ranking, or grouping activities.
- **Video Case:** See management in action through interactive videos.
- **Self-Assessment:** Designed to promote student self-awareness and reflection, these research-based surveys contain detailed feedback for students.
- **Application-Based Activities:** These highly interactive, application- and analysis-based exercises allow students to take on specific roles to complete management related tasks within a real-world context.

✓ **SmartBook 2.0™**—Smartbook 2.0 is an adaptive learning solution that provides personalized learning to individual student needs, continually adapts to pinpoint knowledge gaps and focuses learning on concepts requiring additional study. It fosters more productive learning, takes the guesswork out of what to study, and helps students better prepare for class.

Notes

1. C. Dever, "Managing Up," *The Chronicle of Higher Education*, November 9, 2021; Forbes Coaches Council, "Council Post: 14 Ways 'Managing Up' Can Impact A Professional's Career," *Forbes*, December 17, 2021; "The Essentials: Managing Up," Podcast, *Women at Work* (Harvard Business Review, April 18, 2022); M. Bennett, "10 Managing Up Mistakes and How To Avoid Them," *Niagara Institute* (blog), July 4, 2022; H.L. Kurter, "Employees, Here Are 3 Ways To Skillfully Manage Your Boss," *Forbes*, August 31, 2022.
2. J.R. French and B. Raven, "The Bases of Social Power," in *Studies in Social Power*, ed. D. Cartwright (Ann Arbor: University of Michigan Press, 1959), 150–67; A.D. Galinsky et al., "Power and Perspectives Not Taken," *Psychological Science* 17, no. 12 (2006): 1068–74. Also see H. Mintzberg, *Power in and around Organizations* (Englewood Cliffs, NJ: Prentice Hall, 1983), Chap. 1; J. Pfeffer, *Managing with Power: Politics and Influence in Organizations* (Boston: Harvard Business School Press, 1992), 17, 30; A. Guinote and T.K. Vescio, "Introduction: Power in Social Psychology," in *The Social Psychology of Power*, ed. A. Guinote and T.K. Vescio (New York: Guilford Press, 2010), 1–18.
3. R.A. Dahl, "The Concept of Power," *Behavioral Science* 2 (1957): 201–18; R.M. Emerson, "Power-Dependence Relations," *American Sociological Review* 27 (1962): 31–41; A.M. Pettigrew, *The Politics of Organizational Decision-Making* (London: Tavistock, 1973).
4. J. Pfeffer and G.R. Salancik, *The External Control of Organizations* (New York: Harper & Row, 1978), 52–54; K. Cowan, A.K. Paswan, and E. Van Steenburg, "When Inter-Firm Relationship Benefits Mitigate Power Asymmetry," *Industrial Marketing Management* 48 (2015): 140–48.
5. J.R. French and B. Raven, "The Bases of Social Power," in *Studies in Social Power*, ed. D. Cartwright (Ann Arbor: University of Michigan Press, 1959), 150–67; P.M. Podsakoff and C. Schreisheim, "Field Studies of French and Raven's Bases of Power: Critique, Analysis, and Suggestions for Future Research," *Psychological Bulletin* 97 (1985): 387–411; P.P. Carson and K.D. Carson, "Social Power Bases: A Meta-Analytic Examination of Interrelationships and Outcomes," *Journal of Applied Social Psychology* 23 (1993): 1150–69. Most alternative models of power bases parallel French and Raven's list. See P. Heinemann, *Power Bases and Informational Influence Strategies: A Behavioral Study on the Use of Management Accounting Information* (Wiesbaden, Germany: Deutscher Universitäts-Verlag, 2008). Raven subsequently proposed information power as a sixth source of power. We present information power as forms of legitimate and expert power rather than as a distinct sixth power base.
6. Legitimate power and expert power are also consistently the strongest sources of power that coaches have over players in sports. See P. Rylander, "Coaches' Bases of Power: Developing Some Initial Knowledge of Athletes' Compliance with Coaches in Team Sports," *Journal of Applied Sport Psychology* 27, no. 1 (2015): 110–21.
7. C. Barnard, *The Function of the Executive* (Cambridge, MA: Harvard University Press, 1938), 167–70; B.J. Tepper, "What Do Managers Do When Subordinates Just Say, 'No'? An Analysis of Incidents Involving Refusal to Perform Downward Requests," in *Power and Influence in Organizations*, ed. L. L. Neider and C.A. Schreisheim (Charlotte, NC: IAP/Information Age Publishing, 2006), 1–20.
8. A.I. Shahin and P.L. Wright, "Leadership in the Context of Culture: An Egyptian Perspective," *Leadership & Organization Development Journal* 25, no. 5/6 (2004): 499–511; Y.J. Huo et al., "Leadership and the Management of Conflicts in Diverse Groups: Why Acknowledging versus Neglecting Subgroup Identity Matters," *European Journal of Social Psychology* 35, no. 2 (2005): 237–54.
9. B.H. Raven, "Kurt Lewin Address: Influence, Power, Religion, and the Mechanisms of Social Control," *Journal of Social Issues* 55 (1999): 161–86.

10. A.W. Gouldner, "The Norm of Reciprocity: A Preliminary Statement," *American Sociological Review* 25 (1960): 161–78; P. Belmi and J. Pfeffer, "How 'Organization' Can Weaken the Norm of Reciprocity: The Effects of Attributions for Favors and a Calculative Mindset," *Academy of Management Discoveries* 1, no. 1 (2015): 36–57; D. Gervasi et al., "Reciprocity in Organizational Behavior Studies: A Systematic Literature Review of Contents, Types, and Directions," *European Management Journal* 40, no. 3 (2022): 441–57. One study suggests that the norm of reciprocity is weaker in organizations because coworkers believe that the helping behavior is calculative.

11. G. Yukl and C.M. Falbe, "Importance of Different Power Sources in Downward and Lateral Relations," *Journal of Applied Psychology* 76 (1991): 416–23; B.H. Raven, "Kurt Lewin Address: Influence, Power, Religion, and the Mechanisms of Social Control," *Journal of Social Issues* 55 (1999): 161–86.

12. A.M. Pettigrew, "Information Control as a Power Resource," *Sociology* 6, no. 2 (1972): 187–204; P.L. Dawes, D.Y. Lee, and G.R. Dowling, "Information Control and Influence in Emergent Buying Centers," *Journal of Marketing* 62, no. 3 (1998): 55–68; J. Webster et al., "Beyond Knowledge Sharing: Withholding Knowledge at Work," *Research in Personnel and Human Resources Management* 27 (2008): 1–37; C.E. Connelly et al., "Knowledge Hiding in Organizations," *Journal of Organizational Behavior* 33, no. 1 (2012): 64–88.

13. S.L. Robinson, J. O'Reilly, and W. Wang, "Invisible at Work: An Integrated Model of Workplace Ostracism," *Journal of Management* 39 (2013): 203–31; S. Gallani, "Incentives Don't Help People Change, but Peer Pressure Does," *Harvard Business Review*, March 23, 2017.

14. J.M. Peiro and J.L. Melia, "Formal and Informal Interpersonal Power in Organisations: Testing a Bifactorial Model of Power in Role-Sets," *Applied Psychology* 52, no. 1 (2003): 14–35.

15. C.R. Hinings et al., "Structural Conditions of Intraorganizational Power," *Administrative Science Quarterly* 19 (1974): 22–44. Also see C.S. Saunders, "The Strategic Contingency Theory of Power: Multiple Perspectives," *Journal of Management Studies* 27 (1990): 1–21.

16. A. Einstein, *The Ultimate Quotable Einstein*, ed. A. Calaprice (Princeton, NJ: Princeton University Press, 2011), 161. Originally in a letter to Swiss teacher Jost Winteler on July 8, 1901.

17. W.H. Friedland, "For a Sociological Concept of Charisma," *Social Forces* 43, no. 1 (1964): 18–26; K. Miyahara, "Charisma: From Weber to Contemporary Sociology," *Sociological Inquiry* 53, no. 4 (1983): 368–88; J.D. Kudisch and M.L. Poteet, "Expert Power, Referent Power, and Charisma: Toward the Resolution of a Theoretical Debate," *Journal of Business & Psychology* 10 (1995): 177–95; K.O. Tskhay, R. Zhu, and N.O. Rule, "Perceptions of Charisma from Thin Slices of Behavior Predict Leadership Prototypicality Judgments," *Leadership Quarterly*, 28 (2017): 555–62. One recent review analyzes various definitions and concludes that charisma "is values-based, symbolic, and emotion-laden leader signaling." Although a useful development, even this definition may miss the mark somewhat because all interactions generate emotions, and people can be charismatic by their mere presence (signaling) without conversation and therefore perhaps without values-based interaction. See J. Antonakis et al., "Charisma: An Ill-Defined and Ill-Measured Gift," *Annual Review of Organizational Psychology and Organizational Behavior* 3 (2016): 293–319.

18. R.B. Cialdini and N.J. Goldstein, "Social Influence: Compliance and Conformity," *Annual Review of Psychology* 55 (2004): 591–621; T. Wray, C. Yu, and C. Philbey, "Akrasia and Obedience in Medicine," in *Ethics and Professionalism in Healthcare: Transition and Challenges*, ed. S. Salloch et al. (London: Routledge, 2016), 151–61. Several writers point out methodological limitations in the evidence on this topic. However, they focus on one flawed study (Milgram) and neglect the intricacies of expert, legitimate, and referent power. For example, see: J.M. Burger et al., "Obedience," in *The Oxford Handbook of Social Influence* (New York: Oxford University Press, 2017), 129–45; S.A. Haslam and S.D. Reicher, "50 Years of 'Obedience to Authority': From Blind Conformity to Engaged Followership," *Annual Review of Law and Social Science* 13, no. 1 (2017): 59–78; M. Meyer, "Putting the Onus on Authority: A Review of Obedient Behavior and Why We Should Move On," *New Ideas in Psychology* 60 (2021): 100831.

19. S.D. Farley, D.H. Carson, and T.J. Pope, "'I Would Never Fall for That': The Use of an Illegitimate Authority to Teach Social Psychological Principles," *Teaching of Psychology* 46, no. 2 (2019): 146–52.

20. C. Perkel, "It's Not CSI," *Canadian Press*, November 10, 2007; "Dr. Charles Smith: The Man behind the Public Inquiry," *CBC News* (Toronto), August 10, 2010; J. Chipman, *Death in the Family* (Toronto: Doubleday Canada, 2017). The broader problem of judicial deference to medical experts is discussed in C. Foster, "The Dangers of Deferring to Doctors | Practical Ethics," *Oxford University-Practical Ethics* (blog), July 30, 2018.

21. D.J. Hickson et al., "A Strategic Contingencies' Theory of Intraorganizational Power," *Administrative Science Quarterly* 16 (1971): 216–27; C.R. Hinings et al., "Structural Conditions of Intraorganizational Power," *Administrative Science Quarterly* 19 (1974): 22–44; R.M. Kanter, "Power Failure in Management Circuits," *Harvard Business Review* (1979): 65–75.

22. R.M. Emerson, "Power-Dependence Relations," *American Sociological Review* 27 (1962): 31–41. Emerson uses the term *availability*. For recent applications of nonsubstitutability to specific departments and individuals, see: M. Tremblay, J. Côté, and D.B. Balkin, "Explaining Sales Pay Strategy Using Agency, Transaction Cost and Resource Dependence Theories*," *Journal of Management Studies* 40, no. 7 (2003): 1651–8; I. Roper and P. Higgins, "Hidden in Plain Sight? The Human Resource Management Practitioner's Role in Dealing with Workplace Conflict as a Source of Organisational–Professional Power," *Human Resource Management Journal* 30, no. 4 (2020): 508–24.

23. S. Ragavan, "Is Personal Branding More Important than Qualifications?," *PR Week*, March 30, 2022; B.H. Robb, "Building Your Personal Brand," *Entrepreneur*, May 18, 2022; W. Arruda, "3 Personal Branding Mistakes Job Seekers Must Avoid," *Forbes*, September 20, 2022; M. Avram, "How to Build Your Personal Brand," *The Business of Fashion*, October 13, 2022; K. Fletcher, "Why Personal Branding Is Important for Every Working Adult," *Entrepreneur*, February 28, 2023.

24. J.D. Hackman, "Power and Centrality in the Allocation of Resources in Colleges and Universities," *Administrative Science Quarterly* 30 (1985): 61–77; S.P. Borgatti and D.J. Brass, "Centrality: Concepts and Measures," in *Social Networks at Work*, ed. D.J. Brass and S.P. Borgatti (New York: Routledge, 2020), Chapter 2.

25. A. Caza, "Typology of the Eight Domains of Discretion in Organizations," *Journal of Management Studies* 49, no. 1 (2012): 144–77.

26. B.E. Ashforth, "The Experience of Powerlessness in Organizations," *Organizational Behavior and Human Decision Processes* 43 (1989): 207–42; D.B. Wangrow, D.J. Schepker, and V.L. Barker, "Managerial Discretion: An Empirical Review and Focus on Future Research Directions," *Journal of Management* 41, no. 1 (2015): 99–135.

27. "Great Expectations: Making Hybrid Work," 2022 Work Trend Index: Annual Report (Redmond, WA: Microsoft, March 16, 2022); E. Jacobs, "Middle Managers—on the New Front Line of Office Life," *Financial Times*, September 19, 2022.

28. J. Lammers, J.I. Stoker, and D.A. Stapel, "Differentiating Social and Personal Power: Opposite Effects on Stereotyping, but Parallel Effects on Behavioral Approach Tendencies," *Psychological Science* 20, no. 12 (2009): 1543–49; S. Leach, M. Weick, and J. Lammers, "Does Influence Beget Autonomy? Clarifying the Relationship between Social and Personal Power," *Journal of Theoretical Social Psychology* 1, no. 1 (2017): 5–14; P. Ziemianski, "Identifying and Mitigating the Negative Effects of Power in Organizations," *Journal of Applied Social Science* 16, no. 1 (2022): 140–59.

29. J. Lammers et al., "Power and Morality," *Current Opinion in Psychology* 6 (2015): 15–19.

30. A.D. Galinsky et al., "Acceleration with Steering: The Synergistic Benefits of Combining Power and Perspective-Taking," *Social Psychological and Personality Science* 5, no. 6 (2014): 627–35; A. Cislak et al., "Power Corrupts, but Control Does Not: What Stands Behind the Effects of Holding High Positions," *Personality and Social Psychology Bulletin* 44, no. 6 (2018): 944–57; K. Fousiani and B. Wisse, "Effects of Leaders' Power Construal on Leader-Member Exchange: The Moderating Role of Competitive Climate at Work," *Journal of Leadership & Organizational Studies* 29, no. 3 (2022): 306–24.

31. D.J. Brass et al., "Taking Stock of Networks and Organizations: A Multilevel Perspective," *Academy of Management Journal* vol. 47 no. 6 (2004): S.P. Borgatti, M.G. Everett, and J.C. Johnson, *Analyzing Social Networks*, 2nd ed. (London: SAGE, 2018), Chap. 1; E.B. Smith et al., "Social Networks and Cognition," *Annual Review of Sociology* 46 (2020): 159–74; D.J. Brass, "New Developments in Social Network Analysis," *Annual Review of Organizational Psychology and Organizational Behavior* 9 (2022): 225–46.

32. M. Grossetti, "Where Do Social Relations Come From?: A Study of Personal Networks in the Toulouse Area of France," *Social Networks* 27, no. 4 (2005): 289–300; T.M. Welbourne, S. Rolf, and S. Schlachter, "The Case for Employee Resource Groups: A Review and Social Identity Theory-Based Research Agenda," *Personnel Review* 46, no. 8 (2017): 1816–34; E.G. Foldy, "Employee Resource Groups: What We Know about Their Impact on Individuals and Organizations," *Academy of Management Proceedings* 2019 (August 2019): 10033.

33. J. Barbalet, "Guanxi, Tie Strength, and Network Attributes," *American Behavioral Scientist* 59, no. 8 (2015): 1038–50; B. Dobrucalı, "The Role of Guanxi on International Business-to-Business Relationships: A Systematic Review and Future Directions," *Journal of Business & Industrial Marketing* 35, no. 7 (2019): 1125–40. For problems with guanxi, see: F. Yang, "Guanxi Human Resource Management Practices as a Double-Edged Sword: The Moderating Role of Political Skill," *Asia Pacific Journal of Human Resources* 52, no. 4 (2014): 496–510; J. Zhang and C. Gill, "Leader–Follower Guanxi: An Invisible Hand of Cronyism in Chinese Management," *Asia Pacific Journal of Human Resources* 57, no. 3 (2019): 322–44.

34. A. Portes, "Social Capital: Its Origins and Applications in Modern Society," *Annual Review of Sociology* 24 (1998): 1–24; P.S. Adler and S.W. Kwon, "Social Capital: Prospects for a New Concept," *Academy of Management Review* 27, no. 1 (2002): 17–40; R. Lee, "Social Capital and Business and Management: Setting a Research Agenda," *International Journal of Management Reviews* 11, no. 3 (2009): 247–73.

35. R. Chisholm, *Developing Network Organizations: Learning from Practice and Theory* (Reading, MA: Addison-Wesley Longman, 1998); W.S. Chow and L.S. Chan, "Social Network, Social Trust and Shared Goals in Organizational Knowledge Sharing," *Information & Management* 45, no. 7 (2008): 458–65.

36. R.S. Burt, *Structural Holes: The Social Structure of Competition* (Cambridge, MA: Harvard University Press, 1992).

37. M.T. Rivera, S.B. Soderstrom, and B. Uzzi, "Dynamics of Dyads in Social Networks: Assortative, Relational, and Proximity Mechanisms," *Annual Review of Sociology* 36 (2010): 91–115.

38. R. Cross and R.J. Thomas, *Driving Results through Social Networks: How Top Organizations Leverage Networks for Performance and Growth* (San Francisco: Jossey-Bass, 2009); R. McDermott and D. Archibald, "Harnessing Your Staff's Informal Networks," *Harvard Business Review* 88, no. 3 (2010): 82–89.

39. M. Kilduff and D. Krackhardt, *Interpersonal Networks in Organizations: Cognition, Personality, Dynamics, and Culture* (New York: Cambridge University Press, 2008).

40. D.J. Brass et al., "Taking Stock of Networks and Organizations: A Multilevel Perspective," *Academy of Management Journal* 47, no. 6 (2004): 795–817; D. Melamed and B. Simpson, "Strong Ties Promote the Evolution of Cooperation in Dynamic Networks," *Social Networks* 45 (2016): 32–44.

41. M.S. Granovetter, "The Strength of Weak Ties," *American Journal of Sociology* 78 (1973): 1360–80; B. Erickson, "Social Networks," in *The Blackwell Companion to Sociology*, ed. J.R. Blau (Malden, MA: Blackwell, 2004), 314–26.

42. B. Uzzi and S. Dunlap, "How to Build Your Network," *Harvard Business Review* 83, no. 12 (2005): 53–60.

43. Y. Zenou, "A Dynamic Model of Weak and Strong Ties in the Labor Market," *Journal of Labor Economics* 33, no. 4 (2015): 891–932; C. Gubbins and T. Garavan, "Social Capital Effects on the Career and Development Outcomes of HR Professionals," *Human Resource Management* 55, no. 2 (2016): 241–60.

44. C.C. Su and N.K. Chan, "Predicting Social Capital on Facebook: The Implications of Use Intensity, Perceived Content Desirability, and Facebook-Enabled Communication Practices," *Computers in Human Behavior* 72 (2017): 259–68.

45. S.P. Borgatti and D.J. Brass, "Centrality: Concepts and Measures," in *Social Networks at Work*, ed. D.J. Brass and S.P. Borgatti (New York: Routledge, 2020), 9–22.

46. R.S. Burt, *Structural Holes: The Social Structure of Competition* (Cambridge, MA: Harvard University Press, 1992); D.J. Brass and D.M. Krackhardt, "Power, Politics, and Social Networks in Organizations," in *Politics in Organizations: Theory and Research Considerations*, ed. G.R. Ferris and D.C. Treadway (New York: Routledge, 2012), 355–75.

47. B.R. Ragins and E. Sundstrom, "Gender and Power in Organizations: A Longitudinal Perspective," *Psychological Bulletin* 105 (1989): 51–88; S. McDonald et al., "Frontiers of Sociological Research on Networks, Work, and Inequality," in *Networks, Work and Inequality*, ed. S. McDonald, Research in the Sociology of Work (Bingley, UK: Emerald Group Publishing Limited, 2013), 1–41.

48. "Diversity, Equity, and Inclusion," Franklin Electric, 2023, https://franklin-electric.com/company/diversity,-equity,-and-inclusion/; "Franklin Electric Launches New Employee Resource Group: Franklin Women's Network," *Automation.Com* (International Society of Automation), March 6, 2023.

49. S. Lee et al., "How Do I Get My Way? A Meta-Analytic Review of Research on Influence Tactics," *The Leadership Quarterly* 28 (2017): 210–28.

50. D. Kipnis, S.M. Schmidt, and I. Wilkinson, "Intraorganizational Influence Tactics: Explorations in Getting One's Way," *Journal of Applied Psychology* 65 (1980): 440–52; G. Yukl, "Power and the Interpersonal Influence of Leaders," in *Power and Interdependence in Organizations*, ed. D. Tjosvold and B. Wisse (New York: Cambridge University Press, 2009), 207–23. A recent review includes these influence tactics but divides some of them into narrower subcategories. See S. Lee et al., "How Do I Get My Way? A Meta-Analytic Review of Research on Influence Tactics," *The Leadership Quarterly* 28 (2017): 210–28.

51. B. van Knippenberg, R. van Eijbergen, and H. Wilke, "The Use of Hard and Soft Influence Tactics in Cooperative Task Groups," *Group Processes & Intergroup Relations* 2 (1999): 231–44.

52. R.B. Cialdini and N.J. Goldstein, "Social Influence: Compliance and Conformity," *Annual Review of Psychology* 55 (2004): 591–621; A. Bourgoin, N. Bencherki, and S. Faraj, "'And Who Are You?': A Performative Perspective on Authority in Organizations," *Academy of Management Journal* 63, no. 4 (2020): 1134–65.

53. The most widely applied model or power excludes silent authority. Its closest category is "legitimating tactics," which is an active attempt to demonstrate one's right to the request based on rules or contracts. See G. Yukl, C.F. Seifert, and C. Chavez, "Validation of the Extended Influence Behavior Questionnaire," *The Leadership Quarterly* 19 (2008): 609–21. Several studies identify the importance of silent authority in high power distance cultures. For example, see Y. Zhai, "Values of Deference to Authority in Japan and China," *International Journal of Comparative Sociology* 58, no. 2 (2017): 120–39.

54. C. de Gaulle, *The Edge of the Sword (Le fil de l'epée)*, trans. G. Hopkins (London: Faber, 1960), 59.

55. G. Namie, "2021 WBI U.S. Workplace Bullying Survey" (Workplace Bullying Institute, April 2021); D.A. Mazzone et al., "Report on the National Survey of Staff Experiences of Bullying in Irish Higher Education Institutions: Summary of Survey Findings" (Dublin City University: Anti-Bullying Centre, May 2022); B. Su-Lyn, "Nearly Quarter Of Supervisors In MOH Admit Bullying: HWCITF Report," *CodeBlue* (blog), August 18, 2022; "Roughly a Third of Employees in Japan Have Experienced Workplace Harassment," Nippon.Com, December 6, 2022; "Is It Banter Or Bullying? The Fine Line That Is Affecting the British Workplace" (Sheffield: Irwin Mitchell, February 22, 2023).

56. S. Maitlis, "Taking It from the Top: How CEOs Influence (and Fail to Influence) Their Boards," *Organization Studies* 25, no. 8 (2004): 1275–311. This type of influence is a form of manipulation. See P. Fleming and A. Spicer, "Power in Management and Organization Science," *The Academy of Management Annals* 8, no. 1 (2014): 237–98.

57. J.K. Murnighan, "Organizational Coalition Formation: Process, Consequences and Dominant Coalitions," BEBR faculty working paper, 1985; W.B. Stevenson, J.L. Pearce, and L.W. Porter, "The Concept of 'Coalition' in Organization Theory and Research," *Academy of Management Review* 10, no. 2 (1985): 256–68; F. Liu, O. Dedehayir, and B. Katzy, "Coalition Formation during Technology Adoption," *Behaviour & Information Technology* 34 (2015): 1186–99.

58. A.T. Cobb, "Toward the Study of Organizational Coalitions: Participant Concerns and Activities in a Simulated Organizational Setting," *Human Relations* 44 (1991): 1057–79; E.A. Mannix, "Organizations as Resource Dilemmas: The Effects of Power Balance on Coalition Formation in Small Groups," *Organizational Behavior and Human Decision Processes* 55 (1993): 1–22; K. Rangus and M. Černe, "The Impact of Leadership Influence Tactics and Employee Openness toward Others on Innovation Performance: Leadership Influence Tactics and Employee Openness," *R&D Management* 49, no. 2 (2019): 168–79.

59. A.P. Brief, *Attitudes in and around Organizations* (Thousand Oaks, CA: Sage, 1998), 69–84; D.J. O'Keefe, *Persuasion: Theory and Research* (Thousand Oaks, CA: Sage, 2002); R.H. Gass and J.S. Seiter, *Persuasion: Social Influence and Compliance Gaining*, 5th ed. (New York: Routledge, 2014).

60. These and other features of message content in persuasion are detailed in R. Petty and J. Cacioppo, *Attitudes and Persuasion: Classic and Contemporary Approaches* (Dubuque, IA: W.C. Brown, 1981); D.J. O'Keefe, *Persuasion: Theory and Research* (Thousand Oaks, CA: Sage, 2002), Chap. 9; G. Van Kleef, H. van den Berg, and M. Heerdink, "The Persuasive Power of Emotions: Effects of Emotional Expressions on Attitude Formation and Change," *Journal of Applied Psychology* 100 (2015): 1124–42; E. Falk and C. Scholz, "Persuasion, Influence, and Value: Perspectives from Communication and Social Neuroscience," *Annual Review of Psychology* 69 (2018): 329–56; D. Albarracin and S. Shavitt, "Attitudes and Attitude Change," *Annual Review of Psychology* 69 (2018): 299–327.

61. J.A. Banas and S.A. Rains, "A Meta-Analysis of Research on Inoculation Theory," *Communication Monographs* 77, no. 3 (2010): 281–311; B. Ivanov et al., "Beyond Simple Inoculation: Examining the Persuasive Value of Inoculation for Audiences with Initially Neutral or Opposing Attitudes," *Western Journal of Communication* 81, no. 1 (2017): 105–26.

62. Y. Lim and R.J. Lee-Won, "When Retweets Persuade: The Persuasive Effects of Dialogic Retweeting and the Role of Social Presence in Organizations' Twitter-Based Communication," *Telematics and Informatics* 34, no. 5 (2017): 422–33; P. Briñol and R.E. Petty, "The Impact of Individual Differences on Attitudes and Attitude Change," in *The Oxford Handbook of Personality and Social Psychology*, ed. D. Albarracín and B. Johnson, 2nd ed., vol. 1 (New York: Oxford University Press, 2019), 520–56.

63. M. Bolino, D. Long, and W. Turnley, "Impression Management in Organizations: Critical Questions, Answers, and Areas for Future Research," *Annual Review of Organizational Psychology and Organizational Behavior* 3 (2016): 377–406; J.A. Peck and J. Levashina, "Impression Management and Interview and Job Performance Ratings: A Meta-Analysis of Research Design with Tactics in Mind," *Frontiers in Psychology* 8 (2017): 00201.

64. T. Peters, "The Brand Called You," *Fast Company*, August 1997; C. Johnson, *Platform: The Art and Science of Personal Branding* (New York: Penguin Random House, 2019); L.A. King, *Just Do You: Authenticity, Leadership, and Your Personal Brand* (Toronto: Ingenium Books, 2019).

65. D. Strutton and L.E. Pelton, "Effects of Ingratiation on Lateral Relationship Quality within Sales Team Settings," *Journal of Business Research* 43 (1998): 1–12; R. Vonk, "Self-Serving Interpretations of Flattery: Why Ingratiation Works," *Journal of Personality and Social Psychology* 82 (2002): 515–26.

66. C. A. Higgins, T. A. Judge, and G. R. Ferris, "Influence Tactics and Work Outcomes: A Meta-Analysis," *Journal of Organizational Behavior* 24 (2003): 90–106; L.-Z. Wu et al., "Ingratiation in the Workplace: The Role of Subordinate and Supervisor Political Skill," *Journal of Management Studies* 50, no. 6 (2013): 991–1017; M. Bolino, D. Long, and W. Turnley, "Impression Management in Organizations: Critical Questions, Answers, and Areas for Future Research," *Annual Review of Organizational Psychology and Organizational Behavior* 3 (2016): 377–406; S. Shaheen et al., "Organizational Cronyism as an Antecedent of Ingratiation: Mediating Role of Relational Psychological Contract," *Frontiers in Psychology* 10 (2019): 01609; P. Sanchez-Ruiz, M.S. Wood, and A. Long-Ruboyianes, "Persuasive or Polarizing? The Influence of Entrepreneurs' Use of Ingratiation Rhetoric on Investor Funding Decisions," *Journal of Business Venturing* 36, no. 4 (2021): 106120; F. Danioni and D. Barni, "Value Priorities, Impression Management and Self-Deceptive Enhancement: Once Again, Much Substance and a Little Bit of Style," *The Journal of Social Psychology* 161, no. 2 (2021): 146–59.

67. C.M. Falbe and G. Yukl, "Consequences for Managers of Using Single Influence Tactics and Combinations of Tactics," *Academy of Management Journal* 35 (1992): 638–52.

68. G. Yukl and J. Tracey, "Consequences of Influence Tactics Used with Subordinates, Peers, and the Boss," *Journal of Applied Psychology* 77, no. 4 (1992): 525–35; B. Oc and M.R. Bashshur, "Followership, Leadership and Social Influence," *Leadership Quarterly* 24, no. 6 (2013): 919–34; M.B. Wadsworth and A.L. Blanchard, "Influence Tactics in Virtual Teams," *Computers in Human Behavior* 44 (2015): 386–93.

69. P.P. Fu et al., "The Impact of Societal Cultural Values and Individual Social Beliefs on the Perceived Effectiveness of Managerial Influence Strategies: A Meso Approach," *Journal of International Business Studies* 35, no. 4 (2004): 284–305; A.N. Smith et al., "Gendered Influence: A Gender Role Perspective on the Use and Effectiveness of Influence Tactics," *Journal of Management* 39, no. 5 (2013): 1156–83; C.C. Lewis and J. Ryan, "Age and Influence Tactics: A Life-Stage Development Theory Perspective," *The International Journal of Human Resource Management* 25, no. 15 (2014): 2146–58.

70. This definition is founded on a cluster of definitions with similar core elements, including self-interest, damage to individuals and the organization, and perceived motivation of the political actor. See H. Mintzberg, *Power In and Around Organizations* (Englewood Cliffs, NJ: Prentice Hall, 1983); K. Michele Kacmar and G.R. Ferris, "Politics at Work: Sharpening the Focus of Political Behavior in Organizations," *Business Horizons* 36, no. 4 (1993): 70–74; C.-H. Chang, C.C. Rosen, and P.E. Levy, "The Relationship between Perceptions of Organizational Politics and Employee Attitudes, Strain, and Behavior: A Meta-Analytic Examination," *Academy of Management Journal* 52 (2009): 779–801; A. Bedi and A. Schat, "Perceptions of Organizational Politics: A Meta-Analysis of Its Attitudinal, Health, and Behavioural Consequences," *Canadian Psychology* 54 (2013): 246–59.

71. D.L. Madison et al., "Organizational Politics: An Exploration of Managers' Perceptions," *Human Relations* 33, no. 2 (1980): 79–100; P. Kumar and R. Ghadially, "Organizational Politics and Its Effects on Members of Organizations," *Human Relations* 42, no. 4 (1989): 305–14; D. Buchanan and R. Badham, *Power, Politics, and Organizational Change: Winning the Turf Game* (Thousand Oaks, CA: Sage, 2008), 11; E.M. Landells and S.L. Albrecht, "Positive Politics, Negative Politics, and Engagement: Psychological Safety, Meaningfulness, and Availability as 'Black Box' Explanatory Mechanisms," in *Research in Occupational Stress and Well-Being*, ed. C.C. Rosen and P.L. Perrewé, vol. 15 (Bingley, UK: Emerald Publishing Limited, 2017), 33–49; E.M. Landells and S.L. Albrecht, "The Positives and Negatives of Organizational Politics: A Qualitative Study," *Journal of Business and Psychology* 32 (2017): 41–58.

72. Surveys of employees consistently identify organizational politics as self-serving behavior that is dysfunctional for employee well-being and performance. See, for example, "Sloppy Worker Wake-Up Call: Sweating the Small Stuff Matters," news release (Menlo Park, CA: Accountemps, January 10, 2017); "Indian Millennials Lack Critical Skills: HBR Ascend Survey," *Hindustan Times*, July 18, 2017; Z. Mejia, "These Are the Top 10 Workplace Struggles Employees Face in 2018," *CNBC*, September 19, 2018; "New DDI Research: 57 Percent of Employees Quit Because of Their Boss," news release (Pittsburgh: Development Dimensions International, December 9, 2019).

73. This famous quotation is attributed to both Nicolo Machiavelli and Sun-tzu. None of Machiavelli's five main books (translated) has any statement close to this quotation. Sun-tzu's book *Art of War* (translated) does not have this quotation either, but he makes a similar statement about spies: "Hence it is that with none in the whole army are more intimate relations to be maintained than with spies." See Sun-tzu, *The Art of War*, trans. L. Giles (Mineola, NY: Dover, 2002), 98.

74. "South African Workplace Habits–The Truth Revealed!" *CareerJunction Blog* (blog), April 23, 2019; "Mavenlink Future of Work Survey Shows 47 percent of Employees Feel Lazy Coworkers Are Number-One Pet Peeve," Press Release (Irvine, Calif.: Mavenlink, February 5, 2020); R. Pelta, "FlexJobs Survey Finds Remote Work Remains in Demand," *FlexJobs* (blog), April 19, 2021; "The 2020 UK Workplace Stress Survey" (London, UK: Perkbox, 2021); J. Kelly, "98 percent Of HR Professionals Are Burned Out, Study Shows," *Forbes*, April 14, 2022.

75. C.H. Chang, C.C. Rosen, and P.E. Levy, "The Relationship between Perceptions of Organizational Politics and Employee Attitudes, Strain, and Behavior: A Meta-Analytic Examination," *Academy of Management Journal* 52, no. 4 (2009): 779–801; A. Bedi and A. Schat, "Perceptions of Organizational Politics: A Meta-Analysis of Its Attitudinal, Health, and Behavioural Consequences," *Canadian Psychology* 54 (2013): 246–59; W.A. Hochwarter et al., "Perceptions of Organizational Politics Research: Past, Present, and Future," *Journal of Management* 46, no. 6 (2020): 879–907.

76. L.W. Porter, R.W. Allen, and H.L. Angle, "The Politics of Upward Influence in Organizations," *Research in Organizational Behavior* 3 (1981): 120–22; R.J. House, "Power and Personality in Complex Organizations," *Research in Organizational Behavior* 10 (1988): 305–57.

77. E. O'Boyle et al., "A Meta-Analysis of the Dark Triad and Work Behavior: A Social Exchange Perspective," *Journal of Applied Psychology* 97, no. 3 (2012): 557–79; A. Harrison, J. Summers, and B. Mennecke, "The Effects of the Dark Triad on Unethical Behavior," *Journal of Business Ethics* 153, no. 1 (2018): 53–77; M. Moshagen, B.E. Hilbig, and I. Zettler, "The Dark Core of Personality," *Psychological Review* 125, no. 5 (2018): 656–88; S.M. Spain, "The Dark Side of Personality," in *Leadership, Work, and the Dark Side of Personality*, ed. S.M. Spain (Cambridge, MA: Academic Press, 2019), 41–93.

78. G. Atinc et al., "Perceptions of Organizational Politics: A Meta-Analysis of Theoretical Antecedents," *Journal of Managerial Issues* 22, no. 4 (2010): 494–513; M.L. Ambrose, "It's Fairly Political around Here: Relationship between Perceptions of Organizational Politics and Organizational Justice," in *Politics in Organizations: Theory and Research Considerations*, ed. G.R. Ferris and D.C. Treadway (New York: Routledge, 2012), 133–60; J. Yang, D.C. Treadway, and L.P. Stepina, "Justice and Politics: Mechanisms for the Underlying Relationships of Role Demands to Employees' Satisfaction and Turnover Intentions," *Journal of Applied Social Psychology* 43, no. 8 (2013): 1624–35; G. Blickle, N. Schütte, and A. Wihler, "Political Will, Work Values, and Objective Career Success: A Novel Approach—The Trait-Reputation-Identity Model," *Journal of Vocational Behavior* 107 (2018): 42–56; D.P. Waggoner, "The Use of Political Skill in Organizational Change," *Journal of Organizational Change Management* 33, no. 5 (2020): 753–63; W.A. Hochwarter et al., "Perceptions of Organizational Politics Research: Past, Present, and Future," *Journal of Management* 46, no. 6 (2020): 879–907.

10 Conflict and Negotiation in the Workplace

fizkes/Shutterstock

Learning Objectives

After reading this chapter, you should be able to:

LO10-1 Define conflict and debate its positive and negative consequences in the workplace.

LO10-2 Distinguish task conflict from relationship conflict and describe three strategies to minimize relationship conflict during task conflict episodes.

LO10-3 Diagram the conflict process model and describe six structural sources of conflict in organizations.

LO10-4 Outline the five conflict-handling styles and discuss the circumstances in which each would be most appropriate.

LO10-5 Apply the six structural approaches to conflict management and describe the three types of third-party dispute resolution.

LO10-6 Discuss activities in the negotiation preparation, process, and setting that improve negotiation effectiveness.

conflict The process in which one party perceives that its interests are being opposed or negatively affected by another party

The top management team at Under Armour (UA) experienced considerable frustration and antagonism with each other after the sports apparel company hired several executives from Nike and Adidas. These new hires and UA's long-service executives embraced different strategies, resulting in clashes about which products to develop and how many to produce.

The conflict was compounded by the CEO's apparent bias favoring the insiders' views. "[The CEO] was so loyal to the guys who were there before that when the Nike guys came in, suddenly, they were insiders and we [Nike executives] were outsiders," complained a former Nike executive who left Under Armour after two years. "Why recruit talented, proven people and then not listen to them?"[1]

This discord among executives at Under Armour isn't unusual. Every day, people disagree because they have unique backgrounds, experiences, and perspectives about how to achieve organizational objectives. In many instances, their jobs emphasize competing goals and associated rewards. Some squabbles begin merely because one or more coworkers has an inherently combative interpersonal communication style. These and other conditions are the sources of conflict that we discuss in this chapter.

We begin this chapter by defining conflict and discussing the age-old question: Is conflict good or bad? Next, we look at the conflict process and examine in detail the main factors that cause or amplify conflict. The five styles of handling conflict are then described, including its contingencies as well as gender and cross-cultural differences. This is followed by discussion of the most important structural approaches to conflict resolution. Next, we look at the role of managers and others in third-party conflict resolution. The final section of this chapter reviews key factors to consider when negotiating conflict resolution.

LO10-1 Define conflict and debate its positive and negative consequences in the workplace.

THE MEANING AND CONSEQUENCES OF CONFLICT

Conflict is a fact of life in organizations. Companies are continuously adapting to their external environment, yet there is no clear road map on what changes are best. Every day, employees disagree on which work objectives should receive priority, which norms they should abide by, and how even minor job tasks should be performed. These conflict episodes occur because of clashing work goals, divergent personal values and experiences, and a variety of other reasons that we discuss in this chapter.

Conflict is a process in which one party perceives that its interests are being opposed or negatively affected by another party.[2] It occurs when one party obstructs another's goals in some way, or when one party perceives that the other person or group is likely to do so. Conflict is ultimately based on perceptions; it exists whenever one party *believes* that another might obstruct its efforts, regardless of whether the other party actually has those intentions.

This definition–and the focus of this chapter–is on conflict with others, such as between people on the same team or department, between work units or business divisions, or between the organization and external stakeholders. However, conflict also occurs within each of us (called *intrapersonal conflict*), such as when our behavior conflicts with our beliefs and values (see Chapter 4 on cognitive dissonance), and when we need to reconcile conflicting goals in decision making, such as providing customer service versus working efficiently (see Chapter 6).

Conflict is ultimately based on perceptions; it exists whenever one party *believes* that another might obstruct its efforts, regardless of whether the other party actually intends to do so.
Goodboy Picture Company/Getty Images

Is Conflict Good or Bad?

One of the oldest debates in organizational behavior is whether conflict is good or bad—or, more recently, what forms of conflict are good or bad.[3] The dominant view over most of this time has been that conflict is dysfunctional.[4] This perspective argues that organizations work best through harmonious relations, whereas even moderately low levels of conflict tatter the fabric of workplace relations and sap energy from productive activities.

The "conflict-is-bad" perspective is now considered too simplistic, yet workplace conflict can indeed have negative consequences under some circumstances (see Exhibit 10.1).[5] Conflict potentially threatens personal needs and self-concept, which reduces job satisfaction and increases stress and turnover. It undermines job performance by consuming otherwise productive time, distracting employees from their work, and draining their personal energy.[6]

Conflict also potentially undermines information sharing because employees are less motivated to ask for, pay attention to, and transmit information with discordant coworkers.[7] Disagreements can also fuel organizational politics and thereby waste resources, such as when employees try to undermine the credibility of their opponents. Conflict among team members may hurt team cohesion and performance. Even when conflict occurs between work units or regions (such as when competing for budget funding), the interdepartmental conflict may lead to conflict and power struggles among employees *within* each group.[8]

> "Conflict is the gadfly of thought. It stirs us to observation and memory. It instigates to invention. It shocks us out of sheeplike passivity, and sets us at noting and contriving.[11]"
>
> —John Dewey, educational philosopher/psychologist

Benefits of Conflict In the 1920s, when most organizational scholars viewed conflict as inherently dysfunctional, a few experts argued that conflict can have positive outcomes.[9] But it wasn't until the 1970s that conflict management experts began to embrace this idea that some level of conflict can be beneficial.[10] They formed an "optimal conflict" perspective, which states that organizations are most effective when employees experience neither too much nor too little conflict.

What are the benefits of conflict? First, it potentially improves decision making by energizing people to debate issues and evaluate alternatives more thoroughly. When employees disagree constructively, they probe and test one another's way of thinking to better understand the underlying issues that need to be addressed. They evaluate the logic of the opposing positions and reexamine each party's basic assumptions about the problem and its possible solution. Conflict also motivates creative thinking to discover novel solutions to the disagreement.[12]

A second potential benefit is that moderate levels of conflict maintain vigilance with the external environment. Through disagreement, employees engage in active thinking, and this often involves ongoing questioning about how the organization can be more closely aligned with its customers, suppliers, and other stakeholders.[13] A third benefit occurs when team members experience conflict with external sources, such as competition with other teams or threats from other organizations. People tend to be more motivated to work together when faced with an external threat, which strengthens cohesion within the team (see Chapter 7). However, as we mentioned a few paragraphs ago, interdepartmental conflict sometimes undermines relations within the department.

Exhibit 10.1 Consequences of Workplace Conflict

Negative Consequences	Positive Consequences
• Lower performance • Higher stress, dissatisfaction, and turnover • Less information sharing and coordination • Increased organizational politics • Wasted resources • Weakened team cohesion (when conflict exists among team members)	• Better decision making —Tests logic of arguments —Questions assumptions —Generates creative thinking • More responsive to changing environment • Stronger team cohesion (when conflict exists between the team and outside opponents)

LO10-2 Distinguish task conflict from relationship conflict and describe three strategies to minimize relationship conflict during task conflict episodes.

THE EMERGING VIEW: TASK AND RELATIONSHIP CONFLICT

The "optimal conflict" perspective remains popular and seems to be true in some respects–too much of any conflict is probably dysfunctional.[14] However, the school of thought most widely accepted today is that there are two dominant types of conflict: task conflict and relationship conflict. These represent two distinct ways that people approach and interact with one another during disagreements.[15]

Task Conflict

Task conflict (also called *constructive conflict*) occurs when people focus their discussion around the issue (i.e., the "task") while showing respect for people involved in that disagreement. This type of conflict keeps the spotlight on the merits of the ideas presented. With task conflict, participants examine behavior, ideas, and recommendations in terms of their factual accuracy, logic, and reasonable inferences. The discussion avoids any attention to the qualifications, status, or power of the people involved. Although there is likely an upper limit to the intensity of any disagreement, research indicates that task conflict tends to produce the beneficial outcomes described earlier.[16]

We often hear about workplace conflicts caused by "personality clashes." The problem with this claim is that personalities aren't direct causes of conflict. In fact, we don't directly see personality. Instead, the individual's behavior triggers the disagreement, and their personality is inferred from that behavior. Therefore, we can view a disagreement as a personality clash or as disagreement over appropriate behavior. The latter is task conflict.

Suppose an employee describes a disagreement with a coworker in terms of the latter's reckless personality, which is inferred from their risky statements and behaviors. A task-oriented view of this conflict is possible by focusing on what the allegedly reckless employee does (the logic, ethics, and consequences of those actions) and on the logic and factual foundation of that person's suggestions, not on alleged personal attributes. The point here is that almost all workplace conflicts can be framed as task conflicts, even when some participants try to pin the problem on flaws with the other party's personal characteristics.

task conflict A type of conflict in which people focus their discussion around the issue (i.e., the "task") in which different viewpoints occur while showing respect for people involved in that disagreement

relationship conflict A type of conflict in which people focus their discussion on qualities of the people in the dispute, rather than on the qualities of the ideas presented regarding a task-related issue

Relationship Conflict

In contrast to task conflict, **relationship conflict** occurs when the discussion focuses on the opponent's personal characteristics rather than on the qualities of the ideas presented.[17] The most direct form of relationship conflict is to attack the competence, wisdom, trustworthiness, personality, and other qualities of the opponent, rather than to present logical and factual concerns with the opponent's ideas or arguments (task conflict). This approach infers that an idea should be dismissed because those who propose or support that idea lack credentials or other personal characteristics. In most situations, this *argumentum ad hominem* ("argument about the person") isn't just character assassination. It is a well-known logical fallacy because the characteristics of the person being criticized are not direct evidence (or any evidence at all!) that their idea lacks merit.[18]

> "Task conflict keeps the spotlight on the merits of the ideas presented and avoids any attention to the qualifications, status, or power of the participants."

A second form of relationship conflict occurs when someone relies on their own status or expertise to support or defend an idea ("My recommendation is best because I have the most experience!"). This is an indirect way of attacking others because it implies the inferiority of those who present opposing arguments or recommendations. Once again, it focuses on the relative qualities of the people involved, not the qualities of the ideas presented.

A third form of relationship conflict occurs when someone uses assertive influence to demonstrate the superiority of their position in the disagreement. This aggression inherently demeans others in the conversation.[19] For example, a manager who bangs a fist on the desk while presenting an argument is demonstrating that they are more powerful than the opponents.

Whether directly attacking the other party's personal attributes or doing so indirectly through status or assertiveness,

psychological safety A shared belief that it is safe to engage in interpersonal risk-taking; specifically, that presenting unusual ideas, constructively disagreeing with the majority, and experimenting with new work behaviors will not result in coworkers posing a threat to their self-concept, status, or career

relationship conflict is dysfunctional because it threatens the opponent's self-esteem (see Chapter 3). It usually triggers defense mechanisms and a competitive orientation between the opponents. It also reduces mutual trust by emphasizing interpersonal differences, thereby weakening any bond that might otherwise exist between the parties.[20] Relationship conflict escalates more easily than task conflict because the adversaries become less motivated to communicate and share information, making it more difficult for them to discover common ground and ultimately resolve the conflict. Instead, they rely increasingly on distorted perceptions and stereotypes, which tend to reinforce their perceptions of threat.

Minimizing Relationship Conflict during Task Conflict

The logical recommendation from our discussion so far is to encourage task conflict and minimize relationship conflict. This sounds good in theory, but separating these two types of conflict isn't easy in practice. Research indicates that people experience some degree of relationship conflict whenever they engage in constructive debate.[21] No matter how diplomatically others question our ideas and actions, they potentially threaten our self-esteem and our public image, which usually triggers our drive to defend. The stronger the level of debate and the more the issue is tied to our self-view, the more likely that task conflict will evolve into (or mix with) relationship conflict. Fortunately, three conditions potentially minimize the level of relationship conflict during task conflict episodes.[22]

People experience some degree of relationship conflict whenever they engage in constructive debate, but relationship conflict can be minimized through emotional intelligence, team development, and psychological safety norms.
DragonImages/Getty Images

- *Emotional intelligence.* Relationship conflict is less likely to occur, or is less likely to escalate, when team members have high levels of emotional intelligence, as well as the related attributes of emotional stability (low neuroticism) and trait self-control.[23] Employees with higher emotional intelligence are better at recognizing and regulating their emotions during debate, which reduces the risk of escalating perceptions of interpersonal hostility. They are also more likely to view a coworker's emotional reaction as valuable information about that person's needs and expectations, rather than as a personal attack.
- *Team development.* Team development plays a critical role in suppressing relationship conflict during task conflict.[24] One reason is that as teams develop, their members become better at understanding and anticipating one another, which reduces the risk that a coworker's words or actions will be misinterpreted as a conflict trigger. A second reason is that team development produces higher team cohesion, in which employees feel a strong social identity with the group. Members of cohesive teams are motivated to minimize relationship conflict because these episodes threaten the team's stability and the member's future with that group.
- *Norms supporting psychological safety.* Task conflict is less likely to mutate into chronic relationship conflict when the team or broader organization adopts norms that support psychological safety.[25] **Psychological safety** refers to a shared belief that it is safe to engage in interpersonal risk-taking (see Chapter 7). In other words, employees are confident that presenting unusual ideas, constructively disagreeing with the majority, or experimenting with new work behaviors will not cause coworkers to threaten their self-concept, status, or career. Psychological safety flourishes when team and organizational norms encourage employees to respect and value one another, demonstrate interest in one another, be open-minded about and tolerant with coworkers' opinions, and show positive intentions toward one another. Showing positive intentions involves displaying positive emotions and nonthreatening behavior when discussing different points of view.

LO10-3 Diagram the conflict process model and describe six structural sources of conflict in organizations.

CONFLICT PROCESS MODEL

Now that we have outlined the history and current perspectives of conflict and its outcomes, let's look at the model of the conflict process, shown in Exhibit 10.2.[26] This model begins with the sources of conflict, which we will describe in the next section. The sources of conflict lead one or both parties to perceive that conflict exists. They become aware that one party's statements and actions interfere with or otherwise threaten their own goals or beliefs. These perceptions produce and interact with emotions experienced about the conflict.

Conflict perceptions usually produce negative emotions, including stress, anxiety, fear, frustration, and/or anger.[27] However, some people experience positive emotions through cognitive reappraisal of the conflict, such as by perceiving the situation as a positive challenge, an opportunity to learn about

Exhibit 10.2 Model of the Conflict Process

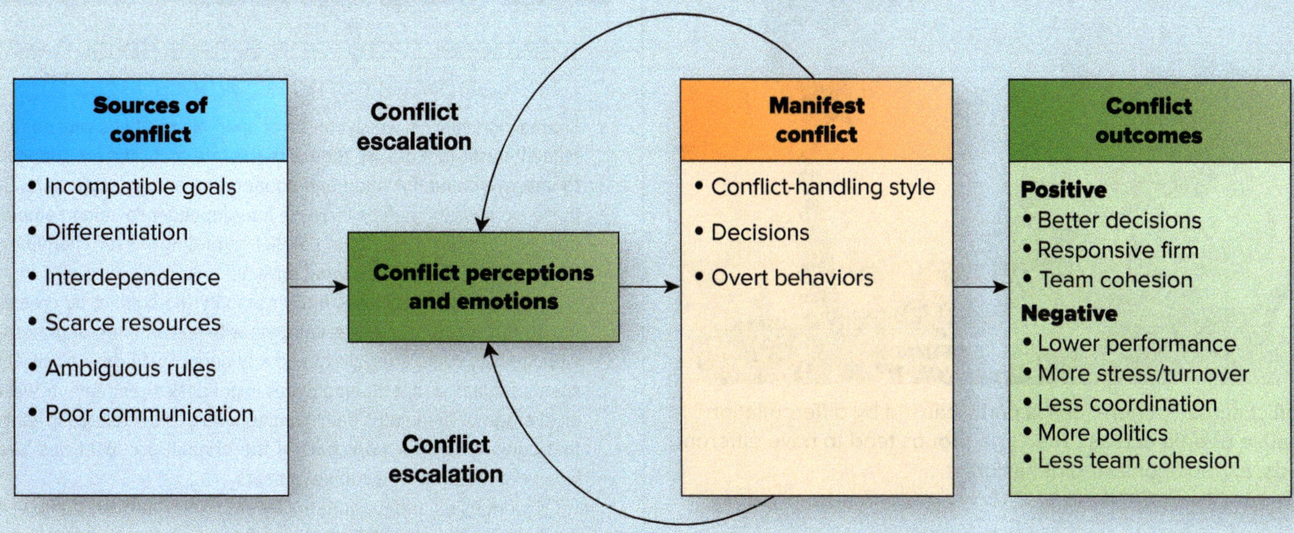

other viewpoints, and a relief that nagging concerns about a possible conflict are out in the open and can now be addressed.

Manifest conflict represents each party's decisions and behaviors toward the other. These *conflict episodes* may range from subtle nonverbal communication to warlike aggression. Manifest conflict incidents are influenced by how the other party perceives and reacts emotionally to them.[28] Conflict is also behaviorally revealed by the style each side prefers using to resolve the conflict. Some people tend to avoid the conflict whereas others try to defeat those with opposing views. We discuss different conflict handling styles later in this chapter.

Exhibit 10.2 shows arrows looping back from manifest conflict to conflict perceptions and emotions. These arrows illustrate that the conflict process is really a series of episodes that potentially cycle into conflict escalation.[29] It doesn't take much to start this conflict cycle—just an inappropriate comment, a misunderstanding, or an action that lacks diplomacy. These behaviors cause the other party to perceive that conflict exists. Even if the first party did not intend to demonstrate conflict, the second party's response may create that perception.

STRUCTURAL SOURCES OF CONFLICT IN ORGANIZATIONS

The conflict model starts with the sources of conflict, so we need to understand these sources to effectively diagnose conflict episodes and subsequently resolve the disagreement or occasionally to generate conflict where it is lacking. The six main conditions that cause conflict in organizational settings are incompatible goals, differentiation, interdependence, scarce resources, ambiguous rules, and communication problems.

Incompatible Goals

Organizations divide work among departments and teams, who divide it further among individuals. Each division of work has associated goals, so employees and departments have different—and often conflicting—work objectives. Goal incompatibility occurs when the goals of one person or department seem to interfere with another person's or department's goals.[30] For example, the production department strives for cost-efficiency by scheduling long production runs whereas the sales team emphasizes customer service by delivering the client's product as quickly as possible. If the company runs out of a particular product, the production team would prefer to have clients wait until the next production run. This infuriates sales representatives who would rather change production quickly to satisfy consumer demand.

Differentiation

Another source of conflict is differentiation—differences among people and work units regarding their beliefs, values, experiences, and preferences. Differentiation is distinct from goal incompatibility; two people or departments may agree on a common goal (serving customers better) but have different beliefs about how to best achieve that goal (such as by introducing new technology versus employee customer service training). Employees form different beliefs, expectations, and worldviews due to their lifelong socialization, gender, ethnicity, occupation, personal values, and personality.[31] Also, conflict is a perception, so before differences are actually apparent, employees form conflict beliefs based on stereotypes and false expectations about coworkers who have different backgrounds.

Conflict across generations is partly caused by differentiation because people across broad age groups tend to have different needs, expectations, and behaviors.[32] One reason is that each generation develops a somewhat unique perspective due to the

Conflict across generations is partly caused by differentiation because people across broad age groups tend to have different needs, expectations, and behaviors.
Michal Kowalski/Shutterstock

technological advances, economic conditions, and other "social forces" they experience throughout their lives. A second reason why generational differentiation exists is that people have somewhat different needs and priorities at each stage of their career and life.

Conflict due to differentiation also exists during corporate mergers and acquisitions.[33] Even when people from both companies want the integrated organization to succeed, they fight over the "right way" to do things because of their unique experiences in the separate companies. A variation of this differentiation occurs when the organization hires a cluster of people from another company whose backgrounds and experiences differ from the long-term staff. This explains the conflict among executives at Under Armour, which was described at the beginning of this chapter. Employees within the organization also have conflicting beliefs and preferences due to regional and national culture diversity.[34] For example, a remote team of employees from different countries might experience friction regarding the expected amount of debate, authority of the team leader, and so forth.

Interdependence

All workplace conflict is caused to some extent by task interdependence. Conflict isn't possible between two people or work units that have no mutual involvement or shared resources (i.e., they are independent entities) because they would not have occasion to interfere with each other. Task interdependence exists when employees must share resources or coordinate work activities to perform their jobs (see Chapter 7). Conflict is inherently about relationships because people and work units are affected by others only when they have some degree of interdependence.

The probability and intensity of conflict increase with the level of interdependence.[35] Conflict is usually lowest when working with others in a pooled interdependence relationship, such as when sharing a common resource. The potential for conflict is higher in sequential interdependence work relationships, such as an assembly line. The highest risk and intensity of conflict tends to occur with reciprocal interdependence because employees in these situations quickly and significantly affect one another (i.e., high centrality).

> **OB THEORY TO PRACTICE**
>
> ### Interdependence and Scarce Resources Fuel Conflict in Shared Workspaces[36]
>
> Shared workspaces, which consist of open-plan settings with nonpermanent desks (hot desks), reduce real estate costs and are supposed to improve communication and cooperation among coworkers. But these work arrangements increase interdependence among employees, which potentially fuels conflict regarding noise, cleanliness, visual movement, and territorial privacy.
>
> Hot desk arrangements further amplify the conflict by creating scarce resources. Employees compete with one another for preferred workspaces; some struggle to find any unoccupied desk at all. One survey estimated that UK employees in hot desk arrangements waste an average of 18 minutes daily hunting for a desk. A related irritant is that coworkers take workspace if the original occupant has been away at a meeting for a couple of hours.
>
> "I work as an auditor and don't want to play musical chairs each day I arrive at work and fix up the settings of my workstation," says an employee at the Australian Taxation Office (ATO) after the government agency introduced hot desks. "When I go and attend a meeting I don't want to come back to a desk I started working on in the morning and find it occupied. Then I have to find another desk." The ATO auditor also experiences conflict with coworkers regarding cleanliness. "I don't want to have to clean up after people who leave a mess at a work station."

Scarce Resources

Resource scarcity generates conflict because each person or department requiring the same resource necessarily interferes with others who also need that resource to fulfill their goals.[37] Budget deliberations within organizations produce conflict because there isn't enough cash flow or debt facility to satisfy the funding aspirations of each work unit. Most labor strikes occur because there aren't enough financial and other resources for employees and company owners to each receive the outcomes they seek, such as higher pay (employees) and higher investment returns (stockholders). The more resources one group receives, the fewer resources other groups will receive. Fortunately, as we discuss later in this chapter, these interests aren't perfectly opposing in complex negotiations, but limited resources are typically a major source of friction.

Ambiguous Rules

Conflict is more common in work settings where rules are ambiguous, inconsistently enforced, or completely missing. This occurs because uncertainty increases the risk that one party will interfere with the other party's goals. Ambiguity also encourages political tactics and, in some cases, employees enter a free-for-all battle to win decisions in their favor. This explains why conflict is more common during mergers and acquisitions. Employees from both companies have conflicting practices and values, and few rules have developed to minimize the maneuvering for power and resources.[38]

Communication Problems

Conflict often becomes dysfunctional when employees lack the ability or motivation to state their disagreement in a diplomatic, nonconfrontational manner. It is difficult to craft a message that communicates dissent with neither too little nor too much assertiveness.[39] Influenced by their own strong feelings about an issue, employees tend to use emotion-laden language and aggressive nonverbal behavior when transmitting their concerns. The stronger the emotive language and other signals, the stronger the perception by receivers that the conflict not only exists, but is a high risk threat. Receivers often reciprocate with a similar response, which further escalates the conflict. Aggressive and emotive communication fuels relationship conflict, which makes it more difficult for the discussants to maintain a task conflict focus.

Poorly crafted communication is a source of conflict, but a lack of communication often amplifies that conflict. Occasionally, lack of communication exists because employees don't have the opportunity to discuss their differences. More often, the quarrel makes the relationship so uncomfortable that the parties actively avoid each other. Unfortunately, less communication can further escalate the conflict because each side increasingly relies on distorted images and stereotypes of the other party. Perceptions are further distorted because people in conflict situations tend to engage in a stronger us-versus-them mindset against opponents (see Chapter 3). This perceived differentiation creates a more positive and re-assuring self-concept and a more negative image of the opponent.[41]

win–win orientation The belief that conflicting parties will find a mutually beneficial solution to their disagreement

win–lose orientation The belief that conflicting parties are drawing from a fixed pie, so the more one party receives, the less the other party will receive

LO10-4 Outline the five conflict-handling styles and discuss the circumstances in which each would be most appropriate.

INTERPERSONAL CONFLICT-HANDLING STYLES

The six sources of conflict described in the previous section lead to conflict perceptions and emotions which, in turn, motivate people to respond in some way to the conflict. More than 70 years ago, organizational behavior pioneer Mary Parker Follett observed that people use a variety of interpersonal conflict-handling styles to address conflict situations. Follett's original list was expanded and refined over the years into the five-category model shown in Exhibit 10.3. This model recognizes that how people respond behaviorally to a conflict situation depends on the relative importance they place on maximizing outcomes for themselves and for the other party.[42]

Flashpoints of Conflict in the Workplace[40]

44% of 2,211 UK employees who experienced a serious conflict with a coworker or manager within the past year say the conflict has been resolved (36% say it has not been resolved).

36% of a large sample of employees say they deal with conflict often, very often, or all the time (29% said this 14 years ago).

67% of 186,882 Canadian government employees say they are not at all stressed by coworker issues (conflicts).

13% of 5,136 UK employees say they have had shouting or very heated arguments at work within the past year.

80% of 1001 U.S. remote work professionals say they have experienced conflicts while working remotely (65% say most of those conflicts were with coworkers).

Donskarpo/Shutterstock

- *Problem solving.* Problem solving tries to find a solution that is beneficial for both parties. This is known as the **win–win orientation** because people using this style believe the resources at stake are expandable rather than fixed if the parties work together to find a creative solution. Information sharing is an important feature of this style because both parties collaborate to identify common ground and potential solutions that satisfy everyone involved.
- *Forcing.* Forcing tries to win the conflict at the other's expense. People who use this style typically have a **win–lose orientation**—they believe the parties are drawing from a fixed pie, so the more one party receives, the less the other party will receive. Consequently, this

Exhibit 10.3 Interpersonal Conflict-Handling Styles

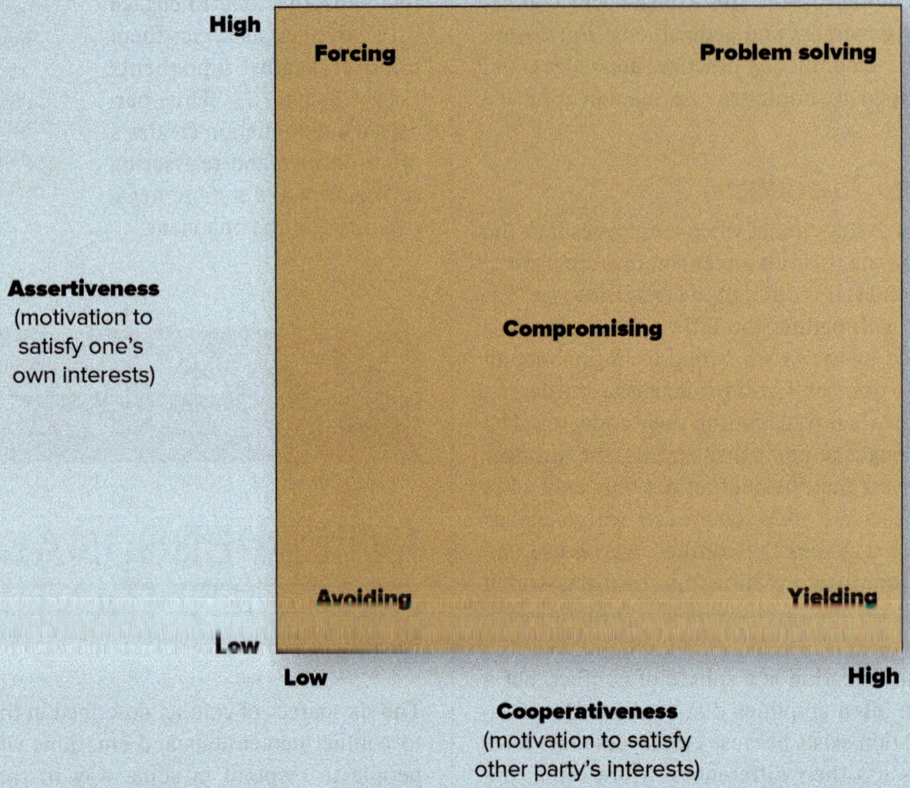

Source: Dreu De, C. K. W., A. Evers, B. Beersma, E. S. Kluwer, and A. Nauta. "A Theory-Based Measure of Conflict Management Strategies in the Workplace." *Journal of Organizational Behavior* 22 (2001): 645–68.

style relies on "hard" influence tactics (see Chapter 9) to get one's own way. Forcing is not necessarily aggressiveness or bullying, however. It also includes moderate degrees of assertiveness, such as when you speak up and show conviction for your idea or request.[43]

- *Avoiding.* Avoiding tries to smooth over or evade conflict situations altogether. A common avoidance strategy is to steer clear of the coworkers associated with the conflict. Another action is to minimize discussion of the sensitive topic when interacting with the other person. Although it is situated in the "low–low" sector of the model, avoidance does not necessarily mean that people always have a low concern for both one's own and the other party's interests. Instead, they might be very concerned about one or both party's interests but conclude that avoidance is the best strategy, at least for the short term.[44]
- *Yielding.* Yielding involves giving in completely to the other side's wishes, or at least cooperating with little or no attention to your own interests. This style involves making unilateral concessions and unconditional promises, as well as offering help with no expectation that the other party needs to reciprocate in the future.
- *Compromising.* Compromising involves actively seeking a middle ground between the interests of the two parties. This involves calculating losses from concessions with equally valued gains, or at least trying to achieve similar levels of how much value each party sacrifices to reach agreement.

connect

SELF-ASSESSMENT 10.1: What Is Your Preferred Conflict-Handling Style?

Choosing the Best Conflict-Handling Style

Chances are that you gravitate toward one or two conflict-handling styles that match your personality, personal and cultural values, and past experience.[45] You might typically use avoiding or yielding because disagreement makes you feel uncomfortable and is contrary to your self-view as someone who likes to get along with everyone. Or perhaps you prefer the forcing and compromising strategies because they reflect your strong need for achievement and to control the situation. However, the best style depends on the situation, so you need to understand and develop the capacity to use each style in the appropriate circumstances.[46]

Exhibit 10.4 summarizes the main contingencies and problems associated with using each conflict-handling style. Problem solving is

Exhibit 10.4 Conflict-Handling Style Contingencies and Problems

Conflict-Handling Style	Preferred Style When ...	Problems with This Style
Problem solving	• Interests are not perfectly opposing (i.e., not pure win–lose) • Parties have trust, openness, and time to share information • Issues are complex	• Involves sharing information that the other party might use to their advantage
Forcing	• Dispute requires a quick solution • Your position objectively has a much stronger logical or moral foundation • Other party would take advantage of more cooperative strategies	• Highest risk of relationship conflict • May damage long-term relations, reducing future problem-solving success
Avoiding	• Conflict has become too emotionally charged • Parties want to maintain a harmonious relationship • Cost of trying to resolve the conflict outweighs the benefits	• Doesn't usually resolve the conflict • May increase uncertainty and frustration
Yielding	• Issue is much less important to you than to the other party • The value and logic of your position isn't as clear • Parties want to maintain a harmonious relationship • Other party has substantially more power	• Increases other party's expectations in future conflict episodes
Compromising	• Single issue conflict with opposing interests • Parties lack time or trust for problem solving • Parties want to maintain a harmonious relationship • Parties have equal power	• Suboptimal solution where mutual gains are possible

the preferred conflict-handling style whenever possible. Why? Because this approach offers the best chance for the conflicting parties to reach a solution that is closest to their needs and goals. Through dialogue and clever thinking, the parties discover a win-win solution. In addition, the problem-solving style tends to improve long-term relationships, reduce stress, and minimize emotional defensiveness and other indications of relationship conflict.[47]

The problem-solving style is not the best conflict-handling style in all situations, however. If the conflict is simple and perfectly opposing (each party wants more of a single fixed pie), then this approach will waste time and increase frustration. It also takes more time and requires a fairly high degree of trust because there is a risk that the other party will take advantage of the information you have openly shared. The problem-solving style can be stressful and difficult when people experience strong feelings of conflict, likely because these negative emotions undermine trust in the other party.[48]

The forcing style is usually inappropriate because a high level of assertiveness tends to generate relationship conflict more quickly or intensely than occurs with other conflict-handling styles. Even so, a moderate degree of assertiveness may be appropriate where the dispute requires a quick solution or your ideas have a significantly and objectively stronger logical or moral foundation. This conflict-handling style may also be preferred when the other party would take advantage of a more cooperative conflict-handling style.

Avoiding is often ineffective as a conflict-handling style because it produces uncertainty and frustration rather than resolution of the conflict.[49] However, avoiding may be the best short-term strategy when the conflict has become emotionally charged, conflict resolution would cost more than its benefits, or the parties prefer superficial harmony over resolving the conflict.

> **The more arguments you win, the fewer friends you will have.[50]**
>
> —Unknown source, popular adage since late 1800s

Steering Clear of Workplace Conflict[51]

39% of people with an introverted personality (measured in a large sample) identify "avoiding" as their most preferred conflict-handling style (approximately 13% of extraverts prefer the avoiding style).

50% of 1001 U.S. professionals who work remotely say they wanted to leave their job, or have actual left their job because of a workplace conflict.

50% of 507 U.S. workers say they do nothing when experiencing conflict with a coworker who does something wrong (from a list of 19 behaviors, including falsely taking credit, being unsanitary, and blocking access to information).

5% of 716 professionals in 36 countries (most in US, Canada, and UK) say they naturally gravitate toward the avoiding style when experiencing workplace conflict (60% say they prefer the collaborating/problem solving style).

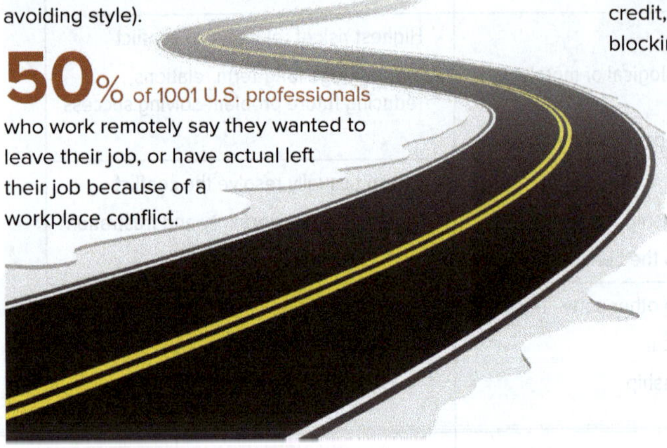

Alhovik/Shutterstock

The yielding style may be appropriate when the other party has substantially more power, the issue is not as important to you as to the other party, and you aren't confident that your position has superior logical or ethical justification.[52] On the other hand, yielding may give the other side unrealistically high expectations and motivate them to seek more from you in the future. In the long run, this style may produce more conflict, not less.

The compromising style may be best where the conflict is simple and perfectly opposing (each party wants more of a single fixed pie). Even if the conflict is sufficiently complex for potential mutual gains, compromising may be necessary when the parties lack time, trust, and openness to apply the problem-solving style. The compromising style is also popular where the parties prioritize harmony in their relationship over personal gains in the dispute.[53] Compromise also tends to occur where both parties have approximately equal power, which prevents one party from gaining advantage over the other. However, many conflicts have the potential for mutual gains through problem solving, whereas the compromise style settles for a suboptimal solution. Research also suggests that employees are less happy with a compromise agreement under some conditions.

Cultural and Male–Female Differences in Conflict-Handling Styles

The preferred conflict-handling style varies from one culture to another.[54] For example, people from high collectivist cultures—where people are expected to support and show allegiance to the group—are motivated to maintain harmonious relations and, consequently, are more likely than those from less collectivist cultures to manage disagreements through avoidance or problem solving. However, collectivism motivates harmony *within* the group, not necessarily with people outside the group.[55] Generally, cultural values and norms represent an important contingency when choosing the preferred conflict-handling approach in that culture.

Males and females rely on different conflict-handling styles to some degree.[56] The clearest difference is that males are more likely than females to use the forcing style, whether as managers or nonmanagement employees. Also, females (whether as managers or employees) are more likely than male counterparts to use the avoiding style. Females are also slightly more likely than males to use problem solving, compromising, and yielding. Overall, except for the male preference for forcing, differences in conflict-handling styles are relatively small, but they have a logical foundation. Compared to males, females pay more attention to the relationship between the parties, so their preferred style tries to protect the relationship. This is apparent in less forcing, more avoiding, and slightly more use of compromising and yielding.

LO10-5 Apply the six structural approaches to conflict management and describe the three types of third-party dispute resolution.

STRUCTURAL APPROACHES TO CONFLICT MANAGEMENT

Conflict-handling styles describe how we approach the other party in a conflict situation. But conflict management also involves altering the underlying structural causes of potential conflict. The main structural approaches parallel the sources of conflict discussed earlier. Six structural approaches to minimize dysfunctional conflict are: emphasize superordinate goals, reduce differentiation, improve communication and understanding, reduce task interdependence, increase resources, and clarify rules and procedures.

Emphasize Superordinate Goals

One of the oldest recommendations for resolving conflict is to increase the parties' commitment to superordinate goals and decrease the importance of the conflicting subordinate goals.[57]

superordinate goals Goals that the conflicting parties value and whose attainment requires the joint resources and effort of those parties

Superordinate goals are goals that the conflicting employees or departments value and whose attainment requires the joint resources and effort of those parties.[58] These goals are called superordinate because they are higher-order aspirations such as the organization's strategic objectives rather than work unit operational goals or individual key performance objectives. Research indicates that the most effective executive teams frame their decisions as superordinate goals that rise above each executive's departmental or divisional goals. Similarly, effective leaders reduce dysfunctional organizational conflict through an inspirational vision that unifies employees and makes them less preoccupied with their subordinate goal differences.[59]

Suppose that marketing staff want a new product released quickly, whereas engineers want more time to test and add new features. Leaders can potentially reduce this interdepartmental conflict by reminding both groups of the company's mission to serve customers or by pointing out that competitors currently threaten sales of the company's existing products. By increasing commitment to companywide goals (customer focus, competitiveness), engineering and marketing employees pay less attention to their competing departmental-level goals, which reduces their perceived conflict with each other.[60]

Reduce Differentiation

Earlier in this chapter, we explained that one of the main sources of workplace conflict is differentiation–differences among people regarding their training, values, beliefs, and experiences. Therefore, reducing differentiation is a logical approach to reducing dysfunctional conflict. As employees develop and recognize more similarities than differences with coworkers in other departments, they increase their trust in them and are more willing to coordinate activities and resolve their disputes through constructive discussion.[61]

Organizations can reduce differentiation among individuals or work units in several ways.[62] One strategy is for employees to have meaningful interaction with people in other groups, such as through participation in multidisciplinary projects.[63] A second strategy is to rotate staff to different departments or regions throughout their career. A third strategy is for leaders to build and maintain a strong organizational culture. Employees have shared values and assumptions and a stronger sense of community in a company with a strong culture (see Chapter 13). Each of these strategies creates common experiences or underlying beliefs that increase employee identification with the organization rather than just with a narrow business function, career specialization, or geographic region.

Improve Communication and Mutual Understanding

A third way to reduce dysfunctional conflict is to give the conflicting parties more opportunities to communicate with and understand each other.[64] These activities don't necessarily reduce differentiation (employees still have divergent beliefs and experiences), but the interaction and discussion may create better awareness of and respect for the other person or group's situation and point of view. The most basic application of this strategy is to change physical or reporting arrangements so employees across departments have more occasions to interact with one another. Employees also develop better mutual understanding with people in other departments through lunch-and-learn or poster session gatherings, in which one group summarizes its current projects to coworkers in other groups. Some companies encourage remote staff to have virtual coffee chats with people in other departments who they rarely speak to directly but are internal clients or dependent on the remote worker's department in other ways.

Some companies improve mutual understanding through a variation of the Johari Window model (see Chapter 3). In seminars with a trained facilitator, individuals disclose to coworkers information about themselves and their self-perceptions as well as feedback to others about how they are perceived.[65] Where conflicts have escalated, some embattled groups have participated in a deeper version of this process, called *intergroup mirroring*.[66]

OB THEORY TO PRACTICE

Minimizing Relationship Conflict through Casual Encounters[67]

A classic strategy for reducing or preventing workplace conflict is to create more opportunities for employees across the organization to communicate with and understand each other. Here are three ways that specific companies are applying this strategy.

Casual Interactions through Workspace Design. Apple Park (Apple headquarters) and the Pixar Animation Studios campus are designed around team pods. However, these firms also encourage casual interactions with people on other teams because employees must travel considerable distance from their isolated pods to fetch their mail, have lunch, or visit the restroom.

Lunch Roulettes. WeWork's Tel-Aviv technology group wanted to preempt dysfunctional conflict when the group expanded to 100 people, so it set up random lunch groups. Employees use an app to sign up for the fortnightly event. A couple of hours before the lunch, participants are organized randomly—like a roulette wheel—into groups of three people. The app creates a private digital space so each luncheon trio can coordinate where to eat and what to order. Attendees can optionally input information about their hobbies and a "talk to me about" topic.

Virtual Coffee Chats and Lotteries. Everyone works remotely at Gitlab, so the technology firm encourages its 1,500 employees to have regular virtual coffee chats with people outside their team. Its guidelines specifically suggests pairing with someone you don't know well but whose group depends on or otherwise works with your team. Many Culture Amp "campers" (employees) also work remotely, so the company created a Camper Coffee Lottery. Every three weeks, participants are randomly organized into pairs with their own chat channel to arrange the casual coffee break conversation.

third-party conflict resolution Any attempt by a relatively neutral person to help conflicting parties resolve their differences

Led by an external consultant, the conflicting groups separately document their perceptions of (1) how the group perceives itself, (2) how it perceives the other group, and (3) how the group believes it is perceived by the other group. The "mirroring" stage follows, whereby each group discusses its three sets of perceptions with the other group. The two sides use this shared information to review their relationship problems and establish joint goals and action plans to improve their relationship.

Although communication and mutual understanding can reduce dysfunctional conflict, there are two important warnings. First, these interventions should be applied only for groups or individuals with moderate or low differentiation. If the parties have overwhelming differences, they tend to focus on information during the interaction that reinforces that view.[68] Consequently, dialogue could escalate rather than reduce relationship conflict. The second warning is that people in some cultures are less comfortable with the practice of resolving differences through direct and open dialogue.[69] This approach threatens harmony and risks loss of face, whereas people in collectivist and high power distance cultures, for example, prefer avoidance, yielding, and compromising to minimize the risk of any manifest conflict.

Reduce Interdependence

Conflict occurs where people are dependent on one another, so another way to reduce dysfunctional conflict is to minimize the level of interdependence among the parties. Three ways to reduce interdependence among employees and work units are to create buffers, use integrators, and combine jobs.

- *Create buffers.* A buffer is any mechanism that loosens the coupling between two or more people or work units. This decoupling reduces the potential for conflict because the buffer reduces the effect of one party on the other. Building up in-process inventory between assembly-line workers is a buffer, for example, because each employee is less dependent in the short term on the previous person along that line.[70]
- *Use integrators.* Integrators are employees who coordinate the activities of multiple work units toward the completion of a shared task or project.[71] Brand managers, for instance, are responsible for coordinating the efforts of the research, production, advertising, and marketing departments regarding a specific product line. Integrators typically reduce the amount of direct interaction required among these diverse work units. Integrators rarely have direct authority over the departments they integrate, so they must rely on referent power and persuasion to manage conflict and accomplish the work.
- *Combine jobs.* Combining jobs is both a form of job enrichment and a way to reduce task interdependence. Consider a toaster assembly system where one person inserts the heating element, another adds the sides, and so on. By combining these tasks so that each person assembles an entire toaster, the employees now have a pooled rather than sequential form of task interdependence and the likelihood of dysfunctional conflict is reduced.

Increase Resources

Resource scarcity is a source of conflict, so increasing the amount of resources available would have the opposite effect.[72] This might not be a feasible strategy for minimizing dysfunctional conflict due to the costs involved. However, these costs need to be compared against the costs of dysfunctional conflict created by the resource scarcity.

Clarify Rules and Procedures

Conflicts that arise from ambiguous rules can be minimized by establishing clear rules and procedures. If two departments are fighting over the use of a new laboratory, a schedule might be established that allocates the lab exclusively to each team at certain times of the day or week.

THIRD-PARTY CONFLICT RESOLUTION

Most of this chapter has focused on people directly involved in a conflict, yet many workplace disagreements are resolved with the assistance of a manager, coworker, or other person outside the dispute. **Third-party conflict resolution** is any attempt by a relatively neutral person to help the parties resolve their differences.[73] There are three main third-party dispute resolution activities: arbitration, mediation, and inquisition. These interventions can be classified by their level of control over the process and control over the decision (see Exhibit 10.5).[74]

- *Arbitration.* Arbitrators have high control over the final decision, but low control over the process. Executives engage in this strategy by following previously agreed rules of due process, listening to arguments from the disputing employees, and making a binding decision. Arbitration is

Exhibit 10.5 Types of Third-Party Intervention

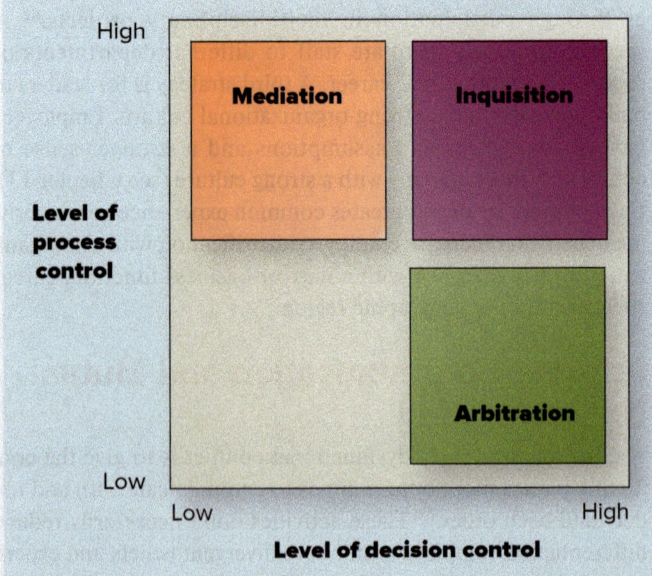

Managers as Third-Party Conflict Handlers[75]

32% of 701 UK employees who've experienced serious conflict over the past year agree that their line manager's involvement made the situation worse (45% disagree).

22% of a large sample of employees say their managers handle conflict poorly over very poorly.

ATIC12/Getty Images

34% of 3,000 Canadian employees say their organization does not provide training, coaching, or support to help deal with workplace conflict and/or aggression.

54% of 1,027 employees surveyed who recently experienced conflict with a coworker took the dispute to their supervisor or human resources staff.

applied as the final stage of grievances by unionized employees in many countries, but it is also applied to nonunion conflicts in organizations with formal conflict resolution processes.

- *Mediation.* Mediators have high control over the intervention process but low control over the decision. Their main purpose is to help the disputing parties progress toward conflict resolution by coaching their interaction and providing a supportive context. The conflicting parties alone make the final decision about how to resolve their differences.[76]
- *Inquisition.* The inquisition approach gives the third party high control over both the process and decision. Like arbitrators, inquisitors have high decision control because they determine how to resolve the conflict. Like mediators, inquisitors also have high process control because they choose which information to examine and how to examine it, and they generally decide how the conflict resolution process will be handled.[77]

Choosing the Best Third-Party Intervention Strategy

Team leaders, executives, and coworkers regularly intervene in workplace disputes. Sometimes they mediate; at other times they serve as arbitrators. Occasionally, they begin with one approach then switch to another. However, research suggests that managers usually adopt an inquisitional approach whereby they dominate the intervention process as well as make a binding decision.[78] They prefer the inquisition approach because it is consistent with the decision-oriented nature of managerial jobs; it gives them control over the conflict process and outcome, and tends to resolve disputes efficiently.

Unfortunately, inquisition is usually the least effective third-party conflict resolution method in organizational settings.[79] One problem is that leaders who take an inquisitional role tend to collect limited information about the problem, so their imposed decision may produce an ineffective solution to the conflict. Another issue is that employees often view inquisitional procedures and outcomes as unfair because they have little control over this approach. In particular, the inquisitional approach potentially violates several procedural justice rules (see Chapter 5).

Which third-party intervention is most appropriate in organizations? The answer partly depends on the situation, such as the type of dispute, the relationship between the manager and employees, and cultural values such as power distance.[80] Also, any third-party approach has more favorable results when it applies the procedural and interactional justice rules described in Chapter 5.[81] Generally, for everyday disagreements between two employees, the mediation approach is usually best because this gives workers more responsibility for resolving their own disputes. The third-party representative merely establishes an appropriate context for conflict resolution. Although not as efficient as other strategies, mediation potentially offers the highest level of employee satisfaction with the conflict process and outcomes.[82] When employees cannot resolve their differences through mediation, arbitration seems to work best because the predetermined rules of evidence and other processes create a higher sense of procedural justice.[83] Arbitration is also preferred where the organization's goals should take priority over individual goals.

negotiation The process in which interdependent parties with divergent beliefs or goals attempt to reach agreement on issues that mutually affect them

LO10-6 Discuss activities in the negotiation preparation, process, and setting that improve negotiation effectiveness.

RESOLVING CONFLICT THROUGH NEGOTIATION

Think back through yesterday's events. Maybe you had to reach consensus with other students about what tasks to complete for a team project. Chances are that you shared transportation with someone, so you had to agree on the timing of the ride. Then perhaps there was the question of who made dinner. Each of these daily events created potential conflict and, most likely, they were resolved through negotiation.

Negotiation occurs when interdependent parties with divergent beliefs or goals attempt to reach agreement on issues that mutually affect them. In other words, people negotiate when they need to work together (mutual dependence), need to reach a consensus on decisions that affect them, and initially don't have identical preferences regarding those decisions.[84] This definition highlights the fact that negotiation skills are vital in organizations and everyday life because they help us achieve our

best alternative to a negotiated agreement (BATNA) The best outcome you might achieve through some other course of action if you abandon the current negotiation

goals, reduce conflict, and build collaborative relationships. In this section, we identify many of the strategies and conditions that effective negotiators consider in organizations and other settings.

Distributive versus Integrative Approaches to Negotiation

Earlier in this chapter, we noted that some conflict-handling styles adopt a win-lose orientation—the view that one party necessarily loses when the other party gains. In negotiations, this is called the *distributive* approach because the negotiator believes those involved in the conflict must distribute portions from a fixed pie. The opposing view is a win-win orientation, known as the *integrative* or *mutual gains* approach to negotiations. This approach exists when negotiators believe the resources at stake are expandable rather than fixed if the parties work creatively together to find a solution.

Distributive negotiation is most common when the parties have only one item to resolve, such as product price or starting salary. Integrative negotiation is more common when multiple issues are open for discussion. Negotiating multiple issues provides greater opportunity for mutual gains because each issue or element in the negotiation has different value to each party. Consider the example of a buyer who wants to pay a low price for a large batch of manufactured items from a seller, doesn't need the entire order at the same time, but does need the payment schedule spread over time due to limited cash flow. The seller would like the buyer to pay a high price, but also values steady production to minimize overtime and layoffs. Through negotiation, the parties learn that spreading out the delivery schedule benefits both of them, and that the buyer would agree to a higher price if payments could be spread out with the delivery schedule.

Negotiating multiple issues provides greater opportunity for mutual gains because each issue or element in the negotiation has different value to each party.
Helder Almeida/123RF

Negotiators usually begin with a cautiously integrative approach to negotiations, but they switch to a distributive approach when they realize that their interests are perfectly opposing. Another factor is the individual's personality and past experience. Some people have a natural tendency to be competitive and think more distributively whereas others more frequently believe that conflicts can result in mutual gains.

Preparing to Negotiate

Preparation is essential for successful negotiations.[85] You can't resolve disagreements unless you know what you want, why you want it, and what power you have to get it. You also need to anticipate the other party for each of these factors.

Develop Goals and Understand Needs Successful negotiators develop *goals* about what they want to achieve from the exchange. Equally important, they reflect on what *needs* they are trying to fulfill from those goals. The distinction between goals and needs is important because specific needs can be satisfied by different goals. For example, an employee might negotiate for a promotion (a goal), but what the employee really wants is more status and interesting work (underlying needs). Effective negotiators try to understand their own needs and avoid becoming locked into fixed goals. Focusing on needs enables negotiators to actively consider different proposals and opportunities, some of which could fulfill their needs better than their original negotiation goals. Preparation also includes anticipating the other party's goals and their underlying needs, based on available information before negotiation sessions begin.

Negotiators engage in a form of goal setting that identifies the three key positions shown in the bargaining zone model (see Exhibit 10.6).[86] The *initial offer point*—each party's opening offer to the other side—requires careful consideration because it can influence the negotiation outcome. If the initial offer is set higher—but not outrageously higher—than the other party expects, it can anchor the negotiation at a higher point along the range by reframing the other party's perception of what is considered a "high" or "low" demand (see Chapter 6).[87] In other words, a high initial offer point can potentially keep the outcome closer to your target point; it may even cause the other side to lower its resistance point.

Exhibit 10.6 Bargaining Zone Model of Negotiations

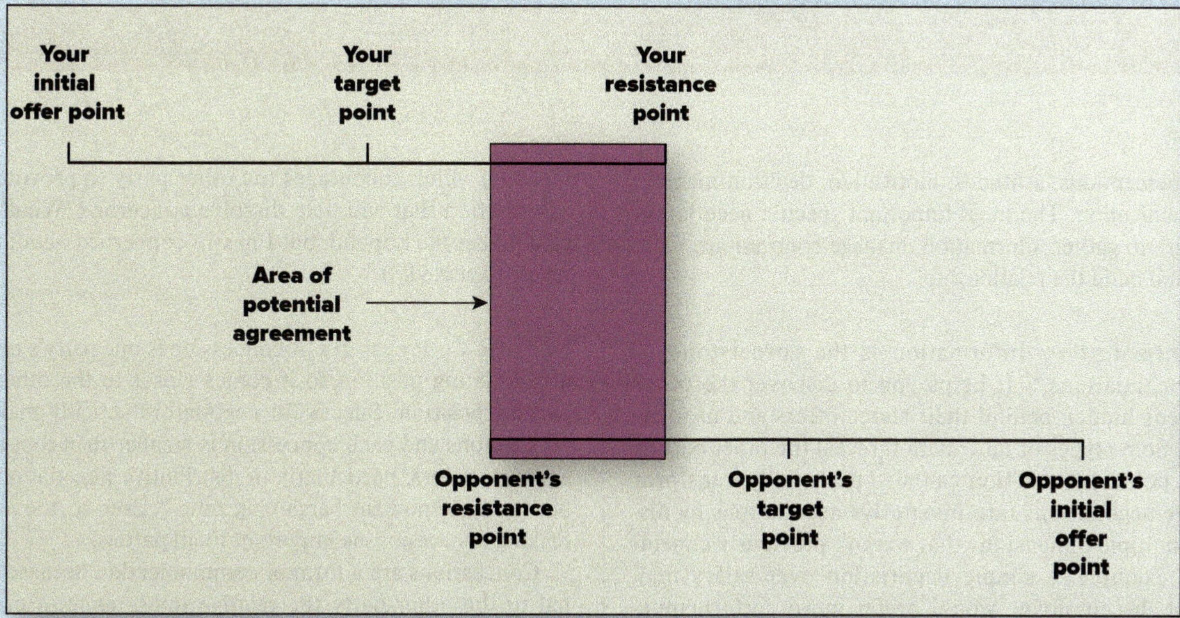

The *target point* is your realistic goal or expectation for a final agreement. This position must consider alternative strategies to achieve those objectives as well as test underlying assumptions about the situation.[88] Negotiators who set high, specific target points usually obtain better outcomes than those with low or vague target points. In this respect, a target point needs to possess the same characteristics as effective goal setting (see Chapter 5). Unfortunately, perceptual distortions cause inexperienced negotiators to form overly optimistic expectations, which can only be averted through careful reflection of the facts.[89]

Know Your BATNA and Power The *resistance point* in the bargaining zone model is the point beyond which you will make no further concessions and, instead, walk away from the negotiations. How do you determine the resistance point? The answer requires thoughtful comparison of how your goals and needs might be achieved through some other means. This comparison is called the **best alternative to a negotiated agreement (BATNA)**.[90] BATNA estimates your power in the negotiation because it represents the estimated cost to you of walking away from the relationship. If people outside the current negotiation are willing to negotiate with you and provide a reasonable agreement, then you have a high BATNA because it would cost you very little to walk away from the current negotiation.

The best alternative to a negotiated agreement (BATNA) estimates your power in the negotiation because it represents the estimated cost to you of walking away from the relationship.
Shao-Chun Wang/123RF

Having more than one BATNA to a negotiation increases your power. A common problem, however, is that people tend to overestimate their BATNA.[91] They wrongly believe there are plenty of other ways to achieve their objective rather than through this specific negotiation. Wise advice here is to actively investigate multiple alternatives, not just assume they exist.

Your power in the negotiation depends on the sources and contingencies of power discussed in Chapter 9. For example, you have more power to negotiate a better starting salary and job conditions if you have valued skills and experience that few other people possess (high expertise with low substitutability), the employer knows that you possess these talents (high visibility), and the company will experience costs or lost opportunities fairly quickly if this position is not filled soon (high centrality). Not surprisingly, BATNA tends to be higher for those with favorable sources and contingencies of power, because they would be in demand in the marketplace.

The Negotiation Process

The negotiation process is a complex human interaction that draws on many topics in this book,

> **Seek first to understand, then to be understood.**[95]
>
> —Stephen Covey, educator and consultant

including perceptions, attitudes, motivation, decision making, and communication. The most important specific negotiation practices are to gather information, manage concessions, manage time, and build the relationship.

Gather Information Information is the cornerstone of effective negotiations.[92] It helps you to discover the other party's needs hidden behind their stated offers and negotiation goals. Some types of information reveal the other party's resistance point. Information can also potentially transform distributive negotiations into integrative negotiations by discovering multiple dimensions that weren't previously considered. For example, a simple negotiation over salary may reveal that the employee would prefer more performance-based pay and less fixed salary. Thus, mutual gains may be possible because there is now more than one variable to negotiate. Information is even more important in integrative negotiations because the parties require knowledge of each other's needs to discover solutions that maximize benefits for both sides.

Skilled negotiators spend most of the negotiation time listening closely to the other party and asking for details.[93] In contrast, inexperienced negotiators mainly talk to the other side about their arguments and justifications. Skilled negotiators draw out more details by presenting open-ended questions, followed by probe questions ("Oh, why is that?"). Nonverbal communication is also observed as an associated source of information during this dialogue.

Skilled negotiators also test how well they understand the other side's facts and position by summarizing the information presented and by asking for clarification on specific points. They also communicate their inner thoughts and feelings, which encourages the other party to provide further information that will help dissolve concerns ("What you just said makes me hopeful, but I'm still concerned about the time frame expected.")

Manage Concessions A concession is one party's revision of a negotiating position so it comes closer to the other party's current position. Successful negotiators actually make fewer concessions and each concession is smaller than those of average negotiators, particularly in distributive negotiations where both parties know the bargaining zone.[96] Even so, the process of making concessions is important to all parties.

Concessions are a form of communication because they signal to the other party the relative importance of each issue being negotiated. This communication of priorities occurs by presenting multi-issue offers rather than one issue at a time. Concessions also symbolize each party's motivation to bargain in good faith. In fact, an important feature of negotiations is that each party reciprocates when the other side makes a concession.[97] Concessions need to be clearly labeled as such and should be accompanied by an expectation that the other party will reciprocate. They should also be offered in installments because people experience more positive emotions from a few smaller concessions than from one large concession.[98] Generally, the best strategy is to be moderately tough and give just enough concessions to communicate sincerity and motivation to resolve the conflict.

Manage Time Negotiators make more concessions as the deadline gets closer.[99] This can be a liability if you are under time pressure, or it can be an advantage if the other party alone is under time pressure. Negotiators with more power in the

OB THEORY TO PRACTICE

Applying Mirroring to Gather Information in Negotiations[94]

Successful negotiators gather information about the opponent's underlying needs and expectations. They do this by listening more than talking but also by encouraging the other party to reveal more information. "It's not just listening, but it's understanding how to get them to talk more," says former FBI hostage negotiator, Chris Voss.

One effective strategy used by the FBI is *mirroring*—repeating back as a question the last few words of what the other person said. If the opponent says "I need to receive your shipment within the next month," you would mirror by asking "Within the next month?" This usually motivates the other person to explain further. "By repeating back what people say, you trigger this mirroring instinct and your counterpart will inevitably elaborate on what was just said and sustain the process of connecting," Voss explains.

relationship sometimes apply time pressure through an "exploding offer" whereby they give the opponent a very short time to accept their offer.[100] These time-limited offers are frequently found in consumer sales ("On sale today only!") and in some job offers. They produce time pressure, which can motivate the other party to accept the offer and forfeit the opportunity to explore their BATNA. Another time factor is that the more time someone has invested in the negotiation, the more committed they become to ensuring an agreement is reached. This commitment increases the tendency to make unwarranted concessions so that the negotiations do not fail.

Negotiators with more power in the relationship sometimes apply time pressure through an "exploding offer," whereby they give the opponent a very short time in which to accept their offer.
Gstockstudio/123RF

Build the Relationship Building and maintaining trust is important in all negotiations.[101] In purely distributive negotiation situations, trust keeps the parties focused on the issue rather than personalities, motivates them to return to the bargaining table when negotiations stall, and encourages the parties to engage in future negotiations. Trust is also critical in integrative negotiations because it motivates the parties to share information and actively search for mutual gains.

Effective negotiators build trust by discovering common backgrounds and interests with the other party, such as places they have lived and favorite sports teams. In addition, trust tends to be higher when team members closely match the backgrounds of the other party. First impressions are also important. People form beliefs and emotions in a fraction of a second, so negotiators need to be sensitive to their nonverbal cues, appearance, and initial statements. Another way to build trust is by keeping promises in the negotiation and identifying shared goals and values with the other party. Trustworthiness also increases by developing a shared understanding of the negotiation process, including its norms and expectations about speed and timing.[102]

Finally, relationship building demands emotional intelligence.[103] This includes managing the emotions each person displays to the other party, particularly avoiding an image of superiority, aggressiveness, or insensitivity. Emotional intelligence also involves managing the other party's emotions. Well-placed flattery, humor, and other methods keep everyone in a good mood and diffuse dysfunctional tension.[104]

The Negotiation Setting

The effectiveness of negotiating depends to some extent on the environment in which the negotiations occur. Location is an important situational characteristic. It is easier to negotiate on your own turf because you are familiar with the negotiating environment and are able to maintain comfortable routines.[105] Also, there is no need to cope with travel-related stress or depend on others for resources during the negotiation. Due to these strategic advantages of home turf, many negotiators agree to neutral territory.

The physical distance between the parties and formality of the setting can influence how they perceive each other and the disputed issues. Seating arrangements have a similar effect. People who sit face-to-face are more likely to develop a win-lose orientation toward the conflict situation.

Most negotiators have audiences—anyone with a vested interest in the negotiation outcomes, such as executives, other team members, or the general public. Negotiators tend to act differently when their audience observes the negotiation or has detailed information about the process, compared to situations in which the audience sees only the end results.[106] When the audience has direct surveillance over the proceedings, negotiators tend to be more competitive, less willing to make concessions, and more likely to engage in assertive tactics against the other party. This "hard-line" behavior shows the audience that the negotiator is working for their interests. With their audience watching, negotiators also have more interest in saving face.

> People form beliefs and emotions in a fraction of a second, so negotiators need to be sensitive to their nonverbal cues, appearance, and initial statements.

Study Checklist

Connect® is available for *M: Organizational Behavior.* Additional resources include:

✓ Exercises:

- **Case Analysis:** Apply concepts within the context of a real-world situation.
- **Click and Drag:** Helps make the connection between theory and application through matching, ranking, or grouping activities.
- **Video Case:** See management in action through interactive videos.
- **Self-Assessment:** Designed to promote student self-awareness and reflection, these research-based surveys contain detailed feedback for students.
- **Application-Based Activities:** These highly interactive, application- and analysis-based exercises allow students to take on specific roles to complete management related tasks within a real-world context.

✓ **SmartBook 2.0™**—Smartbook 2.0 is an adaptive learning solution that provides personalized learning to individual student needs, continually adapts to pinpoint knowledge gaps and focuses learning on concepts requiring additional study. It fosters more productive learning, takes the guesswork out of what to study, and helps students better prepare for class.

©Natthawat Jamnapa/123RF

Notes

1. J. Creswell and K. Draper, "How Under Armour Lost Its Edge," *New York Times,* January 26, 2020.
2. J.A. Wall and R.R. Callister, "Conflict and Its Management," *Journal of Management* 21 (1995): 515–58; M.A. Rahim, *Managing Conflict in Organizations,* 4th ed. (New Brunswick, NJ: Transaction, 2011), 15–17; D. Tjosvold, A.S.H. Wong, and N.Y.F. Chen, "Constructively Managing Conflicts in Organizations," *Annual Review of Organizational Psychology and Organizational Behavior* 1, no. 1 (2014): 545–68.
3. J.A. Litterer, "Conflict in Organization: A Re-Examination," *Academy of Management Journal* 9, no. 3 (September 1966): 178–86; M.A. Rahim, *Managing Conflict in Organizations,* 4th ed. (New Brunswick, NJ: Transaction, 2011), Chap. 1.
4. For example, see L. Urwick, *The Elements of Administration,* 2nd ed. (London: Pitman, 1947); H.L. Sheppard and S. Chase, "The Social and Historical Philosophy of Elton Mayo [with Comment]," *The Antioch Review* 10, no. 3 (1950): 396–406; C. Argyris, "The Individual and Organization: Some Problems of Mutual Adjustment," *Administrative Science Quarterly* 2, no. 1 (1957): 1–24; K.E. Boulding, "Organization and Conflict," *Conflict Resolution* 1, no. 2 (1957): 122–34; R.R. Blake, H.A. Shepard, and J.S. Mouton, *Managing Intergroup Conflict in Industry* (Houston: Gulf, 1964).
5. C.K.W. De Dreu and L.R. Weingart, "A Contingency Theory of Task Conflict and Performance in Groups and Organizational Teams," in *International Handbook of Organizational Teamwork and Cooperative Working,* ed. M.A. West, D. Tjosvold, and K.G. Smith (Chichester, UK: Wiley, 2003), 151–66; S. Rispens, "Benefits and Detrimental Effects of Conflict," in *Handbook of Conflict Management Research,* ed. O.B. Ayoko, N.M. Ashkanasy, and K.A. Jehn (Cheltenham, UK: Edward Elgar, 2014), 19–32; D. De Clercq and I. Belausteguigoitia, "Overcoming the Dark Side of Task Conflict: Buffering Roles of Transformational Leadership, Tenacity, and Passion for Work," *European Management Journal* 35, no. 1 (February 2017): 78–90.
6. F.R.C. de Wit, L.L. Greer, and K.A. Jehn, "The Paradox of Intragroup Conflict: A Meta-Analysis," *Journal of Applied Psychology* 97, no. 2 (2012): 360–90; L.L. Meier et al., "Relationship and Task Conflict at Work: Interactive Short-Term Effects on Angry Mood and Somatic Complaints," *Journal of Occupational Health Psychology* 18, no. 2 (2013): 144–56; N.L. Jimmieson, M.K. Tucker, and J.L. Campbell, "Task Conflict Leads to Relationship Conflict When Employees Are Low in Trait Self-Control: Implications for Employee Strain," *Personality and Individual Differences* 113 (2017): 209–18.
7. J. Meng, J. Fulk, and Y.C. Yuan, "The Roles and Interplay of Intragroup Conflict and Team Emotion Management on Information Seeking Behaviors in Team Contexts," *Communication Research* 42, no. 5 (2015): 675–700; M.-H. Tsai and C. Bendersky, "The Pursuit of Information Sharing: Expressing Task Conflicts as Debates vs. Disagreements Increases Perceived Receptivity to Dissenting Opinions in Groups," *Organization Science* 27, no. 1 (2015): 141–56.
8. L.L. Greer, L. van Bunderen, and S. Yu, "The Dysfunctions of Power in Teams: A Review and Emergent Conflict Perspective," *Research in Organizational Behavior* 37 (2017): 103–24; L. van Bunderen, L.L. Greer, and D. van Knippenberg, "When Interteam Conflict Spirals into Intrateam Power Struggles: The Pivotal Role of Team Power Structures," *Academy of Management Journal* 61, no. 3 (2018): 1100–30.
9. M.P. Follett, "Constructive Conflict," in *Dynamic Administration: The Collected Papers of Mary Parker Follett,* ed. H.C. Metcalf and L. Urwick (Bath, UK: Management Publications Trust, 1941), 30–49.
10. Although the 1970s marked a point when the benefits of conflict became widely acknowledged, a few earlier writers had also expressed this view. See L.A. Coser, *The Functions of Social Conflict* (New York: Free Press, 1956); J.A. Litterer, "Conflict in Organization: A Re-Examination," *Academy of Management Journal* 9 (1966): 178–86; H. Assael, "Constructive Role of Interorganizational Conflict," *Administrative Science Quarterly* 14 (1969): 573–82.

11. J. Dewey, *Human Nature and Conduct: An Introduction to Social Psychology* (New York: Holt, 1922), 300.

12. P.J. Carnevale, "Creativity in the Outcomes of Conflict," in *The Handbook of Conflict Resolution: Theory and Practice*, ed. M. Deutsch, P.T. Coleman, and E.C. Marcus (San Francisco: Jossey-Bass, 2006), 414–35; T.A. O'Neill, N.J. Allen, and S.E. Hastings, "Examining the 'Pros' and 'Cons' of Team Conflict: A Team-Level Meta-Analysis of Task, Relationship, and Process Conflict," *Human Performance* 26 (2013): 236–60; X.-Y. Xie, W.-L. Wang, and K. Luan, "It Is Not What We Have, but How We Use It: Re-exploring the Relationship between Task Conflict and Team Innovation from the Resource-Based View," *Group Processes & Intergroup Relations* 17 (2014): 240–51, P. Petrou, A.B. Bakker, and K. Bezemer, "Creativity under Task Conflict: The Role of Proactively Increasing Job Resources," *Journal of Occupational and Organizational Psychology* 92 (2019): 305–29.

13. K.M. Eisenhardt, J.L. Kahwajy, and L.J. Bourgeois III, "Conflict and Strategic Choice: How Top Management Teams Disagree," *California Management Review* 39 (1997): 42–62; T. Greitemeyer et al., "Information Sampling and Group Decision Making: The Effects of an Advocacy Decision Procedure and Task Experience," *Journal of Experimental Psychology: Applied* 12, no. 1 (2006): 31–42; U. Klocke, "How to Improve Decision Making in Small Groups: Effects of Dissent and Training Interventions," *Small Group Research* 38, no. 3 (2007): 437–68.

14. C.K.W. De Dreu, "When Too Little or Too Much Hurts: Evidence for a Curvilinear Relationship Between Task Conflict and Innovation in Teams," *Journal of Management* 32 (2006): 83–107; J.L. Farh, C. Lee, and C.I.C. Farh, "Task Conflict and Team Creativity: A Question of How Much and When," *Journal of Applied Psychology* 95 (2010): 1173–80; G. Todorova, J.B. Bear, and L.R. Weingart, "Can Conflict Be Energizing? A Study of Task Conflict, Positive Emotions, and Job Satisfaction," *Journal of Applied Psychology* 99 (2014): 451–67; L.R. Weingart et al., "The Directness and Oppositional Intensity of Conflict Expression," *Academy of Management Review* 40 (2015): 235–62.

15. This book adopts the long-held perspective (Fisher & Ury, Tjosvold, etc.) that all conflict can be framed as either (or degrees of) task and relationship conflict. For example employees who refer to a conflict as a "personality clash" have attributed the conflict to problems with the other party's personal characteristics (relationship conflict). Yet others frame the same situation as task conflict by attributing the disagreement to different beliefs and feelings about the issue that need to be understood and analyzed logically. This "framing" perspective contrasts with the view by some writers that task and relationship (along with process and status) conflict are somehow fundamental sources of conflict. This "content" perspective defines the type of conflict by the topic or content of the conflict. One problem is that content-based typologies can expand into an almost infinite list of topics. Furthermore, the content-based view inappropriately assumes that task conflict and relationship conflict cannot co-exist or be perceived in the same conflict episode. This book takes the established view that it is how conflicts are framed–not whether the alleged topic is the task, process, status, or relationship–that affects the key outcomes in conflict episodes. For literature on types of conflict, see: A.C. Amason, "Distinguishing the Effects of Functional and Dysfunctional Conflict on Strategic Decision Making: Resolving a Paradox for Top Management Teams," *Academy of Management Journal* 39, no. 1 (1996): 123–48; R. Fisher and W. Ury, *Getting to Yes: Negotiating an Agreement without Giving In* (Random House, 2012); K.A. Jehn, "Types of Conflict: The History and Future of Conflict Definitions and Typologies," in *Handbook of Conflict Management Research*, ed. O.B. Ayoko, N.M. Ashkanasy, and K.A. Jehn (Cheltenham, UK: Edward Elgar, 2014), 3–18; D. Tjosvold, A.S.H. Wong, and N.Y.F. Chen, "Constructively Managing Conflicts in Organizations," *Annual Review of Organizational Psychology and Organizational Behavior* 1 (2014): 545–68; T.A. O'Neill et al., "The Structure and Function of Team Conflict State Profiles," *Journal of Management* 44, no. 2 (2018): 811–36. One recent review recognizes this distinction between conflict type and how conflict is viewed (focus) or how it is expressed. See: L.R. Weingart et al., "The Directness and Oppositional Intensity of Conflict Expression," *Academy of Management Review* 40, no. 2 (2015): 235–62.

16. F.R.C. de Wit, L.L. Greer, and K.A. Jehn, "The Paradox of Intragroup Conflict: A Meta-Analysis," *Journal of Applied Psychology* 97, no. 2 (2012): 360–90. Earlier meta-analyses reported either nonsignificant or somewhat negative correlations between task conflict and team outcomes. However, the recent meta-analysis and other writers point to several methodological problems with conflict research that explain the mixed findings. For a review, see M.L. Loughry and A.C. Amason, "Why Won't Task Conflict Cooperate? Deciphering Stubborn Results," *International Journal of Conflict Management* 25, no. 4 (2014): 333–58.

17. One of the clearest recent descriptions of relationship versus task conflict is found in L.R. Weingart et al., "The Directness and Oppositional Intensity of Conflict Expression," *Academy of Management Review* 40, no. 2 (2015): 235–62.

18. D. Walton, *Ad Hominem Arguments* (Tuscaloosa: University of Alabama Press, 1998), Chaps 1–2. The ad hominem fallacy is a major concern in academic critiques. See, for example: R.M. Barnes et al., "The Effect of Ad Hominem Attacks on the Evaluation of Claims Promoted by Scientists," *PLoS ONE* 13, no. 1 (2018): e0192025.

19. J.M. Leon-Perez et al., "The Relationship between Interpersonal Conflict and Workplace Bullying," *Journal of Managerial Psychology* 30 (2015): 250–63; K.A. Graham et al., "Too Many Cooks in the Kitchen: The Effects of Dominance Incompatibility on Relationship Conflict and Subsequent Abusive Supervision," *Leadership Quarterly* 30 (2019): 351–64.

20. R.S. Lau and A.T. Cobb, "Understanding the Connections between Relationship Conflict and Performance: The Intervening Roles of Trust and Exchange," *Journal of Organizational Behavior* 31, no. 6 (2010): 898–917.

21. C.K.W. De Dreu and L.R. Weingart, "Task versus Relationship Conflict, Team Performance, and Team Member Satisfaction: A Meta-Analysis," *Journal of Applied Psychology* 88 (2003): 587–604; A.C. Mooney, P.J. Holahan, and A.C. Amason, "Don't Take It Personally: Exploring Cognitive Conflict as a Mediator of Affective Conflict," *Journal of Management Studies* 44, no. 5 (2007): 733–58; K. Choi and B. Cho, "Competing Hypotheses Analyses of the Associations between Group Task Conflict and Group Relationship Conflict," *Journal of Organizational Behavior* 32, no. 8 (2011): 1106–26.

22. J.X. Yang and K.W. Mossholder, "Decoupling Task and Relationship Conflict: The Role of Intergroup Emotional Processing," *Journal of Organizational Behavior* 25 (2004): 589–605; B.H. Bradley et al., "Ready to Rumble: How Team Personality Composition and Task Conflict Interact to Improve Performance," *Journal of Applied Psychology* 98, no. 2 (2013): 385–92; B.H. Bradley et al., "Reaping the Benefits of Task Conflict in Teams: The Critical Role of Team Psychological Safety Climate," *Journal of Applied Psychology* 97, no. 1 (2012): 151–58.

23. P.L. Curseu, S. Boros, and L.A.G. Oerlemans, "Task and Relationship Conflict in Short-Term and Long-Term Groups: The Critical Role of Emotion Regulation," *International Journal of Conflict Management* 23 (2012): 97–107; A. Schlaerth, N. Ensari, and J. Christian, "A Meta-Analytical Review of the Relationship between

Emotional Intelligence and Leaders' Constructive Conflict Management," *Group Processes & Intergroup Relations* 16 (2013): 126–36; N.L. Jimmieson, M.K. Tucker, and J.L. Campbell, "Task Conflict Leads to Relationship Conflict When Employees Are Low in Trait Self-Control: Implications for Employee Strain," *Personality and Individual Differences* 113 (2017): 209–18; H.R. Flores, X. Jiang, and C.C. Manz, "Intra-Team Conflict: The Moderating Effect of Emotional Self-Leadership," *International Journal of Conflict Management* 29 (2018): 424–44.

24. F.R.C. de Wit, L.L. Greer, and K.A. Jehn, "The Paradox of Intragroup Conflict: A Meta-Analysis," *Journal of Applied Psychology* 97, no. 2 (March 2012): 360–90; S.E. Humphrey et al., "Team Conflict Dynamics: Implications of a Dyadic View of Conflict for Team Performance," *Organizational Behavior and Human Decision Processes* 142 (2017): 58–70; T.A. O'Neill and M.J.W. McLarnon, "Optimizing Team Conflict Dynamics for High Performance Teamwork," *Human Resource Management Review* 28 (2018): 378–94.

25. A.C. Edmondson and Z. Lei, "Psychological Safety: The History, Renaissance, and Future of an Interpersonal Construct," *Annual Review of Organizational Psychology and Organizational Behavior* 1, no. 1 (2014): 23–43, https://doi.org/10.1146/annurev-orgpsych-031413-091305; D. Tjosvold, A.S.H. Wong, and N.Y.F. Chen, "Constructively Managing Conflicts in Organizations," *Annual Review of Organizational Psychology and Organizational Behavior* 1, no. 1 (2014): 545–68; A. Newman, R. Donohue, and N. Eva, "Psychological Safety: A Systematic Review of the Literature," *Human Resource Management Review* 27, no. 3 (September 2017): 521–35.

26. L. Pondy, "Organizational Conflict: Concepts and Models," *Administrative Science Quarterly* 2 (1967): 296–320; K.W. Thomas, "Conflict and Negotiation Processes in Organizations," in *Handbook of Industrial and Organizational Psychology*, ed. M.D. Dunnette and L.M. Hough (Palo Alto, CA: Consulting Psychologists Press, 1992), 651–718.

27. E. Halperin, "Emotion, Emotion Regulation, and Conflict Resolution," *Emotion Review* 6, no. 1 (January 1, 2014): 68–76; G. Todorova, J.B. Bear, and L.R. Weingart, "Can Conflict Be Energizing? A Study of Task Conflict, Positive Emotions, and Job Satisfaction," *Journal of Applied Psychology* 99, no. 3 (2014): 451–67; S. Čehajić-Clancy et al., "Social-Psychological Interventions for Intergroup Reconciliation: An Emotion Regulation Perspective," *Psychological Inquiry* 27, no. 2 (2016): 73–88; M. Caldara et al., "A Study of the Triggers of Conflict and Emotional Reactions," *Games* 8, no. 2 (2017): 21; G.A. van Kleef and S. Côté, "Emotional Dynamics in Conflict and Negotiation: Individual, Dyadic, and Group Processes," *Annual Review of Organizational Psychology and Organizational Behavior* 5, no. 1 (2018): 437–64.

28. E. Halperin, "Emotion, Emotion Regulation, and Conflict Resolution," *Emotion Review* 6, no. 1 (2014): 68–76; D. Motro, T. Kugler, and T. Connolly, "Back to the Basics: How Feelings of Anger Affect Cooperation," *International Journal of Conflict Management* 27, no. 4 (2016): 523–46; J. Folger, M.S. Poole, and R.K. Stutman, *Working through Conflict: Strategies for Relationships, Groups, and Organizations*, 7th ed. (Oxon, UK: Routledge, 2016), Chap. 2.

29. G.E. Martin and T.J. Bergman, "The Dynamics of Behavioral Response to Conflict in the Workplace," *Journal of Occupational & Organizational Psychology* 69 (1996): 377–87; K.A. Kennedy and E. Pronin, "When Disagreement Gets Ugly: Perceptions of Bias and the Escalation of Conflict," *Personality and Social Psychology Bulletin* 34, no. 6 (2008): 833–48; L.F. Smyth, "Escalation and Mindfulness," *Negotiation Journal* 28, no. 1 (2012): 45–72.

30. R.E. Walton and J.M. Dutton, "The Management of Conflict: A Model and Review," *Administrative Science Quarterly* 14 (1969): 73–84; S.M. Schmidt and T.A. Kochan, "Conflict: Toward Conceptual Clarity," *Administrative Science Quarterly* 17, no. 3 (1972): 359–70.

31. K.A. Jehn, C. Chadwick, and S.M.B. Thatcher, "To Agree or Not to Agree: The Effects of Value Congruence, Individual Demographic Dissimilarity, and Conflict on Workgroup Outcomes," *International Journal of Conflict Management* 8 (1997): 287–305; A.N. Gorman, D.C. Leach, and N. Spector, "Worldviews in Collision: Conflict and Collaboration across Professional Lines," *Journal of Organizational Behavior* 27 (2006): 829–49; L.L. Greer et al., "Why and When Hierarchy Impacts Team Effectiveness: A Meta-Analytic Integration," *Journal of Applied Psychology* 103 (2018): 591–613; X. "Paul" Zhang et al., "One World, Two Realities: Perception Differences between Software Developers and Testers," *Journal of Computer Information Systems* 58 (2018): 385–94.

32. D.R. Hillman, "Understanding Multigenerational Work-Value Conflict Resolution," *Journal of Workplace Behavioral Health* 29 (2014): 240–57; S. Lyons and L. Kuron, "Generational Differences in the Workplace: A Review of the Evidence and Directions for Future Research," *Journal of Organizational Behavior* 35 (2014): S139–57; M.J. Urick et al., "Understanding and Managing Intergenerational Conflict: An Examination of Influences and Strategies," *Work, Aging and Retirement* 3 (2017): 166–85.

33. J. Joseph, "Managing Change after the Merger: The Value of Pre-Merger Ingroup Identities," *Journal of Organizational Change Management* 27, no. 3 (2014): 430–48; H.E. Yildiz, "'Us vs. Them' or 'Us over Them'? On the Roles of Similarity and Status in M&As," *International Business Review* 25, no. 1, Part A (2016): 51–65; R.M. Sarala, E. Vaara, and P. Junni, "Beyond Merger Syndrome and Cultural Differences: New Avenues for Research on the 'Human Side' of Global Mergers and Acquisitions (M&As)," *Journal of World Business* 54, no. 4 (2019): 307–21.

34. J. Brett, "Intercultural Challenges in Managing Workplace Conflict–A Call for Research," *Cross Cultural & Strategic Management* 25, no. 1 (2018): 32–52.

35. P.C. Earley and G.B. Northcraft, "Goal Setting, Resource Interdependence, and Conflict Management," in *Managing Conflict: An Interdisciplinary Approach*, ed. M.A. Rahim (New York: Praeger, 1989), 161–70; K. Jehn, "A Multimethod Examination of the Benefits and Detriments of Intragroup Conflict," *Administrative Science Quarterly* 40 (1995): 245–82; P.T. Coleman et al., "Navigating Conflict and Power at Work: The Effects of Power and Interdependence Asymmetries on Conflict in Organizations," *Journal of Applied Social Psychology* 43, no. 10 (2013): 1963–83.

36. F. Chung, "'I Don't Want to Play Musical Chairs Each Day': Tax Office Staff Revolt over Hot-Desk Plan," *News.Com.Au*, August 22, 2017; R.L. Morrison and K.A. Macky, "The Demands and Resources Arising from Shared Office Spaces," *Applied Ergonomics* 60 (April 2017): 103–15; "UK Office Workers Waste 'almost Two Weeks' a Year Finding Somewhere to Sit," *Business Matters (UK)*, June 28, 2019; B. Doherty, "Struggling to Focus When Returning to the Office? You Aren't Alone," *Globe and Mail*, January 30, 2023.

37. J.G. March and H.A. Simon, *Organizations* (New York: John Wiley & Sons, 1958), 126.

38. A. Risberg, "Employee Experiences of Acquisition Processes," *Journal of World Business* 36 (2001): 58–84; G. Karamustafa and S.C. Schneider, "Buffering and Bridging: How Leaders Can Make a Difference during the Post-Merger Integration Process," in *Research Handbook of Global Leadership*, ed. L. Zander (Cheltenham, UK: Edward Elgar Publishing, 2020), 288–306.

39. L.R. Weingart et al., "The Directness and Oppositional Intensity of Conflict Expression," *Academy of Management Review* 40 (2015): 235–62; D. Ames, A. Lee, and A. Wazlawek, "Interpersonal Assertiveness: Inside the Balancing Act," *Social and Personality Psychology Compass* 11 (2017): e12317; C. Samba, D. Van Knippenberg, and C.C. Miller, "The Impact of Strategic Dissent on Organizational Outcomes: A Meta-Analytic Integration," *Strategic Management Journal* 39 (2018): 379–402.

40. D. Wheatley and J. Gifford, "UK Working Lives: The CIPD Job Quality Index" (London: Chartered Institute of Personnel and Development (CIPD), July 2019); R. Suff, "Managing Conflict in the Modern Workplace" (London: Chartered Institute of Personnel and Development, January 2020); "2020 Public Service Employee Survey Results for the Public Service" (Ottawa: Government of Canada, Treasury Board of Canada Secretariat, January 2021); J. Pieniazek, "The Blow-By-Blow on Remote Work Conflict [2021 Study]," *My Perfect Resume* (blog), February 21, 2021; K. Wood, "Conflict at Work: What Are Your Options?," *Myers-Briggs Connect with Us* (blog), October 4, 2022.

41. M. Hewstone, M. Rubin, and H. Willis, "Intergroup Bias," *Annual Review of Psychology* 53 (2002): 575–604; T. Yamagishi and N. Mifune, "Social Exchange and Solidarity: In-Group Love or Out-Group Hate?," *Evolution and Human Behavior* 30 (2009): 229–37; N. Halevy, O. Weisel, and G. Bornstein, "'In-Group Love' and 'Out-Group Hate' in Repeated Interaction between Groups," *Journal of Behavioral Decision Making* 25 (2012): 188–95; O. Weisel and R. Böhm, "'Ingroup Love' and 'Outgroup Hate' in Intergroup Conflict between Natural Groups," *Journal of Experimental Social Psychology* 60 (2015): 110–20.

42. M.P. Follett, "Constructive Conflict," in *Dynamic Administration: The Collected Papers of Mary Parker Follett*, ed. H.C. Metcalf and L. Urwick, (Bath, UK: Management Publications Trust, 1941), 30–49; R.R. Blake, H.A. Shepard, and J.S. Mouton, *Managing Intergroup Conflict in Industry* (Houston: Gulf Publishing, 1964); T. Ruble and K. Thomas, "Support for a Two-Dimensional Model of Conflict Behavior," *Organizational Behavior and Human Performance* 16 (1976): 143–55; C.K.W. De Dreu et al., "A Theory-Based Measure of Conflict Management Strategies in the Workplace," *Journal of Organizational Behavior* 22 (2001): 645–68; D. Tjosvold, A.S.H. Wong, and N.Y.F. Chen, "Constructively Managing Conflicts in Organizations," *Annual Review of Organizational Psychology and Organizational Behavior* 1 (2014): 545–68; K.E. Johnson and J.A. Hall, "Validity of Self-Reported Conflict Handling Preferences and the Role of Self-Enhancement," *International Journal of Conflict Management* 29 (2018): 543–63.

43. D. Ames, A. Lee, and A. Wazlawek, "Interpersonal Assertiveness: Inside the Balancing Act," *Social and Personality Psychology Compass* 11, no. 6 (2017): e12317.

44. Q. Wang, E.L. Fink, and D.A. Cai, "The Effect of Conflict Goals on Avoidance Strategies: What Does Not Communicating Communicate?" *Human Communication Research* 38, no. 2 (2012): 222–52.

45. Several studies have identified personal characteristics that predict a person's preferred conflict style. For example, see P.J. Moberg, "Linking Conflict Strategy to the Five-Factor Model: Theoretical and Empirical Foundations," *International Journal of Conflict Management* 12 (2001): 47–68; J.E. Barbuto Jr., K.A. Phipps, and Y. Xu, "Testing Relationships between Personality, Conflict Styles and Effectiveness," *International Journal of Conflict Management* 21 (2010): 434–47; M. Gunkel, C. Schlaegel, and V. Taras, "Cultural Values, Emotional Intelligence, and Conflict Handling Styles: A Global Study," *Journal of World Business* 51 (2016): 568–85; L. Parmer, "Relationships between Philosophical Values and Conflict Management Styles," *International Journal of Conflict Management* 29 (2017): 236–52.

46. D.W. Johnson et al., "Effects of Cooperative, Competitive, and Individualistic Goal Structures on Achievement: A Meta-Analysis," *Psychological Bulletin* 89 (1981): 47–62; G.A. Callanan, C.D. Benzing, and D.F. Perri, "Choice of Conflict-Handling Strategy: A Matter of Context," *Journal of Psychology* 140, no. 3 (2006): 269–88; T.J. Hargrave and A.H. Van de Ven, "Integrating Dialectical and Paradox Perspectives on Managing Contradictions in Organizations," *Organization Studies* 38, no. 3-4 (2017): 319–39.

47. X.M. Song, J. Xile, and B. Dyer, "Antecedents and Consequences of Marketing Managers' Conflict-Handling Behaviors," *Journal of Marketing* 64 (2000): 50–66; L.A. DeChurch, K.L. Hamilton, and C. Haas, "Effects of Conflict Management Strategies on Perceptions of Intragroup Conflict," *Group Dynamics* 11, no. 1 (2007): 66–78; D.G. Oore, M.P. Leiter, and D.E. LeBlanc, "Individual and Organizational Factors Promoting Successful Responses to Workplace Conflict," *Canadian Psychology* 56, no. 3 (2015): 301–10.

48. G.A. Chung-Yan and C. Moeller, "The Psychosocial Costs of Conflict Management Styles," *International Journal of Conflict Management* 21, no. 4 (2010): 382–99.

49. A. Chunyan Peng and D. Tjosvold, "Social Face Concerns and Conflict Avoidance of Chinese Employees with Their Western or Chinese Managers," *Human Relations* 64 (2011): 1031–50; J.B. Bear, L.R. Weingart, and G. Todorova, "Gender and the Emotional Experience of Relationship Conflict: The Differential Effectiveness of Avoidant Conflict Management," *Negotiation and Conflict Management Research* 7 (2014): 213–31; I. Yang, "Perceived Conflict Avoidance by Managers and Its Consequences on Subordinates' Attitudes," *Business Ethics: A European Review* 24 (2015): 282–96; Z.-X. Zhang and X. Wei, "Superficial Harmony and Conflict Avoidance Resulting from Negative Anticipation in the Workplace," *Management and Organization Review* 13 (2017): 795–820.

50. Several variations of this quotation have appeared over the past century. The field of marketing has an even older version of this quotation—Win an argument and lose a sale (or customer). Marketing textbooks and trade publications cited it in the 1890s. The "friends" version of this quotation has occasionally been attributed to Edward Wood, 1st Earl of Halifax, but we could not verify this. In any event, the earliest marketing/sales version appeared before Lord Halifax was an adult. Dale Carnegie definitely popularized the idea behind the notion that winning arguments loses friends. The entire first chapter of Part 3 in his best-selling book *How to Win Friends and Influence People* (1936) is devoted to this topic: "You Can't Win an Argument." The version of the quotation cited here is published in E. Knowles, *Little Oxford Dictionary of Proverbs* (Oxford, UK: Oxford University Press, 2009), 21.

51. J. Pieniazek, "The Blow-by-Blow on Remote Work Conflict [2021 Study]," *My Perfect Resume* (blog), February 21, 2021; "Workplace Conflict Statistics: How We Approach Conflict at Work" (Toronto: Niagara Institute, August 11, 2022); K. Gurchiek, "Wash Your Hands! Clean Your Cubicle!," *SHRM*, October 3, 2022; "Introverts Are Nearly Three Times More Likely to Avoid Conflict Than Extraverts," Press Release (Sunnyvale, Calif.: Myers-Briggs Company, December 29, 2022).

52. A. Ergeneli, S.M. Camgoz, and P.B. Karapinar, "The Relationship between Self-Efficacy and Conflict-Handling Styles in Terms of Relative Authority Positions of the Two Parties," *Social Behavior & Personality: An International Journal* 38, no. 1 (2010): 13–28.

53. K. Leung et al., "Harmony and Conflict: A Cross-Cultural Investigation in China and Australia," *Journal of Cross-Cultural Psychology* 42 (2011): 795–816; W.-F. Lin et al., "We Can Make It Better: 'We' Moderates the Relationship Between a Compromising Style in Interpersonal Conflict and Well-Being," *Journal of Happiness Studies* 17 (2016): 41–57.

54. C.H. Tinsley, "How Negotiators Get to Yes: Predicting the Constellation of Strategies Used across Cultures to Negotiate Conflict," *Journal of Applied Psychology* 86, no. 4 (2001): 583–93; M. Gunkel, C. Schlaegel, and V. Taras, "Cultural Values, Emotional Intelligence, and Conflict Handling Styles: A Global Study," *Journal of World Business* 51, no. 4 (2016): 568–85.

55. F.P. Brew and D.R. Cairns, "Styles of Managing Interpersonal Workplace Conflict in Relation to Status and Face Concern: A Study with Anglos and Chinese," *International Journal of Conflict Management* 15 (2004): 27–57; A. C-Y. Peng and D. Tjosvold, "Social Face Concerns and Conflict Avoidance of Chinese Employees with Their Western or Chinese Managers," *Human Relations* 64 (2011): 1031–50; X. Li, V. Worm, and P. Xie, "Towards an Integrative Framework of Conflict-Handling Behaviour: Integrating Western and Chinese Perspectives," *Asia Pacific Business Review* 24 (2018): 22–36; J. Brett, "Intercultural Challenges in Managing Workplace Conflict–A Call for Research," *Cross Cultural & Strategic Management* 25 (2018): 32–52.

56. J.L. Holt and C.J. DeVore, "Culture, Gender, Organizational Role, and Styles of Conflict Resolution: A Meta-Analysis," *International Journal of Intercultural Relations* 29, no. 2 (2005): 165–96; M. Davis, S. Capobianco, and L. Kraus, "Gender Differences in Responding to Conflict in the Workplace: Evidence from a Large Sample of Working Adults," *Sex Roles* 63, no. 7 (2010): 500–14; B.M. Gayle, R.W. Preiss, and M. Allen, "Where Are We Now? A Meta-Analytic Review of Sex Difference Expectations for Conflict Management Strategy Selection," in *Managing Interpersonal Conflict: Advances through Meta-Analysis,* ed. N.A. Burrell, et al. (New York: Routledge, 2014), 226–47.

57. K. Lewin, *Resolving Social Conflicts* (New York: Harper, 1948).

58. M. Sherif, "Superordinate Goals in the Reduction of Intergroup Conflict," *American Journal of Sociology* 63, no. 4 (1958): 349–56; J.D. Hunger and L.W. Stern, "An Assessment of the Functionality of the Superordinate Goal in Reducing Conflict," *Academy of Management Journal* 19, no. 4 (1976): 591–605.

59. K.M. Eisenhardt, J.L. Kahwajy, and L.J. Bourgeois III, "How Management Teams Can Have a Good Fight," *Harvard Business Review* (July/August 1997): 77–85; O. Doucet, J. Poitras, and D. Chênevert, "The Impacts of Leadership on Workplace Conflicts," *International Journal of Conflict Management* 20 (2009): 340–54; J. DiBenigno, "Anchored Personalization in Managing Goal Conflict between Professional Groups: The Case of U.S. Army Mental Health Care," *Administrative Science Quarterly* 63 (2018): 526–69.

60. R.S. Lau and A.T. Cobb, "Understanding the Connections between Relationship Conflict and Performance: The Intervening Roles of Trust and Exchange," *Journal of Organizational Behavior* 31 (2010): 898–917; D.E. Rast, M.A. Hogg, and D. van Knippenberg, "Intergroup Leadership across Distinct Subgroups and Identities," *Personality and Social Psychology Bulletin* 44 (2018): 1090–103.

61. M.-G. Seo and N.S. Hill, "Understanding the Human Side of Merger and Acquisition: An Integrative Framework," *The Journal of Applied Behavioral Science* 41 (2005): 422–43; H.E. Yildiz, "'Us vs. Them' or 'Us over Them'? On the Roles of Similarity and Status in M&As," *International Business Review* 25, Part A (2016): 51–65; F. Du and K. Xu, "The Path to Independence: Board Cohesion, Cognitive Conflict, and Information Sharing," *Journal of Management Accounting Research* 30 (2018): 31–54.

62. J. Sanchez-Burks, C.-Y. Cheng, and F. Lee, "Taking Advantage of Differences: Increasing Team Innovation through Identity Integration," in *Diversity and Groups*, vol. 11, *Research on Managing Groups and Teams* 11 (Bingley, UK: Emerald Group Publishing Limited, 2008), 55–73; A.M. Carton and B.A. Tewfik, "Perspective—A New Look at Conflict Management in Work Groups," *Organization Science* 27 (2016): 1125–41; H. Rubinstein, "The Importance of Multiple Perspectives," in *Applying Behavioural Science to the Private Sector: Decoding What People Say and What They Do*, ed. H. Rubinstein (Cham, Switzerland: Palgrave Pivot, 2018), 89–106; T. Wei and J. Clegg, "Effect of Organizational Identity Change on Integration Approaches in Acquisitions: Role of Organizational Dominance," *British Journal of Management* 29 (2018): 337–55.

63. J. DiBenigno, "Anchored Personalization in Managing Goal Conflict between Professional Groups: The Case of U.S. Army Mental Health Care," *Administrative Science Quarterly* 63, no. 3 (2018): 526–69.

64. J.F. Dovidio et al., "Reducing Intergroup Bias through Intergroup Contact: Twenty Years of Progress and Future Directions," *Group Processes & Intergroup Relations* 20 (2017): 606–20; R. Böhm, H. Rusch, and J. Baron, "The Psychology of Intergroup Conflict: A Review of Theories and Measures," *Journal of Economic Behavior & Organization*, 178 (October 2020): 947–62.

65. J. Luft, *Of Human Interaction* (Palo Alto, CA: National Press, 1969); E.H. Schein, "Reactions, Reflections, Rejoinders, and a Challenge," *The Journal of Applied Behavioral Science* 45, no. 1 (2009): 141–58; L. Shamoa-Nir, "The Window Becomes a Mirror: The Use of the Johari Window Model to Evaluate Stereotypes in Intergroup Dialogue in Israel," *Israel Affairs* 23, no. 4 (2017): 727–46.

66. R.R. Blake and J.S. Mouton, "Reactions to Intergroup Competition under Win-Lose Conditions," *Management Science* 7 (1961): 420–35; R.R. Blake and J.S. Mouton, *Solving Costly Organizational Conflicts*, 1st ed. (San Francisco: Jossey-Bass Publishers, 1984), Chap. 6; M.L. Marks, "Merger Management HR's Way," *HRMagazine* 36, no. 5 (May 1991): 60; G. Gemmill and M. Elmes, "Mirror, Mask, and Shadow: Psychodynamic Aspects of Intergroup Relations," *Journal of Management Inquiry* 2 (1993): 43–51.

67. S.P. Means, "Playing at Pixar," *Salt Lake Tribune*, May 30, 2003; S. Levy, "Apple's New Campus: An Exclusive Look Inside the Mothership," *Wired*, May 16, 2017; B. Sitbon, "Meet, Eat, Scale, Repeat," *WeWork Technology* (blog), May 29, 2018; S. Nordwall, "How to Use Slack's Donut Bot to Foster Connection in the Workplace," *Culture Amp* (blog), 2020; "Informal Communication in an All-Remote Environment," in *GitLab Guide to All-Remote* (GitLab, 2021).

68. A.-K. Newheiser and J.F. Dovidio, "Individual Differences and Intergroup Bias: Divergent Dynamics Associated with Prejudice and Stereotyping," *Personality and Individual Differences* 53 (2012): 70–74; L. Cosmides and J. Tooby, "Evolutionary Psychology: New Perspectives on Cognition and Motivation," *Annual Review of Psychology* 64 (2013): 201–29.

69. M.A. Von Glinow, D.L. Shapiro, and J.M. Brett, "Can We Talk, and Should We? Managing Emotional Conflict in Multicultural Teams," *Academy of Management Review* 29 (2004): 578–92; X. Li, V. Worm, and P. Xie, "Towards an Integrative Framework of Conflict-Handling Behaviour: Integrating Western and Chinese Perspectives," *Asia Pacific Business Review* 24 (2018): 22–36.

70. J.R. Galbraith, *Organization Design* (Reading, MA: Addison-Wesley, 1977), 132.

71. P.R. Lawrence and J.W. Lorsch, "New Management Job: The Integrator," *Harvard Business Review*, December 1967, 142–51; J.R. Galbraith, *Organization Design* (Reading, MA: Addison-Wesley, 1977), 152–58; R. Cappetta and P. Cillo, "Managing Integrators Where Integration Matters: Insights from Symbolic Industries," *The International Journal of Human Resource Management* 19 (2008): 2235–51.

72. J.G. March and H.A. Simon, *Organizations* (New York: John Wiley & Sons, 1958), 126.

73. A.R. Elangovan, "The Manager as the Third Party: Deciding How to Intervene in Employee Disputes," in *Negotiation: Readings, Exercises, and Cases*, ed. R.J. Lewicki, J.A. Litterer, and D. Saunders, 5th ed (New York: McGraw Hill, 2007), 473–84; D.E. Conlon et al., "Third Party Interventions across Cultures: No 'One Best Choice,'" in *Research in Personnel and Human Resources Management* (Greenwich, CT: JAI, 2007), 309–49. A broader variation of third-party conflict resolution is peacemaking. See X. Zhang et al., "Peacemaking at the Workplace: A Systematic Review," *Negotiation and Conflict Management Research* 11 (2018): 204–24.

74. J.W. Thibaut and L. Walker, *Procedural Justice: A Psychological Analysis* (Hillsdale, N.J.: L. Erlbaum Associates, 1975); B.H. Sheppard, "Managers as Inquisitors: Lessons from the Law," in *Bargaining inside Organizations*, ed. M.H. Bazerman and R.J. Lewicki (Beverly Hills, CA: Sage, 1983).

75. "Co-Worker Conflicts," *Nulab* (blog), October 1, 2019; R. Suff, "Managing Conflict in the Modern Workplace" (London: Chartered Institute of Personnel and Development (CIPD), January 2020); "Twenty per Cent of Canadians Experienced Increased Workplace Conflict or Aggression," Press Release (Toronto: TELUS Health, June 23, 2022); K. Wood, "Conflict at Work: What Are Your Options?," *Myers-Briggs Connect with Us* (blog), October 4, 2022.

76. J.A. Wall and T.C. Dunne, "Mediation Research: A Current Review," *Negotiation Journal* 28 (2012): 217–44; K. Bollen and M. Euwema, "Workplace Mediation: An Underdeveloped Research Area," *Negotiation Journal* 29 (2013): 329–53. Some researchers suggest that there are several forms of mediation, not all of which have high process and low decision control. See D.L. Shapiro and E.N. Sherf, "The Role of Conflict in Managing Justice," in *The Oxford Handbook of Justice in the Workplace*, ed. R. Cropanzano and M.L. Ambrose (New York: Oxford University Press, 2015), 443–60.

77. D.J. Bussel, "A Third Way: Examiners as Inquisitors," *American Bankruptcy Law Journal* 90 (2016): 59–127.

78. B.H. Sheppard, "Managers as Inquisitors: Lessons from the Law," in *Bargaining inside Organizations*, ed. M.H. Bazerman and R.J. Lewicki (Beverly Hills, CA: Sage, 1983). Even in cultures that support managerial mediation, managers slip easily into inquisition and arbitration approaches where conflict has escalated. See M.K. Kozan, C. Ergin, and K. Varoglu, "Bases of Power and Conflict Intervention Strategy: A Study on Turkish Managers," *International Journal of Conflict Management* 25 (2014): 38–60.

79. R. Karambayya and J.M. Brett, "Managers Handling Disputes: Third Party Roles and Perceptions of Fairness," *Academy of Management Journal* 32 (1989): 687–704; B.M. Goldman et al., "The Role of Third Parties/Mediation in Managing Conflict in Organizations," in *The Psychology of Conflict and Conflict Management in Organizations*, ed. C.K.W. De Dreu and M.J. Gelfand (New York: Lawrence Erlbaum Associates, 2008): 291–319.

80. A.R. Elangovan, "Managerial Intervention in Organizational Disputes: Testing a Prescriptive Model of Strategy Selection," *International Journal of Conflict Management* 4 (1998): 301–35; P.S. Nugent, "Managing Conflict: Third-Party Interventions for Managers," *Academy of Management Executive* 16, no. 1 (2002): 139–54.

81. K. Bollen, H. Ittner, and M.C. Euwema, "Mediating Hierarchical Labor Conflicts: Procedural Justice Makes a Difference–For Subordinates," *Group Decision and Negotiation* 21, no. 5 (2012): 621–36; R. Nesbit, T. Nabatchi, and L.B. Bingham, "Employees, Supervisors, and Workplace Mediation: Experiences of Justice and Settlement," *Review of Public Personnel Administration* 32, no. 3 (2012): 260–87.

82. J.P. Meyer, J.M. Gemmell, and P.G. Irving, "Evaluating the Management of Interpersonal Conflict in Organizations: A Factor-Analytic Study of Outcome Criteria," *Canadian Journal of Administrative Sciences* 14 (1997): 1–13; L.B. Bingham, "Employment Dispute Resolution: The Case for Mediation," *Conflict Resolution Quarterly* 22, no. 1/2 (2004): 145–74; M. Hyde et al., "Workplace Conflict Resolution and the Health of Employees in the Swedish and Finnish Units of an Industrial Company," *Social Science & Medicine* 63, no. 8 (2006): 2218–27.

83. W.H. Ross and D.E. Conlon, "Hybrid Forms of Third-Party Dispute Resolution: Theoretical Implications of Combining Mediation and Arbitration," *Academy of Management Review* 25, no. 2 (2000): 416–27; W.H. Ross, C. Brantmeier, and T. Ciriacks, "The Impact of Hybrid Dispute-Resolution Procedures on Constituent Fairness Judgments," *Journal of Applied Social Psychology* 32, no. 6 (2002): 1151–88.

84. L.L. Thompson, J. Wang, and B.C. Gunia, "Negotiation," *Annual Review of Psychology* 61 (2010): 491–515; B. O'Neill, "International Negotiation: Some Conceptual Developments," *Annual Review of Political Science* 21 (2018): 515–33.

85. Several models of negotiations have been developed. Preparation (also called planning) is a key part of these models in organizational settings. See, for example, D. Jang, H.A. Elfenbein, and W.P. Bottom, "More than a Phase: Form and Features of a General Theory of Negotiation," *Academy of Management Annals* 12, no. 1 (2018): 318–56.

86. R. Stagner and H. Rosen, *Psychology of Union-Management Relations* (Belmont, CA: Wadsworth, 1965), 95–96, 108–10; R.E. Walton and R.B. McKersie, *A Behavioral Theory of Labor Negotiations: An Analysis of a Social Interaction System* (New York: McGraw Hill, 1965), 41–46; L. Thompson, *The Mind and Heart of the Negotiator* (Upper Saddle River, NJ: Prentice Hall, 1998), Chap. 2.

87. A. Tversky and D. Kahneman, "Judgment under Uncertainty: Heuristics and Biases," *Science* 185, no. 4157 (1974): 1124–31; J.D. Jasper and S.D. Christman, "A Neuropsychological Dimension for Anchoring Effects," *Journal of Behavioral Decision Making* 18 (2005): 343–69.

88. S. Doctoroff, "Reengineering Negotiations," *Sloan Management Review* 39 (1998): 63–71; D.C. Zetik and A.F. Stuhlmacher, "Goal Setting and Negotiation Performance: A Meta-Analysis," *Group Processes & Intergroup Relations* 5 (2002): 35–52.

89. A. Caputo, "A Literature Review of Cognitive Biases in Negotiation Processes," *International Journal of Conflict Management* 24 (2013): 374–98; A.B.V. Zant and L.J. Kray, "Negotiation and Conflict Resolution: A Behavioral Decision Research Perspective," in *The Wiley Blackwell Handbook of Judgment and Decision Making,* ed. G. Keren and G. Wu (Chichester, UK: John Wiley & Sons, Ltd, 2015), 828–48; M. Schaerer, D.D. Loschelder, and R.I. Swaab, "Bargaining Zone Distortion in Negotiations: The Elusive Power of Multiple Alternatives," *Organizational Behavior and Human Decision Processes* 137 (2016): 156–71.

90. L.L. Thompson, J. Wang, and B.C. Gunia, "Negotiation," *Annual Review of Psychology* 61 (2010): 491–515. Some negotiation experts warn that BATNA is often misunderstood and that "no deal option" may be a better way of viewing such situations. See J.K. Sebenius, "BATNAs in Negotiation: Common Errors and Three Kinds of 'No,'" *Negotiation Journal* 33 (2017): 89–99.

91. R.L. Pinkley et al., "The Power of Phantom Alternatives in Negotiation: How What Could Be Haunts What Is," *Organizational Behavior and Human Decision Processes* 151 (2019): 34–48.

92. L.L. Thompson, "Information Exchange in Negotiation," *Journal of Experimental Social Psychology* 27 (1991): 161–79; R. Fells, *Effective Negotiation: From Research to Results*, 2nd ed. (Melbourne: Cambridge University Press, 2012), Chap. 6.

93. N. Rackham and J. Carlisle, "The Effective Negotiator—Part I: The Behaviour of Successful Negotiators," *Journal of European Industrial Training* 2, no. 6 (1978): 6–11; J.M. Brett, "Managing Organizational Conflict," *Professional Psychology: Research and Practice* 15 (1984): 664–78; R. Fells et al., "Unraveling Business Negotiations Using Practitioner Data," *Negotiation and Conflict Management Research* 8, no. 2 (2015): 119–36.

94. C. Voss and T. Raz, *Never Split the Difference: Negotiating as If Your Life Depended on It* (Random House, 2016), Chap. 2; C. Clifford, "Ex FBI Negotiator Chris Voss: How to Get What You Want," *CNBC*, October 16, 2017.

95. S.R. Covey, *The 7 Habits of Highly Effective People* (New York: Free Press, 1989), pp. 235–60. Covey's statement was likely inspired by a prayer attributed to Saint Francis of Assisi, who lived around 1200. Its translation in part says: "Grant that I may not so much seek ... To be understood as to understand." This prayer has been published in English for more than two centuries. For example, see: Episcopal Church, *The Book of Common Prayer: And Administration of the Sacraments and Other Rites and Ceremonies of the Church ... Together with the Psalter; Or, Psalms of David* (Church Publishing, Inc., 1803), pg. 833.

96. A.R. Herrman and M. Allen, "Hardline versus Softline Bargaining Strategies: A Meta-Analytic Review," in *Managing Interpersonal Conflict: Advances through Meta-Analysis*, ed. N.A. Burrell, et al. (New York: Routledge, 2014), 213–25; J. Hüffmeier et al., "Being Tough or Being Nice? A Meta-Analysis on the Impact of Hard- and Softline Strategies in Distributive Negotiations," *Journal of Management* 40, no. 3 (2014): 866–92.

97. C. Thuderoz, "Why Do We Respond to a Concession with Another Concession? Reciprocity and Compromise," *Negotiation Journal* 33, no. 1 (2017): 71–83.

98. D. Malhotra, "The Fine Art of Making Concessions," *Negotiation* (2006): 3–5.

99. A.F. Stuhlmacher, T.L. Gillespie, and M.V. Champagne, "The Impact of Time Pressure in Negotiation: A Meta-Analysis," *International Journal of Conflict Management* 9 (1998): 97–116; C.K.W. De Dreu, "Time Pressure and Closing of the Mind in Negotiation," *Organizational Behavior and Human Decision Processes* 91 (2003): 280–95; P.J. Carnevale, "Strategic Time in Negotiation," *Current Opinion in Psychology*, 26 (2019): 106–12.

100. As with other forms of time pressure, the exploding offer effects on negotiation outcomes are complex. Those who apply these offers can be worse off in the negotiation under some circumstances. See N. Lau et al., "Exploding Offers Can Blow up in More Than One Way," *Decision Analysis* 11, no. 3 (2014): 171–88; W. Güth and M.G. Kocher, "More Than Thirty Years of Ultimatum Bargaining Experiments: Motives, Variations, and a Survey of the Recent Literature," *Journal of Economic Behavior & Organization* 108 (2014): 396–409.

101. M. Olekalns and P.L. Smith, "Moments in Time: Metacognition, Trust, and Outcomes in Dyadic Negotiations," *Personality and Social Psychology Bulletin* 31, no. 12 (2005): 1696–707.

102. D.W. Choi, "Shared Metacognition in Integrative Negotiation," *International Journal of Conflict Management* 21, no. 3 (2010): 309–33.

103. J.M. Brett et al., "Sticks and Stones: Language, Face, and Online Dispute Resolution," *Academy of Management Journal* 50 (2007): 85–99; D. Druckman and M. Olekalns, "Emotions in Negotiation," *Group Decision and Negotiation* 17 (2008): 1–11; M.J. Boland and W.H. Ross, "Emotional Intelligence and Dispute Mediation in Escalating and De-Escalating Situations," *Journal of Applied Social Psychology* 40 (2010): 3059–105.

104. P.J. Carnevale and A.M. Isen, "The Influence of Positive Affect and Visual Access on the Discovery of Integrative Solutions in Bilateral Negotiation," *Organizational Behavior and Human Decision Processes* 37 (1986): 1–13; L. Thompson, *The Mind and Heart of the Negotiator* (Upper Saddle River, NJ: Prentice-Hall, 1998), Chap. 2.

105. J.W. Salacuse and J.Z. Rubin, "Your Place or Mine? Site Location and Negotiation," *Negotiation Journal* 6 (1990): 5–10; G. Brown and M. Baer, "Location in Negotiation: Is There a Home Field Advantage?" *Organizational Behavior and Human Decision Processes* 114, no. 2 (2011): 190–200.

106. R. Lewicki, B. Barry, and D. Saunders, *Negotiation*, 8th ed. (New York: McGraw Hill, 2020), Chap. 11.

11 Leadership in Organizational Settings

Learning Objectives

After reading this chapter, you should be able to:

LO11-1 Define leadership and shared leadership.

LO11-2 Describe the four elements of transformational leadership and explain why they are important for organizational change.

LO11-3 Compare managerial leadership with transformational leadership, and describe the features of task-oriented, people-oriented, and servant leadership.

LO11-4 Discuss the elements of path–goal leadership theory and leadership substitutes theory.

LO11-5 Describe the two components of the implicit leadership perspective.

LO11-6 Identify eight personal attributes associated with effective leaders and describe authentic leadership.

LO11-7 Discuss cultural and male–female similarities and differences in leadership.

Successful leaders need to engage in different forms of leadership at appropriate times. "On one hand, part of being a leader is cultivating growth which entails convening people under a common purpose and allowing ideas to flourish," advises Leagh Turner, co-CEO of Ceridian and previously global chief operating officer of SAP. Inspiring employees toward a common purpose and encouraging new ideas are two elements of transformational leadership.

"On the other hand, it's about knowing when to jump in and steer the ship which entails helping the team take their ideas and shape them into something meaningful and executable," says Turner. Adapting this more granular approach to guiding teams and individuals toward more effective work practices refers to managerial leadership.

The challenge, Turner warns, is to know how much and when to apply transformational and managerial leadership. "The balance of knowing when to 'fly high' and ensure the overall health of the business, and when to 'dive deep' and run right alongside the teams, is a careful balancing act that is imperative to master for the sustainable health of both the business and the team."[1]

leadership Influencing, motivating, and enabling others to contribute toward the effectiveness and success of the organizations of which they are members

Leagh Turner's comments highlight the fact that there are multiple perspectives of leadership (including transformational and managerial leadership) and that people need to adopt these different approaches under appropriate circumstances. It also recognizes that effective leaders are adept at engaging in multiple forms of leadership; these leadership perspectives are not embodied in different people.

Leadership is one of the most researched and discussed topics in the field of organizational behavior. This topic receives so much attention because we are captivated by the ability of some individuals to influence and motivate beyond expectations a large collective of people. This chapter explores leadership from four perspectives: transformational, managerial, implicit, and personal attributes.[2] Although some of these perspectives are currently more popular than others, each helps us to more fully understand the complex subject of leadership. The final section of this chapter looks at cross-cultural and male-female differences in organizational leadership. But first, we learn about the meaning of leadership as well as shared leadership.

LO11-1 Define leadership and shared leadership.

WHAT IS LEADERSHIP?

Several years ago, dozens of leadership experts from around the world reached a consensus that **leadership** is about influencing, motivating, and enabling others to contribute toward the effectiveness and success of the organizations of which they are members.[4] This definition has two key components. First, leaders motivate others through persuasion and other influence tactics. They use their communication skills, rewards, and capacity to empower others to energize everyone toward the achievement of challenging objectives. Second, leaders are enablers. They allocate resources, redesign physical and organizational structures, minimize external disruptions, and establish other changes that make it easier for employees to achieve aspirational objectives.

The Leadership Report Card[3]

83% of 3,000 full-time American workers say they could do their job without a manager.

78% of 557,778 U.S federal government employees say their immediate supervisor is doing a good job (increasing annually from 70% approval five years earlier).

40% of 13,695 managers in 1,556 firms globally say their company has high-quality leaders.

29% of 1,009 talent acquisition professionals globally say they are confident their organization has the right leaders to guide the company into the future.

57% of 1,257 American workers say managers in their workplace could benefit from training on how to be a better people manager.

70% of 3,000 full-time American workers say they somewhat or strongly enjoy working for their manager.

(Photo): Vasilyrosca/123RF

Shared leadership is the view that leadership is a set of roles, not a formal position; companies are far more effective when everyone performs leadership responsibilities as the occasion arises.
Dragon Images/Shutterstock

Shared Leadership

Shared leadership is the view that leadership is a set of roles, not a formal position assigned to one person; everyone within the team and organization leads one another in various ways and at various times.[5] The formal leader cannot—and should not—try to perform all leadership tasks. Instead, companies are far more effective when everyone performs leadership responsibilities as the occasion arises. Shared leadership exists when an employee persuades coworkers to try out a new work activity or introduce new technology. It exists when employees help one another through social support or organizational citizenship behaviors. Shared leadership also exists when employees keep one another focused on the task and deadlines.

Shared leadership typically supplements formal leadership; that is, employees lead along with the formal manager, rather than as a replacement for that manager. However, W. L. Gore & Associates, Morning Star Company, Valve Corporation, and a few other unique companies rely almost completely on shared leadership because they don't have any formal managers on the organizational chart.[6]

Shared leadership flourishes under specific conditions.[7] It requires formal leaders who are willing to delegate power and encourage employees to take the initiative and risks without fear of failure (i.e., a learning orientation culture). Shared leadership also calls for a collaborative rather than internally competitive culture because employees succeed in shared leadership roles only when their coworkers support them in these roles. Furthermore, shared leadership lacks formal authority, so it operates best when employees learn to influence others through their enthusiasm, logical analysis, and involvement of coworkers in their idea or vision.

LO11-2 Describe the four elements of transformational leadership and explain why they are important for organizational change.

TRANSFORMATIONAL LEADERSHIP PERSPECTIVE

Most leadership concepts and practices can be organized into four perspectives: transformational, managerial, implicit, and personal attributes. By far the most popular leadership perspective today—and arguably the most important in the domain of leadership—is transformational leadership. **Transformational leadership** views leaders as change agents. They move the organization or work unit in a new direction that will provide better opportunities and alignment with the external environment.

There are several models of transformational leadership, but four elements are common throughout most of them and represent the core concepts of this leadership perspective (see Exhibit 11.1).[9] Transformational leaders create, communicate, and model a shared vision for the team or organization. They encourage experimentation so employees discover a better path to the future. Through these and other activities, transformational leaders also build commitment in followers to strive for that vision.

Develop and Communicate a Strategic Vision

The heart of transformational leadership is a strategic *vision*.[10] A vision is a positive image or model of the future that energizes and unifies employees.[11] Sometimes this vision is created by the leader; at other times, it is formed by employees or other stakeholders and then adopted and championed by the formal

> We've abandoned the Great Man model of leadership that long characterized Fiat and have created a culture where everyone is expected to lead.[8]
>
> —Sergio Marchionne, former CEO of Fiat Chrysler Automobiles and Ferrari

Exhibit 11.1 Elements of Transformational Leadership

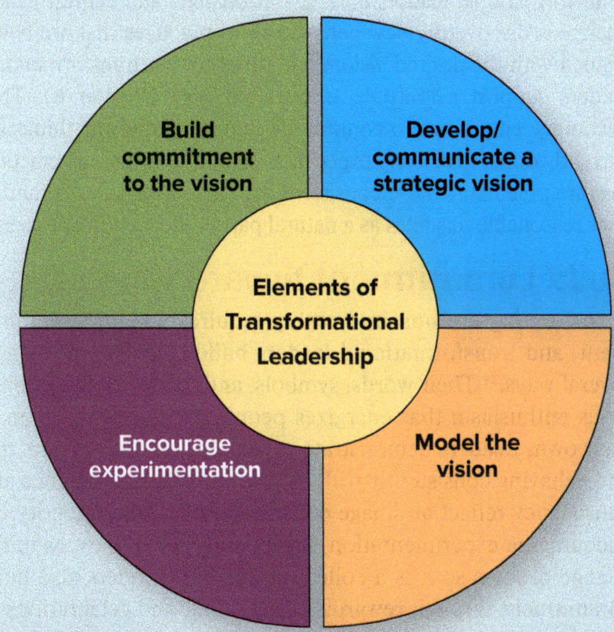

leader. An effective strategic vision has several identifiable features.[12] It describes an aspirational future with a higher purpose. This purpose is associated with personal values that directly or indirectly fulfill the needs of multiple stakeholders. A values-based vision is particularly meaningful and appealing to employees, which motivates them to strive for that ideal.

A strategic vision also engages employees because it is a distant goal that is both challenging and abstract. It is challenging because a vision of the future requires substantial change, such as new work practices and belief systems. A strategic vision is necessarily abstract for two reasons. One reason is that the vision hasn't yet been experienced (at least, not in this company or industry), so it isn't possible to detail exactly what the vision looks like. The other reason is that an abstract description enables the vision to remain stable over time, yet is sufficiently flexible to accommodate operational adjustments in a shifting external environment. As such, a vision describes a broad noble cause related to the fulfillment of needs of multiple stakeholders.

Another feature of an effective vision is that it is unifying. It is a superordinate objective that bonds employees together and aligns their personal values with the organization's values. In fact, a successful vision is a shared vision because employees collectively define themselves by this aspirational image of the future as part of their identification with the organization.

Communicate the Vision The effectiveness of a strategic vision depends on how well leaders communicate it to followers and other stakeholders.[15] Transformational leaders generate

Not Quite Leading with Vision[14]

79% of 5,113 adults in the U.S., U.K., France, and Germany would consider a company's mission/purpose (vision) before applying for a job there.

74% of 615 U.S. organizational leaders say they are inspiring their teams (27% of employees in those organizations agree).

47% of 2,065 employees and executives across 23 countries who successfully went through a transformation say the leader communicated a clear and compelling vision (26% of those in low-performing transformations say this).

25% of 400 private company finance leaders say that their organization's CFO is perceived as an inspirational leader and strong communicator (2nd highest attribute after big thinker/strategist).

22% of 2.2 million employees surveyed worldwide strongly agree that their company's leaders have a clear direction for their organization.

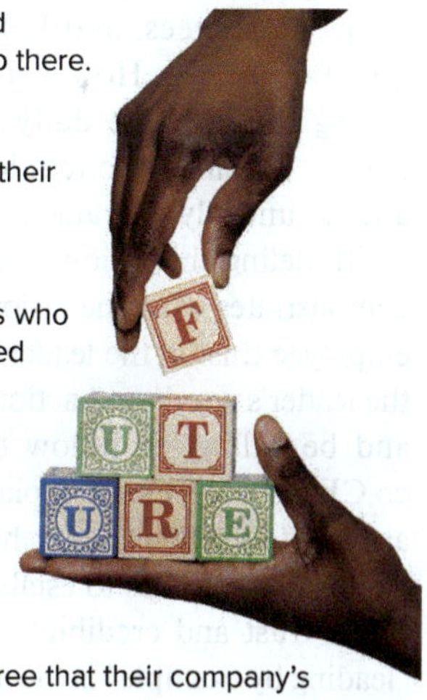

(Photo): Barbara Penoyar/Getty Images

> **The world is made up of those who make things happen, those who watch things happen, and those who ask what happened.[13]**
>
> —Norman Augustine, aerospace business leader

shared leadership The view that leadership is a role, not a position assigned to one person; consequently, people within the team and organization lead one another

transformational leadership A leadership perspective that explains how leaders change teams or organizations by creating, communicating, and modeling a vision for the organization or work unit and inspiring employees to strive for that vision

learning orientation A set of beliefs and norms in which people are encouraged to question past practices, learn new ideas, experiment putting ideas into practice, and view mistakes as part of the learning process

meaning and motivation in followers by relying on symbols, metaphors, stories, and other vehicles that transcend plain language.[16] Metaphors and related communication tools "frame" the vision, meaning that they guide or construct the listener's mental model of the situation. Borrowing images from other experiences creates a richer understanding of the abstract vision that generates emotions and motivates people to pursue the vision.

Transformational leaders also convey the vision using verbal and nonverbal communication practices that show humility, sincerity, and a level of passion that reflects their personal belief in the vision and their optimism that employees can succeed. They strengthen team orientation and employee self-efficacy by referring to the team's strengths and potential. By focusing on shared experiences and the central role of employees in achieving the vision, transformational leaders suppress leader-follower differences, deflect attention from themselves, and avoid any image of superiority over the team.[17]

Model the Vision

Transformational leaders not only talk about a vision; they enact it. They "walk the talk" by stepping outside the executive suite and doing things that symbolize the vision.[18] Leaders model the vision through significant events such as visiting customers, moving their offices closer to (or further from) employees, and holding ceremonies to symbolize significant change. However, they also enact the vision by ensuring that routine daily activities—meeting agendas, dress codes, executive schedules—are consistent with the vision and its underlying values.

Modeling the vision is important because it legitimizes and demonstrates what the vision looks like in practice. It also builds employee trust in the leader. The greater the consistency between the leader's words and actions, the more employees will believe in and be willing to follow the leader. Ceridian chairman and co-CEO David Ossip explains: "When employees are able to see their leadership live by the values that guide them, it helps to establish a sense of organizational trust and credibility."[19] Surveys report that "leading by example" is the most important attribute of effective leaders and is one of the most important characteristics of a company's culture.[20]

Encourage Experimentation

Transformational leadership is about change, and central to any change is discovering new behaviors and practices that are better aligned with the desired vision.[22] In other words, transformational leaders support a **learning orientation** (see Chapter 6). They encourage employees to continuously question the way things are currently done, to actively experiment with new ideas and practices that are potentially more consistent with the vision's future, and to view reasonable mistakes as a natural part of the learning process.[23]

Build Commitment toward the Vision

Transforming a vision into reality requires employee commitment, and transformational leaders build this commitment in several ways.[24] Their words, symbols, and stories create a contagious enthusiasm that energizes people to adopt the vision as their own. Leaders demonstrate a "can-do" attitude by enacting and behaving consistently with their vision. This persistence and consistency reflect an image of honesty, trust, and integrity. By encouraging experimentation, leaders involve employees in the change process so it is a collective activity. Leaders also build commitment through rewards, recognition, and celebrations as employees pass milestones along the road to the desired vision.

Transformational Leadership and Charisma

Some experts describe charisma as an essential ingredient of transformational leadership.[25] However, the emerging view, which this book adopts, is that charismatic leadership is distinct from transformational leadership. Several studies and reviews indicate that charisma is not necessarily part of transformational leadership; in fact, some of its effects on employees may be opposite to the effects of transformational leadership.[26]

Charisma refers to a set of self-presentation characteristics and nonverbal communication behaviors (i.e., signaling) that generate interpersonal attraction and referent power over others as well as follower deference to the charismatic person (see Chapter 9).[27] In contrast, transformational leadership is a set of behaviors that engage followers toward a better future.

Mc Graw Hill connect

SELF-ASSESSMENT 11.1: What Are Your Transformational Leadership Tendencies?

> Great leaders walk the talk. They lead by example. There isn't anything they ask people to do they're not willing to do themselves.[21]
>
> —Mike Perlis, vice chairman of Forbes Media

Transformational leaders are not necessarily charismatic, and charismatic leaders are not necessarily transformational.
Yuganov Konstantin/Shutterstock

Charismatic leadership motivates followers directly through the leader's referent power, whereas transformational leadership motivates followers through behaviors that persuade and earn trust. For instance, communicating an inspiring vision is a transformational leadership behavior that motivates followers to strive for that vision. This motivational effect exists separate from the leader's charismatic appeal.

Being charismatic is not inherently good or bad, but several research studies have concluded that charismatic leadership can produce negative consequences.[28] One concern is that charismatic leadership tends to increase dependence on the leader because, by definition, followers want to be associated with people who have charisma. Transformational leadership has the opposite effect; it builds follower empowerment, which tends to reduce dependence on the leader. Another concern is that leaders who are charismatic may become intoxicated by this power, which leads to a greater focus on self-interest than on the common good.[29] The main point here is that transformational leaders are not necessarily charismatic, and charismatic leaders are not necessarily transformational.

Evaluating the Transformational Leadership Perspective

Transformational leaders make a difference.[30] Subordinates are more satisfied and have higher affective organizational commitment under transformational leaders. They also perform their jobs better, engage in more organizational citizenship behaviors, and make better or more creative decisions. Although transformational leadership is valuable, the theory has a few imperfections.[31] One problem is that some models engage in circular logic. They define and measure transformational leadership by its effects on employees (e.g., inspire employees), then (not surprisingly) report that this leadership is effective because it inspires employees. Instead, transformational leadership needs to be defined purely as a set of behaviors (communicating, modeling, encouraging experimentation, etc.) to lead others through the change process.

A second concern is that some transformational leadership theories combine leader behaviors with the personal characteristics of leaders. For instance, transformational leaders are described as visionary, imaginative, sensitive, and thoughtful, yet these personal characteristics are actually predictors of how easily the individual can engage in transformational leadership behaviors.[32] A third concern is that transformational leadership is usually described as a universal concept, that is, it should be applied in all situations. Only a few studies have investigated whether this transformational leadership is more valuable in some situations than others.[33] Preliminary evidence suggests that the transformational leadership perspective is relevant across cultures. However, there may be specific elements of transformational leadership, such as the way visions are communicated and modeled, that are more appropriate in North America than in other cultures.

managerial leadership A leadership perspective stating that effective leaders help employees improve their performance and well-being toward current objectives and practices

LO11-3 Compare managerial leadership with transformational leadership, and describe the features of task-oriented, people-oriented, and servant leadership.

MANAGERIAL LEADERSHIP PERSPECTIVE

Leaders don't spend all—or even most—of their time transforming the organization or work unit. They also engage in **managerial leadership** (also called *functional leadership*), which are daily activities that support and guide the performance and well-being of individual employees and the work unit toward current objectives and practices. Leadership experts recognize that leading (transformational leadership) differs from managing (managerial leadership).[34] Although the distinction between these two perspectives continues to be debated, each cluster has a reasonably clear set of activities and strong research foundation.

> **Managers are people who do things right and leaders are people who do the right thing.[35]**
>
> —Warren Bennis, leadership scholar (based on earlier writing by Peter Drucker)

One distinction between these two perspectives is that managerial leadership assumes the organization's or department's objectives are stable and aligned with the external environment.[36] In contrast, transformational leadership assumes the organization is misaligned with its environment and therefore needs to change its direction. An often-cited saying is that managers "do things right," which means that managerial leadership focuses on making employees and work units more effective at established objectives and practices. In contrast, leaders "do the right thing," which means that transformational leadership focuses on changing people toward new objectives and practices that are aligned more closely with the external environment.

A second distinction is that managerial leadership is more micro-focused and concrete because it relates to the specific performance and well-being objectives of individual employees and the immediate work unit. Transformational leadership is more macro-focused and abstract. It is directed toward an imprecise strategic vision for an entire organization, department, or team.

Managerial leadership requires transformational leadership to set the right direction (vision); transformational leadership requires managerial leadership to translate the abstract vision into specific operational behaviors and practices.
Rawpixel/Shutterstock

Interdependence of Managerial and Transformational Leadership

Although transformational and managerial leadership are discussed as two leadership perspectives, they are more appropriately viewed as *interdependent* perspectives.[37] In other words, transformational leadership and managerial leadership depend on each other. Transformational leadership identifies, communicates, and builds commitment to a better future for the organization or work unit. But these transformational leadership behaviors are not enough for organizational success. That success also requires managerial leadership to translate the abstract vision into more specific operational behaviors and practices, and to continuously improve employee performance and well-being in the pursuit of that future ideal. Managerial leadership also depends on transformational leadership to set the right direction (i.e., the organization's strategic vision). Otherwise, managers might produce operational excellence toward goals that are misaligned with the organization's long-term survival.

Top-level executives typically engage in more transformational leadership than do middle managers, supervisors, and others further down the hierarchy. This greater emphasis on transformational leadership at higher levels likely occurs because senior leaders are more responsible for the organization's alignment with its environment and because they have more discretion to enable macro-level change. However, managerial and transformational leadership are not embodied in different people or positions in the organization. Every manager needs to apply both transformational and managerial leadership behaviors to varying degrees. Through shared leadership, even frontline employees apply managerial leadership (e.g., helping coworkers through a difficult project) and transformational leadership (e.g., championing more customer-friendly norms in the work unit).

Task-Oriented and People-Oriented Leadership

Managerial leadership research began in the 1940s when several universities launched intensive investigations to answer the question "What behaviors make leaders effective?" They studied first-line supervisors by asking subordinates to rate their bosses on many behaviors. These independent research teams essentially identified the same two clusters of leadership behavior from literally thousands of items (Exhibit 11.2).[38]

Exhibit 11.2 Task- and People-Oriented Leadership Styles

Leaders are task-oriented when they . . .	Leaders are people-oriented when they . . .
• Assign work and clarify responsibilities. • Set goals and deadlines. • Evaluate and provide feedback on work quality. • Establish well-defined best work procedures. • Plan future work activities.	• Show interest in others as people. • Listen to employees. • Make the workplace more pleasant. • Show appreciation to employees for their performance contribution. • Are considerate of employee needs.

One cluster, called *task-oriented leadership,* includes behaviors that define and structure work roles. This leadership style includes assigning work to employees and clarifying responsibilities for those tasks, setting goals and deadlines, evaluating and providing feedback on work quality, establishing the best work procedures, and planning future work activities. The other cluster represents *people-oriented leadership.* This leadership style includes showing interest in staff as individuals, listening to employees for their opinions and ideas, creating a pleasant physical work setting, recognizing and showing appreciation to employees for their work effort, and showing consideration of employee needs.

These early managerial leadership studies tried to find out whether effective managers are more task-oriented or more people-oriented. This proved to be a difficult question to answer because each style has its advantages and disadvantages. In fact, numerous studies now indicate that effective leaders rely on both styles but in different circumstances.[39] When leaders engage in people-oriented leadership behaviors, their employees tend to have more positive attitudes as well as lower absenteeism, grievances, stress, and turnover. When leaders use task-oriented leadership behaviors, their employees tend to have higher job performance. Not surprisingly, employees generally prefer bosses who use more people-oriented behaviors, and they form negative attitudes toward bosses who are mostly task-oriented. However, task-oriented leadership also is appreciated to some degree. For example, college students value task-oriented instructors because those teachers provide clear expectations, well-prepared course outlines, and constructive feedback.[40]

SELF-ASSESSMENT 11.2: What Is Your Preferred Managerial Leadership Style?

Servant Leadership

Servant leadership is an extension or variation of people-oriented leadership because it defines leadership as serving others. In particular, servant leaders selflessly assist others in their need fulfillment, personal development, and growth.[41] Servant leaders ask, "How can I help you?" rather than expecting employees to serve them. They are typically described as selfless, egalitarian, humble, nurturing, empathetic, and ethical coaches. The main objective of servant leadership is to help followers and other stakeholders fulfill their needs and potential, particularly "to become healthier, wiser, freer, more autonomous, more likely themselves to become servants."[42] This description captures three key features of servant leadership:[43]

> Servant leaders selflessly assist others in their need fulfillment, personal development, and growth.

servant leadership The view that leaders serve followers, rather than vice versa; leaders help employees fulfill their needs and are coaches, stewards, and facilitators of employee development

- *Natural desire or "calling" to serve others*. Servant leaders have a deep commitment to help others in their personal growth for that purpose alone. This commitment is not merely an instrument to achieve company objectives. It is a selfless desire to support others that goes beyond the leader's role obligation.
- *Humble, egalitarian, accepting relationship with followers.* Servant leaders do not view leadership as a position of power. Rather, they serve without drawing attention to themselves, without evoking superior status, and without being judgmental about others or defensive of criticisms received.
- *Ethical decisions and behavior*. Servant leaders display sensitivity to and enactment of moral values. They are not swayed by deviant social pressures or expectations. Servant leaders maintain moral integrity by relying on personal values to anchor their decisions and behavior. In this respect, servant leadership relies heavily on authentic leadership, which we discuss later in this chapter.

Servant leadership was introduced several decades ago and has since had a steady following, particularly among practitioners and religious leaders.[44] Scholarly research indicates that servant leaders improve employee well-being, feelings of empowerment, and job performance. However, the concept still faces conceptual hurdles. Although servant leadership writers generally agree on the three features we described here, many have included other characteristics that might confound the concept with its predictors and outcomes.

LO11-4 Discuss the elements of path–goal leadership theory and leadership substitutes theory.

PATH–GOAL AND LEADERSHIP SUBSTITUTES THEORIES

Path–Goal Leadership Theory

The earliest managerial leadership studies not only identified the task-oriented and people-oriented leadership styles; they also concluded that the best leadership style depends on the situation.[45] This "it depends" view is consistent with the contingency

Exhibit 11.3 Path–Goal Leadership Theory

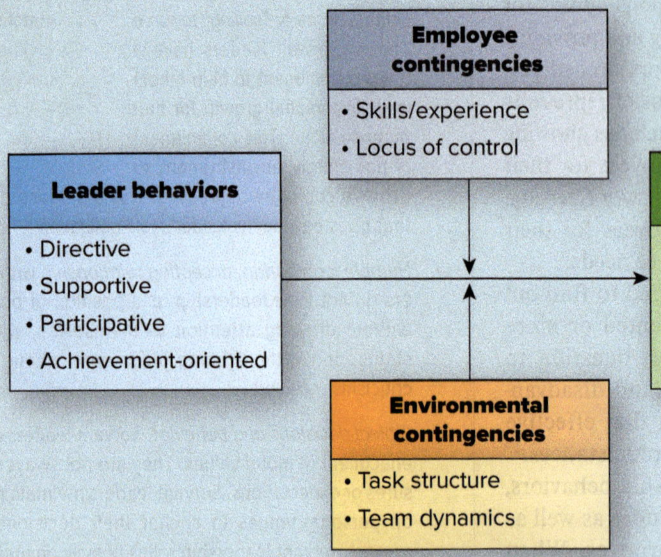

anchor of organizational behavior discussed in Chapter 1. The dominant theory that applies this contingency approach to managerial leadership is **path–goal leadership theory**. The theory states that effective leaders choose one or more leadership styles to influence employee expectations (their preferred *path*) regarding achievement of desired results (their work-related *goals*), as well as their perceived satisfaction with those results (outcome valences). Leaders clarify the link between employee behaviors and outcomes, influence the valence of those outcomes, and provide a work environment to facilitate goal accomplishment.[46] Notice from this description that path-goal theory builds on the expectancy theory of motivation (Chapter 5) and its underlying formula of rational decision making (Chapter 6).[47]

Path–Goal Leadership Styles Exhibit 11.3 presents the path-goal leadership theory model. It highlights four leadership styles and several contingency factors leading to three indicators of leader effectiveness. The four leadership styles are:[48]

- *Directive.* Directive leadership is the same as task-oriented leadership, described earlier. This leadership style consists of behaviors that provide a cognitive structure for subordinates. It includes clarifying performance goals, the means to reach those goals, and the standards against which performance will be judged. Directive leadership also includes judicious use of rewards and disciplinary actions.
- *Supportive.* Supportive leadership is the same as people-oriented leadership, described earlier. This style consists of behaviors that provide psychological support for subordinates. The leader is friendly and approachable; makes the work more pleasant; treats employees with respect; and shows concern for the status, needs, and well-being of employees.
- *Participative.* Participative leadership consists of behaviors that encourage and facilitate employee involvement in decisions beyond their normal work activities. The leader consults with staff, asks for their suggestions, carefully reflects on employee views before making a decision, and at times empowers employees to make the decision. Participative leadership is the same as employee involvement, discussed in Chapter 6.
- *Achievement-oriented.* This leadership style consists of behaviors that encourage employees to reach their peak performance. The leader sets challenging goals, expects employees to perform at their highest level, continuously seeks improvement in employee performance, and shows a high degree of confidence that employees will assume responsibility and accomplish challenging goals. Achievement-oriented leadership applies goal-setting theory as well as positive expectations in self-fulfilling prophecy.

Path–Goal Leadership Theory Contingencies As a contingency theory, path-goal leadership theory states that each of the four leadership styles will be more effective in some situations than in others. The theory also contends that managers are able to apply the most appropriate leadership style (or styles) for each situation. Depending on the circumstances, this skill may involve using two or more leadership styles at the same time. The model specifies two sets of situational variables: (1) employee characteristics and (2) characteristics of the employee's work environment. Several employee and workplace contingencies have been studied, but the following four have received the most attention:[49]

- *Skill and experience.* A combination of directive and supportive leadership is best for employees who are (or perceive themselves to be) inexperienced

OB THEORY TO PRACTICE

Great Bosses Apply Path-Goal Leadership Theory[50]

When asked to describe their favorite boss, employees refer to leadership styles and situations that fit path–goal theory. For example, a junior employee at a pharmaceutical company in London, United Kingdom, praises his boss's supportive style. "She has this magical ability to lead with empathy, compassion and transparency." An experienced community education services worker in Minnesota appreciates participative leadership. "Is he perfect? No. But he listens to others' opinions and always considers them."

A financial services professional in Illinois says his manager is someone "you would walk on coals for" because of his balance of achievement and supportive leadership. "He pushed you but always had your best interest at heart and wanted you to succeed." And a school teacher in Michigan is happy that his current boss doesn't apply too much directive leadership, but instead "trusts that I am a veteran professional and does not micromanage."

FatCamera/E+/Getty Images

and unskilled.[51] Directive leadership involves providing information about how to accomplish the task, whereas supportive leadership offers support to cope with the uncertainties of unfamiliar work situations. This style is detrimental when employees are skilled and experienced because it introduces too much supervisory control (i.e., micromanaging).

- *Locus of control.* People with an internal locus of control believe that they have control over their work environment (see Chapter 3). Consequently, these employees prefer participative and achievement-oriented leadership styles and may become frustrated with a directive style. In contrast, people with an external locus of control believe that their performance is due more to luck and fate, so they tend to be more satisfied with directive and supportive leadership.
- *Task structure.* When tasks are nonroutine (complex, unique, ambiguous), leaders should adopt the directive style for inexperienced employees because it provides guidance and learning. The directive style is redundant and potentially irritating for experienced employees in nonroutine task situations because they have as much knowledge as their supervisor. Instead, participative leadership is preferred for experienced employees because they require more autonomy (fewer rules) to navigate through complex and unusual job assignments.[52] For routine tasks, neither inexperienced nor experienced employees benefit from directive leadership because the work is easily understood without the supervisor's guidance. The participative style is also ineffective for employees in routine tasks because routine tasks tend to lack discretion. Employees performing routine and simple tasks may require supportive leadership to help them cope with the tedious nature of the work and lack of control over the pace of work.
- *Team dynamics.* Cohesive teams with performance-oriented norms act as a substitute for most leader interventions. High team cohesion substitutes for supportive leadership, whereas performance-oriented team norms substitute for directive and possibly achievement-oriented leadership. Thus, when team cohesion is low, leaders should use a supportive style. Leaders should apply a directive style to counteract team norms that oppose the performance objectives assigned to the team. For example, the team leader may need to exert authority if team members have developed a norm to "take it easy" rather than get a project completed on time.

path–goal leadership theory A leadership theory stating that effective leaders choose the most appropriate leadership style(s), depending on the employee and situation, to influence employee expectations about desired results and their positive outcomes

leadership substitutes theory A theory identifying conditions that either limit a leader's ability to influence subordinates or make a particular leadership style unnecessary

Evaluating Path–Goal Theory Path-goal leadership theory has received more research support than other managerial leadership models. In fact, effective leadership is predicted just as well as or possibly even better by path-goal and associated managerial leadership than by transformational leadership.[53] This stronger effect likely exists because managers typically spend more of their time engaging in managerial rather than transformational leadership.[54]

Support for the path-goal leadership model is far from ideal, however. Not all contingencies have sufficient research support and a few haven't been investigated at all.[55] Another concern is that path-goal theory assumes that effective leaders can change managerial styles to fit the situation. In reality, it takes considerable effort to do so because leaders typically prefer one style that is most consistent with their personality and values. Some experts even suggest that leadership styles are hardwired.[56] In spite of these limitations, path-goal leadership theory remains a relatively robust model of managerial leadership.

Leadership Substitutes Theory

Leadership substitutes theory takes a completely different approach to leadership. It suggests that the situation either limits the leader's ability to influence subordinates or renders a particular leadership style unnecessary.[57] The literature identifies several conditions that possibly substitute for task-oriented or people-oriented leadership (see Exhibit 11.4).

Consistent with path-goal theory, task-oriented leadership is likely less valuable for employees as they gain skill and experience in the job. This leadership style also may be unnecessary when performance-based rewards motivate employees to

Exhibit 11.4 Possible Leadership Substitutes

Managerial Leadership Style	Possible Substitutes for That Style
Task-oriented	• Performance-based rewards • Employee is skilled and experienced • Guidance from coworkers • Team norms reinforce task objectives • Work is intrinsically motivating • Employee applies self-leadership
People-oriented	• Coworkers are supportive • Employee is skilled and experienced • Work is intrinsically satisfying • Employee effectively copes with stress

Based on ideas in S. Kerr and J.M. Jermier, "Substitutes for Leadership: Their Meaning and Measurement," *Organizational Behavior and Human Performance* 22 (December 1978): 375–403; P.M. Podsakoff and S.B. MacKenzie, "Kerr and Jermier's Substitutes for Leadership Model: Background, Empirical Assessment, and Suggestions for Future Research," *Leadership Quarterly* 8 (1997): 117–32.

achieve organizational goals, when the work is intrinsically motivating, and when the employee has good self-motivation skills (such as self-set goals, self-reinforcement, and positive self-talk).[58] Teams also substitute for task-oriented leadership under some conditions and to some degree.[59] Task-oriented leadership is substituted by team members who informally train less-experienced employees, and by team members who encourage (or pressure) coworkers to perform their tasks.

Task-oriented leadership may be unnecessary when performance-based rewards motivate employees to achieve organizational goals, when the work is intrinsically motivating, and when the employee has good self-motivation skills.
Maridav/Shutterstock

People-oriented leadership may be less valuable when the work itself is enjoyable and when the employee applies effective coping strategies to minimize stress. This leadership style is also substituted by coworkers who use humor to create psychological safety.[60] Skilled and experienced employees also have higher self-efficacy, which results in less stressful work and therefore less need for people-oriented leadership interaction from the boss.

The leadership substitutes model has intuitive appeal, but the evidence has been mixed. Some studies show that a few substitutes do replace the need for task- or people-oriented leadership, but others do not. The difficulties of statistically testing for leadership substitutes may account for some problems. However, a few writers contend that the weak support for substitutes indicates that formal leadership plays a critical role regardless of the situation.[61] Overall, we can conclude that leadership substitutes might reduce the need for managerial leadership behaviors, but they do not completely replace managers in these situations.

LO11-5 Describe the two components of the implicit leadership perspective.

IMPLICIT LEADERSHIP PERSPECTIVE

Research on transformational and managerial leadership has found that leaders do "make a difference"; that is, leaders significantly influence the performance of their teams, departments, and organizations. However, a third leadership perspective, called **implicit leadership theory**, explains that followers' perceptions also play a role in a leader's effectiveness or, at least, the leader's perceived effectiveness. The implicit leadership perspective has two components: leader prototypes and the romance of leadership.[62]

Prototypes of Effective Leaders

One aspect of implicit leadership theory states that everyone has *leadership prototypes*—preconceived beliefs about the features and behaviors of effective leaders.[63] These prototypes, which develop through socialization within the family and society, shape the follower's expectations and acceptance of others as leaders, and this in turn affects their willingness to remain as a follower. Leadership prototypes not only support a person's role as a leader; they also influence follower perceptions of the leader's effectiveness. In other words, a leader is often perceived as more effective when they look like and act consistently with the prototype of a leader.[64]

Leadership prototypes are preconceived beliefs about the features and behaviors of effective leaders, which shape the follower's expectations and acceptance of someone as a leader.
Syda Productions/Shutterstock

This prototype comparison process occurs because people want to trust their leader before they are willing to serve as followers. However, the leader's actual effectiveness usually isn't known for several months or possibly years, so comparing the leader against a prototype is a quick (although faulty) way of estimating the leader's future success.

The Romance of Leadership

Along with relying on implicit prototypes of effective leaders, followers tend to inflate the perceived influence of leaders on the organization's success. This "romance of leadership" effect occurs for two reasons.[65] First, leadership is a useful way for us to simplify life events. It is easier to explain organizational successes and failures in terms of the leader's ability than by analyzing a complex array of other forces.

The second reason why people inflate their perception of the leader's influence over the situation is that people in the United States and many other cultures want to believe that life events are generated more from people than from uncontrollable natural forces.[66] This illusion of control is satisfied by believing that events result from the rational actions of leaders. In other words, employees feel better believing that leaders make a difference, so they actively look for evidence that this is so.

Attribution errors (see Chapter 3) also explain why followers believe that leaders make a difference. Leaders are often given credit for the company's success because employees do not readily see the external forces that also influence these events (fundamental attribution error). Leaders reinforce this belief by taking credit for organizational successes (self-serving bias).[67]

implicit leadership theory A theory stating that people evaluate a leader's effectiveness in terms of how well that person fits preconceived beliefs about the features and behaviors of effective leaders (leadership prototypes) and that people tend to inflate the influence of leaders on organizational events

The implicit leadership perspective highlights the fact that leadership is influenced by followers' perceptions, not only the actual behaviors and formal roles of people calling themselves leaders. Potential leaders must be sensitive to this fact and be aware of follower expectations. Individuals who do not naturally fit leadership prototypes need to provide more direct evidence of their effectiveness as leaders.

LO11-6 Identify eight personal attributes associated with effective leaders and describe authentic leadership.

PERSONAL ATTRIBUTES PERSPECTIVE OF LEADERSHIP

Since the beginning of recorded civilization, people have been interested in the personal characteristics that distinguish great leaders from the rest of us.[68] One major review in the late 1940s concluded that no valid list of leadership traits could be distilled from previous research. That conclusion was premature; a decade later, an updated review concluded that a few traits are indeed associated with effective leaders.[69] Unfortunately, the earlier review caused many scholars to give up their search for the personal characteristics of effective leaders.

Eight Important Leadership Attributes

Leadership experts have since returned to the notion that effective leaders possess specific personal attributes. Many leadership studies conducted long ago were apparently plagued by methodological problems, lack of theoretical foundation, and inconsistent definitions of leadership. Recent studies have mostly corrected these problems, with the result that several attributes are now consistently identified with effective leadership or leader emergence. Eight important attributes of effective leaders (not in any particular

McGraw Hill connect

SELF-ASSESSMENT 11.3: Do Leaders Make a Difference?

Successful leaders have a complex, internally consistent, and clear self-concept as both a transformational and managerial leader.

order) are personality, self-concept, leadership motivation, drive, integrity, knowledge of the business, cognitive and practical intelligence, and emotional intelligence (see Exhibit 11.5):[70]

Personality Most of the Big Five personality dimensions (see Chapter 2) are associated with effective leadership.[71] However, the strongest predictors are high levels of extraversion (outgoing, talkative, sociable, and assertive) and conscientiousness (careful, dependable, and self-disciplined). With high extraversion, effective leaders are comfortable having an influential role in social settings. With higher conscientiousness, effective leaders set higher goals for themselves (and others), are organized, and have a strong sense of duty to fulfill work obligations.

EXHIBIT 11.5 Personal Attributes of Effective Leaders

Leadership Attribute	Description
Personality	Effective leaders have higher levels of extraversion (outgoing, talkative, sociable, and assertive) and conscientiousness (careful, dependable, and self-disciplined).
Self-concept	Effective leaders have strong self-beliefs and a positive self-evaluation about their own leadership skills and ability to achieve objectives.
Leadership motivation	Effective leaders have a need for socialized power (not personalized power) to accomplish team or organizational goals.
Drive	Effective leaders have an inner motivation to pursue goals.
Integrity	Effective leaders have strong moral principles, which are demonstrated through truthfulness and consistency of words with deeds.
Knowledge of the business	Effective leaders have deep knowledge about the company's environment, enabling them to make more intuitive decisions.
Cognitive and practical intelligence	Effective leaders have above-average cognitive ability to process information (cognitive intelligence) and ability to solve real-world problems by adapting to, shaping, or selecting appropriate environments (practical intelligence).
Emotional intelligence	Effective leaders have the ability to recognize and regulate their own emotions and the emotions of others.

Self-Concept Successful leaders have a complex, internally consistent, and clear self-concept as both a transformational and managerial leader (see Chapter 3).[72] This "leader identity" also includes a positive self-evaluation, which consists of high self-esteem, high self-efficacy, and an internal locus of control. Many people in leadership positions default to daily managerial leadership and define themselves as managers. Effective leaders, on the other hand, view themselves as both transformational and managerial, and they are confident with both of these self-views.[73]

Leadership Motivation Effective leaders are motivated to lead others. They have a strong need for *socialized power*, meaning that they want power to lead others in accomplishing organizational objectives and similar good deeds. This contrasts with a need for *personalized power*, which is the desire to have power for personal gain or for the thrill one might experience from wielding power over others (see Chapter 5).[74] Leadership motivation is also necessary because, even in organizations where managers support one another, they are in contests for positions further up the hierarchy. Effective leaders thrive rather than wither in the face of this competition.[75]

Drive Successful leaders have a moderately high drive, which is variously described as energy, need for achievement, initiative, tenacity, and ambition. Drive is also associated with high conscientiousness, extraversion, and positive self-evaluation. It is the inner motivation that leaders possess to pursue their goals and encourage others to move forward with theirs. Drive inspires inquisitiveness, an action orientation, and measured boldness to take the organization or team into uncharted waters.

Integrity Integrity involves having strong moral principles, which supports the tendency to be truthful and to be consistent in words and deeds. Leaders have a high moral capacity to judge dilemmas using sound values and to act accordingly. They model ethical conduct while also signaling that followers are expected to act with integrity. Notice that integrity is ultimately based on the leader's values, which provide an anchor for authentic leadership The view that effective leaders are aware of, feel comfortable with, and act consistently with their values, personality, and self-concept

Employee Perceptions of Leader Integrity[77]

32% of 13,695 professionals and managers in 1,556 firms globally say they trust senior leaders in their organization to do what is right (46% say this about their immediate manager).

42% of 2,100 leaders and employees identify values/ethics as one of the top three qualities they want in their leaders.

71% of 9,834 working adults across 13 countries say that their line manager sets a good example of ethical business behavior (ranges from 79% in the US to 64% in Portugal).

(Photo): Aquir/Shutterstock

60% of 557,778 U.S. federal government employees say their organization's senior leaders maintain high standards of honesty and integrity.

38% of 332,860 employees, supervisors, and executives identify "displays high integrity and honesty" as one of the four skills that have the greatest impact on a leader's success.

consistency. Several large-scale studies have reported that integrity and honesty are the most important characteristics of effective leaders.[76]

Knowledge of the Business Effective leaders understand the business environment in which they operate, including subtle indications of emerging trends. Knowledge of the business also includes a solid grasp of how their organization works effectively.

Cognitive and Practical Intelligence Leaders have above-average cognitive ability to process enormous amounts of information. Leaders aren't necessarily geniuses; rather, they have a superior ability to analyze a variety of complex alternatives and opportunities. Furthermore, leaders have practical intelligence. This means that they can think through the relevance and application of ideas in real-world settings. Practical intelligence is particularly evident where problems are poorly defined, information is missing, and more than one solution may be plausible.[78]

Emotional Intelligence Effective leaders have a high level of emotional intelligence. They are able to recognize and regulate emotions in themselves and in other people (see Chapter 4).[79] For example, effective leaders can sense how well their conversations are influencing employees and other stakeholders. Also, they can recognize and change their own emotional state to suit the situation, such as feeling optimistic and determined in spite of recent business setbacks.

Authentic Leadership

A few paragraphs ago, we said that successful leaders have a complex, internally consistent, and clear self-concept as a leader, and that they have a strong positive self-evaluation. These characteristics lay the foundation for **authentic leadership**, which refers to how well leaders are aware of, feel comfortable with, and act consistently with their values, personality, and self-concept.[80]

Authenticity is mainly about knowing yourself and being yourself (see Exhibit 11.6). Leaders learn more about their personality, values, thoughts, and habits by reflecting on various situations and personal experiences. They also improve this self-awareness by receiving feedback from trusted people inside and outside the organization. Both self-reflection and receptivity to feedback require high levels of emotional intelligence.

As people learn more about themselves, they gain a greater understanding of their inner purpose, which, in turn, generates a long-term passion for achieving something worthwhile for the organization or society. Some leadership experts suggest that this inner purpose emerges from a life story, typically initiated by a transformative event or experience earlier in life.[81]

Authentic leadership is more than self-awareness; it also involves behaving in ways that are consistent with that self-concept rather than pretending to be someone else. It is difficult enough to lead others as your natural self; to lead others while pretending to be someone else is nearly impossible. To be themselves, great leaders regulate their decisions and behavior in a few ways. First, they develop their own style and, where appropriate, move into positions where that style is most effective. Although effective leaders adapt their behavior to the situation to some extent, they invariably understand and rely on decision methods and interpersonal styles that feel most comfortable to them.

Second, effective leaders continually think about and consistently apply their stable hierarchy of personal values to those decisions and behaviors. Leaders face many pressures and temptations, such as achieving short-term stock price targets at the

Exhibit 11.6 Authentic Leadership

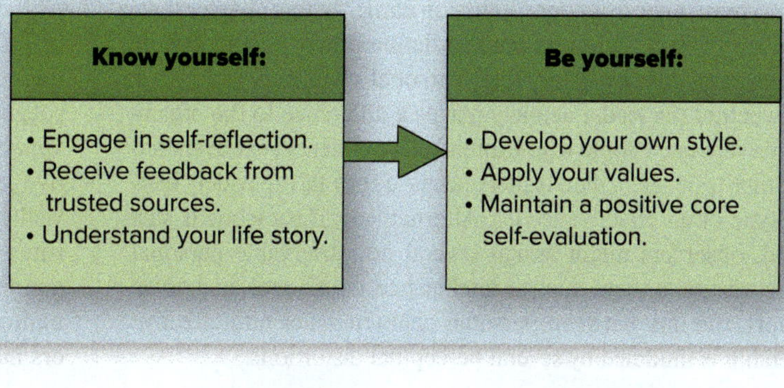

Authentic leadership begins by knowing yourself better through self-reflection and receptivity to feedback from trusted sources.
Michaeljung/Shutterstock

cost of long-term profitability. Experts note that authentic leaders demonstrate self-discipline by remaining anchored to their values. Third, effective leaders regulate their decisions and behavior by maintaining consistency around their self-concept. They have a strong, positive core self-evaluation, consisting of high self-esteem and self-efficacy as well as an internal locus of control (Chapter 3).

Personal Attributes Perspective Limitations and Practical Implications

Personality, experience, self-concept, and other individual characteristics potentially contribute to a leader's effectiveness. Still, the leadership attributes perspective has a few limitations.[82] First, it assumes that all effective leaders have the same personal characteristics that are equally important in all situations. This is probably a false assumption; leadership is far too complex to have a universal list of traits that apply to every condition. Some attributes might not be important all the time. Second, alternative combinations of attributes may be equally successful; two people with different sets of personal characteristics might be equally good leaders. Third, the personal attributes perspective views leadership as something within a person, yet experts emphasize that leadership is relational. People are effective leaders because of their favorable relationships with followers, not just because they possess specific personal characteristics.[83]

Also remember from our discussion earlier in this chapter that, in the short term, followers tend to define others as effective or ineffective leaders based on their personal characteristics rather than whether the leader actually makes a difference to the organization's success. People who exhibit self-confidence, extraversion, and other traits are called leaders because they fit the widely held prototype of an effective leader. Alternatively, if someone is successful, observers might assign several nonobservable personal characteristics to them, such as intelligence, confidence, and drive. In short, the link between personal characteristics and effective leadership is muddied by several perceptual distortions.

One important final point: The personal attributes perspective of leadership does not necessarily imply that leadership is a talent acquired at birth. On the contrary, attributes indicate only leadership *potential*, not leadership performance. People with these characteristics become effective leaders only after they have developed and mastered the necessary leadership behaviors through experience. However, even those with fewer leadership attributes may become very effective leaders by more fully developing their potential.

LO11-7 Discuss cultural and male–female similarities and differences in leadership.

CROSS-CULTURAL AND GENDER ISSUES IN LEADERSHIP

Culture shapes the leader's values and norms, which influence their decisions and actions. Cultural values also shape the expectations that followers have of their leaders. An executive who acts inconsistently with cultural expectations is more likely to be perceived as an ineffective leader. Furthermore, leaders who deviate from those expectations may experience various forms of influence to get them to conform to the leadership norms and expectations of the society. Thus, differences in leadership practices across cultures are partly explained by implicit leadership theory, which was described earlier in this chapter.

Studies in work settings have generally found that male and female leaders do not differ in their levels of task-oriented or people-oriented leadership. The main explanation is that real-world jobs require similar behavior from male and female job incumbents.[84] However, female leaders do adopt a participative leadership style more readily compared to male leaders. One possible reason is that, compared to boys, girls are often raised to be more egalitarian and less status-oriented, which is consistent with being participative. There is also some evidence that, compared to males, females have somewhat better interpersonal skills, and this translates into their relatively greater use of the participative leadership style. A third explanation is that employees are motivated by their own stereotypes that female leaders are more participative. Thus, female leaders comply with follower expectations to some extent.

Several studies report that females are rated higher than males on the increasingly valued leadership qualities of coaching, teamwork, and empowering employees.[85] Yet research also suggests that women are evaluated negatively when they try to apply the full range of leadership styles, particularly more directive and autocratic approaches. Thus, ironically, women may be well suited to contemporary leadership roles, yet they often continue to face implicit leadership challenges due to followers' gender stereotypes and prototypes of leaders.[86] Overall, both male and female leaders must be sensitive to the fact that followers have expectations about how leaders should act.

Study Checklist

Connect® is available for *M: Organizational Behavior.* Additional resources include:

✓ Exercises:

- **Case Analysis:** Apply concepts within the context of a real-world situation.
- **Click and Drag:** Helps make the connection between theory and application through matching, ranking, or grouping activities.
- **Video Case:** See management in action through interactive videos.
- **Self-Assessment:** Designed to promote student self-awareness and reflection, these research-based surveys contain detailed feedback for students.
- **Application-Based Activities:** These highly interactive, application- and analysis-based exercises allow students to take on specific roles to complete management related tasks within a real-world context.

✓ **SmartBook 2.0™**—Smartbook 2.0 is an adaptive learning solution that provides personalized learning to individual student needs, continually adapts to pinpoint knowledge gaps and focuses learning on concepts requiring additional study. It fosters more productive learning, takes the guesswork out of what to study, and helps students better prepare for class.

Notes

1. L. Turner, "Five Tips for Exceptional Leadership," *SAP Community* (blog), November 24, 2014.
2. Many of these perspectives are summarized in R.N. Kanungo, "Leadership in Organizations: Looking Ahead to the 21st Century," *Canadian Psychology* 39 (1998): 71–82; G.A. Yukl, *Leadership in Organizations*, 8th ed. (Upper Saddle River, NJ: Pearson Education, 2013).
3. "Less Than a Third of HR Professionals Are Confident They Have the Right Leaders for the Future," News Release (Los Angeles: Korn Ferry, February 4, 2020); "Survey: 84 Percent of U.S. Workers Blame Bad Managers for Creating Unnecessary Stress," Press Release (Alexandria, VA: SHRM, December 8, 2020); S. Korolevich, "Horrible Bosses: A Survey of the American Workforce," *GoodHire* (blog), January 11, 2022; "2022 Federal Employee Viewpoint Survey" (Washington, DC: United States Government, Office of Personnel Management, November 2022); "Global Leadership Forecast 2023" (Pittsburgh, PA: DDI, January 2023).
4. R. House, M. Javidan, and P. Dorfman, "Project GLOBE: An Introduction," *Applied Psychology: An International Review* 50 (2001): 489–505; R. House et al., "Understanding Cultures and Implicit Leadership Theories across the Globe: An Introduction to Project GLOBE," *Journal of World Business* 37 (2002): 3–10.
5. J.A. Raelin, "We the Leaders: In Order to Form a Leaderful Organization," *Journal of Leadership & Organizational Studies* 12, no. 2 (2005): 18–30; C.L. Pearce, J.A. Conger, and E.A. Locke, "Shared Leadership Theory," *Leadership Quarterly* 19, no. 5 (2008): 622–28; L. D'Innocenzo, J.E. Mathieu, and M.R. Kukenberger, "A Meta-Analysis of Different Forms of Shared Leadership–Team Performance Relations," *Journal of Management* 42, no. 7 (2016): 1964–91.
6. J.A. Raelin, *Creating Leaderful Organizations: How to Bring Out Leadership in Everyone* (San Francisco: Berrett-Koehler, 2003).
7. M.S. Fausing et al., "Antecedents of Shared Leadership: Empowering Leadership and Interdependence," *Leadership & Organization Development Journal* 36, no. 3 (2015): 271–91; A. Ali, H. Wang, and R.E. Johnson, "Empirical Analysis of Shared Leadership Promotion and Team Creativity: An Adaptive Leadership Perspective," *Journal of Organizational Behavior* 41, no. 5 (2020): 405–23. Without the conditions described, shared leadership may have several negative consequences. See: W. Chen and J.-H. Zhang, "Does Shared Leadership Always Work? A State-of-the-Art Review and Future Prospects," *Journal of Work-Applied Management* 15, no. 1 (2022): 51–66.
8. S. Marchionne, "Fiat's Extreme Makeover," *Harvard Business Review* (2008): 45–48.
9. Most or all of these elements are included in: W. Bennis and B. Nanus, *Leaders: The Strategies for Taking Charge* (New York: Harper & Row, 1985); N.M. Tichy and M.A. Devanna, *The Transformational Leader* (New York: Wiley, 1986); B.M. Bass and R.E. Riggio, *Transformational Leadership*, 2nd ed. (Mahwah, NJ: Lawrence Erlbaum Associates, 2006); J.M. Kouzes and B.Z. Posner, *The Leadership Challenge: How to Make Extraordinary Things Happen in Organizations* (Hoboken, N.J.: John Wiley & Sons, 2017). Most transformational leadership elements might also apply to managerial leadership, but with the latter focusing on improving current operational objectives rather than discovering new strategic directions. This is consistent with the recent recommendation to focus more on specific leader activities (modeling, directing, acting symbolically) rather than broad leadership typologies. See: A.M. Carton, "The Science of Leadership: A Theoretical Model and Research Agenda," *Annual Review of Organizational Psychology and Organizational Behavior* 9, no. 1 (2022): 61–93.
10. Strategic collective vision has been identified as a key factor in leadership since Chester Barnard's seminal book in organizational behavior. See C. Barnard, *The Functions of the Executive* (Cambridge, MA: Harvard University Press, 1938), 86–89.
11. W. Bennis and B. Nanus, *Leaders: The Strategies for Taking Charge* (New York: Harper & Row, 1985), 27–33, 89; R.E. Quinn, *Building the Bridge as You Walk on It: A Guide for Leading Change* (San Francisco: Jossey-Bass, 2004), Chap. 11; R. Gill, *Theory and Practice of Leadership* (London: Sage, 2011), Chap. 4; D. O'Connell, K. Hickerson, and A. Pillutla, "Organizational Visioning: An Integrative Review," *Group & Organization Management* 36, no. 1 (2011): 103–25.
12. J.M. Strange and M.D. Mumford, "The Origins of Vision: Effects of Reflection, Models, and Analysis," *Leadership Quarterly* 16 (2005): 121–48; S. Kantabutra, "Toward a Behavioral Theory of Vision in Organizational Settings," *Leadership & Organization Development Journal* 30 (2009): 319–37; S.A. Kirkpatrick, "Lead through Vision and Values," in *Handbook of Principles of Organizational Behavior*, ed. E.A. Locke (Chichester, UK: Wiley, 2010), 367–87; R. Ashkenas and B. Manville, "You Don't Have to Be CEO to Be a Visionary Leader," *Harvard Business Review*, April 4, 2019.

13. N. Augustine, *Augustine's Laws*, 3rd ed. (New York: Viking, 1986), 33.

14. "Global Workforce Study" (London: Willis Towers Watson, September 29, 2016); Gallup Inc., *State of the American Workplace* (Washington, DC: Gallup, February 23, 2017); "Half of Employees Can't Recite Their Organisation's Vision or Values," *Small Business* (London), February 26, 2018; "2019 Edelman-LinkedIn B2B Thought Leadership Impact Study" (New York: Edelman, December 6, 2018); "Mission & Culture Survey 2019" (Mill Valley, CA: Glassdoor, July 9, 2019).

15. J.A. Conger and R.N. Kanungo, *Charismatic Leadership in Organizations* (Thousand Oaks, CA: Sage, 1998), 173–83; M. Venus, D. Stam, and D. van Knippenberg, "Leader Emotion as a Catalyst of Effective Leader Communication of Visions, Value-Laden Messages, and Goals," *Organizational Behavior and Human Decision Processes* 122, no. 1 (2013): 53–68; J. Mayfield, M. Mayfield, and W.C. Sharbrough, "Strategic Vision and Values in Top Leaders' Communications: Motivating Language at a Higher Level," *International Journal of Business Communication* 52, no. 1 (2015): 97–121.

16. D.A. Waldman, P.A. Balthazard, and S.J. Peterson, "Leadership and Neuroscience: Can We Revolutionize the Way That Inspirational Leaders Are Identified and Developed?" *Academy of Management Perspectives* 25, no. 1 (2011): 60–74; S. Denning, *The Leader's Guide to Storytelling: Mastering the Art and Discipline of Business Narrative*, rev. ed. (San Francisco: Jossey-Bass, 2011); J.C. Sarros et al., "Leaders and Their Use of Motivating Language," *Leadership & Organization Development Journal* 35, no. 3 (2014): 226–40; A.M. Carton, C. Murphy, and J.R. Clark, "A (Blurry) Vision of the Future: How Leader Rhetoric about Ultimate Goals Influences Performance," *Academy of Management Journal* 57, no. 6 (2014): 1544–70.

17. J.E. Baur et al., "More Than One Way to Articulate a Vision: A Configurations Approach to Leader Charismatic Rhetoric and Influence," *Leadership Quarterly* 27, no. 1 (2016): 156–71.

18. D.E. Berlew, "Leadership and Organizational Excitement," *California Management Review* 17, no. 2 (1974): 21–30; W. Bennis and B. Nanus, *Leaders: The Strategies for Taking Charge* (New York: Harper & Row, 1985), 43–55; T. Simons, "Behavioral Integrity: The Perceived Alignment between Managers' Words and Deeds as a Research Focus," *Organization Science* 13, no. 1 (2002): 18–35.

19. D. Ossip, "Create a Culture of Engagement for Successful Customer Outcomes," *The CEO Forum* 2015, 30–31.

20. For a discussion of trust in leadership, see C.S. Burke et al., "Trust in Leadership: A Multi-Level Review and Integration," *Leadership Quarterly* 18, no. 6 (2007): 606–32. The surveys on leading by example are reported in J.C. Maxwell, "People Do What People See," *BusinessWeek*, 19 November 2007, 32; "Who's the Boss of Workplace Culture?," News release (Chelmsford, MA: Kronos, 9 March 2016). One recent study found that leading by doing has a positive correlation with employee productivity and service quality. See: L. Eldor, "Leading by Doing: Does Leading by Example Impact Productivity and Service Quality?," *Academy of Management Journal* 64, no. 2 (2021): 458–81.

21. S. Kolesnikov-Jessop, "You're the Conductor: Listen to the Music You Can Create with the Group," *The New York Times*, April 11, 2016.

22. B.M. Bass and R.E. Riggio, *Transformational Leadership,* 2nd ed. (Mahwah, NJ: Erlbaum, 2006), 7; J.M. Kouzes and B.Z. Posner, *The Leadership Challenge: How to Make Extraordinary Things Happen in Organizations* (Hoboken, N.J.: John Wiley & Sons, 2017), Chaps. 7 and 8.

23. W.E. Baker and J.M. Sinkula, "The Synergistic Effect of Market Orientation and Learning Orientation on Organizational Performance," *Academy of Marketing Science Journal* 27, no. 4 (1999): 411–27; Z. Emden, A. Yaprak, and S. T. Cavusgil, "Learning from Experience in International Alliances: Antecedents and Firm Performance Implications," *Journal of Business Research* 58, no. 7 (2005): 883–92.

24. J.M. Kouzes and B.Z. Posner, *The Leadership Challenge,* 6th ed. (San Francisco: Jossey-Bass, 2017).

25. R.J. House, "A 1976 Theory of Charismatic Leadership," in *Leadership: The Cutting Edge*, ed. J.G. Hunt and L.L. Larson (Carbondale: Southern Illinois University Press, 1977), 189–207; J.A. Conger, "Charismatic Leadership," in *The Sage Handbook of Leadership*, ed. A. Bryman et al. (London: Sage, 2011), 86–102.

26. J.E. Barbuto Jr., "Taking the Charisma out of Transformational Leadership," *Journal of Social Behavior & Personality* 12 (1997): 689–97; Y.A. Nur, "Charisma and Managerial Leadership: The Gift That Never Was," *Business Horizons* 41 (1998): 19–26; M.D. Mumford and J.R. Van Doorn, "The Leadership of Pragmatism: Reconsidering Franklin in the Age of Charisma," *Leadership Quarterly* 12, no. 3 (2001): 279–309; A. Fanelli, "Bringing Out Charisma: CEO Charisma and External Stakeholders," *Academy of Management Review* 31, no. 4 (2006): 1049–61; M.J. Platow et al., "A Special Gift We Bestow on You for Being Representative of Us: Considering Leader Charisma from a Self-Categorization Perspective," *British Journal of Social Psychology* 45, no. 2 (2006): 303–20.

27. W.H. Friedland, "For a Sociological Concept of Charisma," *Social Forces* 43 (1964): 18–26; K. Miyahara, "Charisma: From Weber to Contemporary Sociology," *Sociological Inquiry* 53 (1983): 368–88; J. Antonakis et al., "Charisma: An Ill-Defined and Ill-Measured Gift," *Annual Review of Organizational Psychology and Organizational Behavior* 3 (2016): 293–319; K.O. Tskhay, R. Zhu, and N.O. Rule, "Perceptions of Charisma from Thin Slices of Behavior Predict Leadership Prototypicality Judgments," *Leadership Quarterly*, 28 (2017): 555–62.

28. B. Shamir et al., "Correlates of Charismatic Leader Behavior in Military Units: Subordinates' Attitudes, Unit Characteristics, and Superiors' Appraisals of Leader Performance," *Academy of Management Journal* 41, no. 4 (1998): 387–409; R. Khurana, *Searching for a Corporate Savior: The Irrational Quest for Charismatic CEOs* (Princeton, NJ: Princeton University Press, 2002); R.E. de Vries, R.D. Pathak, and A.R. Paquin, "The Paradox of Power Sharing: Participative Charismatic Leaders Have Subordinates with More Instead of Less Need for Leadership," *European Journal of Work and Organizational Psychology* 20, no. 6 (2010): 779–804; J. Vergauwe et al., "The Double-Edged Sword of Leader Charisma: Understanding the Curvilinear Relationship between Charismatic Personality and Leader Effectiveness," *Journal of Personality and Social Psychology* 114, no. 1 (2018): 110–30.

29. J. Lipman-Blumen, "A Pox on Charisma: Why Connective Leadership and Character Count," in *The Drucker Difference: What the World's Greatest Management Thinker Means to Today's Business Leaders*, ed. C.L. Pearce, J.A. Maciariello, and H. Yamawaki (New York: McGraw Hill, 2010), 149–74.

30. A. Mackey, "The Effect of CEOs on Firm Performance," *Strategic Management Journal* 29, no. 12 (2008): 1357–67. However, one study reported that transformational leadership is less effective than authoritarian (command-control with punishment) leadership in resource scarcity environments. See X. Huang et al., "When Authoritarian Leaders Outperform Transformational Leaders: Firm Performance in a Harsh Economic Environment," *Academy of Management Discoveries* 1, no. 2 (2015): 180–200.

31. A. Bryman, "Leadership in Organizations," in *Handbook of Organization Studies*, ed. S.R. Clegg, C. Hardy, and W.R. Nord (Thousand Oaks, CA: Sage, 1996), 276–92; D. van Knippenberg and S.B. Sitkin, "A Critical Assessment of Charismatic–Transformational Leadership Research: Back to the Drawing Board?," *Academy of Management Annals* 7, no. 1 (2013): 1–60.

32. G. Yukl and J.W. Michel, "A Critical Assessment of Research on Effective Leadership Behavior," in *Advances in Authentic and Ethical Leadership*, ed. L.L. Neider and C.A. Schriesheim (Charlotte, NC: Information Age, 2014), 209–30.

33. B.S. Pawar and K.K. Eastman, "The Nature and Implications of Contextual Influences on Transformational Leadership: A Conceptual Examination," *Academy of Management Review* 22 (1997): 80–109; C.P. Egri and S. Herman, "Leadership in the North American Environmental Sector: Values, Leadership Styles, and Contexts of Environmental Leaders and Their Organizations," *Academy of Management Journal* 43, no. 4 (2000): 571–604.

34. A. Zaleznik, "Managers and Leaders: Are They Different?," *Harvard Business Review* 55, no. 3 (1977): 67–78; J.P. Kotter, *A Force for Change: How Leadership Differs from Management* (New York: Free Press, 1990); E.A. Locke, *The Essence of Leadership* (New York: Lexington Books, 1991); G. Yukl and R. Lepsinger, "Why Integrating the Leading and Managing Roles Is Essential for Organizational Effectiveness," *Organizational Dynamics* 34, no. 4 (2005): 361–75; D.V. Simonet and R.P. Tett, "Five Perspectives on the Leadership–Management Relationship: A Competency-Based Evaluation and Integration," *Journal of Leadership & Organizational Studies* 20, no. 2 (2013): 199–213; H. Mintzberg, *Simply Managing: What Managers Do–and Can Do Better* (San Francisco: Berrett-Koehler Publishers, 2013); M. Bresnen et al., "Leadership Talk: From Managerialism to Leaderism in Health Care after the Crash," *Leadership* 11, no. 4 (2015): 451–70; U.Y. Eseryel, K. Crowston, and R. Heckman, "Functional and Visionary Leadership in Self-Managing Virtual Teams," *Group & Organization Management* 46, no. 2 (2021): 424–60.

35. W. Bennis and B. Nanus, *Leaders: The Strategies for Taking Charge* (New York: Harper & Row, 1985), 21. Peter Drucker also is widely cited as the source of this quotation. The closest passage we could find, however, is in the first two pages of *The Effective Executive* (1966) where Drucker states that effective executives "get the right things done." On the next page, he states that manual workers only need efficiency, "that is, the ability to do things right rather than the ability to get the right things done." See P.F. Drucker, *The Effective Executive* (New York: Harper Business, 1966), 1–2.

36. R.J. House and R.N. Aditya, "The Social Scientific Study of Leadership: Quo Vadis?" *Journal of Management* 23, no. 3 (1997): 409–73.

37. G. Yukl and R. Lepsinger, "Why Integrating the Leading and Managing Roles Is Essential for Organizational Effectiveness," *Organizational Dynamics* 34, no. 4 (2005): 361–75; U.Y. Eseryel, K. Crowston, and R. Heckman, "Functional and Visionary Leadership in Self-Managing Virtual Teams," *Group & Organization Management* 46, no. 2 (2021): 424–60.

38. E.A. Fleishman, "The Description of Supervisory Behavior," *Journal of Applied Psychology* 37, no. 1 (1953): 1–6. For discussion on methodological problems with the development of these people-versus-task-oriented leadership constructs, see C.A. Schriesheim, R.J. House, and S. Kerr, "Leader Initiating Structure: A Reconciliation of Discrepant Research Results and Some Empirical Tests," *Organizational Behavior and Human Performance* 15, no. 2 (1976): 297–321; L. Tracy, "Consideration and Initiating Structure: Are They Basic Dimensions of Leader Behavior?," *Social Behavior and Personality* 15, no. 1 (1987): 21–33.

39. A.K. Korman, "Consideration, Initiating Structure, and Organizational Criteria—A Review," *Personnel Psychology* 19 (1966): 349–62; E.A. Fleishman, "Twenty Years of Consideration and Structure," in *Current Developments in the Study of Leadership*, ed. E.A. Fleishman and J.C. Hunt (Carbondale: Southern Illinois University Press, 1973), 1–40; T.A. Judge, R.F. Piccolo, and R. Ilies, "The Forgotten Ones? The Validity of Consideration and Initiating Structure in Leadership Research," *Journal of Applied Psychology* 89, no. 1 (2004): 36–51; D.S. DeRue et al., "Trait and Behavioral Theories of Leadership: An Integration and Meta-Analytic Test of Their Relative Validity," *Personnel Psychology* 64, no. 1 (2011): 7–52; G.A. Yukl, *Leadership in Organizations*, 8th ed. (Upper Saddle River, NJ; Pearson Education, 2013), 62–75.

40. V.V. Baba, "Serendipity in Leadership: Initiating Structure and Consideration in the Classroom," *Human Relations* 42 (1989): 509–25; D. Erdel and M. Takkaç, "Teacher Leadership inside the Classroom: Implications for Effective Language Teaching," *International Journal of Curriculum and Instruction* 12 (2020): 467–500.

41. S.J. Peterson, B.M. Galvin, and D. Lange, "CEO Servant Leadership: Exploring Executive Characteristics and Firm Performance," *Personnel Psychology* 65, no. 3 (2012): 565–96.

42. R.K. Greenleaf, *Servant Leadership: A Journey into the Nature of Legitimate Power & Greatness* (Mahwah, NJ: Paulist Press, 1977; repr., 2002), 27.

43. S. Sendjaya, J.C. Sarros, and J.C. Santora, "Defining and Measuring Servant Leadership Behaviour in Organizations," *Journal of Management Studies* 45 (2008): 402–24; R.C. Liden et al., "Servant Leadership: Development of a Multidimensional Measure and Multi-Level Assessment," *Leadership Quarterly* 19 (2008): 161–77; D. van Dierendonck, "Servant Leadership: A Review and Synthesis," *Journal of Management* 37 (2011): 1228–61; R. VanMeter et al., "In Search of Clarity on Servant Leadership: Domain Specification and Reconceptualization," *AMS Review* 6 (2016): 59–78.

44. R. VanMeter et al., "In Search of Clarity on Servant Leadership: Domain Specification and Reconceptualization," *AMS Review* 6, no. 1 (2016): 59–78; K.E. Mcquade, C. Harrison, and H. Tarbert, "Systematically Reviewing Servant Leadership," *European Business Review* 33, no. 3 (2020): 465–90; Y. Zhang et al., "A Meta-Analytic Review of the Consequences of Servant Leadership: The Moderating Roles of Cultural Factors," *Asia Pacific Journal of Management* 38, no. 1 (2021): 371–400.

45. S. Kerr et al., "Towards a Contingency Theory of Leadership Based Upon the Consideration and Initiating Structure Literature," *Organizational Behavior and Human Performance* 12 (1974): 62–82; L.L. Larson, J.G. Hunt, and R.N. Osborn, "The Great Hi-Hi Leader Behavior Myth: A Lesson from Occam's Razor," *Academy of Management Journal* 19 (1976): 628–41; V.H. Vroom and A.G. Jago, "The Role of the Situation in Leadership," *American Psychologist* 62, no. 1 (2007): 17–24.

46. R.J. House, "A Path Goal Theory of Leader Effectiveness," *Administrative Science Quarterly* 16 (1971): 321–39; M.G. Evans, "Extensions of a Path-Goal Theory of Motivation," *Journal of Applied Psychology* 59 (1974): 172–78; R.J. House and T.R. Mitchell, "Path-Goal Theory of Leadership," *Journal of Contemporary Business* (1974): 81–97; M.G. Evans, "Path Goal Theory of Leadership," in *Leadership*, ed. L.L. Neider and C.A. Schriesheim (Greenwich, CT: Information Age Publishing, 2002), 115–38.

47. For a thorough study of how expectancy theory of motivation relates to leadership, see R.G. Isaac, W.J. Zerbe, and D.C. Pitt, "Leadership and Motivation: The Effective Application of Expectancy Theory," *Journal of Managerial Issues* 13 (2001): 212–26.

48. R.J. House, "Path-Goal Theory of Leadership: Lessons, Legacy, and a Reformulated Theory," *The Leadership Quarterly* 7, no. 3 (1996): 323–52.

49. J. Indvik, "Path-Goal Theory of Leadership: A Meta-Analysis," *Academy of Management Proceedings* (1986): 189–92; J.C. Wofford and L.Z. Liska, "Path-Goal Theories of Leadership: A Meta-Analysis," *Journal of Management* 19 (1993): 857–76.

50. These testimonials are reported in S. Sahadi, "We Asked CNN Business Readers What Makes a Great Boss. Here's What You Said," *CNN Business*, March 27, 2019.

51. J.D. Houghton and S.K. Yoho, "Toward a Contingency Model of Leadership and Psychological Empowerment: When Should Self-Leadership Be Encouraged?," *Journal of Leadership & Organizational Studies* 11, no. 4 (2005): 65–83.

52. R.T. Keller, "A Test of the Path–Goal Theory of Leadership with Need for Clarity as a Moderator in Research and Development Organizations," *Journal of Applied Psychology* 74 (1989): 208–12; M.A.M.G. Hoogeboom and C.P.M. Wilderom, "Advancing the Transformational–Transactional Model of Effective Leadership: Integrating Two Classic Leadership Models with a Video-Based Method," *Journal of Leadership Studies* 13, no. 2 (2019): 23–46.

53. R.P. Vecchio, J.E. Justin, and C.L. Pearce, "The Utility of Transactional and Transformational Leadership for Predicting Performance and Satisfaction within a Path–Goal Theory Framework," *Journal of Occupational and Organizational Psychology* 81 (2008): 71–82; M.A.M.G. Hoogeboom and C.P.M. Wilderom, "Advancing the Transformational–Transactional Model of Effective Leadership: Integrating Two Classic Leadership Models with a Video-Based Method," *Journal of Leadership Studies* 13, no. 2 (2019): 23–46; A. Puni, S.K. Hilton, and B. Quao, "The Interaction Effect of Transactional-Transformational Leadership on Employee Commitment in a Developing Country," *Management Research Review* 44, no. 3 (2020): 399–417.

54. B. Carroll and L. Levy, "Defaulting to Management: Leadership Defined by What It Is Not," *Organization* 15, no. 1 (2008): 75–96; L. Crevani and N. Endrissat, "Mapping the Leadership-as-Practice Terrain: Comparative Elements," in *Leadership-as-Practice*, ed. J.A. Raelin (New York: Routledge, 2016), 21–49; M. Korica, D. Nicolini, and B. Johnson, "In Search of 'Managerial Work': Past, Present and Future of an Analytical Category," *International Journal of Management Reviews* 19, no. 2 (2017): 151–74.

55. C.A. Schriesheim and L.L. Neider, "Path–Goal Leadership Theory: The Long and Winding Road," *Leadership Quarterly* 7 (1996): 317–21.

56. N. Nicholson, *Executive Instinct* (New York: Crown, 2000); T.A. Judge, R.F. Piccolo, and R. Ilies, "The Forgotten Ones? The Validity of Consideration and Initiating Structure in Leadership Research," *Journal of Applied Psychology* 89, no. 1 (2004): 36–51; T.A. Judge, R.F. Piccolo, and T. Kosalka, "The Bright and Dark Sides of Leader Traits: A Review and Theoretical Extension of the Leader Trait Paradigm," *Leadership Quarterly* 20 (2009): 855–75. One pioneering managerial leadership expert specifically argued that managers cannot easily switch leadership styles. See FE. Fiedler, "Engineer the Job to Fit the Manager," *Harvard Business Review* 43, no. 5 (1965): 115–22.

57. S. Kerr and J.M. Jermier, "Substitutes for Leadership: Their Meaning and Measurement," *Organizational Behavior and Human Performance* 22 (December 1978): 375–403.

58. C.A. Schriesheim, "Substitutes-for-Leadership Theory: Development and Basic Concepts," *Leadership Quarterly* 8 (1997): 103–08; R.T. Keller, "Transformational Leadership, Initiating Structure, and Substitutes for Leadership: A Longitudinal Study of Research and Development Project Team Performance," *Journal of Applied Psychology* 91, no. 1 (2006): 202–10.

59. B. Künzle et al., "Substitutes for Leadership in Anaesthesia Teams and Their Impact on Leadership Effectiveness," *European Journal of Work and Organizational Psychology* 19, no. 5 (2010): 505–31; B.A. De Jong, K.M. Bijlsma-Frankema, and L.B. Cardinal, "Stronger Than the Sum of Its Parts? The Performance Implications of Peer Control Combinations in Teams," *Organization Science* 25, no. 6 (2014): 1703–21.

60. W. Potipiroon and M.T. Ford, "Does Leader Humor Influence Employee Voice? The Mediating Role of Psychological Safety and the Moderating Role of Team Humor," *Journal of Leadership & Organizational Studies* 28, no. 4 (2021): 415–28.

61. P.M. Podsakoff and S.B. MacKenzie, "Kerr and Jermier's Substitutes for Leadership Model: Background, Empirical Assessment, and Suggestions for Future Research," *Leadership Quarterly* 8 (1997): 117–32; S.D. Dionne et al., "Neutralizing Substitutes for Leadership Theory: Leadership Effects and Common-Source Bias," *Journal of Applied Psychology* 87, no. 3 (2002): 454–64; J.R. Villa et al., "Problems with Detecting Moderators in Leadership Research Using Moderated Multiple Regression," *Leadership Quarterly* 14, no. 1 (2003): 3–23; S.D. Dionne et al., "Substitutes for Leadership, or Not," *Leadership Quarterly* 16, no. 1 (2005): 169–93.

62. J.R. Meindl, "On Leadership: An Alternative to the Conventional Wisdom," *Research in Organizational Behavior* 12 (1990): 159–203; L.R. Offermann, J.K. Kennedy, and P.W. Wirtz, "Implicit Leadership Theories: Content, Structure, and Generalizability," *Leadership Quarterly* 5, no. 1 (1994): 43–58; P. Jacquart and J. Antonakis, "When Does Charisma Matter for Top-Level Leaders? Effect of Attributional Ambiguity," *Academy of Management Journal* 58, no. 4 (2015): 1051–74; R.G. Lord et al., "Implicit Leadership Theories, Implicit Followership Theories, and Dynamic Processing of Leadership Information," *Annual Review of Organizational Psychology and Organizational Behavior* 7 (2020): 49–74.

63. F.C. Brodbeck et al., "Cultural Variation of Leadership Prototypes across 22 European Countries," *Journal of Occupational and Organizational Psychology* 73, no. 1 (2000): 1–29; O. Epitropaki et al., "Implicit Leadership and Followership Theories 'in the Wild': Taking Stock of Information-Processing Approaches to Leadership and Followership in Organizational Settings," *The Leadership Quarterly* 24, no. 6 (2013): 858–81; G.M. Tavares et al., "Opening the Implicit Leadership Theories' Black Box: An Experimental Approach with Conjoint Analysis," *Frontiers in Psychology* 9 (2018): 0100.

64. S.F. Cronshaw and R.G. Lord, "Effects of Categorization, Attribution, and Encoding Processes on Leadership Perceptions," *Journal of Applied Psychology* 72 (1987): 97–106; J.L. Nye and D.R. Forsyth, "The Effects of Prototype-Based Biases on Leadership Appraisals: A Test of Leadership Categorization Theory," *Small Group Research* 22 (1991): 360–79.

65. R. Meindl, "On Leadership: An Alternative to the Conventional Wisdom," *Research in Organizational Behavior* 12 (1990): 163; B. Schyns, J.R. Meindl, and M.A. Croon, "The Romance of Leadership Scale: Cross-Cultural Testing and Refinement," *Leadership* 3, no. 1 (2007): 29–46; J. Felfe and L.E. Petersen, "Romance of Leadership and Management Decision Making," *European Journal of Work and Organizational Psychology* 16, no. 1 (2007): 1–24.

66. J. Pfeffer, "The Ambiguity of Leadership," *Academy of Management Review* 2 (1977): 102–12.

67. R. Weber et al., "The Illusion of Leadership: Misattribution of Cause in Coordination Games," *Organization Science* 12, no. 5 (2001): 582–98; N. Ensari and S.E. Murphy, "Cross-Cultural Variations in Leadership Perceptions and Attribution of Charisma to the Leader," *Organizational Behavior and Human Decision Processes* 92 (2003): 52–66; M.L.A. Hayward, V.P. Rindova, and T.G. Pollock, "Believing One's Own Press: The Causes and Consequences of CEO Celebrity," *Strategic Management Journal* 25, no. 7 (2004): 637–53; G.T. Fairhurst and D. Grant, "The Social Construction of Leadership: A Sailing Guide," *Management Communication Quarterly* 24, no. 2 (2010): 171–210.

68. L.L. Koppes et al., eds., "Leadership: A Critical Historical Analysis of the Influence of Leader Traits," in *Historical Perspectives in Industrial and Organizational Psychology* (New York: Routledge, 2021), 227–48.

69. R.M. Stogdill, *Handbook of Leadership* (New York: Free Press, 1974), chap. 5.

70. This list is based on S.A. Kirkpatrick and E.A. Locke, "Leadership: Do Traits Matter?," *Academy of Management Executive* 5 (1991): 48–60; G.A. Yukl, *Leadership in Organizations*, 8th ed. (Upper Saddle River, NJ: Pearson Education, 2013), Chap. 6; S.J. Zaccaro et al., "Leader Individual Differences, Situational Parameters, and Leadership Outcomes: A Comprehensive Review and Integration," *The Leadership Quarterly* 29, no. 1 (2018): 2–43.

71. T.A. Judge et al., "Personality and Leadership: A Qualitative and Quantitative Review," *Journal Of Applied Psychology* 87, no. 4 (2002): 765–80; D.S. Derue et al., "Trait and Behavioral Theories of Leadership: An Integration and Meta-Analytic Test of Their Relative Validity," *Personnel Psychology* 64, no. 1 (2011): 7–52; A. Deinert et al., "Transformational Leadership Sub-Dimensions and Their Link to Leaders' Personality and Performance," *Leadership Quarterly* 26, no. 6 (2015): 1095–120. Recent evidence suggests that being a formal leader changes the individual's personality (e.g., conscientiousness increases). See: W.-D. Li et al., "Can Becoming a Leader Change Your Personality? An Investigation with Two Longitudinal Studies from a Role-Based Perspective," *The Journal of Applied Psychology* 106, no. 6 (2020): 882–901.

72. H. Ibarra et al., "Leadership and Identity: An Examination of Three Theories and New Research Directions," in *The Oxford Handbook of Leadership and Organizations*, ed. D.V. Day (New York: Oxford University Press, 2014), 285–301; L. Guillén, M. Mayo, and K. Korotov, "Is Leadership a Part of Me? A Leader Identity Approach to Understanding the Motivation to Lead," *Leadership Quarterly* 26, no. 5 (2015): 802–20; D. Miscenko, H. Guenter, and D.V. Day, "Am I a Leader? Examining Leader Identity Development over Time," *The Leadership Quarterly* 28, no. 5 (2017): 605–20; E. Lanka, A. Topakas, and M. Patterson, "Becoming a Leader: Catalysts and Barriers to Leader Identity Construction," *European Journal of Work and Organizational Psychology* 29, no. 3 (2020): 377–90.

73. B. Carroll and L. Levy, "Defaulting to Management: Leadership Defined by What It Is Not," *Organization* 15, no. 1 (2008): 75–96.

74. L. Guillén, M. Mayo, and K. Korotov, "Is Leadership a Part of Me? A Leader Identity Approach to Understanding the Motivation to Lead," *The Leadership Quarterly* 26, no. 5 (2015): 802–20; K.L. Badura et al., "Motivation to Lead: A Meta-Analysis and Distal-Proximal Model of Motivation and Leadership," *Journal of Applied Psychology* 105, no. 4 (2020): 331–54.

75. J.B. Miner, "Twenty Years of Research on Role Motivation Theory of Managerial Effectiveness," *Personnel Psychology* 31 (1978): 739–60; C.J. Vinkenburg et al., "Arena: A Critical Conceptual Framework of Top Management Selection," *Group & Organization Management* 39, no. 1 (2014): 33–68; B.L. Connelly et al., "Tournament Theory: Thirty Years of Contests and Competitions," *Journal of Management* 40, no. 1 (2014): 16–47; Y. Baruch and Y. Vardi, "A Fresh Look at the Dark Side of Contemporary Careers: Toward a Realistic Discourse," *British Journal of Management* 27, no. 2 (2016): 355–72.

76. S. Giles, "The Most Important Leadership Competencies, According to Leaders around the World," *Harvard Business Review*, March 15, 2016; C. Moore et al., "Leaders Matter Morally: The Role of Ethical Leadership in Shaping Employee Moral Cognition and Misconduct," *Journal of Applied Psychology* 104, no. 1 (2019): 123–45; A.C. Peng and D. Kim, "A Meta-Analytic Test of the Differential Pathways Linking Ethical Leadership to Normative Conduct," *Journal of Organizational Behavior* 41, no. 4 (2020): 348–68; G.C. Banks et al., "Ethical Leadership: Mapping the Terrain for Concept Cleanup and a Future Research Agenda," *The Leadership Quarterly* 32, no. 2 (2021): 101471.

77. S.J. Stowell and S.S. Mead, "What People Want in a Leader: How Do You Measure Up?," *Training Industry Magazine*, March/April 2020, 27–29; "Ethics at Work: 2021 International Survey of Employees" (London: Institute of Business Ethics, November 2021); J. Folkman and J. Zenger, "The Skills Leaders Need at Every Level," *Zenger Folkman* (blog), March 28, 2022; "2022 Federal Employee Viewpoint Survey" (Washington, DC: United States Government, Office of Personnel Management, November 2022); "Global Leadership Forecast 2023" (Pittsburgh, PA: DDI, January 2023).

78. J. Hedlund et al., "Identifying and Assessing Tacit Knowledge: Understanding the Practical Intelligence of Military Leaders," *Leadership Quarterly* 14, no. 2 (2003): 117–40; A. Baczyńska and G.C. Thornton III, "Relationships of Analytical, Practical, and Emotional Intelligence with Behavioral Dimensions of Performance of Top Managers," *International Journal of Selection and Assessment* 25, no. 2 (2017): 171–82.

79. D. Goleman, R. Boyatzis, and A. McKee, *Primal Leaders* (Boston: Harvard Business School Press, 2002); C. Miao, R.H. Humphrey, and S. Qian, "Emotional Intelligence and Authentic Leadership: A Meta-Analysis," *Leadership & Organization Development Journal* 39, no. 5 (2018): 679–90; C.B. Koh and E. O'Higgins, "Relationships between Emotional Intelligence, Perceived and Actual Leadership Effectiveness in the Military Context," *Military Psychology* 30, no. 1 (2018): 27–42; S. Mysirlaki and F. Paraskeva, "Emotional Intelligence and Transformational Leadership in Virtual Teams: Lessons from MMOGs," *Leadership & Organization Development Journal* 41, no. 4 (2020): 551–66.

80. B. George, *Authentic Leadership* (San Francisco: Jossey-Bass, 2004); W.L. Gardner et al., "Authentic Leadership: A Review of the Literature and Research Agenda," *The Leadership Quarterly* 22 (2011): 1120–45; B. Alilyyani, C.A. Wong, and G. Cummings, "Antecedents, Mediators, and Outcomes of Authentic Leadership in Healthcare: A Systematic Review," *International Journal of Nursing Studies* 83 (2018): 34–64; W.L. Gardner et al., "Authentic Leadership Theory: The Case For and Against," *The Leadership Quarterly* 32, no. 6 (2021): 101495.

81. W.G. Bennis and R.J. Thomas, "Crucibles of Leadership," *Harvard Business Review* 80, no. 9 (2002): 39–45; R.J. Thomas, *Crucibles of Leadership: How to Learn from Experience to Become a Great Leader* (Boston: Harvard Business Press, 2008).

82. R. Jacobs, "Using Human Resource Functions to Enhance Emotional Intelligence," in *The Emotionally Intelligent Workplace*, ed. C. Cherniss and D. Goleman (San Francisco: Jossey-Bass, 2001), 161–63; J.A. Conger and D.A. Ready, "Rethinking Leadership Competencies," *Leader to Leader* (2004): 41–47.

83. R.G. Lord and D.J. Brown, *Leadership Processes and Self-Identity: A Follower-Centered Approach to Leadership* (Mahwah, NJ: Erlbaum, 2004); R. Bolden and J. Gosling, "Leadership Competencies: Time to Change the Tune?," *Leadership* 2, no. 2 (2006): 147–63.

84. G.N. Powell, "One More Time: Do Female and Male Managers Differ?," *Academy of Management Executive* 4 (1990): 68–75; M.L. van Engen and T.M. Willemsen, "Sex and Leadership Styles: A Meta-Analysis of Research Published in the 1990s," *Psychological Reports* 94, no. 1 (2004): 3–18.

85. A. H. Eagly, M. C. Johannesen-Schmidt, and M. L. van Engen, "Transformational, Transactional, and Laissez-Faire Leadership Styles: A Meta-Analysis Comparing Women and Men," *Psychological Bulletin* 129 (2003): 569–91; S. Paustian-Underdahl, L. Walker, and D. Woehr, "Gender and Perceptions of Leadership Effectiveness: A Meta-Analysis of Contextual Moderators," *Journal of Applied Psychology* 99, no. 6 (2014): 1129–45.

86. A.H. Eagly, S.J. Karau, and M.G. Makhijani, "Gender and the Effectiveness of Leaders: A Meta-Analysis," *Psychological Bulletin* 117 (1995): 125–45; M.E. Heilman et al., "Penalties for Success: Reactions to Women Who Succeed at Male Gender-Typed Tasks," *Journal of Applied Psychology* 89, no. 3 (2004): 416–27; A.H. Eagly, "Achieving Relational Authenticity in Leadership: Does Gender Matter?," *Leadership Quarterly* 16, no. 3 (2005): 459–74; A.J. Anderson et al., "The Effectiveness of Three Strategies to Reduce the Influence of Bias in Evaluations of Female Leaders," *Journal of Applied Social Psychology* 45, no. 9 (2015): 522–39.

PART 4

12 Designing Organizational Structures

SciStock/E+/Getty Images

Learning Objectives

After reading this chapter, you should be able to:

LO12-1 Describe three types of coordination in organizational structures.

LO12-2 Discuss the role and effects of span of control, centralization, and formalization and relate these elements to organic and mechanistic organizational structures.

LO12-3 Identify and evaluate five types of departmentalization.

LO12-4 Explain how the external environment, organizational size, technology, and strategy are relevant when designing an organizational structure.

organizational structure The division of labor as well as the patterns of coordination, communication, workflow, and formal power that direct organizational activities

Samsung Electronics Co., South Korea's largest business conglomerate, is flattening its organizational structure to become more innovative and nimble. As with most large South Korean organizations, Samsung had a tall, rigid hierarchy with power centralized at the top of the organization. This structure included seven well-defined status titles below the executive level, ranging from an entry-level employee through to division manager. Everyone addressed one another by their rank in the hierarchy rather than by their personal name.

A few years ago, Samsung cut those seven nonexecutive career levels to just four levels. Now, the company is collapsing its entire nonexecutive hierarchy to just two layers with no job titles. Everyone will use the honorific "pro" (professional) or "nim" (a highly respectful variation of Mr./Ms.). Employees will no longer be able to look up coworker ID numbers and other evidence of their seniority and status.

The company hopes this egalitarian setting will encourage more collaboration and coordination through informal communication. "We won't have to worry about what title to refer other employees during business meetings with the change, and we will be able to freely exchange opinions on equal footing," says one Samsung employee.

Samsung is also reducing the number of executive levels. Division head level has been eliminated and two vice-president levels (senior VP and executive VP) will be merged into one "vice-president" level. The company is also removing the minimum years required to be employed at each organizational level. "We are removing qualifications for climbing up the (corporate) ladder and reducing the number of steps to get there, too," says a Samsung Electronics official.[1]

Samsung Electronics Co. is transforming its organizational structure to improve the South Korean conglomerate's creativity and agility. **Organizational structure** refers to the division of labor as well as the patterns of coordination, communication, workflow, and formal power that direct organizational activities. It formally determines what activities receive the most attention as well as financial, power, and information resources. For example, with only two rather than seven nonexecutive levels, Samsung's new structure will likely improve upward and lateral communication, increase power to employees who previously held lower-level positions, and reduce bureaucratic practices found in taller hierarchies.

The topic of organizational structure typically conjures up images of an organizational chart. Organizational structure includes these reporting relationships, but it also includes other features that relate to work standards and rules, team dynamics, power relationships, information flow, and job design. The organization's structure is an important instrument in an executive's toolkit for organizational change because it establishes new communication patterns and aligns employee behavior with the corporate vision. One global survey of 7,000 business and human resources leaders in 130 countries reported that organizational design was their firm's most important trend or priority to improve human capital (leadership and corporate culture were second and third most important, respectively).[2]

This chapter begins by introducing the two fundamental processes in organizational structure: division of labor and coordination. Next, we examine three of the four main elements of organizational structure: span of control, centralization, and formalization. A separate section describes and assesses the fourth element, departmentalization. The last section of this chapter looks at the contingencies of organizational design, including external environment, organizational size, technology, and strategy.

LO12-1 Describe three types of coordination in organizational structures.

DIVISION OF LABOR AND COORDINATION

All organizational structures include two fundamental requirements: the division of labor into distinct tasks and the coordination of that labor so employees are able to accomplish common goals.[3] Organizations are groups of people who work interdependently toward some purpose. To effectively accomplish this common objective, most work is divided into manageable chunks, particularly when there are many different tasks required to complete the work. Employees need to work interdependently, so organizations introduce coordinating mechanisms to ensure that everyone is working in concert toward the same objectives.

Division of Labor

Division of labor refers to the subdivision of work into separate jobs assigned to different people. Subdivided work leads to job specialization because each job now includes a subset of the

All organizational structures include two fundamental requirements: the division of labor into distinct tasks and the coordination of that labor.
Robert Churchill/Vetta/Getty Images

tasks necessary to complete the product or service. Samsung divides its employees into thousands of specific jobs to more effectively design, manufacture, and market new products. As companies get larger, this horizontal division of labor is usually accompanied by vertical division of labor. Some people are assigned the task of supervising employees, others are responsible for managing those supervisors, and so forth.

Why do companies divide the work into several jobs? As we described in Chapter 5, job specialization increases work efficiency.[4] Job incumbents can master their tasks more quickly when work cycles are shorter. Less time is wasted changing from one task to another. Training costs are lower because employees require fewer physical and mental skills to accomplish the assigned work. Job specialization also makes it easier to match people with specific aptitudes or skills to the jobs for which they are best suited. It is almost impossible for one person working alone to competitively design, manufacture, and market new Samsung mobile/cell phones, solid-state drives, or washing machines; instead, hundreds of people with diverse knowledge and skills are required to perform these work activities.

Coordination of Work Activities

When people divide tasks among themselves, they require coordinating mechanisms to ensure that everyone works in concert. In fact, the extent to which work can be effectively divided among several people, teams, and departments depends on how well the divided work can be coordinated. When an organization divides work beyond its capacity to coordinate that work, individual effort is wasted due to misalignment, duplication, and mistiming of tasks. Coordination also tends to become more expensive and difficult as the division of labor increases. Therefore, companies specialize jobs only to the point where it isn't too costly or challenging to coordinate the people in those jobs.[5]

Every organization—from the two-person tax accounting business to the largest corporate entity—uses one or more of the following coordinating mechanisms:[6] informal communication, formal hierarchy, and standardization (see Exhibit 12.1). These forms of coordination align the work of staff within the same department as well as across work units. Coordinating mechanisms are also critical when several organizations work together, such as in joint ventures and humanitarian aid programs.[7]

Coordination through Informal Communication All organizations rely on informal communication as a coordinating mechanism. This process includes sharing information on mutual tasks as well as forming shared and complementary mental models so employees can more effectively synchronize their work activities using the same cognitive road map.[8] Informal communication is vital in nonroutine and ambiguous situations because employees need to exchange a large volume of information through face-to-face communication and other media-rich channels. Samsung's new structure encourages more informal communication because the company relies on

Exhibit 12.1 Coordinating Mechanisms in Organizations

Form of Coordination	Description	Subtypes/Strategies
Informal communication	Sharing information on mutual tasks; forming common mental models to synchronize work activities.	• Direct communication • Liaison roles • Integrator roles • Temporary cross-functional teams
Formal hierarchy	Assigning legitimate power to individuals, who then use this power to direct work processes and allocate resources.	• Direct supervision • Formal communication channels
Standardization	Creating routine patterns of behavior or output.	• Standardized skills • Standardized processes • Standardized output

Sources: Based on information in J. Galbraith, *Designing Complex Organizations* (Reading, MA: Addison-Wesley, 1973), 8–19; H. Mintzberg, *The Structuring of Organizations* (Englewood Cliffs, NJ: Prentice Hall, 1979), Chap. 1; D.A. Nadler and M.L. Tushman, *Competing by Design: The Power of Organizational Architecture* (New York: Oxford University Press, 1997), Chap. 6.

employee involvement and creativity to generate novel ideas for products and work processes.

Coordination through informal communication is easiest in small firms, but digital technologies have further enabled this coordinating mechanism at Samsung and other large organizations.[9] Some companies also support informal communication by limiting the size of each work site. Magna International follows this principle by keeping many of its plants–including its recently opened paint shop in Hoče, Slovenia–to a maximum size of around 200 employees. The global auto-parts manufacturer has found that employees have difficulty remembering one another's names in plants that are any larger, a situation that makes informal communication more difficult as a coordinating mechanism.[10]

Some large firms encourage informal communication through *integrator roles.* These people coordinate a work process by encouraging employees in each work unit to directly share information and coordinate work activities with one another. Brand managers for luxury perfumes are often integrator roles because they ensure that the work of fragrance developers, bottle designers, advertising creatives, production, and other groups are aligned with the brand's image and meaning.[11] Another informal communication coordination strategy is to have *liaison roles.* These employees transmit information between two work units that seldom communicate or coordinate directly with each other. However, liaison roles are likely less common today because digital communication and decentralized decision making have made it easier and more acceptable for the leaders and staff of work units to informally communicate directly with their counterparts in other work units.

Concurrent engineering is another mechanism for supporting coordination through informal communication in large organizations. This approach organizes people across several functional specializations–production engineering, manufacturing, marketing, purchasing, and so on–into temporary cross-functional teams so they can provide immediate feedback to one another as the product is designed and developed. This form of coordination was pioneered by Toyota four decades ago and today is widespread under various labels across many industries. For example, technology companies have introduced "agile" teams to support informal communication coordination when developing or repairing software or production systems. In contrast, traditional product development passes work from one functional department to the next department in a sequential process. Automakers calls this the "over the wall" effect; technology firms call it the "waterfall effect." Both phrases symbolize the notion that traditional product development suffers from inefficient coordination due to the lack of informal two-way communication and feedback.[12]

Concurrent engineering is a form of coordination through informal communication by organizing people across several functional specializations into temporary cross-functional teams.
Cathy Yeulet/Stockbroker/123RF

Coordination through Formal Hierarchy Informal communication is the most flexible form of coordination, but it can become chaotic as the number of employees increases. Consequently, as organizations grow, they rely increasingly on a second coordinating mechanism: formal hierarchy.[13] Hierarchy assigns legitimate power to individuals (typically managers), who then use this power to direct work processes and allocate resources. In other words, work is coordinated through direct supervision–the chain of command. For instance, Walmart stores have managers and assistant managers who are responsible for ensuring that employees are properly trained, perform their respective tasks, and coordinate effectively with other staff.

Coordination through Micromanagement[14]

23% of 2,000 American workers identify micromanaging as their boss's worst trait (top of list, followed by unavailable and incompetence).

17% of Millennials in a survey of 1,274 US workers say that leaders micromanage them (compared to 10% of GenZ and 7% of baby boomers in that sample).

44% of 1,000 US office workers say they have experienced an uptick in micromanaging since returning to the workplace after the pandemic (18% say micromanaging has lessened).

28% of 2,034 knowledge workers in the US, UK, Germany, Italy, the Netherlands, and Australia say that managers at their company are micromanaging the way they work.

23% of 2,800 American office workers say their current supervisor is a micromanager.

(Photo): Steve Hamblin/Corbis

span of control The number of people reporting directly to someone at the next level above in the hierarchy

A century ago, management scholars applauded formal hierarchy as the best coordinating mechanism for large organizations. They argued that organizations are most effective when managers exercise their authority and employees receive orders from only one supervisor. The chain of command—in which information flows across work units only through supervisors and managers—was viewed as the backbone of organizational strength.

Although still important, formal hierarchy is much less popular today. One problem, which Samsung is trying to minimize with its new structure, is that hierarchical organizations are not as agile for coordination in complex and novel situations. Formal communication through the chain of command is rarely as fast or accurate as informal direct communication among employees. Another concern with formal hierarchy is that managers are able to closely supervise only a limited number of employees. As the business grows, the number of supervisors and layers of management must increase, resulting in a costly bureaucracy. A third problem is that today's workforce demands more autonomy over work and more involvement in company decisions. Coordination through formal hierarchy tends to limit employee autonomy and involvement, which increases employee complaints of being "micromanaged."

Coordination through Standardization Standardization, the third type of coordination, involves creating routine patterns of behavior or output. This coordinating mechanism takes three distinct forms:

- *Standardized processes.* Quality and consistency of a product or service often can be improved by standardizing work activities through job descriptions and procedures.[15] Flowcharts represent coordination through standardized processes. This coordinating mechanism works best when the task is routine (such as mass production) or simple (such as stocking shelves), but it is less effective in nonroutine and complex work such as product design or executive decision making.
- *Standardized outputs.* This form of standardization involves ensuring that individuals and work units have clearly defined goals and output measures (e.g., customer satisfaction, production efficiency). For instance, to coordinate the work of salespeople, companies assign sales targets rather than specific behaviors.
- *Standardized skills.* When work activities are too complex to standardize through processes or goals, companies coordinate work effort by ensuring that employees have standardized skills. In-house training programs develop employee knowledge and skills so they perform tasks consistent with company expectations. Organizations also rely on standardized skills by carefully hiring people with the requisite education and past experience.

Division of labor and coordination of work represent the two fundamental ingredients of all organizations. But how work is divided, which coordinating mechanisms are emphasized, who makes decisions, and other issues are related to the four elements of organizational structure that we discuss over the next two sections of this chapter.

LO12-2 Discuss the role and effects of span of control, centralization, and formalization and relate these elements to organic and mechanistic organizational structures.

ELEMENTS OF ORGANIZATIONAL STRUCTURE

Every organizational structure consists of four elements. This section introduces three of them: span of control, centralization, and formalization. The fourth element—departmentalization—is presented in the next section of this chapter.

Span of Control

Span of control (also called *span of management*) refers to the number of people reporting directly to someone at the next level above in the hierarchy. A narrow span of control exists when a manager has very few people reporting directly to them; a wide span exists when a manager has many direct reports.[16] A century ago, French engineer and management scholar Henri Fayol strongly recommended a relatively narrow span of control, typically no more than 20 employees per supervisor and 6 supervisors per manager. Fayol championed formal hierarchy as the primary coordinating mechanism, so he believed that supervisors should closely monitor and coach employees. His views were similar to those of Napoleon Bonaparte, who declared that senior military leaders should have no more than five officers directly reporting to them. These prescriptions were based on the belief that managers would not be able to monitor and control any more subordinates closely enough.[17]

Today, we know better. The best-performing manufacturing plants currently have an average of 38 production employees per supervisor (see Exhibit 12.2).[18] What's the secret here? Did Fayol, Napoleon, and others miscalculate the optimal span of control? The answer is that those who lauded hierarchical control believed that employees should perform the physical tasks, whereas supervisors and other management personnel should make the decisions and monitor employees to make sure they performed their tasks.

In contrast, the best-performing manufacturing operations today rely on self-directed teams, so direct supervision (formal hierarchy) is supplemented with other coordinating mechanisms. Self-directed teams coordinate mainly through informal communication and various forms of standardization (i.e., training and processes), so formal hierarchy has a secondary role in work coordination. Managers can also accommodate a wider span of control when their direct reports coordinate mainly through standardized skills. For instance, nurse managers often have between 25 and 50 direct reports because nurses are professionally trained and have specific protocols to guide most of their work activity.[19]

Exhibit 12.2 Recommended, Actual, Estimated, and Enforced Spans of Control[20]

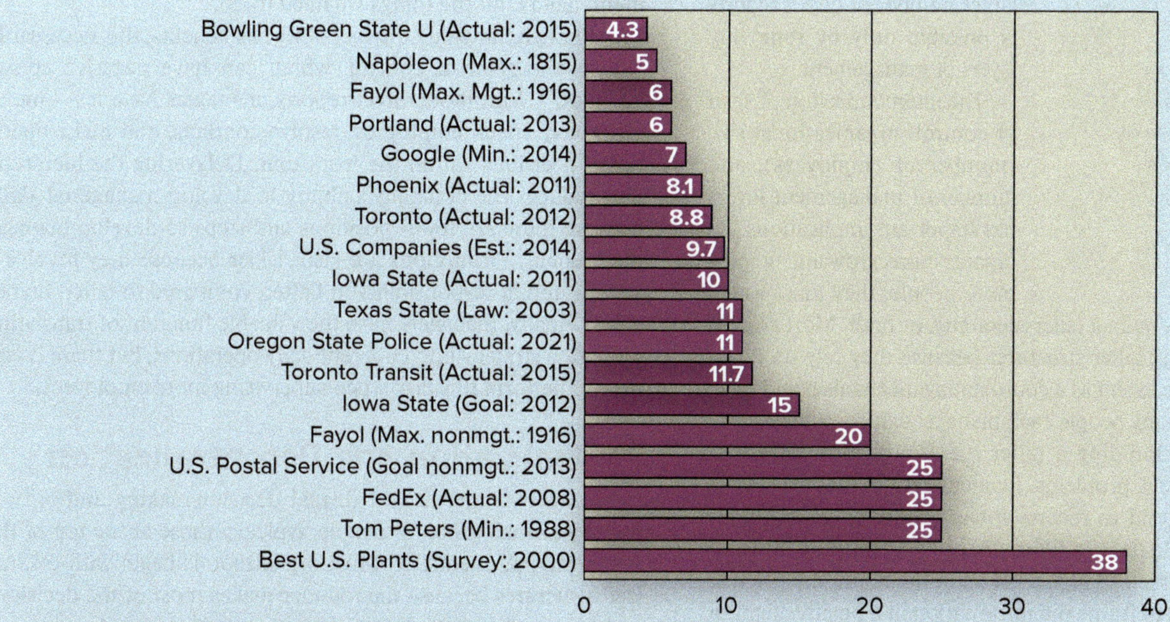

Note: Data represent the average number of direct reports per manager. "Max." is the maximum spans of control recommended by Napoleon Bonaparte and Henri Fayol. "Min." is the minimum span of control applied to teams by Google and recommended by Tom Peters. "Est." is the estimated average span of control across all major U.S. companies, according to consulting firm Deloitte. "Goal" refers to the span of control targets that the U.S. Postal Service and State of Iowa are trying to achieve. (USPS currently exceeds its goal.) The State of Texas number is the span of control mandated by law. The Best U.S. Plants number is the average span of control in American manufacturing facilities identified by *Industry Week* magazine as the most effective. "Actual" refers to the spans of control reported in the cities of Phoenix, Portland, and Toronto; the public service of the U.S. state of Iowa; Bowling Green State University; the Toronto Transit Commission; the Oregon State Police; and FedEx Corporation in the years indicated. The City of Toronto number excludes firefighters and parks, which have unusually high spans of control. When these units are included, Toronto's span of control is 16.3.

A second factor influencing the best span of control is whether employees perform routine tasks. A wider span of control is possible when employees perform routine jobs because they require less direction or advice from supervisors. A narrow span of control is necessary when employees perform novel or complex tasks because these employees tend to require more supervisory decisions and coaching. This principle is illustrated in a survey of property and casualty insurers. The average span of control in commercial-policy processing departments is around 15 employees per supervisor, whereas the span of control is 6.1 in claims service and 5.5 in commercial underwriting. Staff members in the latter two departments perform more technical work, so they have more novel and complex tasks, which requires more supervisor involvement. Commercial-policy processing, on the other hand, is like production work. Tasks are routine and have few exceptions, so managers have less coordinating to do with each employee.[21]

As companies grow and employ more people, they usually build taller structures to enable some degree of direct supervision as a coordinating mechanism.
Rosemary Calvert/Getty Images

A third influence on span of control is the degree of interdependence among employees within the department or team.[22] Generally, a narrow span of control is necessary for highly interdependent jobs because employees tend to experience more conflict with one another, which requires more of a manager's time to resolve. Also, employees are less clear on their personal work performance in highly interdependent tasks, so supervisors spend more time providing coaching and feedback.

Tall versus Flat Structures Span of control is interconnected with organizational size (number of employees) and the number of layers in the organizational hierarchy. Consider two companies with the same number of employees. If Company A has a wider span of control (more direct reports per manager) than Company B, then Company A necessarily has fewer layers of management (i.e., a flatter structure). The reason for this relationship is that a company with a wider span of control has more employees per supervisor,

centralization The degree to which formal decision authority is held by a small group of people, typically those at the top of the organizational hierarchy

formalization Degree to which organizations standardize behavior through rules, procedures, formal training, and related mechanisms

more supervisors for each middle manager, and so forth. This larger number of direct reports is possible only by removing layers of management.

The interconnection of span of control, organizational size (number of employees), and number of management layers has important implications. As organizations grow and employ more people, they must widen the span of control, build a taller hierarchy, or both. Most companies end up building taller structures because they rely on direct supervision to some extent as a coordinating mechanism and there are limits to how many people each manager can coordinate.

Unfortunately, building a taller hierarchy (more layers of management) creates problems. One concern is that executives in tall structures tend to receive lower-quality and less timely information. People tend to filter, distort, and simplify information before it is passed to higher levels in the hierarchy because they are motivated to frame the information in a positive light or to summarize it more efficiently. In contrast, information tends to have less manipulation in flat hierarchies and is often received much more quickly than in tall hierarchies.

A second problem is that taller structures have higher overhead costs. With more managers per employee, tall hierarchies necessarily have more people administering the company, thereby reducing the percentage of staff who are actually making the product or providing the service. A third issue with tall hierarchies is that employees usually feel less empowered and engaged in their work. Hierarchies are power structures, so more levels of hierarchy tend to draw power away from people at the bottom of that hierarchy. Indeed, the size of the hierarchy itself tends to focus power around managers rather than employees.[23]

These problems with tall hierarchies have prompted companies to reduce management layers. For example, Thomson Reuters slashed its hierarchy to a maximum of six layers. The media conglomerate previously had up to 12 layers between the top executive and frontline staff. British personal care products company PZ Cussons also recently flattened its structure by removing regional management layers and decentralizing authority down to individual country teams. Another example is Conagra Foods. CEO Sean Connolly says the packaged food company now has "fewer layers, broader spans of control and the workforce, we believe, is right-sized for speed, empowerment, agility, all the things we need to do."[24]

Although flattening the hierarchy has benefits, this necessarily widens the span of control, which can have negative consequences.[25] With more direct reports, managers have less time to effectively coach employees, resolve conflicts, and make operational decisions within the work unit. Delayering the hierarchy also reduces the company's ability to develop managerial skills because there are fewer positions and steps to develop management talent. Promotions are also riskier because they involve a larger jump in responsibility in flatter, compared to taller, hierarchies. Finally, managers have the valuable function of translating corporate strategy into coherent daily operations, but there is less time to perform this task when supervising more employees.

Centralization and Decentralization

Centralization means that formal decision-making authority is held by a small group of people, typically those at the top of the organizational hierarchy. Most organizations begin with centralized structures because the founder makes most of the decisions and tries to direct the business toward their vision. As organizations grow, however, they diversify and their environments become more complex. Senior executives aren't able to process all the decisions that significantly influence the business. Consequently, larger organizations typically *decentralize*; that is, they disperse decision authority and power throughout the organization.

The optimal level of centralization or decentralization depends on several contingencies that we will examine later in this chapter. However, different degrees of decentralization can occur simultaneously in different parts of an organization. For instance, 7-Eleven centralizes decisions about information technology and supplier purchasing to improve buying power, increase cost-efficiencies, and minimize complexity across the organization. Yet it decentralizes local inventory decisions to store managers because they have the best information about their customers and can respond quickly to local market needs. "We could never predict a busload of football players on a Friday night, but the store manager can," explains a 7-Eleven executive.[26]

Formalization

Formalization is the degree to which organizations standardize behavior through rules, procedures, formal training, and related mechanisms.[27] In other words, companies become more

> Any new idea condemned to struggle upward through multiple levels of rigidly hierarchical, risk-averse management is an idea that won't see daylight . . . until it's too late.[28]
>
> —Sergio Marchionne, former CEO of Fiat Chrysler Automobiles and Ferrari

Large organizations tend to have more formalization because coordinating a large number of people only through direct supervision and informal communication is difficult and costly.
Convisum/123RF

formalized as they increasingly rely on various forms of standardization to coordinate work. Fulfillment by Amazon is well-known–and sometimes infamously identified–for its very high formalization. The warehouse operations for Amazon's third-party sellers relies on standardization of work processes as a coordinating mechanism. Computer algorithms determine how many products employees should pick, move, pack, and store per hour. Even bathroom breaks are apparently timed. As soon as one product is picked, the employee's scanner displays the next item with a countdown of the time allowed to find and scan that item.[29]

Older companies tend to be more formalized because work activities become routinized, making them easier to document into standardized practices. Larger organizations also rely more on formalization because coordinating a large number of people only through direct supervision and informal communication is difficult and costly. External influences, such as government safety legislation and strict accounting rules, also encourage formalization.

Formalization may increase efficiency and compliance, but it also can create problems.[30] Rules and procedures reduce organizational flexibility, so employees follow prescribed behaviors even when the situation clearly calls for a customized response. High levels of formalization tend to undermine creativity. Some work rules become so convoluted that organizational efficiency would decline if they were actually followed as prescribed. Formalization is also a source of job dissatisfaction and work stress. Finally, rules and procedures have been known to take on a life of their own in some organizations. They become the focus of attention rather than the organization's ultimate objectives of producing a product, providing a service, and satisfying stakeholder needs.

Mechanistic versus Organic Structures

We discussed span of control, centralization, and formalization together because they cluster around two broader organizational forms: mechanistic and organic structures (see Exhibit 12.3).[31] A **mechanistic structure** is characterized by a narrow span of control and a high degree of formalization and centralization. Mechanistic structures have many rules and procedures, limited decision making at lower levels, tall hierarchies of people in specialized roles, and vertical rather than horizontal communication flows. Tasks are rigidly defined and are altered only when sanctioned by higher authorities.

Companies with an **organic structure** have the opposite characteristics. They operate with a wide span of control, decentralized decision making, and little formalization. Tasks are fluid, adjusting to new situations and organizational needs. In extremely organic organizations, decision making is decentralized down to teams and individuals, and employees have enough autonomy to adapt their job duties to fit the situation.

As a general rule, mechanistic structures operate better in stable environments because they rely on efficiency and routine behaviors. Organic structures work better in rapidly changing (i.e., dynamic) environments because they are more flexible and responsive to the changes. Organic structures are also more compatible with human capital development (see Chapter 1) because they emphasize information sharing and an empowered workforce rather than hierarchy and status. However, the

mechanistic structure An organizational structure with a narrow span of control and a high degree of formalization and centralization

organic structure An organizational structure with a wide span of control, low formalization, and decentralized decision making

Mc Graw Hill connect

SELF-ASSESSMENT 12.1: Which Organizational Structure Do You Prefer?

Exhibit 12.3 Contrasting Mechanistic and Organic Organizational Structures

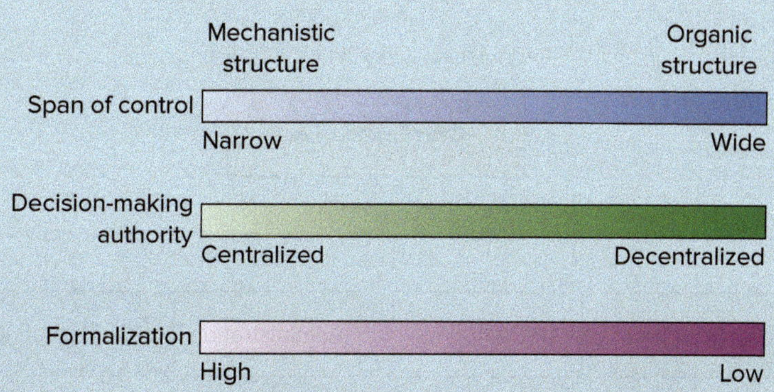

functional structure An organizational structure in which employees are organized around specific knowledge or other resources

effectiveness of organic structures depends on how well employees have developed their roles and expertise.[32] Without these conditions, employees are unable to coordinate effectively with one another, resulting in errors and gross inefficiencies.

LO12-3 Identify and evaluate five types of departmentalization.

FORMS OF DEPARTMENTALIZATION

Span of control, centralization, and formalization are important elements of organizational structure, but most people think about organizational charts when the discussion of organizational structure arises. The organizational chart represents the fourth element in the structuring of organizations, called *departmentalization*. Departmentalization specifies how employees and their activities are grouped together. It is a fundamental strategy for coordinating organizational activities because it influences organizational behavior in the following ways:[33]

- Departmentalization establishes the chain of command—the system of common supervision among positions and units within the organization. It frames the membership of formal work teams and typically determines which positions and units must share resources. Thus, departmentalization establishes interdependencies among employees and subunits.
- Departmentalization focuses people around common mental models or ways of thinking, such as serving clients, developing products, or supporting a particular skill set. This focus is typically anchored around the common budgets and measures of performance assigned to employees within each departmental unit.
- Departmentalization encourages specific people and work units to coordinate through informal communication. With common supervision and resources, members within each configuration typically work near one another, so they can use frequent and informal interaction to get the work done.

There are almost as many organizational charts as there are businesses, but the five most common pure types of departmentalization are simple, functional, divisional, team-based, and matrix.

Simple Structure

The *simple structure* is defined by a lack of complexity.[34] It relies mainly on the business leader's direct supervision of all or most employees rather than more elaborate standardization coordinating mechanisms. Consequently, the simple structure has high centralization (the owner/manager makes most key decisions), a wide span of control (almost everyone reports to the owner/manager), and very little hierarchy (just one or two management layers). It usually exists in organizations with a small number of employees and with a fairly simple product or service offering.

Employees who work in a simple structure tend to perform broadly defined roles because there are insufficient economies of scale to assign them to specialized jobs. As a result, the simple structure is often highly flexible and minimizes the walls that form between work units in other structures. However, this type of structure depends on the owner's direct supervision to coordinate work activities, so it is very difficult to operate as the company grows and becomes more complex.

Functional Structure

As organizations grow, they typically shift from a simple structure to a functional structure. Even after firms adopt more complex organizational structures that we discuss later, they usually have a functional structure at some level of the hierarchy. A **functional structure** organizes employees around specific knowledge or other resources (see Exhibit 12.4). Employees with marketing expertise are grouped into a marketing unit, those with production skills are located in manufacturing, engineers are found in product development, and so forth. Organizations with functional structures are typically centralized to coordinate their activities effectively.

Evaluating the Functional Structure The functional structure creates specialized pools of talent that typically serve everyone in the organization. Pooling talent into one group improves economies of scale compared to dispersing functional specialists over different parts of the organization. The functional structure also increases employee identity with the specialization or profession. Direct supervision is easier in a functional structure because managers oversee people with common issues and expertise.[35]

The functional structure also has limitations.[36] Grouping employees around their skills tends to focus attention on those skills and related professional needs rather than on the company's products, services, or clients. Unless people are rotated through several functional units over time, they might not develop a broader understanding of the business. Compared with other structures, the

Exhibit 12.4 A Functional Organizational Structure

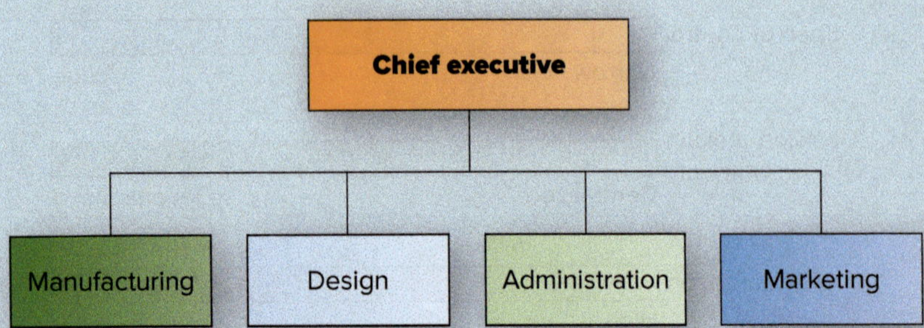

OB THEORY TO PRACTICE

Functional Structure Brings Airbnb Back to Basics[37]

Askar Karimullin/Alamy Stock Photo

Airbnb had a functional structure in its early years (engineering, design, finance, etc.). With rapid growth, the online lodging marketplace company switched to a divisional structure and eventually ballooned to almost a dozen divisions (core host, luxe, business, transportation, etc.). But when the COVID-19 pandemic shut down 80 percent of its business, Airbnb went back to basics.

"The radical thing is we went back to a functional organization," explains CEO Brian Chesky. Large companies tend to be sluggish with a functional structure, but Chesky says the opposite occurred. "When Airbnb became a functional org, suddenly the entire company was on one roadmap. We all had the same exact priorities. There were fewer meetings. Decision-making was faster. Quality was better."

functional structure usually produces more dysfunctional conflict and poorer coordination in serving clients or developing products. These problems occur because employees need to work with coworkers in other departments to complete organizational tasks, yet they have different subgoals and mental models about how to perform the work effectively. Together, these problems require substantial formal controls and coordination when people are organized around functions.

Divisional Structure

The **divisional structure** groups employees around geographic areas, outputs (products or services), or clients. Exhibit 12.5 illustrates these three variations of divisional structure.[38] The *geographic divisional structure* organizes employees around distinct regions of the country or world. Exhibit 12.5(a) illustrates a simplified version of the geographic divisional structure adopted by Kone, the Helsinki-based global elevator and escalator company. The *product/service divisional structure* organizes employees around distinct outputs. Exhibit 12.5(b) illustrates the four product divisions at Medtronic, the medical devices company. The *client divisional structure* organizes employees around specific customer groups. Exhibit 12.5(c) illustrates the client-focused divisional structure at Thomson Reuters, the digital information services company.[39]

divisional structure An organizational structure in which employees are organized around geographic areas, outputs (products or services), or clients

Which form of divisional structure should large organizations adopt? The answer depends mainly on the primary source of environmental diversity or uncertainty.[40] Suppose an organization has one type of product sold to people across the country. If customers have different needs across regions, or if state governments impose different regulations on the product, then a geographic structure would be best so the company can be more vigilant about this diversity. But if the company sells several types of products across the country and customer preferences and government regulations are similar everywhere, then a product structure would likely work best.

Kone, the global elevator and escalator company, is organized mainly around geographic regions; regulations and sales channels for the company's products likely vary much more by region than by product. McDonald's is organized into dozens of countries, which are clustered into three geographic groups led by three top-level executives: USA, International Operated Markets (Canada, Australia, and several developed European countries), and International Developmental Licensee Markets (Asia, Latin America, Middle East, and developing European countries). McDonald's geographic structure makes sense because food preferences and marketing strategies vary around the world; even though it sells the same Big Mac almost everywhere, the fast-food company has more fish products in Hong Kong and more vegetarian products in India, in line with traditional diets in those countries.[41]

Medtronic has numerous country managers to anticipate and respond to unique conditions and decisions in each region. However, the medical devices firm places product groups (cardiac and vascular, diabetes, minimally invasive therapies,

Whether an organization should adopt a geographic, product, or client-focused structure depends mainly on the primary source of environmental diversity or uncertainty.
David Pearson/Alamy Stock Photo

Exhibit 12.5 Three Types of Divisional Structure

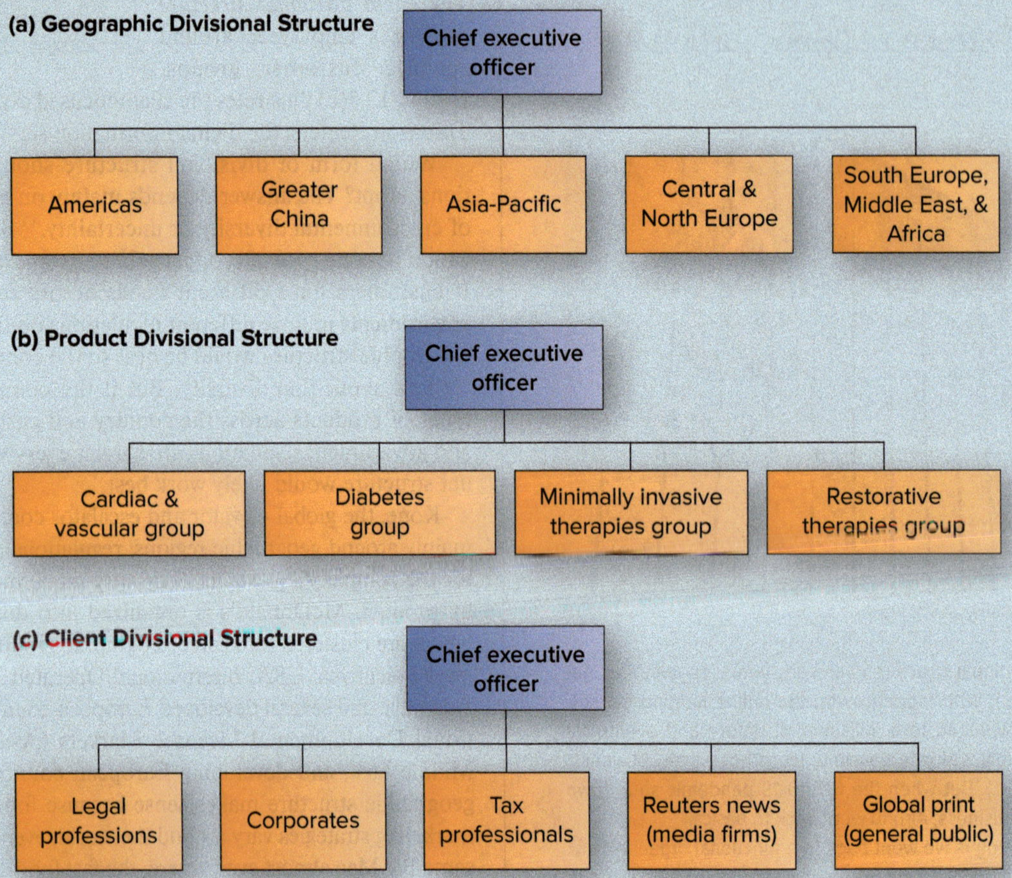

Note: Diagram (a) shows a global geographic divisional structure similar to that of Kone Corporation; diagram (b) depicts the four product divisions of Medtronic; diagram (c) shows the five client divisions of Thomson Reuters. None of these firms has a pure divisional structure. At all three companies the top executive team also includes the heads of some functional units (e.g., finance).

and restorative therapies) at the top of its organizational structure, likely because marketing and manufacturing activities vary much more across product divisions than across regions.

Many companies are moving away from structures that organize people around geographic clusters.[42] One reason is that clients can purchase products online and communicate with businesses from almost anywhere in the world, so local representation is becoming less important. Reduced geographic variation is another reason for the shift away from geographic structures; freer trade has reduced government intervention, and consumer preferences for many products and services are becoming more similar (converging) around the world. The third reason is that large companies increasingly have global business customers who demand one global point of purchase, not one in every country or region.

Evaluating the Divisional Structure The divisional organizational structure is a building-block structure. As the company develops new products, services, or clients, it can sprout new divisions relatively easily. The divisional structure is also outcome-focused. It directs employee attention to customers and products, rather than to their own specialized knowledge.[43]

> **The divisional structure is outcome-focused; it directs employee attention to customers and products, rather than to their own specialized knowledge.**

team-based structure An organizational structure built around self-directed teams that complete an entire piece of work

These advantages are offset by a number of limitations. First, the divisional structure tends to duplicate resources, such as production equipment and engineering or information technology expertise. Also, unless the division is quite large, resources are not used as efficiently as they are in functional structures where resources are pooled across the entire organization. The divisional structure also creates silos of knowledge. Expertise is spread across several autonomous business units, and this reduces the ability and perhaps motivation of the people in one division to share their knowledge with counterparts in other divisions. In contrast, a functional structure groups experts together, thereby supporting knowledge sharing within areas of expertise.

Finally, the preferred divisional structure depends on the company's primary source of environmental diversity or uncertainty. This principle seems to be applied easily enough at Kone and Thomson Reuters, but many global organizations experience diversity and uncertainty in terms of geography, product, *and* clients. Consequently, some organizations revise their structures back and forth or create complex structures that attempt to give all three dimensions equal status. This muddling generates further complications because organizational structure decisions shift power and status among executives. If the company switches from a geographic to a product structure, people who lead the geographic fiefdoms suddenly get demoted under the product chiefs. In short, leaders of global organizations struggle to find the best divisional structure, often resulting in the departure of some executives and frustration among those who remain.

Team-Based Structure

A **team-based structure** is built around self-directed teams that complete an entire piece of work, such as assembling an aircraft engine or developing an electronic game. This type of structure is usually organic. There is a wide span of control because teams operate with minimal supervision. Some team-based structures have no formal leaders within each team, just someone selected by other team members to help coordinate the work and liaise with plant or company management.

Team structures are highly decentralized because almost all day-to-day decisions are made by team members rather than someone further up the organizational hierarchy. Many team-based structures also have low formalization because teams are given relatively few rules about how to organize their work. Instead, executives assign quality and quantity output targets, and often productivity improvement goals, to each team. Teams are then encouraged to use available resources and their own initiative to achieve those objectives.

Team-based structures are usually found within the manufacturing or service operations of larger divisional structures. Several GE aircraft engine plants are organized as team-based structures, but these plants operate within GE's larger divisional structure. A small number of firms apply the team-based structure from top to bottom, including Morning Star Company, W. L. Gore & Associates, and Valve Corporation, where almost all employees work in teams.

Evaluating the Team-Based Structure The team-based structure has gained popularity because it is usually flexible and responsive in turbulent environments.[44] It tends to reduce costs because teams have less reliance on formal hierarchy (direct supervision). A cross-functional team structure improves communication, coordination, and cooperation across traditional specialist boundaries. With greater autonomy, this structure also allows quicker and more informed decision making.[45] For this reason, some hospitals have shifted from functional departments to cross-functional teams. Teams composed of nurses, radiologists, anesthetists, a pharmacology representative, possibly social workers, a rehabilitation therapist, and other specialists work together more efficiently and effectively, thereby reducing delays and errors.[46]

The team-based structure also has several limitations. It can be costly to maintain due to the need for ongoing interpersonal skills training. Teamwork potentially takes more time to coordinate than formal hierarchy during the early stages of team development. Employees may experience more stress due to increased ambiguity in their roles. Team leaders also experience more stress due to increased conflict, loss of functional power, and unclear career progression ladders. In addition, team structures suffer from duplication of resources and potential competition (and lack of resource sharing) across teams.[47]

Matrix Structure

Until a few years ago, Shiseido Company, Limited was heavily dependent on sales in Japan. Most executives at the Tokyo-based cosmetics company were in charge of specialized functions (finance, supply chain, marketing, cosmetics research, etc.). One executive led the company's non-Japanese operations. When Masahiko Uotani became Shiseido's first externally hired CEO, the former Coca-Cola executive recognized that Shiseido

Some hospitals have shifted from functional departments to cross-functional teams to improve communication, coordination, and cooperation across traditional specialist boundaries.
PeopleImages/Getty Images

matrix structure An organizational structure that overlays two structures (such as a geographic divisional and a product divisional structure) in order to leverage the benefits of both

needed to boost the company's global footprint and, at the same time, assign more priority to the company's brands (product groups). To achieve this, he adopted a matrix organizational structure that gave equal power to Shiseido's six global regions and four broad product (brand) groups. Over the next five years, Shiseido's global business soared and the company's share price more than tripled.[48]

Shiseido has a **matrix structure**, which mainly overlays two structures (in this case, a geographic and a product divisional structure) to leverage the benefits of both.[49] Exhibit 12.6 illustrates a matrix structure similar to how Shiseido is organized. The horizontal bars represent the product groups; the vertical bars represent the regions. The "Travel Retail" group represents the global duty-free business.

A common mistake is to assume that everyone in a matrix organizational structure reports to two bosses. In a pure matrix structure of this type, usually only executives at the region-product intersection report to both the regional CEO and to the global brand leader. Employees below the regional head of a product group report to only one manager. Also keep in mind that many matrix structures aren't "pure" because one leader may have somewhat more authority than the other. For instance, Shiseido's regional CEOs likely have more power because the company's revenue and profits are reported by region, not by product.

A global company with a matrix structure most likely has a geographic-product structure. But some global firms have a matrix structure that intersects products (brands) with functions. H&M Group (H&M Hennes & Mauritz AB) has a product-function matrix structure that intersects its store brands (H&M, H&M Home, Monki, & Other Stories, Weekday, COS, ARKET, Afound) with several functional groups (finance, sustainability, human resources, etc.). For instance, COS's head of sustainability likely reports to both the COS managing director and to H&M Group's top executive responsible for sustainability.[50]

A considerably different form of matrix structure, which can be applied to small or large companies, overlays a functional structure with projects.[51] BioWare adopted this project-functional matrix structure soon after the electronic games

One matrix structure overlays functions with projects; employees have a permanent functional unit but are continuously assigned to temporary project teams.

Exhibit 12.6 Matrix Organizational Structure Similar to Shiseido

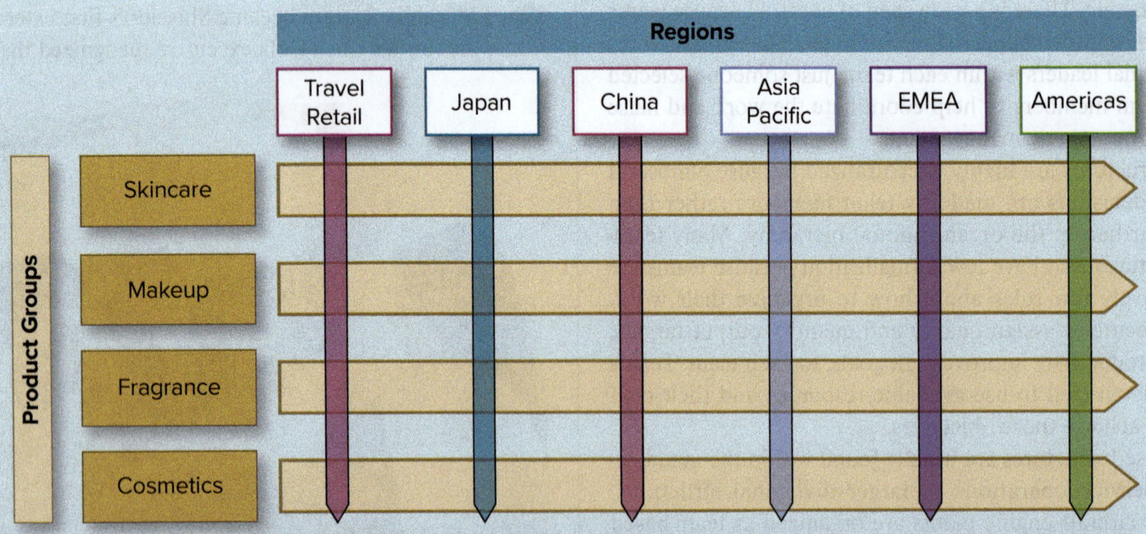

Note: This diagram is a simplified adaptation of Shiseido's most recent matrix structure intersecting geographic regions with products (brands). This diagram shows a pure matrix structure, in which both product leaders and regional leaders have equal power. However, Shiseido's revenue is reported by region, so a regional brand director likely reports to the regional CEO and the global brand executive has only advisory authority over the regional brand director. Also, some products (e.g., cosmetics) are not sold in some regions, so there is no executive for that product in that region. Also not shown is that Shiseido has some degree of matrix structure of headquarters functional departments with regions.

company was born a few decades ago and returned to this matrix structure in recent years. Most employees in a project-functional matrix structure have two managers. One manager leads the specific project to which employees are assigned, such as a specific game, client project, or software app. The other manager is head of the employee's functional specialization, such as engineering, programming, audio, quality assurance, and design.[52] Employees are assigned permanently to a functional unit but physically work with a temporary project team. When the project nears completion, the functional boss reassigns employees in their functional specialization to other projects.

Evaluating the Matrix Structure The project-functional matrix structure usually makes very good use of resources and expertise, making it well-suited for project-based organizations with fluctuating workloads. When properly managed, this form of departmentalization improves communication efficiency, project flexibility, and innovation, compared to purely functional or divisional designs. It focuses employees on serving clients or creating products, yet keeps them organized around their specialization. The result is improved knowledge sharing and more efficient assignment of staff to where they are most needed.

Matrix structures for global organizations are also a logical choice when, as in the case of Shiseido Company, two different dimensions (regions and products) are equally important. Structures determine executive power and what should receive priority; the matrix structure works best when the business environment is complex and two different dimensions deserve equal attention and integration. Executives who have worked in a global matrix also say they have more freedom, likely because their two bosses are more advisory and less oriented toward command-and-control leadership.[53]

In spite of these advantages, the matrix structure has several well-known problems.[54] One concern is that it increases conflict among managers who equally share power. Employees working at the matrix level have two bosses and, consequently, two sets of priorities that aren't always aligned with each other. Project leaders might squabble with functional leaders regarding the assignment of specific employees to projects as well as regarding the employee's technical competence. However, successful companies manage this conflict by developing and promoting leaders who can work effectively in matrix structures. "Of course there's potential for friction," says an executive at IBM India. "In fact, one of the prerequisites to attaining a leadership position at IBM is the ability to function in a matrix structure."[55]

Ambiguous accountability is another challenge with matrix structures. In a functional or divisional structure, one manager is responsible for everything, even the most unexpected issues. But in a matrix structure, the unusual problems don't get resolved because neither manager takes ownership of them.[56] Due to this ambiguous accountability, matrix structures have been blamed for corporate ethical misconduct, such as embezzlement at Hana Financial Group in Korea and massive bribery at Siemens AG in Germany. The combination of dysfunctional conflict and ambiguous accountability in matrix structures also explains why some employees experience more stress and why some managers are less satisfied with their work arrangements.

LO12-4 Explain how the external environment, organizational size, technology, and strategy are relevant when designing an organizational structure.

CONTINGENCIES OF ORGANIZATIONAL DESIGN

Most organizational behavior theories and concepts have contingencies: Ideas that work well in one situation might not work as well in another situation. This contingency approach is relevant when choosing the most appropriate organizational structure.[57] In this section, we introduce four contingencies of organizational design: external environment, size, technology, and strategy.

External Environment

The best structure for an organization depends on its external environment. The external environment includes anything outside the organization, including most stakeholders (e.g., clients, suppliers, government), resources (e.g., raw materials, human resources, information, finances), and competitors. Four characteristics of external environments influence the type of organizational structure best suited to a particular situation: dynamism, complexity, diversity, and hostility.[58]

Dynamic versus Stable Environments Dynamic environments have a high rate of change, leading to unfamiliar situations and a lack of identifiable patterns. Organic structures operate well in dynamic environments. Employees are experienced and

> "The more accountable I can make you, the easier it is for you to show you're a great performer. The more I use a matrix, the easier I make it to blame someone else.[59]"
>
> —Mark Hurd, former Oracle and Hewlett-Packard executive

Mechanistic structures are better suited to stable environments, which have regular cycles of activity, as well as predictable changes in supply for raw materials and demand for finished products.
Monty Rakusen/Getty Images

coordinate well in teams, which enables the organization to adapt more quickly to changes.[60] In contrast, stable environments are characterized by regular cycles of activity, as well as predictable changes in supply for raw materials and demand for finished products. Events are more predictable, enabling the firm to apply rules and procedures. Mechanistic structures are more efficient when the environment is predictable, so they tend to be more profitable than organic structures under these conditions.

Complex versus Simple Environments Complex environments have many elements, whereas simple environments have few things to monitor. As an example, a major university library operates in a more complex environment than a small-town public library. The university library's clients require several types of services, such as book borrowing, online full-text databases, research centers, and course reserve collections. A small-town public library has fewer of these demands placed on it. The more complex the environment, the more decentralized the organization should become. Decentralization is a logical choice for complex environments because decisions are pushed down to people and subunits who possess the information needed to make informed choices.

Diverse versus Integrated Environments Organizations located in an integrated environment have only one type of client and product and serve only one geographic area. In integrated environments, organizations tend to be more effective with a functional structure. Organizations located in diverse environments have a greater variety of products or services, clients, and regions. The more diversified the environment, the more large firms need to adopt a divisional structure aligned with that diversity. If a company sells a single product globally and its design, marketing, or delivery need to be adapted to specific regions, then a geographic divisional structure would align best with that regional diversity. Diverse environments also call for decentralization. By pushing decision making further down the hierarchy, the company can adapt better and more quickly to diverse clients, government requirements, and other circumstances related to that diversity.

Hostile versus Munificent Environments Firms located in hostile environments face resource scarcity and more competition in the marketplace. These conditions are typically dynamic as well because they reduce the predictability of access to resources and demand for outputs. Organic structures tend to be best in hostile environments. However, when the environment is extremely unfavorable–such as during the COVID-19 pandemic or when there is a severe shortage of raw production materials–organizations tend to temporarily centralize so that decisions can be made more quickly and executives feel more comfortable being in control.[61] Ironically, centralization may result in lower-quality decisions during organizational crises because top management has less information, particularly when the environment is complex.[62]

Organizational Size

The organizational structures of large firms differ from those of smaller ones, for good reason.[63] As the number of employees increases, job specialization increases due to a greater division of labor. The greater division of labor requires more elaborate coordinating mechanisms. Thus, larger firms make greater use of standardization (particularly work processes and outcomes) to coordinate work activities. These coordinating mechanisms create an administrative hierarchy and greater formalization. Historically, growing organizations reduced their reliance on informal communication as a coordinating mechanism. However, emerging digital technologies have enabled large firms to coordinate work more through informal communication than was previously possible.[64]

Larger organizations also tend to be more decentralized than are smaller organizations. Executives have neither sufficient time nor expertise to process all the decisions that significantly influence the business as it grows. Therefore, decision-making authority is pushed down to lower levels, where employees are able to make decisions on issues within their narrower range of responsibility.

Technology

Technology is another factor to consider when designing the best organizational structure for the situation.[65] *Technology* refers to the mechanisms or processes an organization relies on to make its products or services. In other words, technology isn't just the equipment used to make something; it also includes how the production process is physically arranged and how the production work is divided among employees.

The two main technological contingencies are task variability and task analyzability, both of which we described as job characteristics in Chapter 5. *Task variability* refers to how predictable the job duties are from one day to the next. In jobs with high

organizational strategy The way the organization positions itself in its environment in relation to its stakeholders, given the organization's resources, capabilities, and mission

Connect

SELF-ASSESSMENT 12.2: Does Your Job Require an Organic or Mechanistic Structure?

> A mechanistic organizational structure is preferred where production work has low task variability and high task analyzability, such as an assembly line.

variability, employees perform several types of tasks, but they don't know which of those tasks are required from one day to the next. Low variability occurs when the work is highly routine and predictable. *Task analyzability* refers to how much the job can be performed using known procedures and rules. In jobs with high task analyzability, employees have well-defined guidelines to direct them through the work process. In jobs with low task analyzability, employees tackle unique situations with few (if any) guidelines to help them determine the best course of action.

An organic structure should be introduced where employees perform tasks with high variability and low analyzability, such as in a research setting. The reason is that employees face unique situations with little opportunity for repetition. In contrast, a mechanistic organizational structure is preferred where production work has low task variability and high task analyzability, such as an assembly line. Assembly work is routine, is highly predictable, and has well-established procedures—an ideal situation for a mechanistic structure to operate efficiently.

Organizational Strategy

Organizational strategy refers to the way the organization positions itself in its environment in relation to its stakeholders, given the organization's resources, capabilities, and mission.[66] In other words, strategy represents the decisions and actions applied to achieve the organization's goals. Although size, technology, and environment influence the optimal organizational structure, these contingencies do not necessarily determine structure. Instead, corporate leaders formulate and implement strategies that shape both the characteristics of these contingencies as well as the organization's resulting structure.

This concept is summed up with the simple phrase "structure follows strategy."[67] Organizational leaders decide how large to grow and which technologies to use. They take steps to define and manipulate their environments, rather than let the organization's fate be entirely determined by external influences (see the open systems view in Chapter 1). Furthermore, organizational structures don't evolve as a natural response to environmental conditions; they are the outcomes of conscious human decisions. Thus, organizational strategy influences both the contingencies of structure and the structure itself.

If a company's strategy is to compete through innovation, a more organic structure would be preferred because it is easier for employees to share knowledge and be creative. If a company chooses a low-cost strategy, a mechanistic structure is preferred because it maximizes production and service efficiency.[68] Overall, organizational structure is influenced by size, technology, and environment, but the organization's strategy may reshape these elements and loosen their connection to organizational structure.

OB THEORY TO PRACTICE

Choosing the Best Organizational Structure

Contingency Variable	Recommendation
Dynamic versus stable environment	Organic structures are better in dynamic environments; mechanistic structures are usually more effective for stable environments.
Complex versus simple environment	Organizations should be more decentralized as environments become more complex.
Diverse versus integrated environment	A functional organizational structure tends to work better in an integrated environment. In diversified environments, large organizations should adopt a divisional structure aligned with the main form of diversity. Also, organizations need to become more decentralized as their environment becomes more diversified.
Hostile versus munificent environment	Organic structures are more suitable for hostile environments; mechanistic structures are usually more effective in munificent environments.
Organizational size	As companies grow, they should make greater use of standardization for coordination and should become more decentralized.
Technology: task variability and task analyzability	Organic structures are better where tasks have high variability and low analyzability; mechanistic structures are better where production involves low variability and high analyzability tasks.
Organizational strategy	An organic structure is better when the company's strategy is to compete through innovation; a mechanistic structure is better when the organization chooses a low-cost strategy.

Study Checklist

Connect® is available for *M: Organizational Behavior.* Additional resources include:

✓ Exercises:

- **Case Analysis:** Apply concepts within the context of a real-world situation.
- **Click and Drag:** Helps make the connection between theory and application through matching, ranking, or grouping activities.
- **Video Case:** See management in action through interactive videos.
- **Self-Assessment:** Designed to promote student self-awareness and reflection, these research-based surveys contain detailed feedback for students.
- **Application-Based Activities:** These highly interactive, application- and analysis-based exercises allow students to take on specific roles to complete management related tasks within a real-world context.

✓ **SmartBook 2.0**™—Smartbook 2.0 is an adaptive learning solution that provides personalized learning to individual student needs, continually adapts to pinpoint knowledge gaps and focuses learning on concepts requiring additional study. It fosters more productive learning, takes the guesswork out of what to study, and helps students better prepare for class.

Notes

1. J.-S. Song, "Samsung's Organizational Culture to Change Like Google," *The Kyunghyang Shinmun*, June 28, 2016; M.-H. Lee, "Samsung to Demolish Rigid, Top-Down Corporate Culture," *Korea Times*, February 11, 2017; E.-K. Choi and T.-H. Lee, "Samsung Electronics May Make Its Org Chart Very Flat," *Korea JoongAng Daily*, November 17, 2021; S.-B. Lee and H.-S. Song, "Samsung to Adopt Flatter Hierarchy to Lure Young Talent," *The Korea Economic Daily*, November 29, 2021.
2. S. Ranson, R. Hinings, and R. Greenwood, "The Structuring of Organizational Structure," *Administrative Science Quarterly* 25 (1980): 1–14; J.E. Johanson, "Intraorganizational Influence," *Management Communication Quarterly* 13 (2000): 393–435; K. Walsh, "Interpreting the Impact of Culture on Structure," *Journal of Applied Behavioral Science* 40, no. 3 (2004): 302–22. The global survey is reported in J. Bersin et al., "The New Organization: Different by Design," in *Global Human Capital Trends 2016* (Westlake, TX: Deloitte University Press, 2016), 1–14.
3. H. Mintzberg, *The Structuring of Organizations* (Englewood Cliffs, NJ: Prentice Hall, 1979), 2–3.
4. E.E. Lawler III, *Motivation in Work Organizations* (Monterey, CA: Brooks/Cole, 1973); M.A. Campion, "Ability Requirement Implications of Job Design: An Interdisciplinary Perspective," *Personnel Psychology* 42 (1989): 1–24.
5. G.S. Becker and K.M. Murphy, "The Division of Labor, Coordination Costs, and Knowledge," *Quarterly Journal of Economics* 107, no. 4 (1992): 1137–60; L. Borghans and B. Weel, "The Division of Labour, Worker Organisation, and Technological Change," *The Economic Journal* 116, no. 509 (2006): F45–F72.
6. H. Mintzberg, *The Structuring of Organizations* (Englewood Cliffs, NJ: Prentice Hall, 1979), Chap. 1; D.A. Nadler and M.L. Tushman, *Competing by Design: The Power of Organizational Architecture* (New York: Oxford University Press, 1997), Chap. 6; J.R. Galbraith, *Designing Organizations: An Executive Guide to Strategy, Structure, and Process* (San Francisco: Jossey-Bass, 2002), Chap. 4.
7. J. Stephenson Jr., "Making Humanitarian Relief Networks More Effective: Operational Coordination, Trust and Sense Making," *Disasters* 29, no. 4 (2005): 337.
8. R.R. Gulati, "Silo Busting," *Harvard Business Review* 85, no. 5 (2007): 98–108; R. Müller and C.H. Antoni, "Individual Perceptions of Shared Mental Models of Information and Communication Technology (ICT) and Virtual Team Coordination and Performance–The Moderating Role of Flexibility in ICT Use," *Group Dynamics: Theory, Research, and Practice* 24, no. 3 (2020): 186–200.
9. L. Borghans and B. Weel, "The Division of Labour, Worker Organisation, and Technological Change," *The Economic Journal* 116, no. 509 (2006): F45–F72.
10. T. Van Alphen, "Magna in Overdrive," *Toronto Star*, July 24, 2006; "Production at Magna Paint Shop Finally under Way," news release (Hoče, Slovenia: Magna Steyr, March 19, 2019).
11. J.R. Galbraith, *Designing Organizations: An Executive Guide to Strategy, Structure, and Process* (San Francisco, CA: Jossey-Bass, 2002), 66–72; D. Aaker, *Spanning Silos: The New CMO Imperative* (Cambridge, MA: Harvard Business Press, 2008), 95–96; A. Pike, *Brands and Branding Geographies* (Cheltenham, UK: Edward Elgar, 2011), 133.
12. S.M. Sapuan, M.R. Osman, and Y. Nukman, "State of the Art of the Concurrent Engineering Technique in the Automotive Industry," *Journal of Engineering Design* 17, no. 2 (2006): 143–57; D.M. Anderson, *Design for Manufacturing: How to Use Concurrent Engineering to Rapidly Develop Low-Cost, High-Quality Products for Lean Management* (Boca Raton, FL: CRC Press/Taylor & Francis, 2014), Chap. 2.
13. A.H. Van De Ven, A.L. Delbecq, and R.J. Koenig Jr., "Determinants of Coordination Modes within Organizations," *American Sociological Review* 41, no. 2 (1976): 322–38.

14. "Survey Reveals Cities Where Workers Are Most (and Least) Happy with Bosses," News Release (Menlo Park, Calif.: Robert Half, October 11, 2018); K. Morris, "Here Are the States Where People Dislike Their Boss the Most—and Why," *Zippia-Advice* (blog), July 16, 2020; "Global Survey: A Leadership Crisis Is Threatening the Future of Work" (Ottawa, Ont.: Alludo (Cascade Parent Ltd.), November 2022); A. Marks, "What Keeps People at Their Jobs? Turns out, It's the Satisfaction of a Job Well Done," *Envoy* (blog), February 22, 2023.

15. Y.M. Hsieh and A.T. Hsieh, "Enhancement of Service Quality with Job Standardisation," *Service Industries Journal* 21 (2001): 147–66.

16. B. Davison, "Management Span of Control: How Wide Is Too Wide?," *Journal of Business Strategy* 24, no. 4 (2003): 22–29; N.A. Theobald and S. Nicholson-Crotty, "The Many Faces of Span of Control: Organizational Structure across Multiple Goals," *Administration Society* 36, no. 6 (2005): 648–60; R.M. Meyer, "Span of Management: Concept Analysis," *Journal of Advanced Nursing* 63, no. 1 (2008): 104–12.

17. D.D. Van Fleet and A.G. Bedeian, "A History of the Span of Management," *Academy of Management Review* 2 (1977): 356–72; H. Fayol, *General and Industrial Management*, trans. C. Storrs (London: Pitman, 1949); D.A. Wren, A.G. Bedeian, and J.D. Breeze, "The Foundations of Henri Fayol's Administrative Theory," *Management Decision* 40, no. 9 (2002): 906–18.

18. D. Drickhamer, "Lessons from the Leading Edge," *IndustryWeek*, February 21, 2000, 23–26.

19. For examples of nurse manager span of control, see: D. Jones et al., "Nurse Manager Scope and Span of Control: An Objective Business and Measurement Model" (AONE 45th Annual Conference, Denver, 2013); R.O. Sherman, "Span of Control in Nurse Leader Roles," *Emerging Nurse Leader* (blog), June 27, 2013; J.M. Kendall, "Nurse Manager Span of Control and the Impact on Employee Engagement," DNP Projects (University of Kentucky, 2018).

20. Iowa State Legislative Services Agency, *Span of Control*, Fiscal Note, Iowa State (Des Moines: Iowa Legislature, March 10, 2011); Western Management Consultants, *Service Efficiency Study Program Management Span of Control Review Report to the City Manager*, City of Toronto (Toronto: October 31, 2012); United States Postal Service, *Supervisor Workhours and Span of Control: Management Advisory* (Washington, DC: United States Postal Service, April 4, 2013); N. Fish and S. Novick, *FY 2013-14 Budget Subcommittee #1 Final Report*, City of Portland, Oregon (Portland, Oregon: April 8, 2013); E. Schmidt and J. Rosenberg, *How Google Works* (New York: Grand Central, 2014), 42–44; S. Stoll, *Accenture Update: Progress Report through August 31, 2015*, Bowling Green University (Bowling Green, OH: September 18, 2015); WMC Consultants, *Toronto Transit Commission Organizational Review Report*, Toronto Transit Commission (Toronto: July 2015); *The New Organization: Different by Design*, Global Human Capital Trends 2016 (New York: Deloitte University Press, 2016); "State of Oregon: Employee Resources and State Workforce–Span of Control," accessed March 13, 2022.

21. J. Greenwald, "Ward Compares the Best with the Rest," *Business Insurance*, August 26, 2002, 16. One recent article also emphasized that claims managers require a narrow span of control. See M.T. Murdock, "Getting Claim Costs under Control: Improve Your Loss Ratio Using These Proven Fundamentals," *Claims Journal*, March 1, 2016.

22. J.H. Gittell, "Supervisory Span, Relational Coordination and Flight Departure Performance: A Reassessment of Postbureaucracy Theory," *Organization Science* 12, no. 4 (2001): 468–83.

23. T.D. Wall, J.L. Cordery, and C.W. Clegg, "Empowerment, Performance, and Operational Uncertainty: A Theoretical Integration," *Applied Psychology: An International Review* 51 (2002): 146–69.

24. Conagra Foods, "Conagra Brands Investor Day," news release (Chicago: CQ FD Disclosure, October 18, 2016); J. Tashea, "With Significant Changes, Thomson Reuters Wants to Be Closer to Its Customers," *ABA Journal*, May 15, 2019; "Building Brands for Life Today and for Future Generations," Annual Report 2021 (Manchester, UK: PZ Cussons, October 2021).

25. Q.N. Huy, "In Praise of Middle Managers," *Harvard Business Review* 79 (2001): 72–79; H.J. Leavitt, *Top Down: Why Hierarchies Are Here to Stay and How to Manage Them More Effectively* (Cambridge: Harvard Business School Press, 2005); "Why Middle Managers May Be the Most Important People in Your Company," *Knowledge @ Wharton*, May 25, 2011; J. Detert, K. Kniffin, and H. Leroy, "Saving Management From Our Obsession With Leadership," *MIT Sloan Management Review* 63, no. 4 (Summer 2022); E. Jacobs, "Middle Managers—on the New Front Line of Office Life," *Financial Times (London)*, September 19, 2022.

26. The variations of decentralization within a company are discussed in G. Masada, "To Centralize or Decentralize?," *Optimize*, May 2005, 58–61. The 7-Eleven example is described in J.G. Kelley, "Slurpees and Sausages: 7-Eleven Holds School," *Richmond* (VA) *Times-Dispatch*, March 12, 2004, C1; S. Marling, "The 24-Hour Supply Chain," *InformationWeek*, January 26, 2004, 43.

27. H. Mintzberg, *The Structuring of Organizations* (Englewood Cliffs, NJ: Prentice Hall, 1979), Chap. 5.

28. S. Marchionne, "Navigating the New Automotive Epoch," *Vital Speeches of the Day* (2010): 134–37.

29. J. Bloodworth, "I Worked in an Amazon Warehouse," *The Guardian*, September 17, 2018; M. Burin, "When You Click 'Buy Now', This Is What Happens inside Amazon Australia's Warehouse," *ABC News (Australia)*, February 27, 2019; M. Zahn and S. Paget, "'Colony of Hell': 911 Calls From Inside Amazon Warehouses," *The Daily Beast*, March 11, 2019.

30. W. Dessein and T. Santos, "Adaptive Organizations," *Journal of Political Economy* 114, no. 5 (2006): 956–95; A.A.M. Nasurdin et al., "Organizational Structure and Organizational Climate as Potential Predictors of Job Stress: Evidence from Malaysia," *International Journal of Commerce and Management* 16, no. 2 (2006): 116–29; C.J. Chen and J.W. Huang, "How Organizational Climate and Structure Affect Knowledge Management—The Social Interaction Perspective," *International Journal of Information Management* 27, no. 2 (2007): 104–18.

31. T. Burns and G. Stalker, *The Management of Innovation* (London: Tavistock, 1961).

32. W.D. Sine, H. Mitsuhashi, and D.A. Kirsch, "Revisiting Burns and Stalker: Formal Structure and New Venture Performance in Emerging Economic Sectors," *Academy of Management Journal* 49, no. 1 (2006): 121–32.

33. H. Mintzberg, *The Structuring of Organizations* (Englewood Cliffs, NJ: Prentice Hall, 1979), 106.

34. H. Mintzberg, *The Structuring of Organizations* (Englewood Cliffs, NJ: Prentice Hall, 1979), Chap. 17; R.M. Burton, B. Obel, and D.D. Håkonsson, *Organizational Design: A Step-by-Step Approach* (Cambridge, UK: Cambridge University Press, 2021), 67–69.

35. J.R. Galbraith, *Designing Organizations: An Executive Guide to Strategy, Structure, and Process* (San Francisco: Jossey-Bass, 2002), 23–25; N. Worren, *Organization Design: Simplifying Complex Systems*, 2nd ed. (Abingdon-on-Thames, UK: Routledge, 2018), Chap. 3; R.M. Burton, B. Obel, and D.D. Håkonsson, *Organizational Design: A Step-by-Step Approach* (Cambridge, UK: Cambridge University Press, 2020), 69–74.

36. E.E. Lawler III, *Rewarding Excellence: Pay Strategies for the New Economy* (San Francisco: Jossey-Bass, 2000), 31–34.

37. N. Patel, "Why the Future of Work Is the Future of Travel, with Airbnb CEO Brian Chesky," *The Verge*, November 16, 2021.

38. The evolutionary development of the divisional structure is described in J.R. Galbraith, "The Evolution of Enterprise Organization Designs," *Journal of Organization Design* 1, no. 2 (2012): 1–13.

39. These structures were identified from corporate websites and annual reports. Most large organizations rely on a mixture of structures (typically functional units along with the divisional units shown here), so the charts shown have been adapted and simplified for learning purposes.

40. M. Goold and A. Campbell, "Do You Have a Well-Designed Organization?," *Harvard Business Review* 80 (2002): 117–24. Others have added factors such as economies of scale and what resources need to be controlled the most. See G. Kesler and A. Kates, *Leading Organization Design: How to Make Organization Design Decisions to Drive the Results You Want* (San Francisco: Jossey-Bass, 2011), Chap. 3.

41. "Our Leadership," McDonald's—Our Company, 2022. The diversity of McDonald's menus in several countries is described in: "Why Is the McDonald's Menu Different in Different Countries?," McDonalds UK-Help-FAQ, May 21, 2018; "The Cultural Marketer: How McDonald's Achieves Brand Success through Cultural Adaptability," *Catalyst Agents* (blog), March 31, 2020; G. Poonia, "Strange McDonald's Menu Items around the World," *Deseret News (Salt Lake City)*, February 18, 2023.

42. J.R. Galbraith, "Structuring Global Organizations," in *Tomorrow's Organization*, ed. S.A. Mohrman et al. (San Francisco: Jossey-Bass, 1998), 103–29; C. Homburg, J.P. Workman Jr., and O. Jensen, "Fundamental Changes in Marketing Organization: The Movement toward a Customer-Focused Organizational Structure," *Academy of Marketing Science Journal* 28 (2000): 459–78; T.H. Davenport, J.G. Harris, and A.K. Kohli, "How Do They Know Their Customers So Well?," *Sloan Management Review* 42 (2001): 63–73; J.R. Galbraith, "Organizing to Deliver Solutions," *Organizational Dynamics* 31 (2002): 194–207.

43. R.M. Burton, B. Obel, and G. DeSanctis, *Organizational Design: A Step-by-Step Approach*, 2nd ed. (Cambridge, UK: Cambridge University Press, 2011), 65–68.

44. J.R. Galbraith, E.E. Lawler III, and Associates, *Organizing for the Future: The New Logic for Managing Complex Organizations* (San Francisco: Jossey-Bass, 1993); R. Bettis and M. Hitt, "The New Competitive Landscape," *Strategic Management Journal* 16 (1995): 7–19.

45. P.C. Ensign, "Interdependence, Coordination, and Structure in Complex Organizations: Implications for Organization Design," *Mid-Atlantic Journal of Business* 34 (1998): 5–22.

46. M.M. Fanning, "A Circular Organization Chart Promotes a Hospital-Wide Focus on Teams," *Hospital & Health Services Administration* 42 (1997): 243–54; B. Cougot et al., "Impact at Two Years of an Intervention on Empowerment among Medical Care Teams: Study Protocol of a Randomised Controlled Trial in a Large French University Hospital," *BMC Health Services Research* 19, no. 1 (2019): 1–13; N. Wellman et al., "Beyond the Pyramid: Alternative Formal Hierarchical Structures and Team Performance," *Academy of Management Journal* 63 (2020): 997–1027.

47. R. Cross, "Looking before You Leap: Assessing the Jump to Teams in Knowledge-Based Work," *Business Horizons* 43, no. 5 (2000): 29–36; M. Fenton-O'Creevy, "Employee Involvement and the Middle Manager: Saboteur or Scapegoat?" *Human Resource Management Journal* 11 (2001): 24–40; G. Garda, K. Lindstrom, and M. Dallnera, "Towards a Learning Organization: The Introduction of a Client-Centered Team-Based Organization in Administrative Surveying Work," *Applied Ergonomics* 34 (2003): 97–105; C. Douglas and W.L. Gardner, "Transition to Self-Directed Work Teams: Implications of Transition Time and Self-Monitoring for Managers' Use of Influence Tactics," *Journal of Organizational Behavior* 25 (2004): 47–65.

48. K. Rozario, "China Closes in on Japan At Beauty Giant Shiseido," *Forbes*, May 14, 2021; "Consolidated Settlement of Accounts for the Fiscal Year Ended December 31, 2021" (Tokyo: Shiseido Company, February 9, 2022). Shiseido may be moving toward a regional structure by giving more power to regions than to brands. See: "WIN 2023 and Beyond: Global Business Transformation" (Tokyo: Shiseido Company, February 2021).

49. S.M. Davis and P.R. Lawrence, *Matrix* (Reading, MA: Addison-Wesley, 1977); J.R. Galbraith, *Designing Matrix Organizations That Actually Work* (San Francisco: Jossey-Bass, 2009); G. Kesler and A. Kates, *Leading Organization Design: How to Make Organization Design Decisions to Drive the Results You Want* (San Francisco: Jossey-Bass, 2011), Chap. 7.

50. "Corporate Governance Report 2022" (Stockholm: H&M Hennes & Mauritz AB, March 2023). Information was also retrieved from LinkedIn accounts of key H&M executives and brands staff.

51. R.C. Ford and W.A. Randolph, "Cross-Functional Structures: A Review and Integration of Matrix Organization and Project Management," *Journal of Management* 18 (1992): 267–94.

52. R. Muzyka and G. Zeschuk, "Managing Multiple Projects," *Game Developer*, March 2003, 34–42; J. Schreier, "BioWare Boss Addresses Studio Issues, Vows To 'Continue Working To Solve Them,'" *Kotaku*, April 4, 2019.

53. J.X.J. Qiu and L. Donaldson, "Stopford and Wells Were Right! MNC Matrix Structures *Do* Fit a 'High-High' Strategy," *Management International Review (MIR)* 52, no. 5 (2012): 671–89; D. Ganguly and M. Mitra, "Survive the Matrix," *Economic Times* (Mumbai, India), March 29, 2013.

54. G. Calabrese, "Communication and Co-operation in Product Development: A Case Study of a European Car Producer," *R&D Management* 27 (1997): 239–52; T. Sy and L.S. D'Annunzio, "Challenges and Strategies of Matrix Organizations: Top-Level and Mid-Level Managers' Perspectives," *Human Resource Planning* 28, no. 1 (2005): 39–48; J. Wolf and W.G. Egelhoff, "An Empirical Evaluation of Conflict in MNC Matrix Structure Firms," *International Business Review* 22, no. 3 (2013): 591–601; R. Sutton and B. Wigert, "Too Many Teams, Too Many Bosses: Overcoming Matrix Madness," *Gallup Workplace*, October 19, 2021.

55. D. Ganguly, "Matrix Evolutions," *Economic Times* (Mumbai, India), February 18, 2012.

56. D.A. Nadler and M.L. Tushman, *Competing by Design: The Power of Organizational Architecture* (New York: Oxford University Press, 1997), Chap. 6; M. Goold and A. Campbell, "Structured Networks: Towards the Well-Designed Matrix," *Long Range Planning* 36, no. 5 (2003): 427–39. The matrix structure problems at Hana Financial and Siemens are discussed in: J.-Y. Lee, "Matrix Structure No Easy Fit for Local Financial Groups," *Korea JoongAng Daily*, February 3, 2012; G. Dietz and N. Gillespie, "Rebuilding Trust: How Siemens Atoned for Its Sins," *The Guardian*, March 26, 2012.

57. L. Donaldson, *The Contingency Theory of Organizations* (Thousand Oaks, CA: Sage, 2001); J. Birkinshaw, R. Nobel, and J. Ridderstråle, "Knowledge as a Contingency Variable: Do the Characteristics of Knowledge Predict Organizational Structure?," *Organization Science* 13, no. 3 (2002): 274–89.

58. P.R. Lawrence and J.W. Lorsch, *Organization and Environment* (Homewood, IL: Irwin, 1967); H. Mintzberg, *The Structuring of Organizations* (Englewood Cliffs, NJ: Prentice Hall, 1979), Chap. 15.

59. D. Ciampa and M. Watkins, "Rx for New CEOs," *Chief Executive*, January 2008.

60. T. Burns and G. Stalker, *The Management of Innovation* (London: Tavistock, 1961); P.R. Lawrence and J.W. Lorsch, *Organization and Environment* (Homewood, IL: Irwin, 1967).

61. B.M. Staw, L.E. Sandelands, and J.E. Dutton, "Threat Rigidity Effects in Organizational Behavior: A Multilevel Analysis," *Administrative Science Quarterly* 26, no. 4 (1981): 501–24; Z. Bakonyi and B. Muraközy, "Centralization of Strategic Decisions during the Great Recession," *Managerial and Decision Economics* 40, no. 4 (2019): 394–413.

62. P. Aghion et al., "Turbulence, Firm Decentralization, and Growth in Bad Times," *American Economic Journal: Applied Economics* 13, no. 1 (2021): 133–69.

63. D.S. Pugh and C.R. Hinings, *Organizational Structure: Extensions and Replications* (Farnborough, UK: Lexington Books, 1976); H. Mintzberg, *The Structuring of Organizations* (Englewood Cliffs, NJ: Prentice Hall, 1979), Chap. 13.

64. G. Hertel, S. Geister, and U. Konradt, "Managing Virtual Teams: A Review of Current Empirical Research," *Human Resource Management Review* 15 (2005): 69–95; J.R. Galbraith, *Designing Matrix Organizations That Actually Work* (San Francisco: Jossey-Bass, 2009), 52–55.

65. C. Perrow, "A Framework for the Comparative Analysis of Organizations," *American Sociological Review* 32 (1967): 194–208; D. Gerwin, "The Comparative Analysis of Structure and Technology: A Critical Appraisal," *Academy of Management Review* 4, no. 1 (1979): 41–51; C.C. Miller et al., "Understanding Technology-Structure Relationships: Theory Development and Meta-Analytic Theory Testing," *Academy of Management Journal* 34, no. 2 (1991): 370–99.

66. R.H. Kilmann, *Beyond the Quick Fix* (San Francisco: Jossey-Bass, 1984), 38.

67. A.D. Chandler, *Strategy and Structure* (Cambridge, MA: MIT Press, 1962).

68. D. Miller, "Configurations of Strategy and Structure," *Strategic Management Journal* 7 (1986): 233–49.

13 Organizational Culture

Fredrick Kippe/Alamy Stock Photo

Learning Objectives

After reading this chapter, you should be able to:

LO13-1 Describe the elements of organizational culture and discuss the importance of organizational subcultures.

LO13-2 Describe four categories of artifacts through which corporate culture is deciphered.

LO13-3 Discuss the importance of organizational culture and the conditions under which organizational culture strength improves organizational performance.

LO13-4 Compare and contrast four strategies for merging organizational cultures.

LO13-5 Describe five strategies for changing and strengthening an organization's culture, including the application of attraction–selection–attrition theory.

LO13-6 Describe the organizational socialization process and identify strategies to improve that process.

organizational culture
The values, norms, and assumptions shared among organizational members

René Lacerte actively created Bill.com's organizational culture when he founded the cloud-based digital business payments company. "The culture of the company was defined and set before we hired our first employee," says Lacerte. "'Humble, Passionate, Dedicated, Authentic and Fun' describes what we at Bill.com all value today and what we'll still value tomorrow."

Bill.com has a strong corporate culture, but Lacerte points out that the San Jose-based company also has subcultures. "As a company grows and scales, it will inevitably develop subcultures. For example, your sales team may have a different working style than your product team."

Lacerte views subcultures as potentially good for the company. "Different leaders might view these subcultures as a threat or somehow diluting the overall culture," says Lacerte "I don't view them that way at all. In fact, I embrace these subcultures and encourage guiding them so they can individually grow and help the larger team thrive by virtue of their differences."

Lacerte says that strong cultures are self-monitoring; they recognize when a subculture is misaligned with the company's core values and with its stakeholder relationships. But most subcultures are beneficial because they provide a unique interpretation and application of the dominant values. Lacerte offers this example: "We have a team with a stronger bias toward urgency than others. While urgency is not one of our values, the principle of speed is how that team expresses their *passion* for moving quickly and *dedication* to the customer. It's their special ingredient."[1]

The phrase "organizational culture" was rarely uttered before 1982.[2] Today, René Lacerte and other leaders monitor and actively try to influence the company's culture, recognizing that it may be an important factor in the firm's survival and success. **Organizational culture** consists of the values, norms, and assumptions that are shared among organizational members.[3] It defines what is important and unimportant in the company and, consequently, directs everyone in the organization toward the "right way" of doing things. You might think of organizational culture as the company's DNA–invisible to the naked eye, yet a powerful template that shapes workplace decisions and behavior.

This chapter begins by identifying the elements of organizational culture and then describing how culture is deciphered through artifacts. Next, we examine the relationship between organizational culture and organizational effectiveness, including the effects of cultural strength, environmental fit, and adaptability. Our attention then turns to strategies for merging organizational cultures. The latter part of this chapter examines ways to change and strengthen organizational culture, and looks more closely at the related topic of organizational socialization.

LO13-1 Describe the elements of organizational culture and discuss the importance of organizational subcultures.

ELEMENTS OF ORGANIZATIONAL CULTURE

Organizational culture consists of shared values, norms, and assumptions. Exhibit 13.1 illustrates how these elements relate to one another and are associated with artifacts, which are discussed in the next section of this chapter. *Values* are stable, evaluative beliefs that guide our preferences for outcomes or courses of action in a variety of situations (see Chapters 1 and 2).[4] They are conscious perceptions about what is good or bad, right or wrong. In the context of organizational culture, values are discussed as *shared values*, which are values that people within the organization or work unit have in common and place near the top of their hierarchy of values.[5]

Organizational culture norms are informal rules and shared expectations of employee behavior (see Chapter 7). These norms are the cultural values translated into more specific behavioral guidelines.[6] A company with a strong performance culture, for example, might have norms that encourage working long hours and being persistent in achieving goals.

Organizational culture also consists of *shared assumptions*–a deeper element that some experts believe is the essence of corporate culture.[7] Shared assumptions are nonconscious, taken-for-granted perceptions or ideal prototypes of behavior that are considered the correct way to think and act toward problems and opportunities. Shared assumptions are so deeply ingrained that you probably wouldn't discover them by surveying employees. Only by observing people, analyzing their decisions, and debriefing them on their actions would these assumptions rise to the surface.

Espoused versus Enacted Values

Most corporate websites have "Careers" web pages for job candidates, and many of these sites proudly list the company's core values. Do these values really represent the organization's culture? Some do, but these websites more likely describe *espoused values*–the values that corporate leaders hope will eventually become the organization's culture, or possibly just the values they want others to believe guide the organization's

Exhibit 13.1 Organizational Culture Assumptions, Values, Norms, and Artifacts

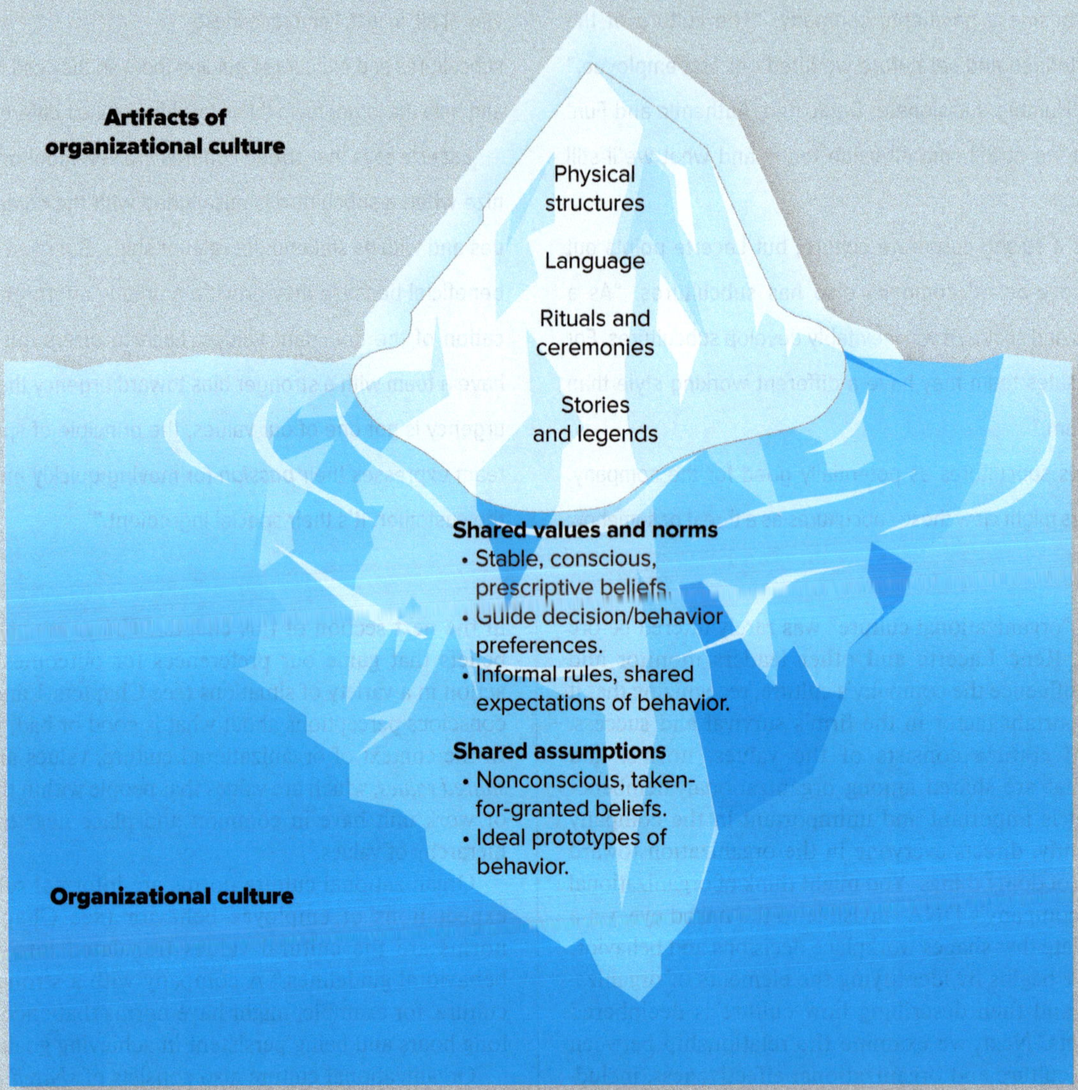

> **The thing I have learned at IBM is that culture is everything.**[8]
>
> —Louis V. Gerstner Jr., former CEO of IBM and RJR Nabisco

decisions and actions.[9] Espoused values are usually socially desirable, so they present a positive public image. Even if top management acts consistently with these values, they are still "espoused" if most employees do not abide by them. Employees bring diverse personal values to the organization, some of which might conflict with the organization's espoused values. Some companies even describe espoused values that are completely different from their actual culture.[10]

An organization's culture is defined by its *enacted values*, not its espoused values. Values are *enacted* when they actually guide and influence decisions and behavior. They are values put into practice. Enacted values are apparent when watching executives and other employees in action, such as where they focus their attention and resources, how they behave toward stakeholders, what decisions they make, and what outcomes occur from those decisions and behavior.

How Important Is Organizational Culture?[11]

74% of 500 CEOs of large firms in 9 countries say their employees are mostly or entirely engaged in applying the company cultural values in their day-to-day work.

72% of 9,464 workers in 12 countries say their company's culture is good or very good (ranges from 55% in Singapore to 87% in India).

67% of 3,243 adults in 42 countries say that their organization's culture is an important topic on the agenda of the company's senior leadership (53% said this 10 years ago; 61% said this 5 years ago).

56% of 5,113 working adults in the U.S., UK, France, and Germany say that company culture is more important than salary when it comes to being satisfied at work.

39% of 1,300 internal communications managers globally (65% from US and UK) identify corporate culture change as one of the top three change programs planned over the next year (second highest after changing work processes).

36% of 752 U.S. executives (most from Fortune 1000 companies) say one of the biggest challenges of hybrid work arrangements is the loss (weakening) of corporate culture.

ozgur_oral/Shutterstock

How many corporate cultures are there? Several models and measures classify organizational culture into a handful of easy-to-remember categories. One model identifies seven corporate cultures: innovation, stability, respect for people, outcome orientation, attention to detail, team orientation, and aggressiveness. Another model identifies four organizational cultures organized in a two-by-two table representing internal versus external focus and flexibility versus control. Other models organize cultures around a circle with 8 or 12 categories. These circumplex models suggest that some cultures are opposite to others, such as an avoidance culture versus a self-actualization culture, or a power culture versus a collegial culture.[14]

Organizational culture models and surveys are popular with corporate leaders faced with the messy business of diagnosing their company's culture and identifying what kind of culture they want to develop. Unfortunately, these models oversimplify the diversity of cultural norms and values within organizations. There are dozens of individual values, and many more combinations of values, so the number of organizational cultures that these models describe likely falls considerably short of the full set.

The diversity of corporate cultures is evident in a study of espoused values at the top 500 American companies.[15] The study distilled these values down to nine categories. Integrity appeared most often, followed by teamwork, innovation, respect, quality, safety, community, communication, and hard work. But each of these categories encapsulates a large number of specific values. The "respect" category, for instance, includes the specific values of diversity, inclusion, development, empowerment, and dignity. As you can see, there are dozens of espoused values, so there would be an equally long list of enacted values.

Another concern is that organizational culture models and measures typically ignore the shared assumptions aspect of culture. This oversight likely occurs because measuring shared assumptions is even more difficult than measuring shared values and norms. A third concern is that many organizational culture models and measures incorrectly assume that organizations have a fairly clear, unified culture that is easily decipherable.[16] In reality, an organization's culture is typically blurry and fragmented. Every employee has a somewhat distinct hierarchy of personal values, so an organization's culture necessarily has noticeable variability. Also, organizations consist of clusters of employees across the organization, and these groups prioritize different

Content of Organizational Culture

Organizations differ in their cultural content, that is, the relative ordering of the culture's dominant values as well as its norms and assumptions.[12] Compare Workday and Netflix, for example. Workday has a collaborative, employee-centered culture. "We believe deeply that if employees feel respected, valued and that what they do matters and they can make an impact, then they will do great things for our customers," says an executive at the financial management and human capital management software firm. In contrast, Netflix's culture seems to prioritize individual performance and undertones of internal competitiveness. For instance, the online streaming media provider reminds employees that "We're a team, not a family," that "Netflix leaders hire, develop, and cut smartly," and that "adequate performance gets a generous severance package."[13]

Mc Graw Hill connect

SELF-ASSESSMENT 13.1: Which Corporate Culture Do You Prefer?

artifacts The observable symbols and signs of an organization's culture

rituals The programmed routines of daily organizational life that dramatize the organization's culture

ceremonies Planned displays of organizational culture, conducted specifically for the benefit of an audience

values than the company's culture. Therefore, many of the popular models and measures oversimplify the variety of organizational cultures and falsely presume that organizations can easily be identified within these categories.

Organizational Subcultures

When discussing organizational culture, we are really referring to the *dominant culture,* that is, the values, norms, and assumptions shared most consistently and widely by the organization's members. The dominant culture is usually supported by senior management, but not always. Cultural values, norms, and assumptions can also persist in spite of senior management's desire for another culture.

As the opening vignette to this chapter highlighted, organizations are also composed of *subcultures* located throughout their various divisions, geographic regions, occupational units, and demographic groups.[17] Some subcultures enhance the dominant culture by espousing parallel values, norms, and assumptions. Others differ from but do not conflict with the dominant culture. Still others are called *countercultures* because they embrace values, norms, and assumptions that directly oppose the organization's dominant culture. It is also possible that some organizations (including some universities, according to one study) consist of subcultures with no decipherable dominant culture at all.[18]

Subcultures, particularly countercultures, may cause conflict and dissension among employees, but they also serve two important functions.[19] First, they maintain the organization's standards of performance and ethical behavior. Employees who hold countercultural values are an important source of surveillance and critical review of the dominant order. They encourage constructive conflict and more creative thinking about how the organization should interact with its environment. Subcultures potentially support ethical conduct by preventing employees from blindly following one set of values. Subculture members continually question the "obvious" decisions and actions of the majority, thereby making everyone more mindful of the consequences of their actions.

Subcultures serve a second valuable function: they are spawning grounds for emerging values, norms, and assumptions that keep the firm aligned with the evolving needs and expectations of customers, suppliers, communities, and other stakeholders. Companies eventually need to revise their existing dominant culture with one that is more appropriate for the changing environment. Those emerging cultural values, norms, and assumptions usually exist in subcultures long before they are ideal for the organization. If subcultures are suppressed, the organization may take longer to discover, develop, and adopt the emerging desired culture.

Some subcultures enhance the dominant culture, whereas others are called *countercultures* because their values, norms, and assumptions oppose the organization's dominant culture.
mediaphotos/Getty Images

LO13-2 Describe four categories of artifacts through which corporate culture is deciphered.

DECIPHERING ORGANIZATIONAL CULTURE THROUGH ARTIFACTS

Shared values, norms, and assumptions are not easily measured through surveys and might not be accurately reflected in the organization's values statements. Instead, as Exhibit 13.1 illustrated earlier, an organization's culture needs to be deciphered through a detailed investigation of artifacts. **Artifacts** are the observable symbols and signs of an organization's culture, such as the way visitors are greeted, the organization's physical layout, and how employees are rewarded.[20] A few experts suggest that artifacts are the essence of organizational culture, whereas most others (including the authors of this book) view artifacts as symbols or indicators of culture. In other words, culture is cognitive–values, norms, and assumptions reside inside people's heads–whereas artifacts are observable manifestations of that culture. Either way, artifacts are important because they represent and reinforce an organization's culture.

Artifacts provide valuable evidence about a company's culture.[21] An organization's ambiguous and fragmented culture is best understood by observing workplace behavior, listening to everyday conversations among staff and with customers, studying written documents and text messages, examining physical structures and settings, and interviewing staff about corporate stories. In other words, to truly understand an organization's culture, we need to sample information from a variety of organizational artifacts. In this section, we review four broad categories of artifacts: organizational stories and legends, language, rituals and ceremonies, and physical structures and symbols.

Organizational Stories and Legends

Stories and legends about the company's founders and past events permeate strong organizational cultures. Some tales recount heroic deeds, whereas others ridicule incidents that deviated from the firm's core values. Organizational stories and legends add human realism to corporate expectations, individual performance standards, and the criteria for getting fired. They also produce emotions, which tend to improve listeners' memory of the lesson within the story.[22] Stories have the greatest effect on communicating corporate culture when they describe real people, are assumed to be true, are known by employees throughout the organization, and convey clear messages about the way things should (or should not) be done.[23]

Organizational Language

The language of the workplace speaks volumes about the company's culture. How employees talk to each other, describe customers, express anger, and greet stakeholders are all verbal symbols of shared values, norms, and assumptions. An organization's culture particularly stands out when employees habitually use customized phrases and labels. For instance, DaVita HealthCare Partners is called the "village" because that word captures the sense of community much more accurately than the "company." Employees at the Denver-based provider of kidney care and dialysis services are "teammates," which conveys the relationship that DaVita staff members have with one another.[24]

Rituals and Ceremonies

Rituals are the programmed routines of daily organizational life that dramatize an organization's culture.[25] They include how visitors are greeted, how often senior executives visit subordinates, how people communicate with one another, how much time employees take for lunch, and so forth. Cultural rituals are repetitive, predictable events that have symbolic meaning of underlying cultural values, norms, and assumptions. For instance, BMW's fast-paced culture is quite literally apparent in the way employees walk around the German automaker's offices. "When you move through the corridors and hallways of other companies' buildings, people kind of crawl, they walk slowly," observes a BMW executive. "But BMW people tend to move faster."[27] **Ceremonies** are more formal artifacts than rituals.

OB THEORY TO PRACTICE

Galvanize Puts the Moose on the Table[26]

YVdavyd/Getty Images

Employees at Galvanize (now part of Diligent Corporation) often utter the phrase "put the moose on the table," which means talking openly about a known problem or issue that everyone has avoided (i.e., the elephant in the room). "It's a symbolic invitation to have the awkward—but necessary—conversation," says Laurie Schultz, who was CEO of the security software company over the past decade and is now a board director or chair of several technology firms. "We say it all the time. It's a huge, huge, huge part of our culture."

As a reminder, Galvanize has stuffed toy moose and moose drawings throughout its offices. Schultz adds: "One thing I've learned is the power of symbols, values, and language when reinforcing a risk-taking culture."

> What we say—and how we say it—can deeply affect a company's culture.[28]
>
> —Tom Kelley and David Kelley, partner (Tom) and founder (David) of IDEO

> **We shape our buildings; thereafter, they shape us.**[31]
>
> —Winston Churchill, former Prime Minister of the United Kingdom

These are planned activities conducted specifically for the benefit of an audience. Ceremonies include celebrating the launch of a new product or newly won contract, as well as publicly rewarding (or punishing) employees.

Physical Structures and Symbols

The size, shape, location, and age of buildings both reflect and influence an organization's culture. Physical structures might support a company's emphasis on teamwork, environmental friendliness, hierarchy, or any other set of values.[29] Even if the building doesn't make much of a statement, there is a treasure-trove of physical artifacts inside. Desks, chairs, office space, and wall hangings (or lack of them) are just a few of the workplace features that might convey cultural meaning.[30] Each physical artifact alone might not say much, but put enough of them together and an image emerges of how they symbolize the organization's culture.

For example, one prominent workspace design and manufacturing company recently identified the workspace features typically found at companies with different organizational cultures. Exhibit 13.2 summarizes the physical space design of collaborative and creative cultures compared to cultures that emphasize efficiency (control) and competition. Collaborative and creative cultures value more teamwork and flexibility, so space design is informal and enables spontaneous group discussion. Controlling and competitive cultures tend to have more structural office arrangements and provide more space for individual work than teamwork.[32]

Exhibit 13.2 Workspace Design and Organizational Culture

Collaborative and Creative Cultures	Controlling and Competitive Cultures

• More team space • Informal space • Low/medium enclosure • Flexible environment • Organic layout	• More individual space • More formal than informal space • High/medium enclosure • More fixed environment • More structured, symmetrical layout

Photos: (Left) PeopleImages/Getty Images; (Right) Westend61 Premium/Shutterstock

Source: Based on information in *How to Create a Successful Organizational Culture: Build It—Literally* (Holland, MI: Haworth Inc., June 2015).

LO13-3 Discuss the importance of organizational culture and the conditions under which organizational culture strength improves organizational performance.

IS ORGANIZATIONAL CULTURE IMPORTANT?

Does a strong organizational culture improve organizational effectiveness? Marty Parker thinks so. "As leaders, we need to put culture at the center of how we do things," says the founder and CEO of consulting and executive search firm Waterstone Human Capital. Tony Guzzi agrees. "I am a firm believer that my job is to define the culture we want, model the culture we want, and nourish the culture we want," says the CEO of EMCOR Group, a *Fortune* 500 company that provides construction, industrial and energy infrastructure, and facilities services. "In the end, the biggest thing you [as CEO] can try to shape is the culture in the organization."[33]

Marty Parker, Tony Guzzi, and many other leaders believe that an organization's success partly depends on its culture. Several popular-press management books similarly assert that the most successful companies have strong cultures.[34] Does OB research support this view that companies are more effective when they have a strong culture? Yes, potentially, but the evidence indicates that the relationship depends on a few conditions.[35]

The Meaning and Potential Benefits of a Strong Culture

Before discussing the contingencies of an effective organizational culture, let's examine the meaning of a "strong" organizational culture and its potential benefits. Culture strength refers to how widely and deeply employees understand and embrace the organization's dominant values, norms, and assumptions. In a strong organizational culture, the company's core values are "shared" by most employees across all subunits. Values are "shared" when employees hold a similar understanding of them and internalize them as part of their personal set of values.

In a strong culture, the company's values, norms, and assumptions are also institutionalized through well-established artifacts, which further entrench the culture. In addition, strong cultures tend to be long-lasting; some can be traced back to personal attributes and behaviors of the company's founder. In contrast, companies have weak cultures when the dominant values are held mainly by a few people at the top of the organization; employees lack awareness or agreement on the meaning of those values; the values, norms, and assumptions are unstable over time or highly varied across the organization; and the culture is difficult to interpret from artifacts.

Under specific conditions, companies are more effective when they have strong cultures because of the three important functions listed in Exhibit 13.3 and described as follows:

- *Control system.* Organizational culture is a deeply embedded form of social control that influences employee decisions and behavior.[36] Culture is pervasive and operates almost invisibly. Think of it as an automatic pilot, nonconsciously directing employees so their behavior is consistent with organizational expectations. For this reason, organizational culture is often described as a compass that points everyone in the same direction.
- *Social glue.* Organizational culture is the social glue that bonds people together and makes them feel part of the collective organizational experience.[38] Employees are motivated to internalize the organization's dominant culture because it fulfills their need for social identity. This social glue attracts new staff and retains top performers. It also becomes the common thread that holds employees together in global organizations.
- *Sense making.* Organizational culture helps employees to make sense of what goes on and why things happen in the company.[39] Corporate culture also makes it easier to understand what is expected of them. As a result, employees in companies with stronger organizational cultures have clearer role perceptions and less role-related stress.

> **Culture is one of the most precious things a company has, so you must work harder on it than anything else.[37]**
>
> —Herb Kelleher, cofounder and former CEO of Southwest Airlines

> **Culture is the X-factor. It's the invisible glue that holds an organization together and ultimately makes the difference between whether an organization is able to succeed in the market or not.[40]**
>
> —Noah G. Rabinowitz, Moderna vice president, learning & development

Exhibit 13.3 Potential Benefits and Contingencies of Culture Strength

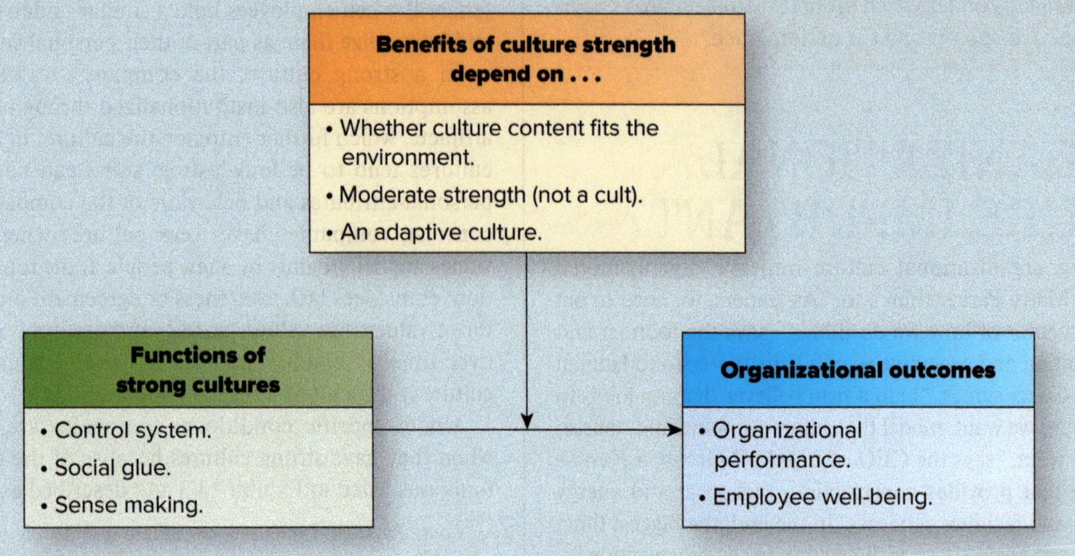

Contingencies of Organizational Culture and Effectiveness

Studies have found only a moderately positive relationship between culture strength and organizational effectiveness. The reason for this weak connection is that strong cultures improve organizational effectiveness only under specific conditions (see Exhibit 13.3). The three main contingencies are (1) whether the culture content is aligned with its external environment; (2) whether the culture is moderately strong, not cult-like; and (3) whether the culture incorporates an adaptive culture.

Culture Content Is Aligned with the External Environment

The benefits of a strong culture depend on whether its content—the relative ordering of the culture's dominant values as well as its norms and assumptions—is aligned with the external environment. If the culture is congruent with the environment, then employees are more motivated and have clearer role perceptions to practice behaviors that improve the organization's interaction with its environment. But when the culture is misaligned with the environment, a strong culture encourages decisions and behaviors that can undermine the organization's connection with its stakeholders.

Consider Microsoft, which has had a strong culture for many years. Until recently, the technology giant's dominant values were noticeably dysfunctional, meaning that they undermined rather than enhanced the organization's capacity to innovate, adapt, and collaborate internally and externally. "Innovation was being replaced by bureaucracy. Teamwork was being replaced by internal politics. We were falling behind," recalls current CEO Satya Nadella. Indeed, some observers predicted that if Microsoft's existing culture continued, the company would be "fading toward irrelevance." Nadella successfully transformed Microsoft's culture by instilling a new set of dominant values around a growth mindset of innovation, information sharing (collaboration), and customer focus—values that are much more aligned with what the technology firm needs to thrive.[41]

Culture Strength Is Not the Level of a Cult A second contingency is the degree of culture strength. Experts suggest that companies with very strong cultures—known as corporate "cults"—may be less effective than companies with moderately strong cultures.[42] One reason why corporate cults tend to undermine an organization's effectiveness is that they lock people into mental models, which can blind them to new opportunities and unique problems. The effect of these very strong cultures is that people overlook or incorrectly define subtle misalignments between the organization's activities and the changing environment.

Corporate cults tend to undermine organizational effectiveness by locking people into mental models, which can blind them from seeing new opportunities and unique problems.
mediaphotos/Getty Images

adaptive culture An organizational culture in which employees are receptive to change, including the ongoing alignment of the organization to its environment and continuous improvement of internal processes

learning orientation A set of beliefs and norms in which people are encouraged to question past practices, learn new ideas, experiment putting ideas into practice, and view mistakes as part of the learning process

The other reason why very strong cultures may be dysfunctional is that they suppress dissenting subcultures. The challenge for organizational leaders is to maintain not only a strong culture but one that allows subcultural diversity. Subcultures encourage task-oriented conflict, which improves creative thinking and offers some level of ethical vigilance over the dominant culture. In the long run, a subculture's nascent values could become important dominant values as the environment changes. Corporate cults suppress subcultures, thereby undermining these benefits.

Culture Is an Adaptive Culture A third condition influencing the effect of cultural strength on organizational effectiveness is whether the culture content includes an **adaptive culture**.[43] An adaptive culture embraces change, creativity, open-mindedness, growth, and learning. It is one in which employees recognize that the organization's survival and success depend on their ability to discover emerging changes in the external environment and to adapt their own behavior to those changes. Thus, employees in adaptive cultures take an open systems view and accept responsibility for the organization's performance and alignment with the external environment.

> You have to create a culture that not only accepts change but seeks out how to change.[46]
>
> —Dan Akerson, former GM CEO

In an adaptive culture, receptivity to change extends to internal processes and roles. Employees believe that satisfying stakeholders requires continuous improvement of internal work processes. They also recognize the importance of remaining flexible in their own work roles. The phrase "That's not my job" is found in nonadaptive cultures. Finally, an adaptive culture has a strong **learning orientation** because being receptive to change necessarily means that the company also supports action-oriented discovery. With a learning orientation, employees welcome new learning opportunities, actively experiment with new ideas and practices, view reasonable mistakes as a natural part of the learning process, and continuously question past practices (see Chapter 6).[44]

Organizational Culture and Business Ethics

An organization's culture influences the ethical conduct of its employees. This makes sense because good behavior is driven by ethical values and norms, which become embedded in an organization's dominant culture. Workday has a strong culture that specifically includes "integrity" as one of its dominant values. "At Workday, integrity is one of our core values, which we define as standing by what we say, being accountable, staying true to our commitments, treating everyone equitably, and being open and honest in how we communicate to our employees and customers," says Christine Fedrow, chief integrity and compliance officer at the financial management and human capital software company. Workday is recognized as one of the world's most ethical companies, based on its culture, environmental and social practices, governance, diversity, and other initiatives. Most Workday employees (94 percent in recent surveys) agree that the company's management is honest and ethical in its business practices.[45]

The opposite is equally true. There are numerous instances where an organization's culture has been the apparent cause of unethical conduct. For instance, until a few years ago, Uber suffered from an organizational culture that resulted in allegations of sexual harassment, bullying, privacy violations, anti-competitive activities, and theft of proprietary technology. It also created an infamously competitive, political, and conflict-ridden workplace. "The culture and approach that got Uber where it is today is not what will get us to the next level," said Dara Khosrowshahi diplomatically, soon after he replaced Uber's founder as CEO. "Our values define who we are and how we work, but I had heard from many employees that some of them simply didn't represent the kind of company we want to be."[47]

LO13-4 Compare and contrast four strategies for merging organizational cultures.

MERGING ORGANIZATIONAL CULTURES

Mergers and acquisitions (M&As) often fail financially when the merging organizations have incompatible cultures.[48] Unless the acquired firm is left to operate independently, companies with clashing cultures tend to undermine employee performance and customer service. Consequently, M&A deals are more often unsuccessful (underperform financial targets) because the merging firms lacked sufficient cultural alignment.[49]

Corporate Culture Risks in Mergers and Acquisitions[50]

60% of 232 senior executives in Fortune 1000 companies include a culture assessment (bicultural audit) during due diligence and make it part of their go/no-go M&A decision.

20% of 1,000 corporate and private equity executives say M&A deals underperform because the parties did not achieve cultural alignment.

30% of 1,438 M&A professionals in 54 countries say that M&A transactions failed to ever meet financial targets due to culture issues.

54% of 1,000 U.S. executives say they would walk away from an acquisition target if its corporate culture is not at all aligned with the acquiring company's culture (10% would value the misaligned firm equally to a similar company with a very aligned culture).

59% of 500 CEOs of large firms in 9 countries say they achieved their corporate culture goals in ensuring the success of a merger or acquisition.

(Photo left): Volodymyr Krasyuk/Shutterstock; (Photo right): Mike Flippo/Shutterstock

Bicultural Audit

Organizational leaders can minimize cultural collisions in corporate mergers and fulfill their duty of due diligence by conducting a bicultural audit.[51] A **bicultural audit** diagnoses cultural relations between the companies and determines the extent to which cultural clashes will likely occur. The process begins by identifying cultural differences between the merging companies. This might occur by surveying employees or through an extended series of meetings where executives and staff of both firms discuss how they think through important decisions in their business. From the survey data or meetings, the parties determine which differences between the two firms will result in conflict and which cultural values provide common ground on which to build a cultural foundation in the merged organization. The final stage involves identifying strategies and preparing action plans to bridge the two organizations' cultures.

Strategies for Merging Different Organizational Cultures

In some cases, the bicultural audit results in a decision to end merger talks because the two cultures are too different to merge effectively. However, even with substantially different cultures, two companies may form a workable union if they apply the appropriate merger strategy. The four main strategies for merging different corporate cultures are assimilation, deculturation, integration, and separation (see Exhibit 13.4).[52]

Assimilation Assimilation occurs when employees at the acquired company willingly embrace the cultural values of the acquiring organization. Typically, this strategy works best when the acquired company has a weak culture or is dysfunctional, whereas the acquiring company's culture is strong and aligned with the external environment. The cultural assimilation

Exhibit 13.4 Strategies for Merging Different Organizational Cultures

Merger Strategy	Description	Works Best When . . .
Assimilation	Acquired company embraces acquiring firm's culture.	Acquired firm has a weak culture and acquiring firm's culture is strong and successful.
Deculturation	Acquiring firm imposes its culture on unwilling acquired firm.	Rarely works—may be necessary only when acquired firm's culture is dysfunctional but its employees aren't yet aware of the problems.
Integration	Merging companies combine the two or more cultures into a new composite culture.	Existing cultures at both firms are relatively weak or have overlapping values and can be improved.
Separation	Merging companies remain distinct entities with minimal exchange of culture or organizational practices.	Firms operate successfully in different businesses requiring different cultures.

Sources: Based on ideas in A.R. Malekzadeh and A. Nahavandi, "Making Mergers Work by Managing Cultures," *Journal of Business Strategy* 11 (May/June 1990): 55–57; K.W. Smith, "A Brand-New Culture for the Merged Firm," *Mergers and Acquisitions* 35 (June 2000): 45–50.

strategy seldom produces cultural clashes because the acquiring firm's culture is highly respected and the acquired firm's culture is fairly easily altered.

Deculturation Assimilation is rare. Employees usually resist organizational change, particularly when they are asked to abide by significantly different corporate values and norms. Under these conditions, some acquiring companies apply a *deculturation* strategy by imposing their culture and business practices on the acquired organization. The acquiring firm strips away reward systems and other artifacts that support the old culture. People who cannot adopt the acquiring company's culture often lose their jobs. Deculturation may be necessary when the acquired firm's culture doesn't work, even when employees in the acquired company aren't convinced of this. However, this strategy is difficult to apply effectively because the acquired firm's employees resist the cultural intrusions from the buying firm, thereby delaying or undermining the merger process.

Integration A third strategy is to combine the cultures of the two firms into one new composite culture that preserves the best features of the previous cultures. Integration is slow and potentially risky because there are many forces preserving the existing cultures. Still, this strategy should be considered when the companies have relatively weak cultures or when their cultures include several overlapping values. Integration works best when the cultures of both merging companies could be improved, which motivates employees to adopt the best cultural elements of the separate entities. This strategy also symbolizes that employees from both firms have meaningful values and norms for the combined organization. "Find one thing in the organization that was good and use it as a cornerstone for a new culture," advises a respected executive who has led several mergers and acquisitions. "People don't want to work for an organization for years and then be told it's rubbish."[53]

Integration works best when the cultures of both merging companies could be improved, which motivates employees to adopt the best cultural elements of the separate entities.
JGI/Blend Images LLC

bicultural audit A process of diagnosing cultural relations between companies and determining the extent to which cultural clashes will likely occur

Separation A separation strategy occurs when the merging companies agree to remain distinct entities with minimal exchange of culture or organizational practices. This strategy is most appropriate when the two merging companies are in unrelated industries because the most appropriate cultural values tend to differ by industry. Separation is also the preferred approach for the corporate cultures of diversified conglomerates. The cultural separation strategy is rare, however. Executives in acquiring firms usually have difficulty keeping their hands off the acquired firm. One ongoing series of surveys reports that only 10 percent of mergers leave the acquired company as a stand-alone unit.[54]

LO13-5 Describe five strategies for changing and strengthening an organization's culture, including the application of attraction–selection–attrition theory.

CHANGING AND STRENGTHENING ORGANIZATIONAL CULTURE

Is it possible to change an organization's culture? Yes, but doing so isn't easy, the change rarely occurs quickly, and often the culture ends up changing (or replacing) corporate leaders. A few scholars argue that an organization's culture "cannot be managed," so attempting to change the company's values, norms, and assumptions is a waste of time.[55] This may be an extreme view, but most experts agree that changing an organization's culture is a monumental challenge. At the same time, the external environment changes over time, so organizations eventually need to shift some aspects of their culture to maintain alignment with the emerging environment.

This section looks at five strategies that have had some success at altering and strengthening corporate cultures. These strategies, illustrated in Exhibit 13.5, are not exhaustive, but each seems to work well in most circumstances.

> There is something only a CEO uniquely can do, which is set that tone, which can then capture the soul of the collective. And it's culture.[56]
>
> —Satya Nadella, chairman and CEO, Microsoft Corporation

Exhibit 13.5 Strategies for Changing and Strengthening Organizational Culture

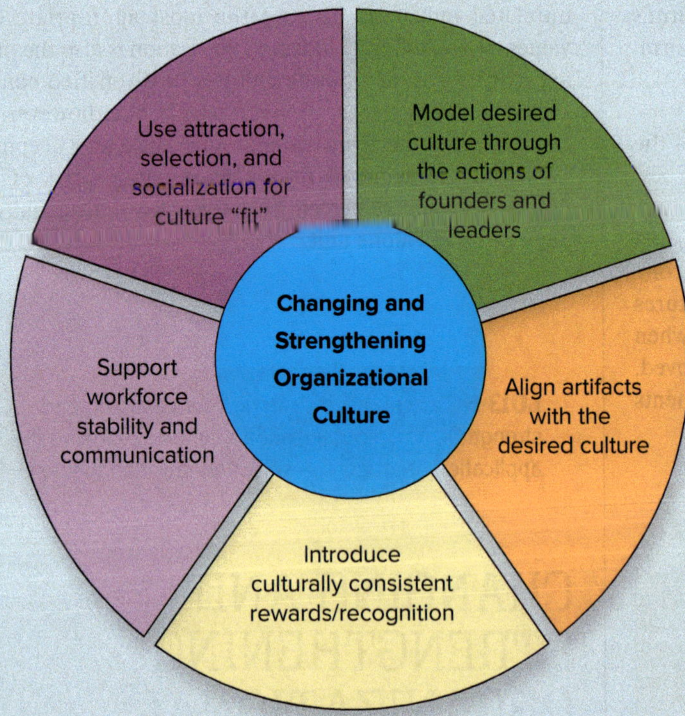

Model Desired Culture through the Actions of Founders and Leaders

Whether deliberately or haphazardly, the company's founder usually forms an organization's culture.[57] The founder's personality, values, habits, and critical events all play a role in establishing the firm's core values, norms, and assumptions. The founder is often an inspiring visionary who provides a compelling role model for others to follow. In later years, organizational culture is reinforced through stories and legends about the founder that symbolize the core values.

Although founders usually establish an organization's culture, subsequent leaders need to actively guide, reinforce, and sometimes alter that culture.[58] The process of leading cultural change is associated with both transformational leadership and authentic leadership (see Chapter 11). In each of those models, leaders base their words and actions on personal values, and those values potentially become a reflection of the organization's values. For instance, one study found that the preferred conflict-handling style of leaders influences the work unit's or organization's cultural expectations on how employees address conflict situations. Another study reported that work units or companies with strong servant leadership were more likely to have a culture that valued providing service to others.[59]

Align Artifacts with the Desired Culture

Artifacts represent more than just the visible indicators of a company's culture. They are also mechanisms that keep the culture in place or shift the culture to a new set of values, norms, and assumptions.[60] Workplace layout, reporting structures, office rituals, and information systems are some of the various organizational systems and structures. And as we discuss in the next chapter, systems and structures are powerful mechanisms for organizational change because they stabilize and reinforce the desired state of affairs. Corporate cultures can also be strengthened through the artifacts of stories and behaviors. According to Max De Pree, former CEO of furniture manufacturer Herman Miller Inc., every organization needs "tribal storytellers" to keep the organization's history and culture alive.[61] Leaders play a role by creating memorable events that symbolize the cultural values they want to develop or maintain.

Introduce Culturally Consistent Rewards and Recognition

Reward systems and informal recognition practices are artifacts, but they deserve separate discussion because of their powerful effect on strengthening or reshaping an organization's culture.[62] Uber created a new reward system to help replace its "toxic"

Artifacts don't just symbolize a company's culture; they also keep the culture in place or shift the culture to a new set of values and assumptions.
Caia Image/Gettyimages

culture with one that is more compatible with societal expectations. The transportation network company previously had an internally competitive (rank-and-yank) merit system and allegedly biased performance review process tied to its original list of dysfunctional values. Uber's new reward system asks employees to document specific performance goals as well as one "citizenship goal" (e.g., helping coworkers, volunteering outside the company). This reward system encourages cooperation, community involvement, and individual development without competing against coworkers. "We're shifting the culture very significantly through this process," says the Uber human resources executive who championed the new reward system.[63]

Support Workforce Stability and Communication

An organization's culture is embedded in the minds of its employees. Organizational stories are rarely written down; rituals and ceremonies do not usually exist in procedure manuals; organizational metaphors are not found in corporate directories. Thus, a strong culture depends on a stable workforce. Workforce stability is important because it takes time for employees to fully understand the organization's culture and how to enact it in their daily work lives. The organization's culture can literally disintegrate during periods of high turnover and precipitous downsizing because the corporate memory is lost with the departing employees.

A strong organizational culture also depends on communication of that culture. One practice is for the executive team through to frontline staff to have ongoing discussions about the company's values and norms, and how they are manifested in decisions and behavior. Redstone Federal Credit Union ensures that these conversations occur at the local level through the assistance of two "cultural ambassadors" at each branch and division of the Huntsville, Alabama financial institution. The ambassadors discuss the company's values with staff as part of their regular huddles.[64] A second way is to communicate corporate culture through casual conversations, so organizations with strong cultures create opportunities for employees to regularly interact with one another. These activities develop shared language, stories, and other artifacts.

Use Attraction, Selection, and Socialization for Cultural Fit

A powerful way to strengthen and possibly change an organization's culture is by recruiting, selecting, and retaining applicants whose values and preferred norms are congruent with the organization's culture. This process is explained by **attraction–selection–attrition (ASA) theory**.[65] ASA theory states that organizations have a natural tendency to attract, select, and retain people with values and personality characteristics that are consistent with the

attraction–selection–attrition (ASA) theory A theory that states that organizations have a natural tendency to attract, select, and retain people with values and personality characteristics that are consistent with the organization's character, resulting in a more homogeneous organization and a stronger culture

Corporate Culture Fit during the Hiring Process[66]

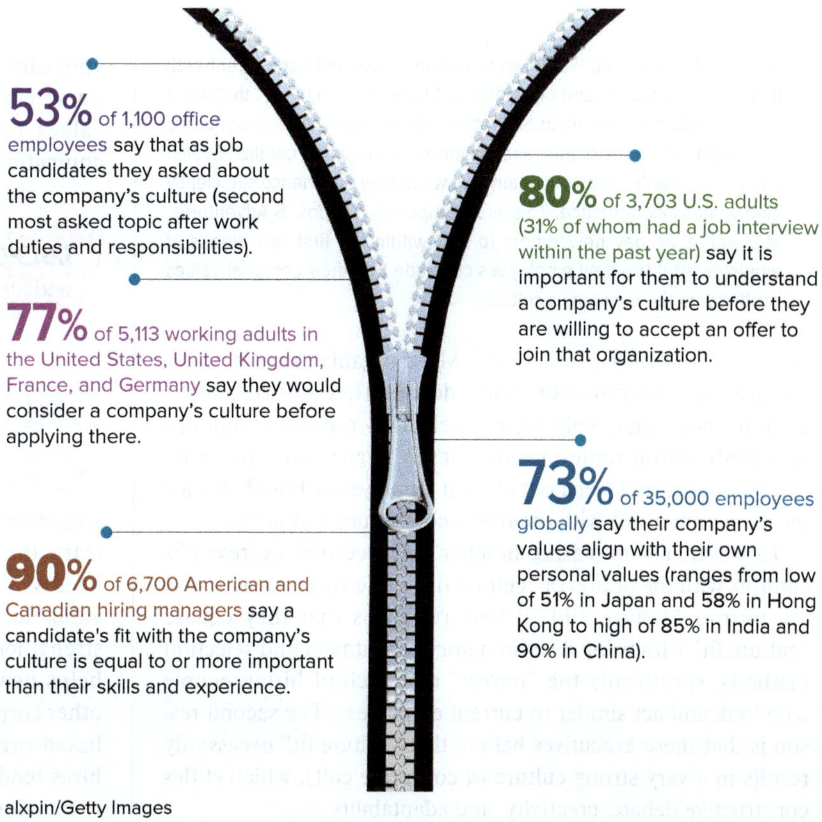

alxpin/Getty Images

organizational socialization The process by which individuals learn the values, expected behaviors, and social knowledge necessary to assume their roles in the organization

organization's character. These activities increase the strength of the organization's culture, but they also produce a more homogeneous organization in other ways.

- *Attraction.* Job applicants engage in self-selection by avoiding prospective employers whose values seem incompatible with their own values.[67] They look for subtle artifacts during interviews and through public information that communicate the company's culture. Some organizations encourage this self-selection by actively describing their cultures.
- *Selection.* Hiring managers increasingly assess how well a job candidate "fits in" with the company's culture when deciding whether to hire that person.[68] IKEA is a values-driven organization, so it determines how well applicants' personal values are compatible with the global retailer's corporate values and how well those applicants are aware of IKEA's values. The idea is that this cultural alignment is good for both the company and the employee. "Be clear of your personal values and connect those with your company values," advises an IKEA human resource manager.[69]

> People seek workplaces that are reasonably congruent with their personal values and are motivated to leave workplaces that are a poor fit.

- *Attrition.* People seek workplaces that are reasonably congruent with their personal values and are motivated to leave workplaces that are a poor fit. This occurs because person–organization values congruence supports their social identity and minimizes internal role conflict. Even if employees aren't forced out, many quit when they experience sufficiently high values incongruence.[70] Several companies (Zappos, G Adventures, etc.) will even pay newcomers to quit within the first few weeks of employment if the new employees conclude that their personal values conflict with the company's culture.

Culture Fit or Culture Add? Most organizations actively manage the ASA process to some degree. They advertise information about their culture, use selection criteria to choose applicants whose values are sufficiently aligned with the company's culture, and weed out current employees whose behavior seems incompatible with the firm's core values and norms.

However, an increasing number of executives express discomfort with the notion of "culture fit," preferring instead to use the phrase "culture add."[71] One reason is that they equate "culture fit" with using discriminatory recruitment and selection methods, specifically the "mirror" approach of hiring people who look and act similar to current employees. The second reason is that these executives believe that "culture fit" necessarily results in a very strong culture (a corporate cult), which stifles constructive debate, creativity, and adaptability.

These concerns are real and have adverse effects on the organization, applicants, current employees, and other stakeholders. But the "culture add" advocates misunderstand the "culture fit" concept. Person–culture fit is well-defined in seminal research as "congruency between an individual's values and those of an organization."[72] Congruence exists when two entities are in harmony, not necessarily identical. On the contrary, as we discussed earlier in this chapter, the most effective organizational cultures are strong, but not corporate cults. Very strong cultures suffocate subcultures, which undermines the organization's effectiveness. Most subcultures bring diverse perspectives and encourage constructive conflict with the dominant culture, which produces more ethical and creative decisions.

Hiring applicants who look and act similar to current employees is also inconsistent with the meaning of culture fit. That mirror approach to hiring is a poor test of values congruence because it screens out people with different backgrounds, even though their personal values may be congruent with the company's culture. Hiring for culture fit requires a careful, valid assessment of an applicant's personal values. In fact, given the challenge of assessing personal values in job applicants, companies might more wisely focus their attention on screening out applicants with significantly incompatible values rather than try to select applicants with the most compatible values.

LO13-6 Describe the organizational socialization process and identify strategies to improve that process.

ORGANIZATIONAL SOCIALIZATION

Organizational socialization is the process by which individuals learn the values, expected behaviors, and social knowledge necessary to assume their roles in the organization.[73] It is a valuable set of practices to help companies change and strengthen their organizational culture. Equally important, it helps newcomers adjust to work procedures, coworkers, and other corporate realities. Research indicates that when evidence-based organizational socialization practices are applied, new hires tend to perform better, have higher job satisfaction, and remain longer with the organization.[74]

Exhibit 13.6 Stages of Organizational Socialization

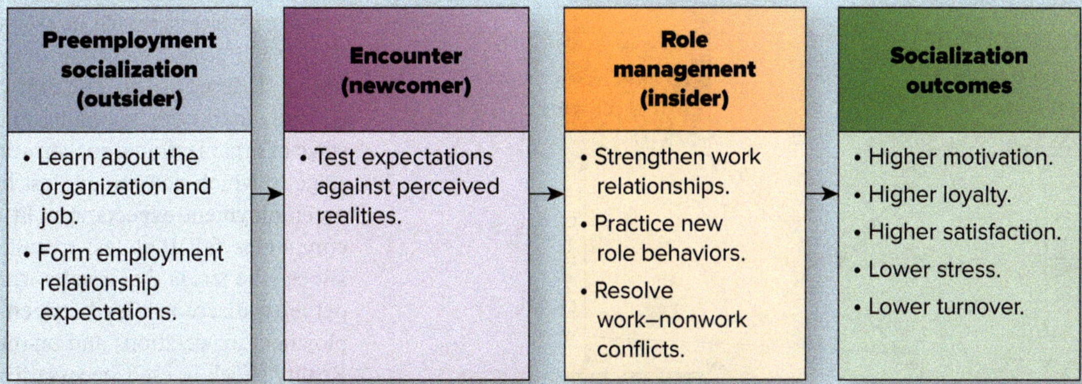

Some writers claim that organizational socialization can change employee values to become more aligned with the company's culture. However, personal values are fairly stable beyond early adulthood and therefore are not so easily altered by short-term training and related socialization events. Instead, effective organizational socialization offers newcomers a clearer understanding about the company's values which, in turn, gives them guidelines to more accurately engage in values-consistent behaviors on the job.[75] Better awareness of the company's culture also motivates new hires to reject the job offer or more quickly leave if their personal values are incompatible with the organization's values and assumptions.

Learning and Adjustment Process

Organizational socialization is a process of both learning and adjustment. It is a learning process because newcomers try to make sense of the company's physical workplace, social dynamics, and strategic and cultural environment. They learn about the organization's performance expectations, power dynamics, corporate culture, company history, and jargon. They also need to form successful and satisfying relationships with other people from whom they can learn the ropes.[76] In other words, effective socialization supports newcomers' *organizational comprehension*. It accelerates development of an accurate cognitive map of the physical, social, strategic, and cultural dynamics of the organization. Ideally, this learning should be distributed over time to minimize information overload.

Organizational socialization is also an adjustment process because individuals need to adopt the organization's and work group's norms, behaviors, and work roles that potentially shift their self-concept.[77] The adjustment process is fairly rapid for many people, usually occurring within a few months. However, newcomers with diverse work experience seem to adjust better than those with limited previous experience, possibly because they have a larger toolkit of knowledge and skills to make the adjustment possible.[78]

Stages of Organizational Socialization

Organizational socialization is a continuous process, beginning before you submit a job application and continuing throughout your career within the company. However, it is most intense during movement across organizational boundaries, such as when first joining a company or getting transferred to an international assignment. These transitions can be viewed as a process with three stages. Our focus here is on the socialization of new employees, so the three stages are called preemployment socialization, encounter, and role management (see Exhibit 13.6). These stages parallel the individual's transition from outsider to newcomer and then to insider.[79]

Stage 1: Preemployment Socialization Think back to the months and weeks before you began working in a new job (or attending a new school). You actively searched for information about the company, formed expectations about working there, and felt some anticipation about fitting into that setting. The preemployment socialization stage encompasses all the learning and adjustment that occurs before the first day of work. In fact, a large part of the socialization adjustment process occurs during this stage.[80]

The main problem with preemployment socialization is that outsiders rely on indirect information about what it is like to work in the organization. This information is often distorted by inherent conflicts that arise during the mating dance between employer and applicant. Exhibit 13.7 illustrates the four main information exchange conflicts (not in any particular order) that result in distorted information exchange during preemployment socialization:[81]

- In Conflict A, the employer's motivation to attract many high-quality job applicants conflicts with the applicant's need to receive complete and accurate information for choosing the best job offer. Many firms describe only positive aspects of the job and company, causing applicants to accept job offers based on misleading expectations about working at that organization.

Exhibit 13.7 Information Exchange Conflicts during Preemployment Socialization

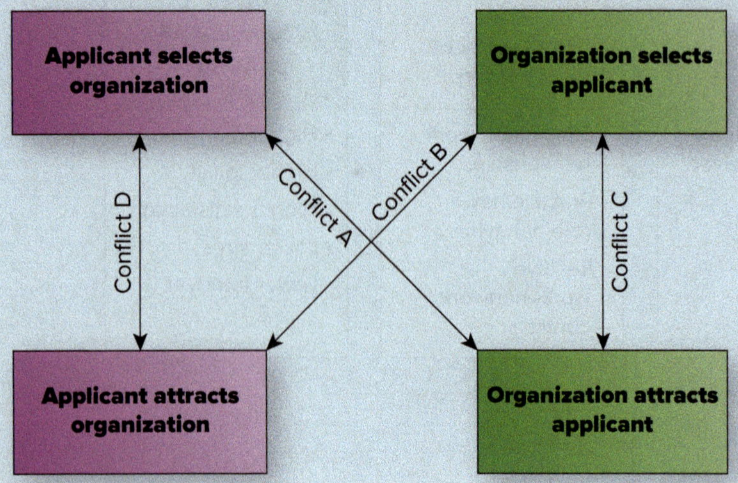

Source: L.W. Porter, E.E. Lawler III, and J.R. Hackman, *Behavior in Organizations* (New York: McGraw Hill, 1975), 134. Reprinted by permission.

- In Conflict B, the job applicant's motivation to receive job offers conflicts with the employer's need to receive complete and accurate information for choosing the best job applicants. Applicants engage in impression management when seeking employment, motivating them to hide negative information, act out of character, and occasionally embellish information about their past accomplishments. Due to this distorted information, the employer chooses applicants that are less qualified or have a poorer culture fit with the organization.
- In Conflict C, employers are motivated to attract many high-quality job applicants, which conflicts with their need to receive complete and accurate information for choosing the best job applicants. Employers are sometimes reluctant to ask some types of questions to applicants or use potentially valuable selection methods because those information-gathering activities might scare off the best job candidates. Without the additional information about applicants, the employer forms inaccurate expectations about job candidates and hires people who might not be sufficiently qualified or compatible with the organization's culture.
- In Conflict D, job applicants are motivated to receive job offers, which conflicts with their need to receive complete and accurate information for choosing the best job offer. Applicants avoid asking important questions about the company because they want to convey a favorable image to their prospective employer. For instance, applicants usually don't like to ask about starting salaries and promotion opportunities because it makes them seem greedy or aggressive. Yet, unless the employer provides this information, applicants might fill in the missing details with false assumptions that produce inaccurate job expectations.

Stage 2: Encounter The first day on the job typically marks the beginning of the encounter stage of organizational socialization. This is the stage in which newcomers test how well their preemployment expectations fit reality. Many companies fail that test, resulting in **reality shock**—the stress that results when employees perceive discrepancies between their preemployment expectations and on-the-job reality.[82] Reality shock doesn't necessarily occur on the first day; it might develop over several weeks or even months as newcomers form a better understanding of their new work environment.

Reality shock is common in many organizations.[83] Newcomers sometimes face *unmet expectations* whereby the employer doesn't deliver on its promises, such as failing to provide challenging projects or the resources to get the work done. However, new hires also experience reality shock due to *unrealistic expectations,* whereby the employee formed overly positive work expectations due to perceptual biases and information exchange conflicts described earlier. Whether due to unmet or unrealistic expectations, reality shock impedes the learning and adjustment process because the newcomer's energy is directed toward managing the resulting stress.[84]

Stage 3: Role Management Role management, the third stage of organizational socialization, really begins during preemployment socialization, but it is most active as employees make the transition from newcomers to insiders. They strengthen relationships with coworkers and supervisors, practice new role behaviors, and adopt attitudes and values consistent with their new positions and the organization. Role management also involves resolving the conflicts between work and nonwork activities, including resolving discrepancies between their personal values and those emphasized by the organizational culture.

Improving the Socialization Process

Companies have a tendency to exaggerate positive features of the job and neglect to mention the undesirable elements. Their

> Newcomers experience reality shock when the employer doesn't deliver on its promises (unmet expectations) and when job applicants inflate the anticipated work arrangements (unrealistic expectations).

Realistic job previews offer a balance of positive and negative information about the job and work context, which helps applicants decide whether their skills, needs, and values are compatible with the job and organization.
Rawpixel.com/Shutterstock

motivation is to attract as many job applicants as possible, which they assume will improve the selection choices. Unfortunately, this flypaper approach often ends badly. Those hired soon discover that the actual workplace is not as favorable as the employer's marketing hype (i.e., unmet expectations), resulting in reality shock. In contrast, a **realistic job preview (RJP)** offers a balance of positive and negative information about the job and work context.[85] This balanced description helps applicants decide for themselves whether their skills, needs, and values are compatible with the job and organization.

reality shock The stress that results when employees perceive discrepancies between their preemployment expectations and on-the-job reality

realistic job preview (RJP) A method of improving organizational socialization in which job applicants are given a balance of positive and negative information about the job and work context

RJPs scare away some applicants, but they also tend to reduce turnover and increase job performance.[86] This occurs because RJPs help applicants develop more accurate preemployment expectations, which, in turn, minimize reality shock. RJPs represent a type of vaccination by preparing employees for the more challenging and troublesome aspects of the work context. There is also some evidence that RJPs increase affective organizational commitment. One explanation is that companies providing candid information are easier to trust. Another explanation is that RJPs show respect and concern for the employee's expectations and welfare.[87]

Socialization Agents If you ask new employees what provided the greatest assistance adjusting to their jobs, they will probably credit helpful coworkers, bosses, or maybe even friends who work elsewhere in the organization. The fact is, socialization agents play a central role in the socialization process.[88] Supervisors tend to provide technical information, performance feedback, and information about job duties. They also improve the socialization process by giving newcomers reasonably challenging first assignments, buffering them from excessive demands, helping them form social ties with coworkers, and generating positive emotions around their new work experience.[89]

Coworkers are important socialization agents because they are easily accessible, can answer questions when problems arise, and serve as role models for appropriate behavior. New employees tend to receive this information and support when coworkers welcome them into the work team. Coworkers also aid the socialization process by being flexible and tolerant in their interactions with new hires.

Organizational socialization is most successful when companies help newcomers strengthen their social bonds with other employees. This can occur casually through immediate involvement with a welcoming team of current employees. It also occurs through various social interaction events, particularly where current staff members help newcomers get acquainted with people elsewhere in the organization. For newcomers who work remotely, the best advice is to have them meet coworkers face-to-face within a few months after joining the company. However, distant workers can also build a sense of community through regular video interactions and access to the internal digital communication platform as soon as they accept the job offer.

OB THEORY TO PRACTICE

Effective Socialization of New Hires at Circles.Life[90]

Circles.Life has an award-winning onboarding process that personalizes the socialization process and gets its new employees quickly and comfortably connected with their coworkers.

A week before their first work day, new employees at the Singapore-based mobile virtual network operator receive a personalized welcome email that includes links to information about the company. They are also invited to say more about themselves. Recruits receive additional pre-onboarding reminders as the first day approaches.

On day one, new hires are welcomed by Circles.Life's people and culture team in person or online and receive a Circles.Life welcome kit (called a "swag") symbolizing that the individual really has been hired and is valued.

"The onboarding journey does not end on day one," explains Jack Ang, Circles.Life's senior human resource business partner. "To ensure that new hires are fully integrated into the Circles.Life culture, we introduced bite-sized modules around rewards, that help with their long-term engagement." This learning process is spread over the first 90 days of employment.

Personalized onboarding has improved the employee socialization process, says Ang. "As a direct impact of utilizing a more personalized approach, we were able to significantly reduce the amount of time spent on set up on day one, resulting in a higher level of engagement amongst new Circles.Lifers."

Study Checklist

Connect® is available for *M: Organizational Behavior.* Additional resources include:

✓ Exercises:

- **Case Analysis:** Apply concepts within the context of a real-world situation.
- **Click and Drag:** Helps make the connection between theory and application through matching, ranking, or grouping activities.
- **Video Case:** See management in action through interactive videos.
- **Self-Assessment:** Designed to promote student self-awareness and reflection, these research-based surveys contain detailed feedback for students.
- **Application-Based Activities:** These highly interactive, application- and analysis-based exercises allow students to take on specific roles to complete management related tasks within a real-world context.

✓ **SmartBook 2.0™**—Smartbook 2.0 is an adaptive learning solution that provides personalized learning to individual student needs, continually adapts to pinpoint knowledge gaps and focuses learning on concepts requiring additional study. It fosters more productive learning, takes the guesswork out of what to study, and helps students better prepare for class.

©Natthawat Jamnapa/123RF

Notes

1. R. Lacerte, "Why Embracing Subcultures Inside Your Company Is Critical to Scaling Your Business," *Fast Company*, January 7, 2022; R. Lacerte, "Creating a Culture (& Why That's So Important from the Start)," *Bill.Com* (blog), accessed March 22, 2022.
2. The terms *organizational culture* and *corporate culture* were popularized in 1982 in T.E. Deal and A.A. Kennedy, *Corporate Cultures* (Reading, MA: Addison-Wesley, 1982); T.J. Peters and R.H. Waternam, *In Search of Excellence: Lessons from America's Best-Run Companies* (New York: Warner, 1982). However, this phrase did appear more than a decade earlier in N. Margulies, "Organizational Culture and Psychological Growth," *The Journal of Applied Behavioral Science* 5, no. 4 (1969): 491–508; S. Silverzweig and R.F. Allen, "Changing the Corporate Culture," *Sloan Management Review* 17, no. 3 (1976): 33–34. The notion that organizations have dominant values can be traced back to P. Selznick, *Leadership in Administration: A Sociological Interpretation* (Evanston, IL: Row, Peterson and Company, 1957), 19–22.
3. A. Williams, P. Dobson, and M. Walters, *Changing Culture: New Organizational Approaches* (London: Institute of Personnel Management, 1989); E.H. Schein, "What Is Culture?," in *Reframing Organizational Culture*, ed. P.J. Frost et al. (Newbury Park, CA: Sage, 1991), 243–53. One of the earliest research papers discussing "organizational culture" explicitly defines the concept in terms of values, attitudes, and norms, which differs from "observable" variables (i.e., artifacts). See: N. Margulies, "Organizational Culture and Psychological Growth," *The Journal of Applied Behavioral Science* 5 (1969): 491–508.
4. B.M. Meglino and E.C. Ravlin, "Individual Values in Organizations: Concepts, Controversies, and Research," *Journal of Management* 24, no. 3 (1998): 351–89; S. Hitlin and J.A. Pilavin, "Values: Reviving a Dormant Concept," *Annual Review of Sociology* 30 (2004): 359–93; L. Sagiv et al., "Personal Values in Human Life," *Nature Human Behaviour* 1, no. 9 (2017): 630–39; S. Arieli, L. Sagiv, and S. Roccas, "Values at Work: The Impact of Personal Values in Organisations," *Applied Psychology* 69, no. 2 (2020): 230–75.
5. N.M. Ashkanasy, "The Case for Culture," in *Debating Organization*, ed. R. Westwood and S. Clegg (Malden, MA: Blackwell, 2003), 300–10.
6. S.J. Hogan and L.V. Coote, "Organizational Culture, Innovation, and Performance: A Test of Schein's Model," *Journal of Business Research* 67, no. 8 (2014): 1609–21.
7. E.H. Schein, *Organizational Culture and Leadership*, 5th ed. (Hoboken, N.J.: John Wiley & Sons, 2017), Chaps 1–2. The notion that shared assumptions are the heart of organizational culture is more strongly stated in the 3rd edition (2004) of Schein's book.
8. M. Lagace, "Gerstner: Changing Culture at IBM," *HBS Working Knowledge*, September 12, 2002.
9. B. Kabanoff and J. Daly, "Espoused Values in Organisations," *Australian Journal of Management* 27, Special issue (2002): 89–104; H. Bourne and M. Jenkins, "Organizational Values: A Dynamic Perspective," *Organization Studies* 34, no. 4 (2013): 495–514.
10. K. Jonsen et al., "Evaluating Espoused Values: Does Articulating Values Pay Off?," *European Management Journal* 33, no. 5 (2015): 332–40; L.W. Lee, D. Hannah, and I.P. McCarthy, "Do Your Employees Think Your Slogan Is 'Fake News?' A Framework for Understanding the Impact of Fake Company Slogans on Employees," *Journal of Product & Brand Management* 29, no. 2 (2019): 199–208.
11. "Mission & Culture Survey 2019" (Mill Valley, Calif.: Glassdoor, July 9, 2019); R. Gailey, I. Johnston, and A. LeSueur, "Aligning Culture with the Bottom Line: How Companies Can Accelerate Progress" (Chicago: Heidrick & Struggles, June 2021); R. Carpenter, "Global Culture Survey 2021: The Link between Culture and Competitive Advantage" (New York: Katzenbach Center, PwC, June 2021); "PwC Pulse Survey: Next in Work," Future of Work (U.S.A.: PwC, August 2021); "State of the Sector 2021/22" (London: Arthur J. Gallagher & Co., January 2022); "Global Culture Research Report 2022: Strengthening Workplace Culture–A Tool for Retaining and Empowering Employees Globally" (Alexandria, VA: SHRM, June 2022).

12. C. Ostroff, A.J. Kinicki, and R.S. Muhammad, "Organizational Culture and Climate," in *Handbook of Psychology*, 2nd ed., ed. I.B. Weiner (New York: Wiley, 2012), 643–76.

13. R. Hastings and P. McCord, *Netflix Culture: Freedom and Responsibility* (Los Gatos, CA: Netflix, August 2009); S. Ramachandran and J. Flint, "At Netflix, Radical Transparency and Blunt Firings Unsettle the Ranks," *Wall Street Journal*, October 25, 2018; B. Murphy Jr., "You Don't Just Get Fired at Netflix," *Inc.* October 27, 2018; E. Hakikat, "How Workday Maintains Employee Experience through Business Growth," *Inside HR*, December 9, 2019; R. Hastings and E. Meyer, *No Rules: Netflix and the Culture of Reinvention* (New York: Penguin Random House, 2020).

14. For reviews of organizational culture survey instruments, see D.E. Leidner and T. Kayworth, "A Review of Culture in Information Systems Research: Toward a Theory of Information Technology Culture Conflict," *MIS Quarterly* 30, no. 2 (2006): 357–99; S. Scott-Findlay and C.A. Estabrooks, "Mapping the Organizational Culture Research in Nursing: A Literature Review," *Journal of Advanced Nursing* 56, no. 5 (2006): 498–513; B. Powell et al., "Measures of Organizational Culture, Organizational Climate, and Implementation Climate in Behavioral Health: A Systematic Review," *Implementation Research and Practice* 2 (2021): 1–29; K.S. Hsiung et al., "Measures of Organizational Culture and Climate in Primary Care: A Systematic Review," *Journal of General Internal Medicine* 36, no. 2 (2021): 487–99.

15. L. Guiso, P. Sapienza, and L. Zingales, "The Value of Corporate Culture," *Journal of Financial Economics* 117, no. 1 (2015): 60–76.

16. J. Martin, P.J. Frost, and O.A. O'Neill, "Organizational Culture: Beyond Struggles for Intellectual Dominance," in *Handbook of Organization Studies*, ed. S. Clegg et al. (London: Sage, 2006), 725–53; N.E. Fenton and S. Inglis, "A Critical Perspective on Organizational Values," *Nonprofit Management and Leadership* 17, no. 3 (2007): 335–47; K. Haukelid, "Theories of (Safety) Culture Revisited—An Anthropological Approach," *Safety Science* 46, no. 3 (2008): 413–26.

17. G. Hofstede, "Identifying Organizational Subcultures: An Empirical Approach," *Journal of Management Studies* 35, no. 1 (1990): 1–12; J. Martin and C. Siehl, "Organizational Culture and Counterculture: An Uneasy Symbiosis," *Organizational Dynamics* (1983): 52–64; E. Carlström and L.-E. Olsson, "The Association between Subcultures and Resistance to Change—in a Swedish Hospital Clinic," *Journal of Health Organization and Management* 28, no. 4 (2014): 458–76.

18. H. Silver, "Does a University Have a Culture?," *Studies in Higher Education* 28, no. 2 (2003): 157–69.

19. A. Sinclair, "Approaches to Organizational Culture and Ethics," *Journal of Business Ethics* 12 (1993); T.E. Deal and A.A. Kennedy, *The New Corporate Cultures* (Cambridge, MA: Perseus Books, 1999), Chap. 10; A. Boisnier and J. Chatman, "The Role of Subcultures in Agile Organizations," in *Leading and Managing People in Dynamic Organizations*, ed. R. Petersen and E. Mannix (Mahwah, NJ: Erlbaum, 2003), 87–112; C. Morrill, M.N. Zald, and H. Rao, "Covert Political Conflict in Organizations: Challenges from Below," *Annual Review of Sociology* 29, no. 1 (2003): 391–415.

20. J.S. Ott, *The Organizational Culture Perspective* (Pacific Grove, CA: Brooks/Cole, 1989), Chap. 2; J.S. Pederson and J.S. Sorensen, *Organizational Cultures in Theory and Practice* (Aldershot, UK: Gower, 1989), 27–29; M.O. Jones, *Studying Organizational Symbolism: What, How, Why?* (Thousand Oaks, CA: Sage, 1996).

21. A. Furnham and B. Gunter, "Corporate Culture: Definition, Diagnosis, and Change," *International Review of Industrial and Organizational Psychology* 8 (1993): 233–61; E.H. Schein, "Organizational Culture," *American Psychologist* (1990): 109–19; M.G. Pratt and A. Rafaeli, "Artifacts and Organizations: Understanding Our 'Object-Ive' Reality," in *Artifacts and Organizations*, ed. A. Rafaeli and M.G. Pratt (Mahwah, NJ: Lawrence Erlbaum Associates, 2006), 279–88.

22. T.E. Deal and A.A. Kennedy, *Corporate Cultures* (Reading, MA: Addison-Wesley, 1982), chap. 5; C.J. Boudens, "The Story of Work: A Narrative Analysis of Workplace Emotion," *Organization Studies* 26, no. 9 (2005): 1285–306; S. Denning, *The Leader's Guide to Storytelling* (San Francisco: Jossey-Bass, 2005).

23. A.L. Wilkins, "Organizational Stories as Symbols Which Control the Organization," in *Organizational Symbolism*, ed. L.R. Pondy et al. (Greenwich, CT: JAI Press, 1984), 81–92; R. Zemke, "Storytelling: Back to a Basic," *Training* 27, no. 3 (1990): 44–50; J.C. Meyer, "Tell Me a Story: Eliciting Organizational Values from Narratives," *Communication Quarterly* 43 (1995): 210–24; W. Swap et al., "Using Mentoring and Storytelling to Transfer Knowledge in the Workplace," *Journal of Management Information Systems* 18 (2001): 95–114.

24. J. Mossman, "Employee-Friendly Workplace Culture a Key to Company Success," *Denver Post*, April 21, 2013; Darden MBA, "'Community First, Company Second': Javier Rodriguez, DaVita Kidney Care" (YouTube, November 18, 2015); Stanford Graduate School of Business, "DaVita CEO Kent Thiry on Building a Signature Company Culture" (YouTube, November 23, 2015); D. Hoerman, "Inside DaVita's Corporate Culture: 'A Community First and a Company Second,'" *Chief Executive*, August 10, 2018.

25. A.C.T. Smith and B. Stewart, "Organizational Rituals: Features, Functions and Mechanisms," *International Journal of Management Reviews* 13 (2011): 113–33.

26. F. Stone, "The Conversation: ACL Services Boss Laurie Schultz Knows Fraud When She Sees It," *BC Business*, February 7, 2017; "5 Questions on Culture with Laurie Schultz, CEO, Galvanize," *Business in Vancouver*, January 2020, pp. 30–31.

27. "The Ultimate Chairman," *Business Times Singapore*, September 3, 2005.

28. T. Kelley and D. Kelley, *Creative Confidence: Unleashing the Creative Potential within Us All* (New York: Random House, 2013), 198.

29. G. Turner and J. Myerson, *New Workspace New Culture: Office Design as a Catalyst for Change* (Aldershot, UK: Gower, 1998); J.C. McElroy and P.C. Morrow, "Employee Reactions to Office Redesign: A Naturally Occurring Quasi-Field Experiment in a Multi-Generational Setting," *Human Relations* 63 (2010): 609–36; T.J. Kallio, K.-M. Kallio, and A.J. Blomberg, "Physical Space, Culture and Organisational Creativity—A Longitudinal Study," *Facilities* 33 (2015): 389–411; S. Zerella, K. von Treuer, and S.L. Albrecht, "The Influence of Office Layout Features on Employee Perception of Organizational Culture," *Journal of Environmental Psychology* 54 (2017): 1–10.

30. K.D. Elsbach and B.A. Bechky, "It's More Than a Desk: Working Smarter through Leveraged Office Design," *California Management Review* 49, no. 2 (2007): 80–101.

31. Churchill apparently made this statement on October 28, 1943, in the British House of Commons, when London, damaged by bombings in World War II, was about to be rebuilt.

32. *How to Create a Successful Organizational Culture: Build It—Literally* (Holland, MI: Haworth Inc., June 2015).

33. G. Forsythe, K. Kuhla, and D. Rice, "The CEO's Role in Shaping an Organization's Culture," *Chief Executive*, February 6, 2018; M. Parker, "Why Leaders Need to Make Corporate Culture the Centre of Corporate Strategy," *CEOWORLD Magazine*, June 19, 2021.

34. J.C. Collins and J.I. Porras, *Built to Last: Successful Habits of Visionary Companies* (London, UK: Century, 1994); T.E. Deal and A.A. Kennedy, *The New Corporate Cultures* (Cambridge, MA: Perseus Books, 1999); R. Barrett, *The Values-Driven Organization*, 2nd ed. (New York: Routledge, 2017); J.M. Kouzes and B.Z. Posner, *The Leadership Challenge*, Sixth ed. (Hoboken, NJ: John Wiley & Sons, 2017), Chap. 3.

35. C. Siehl and J. Martin, "Organizational Culture: A Key to Financial Performance?," in *Organizational Climate and Culture*, ed. B. Schneider (San Francisco: Jossey-Bass, 1990), 241–81; G.G. Gordon and N. Di-Tomaso, "Predicting Corporate Performance from Organizational Culture," *Journal of Management Studies* 29 (1992): 783–98; J.P. Kotter and J.L. Heskett, *Corporate Culture and Performance* (New York: Free Press, 1992); C.P.M. Wilderom, U. Glunk, and R. Maslowski, "Organizational Culture as a Predictor of Organizational Performance," in *Handbook of Organizational Culture and Climate*, ed. N.M. Ashkanasy, C.P.M. Wilderom, and M.F. Peterson (Thousand Oaks, CA: Sage, 2000), 193–210; A. Carmeli and A. Tishler, "The Relationships between Intangible Organizational Elements and Organizational Performance," *Strategic Management Journal* 25 (2004): 1257–78; S. Teerikangas and P. Very, "The Culture–Performance Relationship in M&A: From Yes/No to How," *British Journal of Management* 17, no. S1 (2006): S31–S48.

36. Y. Wiener, "Forms of Value Systems: A Focus on Organizational Effectiveness and Cultural Change and Maintenance," *Academy of Management Review* 13, no. 4 (1988): 534–45; J.A. Chatman and S.E. Cha, "Leading by Leveraging Culture," *California Management Review* 45 (2003): 20–34; M. Alvesson, *Understanding Organizational Culture*, 2nd ed. (London: Sage, 2013).

37. T.E. Deal and A.A. Kennedy, *The New Corporate Cultures* (Reading, MA: Perseus Books, 1999), 22.

38. B. Ashforth and F. Mael, "Social Identity Theory and the Organization," *Academy of Management Review* 14 (1989): 20–39; M. Alvesson, *Understanding Organizational Culture*, 2nd ed. (London: Sage, 2013).

39. M.R. Louis, "Surprise and Sensemaking: What Newcomers Experience in Entering Unfamiliar Organizational Settings," *Administrative Science Quarterly* 25 (1980): 226–51; J.W. Barnes et al., "The Role of Culture Strength in Shaping Sales Force Outcomes," *Journal of Personal Selling & Sales Management* 26, no. 3 (2006): 255–70; M.W. Kramer, "Sensemaking," in *The International Encyclopedia of Organizational Communication*, ed. C.R. Scott and L.K. Lewis (John Wiley & Sons, Ltd, 2017); W.S. Sherman and K.J. Roberto, "Are You Talkin' to Me?: The Role of Culture in Crisis Management Sensemaking," *Management Decision* 58, no. 10 (2020): 2193–2211.

40. "Korn Ferry Global Study: Driving Culture Change Key Leadership Priority," Press Release (Los Angeles: Korn Ferry, February 4, 2016).

41. H. McCracken, "Satya Nadella Rewrites Microsoft's Code," *Fast Company*, September 18, 2017; H. Ibarra, A. Rattan, and A. Johnston, "Microsoft: Instilling a Growth Mindset," *London Business School Review* 29, no. 3 (October 2018): 50–53.

42. C.A. O'Reilly III and J.A. Chatman, "Culture as Social Control: Corporations, Cults, and Commitment," *Research in Organizational Behavior* 18 (1996): 157–200; B. Spector and H. Lane, "Exploring the Distinctions between a High Performance Culture and a Cult," *Strategy & Leadership* 35 (2007): 18–24. Organizational cults are closely associated with high organizational identification, which has several known dysfunctional outcomes for companies and individuals. See S. Conroy et al., "Where There Is Light, There Is Dark: A Review of the Detrimental Outcomes of High Organizational Identification," *Journal of Organizational Behavior* 38 (2017): 184–203.

43. J.P. Kotter and J.L. Heskett, *Corporate Culture and Performance* (New York: Free Press, 1992), Chap. 4; B.M. Bass and R.E. Riggio, *Transformational Leadership*, 2nd ed. (New York: Routledge, 2006), Chap. 7; L.M. Kotrba et al., "Do Consistent Corporate Cultures Have Better Business Performance? Exploring the Interaction Effects," *Human Relations* 65, no. 2 (2012): 241–62; D.P. Costanza et al., "The Effect of Adaptive Organizational Culture on Long-Term Survival," *Journal of Business and Psychology* 31 (2016): 361–81.

44. W.E. Baker and J.M. Sinkula, "The Synergistic Effect of Market Orientation and Learning Orientation on Organizational Performance," *Academy of Marketing Science Journal* 27, no. 4 (1999): 411–27; O. Pesämaa et al., "How a Learning Orientation Affects Drivers of Innovativeness and Performance in Service Delivery," *Journal of Engineering and Technology Management* 30 (2013): 169–87; J.C. Real, J.L. Roldán, and A. Leal, "From Entrepreneurial Orientation and Learning Orientation to Business Performance: Analysing the Mediating Role of Organizational Learning and the Moderating Effects of Organizational Size," *British Journal of Management* 25 (2014): 186–208.

45. Great Place to Work, "Working at Workday," Great Place to Work®, 2020; "Harnessing the Power of Integrity at Workday," *Workday Blog* (blog), March 15, 2022.

46. T. Krisher and D.A. Durbin, "General Motors CEO Akerson Leads Comeback from Bankruptcy by Ruffling Company's Bureaucracy," *Associated Press Newswires*, December 17, 2011.

47. G. Bensinger and J.S. Lublin, "Uber Fires More Than 20 People in Harassment Investigation," *The Wall Street Journal*, June 7, 2017; S. Levin, "Uber's Scandals, Blunders and PR Disasters: The Full List," *Guardian*, June 18, 2017; B. Edelman, "Uber Can't Be Fixed—It's Time for Regulators to Shut It Down," *Harvard Business Review*, June 21, 2017; D. Khosrowshahi, "Uber's New Cultural Norms," Linkedin Blog (blog), November 7, 2017, https://www.linkedin.com/pulse/ubers-new-cultural-norms-dara-khosrowshahi; S. Nicholls, "The Uber Story," transcript, Four Corners (Sydney: ABC Australia, March 13, 2019).

48. M.L. Marks, "Adding Cultural Fit to Your Diligence Checklist," *Mergers & Acquisitions* 34, no. 3 (1999): 14–20; E.H. Schein, *The Corporate Culture Survival Guide* (San Francisco: Jossey-Bass, 1999), Chap. 8; S. Teerikangas and P. Very, "The Culture-Performance Relationship in M&A: From Yes/No to How," *British Journal of Management* 17, no. S1 (2006): S31–S48; G.K. Stahl and A. Voigt, "Do Cultural Differences Matter in Mergers and Acquisitions? A Tentative Model and Examination," *Organization Science* 19, no. 1 (2008): 160–76.

49. "Mercer Survey Reveals Culture Issues Derail M&A Transactions at an Alarming Rate," News Release (New York: Mercer, September 24, 2018); "The State of the Deal: M&A Trends 2019" (New York: Deloitte, December 2018).

50. "Mercer Survey Reveals Culture Issues Derail M&A Transactions at an Alarming Rate," News Release (New York: Mercer, September 24, 2018); "The State of the Deal: M&A Trends 2019" (New York: Deloitte, December 2018); R. Gailey, I. Johnston, and A. LeSueur, "Aligning Culture with the Bottom Line: How Companies Can Accelerate Progress" (Chicago: Heidrick & Struggles, June 2021); J.R. Graham et al., "Corporate Culture: Evidence from the Field," *Journal of Financial Economics* 146, no. 2 (2022): 552–93; G. Nahass and B. Shipman, "Transact to Transform: PwC's 2023 M&A Integration Survey" (U.S.A.: PricewaterhouseCoopers, April 2023).

51. S. Gopalan, J. Dittrich, and R. Nelson, "Analysis of Organizational Culture: A Critical Step in Mergers and Acquisitions," *Journal of Business Strategies* 11, no. 2 (1994): 124–40; C.A. Schorg, C.A. Raiborn, and M.F. Massoud, "Using a 'Cultural Audit' to Pick M&A Winners," *Journal of Corporate Accounting & Finance* (2004): 47–55. These audits (known as cultural audits) also diagnose the need for and risks of organizational culture change within one organization. See: M.R. Testa and L.J. Sipe, "The Organizational Culture Audit: Countering Cultural Ambiguity in the Service Context," *Open Journal of Leadership* 2, no. 2 (2013): 36–44; M. Mitra, M. Brankin, and P. Brankin, "Cultural Audits as Tools for Enabling Processes of Change in the NHS," *British Journal of Healthcare Management* 23, no. 10 (2017): 492–97.

52. A.R. Malekazedeh and A. Nahavandi, "Making Mergers Work by Managing Cultures," *Journal of Business Strategy* (1990): 55–57; K.W. Smith, "A Brand-New Culture for the Merged Firm," *Mergers and Acquisitions* 35 (2000): 45–50.

53. A. Hyland, "Howzat? Wesfarmers and Boral Chairman Bob Every on Career and Overcoming Adversity," *Australian Financial Review*, July 6, 2015.

54. G. Nahass and B. Shipman, "Transact to Transform: PwC's 2023 M&A Integration Survey" (U.S.A.: PricewaterhouseCoopers, April 2023). The percentage of acquisitions that were "stand alone" (the acquired business was operated separately from the rest of the organization) ranged from 6 percent to 13 percent and averaged 10.4 percent in PwC's five M&A surveys in 2010, 2013, 2016, 2019, and 2023. In most recent (2023) survey, stand alones represented 6 percent of all acquisitions.

55. J. Martin, "Can Organizational Culture Be Managed?" in *Organizational Culture*, ed. P.J. Frost et al. (Beverly Hills, CA: Sage, 1985), 95–98.

56. M. Weinberger, "How Microsoft CEO Satya Nadella Did What Steve Ballmer and Bill Gates Couldn't," *Business Insider*, January 31, 2016.

57. E.H. Schein, "The Role of the Founder in Creating Organizational Culture," *Organizational Dynamics* 12, no. 1 (1983): 13–28; A.S. Tsui et al., "Unpacking the Relationship between CEO Leadership Behavior and Organizational Culture," *Leadership Quarterly* 17 (2006): 113–37; Y. Berson, S. Oreg, and T. Dvir, "CEO Values, Organizational Culture and Firm Outcomes," *Journal of Organizational Behavior* 29, no. 5 (2008): 615–33; B. Schneider, M.G. Ehrhart, and W.H. Macey, "Organizational Climate and Culture," *Annual Review of Psychology* 64, no. 1 (2013): 361–88.

58. Y. Berson, S. Oreg, and T. Dvir, "CEO Values, Organizational Culture and Firm Outcomes," *Journal of Organizational Behavior* 29, no. 5 (2008): 615–33; A.S. Klein, J. Wallis, and R.A. Cooke, "The Impact of Leadership Styles on Organizational Culture and Firm Effectiveness: An Empirical Study," *Journal of Management & Organization* 19 (2013): 241–54; D.V. Day, M.A. Griffin, and K.R. Louw, "The Climate and Culture of Leadership in Organizations," in *The Oxford Handbook of Organizational Climate and Culture*, ed. B. Schneider and K.M. Barbera (New York: Oxford University Press, 2014), 101–17.

59. M.J. Gelfand et al., "Conflict Cultures in Organizations: How Leaders Shape Conflict Cultures and Their Organizational-Level Consequences," *Journal of Applied Psychology* 97, no. 6 (2012): 1131–47; R.C. Liden et al., "Servant Leadership and Serving Culture: Influence on Individual and Unit Performance," *Academy of Management Journal* 57, no. 5 (2014): 1434–52.

60. J.C. McElroy and P.C. Morrow, "Employee Reactions to Office Redesign: A Naturally Occurring Quasi-Field Experiment in a Multi-Generational Setting," *Human Relations* 63 (2010): 609–36; S.J. Hogan and L.V. Coote, "Organizational Culture, Innovation, and Performance: A Test of Schein's Model," *Journal of Business Research* 67 (2014): 1609–21; S. Zerella, K. von Treuer, and S.L. Albrecht, "The Influence of Office Layout Features on Employee Perception of Organizational Culture," *Journal of Environmental Psychology* 54 (2017): 1–10.

61. M. De Pree, *Leadership Is an Art* (East Lansing: Michigan State University Press, 1987).

62. J. Kerr and J.W. Slocum Jr., "Managing Corporate Culture through Reward Systems," *Academy of Management Executive* 1 (1987): 99–107; J.M. Higgins et al., "Using Cultural Artifacts to Change and Perpetuate Strategy," *Journal of Change Management* 6, no. 4 (2006): 397–415; H. Hofstetter and I. Harpaz, "Declared versus Actual Organizational Culture as Indicated by an Organization's Performance Appraisal," *International Journal of Human Resource Management* 26, no. 4 (2015): 445–66.

63. A. Griswold, "Uber Is Designed so That for One Employee to Get Ahead, Another Must Fail," *Quartz*, February 27, 2017; M.R. Dickey, "Inside Uber's New Approach to Employee Performance Reviews," *TechCrunch*, August 1, 2017.

64. P. Strozniak, "How Workplace Culture Drives Performance," *Credit Union Times*, February 22, 2022.

65. B. Schneider, "The People Make the Place," *Personnel Psychology* 40, no. 3 (1987): 437–53; B. Schneider et al., "Personality and Organizations: A Test of the Homogeneity of Personality Hypothesis," *Journal of Applied Psychology* 83, no. 3 (1998): 462–70; T.R. Giberson, C.J. Resick, and M.W. Dickson, "Embedding Leader Characteristics: An Examination of Homogeneity of Personality and Values in Organizations," *Journal of Applied Psychology* 90, no. 5 (2005): 1002–10.

66. "More Than One-Third of Workers Would Pass On Perfect Job If Corporate Culture Was Not a Fit, Survey Finds," News Release (Menlo Park, Calif.: Robert Half, November 27, 2018); "Mission & Culture Survey 2019" (Mill Valley, Calif.: Glassdoor, July 9, 2019); "Cappfinity Survey: 80 percent of Job Seekers Want to Understand Company Culture before Accepting Offer," Press Release (New York: Cappfinity, January 27, 2022); "Randstad Workmonitor 2022" (Amsterdam: Randstad Holding nv, April 2022); "Unresponsive Companies, Beware! Survey Finds That 1 in 5 Job Candidates Will Hurt Your Brand If You Don't Follow Up" (New York: The Conference Board, February 14, 2023).

67. T.A. Judge and D.M. Cable, "Applicant Personality, Organizational Culture, and Organization Attraction," *Personnel Psychology* 50, no. 2 (1997): 359–94; D.S. Chapman et al., "Applicant Attraction to Organizations and Job Choice: A Meta-Analytic Review of the Correlates of Recruiting Outcomes," *Journal of Applied*

Psychology 90, no. 5 (2005): 928–44; A.L. Kristof-Brown, R.D. Zimmerman, and E.C. Johnson, "Consequences of Individuals' Fit at Work: A Meta-Analysis of Person–Job, Person–Organization, Person–Group, and Person–Supervisor Fit," *Personnel Psychology* 58, no. 2 (2005): 281–342; C. Hu, H.C. Su, and C.I.B. Chen, "The Effect of Person–Organization Fit Feedback via Recruitment Web Sites on Applicant Attraction," *Computers in Human Behavior* 23, no. 5 (2007): 2509–23.

68. A. Kristof-Brown, "Perceived Applicant Fit: Distinguishing between Recruiters' Perceptions of Person–Job and Person–Organization Fit," *Personnel Psychology* 53, no. 3 (2000): 643–71; A.E.M. Van Vianen, "Person–Organization Fit: The Match between Newcomers' and Recruiters' Preferences for Organizational Cultures," *Personnel Psychology* 53 (2000): 113–49.

69. E. Keating, "'Leadership Is Not Genetics': How IKEA Australia's National Talent Manager D'neale Prosser Puts Authentic Leadership into Practice," *SmartCompany*, March 8, 2018; "We Believe That Your Values Are More Important Than Your CV," *Human Resources Director Australia*, April 11, 2018.

70. D.M. Cable and J.R. Edwards, "Complementary and Supplementary Fit: A Theoretical and Empirical Integration," *Journal of Applied Psychology* 89, no. 5 (2004): 822–34.

71. T. Perkins, "Still Hiring for 'Culture Fit'? It's Time to Think Again," *HR Executive*, September 7, 2021; S. Epstein, "What Does Being a 'Cultural Fit' Actually Mean?," *BBC Worklife*, October 21, 2021; M. Ahmed, "ICYMI: 'Culture Fit' Can Sometimes Be Used to Mask Bias in Hiring," *People Matters*, March 19, 2022.

72. C.A. O'Reilly III, J. Chatman, and D.F. Caldwell, "People and Organizational Culture: A Profile Comparison Approach to Assessing Person–Organization Fit," *Academy of Management Journal* 34 (1991): 487–516.

73. J. Van Maanen, "Breaking In: Socialization to Work," in *Handbook of Work, Organization, and Society*, ed. R. Dubin (Chicago: Rand McNally, 1976).

74. D.G. Allen, "Do Organizational Socialization Tactics Influence Newcomer Embeddedness and Turnover?," *Journal of Management* 32, no. 2 (2006): 237–56; A.M. Saks, K.L. Uggerslev, and N.E. Fassina, "Socialization Tactics and Newcomer Adjustment: A Meta-Analytic Review and Test of a Model," *Journal of Vocational Behavior* 70, no. 3 (2007): 413–46.

75. S.L. McShane, G. O'Neill, and T. Travaglione, "Managing Employee Values in Values-Driven Organizations: Contradiction, Façade, and Illusions" (paper presented at the 21st Annual ANZAM Conference, Sydney, Australia, December 2007); S.L. McShane, G. O'Neill, and T. Travaglione, "Rethinking the Values-Driven Organization Process: From Values Engineering to Behavioral Domain Training" (paper presented at the Academy of Management 2008 Annual Meeting, Anaheim, CA, 2008).

76. G. T. Chao et al., "Organizational Socialization: Its Content and Consequences," *Journal of Applied Psychology* 79 (1994): 450–63; H. D. Cooper-Thomas and N. Anderson, "Organizational Socialization: A Field Study into Socialization Success and Rate," *International Journal of Selection and Assessment* 13, no. 2 (2005): 116–28.

77. N. Nicholson, "A Theory of Work Role Transitions," *Administrative Science Quarterly* 29 (1984): 172–91; A. Elfering et al., "First Years in Job: A Three-Wave Analysis of Work Experiences," *Journal of Vocational Behavior* 70, no. 1 (2007): 97–115; B.E. Ashforth, D.M. Sluss, and A.M. Saks, "Socialization Tactics, Proactive Behavior, and Newcomer Learning: Integrating Socialization Models," *Journal of Vocational Behavior* 70, no. 3 (2007): 447–62; T.N. Bauer, "Newcomer Adjustment during Organizational Socialization: A Meta-Analytic Review of Antecedents, Outcomes, and Methods," *Journal of Applied Psychology* 92, no. 3 (2007): 707–21.

78. J.M. Beyer and D.R. Hannah, "Building on the Past: Enacting Established Personal Identities in a New Work Setting," *Organization Science* 13 (2002): 636–52; H.D.C. Thomas and N. Anderson, "Newcomer Adjustment: The Relationship between Organizational Socialization Tactics, Information Acquisition and Attitudes," *Journal of Occupational and Organizational Psychology* 75 (2002): 423–37.

79. L.W. Porter, E.E. Lawler III, and J.R. Hackman, *Behavior in Organizations* (New York: McGraw Hill, 1975), 163–67; J. Van Maanen, "Breaking In: Socialization to Work," in *Handbook of Work, Organization, and Society*, ed. R. Dubin (Chicago: Rand McNally, 1976), 67–130; D.C. Feldman, "The Multiple Socialization of Organization Members," *Academy of Management Review* 6 (1981): 309–18.

80. B.E. Ashforth and A.M. Saks, "Socialization Tactics: Longitudinal Effects on Newcomer Adjustment," *Academy of Management Journal* 39 (1996): 149–78; J.D. Kammeyer-Mueller and C.R. Wanberg, "Unwrapping the Organizational Entry Process: Disentangling Multiple Antecedents and Their Pathways to Adjustment," *Journal of Applied Psychology* 88, no. 5 (2003): 779–94.

81. L.W. Porter, E.E. Lawler III, and J.R. Hackman, *Behavior in Organizations* (New York: McGraw Hill, 1975), Chap. 5.

82. M.R. Louis, "Surprise and Sensemaking: What Newcomers Experience in Entering Unfamiliar Organizational Settings," *Administrative Science Quarterly* 25 (1980): 226–51.

83. M. Kodama, "Functions of Career Resilience against Reality Shock, Focusing on Full-Time Employees during Their First Year of Work," *Japanese Psychological Research* 59, no. 4 (2017): 255–65; C. Schott, T. Steen, and D.D. Van Kleef, "Reality Shock and Public Service Motivation: A Longitudinal, Qualitative Study among Dutch Veterinary Inspectors," *International Journal of Public Administration* 42, no. 6 (2019): 468–81; T. Voss and M. Kunter, "'Reality Shock' of Beginning Teachers? Changes in Teacher Candidates' Emotional Exhaustion and Constructivist-Oriented Beliefs," *Journal of Teacher Education* 71, no. 3 (2020): 292–306.

84. D.L. Nelson, "Organizational Socialization: A Stress Perspective," *Journal of Occupational Behavior* 8 (1987): 311–24; A. Elfering et al., "First Years in Job: A Three-Wave Analysis of Work Experiences," *Journal of Vocational Behavior* 70 (2007): 97–115; C.-M. Alcover et al., "Understanding the Changing Nature of Psychological Contracts in 21st Century Organizations: A Multiple-Foci Exchange Relationships Approach and Proposed Framework," *Organizational Psychology Review* 7, no. 1 (2017): 4–35.

85. J.P. Wanous, *Organizational Entry* (Reading, MA: Addison-Wesley, 1992); J. E. Baur et al., "A Historical Approach to Realistic Job Previews: An Exploration into Their Origins, Evolution, and Recommendations for the Future," *Journal of Management History* 20, no. 2 (2014): 200–23.

86. J.M. Phillips, "Effects of Realistic Job Previews on Multiple Organizational Outcomes: A Meta-Analysis," *Academy of Management Journal* 41 (1998): 673–90.

87. D.R. Earnest, D.G. Allen, and R.S. Landis, "Mechanisms Linking Realistic Job Previews with Turnover: A Meta-Analytic Path Analysis," *Personnel Psychology* 64, no. 4 (2011): 865–97; S.A. Shibly, "Mapping the Holistic Impact of Realistic Job Preview—Pre-Recruitment Phase, Post-Recruitment Phase and Marketing Spill-over Effect," *Journal of Organizational Psychology* 19, no. 1 (2019): 70–78.

88. C. Ostroff and S.W.J. Koslowski, "Organizational Socialization as a Learning Process: The Role of Information Acquisition," *Personnel Psychology* 45 (1992): 849–74; H.D. Cooper-Thomas and N. Anderson, "Organizational Socialization: A Field Study into Socialization Success and Rate," *International Journal of Selection and Assessment* 13, no. 2 (2005): 116–28; S. Nifadkar and T. Bauer, "Breach of Belongingness: Newcomer Relationship Conflict, Information, and Task-Related Outcomes during Organizational Socialization," *Journal of Applied Psychology* 101, no. 1 (2016): 1–13.

89. S. Nifadkar, A.S. Tsui, and B.E. Ashforth, "The Way You Make Me Feel and Behave: Supervisor-Triggered Newcomer Affect and Approach-Avoidance Behavior," *Academy of Management Journal* 55, no. 5 (2012): 1146–68.

90. "Winning Secrets: How Circles.Life's 90-Day Onboarding Is One Way to Give Power Back to the Employees," *Human Resources Online*, July 13, 2021.

14 | Organizational Change

Juicy SEPTEMBER/Shutterstock

Learning Objectives

After reading this chapter, you should be able to:

LO14-1 Describe the elements of Lewin's force field analysis model.

LO14-2 Discuss the reasons why people resist organizational change and how change agents should view this resistance.

LO14-3 Outline six strategies for minimizing resistance to change, and debate ways to effectively create an urgency for change.

LO14-4 Discuss how leadership, coalitions, social networks, and pilot projects assist organizational change.

LO14-5 Describe and compare action research and appreciative inquiry as formal approaches to organizational change.

LO14-6 Discuss two cross-cultural and three ethical issues in organizational change.

EE ("Everything Everywhere"), the United Kingdom's largest mobile network, has come a long way over the past dozen years. It was born out of the merger of French-owned Orange and German-owned T-Mobile, who sold EE to BT, the United Kingdom's largest Internet service provider.

Communication has been a key ingredient to successful change throughout EE's turbulent transformation. "During change, employee engagement needs to link heavily to internal communications," advises Linda Kennedy-McCarthy, who was EE's chief change officer during and after the merger. "We used every tool we could to keep our messages consistent and ever-present. We even put up posters in all our toilet cubicles! And we monitored closely whether the roadshow messages were being cascaded effectively."

One important purpose of communicating during EE's transformation was to build an urgency for change. "Senior management may jump up and down about burning platforms, but below the surface everyone could be sitting comfortably," warns Kennedy-McCarthy. "If the front line doesn't understand your message or—even worse—never hears it, you'll never be able to deliver real, meaningful change."

EE also relied on ongoing communication to maintain momentum and reduce employee fear of the unknown. "You have to help people see that the change is real and that it applies to them," says Kennedy-McCarthy. "And it's your responsibility to make sure they understand how the change will benefit them or how not changing will cost them."[1]

Whether at the United Kingdom's largest mobile network or at a much smaller business, effective organizational change requires considerable leadership effort and vigilance. As we will describe throughout this chapter, the challenge of change is not just in deciding which way to go; the challenge is in the execution of this strategy. When leaders discover the need for change and identify some ideas about the preferred route to a better future, the change process involves navigating around the numerous obstacles and gaining organization-wide support for that change.

This chapter unfolds as follows. We begin by introducing Lewin's model of change and its component parts. This discussion includes sources of resistance to change, ways to minimize this resistance, and ways to stabilize desired behaviors. Next, the chapter examines two approaches to organizational change–action research and appreciative inquiry. The final section of this chapter considers both cross-cultural and ethical issues in organizational change.

LO14-1 Describe the elements of Lewin's force field analysis model.

LEWIN'S FORCE FIELD ANALYSIS MODEL

Change is the norm, not the exception, in successful organizations. One of the fundamental messages throughout this book is that organizations operate as open systems. As such, they need to continually evolve internally to keep pace with ongoing changes in their external environment, such as consumer needs, global competition, technological advances, community expectations, government (de)regulation, and environmental

Ready for Organizational Change?[2]

38% of 3,500 employees globally are willing to support organizational change (74% were willing to support change in this survey six years ago).

18% of employees globally in a very large Gallup survey say their leaders help them see how changes made today will affect their organization.

80% of government efforts to transform performance don't fully meet their objectives (according to 3,000 government officials surveyed across 18 countries).

38% of 346,957 U.K. civil service employees say that change is managed well in their organization.

58% of human resource leaders in 115 U.K. local government councils say there is a skills gap in the capability of managers to manage change in their organization.

sarahdesign/Shutterstock

force-field analysis Kurt Lewin's model of systemwide change that helps change agents diagnose the forces that drive and restrain proposed organizational change

unfreezing The first part of the change process, in which the change agent produces disequilibrium between the driving and restraining forces

refreezing The latter part of the change process, in which systems and structures are introduced that reinforce and maintain the desired behaviors

standards. Successful organizations monitor their environments and take appropriate steps to maintain a compatible fit with new external conditions. Rather than resist change, employees in successful companies embrace these ongoing changes as an integral part of organizational life.

It is easy to see environmental forces pushing companies to change the way they operate. What is more difficult to see is the complex interplay of these forces on individuals, teams, and work units. Social psychologist Kurt Lewin developed a model to describe this process using the metaphor of a force field (see Exhibit 14.1).[3] Although it was developed more than a half century ago, contemporary reviews of this subject affirm that Lewin's **force field analysis** model remains one of the most widely respected ways of depicting the change process.[4]

One side of the force field model represents the *driving forces* that push organizations toward a new state of affairs. These might include new competitors or technologies, evolving client expectations, or a host of other environmental changes. Corporate leaders also produce driving forces even when external forces for change aren't apparent. For instance, leaders of successful companies urge employees to strive for higher standards or better practices. David Ogilvy, one of the world's most successful advertising executives, stated this view decades ago when describing the culture of his agency: "We have a habit of divine discontent with our performance. It is an antidote to smugness."[5]

The other side of Lewin's model represents the *restraining forces* that maintain the status quo. These restraining forces are commonly called "resistance to change" because they appear to block the change process. Stability occurs when the driving and restraining forces are roughly in equilibrium—that is, they are of approximately equal strength in opposite directions.

Kurt Lewin described how systems (whether individuals or organizations) have transitions between periods of stability and instability, but he never labeled those transition processes, possibly because he generally viewed stability as a brief condition.[6] However, later adaptations of Lewin's force field model refer to these transitions as unfreezing and refreezing. Specifically, the change process begins by **unfreezing** the current situation, moving to a desired condition, and then **refreezing** the system so it remains in the desired state.

> **I've always believed that when the rate of change inside an institution becomes slower than the rate of change outside, the end is in sight.[7]**
>
> —Jack Welch, former General Electric CEO

Exhibit 14.1 Lewin's Force Field Analysis Model

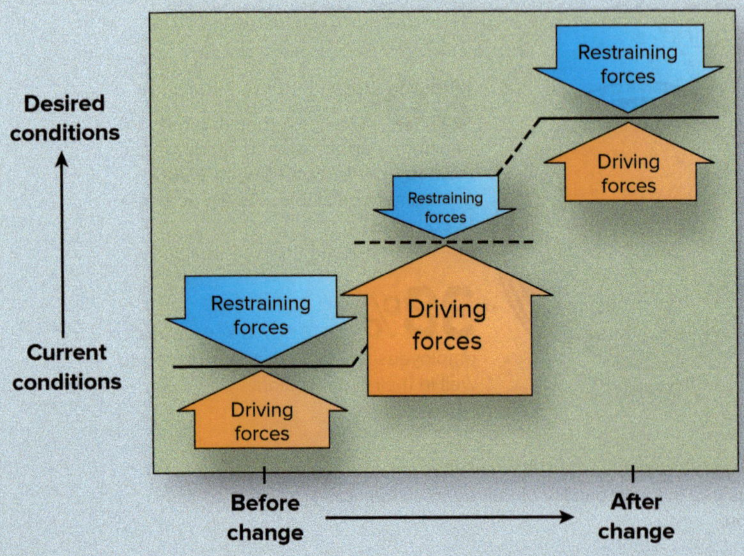

Unfreezing involves producing disequilibrium between the driving and restraining forces. As we will describe later, this may occur by increasing the driving forces, reducing the restraining forces, or doing a combination of both. Refreezing occurs when the organization's systems and structures are aligned with the desired behaviors. They must support and reinforce the new role patterns and prevent the organization from slipping back into the old way of doing things. Over the next two sections of this chapter, we use Lewin's model as well as other change management theories to understand why change is blocked and how the process can progress more smoothly.

LO14-2 Discuss the reasons why people resist organizational change and how change agents should view this resistance.

UNDERSTANDING RESISTANCE TO CHANGE

Mention organizational change to anyone who has attempted to lead these initiatives and the phrase "resistance to change" will inevitably enter the conversation. Resistance to change takes many forms, ranging from overt work stoppages to subtle attempts to continue the old ways.[8] A study of bank employees reported that covert resistance is much more common than overt resistance. Some employees in that study avoided the desired changes by moving into different jobs. Others continued to perform tasks the old way as long as management didn't notice. Even when employees complied with the planned changes, they showed resistance by performing the new task while letting customers know that they disapproved of these changes forced on them![9]

Resistance to change takes many forms, ranging from overt work stoppages to subtle attempts to continue the old ways.
(left): Jacob Wackerhausen/Getty Images; (right): Mark Dierker/McGraw Hill

Most change agents are understandably frustrated by passive or active resistance to their planned change. However, resistance is a common and natural human response. Even when people support change, they typically assume that it is others–not themselves–who need to do the changing. Resistance is a form of conflict, but unfortunately change agents sometimes interpret that disagreement as relationship conflict (see Chapter 10). They describe the people who resist as unreasonable, dysfunctional, and irrational reactionaries to a desirable initiative. By perceiving the situation as relationship conflict, change agents attack the competence of those who resist the change, which further escalates the conflict and generates even stronger resistance to the change initiative.

> People don't resist change. They resist being changed.[12]
>
> —unnamed organizational change consultant, cited by MIT scholar Peter Senge

A more productive approach is to view change resistance as task conflict. From this perspective, opposition is a signal either that the change agent has not sufficiently prepared employees for change or that the change initiative should be altered or improved.[10] Employees might not feel a sufficiently strong urgency to change, or they might believe the change strategy is ill-conceived. Even if they recognize the need for change and agree with the strategy, employees might resist because they lack confidence to change or believe the change will make them worse off than the current situation. Resistance takes many forms, and change agents need to decipher those different types of resistance to understand their underlying causes.[11]

Resistance is also a form of voice, so giving employees an opportunity to discuss their concerns potentially improves procedural justice (see Chapter 5) as well as the quality of decision making about the change (see Chapter 6). By redirecting initial forms of resistance into constructive conversations, change agents can generate a feeling of fairness among employees. Furthermore, resistance is motivated behavior; it potentially engages people to think about the change strategy and process. Change agents can harness that motivational force to ultimately strengthen commitment to the change initiative.

Why Employees Resist Change

Change management experts have developed a long list of reasons why people resist change.[13] Some people inherently oppose change because of their personality and values.[14] Aside from these dispositional factors, employees typically oppose organizational change because they lack sufficient motivation, ability, role clarity, or situational support to change their attitudes, decisions, and behavior.[15] In other words, an employee's readiness for change depends on all four elements of the MARS model. These MARS elements are the foundations of the six most commonly cited reasons why people resist change: (1) negative valence of change, (2) fear of the unknown, (3) not-invented-here syndrome, (4) breaking routines, (5) incongruent team dynamics, and (6) incongruent organizational systems and structures.

SELF-ASSESSMENT 14.1: Are You Ready for Change?

Negative Valence of Change Employees resist change when they believe the post-change situation will have more negative than positive outcomes.[16] In other words, they apply (although imperfectly) the rational choice decision-making model (Chapter 6) to estimate whether the net valence of the change outcomes will be positive or negative. For instance, they consider the cognitive effort of learning new skills, the probability of having more interesting work, the threat of losing job status or work relationships, the opportunity for better career advancement, and the risk of losing their job. In fact, all forms of resistance to change that we describe in this section relate to negative valence of change in some way.

An employee's cost-benefit analysis mainly considers how the change will affect them personally. However, resistance due to negative valence also takes into account the effects of change on the team, organization, or society.[17] Thus, resistance often occurs when employees doubt the planned changes will be worth the risks. They might believe the company is already performing well and that the planned changes will be less effective than the current practices. Or they might view the future practices as confusing and disruptive variations of what employees are currently doing in their jobs.

When you are leading for growth, you know you are going to disrupt comfortable routines and ask for new behavior, new priorities, new skills. Even when we want to change, and do change, we tend to relax and the rubber band snaps us back into our comfort zones.[20]

—Ray Davis, former CEO and chair of Umpqua Bank

Fear of the Unknown Organizational change usually has a degree of uncertainty, and employees tend to assume the worst when they are unsure whether the change will have good or bad outcomes. Uncertainty also is associated with lack of personal control, which is another source of negative emotions. Consequently, the uncertainty inherent in most organizational change is less desirable than the relative certainty of the status quo. This "status quo bias" adds more negative valence to the cost-benefit calculation we described previously.[18]

Not-Invented-Here Syndrome Employees sometimes oppose or even discreetly undermine organizational change initiatives that are introduced by people outside their group. This "not-invented-here" syndrome is most apparent among employees who are usually responsible for the knowledge or initiative.[19] For example, information technology staff are more likely to resist implementing new ideas championed by marketing or finance employees. If the IT staff support the change, they are implicitly acknowledging another group's superiority within IT's own area of expertise. To protect their self-worth, some employees deliberately inflate problems with changes they did not initiate, just to "prove" that those ideas were inferior to their own. As one consultant warned: "Unless they're scared enough to listen, they'll never forgive you for being right and for knowing something they don't."[21]

Employees usually resist change when they believe the post-change situation will have more negative than positive outcomes.
Krakenimages.com/Shutterstock

Breaking Routines People are creatures of habit. They typically resist initiatives that require them to break those automated routines and to learn new role patterns. And unless the new patterns of behavior are strongly supported and reinforced, employees tend to revert to their past routines and habits.

Incongruent Team Dynamics Teams develop and enforce conformity to a set of norms that guide behavior (see Chapter 7). However, conformity to existing team norms may discourage employees from accepting organizational change. For instance, organizational initiatives to improve customer service may be thwarted by team norms that discourage the extra effort

Facing the Challenge of Resistance to Change[22]

71%
of 1,000 U.S. employees
say they are overwhelmed by the amount of change at their job.

38%
of 1,035 U.K. employees
say they resist change due to lack of awareness about the reason for change.

74%
of 1,035 U.K. employees say their leaders need to be doing more to understand why people are resistant to change.

45%
of 2,000 U.S. employed adults
say they don't believe their feedback to management leads to meaningful organizational change (83% of Baby Boomer employees say this).

40%
of 1,737 U.S. HR professionals
identify employee resistance to change as the most common barrier to achieving success in the workplace.

Brand X Pictures/Getty Images

expected to serve customers at this higher standard. Even when employees have positive attitudes about the change, they behaviorally resist the initiative when team norms and associated peer pressure oppose the change.[23]

Incongruent Organizational Systems Rewards, information systems, patterns of authority, career paths, selection criteria, and other systems and structures are both friends and foes of organizational change.[24] When properly aligned, they reinforce desired behaviors. When misaligned, they pull people back into their old attitudes and behavior. Even enthusiastic employees lose momentum after failing to overcome the structural confines of the past.

LO14-3 Outline six strategies for minimizing resistance to change and debate ways to effectively create an urgency to change.

UNFREEZING, CHANGING, AND REFREEZING

Effective change occurs by unfreezing the current situation, moving to a desired condition, and then refreezing the system so it remains in this desired state. Unfreezing occurs when the driving forces are stronger than the restraining forces. This happens by making the driving forces stronger, weakening or removing the restraining forces, or doing both.

The first option is to increase the driving forces, which motivates employees to change through fear or threats (real or contrived). This strategy rarely works, however, because the action of increasing the driving forces alone is usually met with an equal and opposing increase in the restraining forces. A useful metaphor is pushing against the coils of a mattress. The harder corporate leaders push for change, the stronger the restraining forces push back (i.e., employees increase their resistance to the change). This antagonism threatens the change effort by producing tension and conflict between the change leaders and those who are expected to enact the change.

The second option is to weaken or remove the restraining forces. The problem with this strategy is that it provides no motivation for change. To some extent, weakening the restraining forces is like clearing a pathway for change. An unobstructed road makes it easier to travel to the destination but does not motivate anyone to go there. The preferred option, therefore, is to both increase the driving forces and reduce or remove the restraining forces. Increasing the driving forces creates an urgency for change, while reducing the restraining forces lessens motivation to oppose the change and removes obstacles such as lack of ability and situational constraints.

Creating an Urgency for Change

Organizational change is more likely to succeed when employees develop a sufficiently strong urgency for change.[25] In rare situations, employees are motivated (or compliant) to dive into

OB THEORY TO PRACTICE

Diagnosing the Urgency for Change at Rotork Controls[26]

As CEO of Rotork Controls, Kevin Hostetler championed a transformation program that would make the British manufacturer of valve actuators and gearboxes for flow control systems more customer-focused and responsive to emerging technological changes. Early in the change process, Hostetler spoke with many of the global company's 3,200 employees. "I spent much more time on the concrete of factory floors than on the carpet of the boardroom, convincing the organization of the need for change," he recalls.

Rotork's leadership team also diagnosed the company's urgency for change. "We found that we had a senior team with considerable experience in driving change and, two organization levels below, we had a huge body of emerging leaders who longed for organizational improvement," Hostetler reports. But the diagnosis also identified several clusters of staff who resisted the change process. "We had this thick, stuck middle that had been at Rotork for a long time and saw no need to change."

new practices because the forces for change are widely known and worrisome. Most of the time, however, leaders buffer employees from the external environment to such an extent that the prevailing driving forces are hardly felt by anyone below the top executive level. The result is that employees don't understand why they need to change and leaders are surprised when their change initiatives do not have much effect. Consequently, the change process needs to begin by making the external forces for change known to employees and explaining their seriousness for the organization's future. These are the main driving forces in Lewin's model. They push people out of their comfort zone, energizing them to face the risks that change creates.

Some companies fuel the urgency for change by putting executives and employees in direct contact with customers. Dissatisfied customers and other stakeholders represent a compelling driving force for change because the organization's survival typically depends on having customers who are satisfied with the product or service. Personal interaction with customers also provides a human element that further energizes employees to change current behavior patterns.[27]

Creating an Urgency for Change without External Forces Exposing employees to external forces can strengthen the urgency for change, but leaders often need to begin the change process before problems come knocking at the company's door. The challenge is greatest when companies are performing well in their markets. In successful organizations, decision makers tend to be less vigilant about external threats and more resistant to change. "To create a culture that embraces change, rigidity and complacency have no room at the table," warns Josh Schoeller, CEO of health care at LexisNexis Risk Solutions. "Just because something seems to be working, it doesn't mean you should settle into a false sense of security that a particular model, product, or solution will always remain relevant."[28]

Creating an urgency for change when the organization is the market leader requires plenty of persuasive influence that helps employees visualize future competitive threats and environmental shifts. Experts warn, however, that employees may see this strategy as manipulative, which produces cynicism about change and undermines trust in the change agent.[29] Fortunately, the urgency for change doesn't need to originate from problems or threats to the company; this motivation also can develop through the leader's vision of a more appealing future. A future vision of a better organization makes the current situation comparatively less appealing. When the vision connects to employees' values and needs, it can be a motivating force for change even when external problems are insignificant.

Reducing the Restraining Forces

Earlier, we used the mattress metaphor to explain that increasing the driving forces alone will not bring about change because employees often push back harder to offset the opposing forces. To minimize this push-back, change agents need to address each of the sources of resistance. Six of the main strategies for minimizing resistance to change are outlined in Exhibit 14.2. Communication, learning, employee involvement, and stress management should be the first priorities for leading change.[30] However, negotiation and coercion may be necessary for some people who will clearly lose something from the change and in cases where the speed of change is critical.

Communication Communication is the highest priority and first strategy required for any organizational change. The importance of communication in the change process was evident at EE ("Everything Everywhere"), the United Kingdom's largest mobile network, which was described in the opening paragraphs of this chapter.

Communication improves the change process in at least two ways.[31] First, communication generates the urgency for change that we described a few paragraphs ago. Leaders motivate employees to support the change by candidly telling them about the external threats and opportunities that make change so important. The second way that communication minimizes resistance to change is by illuminating the future and thereby reducing fear of the unknown. The more leaders communicate details about the vision as well as milestones already achieved, the more easily employees can understand their own roles in that future.

Learning Learning is an important process in most organizational change initiatives because employees

Mc Graw Hill connect

SELF-ASSESSMENT 14.2: Are You Tolerant of Change?

> The most practical piece of advice I can offer others is to recognize the critical importance of open communication in times of change.[32]
>
> —Chris Catliff, CEO of Blueshore Financial

Exhibit 14.2 Strategies for Minimizing Resistance to Change

Strategy	Example	When Applied	Problems
Communication	Customer complaint letters are shown to employees.	When employees don't feel an urgency for change, don't know how the change will affect them, or resist change due to a fear of the unknown.	Time-consuming and potentially costly.
Learning	Employees learn how to work in teams as company adopts a team-based structure.	When employees need to break old routines and adopt new role patterns.	Time-consuming, potentially costly, and some employees might not be able to learn the new skills.
Employee involvement	Company forms a task force to recommend new customer service practices.	When the change effort needs more employee commitment, some employees need to protect their self-worth, and/or employee ideas would improve decisions about the change strategy.	Very time-consuming. Might lead to conflict and poor decisions if employees' interests are incompatible with organizational needs.
Stress management	Employees attend sessions to discuss their worries about the change.	When communication, training, and involvement do not sufficiently ease employee worries.	Time-consuming and potentially expensive. Some methods may not reduce stress for all employees.
Negotiation	Employees agree to replace strict job categories with multiskilled job clusters in return for increased job security.	When employees will clearly lose something of value from the change and would not otherwise support the new conditions. Also necessary when the company must change quickly.	May be expensive, particularly if other employees want to negotiate their support. Also tends to produce compliance but not commitment to the change.
Coercion	Company president tells managers to "get on board" the change or leave.	When other strategies are ineffective and the company needs to change quickly.	Can lead to subtler forms of resistance, as well as long-term antagonism with the change agent.

Sources: Adapted from P.R. Lawrence, "How to Deal with Resistance to Change," *Harvard Business Review* (May/June 1954): 49–57; J.P. Kotter and L.A. Schlesinger, "Choosing Strategies for Change," *Harvard Business Review* 57 (1979): 106–14.

need new knowledge and skills to fit the organization's evolving requirements. Learning not only helps employees perform better following the change; it also increases their readiness for change by generating more optimism about working successfully in the new situation (called *change self*-efficacy). And when employees develop stronger change self-efficacy, they develop a stronger acceptance of and commitment to the change.[33]

Employee Involvement Employee involvement is often essential in the change process, although only a low level of involvement may be necessary when the change must occur quickly or employee interests significantly conflict with the organization's needs. Change agents who dictate the change initiative experience resistance because employees today feel disempowered and rebel against command-and-control leadership. The potential benefits of employee involvement, which were discussed in Chapter 6, are relevant to organizational change. Rather than being disinterested agents of someone else's decisions, involved employees tend to feel more personal responsibility for successful implementation of the change.[34] This sense of ownership also minimizes the not-invented-here syndrome and fear of the unknown. Furthermore, the work environment is so complex that determining the best direction of the change effort requires ideas and knowledge of many people.

Stress Management Organizational change is a stressful experience for many people because it threatens self-esteem and creates uncertainty about the future.[35] Communication, learning, and employee involvement tend to significantly reduce these stressors.[36] However, research indicates that companies also need to introduce stress management practices to help employees cope with changes.[37] In particular, stress management minimizes resistance by removing some of the negative valence and fear of the unknown about the change process. Stress also saps energy, so minimizing stress potentially increases employee motivation to support the change process.

Negotiation As long as people resist change, organizational change strategies will require a variety of influence tactics. Negotiation is a form of influence that involves the promise of

Applying assertive influence (coercion) is the least desirable way to bring about organizational transformation, but it is sometimes necessary when speed is essential and other tactics are ineffective.
Krakenimages.com/Shutterstock

benefits or resources in exchange for the target person's compliance with the influencer's request. This strategy potentially gains support from those who would otherwise lose out from the change. However, this support usually goes no further than compliance with the change effort. Negotiation rarely produces commitment to change, so it might not be effective in the long term.

Coercion If all else fails, leaders rely on coercion as part of the change process. Coercion includes a range of assertive influence behaviors, such as persistently reminding people of their obligations, frequently monitoring behavior to ensure compliance, confronting people who do not change, and using threats of punishment (including dismissal) to force conformity to the expected changes.

Applying assertive influence on those who will not support the change is the least desirable way to bring about organizational transformation. However, some forms of coercion are sometimes necessary when speed is essential and other tactics are ineffective. It may even be necessary to remove executives who are unwilling or unable to change their existing mental models of the ideal organization. This is a radical form of "unlearning" the organization's past routines that have become dysfunctional.[38] Even so, coercion is a risky strategy because survivors (employees who do not leave) may have less trust in corporate leaders and engage in more political tactics to protect their own job security.

Refreezing the Desired Conditions

Unfreezing and changing behavior won't produce lasting change. People are creatures of habit, so they easily slip back into familiar patterns. Therefore, leaders need to refreeze the new behaviors by ensuring that organizational systems and team dynamics are compatible with the desired changes.[39] Various physical structures and situational conditions need to be realigned. If the change requires more teamwork, then the workplace needs to support team dynamics. Organizational rewards are also powerful systems that refreeze behaviors. If the change process is supposed to encourage efficiency, then rewards should be realigned to motivate and reinforce efficient behavior.

Information systems play a complementary role in the change process, particularly as conduits for feedback.[40] Many companies have discovered significantly better cross-departmental collaboration when enterprise communication platforms such as Slack and Microsoft Teams are introduced with appropriate training and nudging. Feedback systems are also powerful instruments for refreezing change. The organization maintains a stronger customer focus, for example, when people receive ongoing digital feedback regarding customer attitudes and behaviors toward the firm's products and services. The adage "What gets measured, gets done" applies here. Employees concentrate on the new priorities when they receive a continuous flow of feedback about how well they are achieving those goals.

LO14-4 Discuss how leadership, coalitions, social networks, and pilot projects assist organizational change.

LEADERSHIP, COALITIONS, AND PILOT PROJECTS

Kurt Lewin's force field analysis model is a useful template to explain the dynamics of organizational change. But it overlooks four other ingredients in effective change processes: leadership, coalitions, social networks, and pilot projects.

Transformational Leadership and Change

Effective change requires one or more change champions who apply the elements of transformational leadership that were discussed in Chapter 11. Leaders develop a vision of the organization's desired future state, communicate that vision in ways that are meaningful to others, enact decisions and behaviors that are consistent with the vision, and encourage employees to experiment with ways to align work activities more closely with the vision.[41]

Leading change begins with a strategic vision.[42] A leader's vision provides a sense of direction and establishes the critical success factors against which the real changes are evaluated. Furthermore, a vision provides an emotional foundation for the change because it links the individual's values and self-concept to the desired change.[43] A strategic vision also minimizes employee fear of the unknown and provides a better understanding of what behaviors employees must learn for the desired future.

Change initiatives are more successful with a *guiding coalition*—employees who are committed to the transformation, are influencers (highly respected by their peers), and preferably represent various functions and levels of the organization.
ASDF_MEDIA/Shutterstock

Coalitions, Social Networks, and Change

One of the great truths of organizational change is that change agents cannot lead the initiative alone. They need the assistance of several people with a similar degree of commitment to the transformation.[44] Indeed, this group—often called a *guiding coalition*—may be the most important factor in the success of organizational change initiatives.[45]

Membership in the guiding coalition extends beyond the executive team. Ideally, it includes a diagonal swath of employees representing different functions and most levels of the organization. Members of the guiding coalition should also be influencers—highly respected by peers. A guiding coalition is sometimes formed from a special task force that initially investigates the opportunities for change. At other times, the coalition consists of employees who receive special training in the new work practices and then become trainers in their own work units.

Social Networks and Viral Change The change process can be strengthened through *social networks,* which are structures of people connected to one another through one or more forms of interdependence (see Chapter 9). They have an important role in communication and influence, both of which are key ingredients for organizational change. To some extent, coalition members support the change process by feeding into these networks. But social networks contribute to organizational change whether or not the change agent has a formal coalition.[46]

Social networks are not easily controlled, yet some change agents have tapped into them to build a groundswell of support for a change initiative. *Viral change* is a variation of word-of-mouth and viral marketing, whereby information is seeded to a few people and then spread to others through friendship connections.[47] Within organizations, social networks represent the channels through which news and opinions about change initiatives are transmitted. Participants in that network have relatively high trust, so their information and opinions are more persuasive than from more formal channels. Social networks also provide opportunities for behavior modeling—employees observe one another's behavior and eventually adopt that behavior themselves. As key people in the network change their behavior, that behavior is copied by others in the network.

Pilot Projects and Diffusion of Change

Many companies rely on a pilot project, which begins by applying change to one work unit or section of the organization. This cautious approach tests initial employee support for the change as well as the specific methods used to introduce the change (e.g., training, involvement). Furthermore, a pilot project is more flexible and less risky than a companywide initiative.[48] This approach to change also makes it easier to select groups with high readiness for change, thus increasing the likelihood that the transformation will be successful.

How does change get diffused from the pilot project to other parts of the organization? The answer is guided by the MARS model of individual behavior and performance (see Chapter 1). First, employees are more likely to adopt the practices of a pilot project when they are motivated to do so.[49] This occurs when they see that the pilot project is successful and people in the pilot project receive recognition and rewards for changing their previous work practices. Diffusion also occurs more successfully when managers support and reinforce the desired behaviors. More generally, change agents need to minimize the sources of resistance to change that we discussed earlier in this chapter.

Second, employees must have the ability—the required skills, knowledge, and habits—to adopt the practices introduced in the pilot project. According to innovation diffusion studies, people adopt ideas more readily when they have an opportunity to interact with and learn from those who have already applied the new practices.[50]

> **Viral change is a variation of word-of-mouth and viral marketing, whereby information is seeded to a few people and then spread to others through friendship connections.**

action research A problem-focused change process that combines action orientation (changing attitudes and behavior) and research orientation (testing theory through data collection and analysis)

Third, pilot projects get diffused when employees have clear role perceptions; that is, when they understand how the practices in a pilot project apply to them even though they are in a completely different functional or product area. The challenge here is for change agents to provide guidance that is not too narrowly defined around the pilot project setting because it might not seem relevant to other areas of the organization. At the same time, the pilot project intervention should not be described too broadly or abstractly to other employees because this makes the information and role model too vague. Finally, employees require supportive situational factors, including the resources and time necessary to adopt the practices demonstrated in the pilot project.

OB THEORY TO PRACTICE

Strategies for Diffusing Change from a Pilot Project

Motivation

- Widely communicate and celebrate the pilot project's success.
- Reward and recognize pilot project employees as well as those who work at transferring that change to other parts of the organization.
- Ensure that managers support and reinforce the desired behaviors related to the pilot project's success.
- Identify and address potential sources of resistance to change.

Ability

- Give employees the opportunity to interact with and learn from pilot project team members.
- Reassign or temporarily transfer some pilot project employees to other work units, where they can coach and serve as role models.
- Give employees technical training to implement practices identified in the pilot project.

Role Perceptions

- Communicate and teach employees how the pilot project practices are relevant for their own functional areas.
- Ensure that the pilot project is described in a way that is neither too specific nor too general.

Situational Factors

- Give staff sufficient time and resources to learn and implement the pilot project practices in their work units.

LO14-5 Describe and compare action research and appreciative inquiry as formal approaches to organizational change.

TWO APPROACHES TO ORGANIZATIONAL CHANGE

So far, this chapter has examined the dynamics of change that occur every day in organizations. However, organizational change agents and consultants also apply various structured approaches to organizational change. This section introduces two of the leading approaches: action research and appreciative inquiry.

Action Research Approach

Along with introducing the force field model, Kurt Lewin recommended an **action research** approach to the change process. The philosophy of action research is that meaningful change is a combination of action orientation (changing attitudes and behavior) and research orientation (testing theory).[51] The change process needs to be action-oriented because the ultimate goal is to improve workplace behaviors and practices. An action orientation involves diagnosing current problems and applying interventions that correct those problems. At the same time, the change process is a research study because change agents apply a conceptual framework (such as team dynamics or organizational culture) to a real situation. As with any good research, the change process involves collecting data to diagnose problems more effectively and to systematically evaluate how well the theory works in practice.[52]

The philosophy of action research is that meaningful change is a combination of action orientation (changing attitudes and behavior) and research orientation (testing theory).
PeopleImages/iStock/Getty Images

Within this dual framework of action and research, the action research approach adopts an open systems view. It recognizes that organizations have many interdependent parts, so change agents need to anticipate both the intended and the unintended consequences of their interventions. Action research is also a highly participative process because change requires both the knowledge and the commitment of members within that open system. Indeed, employees are essentially co-researchers as well as participants in the intervention. Overall, action research is a data-based, problem-oriented process that diagnoses the need for change, introduces the intervention, and then evaluates and stabilizes the desired changes. The main phases of action research are illustrated in Exhibit 14.3:[53]

1. *Form client–consultant relationship.* Action research usually assumes that the change agent originates outside the system (such as a consultant), so the process begins by forming the client–consultant relationship. Consultants need to determine the client's readiness for change, including whether people are motivated to participate in the process, are open to meaningful change, and possess the abilities to complete the process.
2. *Diagnose the need for change.* Action research is a problem-oriented activity that carefully diagnoses the situation to determine the appropriate change strategy. Organizational diagnosis systematically gathers and analyzes data about an ongoing system, including interviews and surveys of employees and other stakeholders. This diagnosis also involves employees so they help to identify and support the appropriate change method, the schedule for the actions involved, and the expected standards of successful change.
3. *Introduce intervention.* This stage in the action research model applies one or more actions to correct the problem. It may include any of the prescriptions mentioned in this book, such as building more effective teams, managing conflict, building a better organizational structure, or changing the corporate culture. An important issue is how quickly the changes should occur.[54] Some experts recommend *incremental change*, in which the organization fine-tunes the system and takes small steps toward a desired state. Others claim that *rapid change* is often required, in which the system is overhauled decisively and quickly.
4. *Evaluate and stabilize change.* Action research recommends evaluating the effectiveness of the intervention against the standards established in the diagnostic stage. Unfortunately, even when these standards are clearly stated, the intervention's effectiveness might not be apparent for several years or might be difficult to separate from other factors. If the activity has the desired effect, the change agent and participants need to stabilize the new conditions. This refers to the refreezing process that was described earlier in this chapter. Rewards, information systems, team norms, and other conditions are redesigned so they support the new values and behaviors.

The action research approach has dominated organizational change thinking since it was introduced in the 1940s. However, some experts are concerned that the problem-oriented nature of action research—in which something is wrong that must be fixed—focuses on the negative dynamics of the group or system rather than its positive opportunities and potential. This concern with action research has led to the development of a more positive approach to organizational change, called *appreciative inquiry*.[55]

appreciative inquiry A change strategy that directs the group's attention toward the organization's (or work unit's) potential and positive elements and away from its problems

positive organizational behavior A perspective of organizational behavior that focuses on building positive attributes and behaviors within individuals or institutions as opposed to focusing on what is wrong with them

Appreciative Inquiry Approach

Appreciative inquiry tries to break out of the problem-solving mindset of traditional change management practices by reframing relationships around the positive and the possible. It searches for organizational (or team) strengths and capabilities and then applies that knowledge for further success and well-being. Appreciative inquiry is therefore deeply grounded in the philosophy of **positive organizational behavior**, which suggests that focusing on an employee's positive attributes and behaviors rather than on what is wrong with them will improve that individual's well-being and performance. In other words, this approach emphasizes building on strengths rather than trying to directly correct problems.[56]

Exhibit 14.3 The Action Research Process

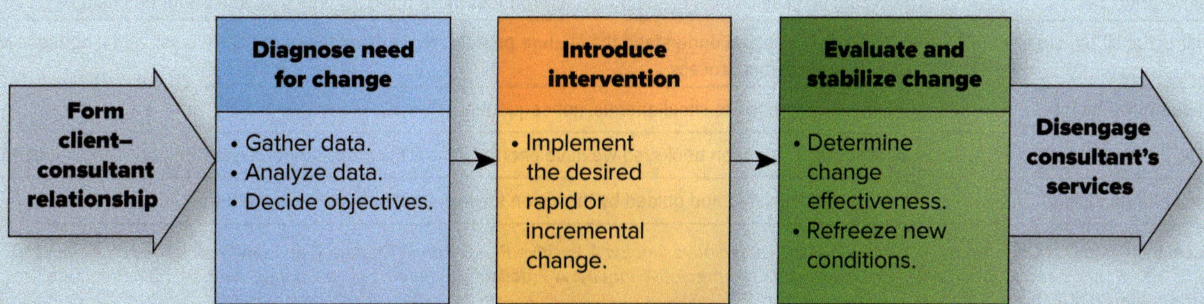

Appreciative inquiry tries to break out of the problem-solving mentality of traditional change management practices by reframing relationships around the positive and the possible.
Colin Anderson/Blend Images LLC

Appreciative inquiry improves open dialogue by redirecting the group's attention away from its own concerns. This is especially useful when participants are aware of their problems or already suffer from negativity in their relationships. The positive orientation of appreciative inquiry enables groups to overcome these negative tensions and build a more hopeful perspective of their future by focusing on what is possible.[57] This positive approach to change also suggests that change agents should adapt an optimistic view of possibilities, such as seeing a glass half full rather than half empty. Therefore, appreciative inquiry actively frames reality in a way that provides constructive value for future development.

Appreciative Inquiry Principles Appreciative inquiry embraces five principles (see Exhibit 14.4). One of these is the positive principle, which we have just described. A second principle, called the *constructionist principle*, recognizes that the questions we ask and the language we use construct different realities. How questions are stated determines the information we receive, which in turn affects which change intervention we choose. A third principle, called the *simultaneity principle*, states that inquiry and change are simultaneous, not sequential. We begin the change process the moment we ask questions because the questions themselves influence those who hear and answer those questions. Consequently, change agents need to be mindful of effects that the inquiry has on the direction of the change process.

A fourth appreciative inquiry principle, called the *poetic principle*, states that organizations are open books, so we have choices in how they may be perceived, framed, and described. The poetic principle encourages change agents to actively frame reality in a way that provides constructive value for future development. The fifth principle, called the *anticipatory principle*, recognizes that people are motivated and guided by an abstract vision of the future that is aligned with their personal values. We noted the importance of visions in our discussion of transformational leadership (Chapter 11) and in the previous section of this chapter.

The Four-D Model of Appreciative Inquiry Appreciative inquiry follows the "Four-D" process shown in Exhibit 14.5. The model's name refers to its four stages, which begins with *discovery*—identifying the positive elements of the observed events or organization.[58] This might involve documenting positive customer experiences elsewhere in the organization. Or it might include directly observing a successful organization elsewhere to discover its fundamental strengths. As participants discuss their findings, they shift into the *dreaming* stage by envisioning what might be possible in an ideal organization. By pointing out a hypothetical ideal organization or situation, participants feel safer revealing their hopes and aspirations than they would if they were discussing their own organization or predicament.

Exhibit 14.4 Five Principles of Appreciative Inquiry

Appreciative Inquiry Principle	Description
Positive principle	Focusing on positive events and potential produces more positive, effective, and enduring change.
Constructionist principle	How we perceive and understand the change process depends on the questions we ask and language we use throughout that process.
Simultaneity principle	Inquiry and change are simultaneous, not sequential.
Poetic principle	Organizations are open books, so we have choices in how they may be perceived, framed, and described.
Anticipatory principle	People are motivated and guided by the vision they see and believe in for the future.

Sources: Based on D.L. Cooperrider and D.K. Whitney, *Appreciative Inquiry: A Positive Revolution in Change* (San Francisco: Berrett-Koehler, 2005), Chap. 7; D.K. Whitney and A. Trosten-Bloom, *The Power of Appreciative Inquiry: A Practical Guide to Positive Change*, 2nd ed. (San Francisco: Berrett-Koehler, 2010), Chap. 3.

Exhibit 14.5 The Four-D Model of Appreciative Inquiry

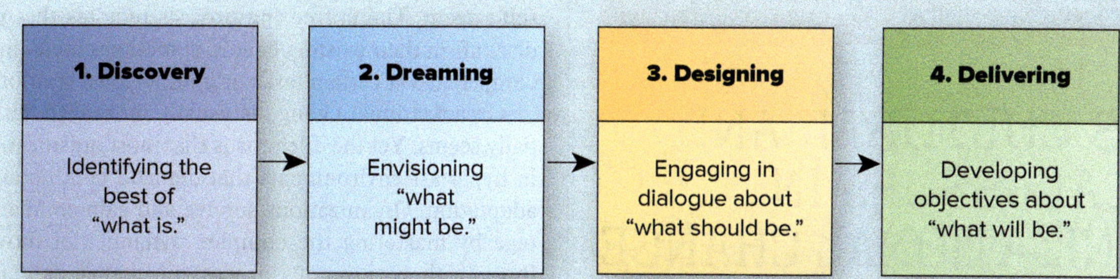

Sources: Based on F.J. Barrett and D.L. Cooperrider, "Generative Metaphor Intervention: A New Approach for Working with Systems Divided by Conflict and Caught in Defensive Perception," *Journal of Applied Behavioral Science* 26 (1990): 229; J.M. Stavros, L.N. Godwin, and D.L. Cooperrider, "Appreciative Inquiry," in *Practicing Organization Development: Leading Transformation and Change*, ed. W.J. Rothwell, J.M. Stavros, and R.L. Sullivan, 4th ed. (John Wiley & Sons, 2016), 96–116.

As participants make their private thoughts public to the group, the process shifts into the third stage, called *designing.* In the designing stage, participants listen with selfless receptivity to each other's models and assumptions, which generates a collective mental model among those participants. In effect, they create a common image of "what should be." As this model takes shape, group members shift the focus back to their own situation. In the final stage of appreciative inquiry, called *delivering* (also known as *destiny*), participants establish specific objectives and direction for their own organization on the basis of their model of "what will be."

Appreciative inquiry has gained popularity since its origins three decades ago. The City of Cleveland recently held the Cleveland Rising Summit, an appreciative inquiry event in which 600 participants developed numerous ideas to improve the region and clarify aspirations for the next decade. Several dozen health professionals at a hospital in Vancouver, Canada, were involved in appreciative inquiry sessions to discover how to improve medical practice for dementia patients. Appreciative inquiry has also been successfully applied across a range of other organizations, including Heidelberg USA, British Broadcasting Corporation, the State of Massachusetts, and Hunter Douglas.[59]

Appreciative inquiry has much to offer, and the evidence to date suggests that it usually has successful outcomes.[60] Still, this type of intervention is not always the best strategy for change. Appreciative inquiry depends on participants' ability to let go of the problem-oriented approach, including the "blame game" of determining who may have been responsible for past failures. It also requires leaders who are willing to accept appreciative inquiry's less structured process. Another concern is that research has not yet examined the contingencies of this approach.[61] In other words, we don't yet know under what conditions appreciative inquiry is useful for organizational change and under what conditions it is less effective. Overall, appreciative inquiry can be an effective approach to organizational change, but we are still discovering its potential and limitations.

OB THEORY TO PRACTICE

Appreciative Inquiry Guides the Future at Lewis County General Hospital[62]

Lewis County General Hospital has adopted appreciative inquiry principles and practices for its long-term strategy development process. "I wanted to focus on what we can do, not on what we can't," says Gerald R. Cayer, CEO of the county-owned medical center in upstate New York.

Instead of focusing on problems, Lewis County General Hospital began with "Discovery and Aspirations" discussion sessions, which reviewed the best practices of rural hospitals around the country. This was followed by the "designing" phase of strategy development. The hospital's appreciative inquiry process involved numerous stakeholders, including hospital administration, employees, labor unions, service providers, the hospital foundation, and community members.

"The point is to bring forward great minds, encourage dialogue, and to think about what can make the most sense for the community and for the hospital," Cayer explains.

Monkey Business Images/Shutterstock

LO14-6 Discuss two cross-cultural and three ethical issues in organizational change.

CROSS-CULTURAL AND ETHICAL ISSUES IN ORGANIZATIONAL CHANGE

Throughout this chapter, we have emphasized that change is inevitable and often continuous because organizations need to remain aligned with the dynamic external environment. Yet, we also need to be aware of cross-cultural and ethical issues with any change process. Many organizational change practices are built around Western cultural assumptions and values, which may differ from and sometimes conflict with assumptions and values in other cultures.[63] One possible cross-cultural limitation is that Western organizational change models, such as Lewin's force field analysis, often assume that change has a beginning and an ending in a logical linear sequence (i.e., a straight line from point A to point B). Yet in some cultures, change is viewed more as a cyclical phenomenon, such as Earth's revolution around the sun or a pendulum swinging back and forth. Other cultures have an interconnected view of change whereby one change leads to another (often unplanned) change, which leads to another change, and so forth, until the change objective is ultimately achieved in a more circuitous way.

Some interventions assume that effective organizational change is necessarily punctuated by tension and overt conflict. Indeed, these events often encourage open conflict. But this direct confrontation view is incompatible with cultures that emphasize harmony (see Chapter 10). These cross-cultural differences suggest that a more contingency-oriented perspective is required for organizational change to work effectively in this era of globalization.

Organizational change practices also need to consider ethical issues.[64] One ethical concern is the risk of violating individual privacy rights. The action research model is built on the idea of collecting information from organizational members, yet this asks employees to provide personal information and reveal emotions they would not normally divulge.[65] A second ethical issue is that some change activities potentially increase management's power by inducing compliance and conformity in organizational members. For instance, action research is a systemwide activity that requires employee participation rather than allowing individuals to get involved voluntarily. A third risk is that some organizational change interventions undermine the individual's self-esteem. The unfreezing process requires that participants disconfirm their existing beliefs, sometimes including their own competence at certain tasks or interpersonal relations.

Organizational change is usually more difficult than it initially seems. Yet the dilemma is that most organizations operate in hyperfast environments that demand continuous and rapid adaptation. Organizations survive and gain competitive advantage by mastering the complex dynamics of moving people through the continuous process of change as quickly as the external environment is changing.

ORGANIZATIONAL BEHAVIOR: THE JOURNEY CONTINUES

More than a century ago, industrialist Andrew Carnegie said: "Take away my people, but leave my factories, and soon grass will grow on the factory floors. Take away my factories, but leave my people, and soon we will have a new and better factory."[66] Carnegie's statement reflects the message woven throughout this book: Organizations are not buildings or machinery; rather, they are the people in those buildings who operate that machinery, and enable the organization to flourish. Organizations are human entities—full of life, sometimes fragile, and always exciting.

Andrew Carnegie
Bettmann/Getty Images

> Some interventions assume that effective organizational change is necessarily punctuated by tension and overt conflict, whereas this practice is incompatible with cultures that emphasize harmony.

Study Checklist

Connect® is available for *M: Organizational Behavior.* Additional resources include:

✓ Exercises:

- **Case Analysis:** Apply concepts within the context of a real-world situation.
- **Click and Drag:** Helps make the connection between theory and application through matching, ranking, or grouping activities.
- **Video Case:** See management in action through interactive videos.
- **Self-Assessment:** Designed to promote student self-awareness and reflection, these research-based surveys contain detailed feedback for students.
- **Application-Based Activities:** These highly interactive, application- and analysis-based exercises allow students to take on specific roles to complete management related tasks within a real-world context.

✓ **SmartBook 2.0**™—Smartbook 2.0 is an adaptive learning solution that provides personalized learning to individual student needs, continually adapts to pinpoint knowledge gaps and focuses learning on concepts requiring additional study. It fosters more productive learning, takes the guesswork out of what to study, and helps students better prepare for class.

Notes

1. O. Blackwell, "How Employee Engagement Helped to Create EE And Turn It into the Number One 'Best Big Company to Work for'," *Engage for Success* (blog), May 20, 2018.
2. T. Allas et al., "Delivering for Success: How to Triple the Success Rate of Government Transformations" (London: McKinsey Center for Government, June 2018); J. Turner, "This New Strategy Could Be Your Ticket to Change Management Success," *Gartner Insights* (blog), November 28, 2022; "Local Government Workforce Survey 2022" (London: U.K. Local Government Association, January 2023); "Civil Service People Survey: 2022 Results" (London: Government of the United Kingdom, March 30, 2023); D. MCLain and R. Pendell, "Why Trust in Leaders Is Faltering and How to Gain It Back," *Gallup Workplace* (blog), April 17, 2023.
3. K. Lewin, *Field Theory in Social Science* (New York: Harper & Row, 1951).
4. D. Coghlan and T. Brannick, "Kurt Lewin: The 'Practical Theorist' for the 21st Century," *Irish Journal of Management* 24, no. 2 (2003): 31-37; B. Burnes, "Kurt Lewin and the Planned Approach to Change: A Re-appraisal," *Journal of Management Studies* 41, no. 6 (2004): 977-1002; S. Cummings, T. Bridgman, and K.G. Brown, "Unfreezing Change as Three Steps: Rethinking Kurt Lewin's Legacy for Change Management," *Human Relations* 69, no. 1 (2016): 33-60.
5. M. Young, *Ogilvy on Advertising in the Digital Age* (London: Goodman Books, 2017), 267. For details about the likely origins of "divine discontent," see the annotation/reference near the end of the "Identifying Problems and Opportunities" section in Chapter 6 (Decision Making and Creativity) of this book.
6. For example, Lewin frequently discusses stable and unstable states in the context of driving and restraining forces in: K. Lewin, *A Dynamic Theory Of Personality* (New York: McGraw Hill, 1935), especially Chap. 3.
7. J. Welch, *Jack: Straight from the Heart* (New York: Warner Business Books, 2001), 432.
8. Some experts suggest that employee "resistance to change" is a misnomer because the resistance isn't to change; it is resistance to the perceived negative outcomes of the change. See E.B. Dent and S.G. Goldberg, "Challenging 'Resistance to Change,'" *Journal of Applied Behavioral Science* 35 (1999): 25-41.
9. S. Chreim, "Postscript to Change: Survivors' Retrospective Views of Organizational Changes," *Personnel Review* 35, no. 3 (2006): 315-35.
10. E.B. Dent and S.G. Goldberg, "Challenging 'Resistance to Change,'" *Journal of Applied Behavioral Science* 35 (1999): 25-41; F.E. Klonek, N. Lehmann-Willenbrock, and S. Kauffeld, "Dynamics of Resistance to Change: A Sequential Analysis of Change Agents in Action," *Journal of Change Management* 14, no. 3 (2014): 334-60.
11. B.J. Tepper et al., "Subordinates' Resistance and Managers' Evaluations of Subordinates' Performance," *Journal of Management* 32, no. 2 (2006): 185-209; J.D. Ford, L.W. Ford, and A. D'Amelio, "Resistance to Change: The Rest of the Story," *Academy of Management Review* 33, no. 2 (2008): 362-77.
12. This quotation is incorrectly attributed to MIT scholar Peter Senge. Senge cites this memorable quotation in his highly regarded book *The Fifth Discipline*, but he states that it originated from an unnamed "seasoned organizational change consultant." See: P.M. Senge, *The Fifth Discipline: The Art and Practice of the Learning Organization* (New York: Doubleday Currency, 1990), 155.
13. D.A. Nadler, "The Effective Management of Organizational Change," in *Handbook of Organizational Behavior*, ed. J.W. Lorsch (Englewood Cliffs, NJ: Prentice Hall, 1987), 358-69; R. Maurer, *Beyond the Wall of Resistance: Unconventional Strategies to Build Support for Change* (Austin, TX: Bard Books, 1996); P. Strebel, "Why Do Employees Resist Change?," *Harvard Business Review* (1996): 86-92; D.A. Nadler, *Champions of Change* (San Francisco: Jossey-Bass, 1998).

14. S. Oreg et al., "Dispositional Resistance to Change: Measurement Equivalence and the Link to Personal Values across 17 Nations," *Journal of Applied Psychology* 93, no. 4 (2008): 935–44.

15. R.R. Sharma, *Change Management: Concepts and Applications* (New Delhi: Tata McGraw Hill, 2007), Chap. 4; I. Cinite, L.E. Duxbury, and C. Higgins, "Measurement of Perceived Organizational Readiness for Change in the Public Sector," *British Journal of Management* 20, no. 2 (2009): 265–77; A.A. Armenakis and S.G. Harris, "Reflections: Our Journey in Organizational Change Research and Practice," *Journal of Change Management* 9, no. 2 (2009): 127–42; S. Jaros, "Commitment to Organizational Change: A Critical Review," *Journal of Change Management* 10, no. 1 (2010): 79–108.

16. A.M. García-Cabrera and F. García-Barba Hernández, "Differentiating the Three Components of Resistance to Change: The Moderating Effect of Organization-Based Self-Esteem on the Employee Involvement-Resistance Relation," *Human Resource Development Quarterly* 25, no. 4 (2014): 441–69; S. Faupel and S. Süß, "The Effect of Transformational Leadership on Employees During Organizational Change – An Empirical Analysis," *Journal of Change Management* 19, no. 3 (2019): 145–66; M.N. Islam, F. Furuoka, and A. Idris, "Employee Engagement and Organizational Change Initiatives: Does Transformational Leadership, Valence, and Trust Make a Difference?," *Global Business and Organizational Excellence* 40, no. 3 (2021): 50–62.

17. R. de la Sablonnière et al., "Profound Organizational Change, Psychological Distress and Burnout Symptoms: The Mediator Role of Collective Relative Deprivation," *Group Processes & Intergroup Relations* 15, no. 6 (2012): 776–90.

18. W. Samuelson and R. Zeckhauser, "Status Quo Bias in Decision Making," *Journal of Risk and Uncertainty* 1, no. 1 (1988): 7–59; K. Lee and K. Joshi, "Examining the Use of Status Quo Bias Perspective in IS Research: Need for Re-Conceptualizing and Incorporating Biases," *Information Systems Journal* 27, no. 6 (2017): 733–52; B.H. Martin, "Unsticking the Status Quo: Strategic Framing Effects on Managerial Mindset, Status Quo Bias and Systematic Resistance to Change," *Management Research Review* 40, no. 2 (2017): 122–41; K.K. Katsaros and A.N. Tsirikas, "Perceived Change Uncertainty and Behavioral Change Support: The Role of Positive Change Orientation," *Journal of Organizational Change Management* 35, no. 3 (2021): 511–26.

19. D. Grosse Kathoefer and J. Leker, "Knowledge Transfer in Academia: An Exploratory Study on the Not-Invented-Here Syndrome," *Journal of Technology Transfer* 37, no. 5 (2012): 658–75; A.L.A. Burcharth, M.P. Knudsen, and H.A. Søndergaard, "Neither Invented nor Shared Here: The Impact and Management of Attitudes for the Adoption of Open Innovation Practices," *Technovation* 34, no. 3 (2014): 149–61.

20. R. Davis, *Leading for Growth: How Umpqua Bank Got Cool and Created a Culture of Greatness* (San Francisco, CA: Jossey-Bass, 2007), 40. Ray Davis also famously pointed out that "change is changing," meaning that the nature and type of change continuously evolves, so leaders need to adapt to new futures. See: S. Gotz, "Ray's List (or What I Learned Working for the CEO of the World's Greatest Bank)," *LinkedIn Pulse* (blog), February 9, 2020.

21. V. Newman, "The Psychology of Managing for Innovation," *KM Review* 9, no. 6 (2007): 10–15.

22. "Employee Feedback Survey Report" (Montreal: Explorance, September 2021); "SHRM Presents State of the Workplace Study," Press Release (Alexandria, VA: SHRM, February 16, 2022); B. Westfall, "Change Fatigue Is Making Employee Burnout Worse," *Capterra* (blog), June 6, 2022; "Experts Reveal Top Tips to Communicate Change in the Workplace," Press Release (Newcastle, UK: Oak Engage, April 20, 2023).

23. R. Borges and C.A. Quintas, "Understanding the Individual's Reactions to the Organizational Change: A Multidimensional Approach," *Journal of Organizational Change Management* 33, no. 5 (2020): 667–81.

24. J. Stouten, D.M. Rousseau, and D. De Cremer, "Successful Organizational Change: Integrating the Management Practice and Scholarly Literatures," *Academy of Management Annals* 12, no. 2 (2018): 752–88.

25. J.P. Kotter, *A Sense of Urgency* (Boston: Harvard Business School Press, 2008); S.H. Appelbaum et al., "Back to the Future: Revisiting Kotter's 1996 Change Model," *Journal of Management Development* 31, no. 8 (2012): 764–82; I. Heim and N. Sardar-Drenda, "Assessment of Employees' Attitudes toward Ongoing Organizational Transformations," *Journal of Organizational Change Management* 34, no. 2 (2020): 327–49.

26. A. Koivuniemi, "An Interview with Rotork's CEO, Kevin Hostetler," *McKinsey & Company: Inside the Strategy Room*, December 13, 2021.

27. L.D. Goodstein and H.R. Butz, "Customer Value: The Linchpin of Organizational Change," *Organizational Dynamics* 27 (1998): 21–35; L. Gill, V. McCarthy, and D. Grimmett, "Voice of the Customer: Creating Client Centered Cultures in Accounting Firms for Retaining Clients and Increasing Profitability," *Journal of Accounting, Business and Management (JABM)* 26, no. 2 (2019): 46-58; L.M. Edinger-Schons et al., "Listen to the Voice of the Customer–First Steps towards Stakeholder Democracy," *Business Ethics: A European Review* 29, no. 3 (2020): 510–27.

28. D. Miller, *The Icarus Paradox: How Exceptional Companies Bring about Their Own Downfall* (New York: HarperBusiness, 1990); S. Finkelstein, *Why Smart Executives Fail* (New York: Viking, 2003). Josh Schoeller's quotation is from: J. Schoeller, "Leading through Change," *Forbes*, March 17, 2021.

29. T.F. Cawsey and G. Deszca, *Toolkit for Organizational Change* (Los Angeles: Sage, 2007), 104.

30. J.P. Kotter and L.A. Schlesinger, "Choosing Strategies for Change," *Harvard Business Review* (1979): 106–14.

31. J.P. Kotter and D.S. Cohen, *The Heart of Change* (Boston: Harvard Business School Press, 2002), 83–98; J. Allen et al., "Uncertainty during Organizational Change: Managing Perceptions through Communication," *Journal of Change Management* 7, no. 2 (2007): 187–210; M. van den Heuvel et al., "Adapting to Change: The Value of Change Information and Meaning-Making," *Journal of Vocational Behavior* 83, no. 1 (2013): 11–21; F. Sguera et al., "Thank You for the Bad News: Reducing Cynicism in Highly Identified Employees during Adverse Organizational Change," *Journal of Occupational and Organizational Psychology* 95, no. 1 (2022): 90–130.

32. Jostle, "Culture Hero Series: Chris Catliff, Blueshore Financial," *The Jostle Blog*, October 30, 2013, http://blog.jostle.me/blog/culture-hero-series-chris-catliff-north-shore-credit-union.

33. D.T. Holt and J.M. Vardaman, "Toward a Comprehensive Understanding of Readiness for Change: The Case for an Expanded Conceptualization," *Journal of Change Management* 13, no. 1 (2013): 9–18; S. Bayraktar and A. Jiménez, "Self-Efficacy as a Resource: A Moderated Mediation Model of Transformational Leadership, Extent of Change and Reactions to Change," *Journal of Organizational Change Management* 33, no. 2 (2020): 301–17.

34. L.K. Lewis and T.L. Russ, "Soliciting and Using Input During Organizational Change Initiatives: What Are Practitioners Doing," *Management Communication Quarterly* 26 (2012): 267–94; F.A. Guzman and A. Espejo, "Introducing Changes at Work: How Voice Behavior Relates to Management Innovation," *Journal of Organizational Behavior* 40, no. 1 (2019): 73–90; C.O. Morain and P. Aykens, "Employees Are Losing Patience with Change Initiatives," *Harvard Business Review*, May 9, 2023.

35. S.G. Bamberger et al., "Impact of Organisational Change on Mental Health: A Systematic Review," *Occupational and Environmental Medicine* 69, no. 8 (2012): 592–98.

36. N.T. Tan, "Maximising Human Resource Potential in the Midst of Organisational Change," *Singapore Management Review* 27, no. 2 (2005): 25–35; A.E. Rafferty and S.L.D. Restubog, "The Impact of Change Process and Context on Change Reactions and Turnover during a Merger," *Journal of Management* 36, no. 5 (2010): 1309–38.

37. M. McHugh, "The Stress Factor: Another Item for the Change Management Agenda?," *Journal of Organizational Change Management* 10 (1997): 345–62; D. Buchanan, T. Claydon, and M. Doyle, "Organisation Development and Change: The Legacy of the Nineties," *Human Resource Management Journal* 9 (1999): 20–37.

38. J.G. Cegarra-Navarro and A. Wensley, "Promoting Intentional Unlearning through an Unlearning Cycle," *Journal of Organizational Change Management* 32, no. 1 (2019): 67–79; S. Sharma and U. Lenka, "On the Shoulders of Giants: Uncovering Key Themes of Organizational Unlearning Research in Mainstream Management Journals," *Review of Managerial Science* 16, no. 6 (2022): 1599–1695. The organizational (un)learning literature focuses mainly on "forgetting" (including voluntary turnover) as well as ways for employees to replace old mental models. That literature has paid limited attention to rapid unlearning through dismissal or motivated turnover (generous separation packages) of staff. It mainly refers only to removal of top executives.

39. D.S. Cohen and J.P. Kotter, *The Heart of Change Field Guide* (Boston: Harvard Business School Press, 2005), 161–77; M.A. Roberto and L.C. Levesque, "The Art of Making Change Initiatives Stick," *MIT Sloan Management Review* 46, no. 4 (2005): 53–60; R.K. Smollan and R.L. Morrison, "Office Design and Organizational Change: The Influence of Communication and Organizational Culture," *Journal of Organizational Change Management* 32, no. 4 (2019): 426–40; G.S. Day and G. Shea, "Changing the Work of Innovation: A Systems Approach," *California Management Review* 63, no. 1 (2020): 41–60.

40. L.D. Goodstein and H.R. Butz, "Customer Value: The Linchpin of Organizational Change," *Organizational Dynamics* 27 (1998): 21–35; R.H. Miles, "Leading Corporate Transformation: Are You up to the Task?" in *The Leader's Change Handbook,* ed. J.A. Conger, G.M. Spreitzer, and E.E. Lawler III (San Francisco: Jossey-Bass, 1999), 221–67.

41. S. J. Stouten, D.M. Rousseau, and D. De Cremer, "Successful Organizational Change: Integrating the Management Practice and Scholarly Literatures," *Academy of Management Annals* 12, no. 2 (2018): 752–88; Oreg and Y. Berson, "Leaders' Impact on Organizational Change: Bridging Theoretical and Methodological Chasms," *Academy of Management Annals* 13, no. 1 (2019): 272–307; M.N. Islam, F. Furuoka, and A. Idris, "Mapping the Relationship between Transformational Leadership, Trust in Leadership and Employee Championing Behavior during Organizational Change," *Asia Pacific Management Review* 26, no. 2 (2021): 95–102; G.B. Onyeneke and T. Abe, "The Effect of Change Leadership on Employee Attitudinal Support for Planned Organizational Change," *Journal of Organizational Change Management* 34, no. 2 (2021): 403–15.

42. M.S. Cole, S.G. Harris, and J.B. Bernerth, "Exploring the Implications of Vision, Appropriateness, and Execution of Organizational Change," *Leadership & Organization Development Journal* 27, no. 5 (2006): 352–67; S. Kirkpatrick, "Leading through Vision and Values," in *Handbook of Principles of Organizational Behavior: Indispensable Knowledge for Evidence-Based Management*, ed. E. Locke (Hoboken: Wiley, 2010), 367–87; V. Lundy and P.P. Morin, "Project Leadership Influences Resistance to Change: The Case of the Canadian Public Service," *Project Management Journal* 44, no. 4 (2013): 45–64.

43. J.P. Kotter and D.S. Cohen, *The Heart of Change* (Boston: Harvard Business School Press, 2002), 61–82; D.S. Cohen and J.P. Kotter, *The Heart of Change Field Guide* (Boston: Harvard Business School Press, 2005).

44. J.P. Kotter, "Leading Change: Why Transformation Efforts Fail," *Harvard Business Review* (1995): 59–67.

45. E.H. Bradley et al., "How Guiding Coalitions Promote Positive Culture Change in Hospitals: A Longitudinal Mixed Methods Interventional Study," *BMJ Quality & Safety* 27, no. 3 (2018): 218–25. The effectiveness of a guiding coalition depends on specific characteristics of its members, some of which we mention here. See: J. Stouten, D.M. Rousseau, and D. De Cremer, "Successful Organizational Change: Integrating the Management Practice and Scholarly Literatures," *Academy of Management Annals* 12, no. 2 (2018): 752–88.

46. J. Stouten, D.M. Rousseau, and D. De Cremer, "Successful Organizational Change: Integrating the Management Practice and Scholarly Literatures," *Academy of Management Annals* 12, no. 2 (2018): 752–88.

47. A. De Bruyn and G.L. Lilien, "A Multi-Stage Model of Word-of-Mouth Influence through Viral Marketing," *International Journal of Research in Marketing* 25, no. 3 (2008): 151–63; J.Y.C. Ho and M. Dempsey, "Viral Marketing: Motivations to Forward Online Content," *Journal of Business Research* 63, no. 9/10 (2010): 1000–06; M. Williams and F. Buttle, "The Eight Pillars of WOM Management: Lessons from a Multiple Case Study," *Australasian Marketing Journal* 19, no. 2 (2011): 85–92.

48. M. Beer, R.A. Eisenstat, and B. Spector, *The Critical Path to Corporate Renewal* (Boston: Harvard Business School Press, 1990).

49. M. Beer, R.A. Eisenstat, and B. Spector, *The Critical Path to Corporate Renewal* (Boston: Harvard Business School Press, 1990), Chap. 5; R.E. Walton, "Successful Strategies for Diffusing Work Innovations," *Journal of Contemporary Business* (1977): 1–22; R.E. Walton, *Innovating to Compete: Lessons for Diffusing and Managing Change in the Workplace* (San Francisco: Jossey-Bass, 1987).

50. E.M. Rogers, *Diffusion of Innovations*, 4th ed. (New York: Free Press, 1995).

51. H. Bradbury et al., "Action Research at Work: Creating the Future Following the Path from Lewin," in *The SAGE Handbook of Action Research: Participative Inquiry and Practice*, ed. P. Reason and H. Bradbury, 2nd ed. (London: SAGE, 2008), 77–92; A.B. (Rami) Shani and D. Coghlan, "Action Research in Business and Management: A Reflective Review," *Action Research* 19, no. 3 (2021): 518–41.

52. V.J. Marsick and M.A. Gephart, "Action Research: Building the Capacity for Learning and Change," *Human Resource Planning* 26 (2003): 14–18.

53. L. Dickens and K. Watkins, "Action Research: Rethinking Lewin," *Management Learning* 30 (1999): 127–40; J. Heron and P. Reason, "The Practice of Co-operative Inquiry: Research 'with' Rather Than 'on' People," in *Handbook of Action Research*, ed. P. Reason and H. Bradbury (Thousand Oaks, CA: Sage, 2001), 179–88.

54. D.A. Nadler, "Organizational Frame Bending: Types of Change in the Complex Organization," in *Corporate Transformation: Revitalizing Organizations for a Competitive World*, ed. R.H. Kilmann, T.J. Covin, and Associates (San Francisco: Jossey-Bass, 1988), 66–83; K.E. Weick and R.E. Quinn, "Organizational Change and Development," *Annual Review of Psychology* 50 (1999): 361–86.

55. T.M. Egan and C.M. Lancaster, "Comparing Appreciative Inquiry to Action Research: OD Practitioner Perspectives," *Organization Development Journal* 23, no. 2 (2005): 29–49.

56. K. Cameron, J.E. Dutton, and R.E. Quinn, eds., *Positive Organizational Scholarship: Foundation of a New Discipline* (San Francisco: Berrett-Koehler, 2003); M.E.P. Seligman et al., "Positive Psychology Progress: Empirical Validation of Interventions," *American Psychologist* 60 (2005): 410–21. On the origins of appreciative inquiry, see G.R. Bushe, "Foundations of Appreciative Inquiry: History, Criticism and Potential," *AI Practitioner* 14, no. 1 (2012): 8–20.

57. D.K. Whitney and D.L. Cooperrider, "The Appreciative Inquiry Summit: Overview and Applications," *Employment Relations Today* 25 (1998): 17–28; J.M. Watkins and B.J. Mohr, *Appreciative Inquiry: Change at the Speed of Imagination* (San Francisco: Jossey-Bass, 2001).

58. F.J. Barrett and D.L. Cooperrider, "Generative Metaphor Intervention: A New Approach for Working with Systems Divided by Conflict and Caught in Defensive Perception," *Journal of Applied Behavioral Science* 26 (1990): 219–39; D.K. Whitney and D.L. Cooperrider, "The Appreciative Inquiry Summit: Overview and Applications," *Employment Relations Today* 25 (1998): 17–28; J.M. Watkins and B.J. Mohr, *Appreciative Inquiry: Change at the Speed of Imagination* (San Francisco: Jossey-Bass, 2001), 15–21.

59. S. Berrisford, "Using Appreciative Inquiry to Drive Change at the BBC," *Strategic Communication Management* 9 (2005): 22–25; G.R. Bushe, "A Comparative Case Study of Appreciative Inquiries in One Organization: Implications for Practice," *Review of Research and Social Intervention* 29 (2010): 7–24; "2013-2015 Massachusetts Joint Statewide Three-Year Electric & Gas Energy Efficiency Plan" (State of Massachusetts, July 2, 2012); T. Wall, J. Russell, and N. Moore, "Positive Emotion in Workplace Impact: The Case of a Work-Based Learning Project Utilising Appreciative Inquiry," *Journal of Work-Applied Management* 9, no. 2 (2017): 129–46; L. Hung et al., "Appreciative Inquiry: Bridging Research and Practice in a Hospital Setting," *International Journal of Qualitative Methods* 17, no. 1 (2018): 1–17; A. Scerri, A. Innes, and C. Scerri, "Using Appreciative Inquiry to Implement Person-Centred Dementia Care in Hospital Wards," *Dementia* 18, no. 1 (2019): 190–209; P. Krouse and M. Kilpatrick, "Cleveland Rising Aspires to Greatness, Needs a Way Forward," *Cleveland.com*, October 31, 2019.

60. A. Merriel et al., "Systematic Review and Narrative Synthesis of the Impact of Appreciative Inquiry in Healthcare," *BMJ Open Quality* 11, no. 2 (2022): e001911.

61. G.R. Bushe, "Five Theories of Change Embedded in Appreciative Inquiry" (paper presented at the 18th Annual World Congress of Organization Development, Dublin, Ireland, July 14–18, 1998); T.F. Yaeger, P.F. Sorensen, and U. Bengtsson, "Assessment of the State of Appreciative Inquiry: Past, Present, and Future," *Research in Organizational Change and Development* 15 (2004): 297–319; G.R. Bushe and A.F. Kassam, "When Is Appreciative Inquiry Transformational? A Meta-Case Analysis," *Journal of Applied Behavioral Science* 41 (2005): 161–81.

62. Based on information in J. Abbass, "Lewis County Hospital Takes a Positive Approach to Planning," *Watertown Daily Times (NY)*, February 25, 2019.

63. T.C. Head and P.F. Sorenson, "Cultural Values and Organizational Development: A Seven-Country Study," *Leadership and Organization Development Journal* 14 (1993): 3–7; R.J. Marshak, "Lewin Meets Confucius: A Review of the OD Model of Change," *Journal of Applied Behavioral Science* 29 (1993): 395–415; C.M. Lau, "A Culture-Based Perspective of Organization Development Implementation," *Research in Organizational Change and Development* 9 (1996): 49–79; C.M. Lau and H.Y. Ngo, "Organization Development and Firm Performance: A Comparison of Multinational and Local Firms," *Journal of International Business Studies* 32, no. 1 (2001): 95–114.

64. M. McKendall, "The Tyranny of Change: Organizational Development Revisited," *Journal of Business Ethics* 12 (1993): 93–104; C.M.D. Deaner, "A Model of Organization Development Ethics," *Public Administration Quarterly* 17 (1994): 435–46.

65. G.A. Walter, "Organization Development and Individual Rights," *Journal of Applied Behavioral Science* 20 (1984): 423–39.

66. This often-cited quotation does not appear, even in other variations, in the books that Andrew Carnegie wrote (such as Gospel of Wealth, 1900; Empire of Business, 1902; and Autobiography, 1920). However, variations of it are found soon after Carnegie's passing. The earliest citations of this exact quotation appeared in the late 1970s (e.g., Wisconsin Career Education Consortium, Autumn 1977). A somewhat different version of this quotation (acknowledged by that author as a variation of the original) appeared in a 1957 Harvard Business Review article: "Take away my factories and my wealth, but leave me my organization, and I will soon regain all that I have lost." Each of these excerpts are possibly derived from a more verbose quotation attributed to Carnegie published since the early 1920s. "You can take away my factories and my plants. Take away my railroads, my ships and my transportation—take away my money—strip me of all of these, but leave me my men, and in two or three years at the most, I will have them all back again." See: F.W. White, "Number of Firms Who Insure Their Officers Growing," *Financial Post (Toronto)*, June 9, 1922, pg. 14; D.S. Sherwin, "The Job of Job Evaluation," *Harvard Business Review* 35, no. 3 (1957): 63–71. One additional observation: The reference to "the grass will grow" in Carnegie's quotation bears an uncanny resemblance to a famous speech by American lawyer and politician William Bryan in 1896 regarding destroying farms versus burning down cities. This is around the same time that Carnegie apparently said that "soon grass will grow on the factory floors."

Organization Index

Name Index

E

F

G

H

M

N

O

P

T

U

V

W

X

Y

Z

Glossary/Subject Index

A

Ability *The natural aptitudes, learned capabilities, and habits required to successfully complete a task*, 18–19

Achievement-nurturing orientation *Cross-cultural value describing the degree to which people in a culture emphasize competitive versus cooperative relations with other people*, 45

Action research *A problem-focused change process that combines action orientation (changing attitudes and behavior) and research orientation (testing theory through data collection and analysis)*, 334–335

Adaptive culture *An organizational culture in which employees are receptive to change, including the ongoing alignment of the organization to its environment and continuous improvement of internal processes*, 309

Adaptive task performance *How well employees modify their thoughts and behavior to align with and support a new or changing work process or work setting*, 20

Affective organizational commitment *An individual's emotional attachment to, involvement in, and identification with an organization*, 88–89

Agreeableness *A personality dimension describing people who are trusting, helpful, good-natured, considerate, tolerant, selfless, generous, and flexible*, 33

Anchoring and adjustment heuristic *A natural tendency for people to be influenced by an initial anchor point such that they do not sufficiently move away from that point as new information is provided*, 141

Appreciative inquiry *A change strategy that directs the group's attention toward the organization's (or work unit's) potential and positive elements and away from its problems*, 335–337

Artifacts *The observable symbols and signs of an organization's culture*, 304–306

Attitudes *The cluster of beliefs, assessed feelings, and behavioral intentions toward a person, object, or event (called an attitude object)*, 79

Attraction-selection-attrition (ASA) theory *A theory that states that organizations have a natural tendency to attract, select, and retain people with values and personality characteristics that are consistent with the organization's character, resulting in a more homogeneous organization and a stronger culture*, 313–314

Attribution process *The perceptual process of determining whether an observed behavior or event is caused largely by internal (personal characteristics) or external (situational) factors*, 62

Authentic leadership *The view that effective leaders need to be aware of, feel comfortable with, and act consistently with their values, personality, and self-concept*, 273–274

Availability heuristic *A natural tendency to assign higher probabilities to objects or events that are easier to recall from memory, even though ease of recall is also affected by nonprobability factors (e.g., emotional response, recent events)*, 141

B

Best alternative to a negotiated agreement (BATNA) *The best outcome you might achieve through some other course of action if you abandon the current negotiation*, 249

Bicultural audit *A process of diagnosing cultural relations between companies and determining the extent to which cultural clashes will likely occur*, 311

Bounded rationality *The view that people are bounded in their decision-making capabilities, including access to limited information, limited information processing, and tendency toward satisficing rather than maximizing when making choices*, 138, 139

Brainstorming *A freewheeling, face-to-face meeting where team members are encouraged to identify crazy ideas, build on the ideas that others have presented, generate as many ideas as possible (because quantity often leads to higher quality ideas), and are prohibited from evaluating or criticizing people or their ideas*, 179

Brainwriting *A variation of brainstorming whereby participants write (rather than speak about) and share their ideas*, 179

C

Categorical thinking *Organizing people and objects into preconceived categories that are stored in our long-term memory*, 60–61

Centrality *A contingency of power pertaining to the degree and nature of interdependence between the power holder and others*, 218–219

Centralization *The degree to which formal decision authority is held by a small group of people, typically those at the top of the organizational hierarchy*, 286

Ceremonies *Planned displays of organizational culture, conducted specifically for the benefit of an audience*, 304, 305–306

Charisma *A set of self-presentation characteristics and nonverbal communication behaviors (i.e., signaling) that generate interpersonal attraction and referent power over others as well as deference to the charismatic person,* 216

Coalition *A group that attempts to influence people outside the group by pooling the resources and power of its members,* 223

Cognitive dissonance *An emotional experience caused by a perception that our beliefs, feelings, and behavior are incongruent with one another,* 82

Collectivism *A cross-cultural value describing the degree to which people in a culture emphasize duty to groups to which they belong and to group harmony,* 44–45

Communication *The process by which information is transmitted and understood between two or more people,* 189

Confirmation bias *The process of screening out information that is contrary to our decisions, beliefs, values, and assumptions, while more readily accepting confirming information,* 59, 141, 145

Conflict *The process in which one party perceives that its interests are being opposed or negatively affected by another party,* 235

Conscientiousness *A personality dimension describing people who are organized, dependable, goal-focused, thorough, disciplined, methodical, and industrious,* 32–33

Contact hypothesis *A theory stating that the more we interact with someone, the less prejudiced or perceptually biased we will be against that person,* 68

Continuance commitment *An individual's calculative attachment to an organization,* 88, 89

Corporate social responsibility (CSR) *Organizational activities intended to benefit society and the environment beyond the firm's immediate financial interests or legal obligations,* 8, 9

D

E

H

I

J

P

R